THE RESPONSA OF PROFESSOR LOUIS GINZBERG

This book was published with the generous assistance of
The Louis Ginzberg Fund for Talmudic Research

Volume XVI in the **Moreshet Series**,
Studies in Jewish History, Literature, and Thought

Prof. Louis Ginzberg (1873-1953)

THE RESPONSA

OF

PROFESSOR LOUIS GINZBERG

Edited

by

David Golinkin

THE JEWISH THEOLOGICAL SEMINARY OF AMERICA
NEW YORK AND JERUSALEM
1996

Contents

Abbreviations

Introduction   **1**

Chapter I General Statements Regarding Jewish Law   **37**
No. 1   An Excerpt from "Zechariah Frankel" (1901)   39
No. 2   "Report, Committee on Authoritative Board for the Interpretation of Jewish Law" (1917)   41
No. 3   An Excerpt from the "Address of the Acting President" (1918)   44
No. 4   An Excerpt from the "Report of the Committee on the Interpretation of Jewish Law" (1921)   46

Chapter II Liturgy   **49**
No. 1   A Statement about Variations in Jewish Liturgy (1918)   51
No. 2   The Reference to the Restoration of Sacrifices in the *Musaf* Service (1923)   52
No. 3   A Prayer for the Government (1927)   54
No. 4   A Prayer for Divine Aid (1944)   56
No. 5   An Excerpt from "A Declaration (Regarding Dr. Mordecai Kaplan's *Siddur*)" (1945)   58
No. 6   A Reaction to Rabbi Silverman's Notes on the *Siddur* (1941) and to his *Siddur* (1946)   64

Chapter III Responsa Related to Orah Haim   **73**
No. 1   May a Cantor Appear in Major Roles at an Opera House? (OH 53:25)   75
No. 2   Covering the Head (OH 91:3 and 2:6)   76
No. 3   Covering the Head During Religious Services (OH 91:3)   77
No. 4   Must a New Synagogue be Built Facing East? (OH 94:2 and 150:5)   78
No. 5   Some of the Technical Terms found in *Pittum Haketoret* (OH 132:2)   81
No. 6   Keeping a *Sefer Torah* in an Army Chapel and Reading from it at Night (OH 135:1 in Mishnah Berurah, par. 1)   84

No. 7 Mixed Pews - 1921 (not in OH) 85

No. 8 An Interview Regarding Mixed Pews - 1926 (?) (not in OH) 88

No. 9 Mixed Pews - 1947-48 (not in OH) 90

No. 10 Is the *Bimah* in the Center a Sephardic Custom? (OH 150:5) 101

No. 11 May the Lower Floor of a Synagogue be used as a *Bet Midrash* and as a Social Hall? (OH 151:1-2) 103

No. 12 May a Synagogue be Sold to a Church? (OH 153) 105

No. 13 May a Synagogue be Sold for Commercial Purposes? (OH 153:7) 107

No. 14 An Interview Regarding Synagogue Construction on *Shabbat* (OH 244:3) 108

No. 15 Are Late Friday Evening Services Permissible? (OH 261:4) 109

No. 16 May Unfermented Wine be Used in Religious Ceremonies? (OH 272:2) 110

No. 17 The Use of a Radio on *Shabbat* and *Yom Tov* (not in OH) 134

No. 18 The Use of the Organ in the Synagogue (OH 338:1-2) 135

No. 19 May Green Peas, String Beans and Tomatoes be Used on Passover? (OH 453:1) 136

No. 20 May a Cracked Shofar be Repaired with Scotch Tape? (OH 586:8-9) 137

No. 21 The Use of New Tunes in Place of Traditional Tunes (OH 619:1) 138

No. 22 Four Questions Regarding the *Shofar* (OH 623:6) 139

Chapter IV Responsa Related to Yoreh Deah **141**

No. 1 "Jewish Sympathy for Animals" (YD 1ff.) 143

No. 2 "The Humaneness of *Shechita*" (YD 1ff.) 146

No. 3 Is Gelatin Kosher? (YD 87:10) 151

No. 4 Art in the Synagogue - 1923 (YD 141) 155

No. 5 Art in the Synagogue - 1927 (YD 141) 157

No. 6 May Jews Who Have Joined a Christian Science Church Be Members of a Synagogue? (YD 158:2 and HM 425:5) 164

No. 7 The Jewish Attitude Towards Spiritualism (YD 179:14) 165

No. 8 Must a Jewish Soldier in the United States Army Retain His Beard? (YD 181:10-11) 166

No. 9 What is Meant by the Expression "born in the Jewish faith"? (YD 268) 167

No. 10 The Conversion of a Gentile Woman Already Married to a Jew and Her Children (YD 268:6-7) 170

No. 11 Euthanasia (YD 339:1) 172

No. 12 The Burial of a Synagogue Member Who was also a Member of a Christian Science Church (YD 345:5 and 362:5) 175

No. 13 The Burial of Jews in a Separate Section of a Non-Jewish Cemetery and the Burial of an Intermarried Jew in a Jewish Cemetery (YD 345:5 and 362:5) 176

No. 14 Seven Questions Regarding Burial (YD 345:5 and 362:5) 178

No. 15 Autopsy (YD 349 and 357) 185

No. 16 Burial in a Mausoleum (YD 362:1) 189

No. 17 Reinterment in Costly Mausoleums (YD 362:1) 190

No. 18 Reinterment from a Mausoleum to a Cemetery (YD 362:1) 191

No. 19 Reinterment in a New Family Plot (YD 363:1) 193

No. 20 Reinterment in a New Family Plot (YD 363:1) 195

No. 21 Reinterment in a New Family Plot (YD 363:1) 197

No. 22 Reinterment in Order to Facilitate Easy Visitation (YD 363:1) 198

No. 23 May a Rabbi Who is a *Kohen* Officiate at Funerals? (YD 369ff.) 199

No. 24 May a *Kohen* Serve in the U.S. Army? (YD 369ff.) 200

No. 25 The Recital of *Kaddish* by a Son Who Bears a Grudge against His Father (YD 376:4) 201

No. 26 The Participation of Children in Mourning in Music Periods and School Assemblies (YD 391) 202

Chapter V Responsa Related to Even Haezer **205**

No. 1 Artificial Insemination by a Donor (EH 1 in Birkei Yosef) 207

No. 2 Marrying a Woman with the Same Name as One's Mother (EH 2 in Pithei Teshuvah, par. 6) 214

No. 3 Should a Rabbi of Uncertain Priestly Status Continue to Behave Like a Kohen? (EH 3) 215

No. 4 Fellatio (EH 23:1 and 25:2 and OH 240:4) 216

No. 5 Does a Couple that Eloped and Spent Several Hours Together Require a *Get*? (EH 26 and 33) 217

No. 6 The History of the Marriage Ring (EH 27:1 and 31:2) 218

No. 7 Weddings on Hol Hamoed Sukkot (EH 64:6 and OH 546:1) 220

No. 8 Weddings on Hol Hamoed Sukkot for Soldiers Leaving for Overseas (EH 64:6 and OH 546:1) 221

No. 9 Remarriage without a Get If the First Wife Was a Transgressor (EH 115:1) 222

No. 10 A Protest against the Laxity with which Jewish Divorce is Practiced (EH 119ff.) 223

No. 11 Giving a Get without Documentary Evidence of a Civil Divorce (EH 119ff.) 224

No. 12 Is a Woman divorced by a Get without a Civil Decree Considered Divorced? (EH 119ff.) 225

No. 13 Agency Appointment for a Soldier Going Off to War (EH 144:5) 226

Chapter VI Miscellaneous Responsa   **229**

No. 1   A Reply to Mr. Paranaitis Concerning the Blood Libel at Kiev
(1913)   231

No. 2   A Reply to Mr. Szacki (1919)   253

No. 3   The Jewish Attitude Towards the Crippled (1938)   263

No. 4   Why was the Palestinian Talmud Never Translated into English?
(1940)   265

No. 5   The Denial of Religious Services to an Unaffiliated Jew (1940)   267

No. 6   Which Midrash Asks Why the Decalogue Does not Mention God's
Role as Creator of the Universe? (1943)   269

No. 7   Women on Synagogue Boards (1944)   270

No. 8   The Languages of the Jews in Ancient Times (1944)   272

No. 9   Ordination in Ancient Times (1946)   273

No. 10   Four Miscellaneous Questions (1947)   277

No. 11   The Legal Responsibility of a Married Woman (1948)   281

No. 12   Impeachment in Talmudic Literature (1949)   283

No. 13   The Inscription on a Parokhet (1949)   284

No. 14   Three Miscellaneous Questions (1950)   286

No. 15   Two Miscellaneous Questions (1951)   287

No. 16   The Numbers in Daniel (1951)   288

No. 17   The Civil Calendar Date of Yom Kippur in 1844 (1952)   289

No. 18   The Fixing of the Jewish Calendar (1952)   290

No. 19   The Renewal of the Sanhedrin (undated)   293

Chapter VII Questions to Which No Answers Have Been Found   **295**

No. 1   Dancing in the Synagogue Basement (1920)   297

No. 2   Reinterment for Various Reasons (1920)   298

No. 3   May a Synagogue be Sold to a Church? (1920 and 1921)   299

No. 4   May a Widow Marry Her Late Husband's Brother? (1921)   302

No. 5   A Reburial Ceremony for a Soldier Whose Body is Being
Brought from Overseas (1921)   304

No. 6   May the Organ be Used in the Synagogue? (1921)   305

No. 7   Is There Any Way to Permit a Halutzah to Marry a Cohen? (1921)   306

No. 8   A Woman and a Non-Jew as Witnesses at a Wedding (1926)   307

No. 9   Shakespeare and the Talmud (1926)   309

No. 10   An Intermarried Woman as a Member of the Ladies Auxiliary
(1927)   311

No. 11   Anaesthetizing Animals Before Shehitah (1928)   313

No. 12   The Use of Hog Intestine Casings for Surgical Gut   314

No. 13   Did the Guests Bring Their Own Food to Chaburah Meals? (1946)   316

No. 14 Did Jews Before the Year 70 C.E. Bless People by the Laying on
      of Hands? (1946)   317
No. 15 The Tosafot of Arvei Pesahim (1949)   318
No. 16 The Source of an Unusual Midrash (1949)   319

Appendix and Indices   321

The Reports of the Committee on the Interpretation of
      Jewish Law, 1917-1926   323
Index of Sources   325
Index of Subjects   338
Index of Names   346
Index of Places   351

Hebrew Section

Hebrew Introduction   א
Hebrew Responsa   יג

Abbreviations

Address	Eli Ginzberg, "Address in Honor of Professor Louis Ginzberg", *PRA* 28 (1964), pp. 109-119
BCA	Boaz Cohen Archives, Archive no. 24, Rare Book Room, Library, Jewish Theological Seminary of America
CJLS Box	a box of Law Committee responsa from ca. 1920-ca. 1945 found in the office of the Committee on Jewish Law and Standards, The Rabbinical Assembly, New York
Cohen	Boaz Cohen, "Bibliography of the Writings of Prof. Louis Ginzberg", in: *Louis Ginzberg Jubilee Volume*, New York 1945, pp. 19-47
EH	Shulhan Arukh, Even Ha'ezer
EJ	*Encyclopedia Judaica*, Jerusalem 1972
ET	*Entziklopedia Talmudit*, Jerusalem 1947-
Exponent	"Professor Ginsburg on Interpretation of Jewish Law", *The Jewish Exponent* 72/21 (February 18, 1921), pp. 1, 9
Five Gates	Jacob Sonderling, "Five Gates: Casual Notes for an Autobiography", *American Jewish Archives* 16 (1964), pp. 107-123
General files	General Files, Series cc, Louis Ginzberg Papers 1904-58, Box 294, Archive no. 1, Rare Book Room, Library, Jewish Theological Seminary of America
HM	Shulhan Arukh, Hoshen Mishpat
JE	*The Jewish Encyclopedia*, New York and London, 1901-06
JNUL	Jewish National and University Library, Jerusalem

Karp	Abraham Karp, *A History of the United Synagogue of America, 1913-63*, New York 1964
Keeper	Eli Ginzberg, *Keeper of the Law: Louis Ginzberg*, Philadelphia 1966
Legends	Louis Ginzberg, *The Legends of the Jews*, 7 vols., Philadelphia 1909-38 and reprints
LG	Louis Ginzberg
LGA	Louis Ginzberg Archives, Archive no. 42, Rare Book Room, Library, Jewish Theological Seminary of America
Nadell	Pamela Nadell, *Conservative Judaism in America: A Biographical Dictionary and Sourcebook*, Westport, Connecticut 1988
New Box	a new box of papers donated to the Rare Book Room, Library, Jewish Theological Seminary of America, by Eli Ginzberg in September, 1992
OH	Shulhan Arukh, Orah Hayyim
PAAJR	*Proceedings of the American Academy for Jewish Research*
PRA	*Proceedings of the Rabbinical Assembly*
Seminary Family	Eli Ginzberg, "The Seminary Family: a View from my Parents' Home", in: ed., Arthur Chiel, *Perspectives on Jews and Judaism in Honor of Wolfe Kelman*, New York 1978, pp. 117-126
Students' Annual	*Students' Annual: Jewish Theological Seminary*
UJE	*Universal Jewish Encyclopedia*, New York 1934-43
USAAR	*United Synagogue of America, Annual Reports*
USR	*The United Synagogue Recorder*
YD	Shulhan Arukh, Yoreh De'ah
[ ]	a source or phrase added or corrected by the editor
( )	a source in the original

Introduction

Prof. Louis (Levi) Ginzberg (1873-1953), one of the outstanding Talmudists of the twentieth century, is well known as the author of *Seridei Yerushalmi, Geonica, Legends of the Jews, Ginzei Schechter,* and *Peirushim V'hidushim Bayerushalmi.* However, very few are aware of the fact that he was an important *posek* (halakhic authority) of the Conservative Movement in North America and that for a period of ten years he was *the posek* of that movement. It is the purpose of this volume to introduce this neglected aspect of his oeuvre and achievements.

Yet Prof. Ginzberg's responsa should not be viewed in a vacuum. In order to understand his legal decisions and approach to *halakhah,* it is essential to place them within the context of his education, ancestry, pious upbringing, genius, academic career, and scientific publications.[1]

If we were to review his education alone, we would find it similar to that of many outstanding Talmudic scholars in the nineteenth and

---

1   Prof. Ginzberg has been the subject of numerous articles as well as two full-length biographies by Eli Ginzberg and David Druck. Since *Keeper of the Law* by Louis Ginzberg's son, Eli, is the most detailed biography to date, we have used it as our starting point, supplementing it with the facts given by Druck and all of the articles listed below. The list which follows appears in alphabetical order by author or title. All subsequent references in this Introduction refer back to this note:

Address; Arzt, Max, "Authentic Judaism", *PRA* 18 (1954), pp. 158-167; Autobiographical Fragment, dictated to his daughter-in-law, Ruth Szold, LGA, Box 16, 52pp.; Cohen; Dash, Joan, *Summoned to Jerusalem: The Life of Henrietta Szold,* New York 1979, pp. 47-100; Druck, David, *R. Levi Ginzberg,* New York 5694, 119pp. (Hebrew); Epstein, Louis, "Dr. Louis Ginzberg, Scholar, Sage and Thinker", *USR* 7/1 (January, 1927), pp. 2-5 (including a bibliography by Abraham Burstein); Finkelstein, Louis, "Necrology: Louis Ginzberg," *PAAJR* 23 (1954), pp. xliv-liii (= *American Jewish Year Book* 56 (1955), pp. 573-579); idem, "Our Teachers", *PRA* 18 (1954), pp. 168-178; idem, "Ginzberg, Louis", in: *Encyclopaedia Britannica,* X, 1958, p. 424; idem, "Professor Louis Ginzberg: An Appreciation", *Conservative Judaism* 28/2 (Winter, 1974), pp. 13-17; Five Gates; Friedman, Theodore, [review of *Keeper of the Law*], *Conservative Judaism* 20/4 (Summer, 1966), pp. 58-60; Ginzberg, Eli, *My Brother's Keeper,* New Brunswick and London 1980, pp. 17-31; idem, "The Last of the First: Mama G", *Conservative Judaism* 33/4 (Summer, 1980), pp. 26-35; idem, *The Eye of Illusion,* New Brunswick and London 1993, pp. 17-28; Goldman, Solomon, "The Portrait of a Teacher", in: *Louis*

twentieth centuries.[2] Born in Kovno on the 15th of Kislev 5634 (November 28, 1873),[3] Levi Ginzberg was educated by a series of private tutors in Kovno, Klin near Moscow, and Neustadt on the Lithuanian-German border.[4] From age eleven to fourteen he studied at Telz and Slobodka, two of the most important *yeshivot* in Lithuania.[5] At Telz, he was caught reading some *Haskalah* literature, for which he was sorely reprimanded by his father.[6] Nonetheless, young Levi's *bar mitzvah* was attended by ten prominent rabbis who marvelled at his learned *pilpul* regarding the laws of

---

Ginzberg Jubilee Volume, New York 1945, pp. 1-18; idem, "Glimpses of Professor Louis Ginzberg", *Jewish Book Annual* 8 (5710), pp. 97-100 (an abbreviated version of the previous article); Golinkin, David, "Prof. Levi Ginzberg as a Halakhic Authority: a Preliminary Survey of His Responsa", *Proceedings of the Eleventh World Congress of Jewish Studies*, Division C, Volume 1, Jerusalem 1994, pp. 251-258 (Hebrew); Gould, Sophie Ginzberg, "Letters from My Father", *Conservative Judaism* 28/2 (Winter, 1974), pp. 18-24; Haneman, Frederick, *JE*, V, p. 671; Hertzberg, Arthur, *EJ*, VII, cols. 584-585; *Keeper* (the second edition entitled: *Louis Ginzberg: Keeper of the Law*, Philadelphia, 1996, contains a new postscript by Eli Ginzberg); Klein, Isaac, "Professor Louis Ginzberg" etc., *Jewish Book Annual* 30 (5733), pp. 90-94; Kohut, George A., "Semitic Silhouettes XVII - The Jewish Scholar", *Opinion* 4/3 (January, 1934), pp. 20-22; Kraemer, David, "The Scholar's Dilemma" etc., *PRA* 48 (1986), pp. 153-166; Landman, Isaac, *UJE*, IV, pp. 613-614; Lieberman, Saul, *Mehkarim B'torat Eretz Yisrael*, Jerusalem 5751, pp. 612-614 (my thanks to Prof. Ya'akov Sussmann of the Hebrew University for this reference); Mayer, Harry, "What Price Conservatism? Louis Ginzberg and the Hebrew Union College", *American Jewish Archives* 10/2 (October, 1958), pp. 145-150; Minkin, Jacob, "Luis Ginzberg", *Davar: Revista Literaria* 54 (September-October, 1954), pp. 110-116 (Spanish); Nadell, pp. 98-102; Parzen, Herbert, "Louis Ginzberg - The Proponent of the Halakhah", *Conservative Judaism* 8/2 (January, 1952), pp. 16-35 (= *Architects of Conservative Judaism*, New York 1964, pp. 128-154, 227-229); "Prof. Louis Ginzberg Called by Hebrew University in Palestine", *USR* 4/4 (October, 1924), p. 18; Raphael, Yitzhak, *Rishonim V'aharonim*, Tel Aviv 1957, pp. 410-416; Rosenblum, Herbert, *Conservative Judaism: A Contemporary History*, New York 1983, pp. 114-118; Seminary Family; Spiegel, Shalom, "Introduction" to Louis Ginzberg, *Legends of the Bible*, New York 1968, pp. xv-xix; "Tribute to Professor Louis Ginzberg", *PRA* 8 (1941-44), pp. 377-401; Twersky, Yohanan, in: Levi Ginzberg, *Al Halakhah Ve'aggadah*, Tel Aviv 1960, pp. 9-10; Urbach, Ephraim E., *Ha'entziklopedia Ha'ivrit*, X, cols. 714-715.

2   Compare, for example, the biographies of Ya'akov Nahum Epstein: S. Abramson, *Y.N. Epstein* etc., Jerusalem 5702, pp. 4-6; Simcha Asaf, *L'zikhro shel Prof. Y.N. Epstein*, Jerusalem 5712, pp. 9-13; Gedaliah Alon: Z. Dimitrovsky, in: *Kiryat Sefer* 26 (1949-50), p. 311; and Saul Lieberman: Tuvia Preshel, *R. Shaul Lieberman U'foalo Hamada'i*, New York 5723, pp. 1-16 and Saul Lieberman, in: *Mehkarim B'torat Eretz Yisrael*, Jerusalem 5751, pp. 608-611.

3   *Keeper*, p. 12; and Druck, p. 17, who mistakenly writes 5633.

4   *Keeper*, pp. 18-25; and Druck, pp. 17-21.

5   *Keeper*, pp. 25-32; and Druck, pp. 31-40. Regarding these two famous *yeshivot*, see Shaul Stampfer, *The Lithuanian Yeshiva*, Jerusalem 1995, pp. 221-292 (Hebrew).

6   *Keeper*, pp. 29-30 (= Autobiographical Fragment, unnumbered page, dated January 25); Druck, pp. 34-35.

tefillin.[7] He proceeded to study at the Slobodka *yeshiveh* on the outskirts of Kovno, which was the center of the Mussar Movement.[8] At age fourteen he moved in with his uncle, Rabbi Aryeh Leib Rashkes, of Shnipishok, a suburb of Vilna. There he was first introduced to the Palestinian Talmud by his learned uncle.[9] At age fourteen, due to poor health, he joined his parents who had recently relocated to Amsterdam.[10]

Upon recovering one year later, Louis Ginzberg began his secular education. He moved to Frankfurt am Main, where he prepared for his university entrance exams in two years. He began to study mathematics and physics at the University of Berlin, yet after one year switched to Orientalia after it was pointed out to him that a Russian Jew would never get an appointment in these fields at a German university.[11] At age 21, at the end of his second year, Ginzberg transferred to the University of Strassburg in order to study with Theodore Noeldeke, the greatest Orientalist of his day.[12] However, at the advice of his father, he returned briefly to Lithuania in order to secure his official release from the Russian army. On that trip, he also obtained *semikhah* from three rabbis just in case he ever wanted to pursue a rabbinical career.[13] Upon returning to Strassburg, he studied with Noeldeke for four years. In several courses, he was the only student and would arrive at the professor's home at 7 a.m. for private instruction. In 1897, Louis Ginzberg was ready to earn his doctorate, but when his professor of Assyriology moved away, he was counseled by Noeldeke to transfer to Heidelberg and take the degree there. His major was Semitics and he minored in Assyriology and Philosophy. Ginzberg's dissertation was entitled,

---

7   *Keeper,* p. 30; and Druck, p. 35.

8   *Keeper,* pp. 30-32; and Druck, pp. 36-40.

9   *Keeper,* pp. 32-33; Druck, pp. 41-43; and Finkelstein, *PAAJR,* p. xlvii. Prof. Ginzberg clearly had great respect for his uncle. He wrote some notes to Rashkes's edition of *Sefer Ra'avan,* which appeared on fols. 27-28 and at the end of Vol. 3, Jerusalem 1915, and he dedicated his lengthy Hebrew responsum on unfermented wine to the memory of Rabbi Rashkes - see note 1 to that responsum on the Hebrew side of this volume. Rabbi Rashkes in turn thanked Levi and his brother Asher for financial help in his Introduction to Vol. 2, Jerusalem 1913, and he dedicated Vol. 3 to Levi's parents, Isaac and Sarah Zippah. For six of Rashkes's responsa, see Avraham Ever Hirschowitz, *She'elot U'teshuvot Bet Avraham,* Jerusalem 5683, pp. 2-5, 13-19, 31, 41-47, and 56-57.

10   *Keeper,* pp. 33-36; and Druck, pp. 44-47.

11   *Keeper,* pp. 37-42; and Druck, pp. 48-50. Druck, however, says that Ginzberg decided that a person with his background should not abandon the study of Judaica for the sake of mathematics.

12   *Keeper,* p. 45; and Druck, pp. 52ff.

13   *Keeper,* pp. 45-46; and Druck, pp. 50-51, who gives their names.

Die Haggada bei den Kirchenvätern, which examined the *midrashim* preserved by the Church Fathers.[14]

These, then, are the bare bones of Louis Ginzberg's education and upbringing. However, in order to understand what made Ginzberg unique, one must examine three other aspects of his biography: his ancestry, his pious upbringing, and his own innate genius. These combined with his education to make him one of a kind. He himself emphasized his lineage and education on at least two occasions.

In 1932, Louis Ginzberg was awarded an honorary doctorate by the Jewish Institute of Religion. He wrote to the President, Rabbi Stephen S. Wise, as follows:

> You were gracious to add to your official communication a few words of a personal touch. May I comment on them? I never considered humility a virtue – it is a demand of common sense. The part one contributes to his own making, bodily or spiritually, is infinitesimal. The greater part of what we are is due to heredity and to the atmosphere of the time and place into which we are born. If I have rendered any service to Jewish learning, there is no reason whatsoever for me to be proud. A descendant of a long line of Jewish intellectuals, brought up in Lithuanian *Yeshivot* and educated at German universities, could not help contributing something to Jewish learning.[15]

Towards the end of his life, Prof. Ginzberg returned to this theme in a similar letter to Dr. Abram Sachar, President of Brandeis University, upon receiving an honorary doctorate:

> I lately read...a book published in England with the title *The History of Science*, a popular, but rather well-written symposium by the leading English scientists. In the two chapters on Darwin, the point is made that he was a third generation scientist and hence grew up in the scientific atmosphere. Your praise of my acumen and devotion to learning, even if it were to be taken literally, would be nothing extraordinary, in view of the fact that I belong to a

---

14   *Keeper*, pp. 48-58; and Druck, pp. 52-56. His dissertation was published in Amsterdam in 1899; in serial form in *Monatschrift fur Geschichte und Wissenschaft des Judentums* 42-43 (1898-99); and in Berlin in 1900. For its importance, see Druck, pp. 74-75.

15   *Keeper*, p. 289.

family [which] for the last five centuries [has] furnished German, Italian, Polish, and Lithuanian Jewry with outstanding intellectuals and saints. One must never forget the great part heredity and environment play in our makeup. When I think of the phenomenal achievements of the *Gaon* of Vilna, one of my ancestors, my own achievements look to me rather picayune. At the same time, one is not to forget that he was not only a great intellect, but also a great saint, and nobody would classify me as such.[16]

Let us therefore examine his ancestry, his family's piety, and his own personal genius.

Louis Ginzberg's ancestry was impressive indeed. His father, Rabbi Isaac Elias Ginzberg, could trace his ancestry back to Rabbi Yechiel, who lived in Porto, Italy in the fifteenth century.[17] Dozens of his ancestors were rabbis in Italy, Germany, and Eastern Europe. The founder of the Kovno branch was Rabbi Eliezer Ginzberg, Louis's great-great-grandfather.[18] As impressive as this lineage may seem, it is clear that Levi Ginzberg took even greater pride in his mother's family tree, for Zippe Jaffe Ginzberg was a great-great-granddaughter of the Vilna *Gaon's* brother, Abraham. Louis and his family took this fact very seriously:

It was family tradition that a future *Gaon* would have blue eyes like the *Gaon* of Vilna, and Louis' eyes were the deepest blue. My first memory is of when I was between three and four when I got an apple from my mother. I was a little boy, so I bit into it without saying a *Beroche*. My mother rebuked me, since the saying of the *Beroche* is taught to children at the very beginning of their Jewish education. She said: "The *Gaon* would have said it". I asked her how she knew, and she said, "You are a silly boy. The *Gaon* would have said it even when he suckled". In our family what the *Gaon* would have done was thrown at our heads every other minute.[19]

---

16 Ibid., p. 330. It is worth noting that Finkelstein, *PAAJR*, p. liii, and again in *Conservative Judaism*, p. 16, and Mayer, p. 145, do indeed classify Prof. Ginzberg as a saint.

17 *Keeper*, p. 14; and cf. Druck, pp. 5-12. Prof. Ginzberg himself stressed this fact - see *Keeper*, p. 279. For a partial family tree, see *JE*, VI, p. 110. For a full family history and family tree, see Hillel Noah and David Maggid, *Toledot Mishpehot Ginzberg*, St. Petersburg 1899.

18 *Keeper*, p. 15.

19 Ibid., pp. 17-18. The first sentence is based on Finkelstein, *PAAJR*, p. xiv, while the remainder is taken from the Autobiographical Fragment, pp. 22-23.

Louis Ginzberg refers to the Vilna *Gaon* on numerous occasions in his writings. In Hebrew he always calls him דודי זקני[20] while in English he calls him "the pride of our family", "my famous ancestor," and the like.[21] Ginzberg devoted an entire chapter to the *Gaon* in his *Students, Scholars and Saints*[22] and he dedicated the first volume of *Peirushim V'hidushim Bayerushalmi* to him:

לגאון משפחתנו ולגאון כל בית ישראל רבינו אליהו מווילנא זכר צדיק וקדוש

לברכה אשר האיר עיני הגולה בתורתו

המחבר

דור ששי להגאון ר' אברהם זצ"ל אחי הגר"א

To the *gaon* of our family and the *gaon* of the entire House of Israel, Rabbi Eliyahu of Vilna whose righteous and holy memory is a blessing, who lit up the eyes of the exile with his Torah. The author, the sixth generation of the *gaon* Abraham, brother of the Gr"a.[23]

Thus, Louis Ginzberg set a lot of store by his own ancestry, and we can therefore concur with his son Eli's assessment:

My father, with his customary skepticism, was disinclined to ascribe the long generations of excellence solely to heredity. He placed a heavy weight on family tradition, superior opportunities for education, and strong motivation. But he never forgot his own lineage, and there was no influence in his own life more powerful than that of his family's tradition.[24]

A second factor which molded Louis Ginzberg's character and personality was the pious upbringing which he received until age fifteen, when he moved to Frankfurt am Main. His maternal grandmother was so pious that she moved from Amsterdam back to Lithuania in her late eighties. While she trusted her son-in-law, she did not trust the *shehitah* and the preparation of bread and other food in Amsterdam.[25] But Levi's main model

---

20   See, for example, his responsum on unfermented wine in the Hebrew section of this volume, in the final summary, par. *"ו"*.

21   *Keeper*, pp. 290, 296.

22   Philadelphia 1928, Chapter VI.

23   *Peirushim V'hiddushim Bayerushalmi*, I, New York 5701, dedication page. Regarding Rabbi Abraham, see Druck, p. 11.

24   *Keeper*, p. 14.

25   Ibid., p. 47.

in this regard was undoubtedly his own father, Rabbi Isaac Elias Ginzberg. As Louis Ginzberg later recalled: "My father was an unusually saintly man".[26] As a youth, Isaac had had the privilege of studying with Rabbi Israel Salanter, the founder of the *Mussar* Movement,[27] but that was clearly not the only source of his *frumkeit*. A few characteristic stories will serve to illustrate just how observant Rabbi Isaac was.

The first story was recounted by Louis Ginzberg himself over sixty years after the fact:

Since we were one of the wealthiest families in Klin, we always had a samovar ready to serve any visitor. One day the *shammash*, a man named Hirshel, came to call. He was a dirty old man with a big long beard, and I couldn't stand him. He used to take snuff, and it was always all over his beard. He used to sit in our house and yawn, and I was tremendously repelled. One day, I gathered a handful of flies, and as he yawned I threw them into his mouth. This was the first time my father beat me. He was furious with me – not because I had been naughty but because I had made Hirshel transgress six laws. Flies belong to the lowest family and there are six prohibitions in the Bible against eating them.[28]

Similarly, in Eastern Europe they still maintained the laws of *bekhorot*. As a result, first-born goats were permitted to run wild so they would develop a blemish and then be permitted for use. Young Levi and his friends once caught and rode such a goat. He was caught by his father and reprimanded for deriving benefit from a first-born goat.[29]

Rabbi Isaac's piety is further illustrated by the fact that from age thirteen on he never *davened* without a *minyan*. Thus, when he took Levi from Neustadt to the Telzer Yeshiveh in 1884 the six-day trip had to be arranged so they would find a *minyan* every morning and every evening.

26 Autobiographical Fragment, p. 9.

27 *Keeper*, p. 16; and Druck, p. 15. Louis Ginzberg devoted an entire chapter (VII) of *Students, Scholars and Saints*, Philadelphia 1928, to Rabbi Salanter which is based in part on stories he heard from his father - see ibid., notes 3, 17, and 19.

28 *Keeper*, pp. 21-22 (= Autobiographical Fragment, pp. 27-28). For the six prohibitions against eating flies, see *Makkot* 16b; Rambam's *Sefer Hamitzvot*, Lo Ta'aseh, no. 179; and idem, Ma'akhalot Assurot 2:23.

29 *Keeper*, p. 22, which is based on Epstein, p. 3. For the laws of *bekhorot*, see Yoreh De'ah 306:1, 5.

At one inn, Rabbi Isaac was able to assemble only nine; there was a tenth Jew in the neighborhood who ran another inn. But the two innkeepers were mortal enemies and had not spoken to each other for many years. Yet Rabbi Isaac was so intent, that he finally prevailed on the keeper of the inn where he had stopped to go after his competitor and to bring him to the service.[30]

On the same trip, Rabbi Isaac and young Levi arrived late one night in the town of Plunge. They had not eaten for many hours, but Rabbi Isaac refused to eat the bread at the inn in case it had been made from *hadash* or new grain, even though many authorities hold that this law is not applicable in the Diaspora.[31] The story continues:

When Rabbi Isaac discovered that the rabbi in this small community had been a classmate of his, he decided to seek him out. Young Louis tagged along since he was more hungry than tired.

The visitors found a light on in the rabbi's house, suggesting that he was still studying, and they did not hesitate to knock and seek entrance. But for a long time their knocking went unanswered. It took a considerable time for the rabbi to decide that he should take some action; then he had to wake his wife, and she in turn had to wake the maid, who then had to get dressed. No rabbi could awaken the maid! The former classmates found much pleasure in their reunion, and they were soon engrossed in a heated discussion about the passage in Maimonides that the rabbi had been studying when his unexpected visitors arrived. Young Louis helped himself to the bread, jam and tea that the lady of the house provided, but his father was too involved in the argument to take time off to eat. The argument continued until after sunrise. And then Rabbi Isaac still could not eat. He first had to say his morning prayers.[32]

---

30   *Keeper*, p. 26. According to Druck, pp. 23-24, Rabbi Isaac himself went to fetch the rival innkeeper.

31   For the laws of *hadash*, see Leviticus 23:14; Rambam, Ma'akhalot Assurot 10:1-5; Yoreh De'ah 293; and *ET*, XII, cols. 622-645. For conflicting opinions regarding *hadash* in the Diaspora, see ibid., cols. 626-628. Rabbi Isaac was no doubt following his ancestor, the Vilna *Gaon* - see Beiur Hagra to Yoreh De'ah 293, subpar. 2.

32   *Keeper*, p. 27, which is based on Druck, pp. 24-26. Regarding eating before *Shaharit*, see Orah Hayyim 89:3-4.

Rabbi Isaac's piety was not limited to *mitzvot* between man and God. When he moved to Amsterdam in the 1880s, he was faced with a problem. According to the Lithuanian custom, one may not sit down to eat on Friday night without inviting a needy Jew.[33] There were not many poor Jews in Amsterdam at that time, but he would nonetheless not sit down to eat on Friday night unless there was a poor Jew at his table.[34]

Finally, there is an episode which occurred when Rabbi Isaac was close to seventy years old. He and his wife were traveling by second class train from Bad Homburg near Frankfurt to Amsterdam. Since the carriages had upholstered seats, he stood for eight hours on the outside chance that he might violate the rabbinic prohibition of *sha'atnez* by sitting down![35]

Given these role models, it is not surprising that young Levi Ginzberg was also very pious before he moved away from home and came under the influence of secular society. This period of his life was climaxed by his sojourn at the Slobodka *mussar yeshiveh* located on the outskirts of Kovno. The students devoted two periods a day to private devotion and select pupils would spend the month of Elul at a spiritual "retreat" with Rabbi Itzile Blaser (Peterburger), one of Rabbi Salanter's successors.[36] Shortly before his fourteenth birthday, young Levi entered upon a forty-day period of silence. When his mother came to visit him in Slobodka, he refused to answer, explaining to her in writing that he was observing a period of silence. When reprimanded by a relative for disrespect to his mother, Levi said in writing that his obligations to God took precedence over *kibbud av va'em*. Needless to say, his mother was distressed and, as a result, Levi was given over to the care of his uncle, Rabbi Rashkes, as mentioned above.[37]

After Louis left home for Frankfurt, he became much more liberal. This is evident both in some of his responsa[38] and from certain episodes in his life.

---

33   In general, see Rambam, Yom Tov 6:18 and Rabbi Gedalia Felder, *Yesodei Yeshurun,* III, Toronto 5718, p. 272.

34   *Keeper,* p. 47. For other examples of Rabbi Isaac's saintly behavior, see Druck, p. 19; and Autobiographical Fragment, p. 9.

35   *Keeper,* p. 47. For this prohibition, see Leviticus 19:19; Deuteronomy 22:11; and Yoreh De'ah 301:2.

36   *Keeper,* p. 31. Regarding these phenomena and Rabbi Blaser, see *EJ,* IV, cols. 1072-1073; Druck, pp. 37-39; Dov Katz, *Tenuat Hamussar,* II, Tel-Aviv 1954², pp. 227-239; and Stampfer, *Lithuanian Yeshiva* (above, note 5), pp. 143-152. Also see Louis Ginzberg himself in *Students, Scholars and Saints* (above, note 27), pp. 157-158, 161-163, 182-184 and note 3, who describes Rabbi Israel Salanter's influence on Kovno.

37   *Keeper,* pp. 31-32; and Druck, pp. 39-42.

38   See below, note 136 and ff.

For example, he used the telephone and the elevator on *Shabbat*,[39] he once forgot to remove some guilder from his pocket before *Shabbat*,[40] he did not allow his wife Adele to wear a *sheitel*,[41] and he was willing to attend the christening of a good friend's baby at Riverside Church on a *Shabbat* afternoon.[42]

Nonetheless, Louis Ginzberg always remained an observant, halakhic Jew. This is evident both from his responsa[43] and from other episodes in his life. One summer, while still a student in Strassburg, he, together with seven non-Jewish friends, walked from Basel over the Alps to Milan. It was agreed at the outset that they would rest on *Shabbat* and whenever they arrived at a new town they would scatter in order to find a Jewish family to provide Ginzberg with a kosher meal.[44] In the summer of 1908, he arrived in Oslo on *Erev Tisha B'av* on his way to an international conference of Orientalists in Copenhagen. His first act was to look for a synagogue and a place to eat before the fast.[45] Later, in New York, the Ginzberg family used to ask the elevator man to turn their lights on and off on *Shabbat*.[46] Finally, for many years Louis Ginzberg served as the *hazzan* at *Neilah* at the Seminary synagogue. This is the way Louis Finkelstein remembered that annual event:

> A tremor, almost palpable, passed through the congregation when toward the end of the fast on the Day of Atonement he would approach the reader's desk to recite the *Neilah* service. The ancient melodies rendered with beauty and skill, combined with the stirring words and his obvious absorption in the prayers, communicated to all a profound sense of the ineffable holiness of the place and the

39 *Keeper*, pp. 214-216.

40 Ibid., p. 122.

41 Ibid., p. 245.

42 Ibid., p. 302. Ginzberg also visited the Cathedral of Ulm on at least three occasions - see *Keeper*, p. 100 (= Autobiographical Fragment, p. 19).

43 See below, notes 134-139.

44 *Keeper*, p. 55 (= Autobiographical Fragment, pp. 11-12). *Keeper* says four friends, but the Fragment says eight. For another episode involving his observance of *kashrut*, see Druck, p. 53.

45 *Keeper*, p. 98 (= Autobiographical Fragment, pp. 11-12); and cf. below, note 79, for a partial quotation.

46 Ginzberg, *My Brother's Keeper*, p. 28.

time....The modern scholar, trained in German universities, would disappear in the intimacy of the ancient service; and before the Ark of the Torah there would stand the successor to the authors of the *Sha'agat Aryeh* and the *Lebush*.[47]

Even so, despite his own observance, Louis Ginzberg felt a certain ambivalence about the path he had chosen and a certain guilt about abandoning the *frumkeit* of his father. This is evident from his letters to Henrietta Szold from Amsterdam in July, 1907, shortly after the death of his father:

I do not mourn, but suffer indescribably. My father was the embodiment of all the noble and great Rabbinical Judaism has produced and his death takes away from me the concreteness of my *Weltanschaung*. You see how selfish my mourning is. Do you remember our frequent conversations about my relation to my father as a typical case for the relation between old and young Israel? Now I never realized the depth of the chasm as I did in the last three months....But I cannot help thinking that my presence partly increased the mental suffering of my father. My father was a great admirer of mine, not in that usual foolish ways of parents but in that of a *connoisseur*, so that he never allowed me to perform the smallest service for him because it is against the (law) to be served upon by a great scholar. And yet how many a time did he suppress a sigh that his son did not become a *gaon* as he could, but a scholar! In this summer, he also realized more and more that I am not *frum*....I know my poor father did not die peacefully on account of my becoming a scholar instead of a *gaon* and on account of my bachelorship, and I can assure you that I do not regret that I did not become a Polish *gaon*, and I only mention those facts to you to show you how much our individual happiness has to do with our relation to Judaism.[48]

---

47 Finkelstein, *PAAJR*, p. liii; cf. Finkelstein, *Conservative Judaism*, p. 17. Also see Kohut, p. 22, who describes Ginzberg weeping while chanting the *El Malei Rahamim* for the victims of the Kishinev massacres; Address, p. 119; and Goldman, "Portrait", p. 13, who describe the tears which streamed down Ginzberg's face as he read *kinot* on *Tisha B'av*.

48 *Keeper*, pp. 121 and 124. The *halakhah* regarding a scholar honoring his father appears in *Yoreh De'ah* 240:7.

These feelings of self-doubt returned to Ginzberg over forty years later, in the summer of 1948. Eli Ginzberg relates:

During those days and weeks, which coincided with the anniversary of the death of his father and the Fast of *Ab*, he revealed more and more of the doubts that had begun to plague him anew about the road that he had taken in pursuing a "scientific" approach to the study of Rabbinics. Not that he had had any choice in the matter. He knew that. But he was concerned about the breach which his approach and method had caused between his father and his father's father and himself. He told me regretfully that he could never have published his Commentary [to the Palestinian Talmud] during his father's lifetime.[49]

These doubts were brought to a head by an extremely nasty anonymous letter from a former classmate which arrived that summer:

Levi of Neistadt:

Your life has been a failure. Not only have you made the Torah a *Kardom Lachpor Bo*, and you glory in the designation of Professor of Talmud and great authority on "*Halakhah*", when you know that there are scores of men superior to you in Talmud in this city; not only have you helped produce "Rabbis" who are in almost every single case *Bo'ale Niddot* and *Chot'im* and *Machti'im et Harabim*; not only are you a *Poresh Min Hatzibur* of the real *Talmidei Chachamim* who toil for the welfare of *K'lal Yisroel*; but you have cast aspersion on the Talmud and supported the *Kofrim*; you declared at least twice (once in your *Legends* and once in your *Students*, etc.) that the Rabbis of the Talmud uttered their Hagadic statements on the spur of the moment (May the Almighty forgive you), and you support Weiss[50] in his denial of the authenticity of a great part of the *Torah Sheba'al Peh*. Your works are full of echoes of the *Kofrim*. Remember your childhood hopes, and now see yourself not only as an associate of M. Kaplan (*Yimach Sh'mo*) but also in part responsible for him and for others like him. For you,

---

49   *Keeper*, p. 265.

50   I.e., Isaac Hirsch Weiss, in his classic *Dor Dor V'dorshav*, which was the frequent target of Orthodox attacks. His most vociferous opponent was Yitzhak Isaac Halevy, in his *Dorot Harishonim*, Frankfurt am Main 1918.

the authority, have undermined the faith of these *Am Ha'aretz*. May the Almighty open your eyes and help you to recant, to recall the harmful books, to repudiate your associates the *Kofrim*, and to return to the *Tzibbur* of *Talmide-Chachamim*.

Yours sincerely,
A Friend[51]

Within twenty-four hours, Louis Ginzberg came down with a severe case of shingles which left him with aggravated neuralgia which would plague him day and night for the rest of his life.[52]

Thus, Louis Ginzberg was brought up in an extemely pious enviroment and, though he remained observant throughout his lifetime, he never came to terms with his self-perceived break with piety and family tradition.[53]

The third fact which molded Ginzberg's character and achievements was his own innate genius. His intellectual abilities were truly astounding. He taught himself to read Hebrew at age five by listening to his older brother's private lessons.[54] Young Levi began studying Talmud at age six and he himself recalled what happened. His uncle, Herman Jaffe, who was also his brother-in-law,

...said he would give me ten kopeks if I would repeat by heart the first page that I had studied. I did this, but when I finished, he said he wouldn't pay me because I had made three mistakes. Whether I did make any mistakes or not I don't know, but I felt he owed me the money. He was to leave for Moscow the next day and when my sister was packing for him, I grabbed a shirt out of his suitcase and ran off with it. Since he really needed it, he was forced to pay me ten kopeks.[55]

Eli Ginzberg relates that his father knew most of the Bible by heart by age seven.[56] When Levi reached the Telzer *Yeshiveh* at age eleven, Rabbi Abel was amazed by his brilliance and put him in the middle class even though he

---

51 *Keeper*, pp. 265-266.
52 Ibid., p. 266.
53 Cf. Friedman, pp. 59-60, for a similar assessment.
54 *Keeper*, p. 18 (= Autobiographical Fragment, p. 23); and Druck, p. 17.
55 *Keeper*, p. 22 (= Autobiographical Fragment, pp. 23-24); and Druck, pp. 18-19.
56 *Keeper*, p. 35; cf. Druck p. 18; Friedman p. 59; and Ginzberg, *My Brother's Keeper*, p. 17.

was the youngest boy in the *yeshiveh*.[57] At age thirteen, as mentioned above, ten rabbis came to hear his *bar mitzvah derasha* and they, too, were amazed by his brilliance.[58] By age fourteen, he had mastered much of rabbinic literature,[59] so much so that he was able to stump Rabbi Eliezer Gordon, the head of the Telzer *Yeshiveh*, by asking him a question related to *kodashim* and *tohorot*.[60]

All of this served as a prelude to his *magnum opus, The Legends of the Jews*. Ginzberg himself relates that it contained 36,000 references, all of which he kept in his head![61] Prof. Saul Lieberman added that Ginzberg never used a Talmudic dictionary.[62] His phenomenal memory is illustrated by an episode related by one of Prof. Ginzberg's students. He was present when Prof. Zvi Diesendruck of Hebrew Union College was discussing a Hebrew document with Prof. Ginzberg. After perusing the document, Prof. Diesendruck said:

"Isn't it strange, in this document written in the rabbinic idiom of the sixteenth century, to find a phrase like this (regretfully, I do not recall the phrase!) which is found only in modern Hebrew". Whereupon your father smiled and said, "I think you are mistaken, Professor. If my memory serves me correctly, this phrase was current in the rabbinical contracts of the sixteenth century". When Professor Diesendruck expressed doubt, your father went to his bookshelves, and without a pause, picked out a slender volume, unerringly turned to a particular page, glanced at it for a moment and then said: "Here it is, look". And sure enough, in this little volume which was written in the sixteenth century, and which dealt with rabbinic contracts, the phrase was there. Professor Diesendruck shook his head and then said, "Tell me, Professor Ginzberg, when did you last have occasion to look into this book?" And with that subtle, quizzical smile which we all loved so much, your father said, "about forty years ago".[63]

---

57 *Keeper*, p. 28; and Druck, p. 31.
58 *Keeper*, p. 30; and Druck, p. 35.
59 *Keeper*, p. 35.
60 Ibid., pp. 35-36; and Druck, pp. 69-71.
61 *Keeper*, p. 23 (= Autobiographical Fragment, p. 24).
62 *Keeper*, p. 306.
63 Ibid., p. 270. Regarding Ginzberg's photographic memory, cf. Kohut, p. 20.

In light of these facts, it is not surprising that Prof. Ralph Marcus of the University of Chicago called Ginzberg "a walking encyclopedia".[64] Yet Ginzberg's brilliance was not limited to Talmud and Rabbinics. As mentioned above, he minored in Philosophy at Heidelberg. His final examination was with Kuno Fischer, a world-famous philospher. Eli Ginzberg describes the exam as follows:

> As an opening gambit, Fischer inquired where my father had spent the vacation that had just come to an end, and when my father told him that he had visited his parents in Amsterdam, Fischer said, "Good, we will talk about Spinoza". He asked my father to trace the principal elements in Spinoza's system. My father replied at length, concluding with the comment, "as you recently outlined the issues in your two-volume work on Spinoza". Professor Fischer, catching the nuance, inquired whether my father had some other ideas on the subject. My father said yes, he did, and for the next three-quarters of an hour launched into an analysis of Spinoza's system of thought in relation to medieval Jewish philosophy and to the *Cabbala*, about which Fischer knew very little and about which he had written even less.[65]

Prof. Fischer was so impressed that he voted to grant Ginzberg his degree *cum laude superate*, a distinction that had been awarded to only a handful of students during the preceding century.[66]

Ginzberg also loved mathematics. The Talmud contains many mathematical problems which his teachers would have liked to have skipped, but young Levi insisted that they all be covered thoroughly.[67] As mentioned above, when he entered the University of Berlin in 1890 he initially studied mathematics and physics. At the end of his first year, Ginzberg bumped into his former teacher, Dr. Heinemann, in Berlin who convinced him that a Russian Jew would never receive an appointment in these fields at a German university. Louis returned to Berlin and reluctantly switched to the field of Orientalia.[68] He later recalled:

---

64   *Keeper*, p. 276. Druck, p. 60, also calls Ginzberg "a living encyclopedia".
65   *Keeper*, p. 57; and cf. Druck, pp. 55-56.
66   See above, note 65.
67   *Keeper*, p. 24 (= Autobiographical Fragment, p. 26). For mathematics in the Talmud, see W.M. Feldman, *Rabbinical Mathematics and Astronomy*, New York 1978[3], Part II.
68   See above, note 11.

My decision to give up mathematics was probably the most difficult
one I ever made....I knew I had a mathematical mind, but I
certainly do not know today whether I would have been a great
mathematician. I have used the mathematical approach even in my
philological work. For instance, I have distinguished between a
theory which *can* be proved and a theory that *must* be proved.[69]

Nonetheless, Prof. Ginzberg continued to keep abreast of the latest
mathematical discoveries. When he met Einstein for the first time, they got
involved in a detailed discussion of mathematics. Some time later, Einstein
ran into his good friend, Judge Irving Lehman, who was on the Seminary
board. In all innocence, he asked Lehman why the Seminary needed a
Department of Mathematics. He had gotten the impression from their
conversation that this was Ginzberg's specialty.[70]

Around 1940, Rabbi David Aronson, one of Ginzberg's former pupils,[71]
introduced his son Raphael to Prof. Ginzberg. Raphael had just finished his
thesis in physics at Harvard on "Proton Isobars and High Energy Proton
Scattering", and they soon became involved in a discussion of mathematical
theories. On the way home, Raphael said to his father: "Daddy, that man
knows his math. He is familar with the latest scientific work."[72]

Finally, Louis Ginzberg was a gifted linguist.[73] As a child in Eastern
Europe, his first languages were Yiddish and Hebrew. In Amsterdam he
learned Dutch; indeed, one of his first articles was published in that
language.[74] Before moving to Frankfurt am Main at age fifteen, he began to
study German with a private tutor.[75] Five years later, he was supplementing
his income by writing dramatic criticism and lyric poetry for the *Frankfurter
Zeitung*. As a matter of fact, his very first book was a volume of lyric poetry

69   *Keeper*, p. 42 (= Autobiographical Fragment, p. 5).

70   Finkelstein, *Conservative Judaism*, p. 15.

71   See Nadell, pp. 35-37; *PRA* 51 (1989), pp. 295-297; and David Golinkin, "The Movement
for Equal Rights for Women in Judaism as Reflected in the Writings of Rabbi David Aronson",
American Jewish Archives (in press). It is interesting to note that he, too, was a direct descendant
of the Vilna *Gaon*, a fact which he mentioned in his "Hadran" in honor of Louis Ginzberg's
seventieth birthday, in: *PRA* 8 (1941-44), pp. 388-389.

72   *Keeper*, p. 43.

73   Ginzberg, *My Brother's Keeper*, p. 20, and *The Eye of Illusion*, p. 20, says that his father
wrote in eight languages. He apparently is referring to Hebrew, Yiddish, Dutch, German,
English, French, Italian, and Latin.

74   "Het Zionisme", *Niewe Israelitische Weekblad* 34/50 (June 2, 1899), p. 2, listed by Cohen,
p. 19.

75   *Keeper*, p. 37.

entitled *Gedichte*, published in Basel in 1894.[76] Years later, he could still recite reams of German poetry by heart.[77]

Ginzberg learned Latin in Frankfurt in order to pass the matriculation exam.[78] Years later, in 1908, this knowledge stood him in good stead. As mentioned earlier, he was in Oslo on *Erev Tisha B'av* and wanted to eat a substantial meal before the fast. Prof. Ginzberg later recalled:

> I walked through the streets of Oslo and saw a store with a sign announcing that the proprietor was named Abramsen. I didn't know then that "sen" is a typically Nordic suffix, but I went in. I asked the storekeeper if there was a synagogue around. He looked blank. At that moment his son walked in. He was about sixteen and was obviously coming home from school. He threw his books on the table, and I noticed that one of them was a Latin book. I addressed him in Latin, and he indicated that I should write it down. He got out a dictionary and I wrote down, "Are you a Jew?" He said, "No". I asked, "Is there a synagogue in town?" He said, "Yes". I asked him, "Where?" He said he didn't know exactly and asked his father. He then wrote down that his father had a friend who was Jewish and who would surely know. His father told him to take me to his friend. We found the synagogue but it was locked, so I wrote down that there must be some indication at the synagogue of where the sexton lives. The boy looked and found it and we found the sexton was a *Landsman* from Vilna. I had a very good meal with him and the following day, I went to synagogue.[79]

Prof. Ginzberg also learned Greek in Frankfurt. He later recalled learning enough Greek in fourteen weeks, including the 280 irregular verbs, to write an essay in Greek for the final exams.[80]

As mentioned above, Ginzberg studied Oriental languages and literatures with Theodore Noeldeke for four years at Strassburg. There he mastered Syriac, Mandaic, Arabic, Akkadian, and other ancient languages, as is

---

76   Ibid., p. 42; and also listed by Cohen, p. 19. He continued to write for the *Frankfurter Zeitung* in America - see *Keeper*, p. 69. Regarding his fluency in German, see ibid., p. 254.

77   Ibid., p. 40. For Ginzberg's knowledge of French, see ibid., p. 261.

78   Ibid., p. 37.

79   Ibid., p. 98 (= Autobiographical Fragment, pp. 11-12). For another story related to Ginzberg's knowledge of Latin, see *Keeper* pp. 99-100 (= Autobiographical Fragment, pp. 19-20).

80   *Keeper*, p. 38 (= Autobiographical Fragment, unnumbered pages, dated January 25).

evident in his philological studies.[81] In 1928-29, while on sabbatical in Israel, he used to read the daily papers in Arabic,[82] and in 1948 he was still able to quote a ninth-century Arabic proverb.[83] He also studied Egyptology and was able to discuss the etymology of the word "pyramid" half a century later.[84]

Last but not least, Louis Ginzberg mastered the English language. When he stepped off the boat in New York in August, 1899,[85] he did not know a word of English. Yet, within three years he had written over four hundred articles for the *Jewish Encyclopedia*. His general love of language is epitomized by the following paragraph written to his friend, Fred Fassett, in 1948:

Amicissimus:

The first language I was taught was Hebrew and, as you well know, the Semitic languages do not permit any *septempedalian* forms of a noun. The best I could do to match your *caritativissimus* is a *quintopedalian*. I assure you, however, that this shorter form wishes to express the same feeling for which you used a longer form.[86]

These, then, are four factors which molded Ginzberg's intellect and personality: his education, his ancestry, his pious upbringing, and his innate genius. With this background in mind, we may proceed to examine his academic career and achievements.

Louis Ginzberg came to America in 1899 at the invitation of Rabbi Isaac Mayer Wise, who assured him that he would be appointed a preceptor in biblical exegesis at Hebrew Union College in Cincinnati. But when he arrived in New York, his brother handed him a letter to the effect that the Board of Governors had not confirmed the recommendation of President Wise that he be appointed to the faculty. We now know that Wise himself changed his

81   See, for example, his "Beitraege zur Lexikographie des Aramaischen", which appeared in three installments (Cohen, nos. 52, 93, and 100), and his notes to the *Arukh* in Samuel Krauss, ed., *Tosafot Le'arukh Hashalem*, Vienna 1937, pp. 417-437.

82   *Keeper*, p. 205.

83   Ibid., p. 313. Also see below, Chapter VI, No. 10, note 8, for his knowledge of Antar, an ancient Arabic saga.

84   *Keeper*, p. 318.

85   Ibid., p. 59.

86   Ibid., p. 299; *amicissimus* = good friend; *septempedalian* = seven-foot, i.e., seven-syllable; *caritativissimus* = great affection; and *quintopedalian* = five-foot i.e., five-syllable.

mind for two different reasons. On the one hand, he had heard that Ginzberg was an adherent of higher criticism of the Bible, which Wise opposed. On the other hand, he was afraid that Ginzberg was too observant and would try to influence Hebrew Union College students in that direction.[87]

Undaunted, Louis Ginzberg soon found employment at the *Jewish Encyclopedia*, as mentioned above. This arrangement, however, was precarious and offered little financial security.[88] Thus, he jumped at the chance when Solomon Schechter offered him the position of Professor of Talmud at the newly re-organized Jewish Theological Seminary in 1902.[89] It is there that Ginzberg made his academic and spiritual home for the next fifty-one years. It is there that he played a major role in training and ordaining 650 rabbis.[90]

Yet he did not limit himself to teaching. First of all, he played a major role in selecting the Seminary's faculty. It was he who discovered Israel Friedlander, H.L. Ginsberg, Saul Lieberman, Shalom Spiegel, and Abraham Joshua Heschel and brought them to the Seminary.[91] Secondly, Prof. Ginzberg played a major role in the development of Jewish Studies in the United States. He was one of the founders of the American Academy for Jewish Research in 1919 and served as its President until 1947.[92] In that capacity, he served as the financial midwife for many of the major projects in Jewish Studies at the time. He raised substantial sums of money for classics such as Kasovsky's concordances of the *Mishnah* and *Tosefta*, Lewin's *Otzar Hageonim*, and Schreiber's *Meiri*.[93] He also did his best to assist and further the careers and publications of friends and colleagues such as Arnold Ehrlich, Solomon Gandz, Hyman Enelow, Harry Wolfson, and Ralph Marcus.[94] He

---

87 *Keeper*, pp. 59-64, which is based on Harry Mayer, "What Price Conservatism?"; and cf. Druck, pp. 57-59.

88 *Keeper*, pp. 65-79; Autobiographical Fragment, pp. 44-46; Druck, pp. 59-63; and see now: Shuly Rubin Schwartz, *The Emergence of Jewish Scholarship in America: The Publication of the Jewish Encyclopedia*, Cincinnati 1991, pp. 55-56, 62, 68-70, 75-77, 88-90, and Index.

89 *Keeper*, pp. 80ff.; and Druck, p. 67.

90 *Keeper*, p. 5.

91 Ibid., pp. 84, 139-142; and Finkelstein, *Conservative Judaism*, pp. 15-16.

92 *Keeper*, pp. 165ff.

93 Ibid., pp. 173-179. The LGA are filled with fundraising letters which Prof. Ginzberg sent to congregational rabbis. He even raised money to help publish Rabbi Shlomo Gorenchik's (later Goren, Chief Rabbi of Israel) *Hayerushalmi Hameforash* to *Berakhot*, which finally appeared in 5721 - see LGA, Box 1, "G" file.

94 *Keeper*, pp. 64-65, 176-177, 184-185, 272-273, 275-279, and 288. Finkelstein, *PAAJR*, p. lii, emphasizes Ginzberg's help to scholars "whether in research, in subsistence, or in funds for publication of their books".

frequently worked behind the scenes to help a younger colleague succeed. For example, he urged George A. Kohut to bring Gershom Scholem to the Jewish Institute of Religion in New York for a semester.[95] Scholem was eventually invited in 1938 and the result was his now classic *Major Trends in Jewish Mysticism.*[96]

Thirdly, Prof. Ginzberg played an important role in the founding of the Institute for Jewish Studies at the Hebrew University. Beginning in 1922, he maintained an active correspondence regarding the nature and goals of the Institute and eventually succeeded in having the American Academy for Jewish Research designated the official American Consulting Committee for the Institute.[97] In 1928-29, he spent his one and only sabbatical occupying the Chair of *Halakhah* at the fledgling Institute which gave it some badly-needed prestige.[98] Finally, in December of 1933, Ginzberg participated in the Hartog Commission which recommended reforms in the administration of the Hebrew University and ways of absorbing a large number of German Jewish scholars who had just then been excluded by Hitler from German universities.[99]

In light of Prof. Ginzberg's scholarship and academic activities, it is not surprising that he was honored on numerous occasions.[100] Yet, the greatest honor was his selection by Harvard University as one of the sixty scholars to recieve an honorary doctorate on the occasion of its tercentenary activities in 1936. The citation calls him "a profound scholar of the laws and legends in talmudic literature".[101]

Before turning to Ginzberg's responsa, it remains for us to briefly outline Prof. Ginzberg's major contributions to "Jewish Law and Lore".[102] He devoted the bulk of his scholarly output to three fields: *Aggadah*, the Palestinian Talmud, and Geonica. In the realm of *Aggadah*, his *Legends of the Jews* remains unsurpassed. As Prof. Boaz Cohen wrote in 1938:

---

95   *Keeper*, p. 183.
96   See Gershom Scholem, *Major Trends in Jewish Mysticism*, New York 1961, in the preface, where Scholem thanks Stephen S. Wise but not Ginzberg. It could be that he did not know of Ginzberg's role in having him invited. For an interesting vignette regarding the genesis of *Major Trends*, see Moshe Davis, *Hashanah Hame'azevet*, Jerusalem 1993, pp. 30-31.
97   *Keeper*, pp. 191-202.
98   Ibid., pp. 202-206.
99   Ibid., pp. 208-211.
100 Ibid., pp. 289, 327, 330.
101 Ibid., pp. 259-262.
102 This is the title of a collection of Prof. Ginzberg's essays reprinted posthumously in Philadelphia, 1955.

Suffice it to say that this work represents the greatest single contibution to the study of the *Agada* within a century. Its significance lies not only in its unsurpassed collection of materials from all out-of-the-way sources, but also in the fact that it paves the way for numerous monographs in the various fields of theology, folklore, superstition, customs and legends.[103]

In addition to his *Legends*, Ginzberg devoted his dissertation to *Die Haggada bei den Kirchenvätern*, one of the first attempts to collate the numerous *midrashim* quoted by the Church Fathers.[104] In 1928, he published volume I of *Ginzei Schechter*, which contains over forty *midrash* fragments from the Cairo Genizah.

In the realm of Talmud, Ginzberg authored two of the classic works on the Palestinian Talmud. His *Seridei Yerushalmi*, published in 1909, was the first, and remains the only, volume of *Genizah* fragments of the Palestinian Talmud.[105] Many of the variant readings from this work were later incorporated into the Vilna edition of the Palestinian Talmud in 1922, though without any acknowledgement of Ginzberg's efforts, a fact which he deeply resented.[106] His *Peirushim V'hidushim Bayerushalmi* on *Berakhot*, Chapters I-V, remains one of the only scientific commentaries to the Yerushalmi. Louis Ginzberg himself viewed it as his "lifework", of more importance than any of his earlier scholarly efforts.[107]

In the realm of Geonica, Ginzberg made three major contributions. The first volume of *Geonica*, published in 1909, remains the only English language introduction to the gaonate and to the halakhic literature of the *geonim*. The second volume of *Geonica*, as well as *Ginzei Schechter*, Volume II, contain over one hundred *Genizah* fragments of geonic responsa and commentaries, early Karaite works, and the writings of Pirkoi ben Baboi.[108]

---

103 *Legends*, VII, p. ix. Also see Druck, pp. 76-78; Goldman, "Portrait", pp. 4-7; Arzt, "Authentic Judaism", pp. 158-159; Finkelstein, *Conservative Judaism*, p. 13; Nadell, p. 99; and Shalom Spiegel, "Introduction", pp. xix, who adds that Ginzberg's *Legends* "easily rank as the most significant work on Jewish lore ever published in the English language".

104 See above, note 14.

105 See Druck, pp. 89-92; and Lieberman, *Mehkarim*, p. 612.

106 See above, note 105; and *Keeper*, p. 120.

107 Druck, p. 92 and Finkelstein, *Conservative Judaism*, p. 14. For a very favorable review, see S. Zeitlin, in: *JQR* 33 (1942-43), pp. 83-88 and 419-434, who calls the work "epoch-making" and compares Ginzberg to Rashi and the *Gaon* of Vilna.

108 Druck, pp. 93-100.

Lastly, Ginzberg made important contributions to a number of other areas of Jewish studies such as biography, lexicography, and the Zadokite Fragment which was later determined to be one of the Dead Sea Scrolls.[109] However, there is one area of Ginzberg's scholarly output that has received scant attention: his responsa.[110] Although Lieberman, Finkelstein, and others have heaped praise upon his responsum regarding the use of unfermented wine for Jewish ceremonies which was published in 1922 (III, 16),[111] and others made posthumous use of his final responsum regarding mixed pews in the synagogue (III, 9),[112] most of Ginzberg's responsa were never published and have remained "as an unturned stone". As a result, nine years ago I took upon myself the task of systematically searching for his responsa.[113] I am pleased to say that I have learned the truth of the Talmudic dictum, "If one says that I have labored and found - believe him" (*Megillah* 6b), for I have found all or part of over one hundred of the responsa that Ginzberg wrote over a period of forty years (1913-1953).[114] They are now incorporated in the present volume.

Before we explain Professor Ginzberg's motives for writing responsa, it is worth stressing the general significance of this discovery. In 1986, Chancellor

109 For biography, see *Students, Scholars and Saints* (above, note 27). For lexicography, see above, note 81. For the Dead Sea Scrolls, see *Eine unbekannte judische Sekte*, New York 1922, and *An Unknown Jewish Sect*, New York 1976; and cf. Druck, pp. 103-105.

110 His responsa are mentioned by Louis Finkelstein, *PAAJR*, p. li; Druck, p. 118; and especially by Eli Ginzberg, in: *Keeper*, Chapter 10, and Seminary Family, p. 125. Herbert Parzen, *Architects*, accuses LG of "devoting himself completely to scientific scholarship" (p. 143), withdrawing "to his study" (ibid.), and using "his prestige through the Law Committee of the Rabbinical Assembly to maintain the status quo" (p. 145). These assertions are thoroughly disproved by this entire volume. Parzen further states that Ginzberg "assumed the chairmanship of the Committee on Jewish Law of the United Synagogue" in 1916 (p. 149) but both the name of the committee and the date are inaccurate (see below, after note 128). Finally, Parzen knows of only one responsum by Ginzberg - that on grape juice written in 1922 (pp. 151-152). Thus Parzen's account is totally inaccurate, and it is unfortunate that later scholars were misled by his article - see Kraemer, pp. 153-154, 165; and Nadell, pp. 100-101.

111 Saul Lieberman, *Mehkarim*, pp. 613-614; Finkelstein, *PAAJR*, p. li; and idem, *PRA*, p. 172. All references in parentheses refer to the chapter and responsum number in this volume.

112 It was published in *Conservative Judaism* 11/1 (Fall, 1956), p. 39. It should, however, be emphasized that that letter gives only a partial picture of his views on the subject - see III, 9 for the full correspondence as well as ibid., 7-8 for his earlier responsa.

113 On the importance of publishing Conservative responsa, see my remarks in *An Index of Conservative Responsa and Practical Halakhic Studies: 1917-1990*, New York 1992, p. 4 and note 12.

114 A few of the items are obviously not responsa, but have been included in this book because they indicate Prof. Ginzberg's active involvement in the halakhic life of American Jewry. I have also included a number of his popular articles (e.g., IV, 1-2) for the same reason.

Ismar Schorsch of the Jewish Theological Seminary of America made the following remarks:

> The...Seminary...inherited from Breslau a tradition that abdicated the responsiblity to provide halakhic guidance for its own day. The twin model of the Rosh Yeshiva and the German professor combined to raise the academic at Breslau or New York above the level of a mere *moreh hora'ah* or halakhic decisor. No discrepancy was felt between devoting the bulk of the curriculum to the study of rabbinic literature and ignoring the halakhic needs of the contemporary community.[115]

I myself concurred with this thesis in a lecture delivered in 1989 which was later published, though I pointed out in a footnote that there were two exceptions to this rule - Prof. Louis Ginzberg and Prof. Boaz Cohen, who were both active members of law committees of the Conservative Movement and who both published a number of responsa.[116] However, in light of the discovery of over one hundred responsa by Prof. Ginzberg, and hundreds of responsa written by Prof. Cohen and his law committee which I hope to publish in the near future, we can now state the following:[117]

The professors at the Rabbinical Seminary of Breslau may not have engaged in *pesak halakhah*,[118] but at the Jewish Theological Seminary of America there were professors in every generation who wrote responsa and gave halakhic guidance to the public at large: Prof. Louis Ginzberg in the first generation; Prof. Boaz Cohen[119] and Dr. Michael Higger[120] in the second generation; Profs. Seymour Siegel and Edward Gershfield[121] in the

---

115 *PRA* 48 (1986), p. 83.

116 *Et La'asot* 2 (5749), p. 38 (= *Conservative Judaism* 46/3 [Spring, 1994], pp.37-38).

117 Prof. Schorsch and I arrived at this conclusion together in a discussion we had in Jerusalem on July 23, 1992.

118 Though they, too, may have written responsa which were never published.

119 Cohen served on the Committee on Jewish Law from 1932-48; he was Secretary in the 1930s and Chairman from 1940-48. Regarding his halakhic activity, see Edward Gershfield, *PRA* 33 (1969), p. 174; and Nadell, pp. 53-54; and my article cited below in note 123.

120 Higger was not actually a member of the Seminary faculty, but he lived in the dormitory for over thirty years and therefore had a tremendous influence on generations of rabbinical students. He served on the Committee on Jewish Law and its successor, the Committee of Jewish Law and Standards (CJLS), from 1932 until his death in 1953, including periods in which he was the Secretary of the Committee. Regarding his halakhic activity, see *PRA* 17 (1953), p. 39, and cf. *PRA* 40 (1978), p. 169.

121 Siegel served on the CJLS from 1964 until his death in 1987 and was Chairman from 1973-80. Gershfield served on the CJLS from 1961-63 and 1968-84.

third generation; and Profs. Joel Roth and Mayer Rabinowitz[122] in the fourth generation. This conclusion has important implications for the Seminary's self-image both in the past and in the present.[123]

Another interesting feature of Prof. Ginzberg's responsa is that all of them, except for two (III, 16 on unfermented wine and V, 1 on artificial insemination), were written in English.[124] There are, of course, precedents from the past for writing responsa in languages other than Hebrew: in Aramaic (the *geonim*), in Arabic (the *geonim*, the Rif and the Rambam), in Yiddish (R. Israel Isserlein),[125] and in German (Orthodox and Reform rabbis in the nineteenth century).[126] However, Prof. Ginzberg is one of the first to write most of his responsa in English.[127] By so doing, he set the norm for all subsequent Conservative law committees in the United States which wrote and continue to write most of their responsa in English.[128]

It is also worth noting the breakdown of the questioners. Of the 93 questioners, thirty-six were rabbis, twenty-four were laymen, seventeen were unidentified Jews, and sixteen were Christians. We can deduce three general

122 Roth and Rabinowitz have served on the CJLS since 1978 and 1979 respectively, and Prof. Roth was the Chairman from 1984-92. My thanks to Rabbi Daniel Nevins, former Secretary of the Committee on Jewish Law and Standards, who supplied most of the dates in notes 121-122.

123 See my article "The Influence of Seminary Professors on Halakhah in the Conservative Movement: 1902-1968" in : Jack Wertheimer, ed., *A History of the Jewish Theological Seminary of America*, New York, 1997 (in press), in which I explore the thesis stated here.

124 It should be pointed out that his English responsa were typed on a typewriter by his secretary and were therefore preserved in the form of carbon copies. On the other hand, he does not seem to have had a Hebrew secretary so there may have been additional Hebrew responsa which he wrote by hand and of which no copy was preserved.

125 See *Leket Yosher*, Yoreh De'ah, Berlin 1904, pp. 19-20, for a complete responsum in Yiddish. For Yiddish words, sentences, and entire paragraphs within the responsa literature, see Zalman Shazar, *Orei Dorot*, Jerusalem 5731, pp. 239-319 (my thanks to Dr. Elhanan Reiner for this reference) and Yosef Bar-El, *A Yiddish-Hebrew Dictionary to the Responsa of the Great Rabbis of Ashkenaz*, Ramat Gan 5737 (Hebrew).

126 For Orthodox responsa, see Rabbi David Zvi Hoffman, *Melamed L'ho-il*, II, Frankfurt am Main 1927, no. 113 and elsewhere. Also see Rabbi Salomon Abraham Trier, ed., *Rabbinische Gutachten über Beschneidung*, Frankfurt am Main 1843, an entire collection devoted to the defense of circumcision against its Reform detractors. (My thanks to Dr. Ira Robinson for the second reference.) For Reform responsa, see Peter Haas, in: Walter Jacob, ed., *Liberal Judaism and Halakhah*, Pittsburgh 1988, pp. 39, 43-52, who describes two collections in detail.

127 For a survey of Reform responsa in English beginning in 1891, see Haas, ibid.; Walter Jacob, ed., *American Reform Responsa*, New York 1983, pp. xvi-xviii; and idem, in: Walter Jacob and Moshe Zemer, eds., *Progressive Halakhah: Essence and Application*, Tel-Aviv and Pittsburgh 1991, pp. 87-105.

128 For proof of this assertion, see the responsa listed in my Index (note 113 above).

conclusions from these figures: (1) They indicate active halakhic interest among both rabbis and laymen; (2) about one-sixth of Prof. Ginzberg's responsa were written to non-Jews! This is undoubtedly the first time in history that a *posek* wrote formal responsa to questions posed by Christians; and (3) aside from the Orthodox community, the general public in the United States - Conservative and Reform rabbis, laymen and Christians - saw in Ginzberg the highest halakhic authority or the most prominent halakhic figure who should be turned to in order to solve disputes between rabbis and rabbis and between rabbis and congregants or to determine the authoritative "Jewish position" on the question under discussion.

Lastly, Prof. Ginzberg set a precedent which has been maintained until today in the Conservative Movement. In a speech delivered at the United Synagogue convention in 1917 (I, 2), he proposed setting up a "Committee on the Interpretation of Jewish Law...to consist of five members learned in the law...to advise congregations and associates of the United Synagogue in all matters pertaining to Jewish law and custom." This suggestion is surprising. Did Prof. Ginzberg really need assistance? After all, he could have rendered halakhic decisions alone and, in fact, he apparently wrote all of the responsa of that Committee by himself![129] Perhaps he wanted to include other qualified rabbis in the halakhic process or he may have wanted to curb criticism that one rabbi is the *posek* for an entire movement. On the other hand, he may have been influenced by the Reform movement which set up a similar law committee in 1911.[130] Regardless of his reasons, this practice of relying on law committees has persisted until today.

Now that we understand the general significance of this discovery, we should explain why Prof. Ginzberg decided to become an active *posek* and to write responsa. We need not speculate in answering this question since he himself explained why in the above-mentioned speech (I, 2). He laments the breakdown of halakhic authority in modern times, especially in the United States:

It is seen here in the appalling religious anarchy of the Jews where 'Every man does that which is right...in his own eyes' [Judges 17:6]....In no other country where some respect for legitimate authority still lingers among the Jews, are the religious conditions as chaotic as in ours. *Geonim* by the grace of butchers, Rabbis by

---

129 The reports of that Committee listed in the Appendix to this volume point to this conclusion, which is also emphasized by Rabbi Burstein in item No. 8, ibid., p. 1.
130 See the literature cited above, note 127.

the authorization of successful wholesale dealers or manufacturers, theologians by the acclamation of still more successful bankers or lawyers and Academicians with degrees from nowhere, are only found in our country. Such a condition will exist as long as lack of authority will continue.[131]

Prof. Ginzberg goes on to say that the true solution would be to appoint an "authoritative council...for the interpretation of Jewish law". But this is not feasible at present since the United Synagogue allows its members a good deal of autonomy so there would be no way for the committee to enforce its authority. He therefore recommends the formation of a Committee on the Interpretation of Jewish Law as explained above. Indeed, this Committee was appointed in 1917 and Prof. Ginzberg served as its Chairman until 1927, when it was dissolved and replaced by the Committee on Jewish Law of the Rabbinical Assembly.[132]

It is worth asking: if *pesak halakhah* was so important to Louis Ginzberg, why did he not publish his numerous responsa? There is no clear-cut answer to this question, but it should be stressed that he *did* publish or summarize part of the responsa of the Committee mentioned above in articles and annual reports which appeared in the *United Synagogue Recorder* and elsewhere in the 1920s.[133] As for the majority of his responsa, which were never published, he may have refrained from doing so because they were written in English, as explained above. This hypothesis is supported by the fact that he did publish his lengthy responsum in Hebrew on unfermented wine (III, 16). On the other hand, perhaps he did not want to take time away from his research projects and he was therefore satisfied with writing the responsa and did not take the time to edit them for publication. Finally, he may have been hurt by the decision to set up an

---

131 Epstein, p. 3, also stresses Ginzberg's emphasis on "the authority of the law". For a similar lament regarding American Jewry penned by Rabbi Jacob David Wilowsky in Chicago in 1904, see Abraham Karp, in: Arthur Chiel, ed., *Perspectives on Jews and Judaism: Essays in Honor of Wolfe Kelman*, New York 1978, p. 228.

132 The latter committee was formed in September 1927 - see *PRA* 3 (1929), pp. 57, 151. Ginzberg, *My Brother's Keeper*, p. 25, states that Prof. Ginzberg resigned from the Committee after concluding that most of the members were unqualified to participate in such deliberations. It seems much more likely that the Committee was reorganized in order to exclude him - see below, note 134.

133 See the reports of the Committee listed in the Appendix to this volume.

alternative law committee in 1927 and may have therefore stopped publishing his responsa.[134]

By examining the entire corpus of Louis Ginzberg's responsa it is possible to ascertain the general outlines of his approach to *halakhah*. First of all, he was quite strict with regard to liturgical and synagogue-related issues, and here he was no doubt influenced by his pious, Lithuanian upbringing described above.

In 1945, Mordecai Kaplan and three of his colleagues published the controversial *siddur*, *The Sabbath Prayer Book*. In June of that year, the Orthodox *Agudass Harabonim* excommunicated Kaplan and one of the young Orthodox rabbis burned a copy of the *siddur* in public. In October of that year, Louis Ginzberg - along with Alexander Marx and Saul Lieberman - published a "Declaration" in a number of Hebrew and English periodicals, in which they both opposed the *herem* and the burning of the *siddur*, but, at the same time, condemned the *siddur*. They lamented the abbreviation of the *Shema*, the changes in the *Amidah*, the insipid Introduction, the editing of the chapters of the Psalms and of *Lekha Dodi*, and more, and suggested a much more conservative alternative:

We do not deny the need of the hour to attract the youth to the synagogue. But the royal road to the synagogue is the house of study and the dissemination of the Torah. However, as a temporary measure, it is proper to improve the externals of the *siddur*, to append at the conclusion of the service prayers in the vernacular, and even to repeat the *Shema* in English after the service.... (II, 5)

In 1946, the Rabbinical Assembly published the *Sabbath and Festival Prayer Book* edited by Rabbi Morris Silverman. The latter sent Professor Ginzberg a copy along with a dedication thanking him for his assistance. He replied:

I deeply appreciate your inscription in which you thanked me for my counsel and assistance. I wish, however, my counsel would have

134 See the remarks of Rabbi Israel Goldstein in *PRA* 1 (1927), p. 36, who said: "It is one thing to address a She'ela and to receive a Teshuba from an authority. It is quite another thing to be able to discuss...them in the company of peers *and not in the dumbfounding presence of a towering superior*". He is no doubt referring to Prof. Ginzberg who was present at that convention - see ibid., p. vii. Regarding the power struggle which led to the reconstruction of the law committee in 1927, see "The Influence of Seminary Professors" (note 123 above), notes 68-75.

been more effective. Then the prayer book would have had less omissions and commissions of which I cannot approve. (II, 6)

In 1949, Prof. Ginzberg was asked to explain the phrase *mei raglayim* in *Pittum Haketoret*. At the beginning of his reponsum, he remarks:

Let me first tell you that your letter gave me a good deal of pleasure for the reason that I often have been asked by congregations whether this or that part of the Prayer Book might be left out. I am, therefore, particularly happy to see that you have in your congregation, people whose interest is in understanding the Prayer Book and not in changing it. (III, 5)

Lastly, in 1947, he reluctantly allowed one section of mixed pews in Chizuk Emunah synagogue in Baltimore in order to prevent the breakup of the synagogue, but, after the fact, he wrote to the rabbi of the synagogue (in Hebrew):

I am having second thoughts as to whether I should have interfered in the dispute in your synagogue. For you know that I am not one of those who likes "new things", and I have a special aversion to changes in the customs of the synagogue. (III, 9)[135]

Eli Ginzberg writes in *Keeper of the Law* that his father "hesitated at change" and elsewhere he speaks of his "growing conservatism".[136] These assessments bear revision in light of the responsa being published below. Aside from liturgy, where he was clearly a conservative, Prof. Ginzberg seems to have judged each case on its own merits and frequently arrived at a lenient decision. He permitted late Friday evening services as was customary in many congregations (III, 15). He disproved the approach of the Magen Avraham and allowed the use of grape juice for *kiddush* in order to prevent the desecration of God's Name caused by rabbis who became rich from selling wine during Prohibition (III, 16). He permitted the use of a radio that had been turned on before *Shabbat* (III, 17). He asserted that peas and green beans are not *kitniyot* and may be eaten on Passover (III, 19). He allowed the

135 For other strict rulings with regard to synagogue-related issues, see III, 4, 11, 12 and IV, 4-5.
136 *Keeper*, pp. 241-242, and Seminary Family, p. 125; and cf. Address, p. 114 and Parzen's opinion quoted above in note 110.

alteration of synagogue melodies, ignoring the opposition of the Maharil and the Rema (III, 21). He allowed the conversion of a gentile woman who was already married to a Jew and permitted the woman to immerse in the *mikveh* while wearing a loose-fitting bathing suit (IV, 10). He allowed children in mourning to attend music classes and assemblies at their public schools (IV, 26). He forbade performing weddings on *Hol Hamoed* as decreed by the *Mishnah*, but allowed it in a case where the groom was a soldier setting sail for combat in Europe (V, 7-8). He also helped Prof. Boaz Cohen prepare an "agency appointment" which would enable a *bet din* to write a *get* should a husband disappear in battle (V, 13). Finally, he allowed women to serve on synagogue boards despite the opposition of the Rambam to women holding public office (VI, 7).

On the other hand, Prof. Ginzberg occasionally prohibited something not because it is technically forbidden by Jewish law, but in order to preserve the "spirit of the law" or to prevent improper behavior such as *marit ayin* or *hillul hashem*.[137] He therefore prohibited a cantor - in this case, Richard Tucker - from working simultaneously as an opera singer because of *marit ayin*. Or, as he put it:

There is no law prohibiting a rabbi from appearing in a cabaret, but do you think that any congregation would seriously consider having a cabaret singer as a rabbi?...I am...sure that people would find it quite strange to see their cantor one day recite the *Neilah* prayer and the following day, sing a love duet with some lady.... (III, 1)[138]

Similarly, Prof. Ginzberg prohibited building a synagogue on *Shabbat* with the help of a gentile contractor even though, technically, one can find a way around this prohibition:

But I object to any synagogue group taking such advantage of legal loopholes....[We must consider] the effect of such conduct on all beholders, Jews and Gentiles alike....My decision, therefore, becomes not a matter of the letter, but of the spirit, and I urge the questioners not to allow this obvious desecration of our day of rest. (III, 14)

---

137 "Appearance of impropriety" and "the desecration of God's Name", respectively.
138 Ginzberg's reference to *Neilah* is apparently not accidental - see above, note 47.

He permitted the United States Army to require a Jewish soldier to cut off his beard with a scissor so that observant Jews would not use this as an excuse to avoid army service (IV, 8). Finally, and for the very same reason, he allowed a *Kohen* to serve in the U.S. army despite the fear of coming into contact with dead bodies (IV, 24).

Prof. Ginzberg was also concerned about the unity of the Jewish people. On two occasions he expressed opposition to the use of an organ in the synagogue and in both cases he explained that, in addition to the halakhic problems involved, he is afraid that American Jewry will cut itself off from world Jewry and therefore this innovation should be avoided (I, 4 and III, 18).

In his classic portrait of his beloved ancestor, the Vilna *Gaon*, Prof. Ginzberg quotes him as saying: "Do not regard the views of the *Shulhan Aruk* as binding if you think that they are not in agreement with those of the Talmud".[139] It is obvious from many places in his reponsa that Louis Ginzberg took this advice to heart. In his opinion, the *halakhah* is determined by the Talmud and the *rishonim* and not by *midrashim*, later customs or the *aharonim*. In his responsum on artificial insemination, Prof. Ginzberg writes at the end of the question: "And the rabbi who asked me replied at length on the basis of the *aharonim*...but since it has always been my practice to base myself on the words of the Talmud and *rishonim*, I have avoided quoting his words and discussing them" (excerpt from the Hebrew section of this volume). This approach is echoed at the end of the same responsum: "All of the above is sufficient to prove that we have not found a peg in the Talmud or in the *Rishonim* on which to hang a lenient ruling in this serious matter (ibid., par. 14). Previously, in the same responsum, he rejects using the *Alpha Beta d'ven Sira* as a halakhic source: "Yet, in any case, one cannot decide *halakhah* on the basis of this legend...for we have learned in Yerushalmi Peah 2:6 [fol. 17a]...'One does not learn [*halakhah*]...from *haggadot* [= legends or non-legal material]'. If they said this about Talmudic *haggadot*, how much moreso is it true regarding a legend from *Alpha Beta d'ven Sira* which is a late work..." (ibid., par. 6). And he continues: "After we have seen that it is difficult to rely on a legend from *Ben Sira* in such a serious matter...let us see what the [Babylonian] Talmud has to say [on our subject] because 'we are dependent on its word'".

A similar approach lies behind his permission for a man to marry a woman whose name is identical to his mother's: "There is nothing in Jewish law prohibiting a man to marry a woman whose name is the same as the

---

139 *Students, Scholars and Saints* (above, note 27), p. 141.

man's mother" (V, 2). This particular custom is based on the Testament attributed to Rabbi Judah the Pious and from there it passed to *Pithei Teshuvah* and other authorities,[140] but in Prof. Ginzberg's opinion these sources are clearly not "Jewish law". His lengthy responsum on the use of unfermented wine for *kiddush* is based primarily on the Talmud and the *rishonim* and opposes the opinion of the *Magen Avraham* by a careful analysis of the *rishonim* (III, 16). Indeed, after refuting the *Magen Avraham* by quoting three earlier works on customs, he explicitly states: "And even though these three are worthy of being relied upon even when there is no emergency, it is not the way of the Torah to decide *halakhah* according to books of customs in cases where we have strong support in the words of the *rishonim*..." (ibid., Hebrew version, beginning of par. 3). Finally, he states in his address of 1921: "The Talmud, though never promulgated as a code of law, became the standard of Jewish law....After the Talmud, there is no authority in the real sense of the word..." (I, 4).[141]

Louis Ginzberg's responsa are also a good source for biographical data about him. For the most part, they do not reveal many new biographical details, but they do confirm some of the facts and characteristics described by Eli Ginzberg and others.

The responsa reflect his poor health towards the end of his life,[142] lively sense of humor,[143] pride in his roots,[144] respect for his teacher, Theodore Noeldeke,[145] desire to help other scholars with their personal problems,[146] and willingness to answer any question no matter how foolish.[147] Prof. Ginzberg also appears here as a passionate defender of his people, willing to engage in lengthy apologetics against anti-Semites.[148] One is impressed anew by the breadth of his knowledge and by his prodigious memory.[149] One is

---

140 See the literature listed in note 2 of the responsum.

141 For additional statements by Prof. Ginzberg stressing the centrality of the Talmud, see *Keeper*, p. 219 and the undated address listed below in the Appendix, No. 9, p. 6.

142 See III, 9 in the final Hebrew letter; IV, 9; VI, 10 (end), 16, 17, 18 (end); and cf. *Keeper*, pp. 257-259, 266-268, 305, 316, etc.

143 VI, 10, 13. Regarding his sense of humor, see Epstein, p. 2; Finkelstein, *Conservative Judaism*, p. 16; and *Keeper*, pp. 18ff., 44-45, 100-101, and 267, which is based in part on the Autobiographical Fragment, pp. 17, 34-35.

144 III, 10; IV, 3; and cf. above, note 15ff.

145 VI, 10; and cf. *Keeper*, pp. 45-46, 269; and Address, p. 111.

146 III, 10; and cf. above, notes 93-96.

147 IV, 9; VI, 4, 10, 15. Finkelstein, *Conservative Judaism*, p. 15, commented upon "his uncanny patience with everyone..."; and cf. Kohut, p. 22.

148 IV, 1, 2; VI, 1, 2.

149 III, 16; V, 6; VI, 1, 6, 14, 15; and cf. above, notes 54-86.

touched by his ability to write a responsum which is truly pastoral in tone.[150] Lastly, Prof. Ginzberg is one of the first *poskim* whose responsa are clearly influenced by Jewish *Wissenschaft* both in form as well as in content.[151]

Many scholars have shown that the responsa literature is a goldmine for historians and sociologists.[152] The responsa of Louis Ginzberg are no exception. They supply the historian with much important data about American Jewry between the years 1913-53. Interestingly enough, "there is nothing new under the sun" and many of the questions asked then continue to be asked today.

Prof. Ginzberg was asked about the sale of a synagogue[153] synagogue construction on Shabbat,[154] women in the synagogue,[155] the organ,[156] art in the synagogue,[157] the direction of the synagogue,[158] dances in the synagogue basement,[159] and the dual use of a synagogue basement as a *beit midrash* and social hall.[160] He received many enquiries about intermarriage,[161] apostates,[162] and unaffiliated Jews.[163] Then, as now, American Jews were greatly influenced by non-Jewish funeral customs and Prof. Ginzberg attempted to combat this phenomenon.[164] Many Jews served in the United States Army and thus he dealt with halakhic problems arising in connection

---

150 IV, 25.

151 In form, some of his responsa read like scientific articles - see especially III, 16. Regarding content, see III, 4, 5, 7-9; IV, 4-5; V, 6, and much of Chapter VI. It is interesting that Lieberman, *Mehkarim*, pp. 613-614, praises Ginzberg's responsum on grape juice (III, 16): "...that even one of the *yeshivah* students who have nothing to do with *Hokhmat Yisrael* would see in him one of their own...". Indeed, that responsum contains features that would be appreciated by a *yeshivah* student, but, in general, its questions, sources, structure, contents, and style all bear the indelible impression of *Hokhmat Yisrael*.

152 See B.D. Weinryb, in: H. J. Zimmels et al., eds., *Essays Presented to Chief Rabbi Israel Brodie*, London 1967, pp. 399-417, and the literature cited there; and Haym Soloveitchik, *The Use of Responsa as Historical Source*, Jerusalem 1990 (Hebrew). There are over fifty historical monographs based primarily on the responsa literature.

153 III, 12-13; VII, 3.

154 III, 14.

155 III, 7-9; VI, 7; VII, 3.

156 I, 4; III, 18; VII, 6.

157 IV, 4-5.

158 III, 4.

159 VII, 1.

160 III, 11.

161 IV, 9, 10; VII, 10.

162 IV, 6, 12, 14.

163 VI, 5.

164 IV, 16-22; VII, 2.

INTRODUCTION 33

with World War One, World War Two, and the Korean War.[165] Then, as now, there were tensions between the need for a *get* and a civil divorce.[166] Then, as now, there were ignorant rabbis or rabbis who openly transgressed Jewish law.[167] Then, as now, there were laymen who did not trust their rabbi and therefore addressed their questions to a higher authority.[168] Finally, these responsa teach us that the term "Conservative Judaism" was in use as early as 1924.[169]

In conclusion, we have uncovered here a new facet of Prof Louis Ginzberg's contribution to Jewish scholarship. This discovery contributes much to our understanding of his approach to Jewish law, his biography, the history of Conservative *halakhah*, and the history of American Jewry in the first half of the twentieth century. But, above all, this volume of responsa places before us a model of a leading Talmudic scholar who did not hide in his ivory tower but rather came down to his people and guided it through the complicated halakhic problems of modern times. This is, in my opinion, a model worthy of admiration and emulation.

* * *

It is said of Rabbi Judah ben Beteira that he lived in Netzivin in Babylonia yet his net was spread over Jerusalem (*Pesahim* 3b). I was reminded of that saying many times as I worked on this book, which is based primarily on archival sources in New York, via long distance from Jerusalem. On two occasions (September 1991 and 1992) I searched through the LGA myself, yet I could not have located and photocopied many of the responsa in this volume without the help of three people: At my request, Dr. Baila Shargel compiled a preliminary list of the responsa in the LGA in the course of researching a book about Prof. Ginzberg's relationship with Henrietta Szold. David L. Cohen photocopied most of the responsa in that list. Finally, Rabbi Nechama Goldberg did all subsequent photocopying and searched for the answers to the questions in Chapter VII.

---

165 World War One: IV, 24; VII, 5; World War Two: III, 6; V, 13; Korean War: IV, 8.
166 V, 10-12.
167 IV, 9, 23; V, 7, 8; VII, 4, 8.
168 III, 1, 7, 9; IV, 23; V, 3.
169 "Conservative Synagogues": III, 22 (in 1933); "Orthodox Conservative Congregation" (sic!): IV, 23 (undated); "Conservative Judaism": V, 7 (in 1924); "Conservative rabbis": V, 8 (after World War Two). Regarding the term "Conservative Judaism", see Rosenblum, *Conservative Judaism*, pp. 3, 20, 22, 32, and the literature cited there.

The initial typing of the responsa was done by Chana Golinkin, Philipa Bakall, Advah Hayam, Irit Babad, Dalya Lev, and Chaya Golinkin. My secretary, Ellen Cohen, typed my notes and carried out all subsequent revisions with infinite patience and good cheer. Yisrael Hazzani edited the Hebrew section of the book, Hani Davis edited the English section, and Donny Finkel, together with the staff at Leshon Limudim, typeset the book and saw it through the press. Dr. Shmuel Glick, director of Seminary publications in Israel, oversaw the publication of the book.

Drs. Mayer Rabinowitz and Jerry Schwarzbard and the other librarians at the Jewish Theological Seminary of America facilitated my access to the Rare Book Room. Dr. David Novak referred me to Rabbi Alan Iser, who very graciously furnished some of the material on artificial insemination as well as his own paper on the subject.

Last by not least, I benefited greatly from the assistance of Prof. Eli Ginzberg, Chancellor Ismar Schorsch, and Prof. Ivan Marcus. Prof. Ginzberg showed me just what it means for a son to honor his father after his death (see *Kiddushin* 31b). He paid for some of the initial expenses, shared his own personal recollections, and was a constant source of encouragement from July, 1987, when I first wrote to him until the book was completed. Chancellor Schorsch arranged for the payment of photocopying expenses and was an excellent sounding board for my thoughts on the meaning and importance of Louis Ginzberg's responsa. Prof. Ivan Marcus also offered me sound advice and accepted the book for publication when he was Vice Chancellor for Academic Affairs at the Seminary.

To all those who assisted me in the preparation of this book I say: גדול״ המעשה יותר מן העושה״ - "Greater is he who helps others do than he who does [a *mitzvah*] himself" (Bava Batra 9a).

In conclusion, it is clear that this book does not contain all of the responsa ever written by Prof. Louis Ginzberg. This is amply proven by the questions in Chapter VII to which the answers have yet to be found. On the other hand, the extensive searches made for some of those answers[170] seem to indicate that most of those answers are no longer extant. In any case, as we learn in *Pirkei Avot* (2:16), ours is not to finish the task. We can therefore conclude by saying, תם ולא נשלם.

David Golinkin
The Seminary of Judaic Studies
Jerusalem
Rosh Hodesh Elul 5756

170 VII, 1, 3, 5, 12.

THE RESPONSA

I. General Statements Regarding Jewish Law

No. 1 An Excerpt from "Zechariah Frankel" (1901)   39

No. 2 "Report, Committee on Authoritative Board for the
Interpretation of Jewish Law" (1917)   41

No. 3 An Excerpt from the "Address of the Acting President"
(1918)   44

No. 4 An Excerpt from the "Report of the Committee on the
Interpretation of Jewish Law" (1921)   46

No. 1 An Excerpt from "Zechariah Frankel"[1] (1901)

Source: Louis Ginzberg, *Students, Scholars and Saints*, Philadelphia 1928, pp. 205-207

...Frankel never deduced the authority of the Law from the plenary inspiration of the Bible as the word of God, and the foremost representative of the positive-historical school next to Frankel was a man who, upon this point, may fairly be stylized almost radical. Neither for Frankel nor for Graetz[2] was Law identical with Bible; but in the course of time, whether for weal or for woe, in the development of Jewish history, the former became the specifically Jewish expression of religiousness. The dietary laws were not incumbent upon us because they conduce to moderation, nor the family laws because they further chastity and purity of morals. The law as a whole is not the means to an end, but the end in itself; the Law is active religiousness, and in active religion must lie what is specifically Jewish. All men need tangible expression to grasp the highest ideas and to keep them clearly before them, to say nothing of the ordinary masses for whom abstract ideas are merely empty words. Our need of sensuous expressions and practical ceremonies brings with it the necessity for the material incorporation of religious conceptions, and various peoples have given them varying forms. The Law is the form in which the Jewish spirit satisfies this need. In the precepts, which are the dramatic representations of the inward feelings, Judaism found a material expression of its religious ideas; through them its abstractions became realities and in them the essential needs themselves, reverence and recognition of the divine will, were expressed. Every form became thus spiritualized and living, bearing within itself a lofty conception.

We may now understand the apparent contradiction between the theory and practice of the positive-historical school. One may for instance conceive of the origin and idea of Sabbath rest as the Professor of Protestant theology at a German University would conceive it, and yet minutely observe the smallest detail of the Sabbath observances known to strict Orthodoxy. For an adherent of this school, the sanctity of the Sabbath reposes not upon the fact that it was proclaimed on Sinai, but on the fact that the Sabbath idea found for thousands of years its expression in Jewish souls. It is the task of the historian to examine into the beginnings and developments of the numerous customs and observances of the Jews; practical Judaism on the other hand is not concerned with origins, but regards the institutions as they have come to be. If we are convinced that Judaism is a religion of deed, expressing itself in observances which are designed to achieve the moral elevation of man and give reality to his religious spirit, we have a principle in obedience to which reforms in Judaism are possible. From this point of view, the evaluation of a law is independent of its origin, and thus the line of demarcation between biblical and rabbinic law almost disappears....

1   Zechariah Frankel (1809-75) was the founder of the positive-historical school in Germany which was the forerunner of the Conservative Movement in the United States. See LG's article and *EJ*, VII, cols. 80-82.

2   Heinrich Graetz (1817-90), the noted historian, taught at Frankel's Jewish Theological Seminary at Breslau - see ibid., cols. 845-850

No. 2 "Report, Committee on Authoritative Board for the Interpretation of Jewish Law" (1917)

Source: *USAAR* 5 (1918), pp. 43-45[1]
Secondary Reference: Cohen, p. 27, no. 53

Afternoon Session
Report, Committee on Authoritative Board for the Interpretation of
Jewish Law (1917)
Professor Louis Ginzberg, Chairman

Democracy, we are often told, is the main characteristic of our age. In discussing today the advisability of forming an authoritative council for the interpretation of Jewish Law, we therefore lay ourselves open to the accusation that we are out of touch with modern progress of thought. But democracy and authority are contrasts to him who sees only the surface of things without being able to penetrate below it. He who knows how to distinguish externals from substance knows that democracy, far from being opposed to authority, insists on the subordination of the individual to authority, and that no democracy is possible without the willingness of the individual to submit to restraints put upon him by wise tradition, sound precedents and the accumulated wisdom of the past. The fight of democracy is not for lawlessness against authority but for authority against those who usurp it. Judaism, being truly democratic, always insisted upon authority. "Yes", we hear some people say, "upon the authority of the law but not upon the authority of men." Now it is true that we who stand on the firm ground of historical Judaism must insist on the immutability of the Torah. But the conception of the Torah as a transcendental automaton which, once wound up, would go on forever without any human intervention, is from a philosophical point of view, absurd, and from a theological one, dangerous. Neither the physical nor the spiritual world presents us with any instance of absolute fixities or absolute mobilities and to eliminate human agency from the workings of Jewish Law would lead to Karaism of the worst kind.

What constitutes Jewish Law is the interpretation and application of the words of the Torah by an authoritative body. This is best illustrated by the following legend [*Bava Metziah* 59a-b]: In the great dispute between the famous *Tanna* Rabbi Eliezer ben Hyrcanos and the majority of scholars concerning certain questions of law, a heavenly voice pronounced its agreement with the views of this *Tanna*. His colleagues, however, were not at all awed by it and insisted on deciding the law in accordance with the view of the majority. Elijah, who often reveals to the saints the heavenly mysteries, told one of them that the Lord, blessed be His name, rejoicing at the decision of the scholars, exclaimed: "My children have prevailed over Me."

But what need is there to refer to legend, if history supplies us with abundant proof that as long as Judaism led a normal life, it never lacked organized authority for the interpretation and regulation of Jewish law. Who has not heard of the great Sanhedrin, the highest authority for religious and civil law, during the first and second commonwealths of the Jews? The decision of this supreme court was binding upon all Jews who are admonished in the Torah never to turn from the laws passed by this authoritative body "To the right hand nor to the left" [Deut. 17:11]. The Rabbis, commenting upon these words of scripture, remark: "Even if the Sanhedrin tells you that the right is left or that the left is right, you must heed them."[2] The destruction of Jewish independence in 70 C.E. did curtail the functions of the great Sanhedrin, but it nevertheless continued in a modified form to exist for many centuries as the supreme seat of authority for all Israel. The academies in Palestine and in Babylonia, [and] later those in European countries, took the place of the old Sanhedrin after it was abolished by the hand of an unmerciful enemy. Not till very recent times did the last mark of organized authority disappear from among the Jews. The havoc caused by the disappearance of organized authority was nowhere as ruinous as in our country. It is seen here in the appalling religious anarchy of the Jews where "Every man does that which is right" - and sometimes even that which is not right - "in his own eyes" [Judges 17:6] as well as in the intellectual anemia prevailing here. This is not said in the spirit of querulous fault-finding but rather in that of a sympathetic physician who often gives his diagnosis with a heart full of pity and sorrow. In no other country where some respect for legitimate authority still lingers among the Jews, are the religious conditions as chaotic as in ours. *Geonim* by the grace of butchers, Rabbis by the authorization of successful wholesale dealers or manufacturers, theologians by the acclamation of the still more successful bankers or lawyers and Academicians with degrees from nowhere, are only found in our country. Such a condition will exist as long as lack of authority will continue.

The correct diagnosis of an evil is a necessary step to its cure but not yet the cure itself. The committee appointed by your president to consider the advisability of forming an authoritative council under the auspices of the United Synagogue for the interpretation of Jewish law, while deploring the lack of an organized authoritative body and recognizing that the formation of such a Council would be very beneficial to the religious life of American Jewry, is fully aware of the great, for the present insurmountable, difficulties lying in the way of the realization of such a plan. Of course, I do not refer to the attacks from "the right and the left" to which the United Synagogue would lay itself open by forming an authoritative Council. There is very little in life worth doing for which one would expect only praise and no blame. The main difficulty is that the United Synagogue as it is composed at present permits a good deal of autonomy to its members, the individual Congregations, and the first condition for the successful working of an authoritative body is its power to enforce its authority. We fervently hope that the time will come, and this not in the far future, when the United Synagogue will be of such a uniform nature that the formation of an authoritative Council for the interpretation of Jewish Law will be feasible and practical.

For the present, your Committee begs to recommend the formation of a standing Committee of the United Synagogue to be known as the Committee on the Interpretation of Jewish Law. Such Committee, to consist of five members learned in the law, shall have the function to advise congregations and associates of the United Synagogue in all matters pertaining to Jewish law and custom. A good deal of religious anarchy prevailing at present among us is due to the fact that congregations as well as individuals do often apply for guidance to irresponsible persons who lack the necessary knowledge, even the religious seriousness required in deciding questions of law and custom. An advisory body for the interpretation of Jewish law, as recommended by your committee, would be the first step in the direction of the formation of an authoritative Council which will have to come sooner or later. We hope that of this advisory board will be said "And though thy beginning was small, thy end shall greatly increase" [Job 8:7].[3]

1   This report was presented at the United Synagogue convention in 1917 and published in 1918.
2   Sifre Devarim, par. 154, ed. Finkelstein, p. 207.
3   This recommendation was debated and approved - see *USAAR* 5 (1918), pp. 45-51.

No. 3 An Excerpt from the "Address of the Acting President" (1918)

Source: *USAAR* 6 (1919), pp. 23-24[1]
Secondary Reference: Cohen, p. 27, no. 54

...The Executive Council, acting on your recommendation at the last
year's convention, has formed a new Standing Committee, to be known as
the Committee on the Interpretation of Jewish Law. It is certainly one of the
most grievous misfortunes of modern Judaism, that the cobbler will not stick
to his last and will imagine himself to be able to judge all things in heaven
and on earth. We Jews glory in the fact that we have no privileged class or
caste which is the sole possessor of truth. A promise is made in Scripture to
Israel that "all His children shall be taught of the law so that great shall be
the peace" [Isaiah 54:13]. As long, however, as this promise is not fulfilled,
we must be guided in questions of law and doctrine by those who know.
Judaism never taught that "ignorance is bliss" or that "the majority cannot
be wrong." The conception that in religious matters anyone however
ignorant can judge for himself, is the direct denial of the old Jewish maxim:
"The ignorant cannot be pious" [*Avot* 2:5]. Abraham, our Sages say, has
been called in Scriptures "The Hebrew," literally, the one on the other side,
by which name he is described as the man standing on one side with the rest
of the world opposing him on the other side.[2] Yet Abraham was right and
the rest of the world wrong. A majority vote of a Board of Directors of a
synagogue is, after all, a negligible quantity when it is in opposition to the
vote of historical Judaism with its myriads of Saints and thousands of Sages.
We have a vast inheritance but no inventory of our treasures transmitted to
us by the past. The sorting, distributing, selecting, harmonizing and
completing can only be done by experienced hands.

In my native country they used to tell the following anecdote. The famous
scholar Rabbi Izel of Slonim once came across a large body of *Chassidim*
leading their rabbi in a triumphal procession. Knowing the chassidic rabbi to
be rather an ignoramus, Rabbi Izel asked him by which merits he claimed to
be a leader in Israel. The other answered: "Master, one grain of wheat is like
the other, but only that is holy which is set aside as *terumah*; I am a holy man
since the people declared me to be one." "You," replied Rabbi Izel, "do not
know the law given in the *Mishnah* which reads,'*Terumah* set aside by people

of unbalanced mind or minors is not holy'" [Terumot 1:1]. We in our days must guard against authorities set up by irresponsible people or who owe their existence to sophomoric wisdom....

1   This speech was delivered at the United Synagogue convention in 1918 and published in 1919.
2   Genesis Rabbah 41:8, eds. Theodor-Albeck, p. 414.

No. 4 An Excerpt from the "Report of the Committee on the Interpretation of Jewish Law" (1921)

Source: LGA, Box 17, "Questions and Answers" file = *Exponent*
Excerpt: *Keeper*, p. 231

...It is useful to turn from time to time from the abstract to the concrete in order to steady and purge our mental vision. Accordingly, I thought it advisable to preface the report of the Committee on the Interpretation of Jewish Law with a few concrete examples of its work. And now let me add a few remarks on the principles guiding the members of the Committee in their work.

The members of your Committee never considered it to be within their function or within their power to improve or change the law. The nature of law requires it to be certain, uniform, and free from personal bias. This, however, in no way justifies the assumption that the human element can be eliminated altogether from the law. The conception of law as a sort of transcendental automaton which once wound up will go on forever without any human intervention, is one of the vainest illusions. The Torah is declared in Scripture to be perfect, but not complete, and it is the pride and glory of Rabbinic Judaism to have prevented the Torah from becoming a mere relic of antiquity, but to have made it the well of life [from] which all Israel in all future ages would be able to draw. We strongly object to Karaism in any form or shape, even if it claims to be based on the *Shulhan Aruk*. But, let me add, a merchant who would start taking stock while his store is in flames would be adjudged insane. For Jews standing upon the ground of historical Judaism to start a revision of Jewish law at the time of the present conflagration of the house of Israel, would be short of suicide.

I do not think I should be accused of vainglory if I say that the history of [the] development of Jewish law is a matter to which I [have given] as much thought and time as any living person today. Yet in the entire expanse of Jewish history spreading over thousands of years, I fail to find any instance of Jewish law having been changed by promulgations issuing from a committee room.[1] Laws have been modified, changed and even abrogated, yet by whom and how? The first requirement of dealing with law is Authority. Leaving aside the theological question of the infallibility of Jewish law - which, by the way, was strongly developed under the influence of [a] philosophy which is extremely realistic, that of Aristotle - the facts are as follows: The Bible became the basis of Jewish Law at the Constitutional Assembly held by Ezra and Nehemiah [Nehemiah, Chapter 8]. The Talmud, though never promulgated as a code of law, became the standard of Jewish law through the authority invested in the great academies of Palestine and Babylonia. After the Talmud, there is no authority in the real sense of the word. Does American Israel have men invested with an authority comparable to that of the authors of the Talmud? Name the men who could impose their opinion as law on others! This is authority. It is of no use to permit a person to take the car to the synagogue on *Shabbos*, as long as you cannot stop him from taking [it] to his shop, still less close the shop. It is easy to make people work on the second day of the Festivals, but difficult to make them rest on the first. And another question: Are you prepared to create a Judaism sui generis, an American Judaism? The great failure of Reform - and today there are very few even among Reformers who would be audacious enough to proclaim it a success - was partly due to the fact that it was provincial. Reform Judaism was an attempt of a certain section of German Jewry to adapt itself to its political and cultural surroundings, but it was never an expression of the soul of כלל ישראל.

Reform was imported to America as many another German article. Any attempt to adapt Judaism to modern life must and will fail as long as it is only an expression of the Jews of a certain country and not of World Jewry. A great part of Jewry, great in number and in intellect, is at present cut off from all communication with the world outside of Russia. Are we to embark on an undertaking of such magnitude as the modification of Jewish law without them? Let me give you a concrete illustration. The question of the organ in the synagogue was as hotly debated at the time of the beginning of the Reform movement in Germany as it is today in some parts of the country. I am at present not interested in the question of whether Jewish Law sanctions the organ or not. But far more important is the fact that the question of the organ does not and will not exist in those countries where the non-Jewish mode of worship knows of no instrumental music. In other words, the Jews living in Greek-Catholic Russia and in Mohammedan countries would never admit the necessity or even the desirability of the organ in the synagogue.[2] You, who I am firmly convinced, have outgrown provincial Judaism and are working for United Israel, could never solve the question of Jewish Law satisfactorily as long as you approach it from the point of view of American Jewry. For the present, we cannot but say "Hands Off" of Jewish Law!...

1   He probably means a committee room of laymen. Rabbis frequently issued takkanot "from a committee room".
2   Regarding the organ, see below, Chapter III, No. 18 and Chapter VII, No. 6.

II. Liturgy

No. 1 A Statement about Variations in Jewish Liturgy (1918)   51

No. 2 The Reference to the Restoration of Sacrifices in the
    Musaf Service (1923)   52

No. 3 A Prayer for the Government (1927)   54

No. 4 A Prayer for Divine Aid (1944)   56

No. 5 An Excerpt from "A Declaration (Regarding
    Dr. Mordecai Kaplan's *Siddur*)" (1945)   58

No. 6 A Reaction to Rabbi Silverman's Notes on the
    Siddur (1941) and to his *Siddur* (1946)   64

No. 1 A Statement about Variations in Jewish Liturgy (1918)
Source: "Address of the Acting President", *USAAR* 6 (1919), p. 20[1]

...Variety, a famous writer remarks, is a great source of beauty and richness in the system both of nature and religion, provided the true foundation is preserved throughout. Judaism always abhors the identity of the narrow, absolute, formal kind. Alexandrian Judaism differed from Palestinian during the second commonwealth, and so did Spanish Judaism differ from Franco-German Judaism in the twelfth century. Nothing illustrates better the liking of the Jew for variation than the history of the prayer book. Within the brotherhood of the Jewish people, the prayer book in Hebrew became the symbol of a closer and more intimate bond of union, fostered and guarded no less loyally and tenaciously than the grand treasures of the race. At the same time, the prayer book became a species of religious dialect which varied with locality and which communities could not forget or abandon even in exile. The secret of this seeming contradiction lies herein, that the unity of type must not be pressed to the extent of denying all variations. Judaism always recognized the fact that there are greater truths and lesser truths, catholic truths and individual opinions, forms which are essential and forms which are not essential. The policy of the United Synagogue is to apply this principle effectively....

1   This address was delivered at the United Synagogue Convention in 1918 and published in 1919.

No. 2 The Reference to the Restoration of Sacrifices in the Musaf Service (1923)

Source: "Current Aspects in Judaism", *USR* 3/2 (April, 1923), pp. 2-3
Excerpt: *USAAR* 11 (1923), p. 12
Secondary Reference: Alexander Marx, "Report of the Prayer Book Committee", *USAAR* 15 (1927), pp. 28-29

...As I am now dealing with matters related to the Synagogue, I shall state in this connection the opinion rendered by your Committee [on the Interpretation of Jewish Law] on a very important question addressed to it by the Committee on the Prayer Book. I must beg your permission to preface this statement by a few remarks which I deem necessary for a correct understanding of the matter.

Of all the institutions that man has ever devised, the one with the longest continuous history is the Synagogue. It is, at the same time, the most original contribution of the Post-Biblical Jew towards religion. Judaism, Christianity and Islam are unthinkable without this institution created by the religious genius of the Jew. The originality of this contribution by the Jew consists chiefly therein that, as far as we know, there had never been in the world's history any form of Congregational worship till the Synagogue appeared. And this characteristic of the Synagogue is best expressed in its liturgy, which is the prayer of the individual Jew for all Israel. The memories of the past and the hopes for the future make up the main body of our liturgy, which, accordingly, may well be described as a national treasure. The mutilation of the Prayer Book is for us an act of vandalism comparable with the worse than wanton destruction of an historical monument.

"To maintain the Traditional character of the liturgy with Hebrew as the language of prayer" and "To preserve in the service the reference to Israel's past and the hope for Israel's restoration" is one of the chief aims of the United Synagogue.[1] That the Prayer Book which the United Synagogue is preparing for publication will preserve in all essentials the traditional character, you have the solemn promise of the Committee on the Prayer Book as well as that of the Committee on the Interpretation of Jewish Law.

The United Synagogue always maintained the view that variety is a great source of beauty and richness in the system, both of nature and religion, provided the true foundation is preserved throughout.

It therefore allows liberty of interpretation as to the meaning of its formulated principles. Our principles are broad, but not flat. There is no room in the United Synagogue for those who do not strongly believe in the restoration of Israel. But the reference to the restoration of sacrifice in the Prayer Book is one of the many ways of expressing our hope for Israel's restoration and not the only one. In view of the fact that some individuals and Congregations have conscientious scruples about perpetuating the petition for the restoration of sacrifices, though they cling with heart and soul to the great aspiration of Israel, your committee gave its consent to the following proposition: That the United Synagogue publish an edition of the Traditional Prayer Book without any changes whatsoever, without, however, opposing another edition by those Congregations who desire to change a word or two in the Musaf Service, by which change the petition for the restoration of sacrifice would be transferred to an historic reference to same; the latter edition to contain on the title page, in addition to the general title, "Festival Prayer Book, published by the United Synagogue of America", the note: "Adapted to the use of certain conservative Congregations by Rabbi...", who would assume personal responsibility of same.[2] I may add that by retaining the historical reference to the sacrificial system of the Temple, the great religious importance of this ceremony is emphasized. Its very purpose was to combat the wrong idea of sacrifice and establish the right. It was to oppose the idea of sacrifice as offerings to appease the gods and establish in a very material way the Jewish ideal of a man's surrender of himself to God.

1   "Preamble to the Constitution of the United Synagogue", reprinted in: Mordechai Waxman, ed., *Tradition and Change*, New York 1958, p. 173.
2   This proposal was carried out. See Marx, who writes: "At the request of certain conservative congregations, Dr. Jacob Kohn was authorized to prepare a special edition in which some references to the sacrificial service are changed into historical reminiscences instead of prayers for the future". The title page of the copy of the *Festival Prayer Book*, New York 1927, which I examined at the JNUL in Jerusalem contains the following sentence: "Adapted for the use of certain conservative congregations by Doctor Jacob Kohn".

No. 3 A Prayer for the Government (1927)

Source: *Festival Prayer Book*, New York 1927, p. 201. Reprinted in:Morris Silverman, ed., *Sabbath and Festival Prayer Book*, New York 1946, p. 130

Secondary References:

1. *Festival Prayer Book*, p. iv; *Sabbath and Festival Prayer Book*, p. 387
2. Cohen, p. 31, no. 78

Background Reading:

1. Shem Tov Gaguine, *Keter Shem Tov*, Kaidan 1934, pp. 417-420
2. Barry Schwartz, "*Hanoten Teshua*': The Origin of the Traditional Jewish Prayer for the Government", *HUCA* 57 (1986), pp. 113-120
3. Simeon Singer, "The Earliest Jewish Prayers for the Sovereign", *Transactions of the Jewish Historical Society of England* 4 (1899-1901), pp. 102-109

תפלה בעד הממשלה

אלהינו ואלהי אבותינו

קבל נא ברחמים את-תפלתנו בעד ארצנו וממשלתה. הרק את-ברכתך על הארץ הזאת על נשיאה שופטיה שוטריה ופקידיה העוסקים בצרכי צבור באמונה. הורם מחקי תורתך הבינם משפטי צדקך למען לא יסורו מארצנו שלום ושלוה אשר וחפש כל-הימים. אנא ה' אלהי הרוחות לכל-בשר שלח רוחך על כל-תושבי ארצנו וטע בין בני האמות והאמונות השונות השוכנים בה אהבה ואחוה שלום ורעות. ועקר מלבם כל שנאה ואיבה קנאה ותחרות. למלאות משא נפש בניה המתימרים בכבודה והמשתוקקים לראותה אור לכל-הגוים.

וכן יהי רצון שתהא ארצנו ברכה לכל-יושבי תבל ותשרה ביניהם רעות וחרות וקים במהרה חזון נביאיך לא "ישא גוי אל-גוי חרב ולא-ילמדו עוד מלחמה" [ישעיהו ב:ד] ונאמר "כי כולם ידעו אותי למקטנם ועד גדולם" [ירמיהו לא:לג]. אמן.

Prayer for the Government[1]

Our God and God of Our Fathers

We invoke thy blessing upon our Country, on the government of this Republic, the President of these United States and all who exercise just and rightful authority. Do thou instruct them out of thy Law, that they may administer all affairs of state in justice and equity, that peace and security, happiness and prosperity, right and freedom may forever abide in our midst.

Unite in loyal and loving accord all the inhabitants of our country, so that men of all races and creeds may find in their common citizenship the bond of a true brotherhood which shall banish all hatred and bigotry and shall safeguard the ideals and free institutions which are our country's pride and glory.

May this land under thy Providence be an influence for good throughout the world, uniting men in peace and freedom and helping to fulfill the vision of thine inspired Seers: "Nation shall not lift up sword against nation, neither shall men learn war any more" [Isaiah 2:4]. Amen.[2]

1   This translation is copied from the *Festival Prayer Book* and was presumably done by the editor, Dr. Maurice Farbridge, or by one of the members of the Prayer Book Committee. The translation found in the *Sabbath and Festival Prayer Book* contains quite a few variations.

2   The final verse is missing from the English translation.

No. 4 A Prayer for Divine Aid (1944)

Source:

1. תפילה לימי המלחמה, *A Prayer for Divine Aid (to be recited during the war)*, The Jewish Theological Seminary [New York 1944], 7 pp.[1]
2. Hebrew text reprinted in *Hadoar* 23/33 (June 30, 1944), p. 626
3. English text reprinted in Women's League *Outlook*, 15/1 (September, 1944), p. 1 (copy in LGA, Box 14, "Articles Published" file) and again in Keeper, pp. 310-311

Secondary References:

1. Cohen, p. 35, no. 108
2. *PRA* 8 (1941-44), p. 377.
3. A letter of thanks from Chaplain Joseph Shubow, Sept. 29, 1944, LGA, Box 11, "Shubow" file[2]

Background Reading:

1. ר' יוסף אונא, בית הכנסת, ג/8-10 (אייר-אב תשי"ח), עמ' 329
2. יהודית באומל, קול בכיות: השואה והתפילה, רמת-גן, 1992, עמ' 134-136

אלהינו ואלהי אבותינו

קבל נא ברחמים את תפילתנו בעד ארצנו וממשלתה. הרק את ברכתך על הארץ הזאת על נשיאה שופטיה שוטריה ופקידיה העוסקים בצרכי ציבור באמונה. הורם מחוקי תורתך הבינם משפטי צדקך למען לא יסורו מארצנו שלום ושלוה, אשר וחפש כל הימים.

אנא ה' אלוהינו אשר בידך נפש כל חי, ורוח כל בשר איש, באנו לפניך בתפלה בצוק העתים, כאשר המו גוים מטו ממלכות ותמוג ארץ, ומפילים אנחנו תחנונינו על כל אלה, אשר חרפו נפשם למות על שדי מלחמה בעד ארצנו האהובה. עשה עמהם כאשר הבטחת, "כי תעבור במים אתך אני, ובנהרות לא ישטפוך, כי תלך במו אש לא תכוה, ולהבה לא תבער בך" [ישעיהו מג:ב]. תשלח ידך ממרום ותושיעם ימינך, והשיבם בשלום לארצם ולמשפחותיהם ולבתיהם, ששים ושמחים כי כלה עריץ, ורשעים עוד אינם.

ועוד אנחנו עומדים בתפלה, יהי רצון מלפניך למנוע כל חלי וכל מכה מצבאותינו והמכים והנפצעים מידי אויביהם אתה ה' תסעדם על ערש דוי, ותשלח להם מהרה רפואה שלמה כי רופא נאמן ורחמן אתה.

על הגבורים אשר הערו נפשם למות יהמו נא רחמיך. תהי מנוחתם תחת כנפי שכינתך ותצרר את נשמותיהם בצרור החיים, כי עמך מקור חיים.

וכן יהי רצון מלפניך שתהא ארצנו ברכה לכל יושבי תבל, ותשרה ביניהם רעות וחרות, וקים במהרה חזון נביאך, "לא ישא גוי אל גוי חרב ולא ילמדו עוד מלחמה" [ישעיהו ב:ד], ונאמר, "כי כלם ידעו אותי למקטנם ועד גדולם" [ירמיהו לא:לג]. אמן.

Our God and God of Our Fathers

We invoke thy blessing upon our Country, on the government of this Republic, the President of these United States and all who exercise just and rightful authority. Do Thou instruct them out of Thy Law, that they may administer all affairs of state in justice and equity, that peace and security, happiness and prosperity, right and freedom may forever abide in our midst.

O God, Our Father, in Thy hand is the soul of all Life and the spirit of all flesh. In these times of distress, we come before Thee in prayer.

When nations roar, sovereignties totter, and the earth crumbles, we bring before Thee our humble supplications in behalf of all who expose their lives on the fields of battle in defense of our beloved country. Do Thou unto them as Thou hast promised saying, "When thou passest thru the waters I will be with thee, and thru the rivers they shall not overflow thee; When thou walkest thru the fire thou shall not be burned, neither shall the flame kindle upon thee" [Isaiah 43:2]. Send Thy power from on high; may Thy right hand be their salvation. Return them to their land, to their homes, and to their loved ones, rejoicing in the knowledge that tyranny is destroyed, and that doers of evil are no more.

May it be Thy will to protect our armies from all manner of pestilence and disease.

We pray for those who have been wounded in performance of their duty. Do Thou, O Lord, support them on their bed of illness that they may rise with greater strength and with a stronger Faith in Thee, for Thou art a true and merciful Healer.

Have compassion, O Lord, on our heroic dead, who have valiantly made the supreme sacrifice. May they rest under the wings of Thy glory and their souls be bound in the bond of life.

May this land under Thy Providence be an influence for good throughout the world, uniting men in peace and freedom and helping to fulfil the vision of Thine inspired Seers. "Nation shall not lift up sword against nation, neither shall men learn war any more" [Isaiah 2:4]. Amen.[3]

1   This pamphlet is very rare. The Seminary library and the JNUL in Jerusalem do not possess copies. I used the copy in the LGA, Box 16, "Prayer for Divine Aid" file.

2   The letter says, among other things: "I write to inform you that as an Army Chaplain I have found your 'Prayer for Divine Aid' a source of superb religious inspiration. I read your prayer to to my G.I. congregation which numbered over five hundred and packed the Chapel beyond its normal capacity both at the *Kol Nidre* Service and at the *Yizkor* service. I read the prayer in Hebrew and in English translation. I received a most excellent reaction from the men who were present. I told them something about you and your work." For biographical details about Rabbi Shubow, see below, Chapter IV, No. 9, note 1.

3   The final verse is missing from the English translation.

No. 5 An Excerpt from "A Declaration (Regarding Dr. Mordecai Kaplan's Siddur)" (1945)

Source:
1. *Hadoar* 24/39 (October 5, 1945), pp. 904-905 = *Bitzaron* 13 (Tishrei-Adar, 5706), pp. 208-211
2. English translation: *The Jewish Forum* 29/1, (January, 1946), pp. 7-8, 16

Secondary References (in chronological order):
1. *Der Morgen Journal,* June 13, 1945, pp. 1, 3 (in Yiddish)
2. *The New York Times,* June 15, 1945, p. 11
3. *Hadoar* 24/31, June 22, 1945, p. 685
4. Ibid., 24/33, July 13, 1945, pp. 739-740
5. *PRA* 9 (1945), pp. 28-29
6. *A Challenge to Freedom of Worship: A Statement,* Jewish Reconstructionist Foundation; New York 1945, 30 pp.
7. Zvi Matt, *Niv* 7/4 (Sivan-Tammuz, 5705), pp. 15-16
8. *The New York Times,* September 6, 1945, p. 12
9. Rabbi Herman Halperin, LGA, Box 4, "Finkelstein" file (a letter protesting this "Declaration")
10. *Keeper,* p. 144
11. Nadell, p. 152
12. Jack Wertheimer, "Kaplan vs. 'The Great Do-Nothings': The Inconclusive Battle over 'The New Haggadah'", *Conservative Judaism* 45/4 (Summer, 1993), pp. 20-37
13. Ira Eisenstein, Letter to the Editor, ibid., 46/2 (Winter, 1994), p. 94

Comment: In 1945, Rabbi Mordecai Kaplan and three of his colleagues published *The Sabbath Prayer Book,* which contains quite a number of revisions and innovations of the traditional liturgy. On June 12, 1945, two hundred members of Agudass Harabonim of the United States and Canada held a special meeting at the McAlpin Hotel in New York City for the express purpose of dealing with the new prayerbook. They excommunicated Rabbi Kaplan (put him in *"herem"*), and one of the younger rabbis, Rabbi Joseph Ralbag, of Ohev Shalom Congregation (*sic!*) publicly burned a copy of the siddur. This "declaration" is a reaction to those events. The footnotes are part of the original article. The middle section, which is a detailed reaction to Prof. Kaplan's pamphlet attacking the *herem,* has been omitted since it is not directly related to the subject of liturgy. The English translation which appeared in *The Jewish Forum* is not accurate and has been thoroughly revised.

גילוי-דעת
(בענין סידורו של ד"ר מרדכי קאפלאן)

יואל נא כ' העורך לתת מקום בעתונו הנכבד לחוות דעתנו על פרשת הסידור של ד"ר קאפלאן ועל מאמרו בחוברת שהוציא המוסד לחידוש היהדות.[1] אנו נמנענו עד עכשיו מלפרסם גילוי דעת בענין מכאיב זה כדי שלא להתווכח בעידן דריתחא ובשעת התרגזות. חכינו עד שישתקע הפולמוס ונוכל לומר מה שנאמר מתוך ישוב-הדעת וכובד-ראש גמור.

במותב תלתא כחדא הוינא ודרשנו וחקרנו בפרשה עגומה זו לכל פרטיה ודקדוקיה ומצאנו שאין שום תירוץ ואמתלה לשריפת ה"סידור" בפומבי. בזמננו אנו, ביחוד אחרי שריפת הספרים בגרמניה ההיטלרית, העלאת ספרים על המוקד אינה אלא מעשה תועבה, ואנו שמחים לשמוע שאגודת הרבנים מנערת את חצנה ממעשה מגונה זה. ולחרם עצמו, הרי מוסד החרם הביא תכופות ברכה להגנת האומה בשעות חירום. קהילת ימי-הבינים, שהתקיימה בתנאים בלתי-נורמאליים, היתה מוכרחה לשמור על קיומה. החרם היה לבית-הדין היהודי הדרך היחידה לכפיה, ובכמה מקרים שמר החרם על שלימות הקהילה והצילה מהריסה והתפוררות מבפנים. ברם בזמננו אנו ובתנאים שלנו יש להמנע מדרך-כפיה זו. כבר הורונו רבותינו:[2] "וכן יש לדיין לנדות ולהחרים מי שאינו בן נידוי כדי לגדור פרץ כפי מה שיראה לו והשעה צריכה לכך". קל וחומר בן בנו של קל וחומר שיש להמנע מלנדות את הראוי לנידוי אם השעה צריכה לכך ואם הפרצה תגדל על-ידי הנידוי, ומכל שכן במקום שיש לחשוש לחילול השם ולבזיון התורה ונושאיה, והרי דרכיה דרכי נועם כתיב, וכל נתיבותיה שלום.

במקום חרם היה צורך להתריע על הזלזול בקדשי האומה; על הקיצוץ הגס בקריאת שמע, שבקריאתה יצאה נשמתם של קדושי ישראל בשעה שמסרו את עצמם על קידוש השם, קריאה העולה באזנינו מתוך פיותיהם של קדושים שדמם עדיין לא נקרש. היה צורך למחות כנגד השינויים והסירוסים במטבע התפילות שטבעו חכמים ובפרט בתפילת "שמונה עשרה" שנתקדשה בפיות עם ישראל באלפי שנים, ומכל שכן כנגד ההקדמה התפלה לסידור זה. ועוד היה צורך לנהל הסברה רחבה על חוסר הטעם שבסידור זה, "סידור" המלא ניגודים וסתירות מיניה וביה והמעורר צער וגיחוך גם יחד. העורכים קבלו על עצמם לערוך את ספר תהלים, לקצץ בו ולסרס אותו, ועשו בו כאדם העושה בתוך שלו, ולא חסו גם על שירתם של פייטנים מאוחרים (ב"לכה דודי" של ר"ש אלקבץ, במקום "על יד איש בן פרצי" תיקנו העורכים "ובישועתו תדוצי" וכן הלאה). הלשון הפשוטה של התפילות שיצאו מעמקי לבם של חסידים ואנשי מעשה שהתחננו והתרפקו על קונם הוחלפה בעברית נלעגת ומגומגמת. שלושה-עשר "אנו מבקשים" של העורכים (עמוד 562 ואילך) מעליבים את הטעם האסתטי של כל אדם מישראל שטעם טעם עברית מימיו. הסברה כזאת היתה מבטלת ומחרימה מאליה את הסידור; מה שאין כן החרם, שהשביח בעיני רבים מעשה הדיוט כמעשה אומן.

אין אנו מתעלמים מדרישת השעה למשוך את הנוער לבית-הכנסת. דרך-המלך
לבית-הכנסת הוא בית-המדרש, הפצת התורה; אבל לפי שעה מן הראוי הוא לשפר
את החיצוניות של הסידור, להוסיף בסוף התפילה תפילות בלשון המדוברת, ואפילו
לקרוא אחר כך (אחרי התפילה) שנית את "שמע" באנגלית. ידעו ילדי ישראל מה הם
מתפללים ולמי הם מתפללים. ברם סידור כזה צריך לצאת מידי תלמידי-חכמים
מומחים...

שנואים עלינו דברי ויכוח ופולמוס ממין זה. ברם יצאנו מגדרנו, כדי שלא יאמרו
הבריות: מדשתקי רבנן שמע מינה ניחא להו. ואמנם זה כמה שנים שהשתדלנו
להשפיע על ד"ר קאפלאן שיחזור בו. כשפרסם את ההגדה לפסח מחינו כנגד סטיותיו
מן המסורת ושינוייו ממטבע שטבעו חכמים. כתבנו לו מכתב פרטי בחתימת כל חברי
הפאקולטה של בית-המדרש לרבנים והוכחנו אותו על השימוש המוטעה במקורות
חז"ל. רמזנו לו ולא נרמז, עקצנוהו ולא נעקץ. מעשיו האחרונים לא הניחו לנו דרך
אחרת לחוות את דעתנו בפומבי. לא עת לחשות היא, ואנו אומרים לד"ר קאפלאן:
"מה לך אצל הלכה? כלך לך אצל אגדה".

לוי גינצבורג,
אלכסנדר מארכס,
שאול ליברמאן

מוצאי יום הכיפורים תש"ו

נחזיק טובה לעתונות העברית והאידית בארץ ובגולה אם תואיל להעתיק מכתב זה.

---

1   *A Challenge to Freedom of Worship*, New York 1945, pp. 7-11
2   רמב"ם, פרק כ"ד מהלכות סנהדרין, הלכה ז...

A Declaration
(Regarding Dr. Mordecai Kaplan's Siddur)

Esteemed Editor: May we ask that you give space in your esteemed newspaper to a statement of our opinion regarding the new siddur of Dr. Kaplan and regarding his pamphlet[1] published by the Society for the Advancement of Judaism.

We have refrained from making a public statement in this painful matter until now, in order not to enter into a debate at a time of hysteria. We therefore waited until the heated polemics would abate, so as to be able to state our case in a calm and weighty manner.

The three undersigned have given this sorry episode considerable deliberation in every particular and we have concluded that there was absolutely no excuse for burning the "*siddur*" publicly.

In our day, especially after the burning of books in Hitlerite Germany, such an act is an abomination and we are glad to hear that the Agudass Harabonim disavows responsibility for this disgraceful action.

As to the "*herem*" itself, in times of emergency the institution of the *herem* frequently helped protect the Jewish people. The medieval Jewish community, which existed under abnormal conditions, was compelled to protect its existence. Excommunication was the only method of coercion a Jewish court had and in some cases it preserved the integrity of a community and kept it from internal disintegration. But in our day and under present conditions, we should avoid this type of coercion. As our Sages have taught:[2] "And so, too, a judge should ban and excommunicate a person who legally speaking is not deserving of excommunication in order to 'fence in a breach' according to his judgement and the needs of the hour." So much the more, however, should a court avoid excommunicating one who incurred it if the hour demands it and if the breach will grow as a result of the excommunication and especially when there is reason to fear the desecration of God's name and the disgrace of the Torah and its bearers. For "the ways of the Torah are pleasantness and all its paths are peace".

Instead of a *herem*, an alarm should have been sounded against the profanation of the sanctities of our people, against the crude abbreviation of the *Shema* in the recital of which Jewish martyrs gave up their lives for the sanctification of God's name, a cry which now reaches our ears from the mouths of martyrs whose blood is yet warm. There was a need to protest against the changes and omissions of prayer formulas established by our sages, particularly in the *Shemoneh Esreh* which was sanctified by the mouths of our people for thousands of years and even more so against the insipid introduction to this siddur.

There was also a need to conduct a widespread campaign regarding the tastelessness of this *"siddur"* which overflows with contradictions and inconsistencies, inducing both pain and laughter.

The editors even undertook to edit the Book of Psalms, to abbreviate and emasculate it, doing with it as they pleased, not sparing even the work of later poets (in "Lekhah Dodi" of R. Solomon Alkabetz, the editors changed "על יד איש בן פרצי" to "ובישועתו תדוצי" and so on and so forth).

The simple language of the prayers that flowed from the hearts of pious men and saints who supplicated and yearned for their Creator was changed to a confused and ridiculous Hebrew. The thirteen "Wants" of the editors (pp. 562ff.) insult the aesthetic taste of every Jew who ever tasted the flavor of Hebrew. Such a campaign would in and of itself have nullified and banned this *siddur*, unlike the *herem* which made many regard this amateur effort as a work of skilled craftsmanship.

We do not deny the need of the hour to attract the youth to the synagogue. But the royal road to the synagogue is the house of study and the dissemination of the Torah. However, as a temporary measure, it is proper to improve the externals of the siddur, to append at the conclusion of the service prayers in the vernacular, and even to repeat the Shema in English after the service. It is well that Jewish children should know what they are praying and to Whom they are praying. But such a siddur must be issued by expert scholars...

Disputes and polemics of this kind are extremely disagreeable to us. However, we made this exception in order that people should not say: since the scholars are silent, they probably acquiesce. Indeed, for a number of years we have tried to influence Dr. Kaplan to recant. When he published his new *haggadah* for Passover, we protested against his deviations from tradition and the changes of the formulas established by our sages. We wrote him a private letter signed by all the members of the Seminary faculty and reproved him for the erroneous usage of the words of our sages. "We gave him a hint, but he disregarded it; we pricked him but he ignored the stinging." His latest acts left us no other alternative than to express our views publicly. This is not a time to be silent, and we say to Dr. Kaplan: "What have you to do with *Halakhah*? Stick to *Aggadah*!"

Louis Ginzberg
Alexander Marx
Saul Lieberman

The day after Yom Kippur, 5706

We would be grateful to the Hebrew and Yiddish press in Israel and the Diaspora if they would agree to print this letter.

1 *A Challenge to Freedom of Worship*, New York 1945, pp. 7-11.
2 Maimonides, Laws of the Sanhedrin 24:7.

No. 6 A Reaction to Rabbi Morris Silverman's Notes on the Siddur (1941) and to his Siddur (1946)

Source of Notes: LGA, Box 15, "Memoirs" file
Source of Letter from 1946: LGA, Box 11, "Silverman" file
Excerpts: *Keeper*, p. 310
Secondary References:
1. Morris Silverman, ed., *Sabbath and Festival Prayer Book*, New York 1946, p. v
2. Letter of November 8, 1945 from Robert Gordis to members of the Prayer Book Commission, inviting them to a meeting with Louis Ginzberg and Alexander Marx: LGA, Box 5, "Gordis" file

RABBI MORRIS SILVERMAN[1]
195 RIDGEFIELD STREET
HARTFORD 12, CONN.

December 14, 1963

Professor Eli Ginzberg
609 Business Building
Columbia University
New York, New York

Dear Professor Ginzberg:

I was delighted to learn that you are compiling an autobiographical memoir about your beloved father and my revered teacher.[2]

Enclosed you will find photostatic copies concerning the Prayer Book which [were] of tremendous help to me in editing the "Sabbath and Festival Prayer Book" as well as the "High Holiday Prayer Book".[3] These notes are remarkable not only because they were written by hand while your father was on vacation,[4] but also because they were written from memory, without the aid of reference books.

Acknowledgment of your father's aid was made in the preface of the Prayer Book. If you do not have copies of them, I shall be pleased to send them to you....[5]

As a Seminary student, I had dinner at your home when you and your sister were little children. I shall never forget that pleasant Sabbath. I shall be looking forward to reading this book that you are compiling. Kindest wishes and *Hanukkah* greetings!

Sincerely yours,

Morris Silverman, Rabbi

~ ~ ~

JEWISH THEOLOGICAL SEMINARY OF AMERICA
NORTHEAST CORNER, BROADWAY AND 122D STREET
NEW YORK CITY

Oakland Maine
August 29, 194[1][6]

Dear Rabbi Silverman,
Enclosed please find a few remarks I jotted down. As I have no books with me dealing with liturgy, I had to limit myself.
May I add the following few remarks.
1. The notes for the Prayerbook seem to me to lack a definite principle. F[or] e[xample], you have a note on ישתבח but not on ברוך שאמר, on אל אדון but not on the following לאל אשר שבת. The same lack of principle I notice with regard to references. You sometimes refer to a passage in the Talmud, sometimes not.
2. The transliteration is not consistent. I think the best would be to be follow the system used in the *Jewish Encyclopedia* - of course, you might disregard the use of the diacritical points.
With kindest regards to you and Mrs. Silverman in which Mrs. Ginzberg joins me.

Very truly yours,

Louis Ginzberg

p. 3 line 6) [*Mizmor Shir L'yom Hashabbat*] was, according to mishnaic tradition, sung by the Levites on [the] Sabbath.[7] Maimonides in one of his Responsa refers to the custom of reciting this Psalm before evening services of the Sabbath.[8]

p. 3 line 9) I would leave out the word "*prayers*" - the Shema is not a part of the prayers.

p. 4 line 3) The Amidah consists now of 19 benedictions. Change, therefore, "*consists*" to "*originally consisted.*"[9]

p. 4 line 9) The origin of *Magen Abot* is very likely different [than the] one given by you in accordance with [the] traditional explanation based upon a statement of the Babylonian Talmud.[10] It is more likely that for the Sabbath, at least, an *abbreviated* form of the Amidah by the was insisted upon while on weekdays the Amidah in the evening was not repeated at all. I deal with this problem in my work on the Yerushalmi [which] will be available in a few weeks.[11]

p. 4 line 14) I am not quite sure about the origin of the *kiddush* in the synagogue. I have somewhere - if I am not mistaken in an article by Dr. Finkelstein - expressed the view that originally the *kiddush* was recited in the synagogue and then transferred to the home.[12] The reverse order would be rather strange.

p. 4 line 21) I am not particularly fond of *making* prayers - they ought to flow from the heart of the inspired poets! But, in a Sabbath prayer, the three aspects of the Sabbath ought to [be] expressed: 1) God the creator as manifested - according to Jewish belief - in the *creatio ex nihilo* 2) God the ruler of the world especially [as] manifested in [the] history of Israel זכר ליציאת מצרים; and 3) God the father of all men and _____ _____ His Command of the Sabbath - the day of rest for those who need it most - the social *significance* of the Sabbath.

p. 6 line 6) On *Festivals* some reference to the particular festival ought to be made as, f[or] e[xample], Passover, the feast of Israel's birth as a nation, *Shabuot*, the revelation of the Torah etc.

p. 7 line 6) This very likely refers [to the] *baraita* of ר' ישמעאל אומר, a passage found at the beginning of the *Sifra* (the *tannaitic* is more correct than the *midrashic* commentary - the latter description would rather point to Leviticus Rabba!), but is not a selection from it but later added to it. The Midrashic rules of R. Ishmael are quite different than those used in the *Sifra*, a product of the School of R. Akiba.[13]

p.7 line 10) [*Birkhot Hashahar*] It is not a matter of idealization but for *practical* reasons - many a person did not know them or would forget to recite them [so they] were introduced in the syn[agogue] service.

p. 8 line 6) [*L'olam Yehei Adam*] The *Tanna* [*d'vei*] *Eliyahu Rabbah*, as we know now, is much older - it is quoted by the *Gaon* Natronai in the 9th century. As its date is rather doubtful (according to my theory, explained in

Ginzei Schechter, I, the groundwork is of tannaitic-amoraic times) I would not try to give any date.[14]

p. 9 line 14) The text of קדיש דרבנן has hardly any similarity with יקום פורקן - which, by the way, is Palestinian, while the former seems to be of Babylonian origin[15] - except for the three words ותלמידי תלמידיהון תלמידיהון, which [appear] in the first but not in the second *Yekum Purkan*. It would be more correct to say _____ _____ in both of these prayers special reference is made to the scholars.

p. 9 line 22) The פסוקי דזמרה are found in the Siddur of R. Sa'adia (500 years before R. Meir of Rothenberg!) *only* for "public" services while the יחיד begins with יוצר אור[16] and I do not know to what you refer by saying that the famous German Rabbi [i.e., Rabbi Meir] introduced some changes.[17] Perhaps you mean that הודו *after* שאמר ברוך was [formerly] recited *before* the blessing as is still the Sephardic *minhag*. I have no books here to establish the facts to which you refer. Perhaps you should mention the fact that the recital of אשרי is mentioned in the Talmud[18] while the following psalms are first referred to by the *Geonim*.

p. 10) *Shir Hakabod* In justice to the author (more likely R. Samuel he-Hasid, the father of R. Judah), it should be pointed out that he often emphasizes the incorporeality of God, by which [I] wish to point out that his anthropomorphisms are poetical license.[19]

p. 11) *El Adon* is *undoubtedly* not earlier than late Geonic times - Saadia does know it! - and it is quite ridiculous to ascribe it to the Essenes. I do not find in it anything mystical - the references to חיות and מרכבה are purely literary form.[20]

p. 12) Before *Amidah* There is nothing in the old sources, *Mishnah*, *Tosefta* and both *Talmudim*, to warrant the statement that Rabban Gamliel introduced any changes. What the sources have to say about the contoversy between R.G. and his colleagues is just the opposite.[21] R.G. maintains that one who has listened carefully to the recital of the prayer by the Reader has no need to say the silent prayer, while his colleagues are of the opinion that every individual man must [recite] the silent prayers. The discussions between these authorities show quite clearly that the "silent" prayer was recited and the controversy is how to interpret the "double" prayer. According to R.G., the recital of the reader is *the* prayer, while the prayer preceding it by the congregation is only "preparatory", while according to his colleagues the prayer by the community is *the* prayer, [and] the recital by the reader has only the purpose to "satisfy the need" of the ignorant who are unable to recite prayers by themselves. By the way, the *silence* is a Babylonian custom only. In Palestine there was no objection to *loud* praying, as long as it was not too loud! I have a lengthy essay on the problem in the third volume of my Commentary.[22]

p. 13) Before *Rezeh* The Talmud refers to the insertions on New Moons and *Hanukah*.[23] The exact texts of these insertions are not given and יעלה ויבוא as well as על הנסים are very likely of Geonic origin.[24] At all events, there is no distinction between them.

[*Elohay Netzor*] "*Rabbinic prayers*" is a queer phrase, for very likely [you] mean prayers by individual Rabbis which later were added to the fixed form of the *Amidah*.[25]

p. 14 line 4) [*Hallel*] "Composed and recited on Festivals". What [does] it mean? Did you wish to say that they were composed to be recited on Festivals? This can only be maintained for Psalm 114 - [a] Passover hymn! - with certainty.

p. 15) Psalm 118: This Psalm is not a dedication psalm and the fixing of the date is [no] more than guesswork.

p. 15) Before *Ein Kamoka* In some countries still today the one called to the scroll reads the Torah, as, f[or] e[xample], among the Yemenites.[26]

p. 16) [Before *Birkat Hahodesh*] The Babylonians no later than [the] eighteenth century B.C. had the intercalation of the year עבור and hence its origin has nothing to do with the specific problem of the Jewish festivals! I would also modify the statement about the date of the fixing of the Calendar by a phrase [that] "the *principal* rules and regulations [were fixed]" or something like it. There were as late as the 9th century many points in dispute.[27]

p. 17 line 3) [Before *Birkat Hahodesh*] *Arika* not Areka![28]

p. 17) The *Musaf* prayer originally did not *"deal"* with sacrifices (a very queer description of a prayer!) but of course had a reference to the restoration of the Temple and its services.[29]

p. 18) The source of the *Kedusha* is *not Pirkei d'rabi Eliezer*. You mean very likely that this *Midrash* has a reference to its use. But Yannai is a much older source![30]

Ein Keloheinu was still recited daily by the *Ashkenazim* - at least among some of them - as late as the 15th century.[31]

p. 19 line 7) It is not quite accurate to speak of *Mahzor Vitry* as compiled under the direction of Rashi. The most one might say is that the *Mahzor* is a product of Rashi's school.[32]

p. 20 line 2) That the *Kaddish* existed in the time of the Temple is an assumption without any basis. The doxology יהא שמיה רבא is of comparatively late date.[33] In Amoraic times (at least in Palestine!) the Hebrew יהי שמו גדול was used.[34] I doubt the correctness of the statement that the קדיש יתום was originally recited only at the death of a scholar. By far more likely is the assumption that at the end of the daily prayers in the house of the mourners - they were not supposed to go to the synagogue - the "honor" of reciting the Kaddish was given to one of the mourners. Likewise the mourner was given the honor of reciting ברכו at the beginning of the prayer.[35]

p. 22) *Adon Olam* is a metrical composition and hence *cannot* be dated before the tenth century, when meter was first introduced. Tradition ascribes it to Solomon Ibn Gabirol.

Notes on p. 99) In discussing the Chosen People, it ought to be pointed out that Judaism was the first proselytizing religion - which reflects a claim of moral superiority. The proselyte of whatever race he was became a member of the Jewish nation.

~   ~   ~

November 5, 1946

Dear Rabbi Silverman,

Many thanks for your kindness for forwarding to me a copy of the prayer book published under your editorship by the Rabbinical Assembly and the United Synagogue.

I deeply appreciate your inscription in which you thanked me for my counsel and assistance. I wish, however, my counsel would have been more effective. Then the prayer book would have had less omissions and commissions of which I cannot approve.

Kindest regards,

Very sincerely yours,

Louis Ginzberg

Rabbi Morris Silverman
195 Ridgefield Street
Hartford, Connecticut

1   Rabbi Morris Silverman (1894-1972) was one of the foremost liturgists in the Conservative Movement - see Nadell, pp. 239-240.

2   I.e., *Keeper of the Law*. Eli Ginzberg solicited memoirs from LG's students in order to help him write the book.

3   Rabbi Silverman's memory seems to have deceived him. *The High Holiday Prayer Book* was published in 1939, before LG's notes were written.

4   LG's handwriting is very difficult to decipher; a blank space indicates an undeciphered word. In addition, since Rabbi Silverman's notes are missing from the LGA, it is not always clear to what LG is reacting. It should be noted that most of Rabbi Silverman's notes were omitted from the *Sabbath and Festival Prayer Book*. See the Notes, ibid., pp. 376-385, which do not contain any of the notes mentioned here other than that regarding the Chosen People on p. 383. My thanks to Professors Eli Ginzberg and Menachem Schmelzer who deciphered a number of phrases using the original documents in the LGA.

5   For the middle of this letter, see below, Chapter III, No. 14, note 3.

6   The last digit is illegible, but LG mentions that his *Commentary on the Palestinian Talmud*, which appeared in 1941, "will be available in a few weeks". Hence this letter was written on August 29, 1941. Regarding the date of the publication of the Commentary, see *Keeper*, pp. 154-155. For other responsa written in Maine, see below, Chapter IV, No. 10; Chapter V, No. 13; and Chapter VII, No. 12 and see, in general, *Keeper*, Index, s.v. Maine.

7   *Mishnah Tamid* 7:4. This is actually a *baraita* which was added at a later date - see Yaakov Nahum Epstein, *Mevo L'nusah Hamishnah*, Jerusalem 5708, p. 979; and LG himself, in his article on *Tamid*, Journal of *Jewish Lore and Philosophy* 1 (1919), p. 283.

8   *Teshuvot Harambam*, ed. J. Blau, No. 178, II, Jerusalem 5720, pp. 326-327.

9   Rabbi Silverman must have written that "the Amidah *consists* of eighteen benedictions". Regarding the additional benediction, see, for example, Ismar M. Elbogen, *Jewish Liturgy: A Comprehensive History*, Philadelphia 1993, pp. 33-35.

10   *Shabbat* 24b and Rashi ad loc. For a recent study, see Yosef Heinemann, *Iyunei Tefilah*, Jerusalem 5741, pp. 36-43.

11   *A Commentary on the Palestinian Talmud*, III, New York 1941, p. 319, but the opinion expressed there is not identical to that expressed here.

12   I do not know to which article LG is referring. Regarding the kiddush in the synagogue, see now Yisrael Ta-Shema, *Minhag Ashkenaz Hakadmon*, Jerusalem 5752, pp. 157-170.

13   On this topic, see now Louis Finkelstein, *Sifra*, I, New York 1989, pp. 186-187.

14   See *Ginzei Schechter*, I, New York 1928, pp. 189-190. For a summary of the various dates proposed for *Eliyahu Rabbah*, see William G. Braude and Israel I. Kapstein, *Tanna Debe Eliyahu*, Philadelphia 1981, pp. 3-11.

15   The origin of *Yekum Purkan* is unknown. It is mentioned by Rabbi Zerahiah Halevi (Provence, 12th century) and appears in *Mahzor Vitry* (France, 12th century). See Israel Davidson, *Otzar Hashira Vehapiyyut*, II, New York 1929, pp. 424-425 and the literature cited there. As for *Kaddish d'rabbanan*, see *EJ*, X, cols. 660-663, as well as David de Sola Pool, *The Kaddish*, Leipzig 1909, pp. 89-96, who shows that *kaddish d'Rabbanan* and *Yekum Purkan* contain many of the same themes.

16   LG was mistaken here because he had no access to the *siddur* in question. It is true that in *Siddur Rav Sa'adia Gaon*, Jerusalem 1941, p. 13, the prayers of the individual begin with *Yotzer Or*. But later on (pp. 32-34) Rav Sa'adia says that the individual must also recite *Pesukei d'Zimra*.

17   Rabbi Silverman probably based himself on Abraham Berliner's *Randbemerkungen zum taeglichen Gebetbuch*, Berlin 1909 = *Ketavim Nivharim*, I, Jerusalem 1945, p. 17, who says that

the Maharam transferred *Birkhot Hashahar* (not *Pesukei d'Zimra*) to the synagogue. Berliner, in turn, based himself on the *Tashbatz* of Shimshon bar Tzadok, par. 217.

18 Berakhot 4b.

19 Berliner (above, note 17), p. 155, adduces proof that *Shir Hakavod* was written by R. *Judah* he-Hasid. For a recent analysis of this poem, see Ismar Schorsch, *Judaism* 37/1 (Winter, 1988), pp. 67-72.

20 S.Y. Rapoport, *Bikkurei Ha-ittim*, 10 (1830), p. 119, ascribed *El Adon* to the Essenes, and LG is certainly correct in rejecting that hypothesis. On the other hand, manuscripts of "Ma'aseh Merkavah" published after these Notes were written prove that *El Adon* was directly influenced by that early mystical work - see Meir Bar-Ilan, *Sitrei Tefilah V'heikhalot*, Ramat Gan 1987, pp. 115-120.

21 *Mishnah Rosh Hashanah* 4:9; *Tosefta* ibid. 2:18, ed. S. Lieberman, p. 321; *Bavli* ibid. 34b.

22 See LG's *Commentary* (above, note 11), pp. 8-22. The basic sources are *Yerushalmi Berakhot* 4:1, fol. 7a and *Hahilukim Shebein Anshei Mizrah U'venei Eretz Yisrael*, ed. M. Margaliot, Jerusalem 1938, No. 43 and pp. 165-167.

23 *Shabbat* 24a.

24 For *Ya'aleh V'yavoh* and *Al Hanissim*, see Elbogen (above, note 9), pp. 51-52, 105, 108-110.

25 *Elohay netzor* and similar individual prayers are found in *Bavli Berakhot* 16b-17a and *Yerushalmi Berakhot* 4:2, fol. 7d.

26 See Rabbi Yosef Kafah, *Halikhot Teiman*, Jerusalem 1982[3], pp. 67-68.

27 See below Chapter VI, No. 18.

28 *Birkat Hahodesh* is actually a private prayer composed by Rav whose real name was Abba *Arikha*. It is taken from Berakhot 16b.

29 For LG's attitude to *Musaf*, cf. above in this chapter, No. 2. Also see LG's *Commentary* (above, note 11), p. 434, where the development of the *Musaf* is described in a different fashion.

30 The *kedushah* is mentioned in *Pirkei d'rabi Eliezer*, Warsaw 1852, Chapter 4 (end), fols. 11a-b. For the many *kedushtot* of Yannai, see Menachem Zulay, ed., *Piyyutei Yannai*, Berlin 1938, pp. XIII-XVI.

31 See, for example, *Sefer Haminhagim L'rabeinu Isaac Tirna*, ed. Spitzer, Jerusalem 5739, p. 13: "There are places where they recite *Ein Keloheinu* [every day]". Also see Tur OH 133 and the Rema to *Shulhan Arukh* OH 132:2.

32 For the author and date of *Mahzor Vitry* see now *Alei Sefer* 11 (5744), pp. 81-89, and 12 (5746), pp. 129-132.

33 See Berakhot 3a, Shabbat 119b, and Sotah 49a.

34 See Kohelet Rabbah to 9:15, ed. Vilna, fol. 25c.

35 This is evident from certain versions of the story about Rabbi Akiva and the orphan. See for example *Mahzor Vitry*, pp. 112-113; *Or Zarua*, II, *Hilkhot Shabbat*, par. 50, fol. 11c-d; and the version published by LG in *Ginzei Schechter* (above, note 14), I, pp. 238-240. For discussion, see ibid., pp. 235-237; and M.B. Lerner, *Assufot* 2 (5748), pp. 29-70.

III. Responsa Related to Orah Haim

No. 1 May a Cantor Appear in Major Roles at an Opera
        House? (OH 53:25)   75

No. 2 Covering the Head (OH 91:3 and 2:6)   76

No. 3 Covering the Head During Religious Services (OH 91:3)   77

No. 4 Must a New Synagogue be Built Facing East?
        (OH 94:2 and 150:5)   78

No. 5 Some of the Technical Terms found in *Pittum Haketoret*
        (OH 132:2)   81

No. 6 Keeping a *Sefer Torah* in an Army Chapel and Reading
        from it at Night (OH 135:1 in Mishnah Berurah, par. 1)   84

No. 7 Mixed Pews - 1921 (not in OH)   85

No. 8 An Interview Regarding Mixed Pews - 1926 (?) (not in OH)   88

No. 9 Mixed Pews - 1947-48 (not in OH)   90

No. 10 Is the *Bimah* in the Center a Sephardic Custom? (OH 150:5) 101

No. 11 May the Lower Floor of a Synagogue be used as a
        Bet Midrash and as a Social Hall? (OH 151:1-2)   103

No. 12 May a Synagogue be Sold to a Church? (OH 153)   105

No. 13 May a Synagogue be Sold for Commercial Purposes?
        (OH 153:7)   107

No. 14 An Interview Regarding Synagogue Construction on
        Shabbat (OH 244:3)   108

No. 15 Are Late Friday Evening Services Permissible? (OH 261:4)   109

No. 16 May Unfermented Wine be Used in Religious
        Ceremonies? (OH 272:2)   110

No. 17 The Use of a Radio on *Shabbat* and *Yom Tov* (not in OH)   134

No. 18 The Use of the Organ in the Synagogue (OH 338:1-2)   135

No. 19 May Green Peas, String Beans and Tomatoes be Used
       on Passover? (OH 453:1)   136

No. 20 May a Cracked Shofar be Repaired with Scotch Tape?
       (OH 586:8-9)   137

No. 21 The Use of New Tunes in Place of Traditional Tunes
       (OH 619:1)   138

No. 22 Four Questions Regarding the *Shofar* (OH 623:6)   139

No. 1 May a Cantor Appear in Major Roles at an Opera House? (OH 53:25)

Source: General Files, File 13 (1944)

October 16, 1944

Dear Doctor Levinthal:[1]

I am in receipt of your letter of October 12, in which you ask my advice whether it would be proper for your Congregation to have its Cantor appear in important roles at the Metropolitan Opera House.

There is, of course, no special law incumbent upon a cantor.[2] He is to be a good Jew, but so also are his Congregants. Yet, while there is no specific prohibition in Jewish law which would prevent a cantor from serving in the synagogue while at the same time appearing in the opera, I do not think that the combination of a cantor and an opera singer is a very healthy one. There is no law prohibiting a rabbi from appearing in a cabaret, but do you think that any congregation would seriously consider having a cabaret singer as a rabbi? Of course, I am quite aware of the fact that certain music may serve very high cultural purposes. Yet, I am, at the same time, sure that people would find it quite strange to see their cantor one day recite the *Neilah* prayer and the following day sing a love duet with some lady. My advice is therefore that you try your utmost to prevent your Cantor from accepting the offer made to him by the Metropolitan.[3]

With kindest regards to you, Mrs. Levinthal, and to the children in which Mrs. Ginzberg joins me, I am

Very sincerely yours,

Louis Ginzberg

Doctor Israel Levinthal
Brooklyn Jewish Center
667 Eastern Parkway
Brooklyn, New York

---

1   Rabbi Israel Levinthal (1888-1982) was ordained by the Seminary in 1910 and served the Brooklyn Jewish Center from its founding in 1919 for over sixty years. See *EJ*, XI, col. 121; Nadell, pp. 174-176; and Elliot Gertel, *PRA* 45 (1983), pp. 119-137. He appears in a photo with LG in *Keeper*, on the seventh page of photos after p. 214.

2   This is not entirely accurate. See OH 53:4ff. and Leo Landman, *The Cantor: an Historic Perspective*, New York 1972, pp. 58-64, 110-113, for the attributes sought in a cantor.

3   The cantor in question was Cantor Richard Tucker (1913-75), who served as cantor at the Brooklyn Jewish Center between 1943 and 1945. In 1945 he made his debut at the Metropolitan Opera House. "...Tucker wanted to remain as cantor at the Brooklyn Jewish Center. But, on the recommendation of a panel of five rabbis (by a vote of three to two), he resigned his post there" (Darryl Lyman, *Great Jews in Music*, New York 1986, pp. 229-230). LG was apparently one of the five rabbis asked.

No 2. Covering the Head (OH 91:3 and 2:6)

Source: CJLS Box, "Bet Knesset" file = BCA, Box 5, "Miscellaneous Questions and Answers" File

Question: Kindly advise a layman whether it is permitted to walk bareheaded, in the street or house. If it is permissible according to Jewish laws and traditions, kindly advise [as to the] source.

Answer: (by Irving H. Fisher)[1] In response to your inquiry, I beg to say that I have consulted Professor Louis Ginzberg, the Chairman of our Committee on Interpretation of Jewish Law. He stated as follows: "It is against Jewish law and custom to pray, study religious works, or perform a religious ceremony while bareheaded. Some pious men refrain from having their heads uncovered at any time, and while this is, or at least was, a widespread custom, it never was considered binding. It is not clear to me whether the writer wishes references to Hebrew sources, or whether in other languages. The *Jewish Encyclopedia*, s.v. Bareheadedness, contains some literature on the subject".[2]

1   He was apparently a layman connected to the United Synagogue, since reference is made to the Committee on Interpretation of Jewish Law, which was under the aegis of the United Synagogue. He is not listed as a rabbi or Seminary graduate in any of the standard lists.

2   The literature is vast. See, for example, *EJ* VIII, cols. 1-6, s.v. Head, Covering of the; Samuel Krauss, *HUCA* 19 (1945-46), pp. 121-154; Jacob Z. Lauterbach, in: Walter Jacob, ed., *American Reform Responsa*, New York 1983, pp. 8-20; and Eric Zimmer, in: Jacob Schacter, ed., *Reverence, Righteousness and Rahmanut: Essays in Memory of Rabbi Dr. Leo Jung*, Northvale, N.J. 1992, pp. 325-352 = *Olam K'minhago Noheg*, Jerusalem 1996, pp. 17-42 (Hebrew).

No. 3 Covering the Head During Religious Services (OH 91:3)
Source: General Files, File 2 (1931-33)

February 5, 1932

My dear Mr. Zwerin:

Because of pressure of work I was unable to reply to your letter of January 15th sooner. I hope, however, that the following few remarks will reach you in time before the completion of your article on "The Custom of Wearing a Hat During Religious Services."

I take it for granted that the origin of the custom is known to you. In eastern countries no man without a head cover is considered properly dressed, and, of course, the decorum of [the] service requires that one appear correctly attired for public service. The synagogue and its historical development of thousands of years has always tried to express in concrete form its continuity. As a product of Palestinian life,[1] it intends to perpetuate, as far as possible, the form of worship created by the religious genius of the Jew. It is, therefore, not at all surprising that an overwhelming majority of Jews vehemently object to the abolishment of this old Jewish custom, especially as the desire for the change was dictated exclusively by the wish to imitate Christian worship in the synagogue.

Sincerely yours,

LOUIS GINZBERG

Mr. Kenneth Carlton Zwerin[2]
International House
Berkeley, Calif.

---

1   But it appears that in Palestine, Jews prayed with *uncovered* heads whereas in Babylon they covered their heads. See the many sources cited by Jacob Z. Lauterbach, in: Walter Jacob, ed. *American Reform Responsa*, New York 1983, pp. 10-16.

2   Zwerin later published a pamphlet entitled *Some Aspects of Jewish Ethics*, Berkeley 1936, 20pp., where he is described as "Formerly Minister Congregation Beth Jacob, Palo Alto, California; Sometime Lecturer, Adult Education Division, University of Hawaii; Member State Bar of California".

No. 4 Must a New Synagogue be Built Facing East? (OH 94:2 and 150:5)

Source: LGA, Box 19, "Cyrus Adler to LG" file
Summary: LGA, Box 17, "Questions and Answers" file = *Exponent*
Excerpt: *Keeper*, pp. 228-229

ALBERT S. GOTTLIEB
Architect
101 Park Avenue, New York.

December 21, 1920

Dr. Cyrus Adler,[1]
2041 North Broad St.,
Philadelphia, Pa.

Dear Sir:

Rabbi Samuel Rosinger of Temple Emanuel, Beaumont, Texas,[2] has suggested to me that I write you in regard to a question that has arisen in connection with a proposed new Temple building for his Congregation and for which I have been making plans.

The point in question relates to the direction in which the Congregation should be seated, that is to say, whether it is mandatory that they should face the East. Rabbi Rosinger was of the opinion that this is so, but unfortunately the people who bought the lot on which the Temple is to be erected evidently gave this point no consideration and have purchased a piece of property on which it is next to impossible to plan a building in which the seats shall face the East and still have a good arrangement for the building, not only from an architectural standpoint but also from a practical one. The longest dimension of their lot is north and south and it would give much better results if the Congregation could face north, the entrance to the Temple being at the southern end.

Rabbi Rosinger's reason for suggesting that I write you directly was in order to save time and I shall feel very grateful to you if you will be kind enough to give me your opinion on this matter. I designed a large Temple for [Rabbi Solomon Foster in the City of Newark, N. J.][3] and in that building, although it was at first suggested that the auditorium be so arranged that the Congregation should face the East, it was not insisted on and the seats as built actually face the West.

I am taking advantage of this occasion to send you under separate cover a booklet on Synagogue and Sunday School Architecture that I have issued and hope that it may prove of interest to you.[4]

Thanking you in advance for any consideration you may give this question and awaiting your reply, I am

Very truly yours,

s/d Albert S. Gottlieb

[Handwritten] Please send answer to Dr. C. Adler.[5]

~ ~ ~

January 10, 1921

Dear Doctor Adler:

Returning home from Chicago, I found your letter of December 23, 1920[6] in which you ask my opinion as to whether it is mandatory that the Congregation should face the East.

After a careful study of the subject, I came to the conclusion that it would be very inadvisable to permit any deviation of the old established custom to have the Congregation face the East. The high antiquity of this custom can be seen from Daniel 6:11 which biblical passage forms the basis for the regulation found in the Talmud and in the later Codes. See, for instance, *Mishnah Berakot* [4:5];[7] Talmud [ibid.] 30a;[8] *Tosefta Megillah* 4,15[9] and *Shulhan Aruk Orah Hayyim* 150,4.[10] It is also highly interesting to notice that the old church has adopted this custom; see Rietschel, *Liturgik* 1,88,124.[11] That this custom was strictly and generally observed among the Jews of antiquity and the middle ages can be seen by [the] fact that Mohammed at the beginning of his career ordained to have the Kibla facing Palestine as a concession to the Jews.[12]

Very sincerely yours,

LOUIS GINZBERG

1   Dr. Cyrus Adler (1863-1940) was Acting President and later President of the Jewish Theological Seminary from 1915 to 1940. See *EJ*, II, cols. 272-274; and Nadell, pp. 27-31.

2   Rabbi Samuel Rosinger (1877- after 1947) was ordained by the Seminary in 1908 and served as rabbi of Temple Emanuel in Beaumont for over thirty years - see *Students' Annual* 3 (1916), p. 195; *PRA* 11 (1947), p. 406; and *Conservative Judaism* 47/3 (Spring 1995), pp. 55-56.

3   This was probably a Reform Temple since Rabbi Foster was not a Seminary graduate. I have rephrased the sentence for the sake of clarity.

4   Albert S. Gottlieb, *Synagogue and Sunday School Architecture*, New York 1919(?), 22 pp., which was previously read as a paper before the Central Conference of American Rabbis at Wildwood, New Jersey on July 3, 1916. Both items are listed in the *Dictionary Catalogue of the Klau Library*, X, Boston 1964, p. 337.

5   This note was probably written by Dr. Adler's secretary who forwarded the letter to LG.

6   The cover letter is missing from the LGA.

7   The source is illegible in the original.

8   See Tosefta Berakhot 3:15-16, ed. S. Lieberman, pp. 15-16 and the parallels cited there.

9   He is referring to the Zuckermandel edition, 4:22, p. 227. He inadvertently wrote the number of the *line* instead of the number of the *halakhah*. In the Lieberman edition it is 3:22, p. 360.

10   It should read 150:5.

11   Georg Rietschel, *Lehrbuch der Liturgik*, I, Berlin 1900, pp. 88 and 124. I was not able to consult the book but it is listed in the *Dictionary Catalogue* (above, note 4), XXI, p. 571. For a thorough discussion, see Franz Landsberger, *HUCA* 28 (1957), pp. 193ff. and, in general, Marilyn Chiat, *Handbook of Synagogue Architecture*, Chico, California 1982, p. 338; *EJ*, s.v. Mizrah; Landsberger, op. *cit.*, pp. 181-203; and John Wilkinson, *Palestine Exploration Quarterly* 116 (January-June, 1984), pp. 16-30. My thanks to Prof. Lee Levine of the Hebrew University and the Seminary of Judaic Studies for the last reference.

12   The Koran, Sura 2:142-150 and cf. *The Shorter Encyclopedia of Islam*, Leiden 1953, s.v. Kibla, pp. 260-261.

No. 5 Some of the Technical Terms found in Pittum Haketoret (OH 132:2)
Source: LGA, Box 8, "Lasker" file

Congregation Beth Israel
735 McFarlan Street, Flint 4, Michigan
Phone 3 - 3586

Arnold A. Lasker[1]
Rabbi
May 3, 1949
Prof. Louis Ginzberg
Jewish Theological Seminary of America
3080 Broadway
New York 27, N.Y.

Dear Doctor Ginzberg:
There has been something of a controversy raging among some of our worshippers on a Talmudic question. It is so gratifying to have such interest, that I thought I might presume to ask you to settle the question.

The problem involves the *Pittum he-Ketoret*[2] and revolves around the use of the words *mei raglayim*. From every indication it seems to me and to a number of others that it means "urine", but a couple of men have brought siddurim which actually forbid the reader to think that it could possibly mean *mei raglayim mamash*.[3] One source suggests that it is a herb with that name and because of the name it was regarded as unseemly to bring it into the *azarah*.[4] In any case, what is the actual effect of soaking onycha[5] in the "mei raglayim"?

What is the basis for translating the Biblical *shehelet*[6] and the Talmudic *tziporen* as onycha? Further, how was it permitted to utilize part of an unclean shellfish for such a sacred purpose?

Does the term *memulah* in the Bible[7] mean salted (with the *melah sedomit*) or spiced in general? Is the latter the proper interpretation of Onkelos' *me-orav*?[8]

Has there been any progress made in identifying *ma'aleh ashan* and *kipat ha-yarden*?

Thank you very much for your attention to these questions.
I trust that you, Mrs. Ginzberg, Sophie and Eli are well.

Sincerely yours,

Arnold A. Lasker

This Year We Build!

~ ~ ~

June 8, 1949

Dear Rabbi Lasker:
Your letter of May 4th reached New York during my absence for several
weeks from the city and on my return a sudden inflammation of the eyes got
hold of me, which made it quite impossible for me to read a line. Hence the
delay in my reply to your letter.

Let me first tell you that your letter gave me a good deal of pleasure for
the reason that I often have been asked by congregations whether this or that
part of the Prayer Book might be left out. I am, therefore, particularly happy
to see that you have in your congregation, people whose interest is in
understanding the Prayer Book and not in changing it.[9]

Actually [regarding] the meaning of [מי רגלים] there can be no doubt that
it is to be taken literally. As early as the 12th century, attempts have been
made to take the phrase in an applied sense, either the name of a particular
well or of a certain kind of a vegetable,[10] but the contents speak definitely
against all these explanations. My son-in-law, who is a professor of bio-
chemistry at the Massachusetts Institute of Technology at Cambridge,[11]
informed me that recently urea has been used in toothpaste with great
success. There is, therefore, nothing strange about the statement that they
knew in olden times to make some use of the alkaline contents of urea for the
purpose mentioned in the *Baraita* about the preparation of the spices.

The most reliable description of the spices used in the Temple is given by
Immanuel Low in *Die Flora Der Juden*, IV [Vienna 1934], pp. 99[-102]. As
this is very likely unavailable in Flint, I am enclosing, herewith, a short
paragraph from this book which I think you might find very useful.

With kindest regards.

Very sincerely yours,

Louis Ginzberg

Rabbi Arnold Lasker
735 McFarlan Street
Flint 4, Michigan

1   Rabbi Arnold Lasker was ordained by the Seminary in 1936 - see *PRA* 5 (1933-38), p. 497. In recent years, he and his son, Daniel, have published a series of articles about the Jewish calendar. He passed away in July 1996.

2   The passage is taken from Keritot 6a = Yerushalmi Yoma 4:5, fol. 41d and is found in all traditional prayerbooks e.g., Philip Birnbaum, ed., *Daily Prayer Book*, New York 1949, p. 407.

3   "Real urine" - see, for example, Seligman Isaac Baer, ed., *Seder Avodat Yisrael*, Rodelheim 1868, p. 246, who is quoting from *Kol Bo*, Lemberg 1860, fol. 39d, par. 38.

4   See, for example, *Mahzor Vitry*, Berlin 1889, p. 46.

5   Onycha is usually explained as the operculum or lid of a type of snail - see Immanuel Low quoted here by LG.

6   Exodus 30:34 in the biblical description of the incense.

7   Exodus 30:35 in the biblical description of the incense.

8   To Exodus, ibid.

9   Compare this paragraph to various statements in Chapter II above.

10   See *Kol Bo* and *Mahzor Vitry*, loc. cit.

11   He is referring to Bernard Gould - see *Keeper*, p. 263.

No. 6. Keeping a Sefer Torah in an Army Chapel and Reading from it at Night (OH 135:1 in the Mishnah Berurah, par. 1)[1]

Source: CJLS Box, "Bet Knesset" file
Summary: Boaz Cohen, *PRA* 8 (1941-44), pp. 142-143

Question: The Government is now erecting [a chapel] at every fort which is used by all denominations. It is provided with an *Aron Kodesh* for a *Sefer Torah* for the Jewish services.

However, because of many reasons, services cannot be held on Saturday or any other morning when the Torah can be read. Services are held here primarily during the week, in the evening. The questions, therefore, are:

1) May we deposit a *Sefer Torah* in the *Aron Kodesh* at the Fort Chapel here without using it?[2]

2) [If we deposit it,] is there any possible way of allowing the *Sefer Torah* to be read in the evening during the week at services?

Answer: With regard to the question of keeping a *Sefer Torah* in government fort chapels and the reading from the Torah at evening services during the week, I consulted Professor Ginzberg. He was of the opinion that it would be improper to keep the *Sefer Torah* in the same place where Catholic services are held.[3] However, if it were convenient, he suggested that the *Sefer Torah* be brought to the chapel especially for the services. If the services were held on Sunday or Wednesday evenings, one might read the first *Parashah* from the weekly *Sidra* and call up three persons, since Sunday evening is considered, according to the Jewish calendar, as part of Monday, and Wednesday evening as part of Thursday.

---

1   The second question is discussed in the *Mishnah Berurah*; the first question is not in the *Shulhan Arukh*. The question may have been addressed to Prof. Boaz Cohen, Chairman of the Committee on Jewish Law, who consulted with LG.

2   The last three words are ambiguous. They either mean "without using the chapel" or "when the Sefer Torah is not in use".

3   This is because many authorities view Catholicism as a form of idolatry. See, for example, the Rambam's commentary to *Mishnah Avodah Zarah* 1:3 (Kafah edition) and again in *Hilkhot Avodah Zarah* 9:4 (uncensored editions); and cf. below, No. 12, note 3 and Chapter VI, No. 1, note 31. It is worth noting, however, that LG visited churches on a number of occasions - see above in the Introduction, note 42.

No. 7 Mixed Pews - 1921 (not in OH)[1]

Source of Question: LGA, Box 4, "Nathan Finkelstein" file

Source of Answer: *USR* 1/3 (July 1921), p. 8 = "Responsum of Prof. Ginzberg on Family Pews for Both Sexes", LGA, Box 17, "Questions and Answers" file = "Mixed Pews" ibid. (with a different ending) = Abraham Karp, in: *American Jewish Year Book* 86 (1986), p. 32

Excerpt of Answer: Karp, p. 45

Secondary References:
1. Joseph Goldberg, in: *Jubilee Book of the Brooklyn Jewish Center*, New York 1946, p. 12
2. Five Gates, p. 115
3. *Keeper*, pp. 229-230
4. Seminary Family, pp. 123-124
5. Jonathan Sarna, "The Debate over Mixed Seating in the American Synagogue", in: Jack Wertheimer, ed., *The American Synagogue: A Sanctuary Transformed*, Cambridge Mass. 1987, pp. 380 and 392
6. Letter From Eli Ginzberg, Sept. 11, 1992

Comment: There is conflicting testimony about LG's own personal practice. LG normally prayed at the Seminary synagogue. Eli Ginzberg, Seminary Family, says that LG would not pray in a synagogue with mixed pews even in inclement weather. But Jacob Sonderling, Five Gates, says that LG attended Sonderling's synagogue with mixed pews when it was raining. According to Sonderling, when asked why, LG explained: "When you live long enough in America, you will realize that the status of womanhood has changed so much that separating women from men has become obsolete". When informed about Sonderling's account, Eli Ginzberg replied: "I cannot place Jacob Sonderling, but I suspect he is right. My father would not worship in a synagogue that used an organ, but he probably made his peace on occasion with mixed pews".

Nathan B. Finkelstein   Tel. Worth 360
Counselor at Law
51 Chambers St.
New York

March 22nd, 1921

Prof. Louis Ginsberg,
Jewish Theological Seminary,
531 W. 123rd St.,
N. Y. City.

Dear Prof. Ginsberg:

The Brooklyn Jewish Centre has almost completed its building. Among our members there is a difference of opinion regarding the future policy of the Institution. Our Constitution provides that the Institution shall always be governed by the laws and customs of "Traditional Judaism".

The first matter of dissension among us is whether our synagogue shall contain mixed pews. Those of us who are opposed to mixed pews maintain that such an innovation in our synagogue would be a departure from traditional Judaism. There are, however, some among us who claim that traditional Judaism is not concerned with the question at all.

The advice of a number of the leaders of thought in Jewry is sought in order to enable us to determine this question correctly.

May I ask you to kindly give me your views in this matter. I shall grealy appreciate your interest, which I feel certain will assist us materially in the determination of this question.[2]

Respectfully yours,

Nathan B. Finkelstein

Family Pews for Both Sexes

The question is asked as to whether family pews would be a departure from traditional Judaism, to which the Chairman of the Committee on the Interpretation of Jewish Law replied as follows: The earliest reference to separating the sexes in the houses of worship is found among the Jewish Therapeutae[3] of which Philo tells us that the women were separated from the men by a wall 3 to 4 cubits in height so that they might listen to the service without infringing the rules of modesty becoming to women.[4] As we otherwise do not lead the life of these Jewish "monks and nuns" there does not seem to be any valid reason why we should attempt to imitate their synagogue regulations. Of greater importance is the fact that in Talmudic times the sexes were separated in the synagogue[5] and this custom must have been so general that the old church adopted it.[6] But we also know that both sexes worshipped then in the same hall and were not separated by any partition, only that the men had their places on one side, and the women on the other. This custom continued till late into the Middle Ages; the women's gallery is, comparatively speaking, a modern invention.[7] It owes its origin not to the desire for a stricter separation of the sexes, but to purely economic and social conditions. Many a congregation would often not be in a position to build a synagogue large enough to accommodate men and women, as the latter were not as frequent visitors of the synagogue as the former - one must not forget that the synagogue was in most cases at the same time a house of study, thus exclusively used by men - they would have to manage for a time without a place to worship. With the expansion of the community the synagogue would keep pace and the women would get their annex to the synagogue or their gallery over the synagogue.[8] Taking into consideration the conditions of today, I do not see any reason for insisting on continuing the women's gallery, but the separation of the sexes is a Jewish custom well established for about 2,000 years, and must not be taken lightly. [And now one word about mixed pews. The synagogue is the place where the Jew is expected to be nothing else but a member of the House of Jacob and the family of Abraham. Mixed pews would rob the synagogue of its democratic character and transfer the snobbishness of the home to the house of God.][9]

1   This question was also asked in brief by Rabbi Samuel Benjamin on Feb. 18, 1920. See Chapter VII, No. 3.

2   LG's responsum was not followed. According to Goldberg, it was decided that men and women should sit together in the two center aisles while the extreme left section was reserved for men and the extreme right section for women. This fact is corroborated below by No. 9, note 11.

3   This was an ascetic sect which lived in the desert of Egypt in the first century C.E.

4   Philo, *On the Contemplative Life or Suppliants*, translated by F.H. Colson, IX, Loeb Classical Library, Cambridge, Mass. 1941, pp. 130-133, paragraphs 32-33.

5   This is an assumption, not a fact, as LG states in No. 8 below. Also see David Golinkin, "A Responsum Regarding the Mehitzah in the Synagogue", *Responsa of the Va'ad Halakhah of the Rabbinical Assembly of Israel*, II: 5747, Jerusalem 5748, pp. 5-20, (in Hebrew), where all possible sources are examined and rejected.

6   This statement has yet to be proved. It appears that some ancient churches had separate seating while others had mixed seating. For separate seating, see Heinrich Kohl and Carl Watzinger, *Antike Synagogen in Galilaea*, Leipzig 1916, p. 221 and note 5; and Solomon Zeitlin, *Jewish Quarterly Review* 38 (1947-48), pp. 306-307. For conflicting evidence see Bernadette Brooten, *Women Leaders in the Ancient Synagogue*, Chico, California 1982, p. 135.

7   This must have been a slip of the pen. The women's gallery is mentioned in many sources beginning in the eleventh century - see Golinkin, p. 14 and note 7.

8   This scenario has yet to be proved.

9   The bracketed section only appears in the typed version entitled "Mixed Pews" in Box 17.

No. 8 An Interview Regarding Mixed Pews - 1926 (?)[1] (not in OH)

Source: CJLS Box, Rabbi Abraham Burstein,[2] "The Decisions of Professor Louis Ginzberg", "Bet Knesset" file = BCA, Box 4, "Burstein, Abraham" file = LGA, Box 17 (p. 1 missing)
Secondary References: Same as above, No. 7

"How, then," was the ensuing query, "if you are to judge without hard and fast legalism, would you decide the matter of mixed pews now agitating so many American congregations?"

"Ah, that," spoke Professor Ginzberg, "is a more frequently presented problem than the matter of Sabbath desecration. Any number of individuals and congregations are writing in all the while for a set decision in the matter."

"I understand," interposed the questioner, "that, as law, the matter of separation of the sexes bears many elements of doubt."

"It does," was the answer. "But here again the question is not entirely a question of law, but also of propriety and liberalism."

"Historical reasons? As a matter of fact, we have no reference in Talmudic lore to the use of special rooms for men and women at worship. We may well assume that in Talmudic days the same room was used for both, with an aisle separating the masculine and feminine worshippers.[3] An amusing incidental of this custom is the story of the famous scholar Abbaye, who, to prevent the young men from encroaching on the ladies' side - or probably vice versa - placed breakable vessels in the aisle, so that any such attempt would entail an unseemly and incriminatory clatter.[4] In the ruins of old synagogues in Galilee, dating from early centuries, there have been discovered no separate rooms for feminine worship.[5] In fact, Philo is the only old authority who mentions the action of the Therapouts – an Egyptian Jewish sect – of using different rooms, separated by a high wall, as a custom of unusual oddity."[6]

"And you say, therefore," the Professor was asked, "that this problem has become in some measure a question of propriety, of liberalism?"

"Most assuredly," was the reply. "The true liberal is he who respects views differing from his own. One may respect views similar to one's own and still remain a thorough bigot. In every congregation so troubled there are parties for or against mixed pews. The man who insists on comingling the sexes has arguments of expediency only, not of religion. He believes more young people will then attend; or that women desiring to remain with their families will be satisfied; or that some vague spirit of modernism may thus be expressed. The believer in separation, however, finds the mixed pew incompatible with his religious convictions – a far more potent impulse than mere expediency. Many Jews would refuse to read the Shema in a pew containing both men and women.[7] It is a matter of earnest principle with such men. Hence, where there is a minority in a congregation which protests against such an innovation, the others should respect their wishes, not on the grounds of law but of true liberalism. The question is out of the realm of law; it is a matter of sympathetic judgment of conditions."

1   Rabbi Burstein states: "It is probable that the Professor will attend the coming convention, to be held in Baltimore and Washington, April 18th to 21st" and in 1926 the United Synagogue convention was held in Baltimore - see Karp, p. 55.

2   Rabbi Abraham Burstein (1893-1966) who was ordained by the Seminary in 1917, was a prolific editor and author who edited *USR* from 1924-29. See *PRA* 31 (1967), pp. 169-171; Nadell, pp. 46-47; and *Conservative Judaism* 47/3 (Spring 1995), pp. 63-65.

3   See above, No. 7, note 5.

4   *Kiddushin* 81a, but the passage makes no mention of a synagogue. According to Rashi, ad loc., Abbaye is dealing with "a place where men and women gather for a *derasha* (sermon) or a wedding". Furthermore, the Talmud is describing there the acts of individual rabbis without ruling in their favor and, indeed, Abbaye's practice was not codified by later authorities.

5   See Golinkin (above, No. 7, note 5), p. 13.

6   See above, No. 7, notes 3-4.

7   See OH 75:1-3 for *halakhot* that could be used to justify such a position.

No. 9 Mixed Pews - 1947-48 (not in OH)

Source: LGA, Box 4, "Fleischer" file. The last letter from Dec. 5, 1947 was published in full in *Conservative Judaism* 11/1 (Fall, 1956), p. 39.
Source of Hebrew letter: Box 17, "Questions and Answers" file
Secondary References: Same as above, No. 7
Comment: Some have assumed (*Keeper; Sarna*) on the basis of the last letter, that LG changed his mind regarding mixed pews between 1921 and 1947, but this assumption is now disproved by the complete correspondence which is being published here for the first time. It is clear that he was still opposed to mixed pews, but allowed them for the sake of congregational unity.

Telephones:
Lafayette 2446
Lafayette 6406
Madison 4778

Joseph Weinstein, Executive Secretary
Res. Telephone:
Lafayette 2210

CHIZUK AMUNO CONGREGATION
EUTAW PLACE AT CHAUNCEY AVENUE
BALTIMORE 17, MARYLAND

November 25, 1947

Prof. Louis Ginzberg
514 West 114th Street
New York 25, N.Y.

Dear Professor Ginzberg:

We would greatly appreciate an answer from you to the following question: "Is there a written prohibition against the mixing of the sexes during worship?"

We expect to have a meeting of our Board within a few days, and we would be grateful for a reply at your earliest convenience.

Cordially yours,

Milton Fleischer, President
Chizuk Amuno Congregation

[Handwritten]: Kindly address your reply to my home: 2401 Eutaw Place, Baltimore - 17 - Md.[1] Many many thanks and may I also extend *Shabos* greetings.

~ ~ ~

December 2, 1947

Dear Mr. Fleischer:

I am in receipt of your letter of November 25th, in which you asked my answer to the following question:

"Is there a written prohibition against the mixing of [the] sexes during worship?"

Let me first remark that as far as I can see, the formulation of the question was done hastily. Your congregation, which is proud, and justly so, of its staunch adherence to historical Judaism, surely does not, in Karaitic fashion, consider only the written word as binding. Scripture speaks of the "Torah which Moses commanded us as [an] inheritance of Israel"[2]. We are thus taught that the Torah is law to Jewish consciousness and Jewish consciousness is law to the Torah. I am, therefore, quite sure that it never occurred to your congregation to introduce worshipping without head-cover, though there are no authoritative writings which prohibit it.[3] Nor can I conceive of your congregation considering abolishing prayer in Hebrew on the basis of written statements according to which one may pray in any language.[4]

The problem of mixing pews confronting you must, therefore, likewise be approached by you and by all to whom historical Judaism is dear, in reverence to Jewish tradition. I would especially warn against that twaddle indulged by many about the contrast between Orientalism and Occidentalism. He who maintains that the separation of sexes in the Synagogue is nothing but the expression of the Oriental concept considering the inferiority of women, shows impartial ignorance of Jewish as well as Oriental history. The Oriental neighbors of the old Hebrews, the Phoenicians and Assyro-Babylonians, to whom they were closely related by race, culture and language, not only did not separate the sexes in their Temples but, on the contrary, had established sexual immorality as an important feature of their worship.[5] It is just this Oriental form of worship against which the Law-Giver and the Prophets carried on an incessant struggle for centuries. It is very likely, therefore, that it was the opposition to Orientalism which led our ancestors during the Second Commonwealth to insist upon separation of the sexes in the Temple. This is, at least, the most likely explanation of the

"Women's Court" in the Second Temple,[6] hence also the women's gallery or women's section in the Synagogue.

The newly discovered ruins of Synagogues in Palestine as well as in the Diaspora dating from the first century of the Common Era clearly indicate that wherever there existed Jewish places of worship, they had separate compartments or sections for men and women.[7] The great philosopher, Philo, a Westerner of the Westerners, but at the same time a very devout Jew, has left us a description of the places of worship of the Jewish Therapeutae - ascetics and religious devotees about 2000 years ago - according to which the females were separated from the males by a wall.[8] He very likely smiled slightly at this rigorous separation, but he found nothing to criticize in it because it was essentially in conformity with established Jewish custom. The references in both Talmudim, the Palestinian and the Babylonian, to synagogues likewise show that this custom was prevailing all over Jewry in Talmudic times.[9] By the time Paganism disappeared in the countries in which the Jews lived, the separation of the sexes in the Synagogue had become a characteristic feature of the Jewish mode of worship and, therefore, continued to be cherished though the original reason for its existence had lost its validity.

Strange to say, the desire for family pews which is said to be so strong in our day, not only did not exist in olden times, but, on the contrary, the Jewish sentiment was strongly against it, and it was this sentiment that greatly contributed to the continuation of the separation of the sexes. The Synagogue was to them the "little sanctuary" [*Megillah* 29a] and [just] as the Sanctuary in Jerusalem was the common property of all Israel, so was the Synagogue. To the Jew of olden times, the conception of a community Synagogue, and still less of a congregational one, was extremely distasteful. The Synagogue threw its gates open to every Jew who wanted to worship and family pews would have robbed it of its true purpose.

The gist of this rather lengthy exposition is, as I hope, an answer to your question but, to be concise, I would like to make these brief statements: While there is no written prohibition against the mixing of the sexes during worship, there can be no doubt that for thousands of years the separation of [the] sexes in the Synagogue was an established custom all through Jewry.

I am sure that my answer will find favor with neither faction of your congregation, but as a student of Israel's past for more than half a century, I consider it my foremost duty to give people the information I have about the past and leave it to them to draw their conclusions from it for the present.

Very sincerely yours,

Louis Ginzberg

Mr. Milton Fleischer
2401 Eutaw Place
Baltimore 17, Maryland

~   ~   ~

Baltimore, Maryland
December 4, 1947

Professor Louis Ginzberg
514 West 114th Street
New York, New York

Dear Dr. Ginzberg:

I am writing this letter from my office which accounts for its not being written on Chizuk Amuno stationery.[10] I want to thank you for the great trouble to which you certainly went in order to furnish me with your comprehensive letter of December 2nd. I regret to have to tell you, however, that undoubtedly it will not serve the purpose of solving the problem that is troubling a large part of our membership.

As I told you on our visit with you, *more than* 85% of our present membership desires that mixed seating be instituted in our Congregation. This is opposed by a minority, small, but protected by a constitutional provision. The request of the majority has been a constant one for the past ten years, and has culminated in a demand which carries the threat that unless the change is instituted, many of those now affiliated will leave our Congregation. We have already had resignations definitely on this account. To put the situation before you as it actually exists, I can say that we are faced with disintegration, and with the loss of some of the most important members of our synagogue.

Let me assure you at the outset, that the change we are contemplating is not being attempted merely for the sake of tinkering and breaking away from the traditions of our faith. Neither are we desirous of alienating the loyalty and sympathy of the small minority which opposes our program. The fact that nothing has been done up to now, even though the agitation has been on for many years, must indicate to you that we are primarily interested in the *peace* of our group and in preserving its *unity*.

In our contemplated change, we insist that provision will be made for those who wish to worship separately, and to this group will be assigned a part of the synagogue on the sides, such as is the practice, let's say, at Rabbi Levinthal's synagogue in Brooklyn.[11] We feel that the minority group would be satisfied to go along with the change, provided they were assured that it is not forbidden to worship in such a set-up; or, let us say, it is permitted to worship where such an arrangement exists.

If this compromise can be agreed on and has your sanction, we shall be able to retain our entire membership within the fold of traditional Judaism, thus forestalling the very definite defection of many of our members to the Reform temples and to Conservative synagogues where the practice of mixed seating is already established.

The enclosed resolution, with especial emphasis on the sections blue-pencilled, is of the utmost importance, and indicates our desire to save the major structure of traditional worship by making the necessary sacrifice of only a small part.

I know it is an imposition on your time and your health to bring you into this controversy, yet in the interest of our unity, we must ask you to make this sacrifice and advise us. May I hear from you promptly, inasmuch as we shall hold our next Board meeting on Tuesday, December 9th.

With best wishes for your good health and extending Shabbos greetings, I am

Cordially yours,

Milton Fleischer

P.S. Kindly address your reply to my home - 2410 Eutaw Place, Baltimore 17, Maryland.[12]

WHEREAS, more than eighty-five per cent (85%) of the members of Baltimore Hebrew Chizuk Amuno Congregation of Baltimore City have, to date, expressed in writing the wish to worship in family pews; and

WHEREAS, it is the opinion of the Board of Directors and Officers of the Congregation, after careful consideration and investigation, that, under modern conditions, it is extremely important to make it possible for parents, during religious services, to assist their children, and for husband and wife to assist each other in the comprehension and appreciation of the prayers and the religious ritual and ceremonies, and that, consequently, the continued separation of family units during services presents a great danger to the present welfare and future life of our Congregation; and

WHEREAS, the Board of Directors of the Congregation has been advised by Dr. Adolph Coblenz, the esteemed and scholarly Rabbi of the Congregation,[13] that there is no specific injunction against family pews contained in the Torah;[14] and

WHEREAS, out of the total membership of three hundred and seventy six (376) congregations in the United Synagogue of America, of which organization, founded thirty-four (34) years ago, our Congregation is a charter member, three hundred and seventy two (372) of the members, or practically ninety-nine per cent (99%), worship in family pews; and

WHEREAS, the Board of Directors and Officers of the Congregation, in recognition of the opposition to family pews of a small minority of the members of the Congregation, are of the opinion that the views of such minority should be respected by providing space in the main auditorium of the Synagogue for the separate seating of the men and women of the families of such members.

NOW, THEREFORE, BE IT RESOLVED, that the Board of Directors of Baltimore Hebrew Chizuk Amuno Congregation of Baltimore City DOES HEREBY RECOMMEND to the general membership of the Congregation that family pews be authorized in the main auditorium of the Synagogue, from and after the _____ day of _____ 19__ ;

PROVIDED, HOWEVER,[15] that space be provided in the main auditorium of the Synagogue for the separate seating of the men and women of the families of those members of the Congregation who may be opposed to family pews; and

PROVIDED FURTHER, that this recommendation be adopted by the members of the Congregation in conformity with the provisions of Section 2 of Article II of the Constitution of the Congregation.

AND BE IT FURTHER RESOLVED,[16] that the adoption of this resolution shall not be considered as a precedent or as authority for deviating from the prayers, ceremonies, and customs of traditional Judaism, and shall be regarded as a confirmation of the existence in full force and effect of the requirements of Section 2 of Article II of the Constitution of the Congregation, with respect to the procedure for making alterations in the prayers, ceremonies or religious customs of the Congregation, and we reaffirm our opposition to any deviation from the prayers, ceremonies and customs of traditional Judaism [handwritten: such as worship with uncovered head, mixed sexes in our Choir, organ music at religious services] [different handwriting: but to continue to worship with *Taleisim* same as we have been and are doing and will continue to do.]

AND BE IT FURTHER RESOLVED, that the Board of Directors submit this resolution for adoption, in conformity with provisions of Section 2 of Article II of the Constitution of the Congregation, at the regular semi-annual meeting of the members of the Congregation, to be held on the 29th day of December, 1947; and that a copy of this resolution be incorporated in the notice of said meeting, which shall be mailed to the members no later than the day of _____ December, 1947.

~   ~   ~

December 5, 1947

Dear Mr. Fleischer:

I hasten to reply to your letter of December 4th, which reached me early this morning, but I shall do it as briefly as possible because of the poor state of my health. My physician strongly insists upon complete rest.

1. While there is no written prohibition against the mixing of the sexes during worship, there can be no doubt that for thousands of years the separation of [the] sexes in the Synagogue was an established custom all through Jewry.

2. The origin of this custom was to emphasize Jewish opposition to the Pagan immorality which held sway over the idolatrous neighbors of the Old Hebrews like the Phoenicians and Assyro-Babylonians.

3. The custom of separating the sexes in the Synagogue was modeled after that of the Temple, yet occasionally, even in the Temple, this rule had its exceptions. For instance, in one of the most solemn ceremonies, on the most solemn day of the year, the Day of Atonement, the High Priest read the Biblical section of the day in the "Women's Court" before men and women.[17] Similarly, the reading of the law by the King at the end of the Sabbatical year took place in the "Women's Court".[18]

4. If, therefore, conditions of a congregation are such that continued separation of family units during services presents a great danger to its spiritual welfare, the minority ought to yield to the spiritual need of the majority.

If you intend making use of my letter, I would be obliged to you if you would put it in its entirety before your members. Quotations are sometimes misleading.

It is my sincerest hope that your Congregation will be led by the words of the Prophet: "Therefore love ye truth and peace".[19]

With kindest regards,

Very sincerely yours,

Louis Ginzberg

Mr. Milton Fleischer
2401 Eutaw Place
Baltimore 17, Maryland.

~   ~   ~

Telephones   Joseph Weinstein, Executive Secretary
Lafayette 2446   Res. Telephone:
Lafayette 6406   Lafayette 2210
Madison 4778
                  CHIZUK AMUNO CONGREGATION
                 EUTAW PLACE AT CHAUNCEY AVENUE
                    BALTIMORE 17, MARYLAND

December 11, 1947

Professor Louis Ginsberg
514 West 114th Street
New York, New York

Dear Dr. Ginsberg,

I desire to thank you most profusely for your prompt reply to my letter of the 4th. Your letter was presented and read at a meeting of our Board of Directors held last evening, and I believe that its contents will have the desired effect of continued *sholom* within the midst of our Congregation as this is of the greatest importance in Congregational life.

I sincerely trust that your health will improve. Permit me to extend *Shabbos* greetings in which our entire Board of Directors join me.

With kindest personal regards, I remain,

Very sincerely yours,
CHIZUK AMUNO CONGREGATION

MILTON FLEISCHER
PRESIDENT

~   ~   ~

January 6, [1948][20]

Dear Mr. Fleischer:

I was very happy to know from your letter of December 30th that, at the semi-annual Congregation meeting, the resolution as submitted by you was adopted by an overwhelming majority. You know, of course, that I am not particularly fond of changes in the Synagogue, yet peace and harmony in the Congregation are too important to consider minor matters.

The majority vote clearly indicates that it wanted and, very likely, needed the proposed changes. Let's hope that your Congregation will continue to uphold Jewish tradition and Jewish law, doing justice to its name חזוק אמונה.[21]

With kindest regards,

Very sincerely yours,

Louis Ginzberg

Mr. Milton Fleischer
N.E. Corner Eutaw Pl. & Chauncey Avenue
Baltimore 17, Maryland

~   ~   ~

יום ד׳: כ״ד שבט, שנת גאולה, ישע וכל ברכה.[22]

(2.5.48)

לר׳ אברהם קובלנץ, שליט״א.[23]

ידידי וחביבי:

שמחתי על קבלת מכתבך מהרה נהפכה לתוגה כשקראתי שאתה מוטל על ערש-דוי. הרופא חולים ישלח לך מהרה רפואה שלמה בתוך שאר חולי ישראל הצריכים רפואה ובתוכם גם אני.

לבי נוקפני אם צדקתי להתערב בסכסוכי הקהלה שלך.[24] הלא תדע כי אני אינני מאוהבי ״חדשות״ וביחוד נפשי מואסת בשנויי מנהגים שבבית-הכנסת. אמנם כן, כאשר נדרשתי לחוות דעתי אם א ס ו ר על-פי הדין להתפלל במקום שאנשים ונשים יושבים על ספסל אחד, לא ראיתי לי דרך אחרת אלא לאמר שאין שום איסור בדבר אבל כך נהגו אבותינו זה כאלפים שנה שבבית-תפלה, האנשים לבד והנשים לבד, וגדול השלום לעבור על מנהג בשבילו. ואני מקוה שלא יאמרו הבריות ״התירו פרושים״[25] לשנות ולהחליף מנהגי ישראל.

בברכת כל טוב וביחוד בריאות טובה,

ידידך,
לוי גינצבורג

1   The President may have been trying to bypass the Rabbi. See below the final letter in Hebrew and note 24.

2   A paraphrase of Deuteronomy 33:4.

3   This is not entirely accurate. See above, Nos. 2-3 and the literature cited there.

4   See *Mishnah Sotah* 7:1 and OH 101:4.

5   See *Entziklopedia Mikra'it*, s.v. Kedeisha; Louis Epstein, *Sex Laws and Customs in Judaism*, New York 1948, pp. 152-155; and Jeffrey Tigay, *The JPS Torah Commentary: Deuteronomy*, Philadelphia and Jerusalem, 1996, pp. 480-481.

6   I have shown in my responsum on mixed seating (above, No. 7, note 5, pp. 6-8) that men and women were only separated in the Temple during the Festival of Drawing the Water on Sukkot. Throughout the year, men and women circulated freely in the Women's Court (ibid., pp. 10-11) and the name of the court can be explained in other ways (ibid., note 4).

7   This was the opinion of many archaeologists at the beginning of the century after the first few synagogues were excavated. This, however, is no longer the majority view since evidence of a gallery has been discovered in only five of the 110 synagogues excavated. See my responsum, above, No. 7, note 5, p. 13. Also see above, No. 8, note 5, where LG says the opposite.

8   See above, No. 7, notes 3-4.

9   I know of no evidence for this assertion.

10   See above, note 1.

11   See above No. 7, note 2.

12   See above, note 1.

13   Rabbi Adolph Coblenz (1887-1949 or 1950) was ordained by the Seminary in 1912 and was rabbi of Chizuk Amuno Congregation for almost thirty years. See *Students' Annual* 3, (1916), p. 189 and *PRA* 14 (1950), pp. 318-320.

14   See below the Hebrew letter from LG to Rabbi Coblenz.

15   This entire paragraph is underlined by hand in the original, as mentioned above.

16   This entire paragraph is bracketed by hand in the original, as mentioned above.

17   *Yoma* 69a-b.

18   *Sota* 40b-41a and parallels.

19   *Zechariah* 8:19.

20   The secretary inadvertently typed 1947, as frequently occurs at the beginning of a new calendar year.

21   I.e., "strengthening of the faith".

22   This is probably a reference to the events of 1947-48 in Israel. On LG's Zionism, see *Keeper*, Index, s.v. Israel.

23   See above, note 13.

24   It is not clear whether LG is reacting to a complaint from Rabbi Coblenz about interfering in his synagogue's affairs or trying to justify his ruling to himself. The second interpretation seems more likely since Rabbi Coblenz's approach as quoted in the resolution above was similar to LG's.

25   The expression is from *Sanhedrin* 82b.

No. 10 Is the Bimah in the Center a Sephardic Custom? (OH 150:5)

Source: LGA, Box 3, "Bosniak" file
Comment: Rabbi Bosniak was born in Gorodetz, Russia.[1] He apparently wanted to know if the fact that the *bimah* there was in the center of the synagogue proved the Sephardic origin of his native community.

May 12, 1947

Dear Rabbi Bosniak:

I quite often attended services at the famous Sephardic Synagogue in Amsterdam, and previous to it I was a frequent worshipper in the no less famous synagogue of Vilna. In both synagogues the *Bimah* was not located in the center. As a matter of fact, in the synagogue in Vilna, the *Bimah* was closer to the entrance than in the synagogue of Amsterdam.[2] You will, therefore, need stronger support for the Sephardic origin of the Jewish community of your native town than that based upon the position of the *Bimah*.

The truth of the matter is that very few old synagogues have the *Bimah* exactly in the center. Not even the old synagogues of the early centuries discovered in modern times.[3] The reason for the rule laid down by the codifiers to place the *Bimah* in the center is to have the reader's place at an equal distance from East, West, North, [and] South.[4] Since the *Bimah* occupied a good deal of space, they did not want to have its back part exactly in the center.

The two greatest Talmudists of the last five centuries, the author of the *Shulhan Aruk* and the *Gaon* of Vilna both call attention to the deviation of the customary place of the *Bimah* from the prescribed rule to have it in the center; comp. *Kesef Mishneh* on Maimonides, *Tefillah* 11:3 [towards the end] and the commentary of the *Gaon* on *Shulhan Aruk* [OH] 150. It is highly interesting that the Gaon speaks of the Bimah being at the "end". He very likely had before his mind the great synagogue of his town, Vilna, where the *Bimah* is very close to the entrance.[5]

May I on this occasion ask of you a great favor. My friend and colleague, Doctor Abraham Heschel, told me that he had written to you asking you to use your influence with the HIAS. Doctor Heschel is not only a great scholar,

but a very close friend of mine and any favor shown to him I would consider
as shown to me.[6]
Kindest regards.

Very sincerely yours,

Louis Ginzberg

Rabbi Jacob Bosniak
450 Ocean Parkway
Brooklyn, New York

1   According to Nadell, pp. 44-46. Rabbi Jacob Bosniak (1887-1963) was ordained by the
Seminary in 1917 and was rabbi in Flatbush for many years (1921-49).
2   For illustrations of the interior of the great Sephardic synagogue of Amsterdam, see *EJ*,
II, cols. 897-898 and XV, col. 616. These illustrations corroborate LG's recollection. For
illustrations of the interior of the great synagogue of Vilna, see George Loukomski, *Jewish Art in
European Synagogues*, London 1947, p. 95 (though the caption there is incorrect; only the *bimah*
is shown); Rachel Wischnitzer, *The Architecture of the European Synagogue*, Philadelphia 1964,
p. 119 (an exaggerated illustration from ca. 1800); Leyzer Ran, *Jerusalem of Lithuania*, I, New
York 1974, pp. 104, 109; Carol Herselle Krinsky, *Synagogues of Europe*, Cambridge, Mass. 1985,
pp. 223-225. None of the illustrations from Vilna show the entire interior of the synagogue but,
taken together, they seem to corroborate LG's recollection.
3   We now know that some do and some do not. For a good summary of recent findings see
Yisrael Levine, *Cathedra* 60 (March, 1990), pp. 57-59 (Hebrew).
4   "One makes a *bimah* in the middle of the synagogue for the Torah reader to stand on...so
that all can hear" - Rambam, *Hilkhot Tefillah* 11:3 = *Tur* OH 150 = Rema in OH 150:5.
5   See the illustrations cited above, note 2.
6   A.J. Heschel came to the United States in 1940 and became a U.S. citizen in 1945 (Nadell,
pp. 138-139), so it is not clear why he needed help with the Hebrew Immigrant Aid Society
(HIAS) in 1947. Perhaps he was trying to help one of the thousands of displaced persons who
arrived in the United States beginning in May, 1946 - see Mark Wischnitzer, *Visas to Freedom:
The History of HIAS*, Cleveland & New York 1956, pp. 211ff.

No. 11 May the Lower Floor of a Synagogue be Used as a Bet Midrash and as a Social Hall? (OH 151:1-2)

Source of Question: LGA, Box 7, "Kleinman" file
Source of Answer to second question: *USR* 1/3 (July, 1921), pp. 7-8 = LGA, Box 17, "Questions and Answers" file

PHILIP KLEINMAN[1]
RABBI
TEMPLE AARON
ST. PAUL, MINN.

3/29/20

Dear Dr. Ginzberg,

I am addressing this communication to you as Chairman of the Committee on the Interpretation of Jewish Law to answer the following two questions.

First, what shall be the Rabbi's procedure in cases of conversion where the fact is known that the party seeking conversion does so because of a desire to marry a member of the Jewish faith? I know that the old Orthodox Rabbis are not in agreement as to the proper procedure. Those in St. Paul decide each case on its own merits - the family's status in the community determining their procedure. They also do not require any preparation on the part of the party to be converted in the fundamentals of Jewish law and life. They are satisfied with the minimum. What shall be our procedure in such cases?

I would appreciate a detailed answer to cover the entire question of Conversion, with special emphasis upon the laws of conversion of women, since the latter are not fully dealt with in the שע [= *Shulhan Arukh*]. Also describe the manner of the conversion ceremony. I am sure that this is a question that each one of our own men are vitally interested in since the sin of intermarriage is national in scope.[2]

The second question is as follows. We have been using the lower floor of our synagogue for services whenever there was a *Yahrzeit* or on some very cold שבת when we could not properly heat the synagogue. At the same time, the lower floor was used for social affairs of every description. Until recently these affairs have been rare. But lately, owing to the growth of the synagogue, the social activities have multiplied. I have therefore insisted that a special בית מדרש be set aside downstairs that won't be used for any other purpose.

Some of the worshippers maintain that the lower floor was originally built for a בית מדרש and cannot now be turned over into a place of social amusement. They claim that one of the officials of the congregation specifically stated that the downstairs will be for them - the old people.

On the other hand, the members of the executive board claim that the lower floor was especially planned for social activities only. They point out the fact that because of that a coat room and kitchen were built near it. They maintain that services were only held there because there was no other place to hold them. They are satisfied to set aside a certain part of the lower floor for a בית מדרש. Thus we have two opposing views, one party claiming that the lower floor was built for a בית מדרש and therefore no social activities can be conducted there, the other party maintaining that it was built for social activities and therefore services may be held there.

I have always opposed the holding of services there and insisted upon a special בית מדרש to be constructed. That has already been planned for. Would you kindly enlighten us on this question. The first party will not yield until they hear an authoritative opinion. I told them I would write to you.

Hoping to receive replies to the above without fail and with kindest regards to the members of the faculty and your dear family.

I remain

Most Sincerely Yours,

Philip Kleinman

The Synagogue and Social Center

A Rabbi requested a decision as to whether a part of the lower floor of a synagogue could be set aside as a social center, and whether that part could then be used at other times for prayer.

The decision is that to use the same room for social activities and prayer is contrary to good taste.[3] If the Executive Committee of the Board decided when the synagogue was built that that part of the building is to be used for social activities, it is permitted to do so, but in that case the room should not be used for prayer. If, on the other hand, it was decided originally that that part of the building be used for prayer, then it [should] not be used for other purposes.

---

1   Rabbi Philip Kleinman (1890- after 1960) was ordained by the Seminary in 1918 and was rabbi in St. Paul, Minnesota and Portland, Oregon. See W. Gunther Plaut, *The Jews in Minnesota*, New York 1959, pp. 200-201 as well as *Students' Annual* 3 (1916), p. 203; *PRA* 5 (1933-38), p. 497; and PRA 24 (1960), p. 339.

2   The answer to this question was not found. For LG's response to a similar question, see below, Chapter IV, No. 10.

3   It is also contrary to Jewish law - see OH 151:1-2.

No. 12 May a Synagogue be Sold to a Church? (OH 153)[1]

Source: CJLS Box, "Bet Knesset" file = BCA, Box 5, "Miscellaneous Questions and Answers" file
Summary: Boaz Cohen, PRA 8 (1941-44), pp. 35-36

Question: I want to consult you on a problem which might arise in my congregation. We are occupying an old building and have purchased a lot for a new synagogue in the residential section of town. The only way in which we shall ever be able to undertake a new structure is in the event we can sell the present property. In the open market, our property is not worth much, barely enough to cover our present indebtedness. Two different church organizations have shown an interest in our property. I don't know what will come of the present negotiations, but we might make a deal with them. Only for a church will the building have sufficient value. There may be objection raised to the sale of the building under any circumstances. We have a few members who are waiting for an opportunity of invoking by-laws passed about 30 years ago which prohibited changes in ritual from Orthodox prescription, but which permitted sale of property [by] a two-thirds vote. They will surely not miss the opportunity of objecting to a sale for a church. Now the *Mishnah Megilla* 3:2, which is quoted in the *Tur Orah Hayim* 153 and in the *Yad, Tefilla* 11:17 does not list a church among the objectionable uses to which a synagogue may not be sold for. I recall that a synagogue on the East Side was actually sold some years ago for a Greek Orthodox church. Do any of the responsa deal with this problem? What is the predominant attitude? Is the expedient of selling the property to an individual resorted to? If so, is it preferable that the individual be a Jew or a non-Jew?

Answer: In reply to your letter in which you inquire whether your synagogue may be sold for the purpose of having it converted into a church, I wish to inform you that this question did not come up in early times and therefore it is difficult to give you citations of precedents. It is possible that in very recent times such questions have been discussed by modern authorities in Responsa literature but, at present, I cannot locate any.[2] I consulted Professor Ginzberg on this question and he informed me that it is contrary to Jewish law to sell a synagogue for the purpose of converting it into a church because it is improper for a Jew even to rent out premises to be used for idolatrous purposes.[3] However, as a practical way out he suggested that it could be sold to a Gentile with the understanding that the synagogue not be used for any improper purposes.[4]

1   For two similar questions, see below, Chapter VII, No. 3.
2   For some recent responsa see *Otzar Ha-she'elot U'teshuvot*, II, Jerusalem 5736, p. 147.
3   According to *Mishnah Avodah Zarah* 1:9, but see YD 151:10, where the later authorities have watered down this restriction. For Catholicism as a form of idol worship, see above, No. 6, note 3 and Chapter VI, No. 1, note 31. Also see the summary in *PRA* where Boaz Cohen refers to Tosefta Avodah Zarah 6:2, ed. Zuckermandel, p. 469, which prohibits selling a house to an idol worshipper.
4   I.e., that it not be used as a church. For a similar stipulation, see below, Chapter VII, No. 3, note 4.

No. 13 May a Synagogue be Sold for Commercial Purposes? (OH 153:7)

Source: *USR* 1/3 (July, 1921), pp. 7-8 = LGA, Box 17, "Questions and Answers" file = *Keeper*, p. 229
Excerpt of Answer: Karp, p. 45

Interesting Decisions by the Committee on Interpretation of Jewish Law

There have been a number of interesting questions propounded to the Committee on the Interpretation of Jewish Law, and the decisions rendered are of interest not only to the congregations and individuals involved, but also to the whole of the Jewish community. Some of the interesting responsa, written by the Chairman of the Committee, Professor Louis Ginzberg, are here given.

Sale of Synagogue for Business Purposes

A congregation about to build a larger and more commodious synagogue desires to sell its old building for commercial purposes in order that it may have the wherewithal to go on with the work on the new building. The response is as follows: In reply thereto I would say that Jewish Law is explicit on this point, discriminating between a community synagogue and a congregational synagogue. A community synagogue cannot be sold for commercial purposes; a congregational synagogue may.[1] By the first, we understand a synagogue erected by the contributions of the Jewish inhabitants of a city or town for the use of all. A congregational synagogue is one which is erected by the contributions of members of a society primarily for their own use. Although I know nothing about the history of your synagogue, I assume that it is a congregational synagogue, as there are hardly any community synagogues in the sense of the law in this country. If my assumption is correct, there is nothing against the sale of the synagogue building for commercial purposes.

1. OH 153:7.

No. 14 An Interview Regarding Synagogue Construction on Shabbat (OH 244:3)[1]

Source: CJLS Box, Rabbi Abraham Burstein, "The Decisions of Professor Louis Ginzberg," "Bet Knesset" file = BCA, Box 4, "Burstein, Abraham" file = LGA, Box 17 (p. 1 missing).

"And you decided, of course," was the rejoinder, "that it may not?" "The answer is not so obvious and simple as that," smiled the Professor. "If I were to be purely legalistic, I could find law and precedent to permit it. The situation generally presented is that where a contract is given to a non-Jewish builder, who thereupon assumes his labors entirely beyond the immediate jurisdiction of the congregation. They merely pay the cost and accept the finished structure. But I object to any synagogue group taking such advantage of legal loopholes. From a broader point of view, building of synagogue structures on the Jewish Sabbath should never be permitted. It is not a matter of seeking excuses, but of considering the effect of such conduct on all beholders, Jews and Gentiles alike.[2] We are constantly admonishing our people, from the pulpit and in our schools, to make sacrifices for Jewish observance; shall the congregation itself refuse to sacrifice a sum of money for the maintenance of our most important ceremonial observance? The non-Jew certainly will accept some legalistic twisting as excuse for a Jewish religious body openly flaunting its religious principles. My decision, therefore, becomes not a matter of the letter, but of the spirit, and I urge the questioners not to allow this obvious desecration of our day of rest."[3]

---

1   For more details about this interview and about Rabbi Burstein, see above, No. 8, notes 1-2.

2   He is worried about *mar'it ayin* and *hashad* - see *ET*, XVII, col. 686ff.

3   LG gave a similar ruling in 1921. It was recalled by Rabbi Morris Silverman in 1963 (in a letter partially printed above, Chapter II, No. 6): "...Several months before your father died, he recalled to me an incident which I had completely forgotten. It was in 1921, I believe, while I was still a student at the Seminary and at the same time rabbi of Temple Israel of Washington Heights. When I heard that the contractors would be permitted to build our Synagogue on the Sabbath in order that the building would be ready for the High Holidays, I strenuously objected. The President of the congregation told me that, according to the contract, the building would not be in our possession until it was completed. At that time, the five-day week was not prevalent. I discussed the matter with your father, and he said [that] although legally it could be done, I was right in my position because the public would not know of this 'legal fiction'. Reinforced with your father's opinion, I persuaded the board to insert a clause in the contract that no work on the building should be done on the Sabbath. It was finished just one day before the High Holidays."

No. 15 Are Late Friday Evening Services Permissible? (OH 261:4)

Source: LGA, Box 17, "Committee on Interpretation of Jewish Law" file = *Exponent* = *Keeper*, pp. 230-231

...I have, however, no doubt that you will all be gratified to know that the number of questions addressed to your committee is increasing with such rapidity as to cause alarm to the treasurer, for your committee might soon apply for a secretary and a stenographer to assist in its business. Your committee had to deal with questions relating to the synagogue, marriage and divorce, proselytism, burial, and many other matters of Jewish law and practice.

To mention only a few instances, a matter frequently referred to your committee, is the question of late Friday evening services. I understand that in some places voices of protest have been raised against this so-called innovation. This only corroborates the truth of the observation made by many that humanity could easily be divided into two main classes, those who maintain that whatever was good enough for our fathers is not good enough for us, and those who proclaim that whatever was not good for our fathers cannot be good for us. There is not the least objection to late Friday evening services even from the strictest point of view of the law,[1] but certain people will nevertheless object to it because it was not known in the time of their fathers. Yet, they forget that what might have been unnecessary and even obnoxious in the times past, may become very necessary and advisable in our days.

---

1   Even so, it goes against the standard practice of "accepting Shabbat" when *barekhu* is recited at the beginning of the *Ma'ariv* service - see OH 261:4, 263:10, and 267:2.

No. 16 May Unfermented Wine be Used in Religious Ceremonies? (OH 272:2)

Source of complete Hebrew responsum: תשובה בדבר יינות הכשרים והפסולים למצוה, נויארק תרפ״ב. The Hebrew responsum has been reprinted in the Hebrew section of this volume.

Source of abbreviated English version of the responsum: *The American Jewish Year Book* 25 (5684), Philadelphia 1923, pp. 401-425

Excerpt of the Hebrew version: *Conservative Judaism* 8/3 (April, 1952), pp. 24-23 (*sic!*)

Summaries:
1. *USR* 2/2 (April, 1922), pp. 3-4
2. *USR* 3/2 (April, 1923), p. 3

Secondary References:
1. Letter from National Grape Juice Company, Dec. 30, 1921, LGA, Box 9, "National Grape Juice" file
2. Letter from The Welch Grape Juice Company, January 12, 1922, LGA, Box 12, "Welch" file
3. Max Drob, *USR* 5/2 (April, 1925), p. 15
4. שאול ליברמן, מחקרים בתורת ארץ ישראל, ירושלים תשנ״א, עמ׳ 613-614 = הארץ, כ׳ בכסלו, תרצ״ד
5. Herbert Parzen, *Conservative Judaism* 8/2 (January 1952), p. 31 = *Architects of Conservative Judaism*, New York 1964, pp. 151-152
6. Louis Finkelstein, *PAAJR* 23 (1954), p. li and *PRA* 18 (1954), p. 172
7. "Five Gates", pp. 112-113
8. Address, pp. 113, 115
9. *Keeper*, pp. 219-221
10. Seminary Family, p. 123
11. Jenna Joselit, *Our Gang: Jewish Crime and the New York Jewish Community, 1900-1940*, Bloomington 1983, Chapter 5 and esp. p. 90
12. Hannah Sprecher, "'Let Them Drink and Forget Our Poverty': Orthodox Rabbis React to Prohibition", *American Jewish Archives* XLIII/2 (Fall-Winter, 1991), pp. 134-179, esp. pp. 154ff.

A Response to the Question
Whether Unfermented Wine May Be Used In Jewish Ceremonies
By LOUIS GINZBERG
Professor of Talmud,
the Jewish Theological Seminary of America
(Translated from the Hebrew original)[1]

The Questions

1. Is there any reason why fermented wine should be preferred to unfermented in the performance of Jewish religious ceremonies?

2. Is there any reason why grape juice may not be used in the performance of those ceremonies?

The Response

The above questions were referred to me by the Rabbinical Assembly of the Jewish Theological Seminary of America. They have become of more than theoretical importance because of the prohibition by the Eighteenth Amendment to the Constitution of the United States of the "manufacture, sale or transportation within" the United States of intoxicating liquors "for beverage purposes". Under the Volstead Act and the Regulations of the Department of Internal Revenue, Jews are permitted to buy wine for the performance of their religious customs. This privilege has given rise to widespread abuse which has attracted attention from many quarters. Many people, not Rabbis, have presumed to exercise the functions of Rabbis, in order to procure and help others procure wine not at all for religious purposes, but for "beverage purposes". The Rabbinical Assembly has been moved by the discovery of these scandals to ask whether fermented wine is indeed essential to the performance of any Jewish religious ceremony.

I. THE HISTORICAL DEVELOPMENT OF THE USE OF WINE IN JEWISH CUSTOM

1. The Origin of the Use of Wine in Jewish Ritual - In order to understand fully the laws regarding the use of wine in Jewish ceremonies it is neccessary to know some of the facts concerning the development of these customs. The sages of Israel never introduced the drinking of wine as a religious custom. They merely gave a religious sanctification to the use of wine which before their times had been drunk in a purely secular way after the fashion of other Oriental peoples. It is a general tendency of rabbinic Judaism to give religious sanction to purely secular actions. By adding a prayer to the drinking of the wine, and by reducing the amount used to a

single cup, wine-drinking ceased to be merely indulgence of the appetite, and its use became a religious rite. This is the origin of the use of wine in every case where it has become part of Jewish ceremonial.

2. The Use of Wine in Religious Ceremonies as Recorded in Scripture - In the Pentateuch the use of wine in the performance of religious ceremonies is mentioned only in connection with libations. The sacrifice being a symbolic way of communing with God, it was composed of all the elements of a Palestinian festival meal: meat, bread, wine, and oil. See Exodus 29:40, Numbers 28:7, 14, and other passages.

3. The Passover Meal - The first reference to the use of wine in a religious ceremony outside the Temple occurs in the Book of Jubilees 49:6, which was composed about the year 100 before the Common Era. Wine is there mentioned as part of the Paschal feast. A similar reference occurs in the early Christian writings (Matthew 26:27). In the tenth chapter of the treatise Pesahim, which has been shown (Hoffmann, *Die Erste Mischna*, pp. 8-9, 16-17)[2] to have been composed before the Fall of the Second Jewish Commonwealth, wine is referred to as an integral part of the Passover meal.

Four cups of wine are drunk in connection with the Passover service. In order to understand the origin of these four cups we must bear in mind that at first the meal, which now follows the recital of the Passover service, preceded it. The Passover home service began with a meal, which consisted of the Paschal lamb, the unleavened cakes, the bitter herbs, and, of course, of wine. As at every other festival meal, wine was drunk before the meal and after it. The wine drunk before the meal was reduced by the sages to a single cup over which was pronounced the benediction for the Sanctification of the Day (*kiddush*); the wine drunk after the meal was again reduced to a single cup, over which [the] grace after the meal was recited. This *kiddush* cup was common to all festivals, and the custom of reciting grace after the meal over a cup of wine was continued even on weekdays till our own times.

After the meal the child would ask for the meaning of the strange customs observed on that night and the reply to it would form the service of the evening (the modern *Haggadah*). After the service, the people would indulge in festive songs, beginning with the great Jewish paean, the Hallel, which consists of Psalms 113-118. This singing was accompanied by drinking which the Rabbis limited to two cups, one before the *Hallel* and one after it. There thus arose the custom of drinking four cups of wine on Passover night, and even in later times, when the *Haggadah* for various reasons was recited before the meal, the four cups continued as an integral part of the service of the evening.

4. *Kiddush* and *Habdalah* - We have seen how the wine ordinarily drunk before the festival meal was sanctified by the Rabbis into a religious ceremony, and the benediction ushering in the holy day pronounced over it. The same development took place regarding the ushering in of the Sabbath. There thus arose the custom of reciting the *kiddush* both for the Sabbath and other festivals over a cup of wine. This ceremony was well established by the first century, since the schools of Shammai and Hillel who flourished in that century differed at that early period as to the proper method of performing the ceremony under various conditions.

Just as at the beginning of the Sabbath and the festivals a benediction was pronounced, so there developed the custom of reciting a benediction at their termination. The final meal, like all festival meals in Palestine, was followed by the drinking of wine. The Rabbis made the cup of wine drunk at that time, the occasion of the pronouncing of a benediction for the termination of the Sabbath or festival. This was called the *Habdalah*, the prayer dividing the holy day from the week-day.

5. Nuptial Benedictions - The Jewish marriage ceremony in early times consisted of two distinct festive occasions: the *erusin* or betrothal, which in Jewish law has legal validity and cannot be dissolved except by due ceremony of divorce; and the *nissuin* or wedding ceremony. These two ceremonies were merged in [medieval] times into one,[3] the passing of the ring from the bridegroom to the bride being performed at the same time as their entrance into the canopy, although the first is the legal *erusin* and the second the theoretical *nissuin*.

Each of these ceremonies has its own benedictions, and in modern times each is recited over a cup of wine. Two cups of wine are thus needed for every marriage ceremony.

There is no mention of the need of a cup of wine for either ceremony in the Talmud or the early geonic works. R. Isaac of Vienna (thirteenth century) in his code (*Or Zorua*, I, par. 752) declared that the use of wine in connection with the marriage benedictions was ordained by the Rabbis, as is "stated in the treatise *Sotah* of the Talmud of Jerusalem, chapter *Keshem*" (i.e., chapter 5). Now in the chapter of *Sotah* mentioned there is no reference to the use of wine at weddings, and the word "כשם" must therefore be emended to "משי״ם", which is an abbreviation for the words *Meshuah Milhamah* or chapter 8 of *Sotah*.[4] In that chapter there occurs a tannaitic statement discussing the question whether wine with a pungent taste may be used for various religious ceremonies. It is mentioned [there] that such wine may be used "to sanctify a bride in marriage".

This expression is ambiguous since it may mean either that the wine may be used as a gift to the bride in consideration of which she becomes sanctified in marriage, or that it may be used to recite the benedictions of the nuptial ceremony. While R. Isaac of Vienna seems to adopt the second interpretation, there is no parallel for the use of the expression in that sense. In speaking of the nuptial benedictions, the Talmud refers to them as "the benedictions of the bridegroom" but never as the "benedictions of the bride".

The first interpretation receives some support from a statement of R. Sa'adja Gaon (Babylon, first half of the tenth century) in his *Seder* (quoted in *Seder R. Amram*, ed. Frumkin, II, p. 196a)[5] that, after the benedictions of *erusin*, the bridegroom says to the bride, "Be thou sanctified to me in marriage in consideration of this cup and its contents". This expression implies that the cup of wine is the actual means whereby the bride is married to the bridegeroom and not the cup over which the benediction is pronounced. The custom of giving a cup of wine to the bride was extant among the Singali Jews, as can be seen from their prayer-book (Amsterdam, 1769, p. 45b).[6] In spite of this support, it is difficult to assume that already in talmudic times the custom of giving a bride a cup of wine in consideration of the marriage had already been established.

Far more likely is it that the passage should be emended by omitting the words "the bride". Thus instead of our text, "and one may sanctify the bride with it", we should read: "and one may sanctify with it". The sanctification would then refer to the Sabbath and the festivals, for which the words are used without particularization. The insertion of the words "the bride" which misled the commentators was due, no doubt, to an error of some scribe who noticed that the previous item was "and one may console the mourners", and therefore thought that the parallel to it ought to be "and one may sanctify the bride". (For the use of wine in the consolation of mourners, see below, paragraph 8.)

The assumption that our text of the Jerusalem Talmud is corrupt gains color from the fact that Maimonides refers to the use of wine at weddings as being merely a custom (Laws of *Ishut* 3:24). Similarly, R. Nissim b. Jacob (North Africa, eleventh century) speaks of the cup of wine as being an essential part of the *nissuin* or wedding ceremony, but claims that it is not essential to the *erusin* or betrothal. (His view is quoted by the Asheri to *Ketubot* 8b.) In view of the fact that R. Nissim and Maimonides were more intimately acquainted with the Talmud of Jerusalem than any of the other earlier scholars, it follows that their failure to take cognizance of the passage under discussion implies that it read differently in their copies. Our text may therefore be assumed to be corrupt.

Some of the early German codifiers mention another passage from the Talmud of Jerusalem which deals with the need [for] wine at weddings, but the passage is not found in our texts and is doubtless a later addition.[7] See R. Eleazar of Worms (thirteenth century), *Rokeah*, par. 352, and R. Eliezer B. Joel Ha-Levi also called Rabiah (Germany, thirteenth century) in *Abi-ezri*, par. 98.

The oldest passage in which reference is made to the use of wine in connection with the wedding ceremony is the *Masseket Soferim* 19:9 [ed. Higger, pp. 334-335] and *Masseket Kallah*, Chapter 1, Gemara [ed. Higger, pp. 170, 172] both of which were compiled in geonic times. See also R. Menahem Meiri (Provence, thirteenth century) in his *Magen Abot*, pp. 30-32.[8]

6. The Use of Wine in Connection with the Rite of Circumcision - That the rite of circumcision was in early times accompanied by a feast follows from [the] Talmud (*Shabbat* 130a).[9] But there is no reference made either there or elsewhere in the Talmud to the pronouncing of a benediction at the ceremony over a cup of wine. Nor is it mentioned in the early codes like that of R. Isaac Alfasi (N. Africa and Spain, eleventh century) or Maimonides. Nevertheless, the use of wine in connection with this ceremony is an old custom, which already prevailed in geonic times; witness R. Natronai *Gaon* and other *Geonim* (*Halakot Gedolot*, ed. Hildesheimer, p. 106.[10] The passage is not found in the older [version].)[11]

7. The Use of Wine in Connection with the Rite of Redemption of the First-Born - As is well-known, the first-born male son of an Israelite is redeemed from a priest on the thirty-first day of his life. While there is no mention made in the Talmud or the early codes regarding the use of wine in connection with this ceremony, its use had become customary in geonic times according to Asheri (b. Germany, c. 1250; d. Spain, 1328), in his code [to] Kiddushin, chapter 1, [par. 41]. See also the *Tur* by R. Jacob son of Asheri, *Yoreh De'ah* 305, and R. Joseph Caro (Palestine, sixteenth century), in the *Shulhan 'Aruk, Yoreh De'ah* 305.

8. The Use of Wine in the Consolation of Mourners - In talmudic times it was customary for the friends of a bereaved person to provide the first meal after the funeral of the deceased. It seems that at first it was customary to provide wine at this meal. But to this custom, there developed objections, so that in many places lentils and eggs were substituted for wine (see Talmud of Jerusalem, *Berakot* 3:1, [fol. 6a]. Concerning the abuse of the drinking of wine in the house of mourners, see *Ketubot* 8b, and *Semahot*, end.

Nevertheless, it is to be noted that the passage in the Talmud of Jerusalem cited above concerning the use of wine in consoling the mourners refers not to this custom, but to the use of wine in reciting the benediction of consolation. The benediction of consolation, [which is] mentioned in so early a source as *Yerushalmi Pesahim* 8:8, [fol. 36b] and *Sanhedrin* 6:11, [fol. 23d], was recited over a cup of wine in some communities as late as the time of R. Paltoi *Gaon* and R. Natronai *Gaon* (*Geonim Kadmonim* 35).[12] In view of the fact that this benediction must be pronounced over a cup of wine, it was relevant for the Talmud of Jerusalem to discuss whether it may be recited over wine with a pungent taste. The custom has, however, fallen into desuetude. The friends of the mourners supply food for a meal rather than wine, and no special benediction is pronounced.

II. THE MAIN PASSAGES IN THE BABYLONIAN TALMUD
BEARING ON THE GRADE OF WINE TO BE USED IN
RELIGIOUS CEREMONIAL

1. The passage in *Baba Batra* 97a - Having examined the history of the development of the various Jewish customs in which wine is used, we shall now proceed to study the passages in the Babylonian Talmud that bear on the status of the various grades of wine that may be used in these ceremonies. Before entering on this discussion, it will simplify matters if a few definitions are prefaced.

There are three conceptions in Jewish ritual law regarding the importance of performing a commandment in a certain way. There are details which are essential to the fulfilment of a commandment. If any one of these is omitted, the action is not regarded as valid and, generally speaking, must be repeated. This is called unfit *bedi'abad* or after the fact. There are some details which are only necessary *lekatehillah*. That is, they ought to be observed, but if they have been omitted, their omission does not render the act itself invalid. Thus, on the evening of the New Moon, mention ought to be made of the festival in a special prayer. The omission of the prayer does not, however, necessitate the repetition of the entire prayer, because the mention of the New Moon in the evening prayer is important only *lekatehillah*. If the mention is omitted from the morning or afternoon prayer, the prayer must be repeated, because then even *bedi'abad*, the prayer is unacceptable.[13]

An important question is then whether the use of fermented wine, if it be found to be preferable, is a matter of *lekatehillah*, that is, whether its use is unessential to the validity of the ceremony, or if it is also *bedi'abad*, that is, whether the failure to use it would render the ceremony invalid.

If, as I expect to show, the use of fermented wine is neither *lekatehillah* nor *bedi'abad*, that is, if it is not at all important from the legal point of view, there may still remain a reason for using it under the principle of *mitzwah min ha-mubhar*. This principle is that any commandment should be fulfilled in the best possible way. There are some details in the observance of the law which are not essential either *lekatehillah* or *bedi'abad*, and are nevertheless observed by the most pious as being the most appropriate form of observing the ceremony. We will, therefore, first discuss the legal necessity of the use of fermented wine, and then the question of *mitzwah min ha-mubhar*.

Since the use of wine in religious ceremonial is in Scripture exclusively connected with the Temple service, all Talmudic discussion of the need of wine in any service necessarily centers about the regulations concerning its use in libations. The earliest reference to the quality of wine to be used in the Temple service is to be found in the words of R. Judah b. Baba who was a young man at the time of the Fall of Jerusalem. He is reported (*'Eduyyot* 6:1) to have said: "Wine, forty days old, may be used for libations."

This statement is ambiguous as it does not tell us whether wine less that forty days old is unfit for altar-use *lekatehillah* or *bedi'abad*. The *Mishnah* is therefore interpreted by a statement in the *Tosefta* (*Menahot* 9:12, ed. Zuckermandel, p. 526) where we read: "One ought not to use wine less than forty days old for the libations; nevertheless if one has used it, the service is valid". The law is thus laid down that wine less than forty days old is unfit *lekatehillah*, but acceptable *bedi'abad*.

The importance of this statement of the Tosefta to an understanding of the questions relating to the use of various grades of wine in Jewish ritual will become evident upon an examination of the main passage in the Talmud dealing with the problem, the one found in the treatise *Baba Batra* 97a.

It reads: "R. Zutra b. Tobiah said in the name of Rab: One may pronounce the *kiddush* only over such wine as may be offered on the altar. Question: Which wine is excluded by Rab's statement? Is it wine from the press? Have we not a *Baraita* of R. Hiyya: 'One should not use wine from the press *lekatehillah*, but it is acceptable *bedi'abad*'. But since the wine from the press is acceptable for libations *bedi'abad*, it is acceptable for *kiddush lekatehillah*. Moreover, Raba has explicitly stated: 'one may press out a cluster of grapes and pronounce the *kiddush* over its juice immediately'".

It is necessary to point out here that the Talmud uses the expressions "wine from the press"and "wine less than forty days old" interchangeably for unfermented wine. The expression "new wine"in the Talmud refers to wine of the same year, as shall be seen below. In the medieval codes, the expression "new wine" is, however, often used of unfermented wine. The word "tirosh" is often used in the Talmud as well as in later writings, as it is always used in Scripture, to designate unfermented wine. From this statement it will appear that the quotation of the *Baraita* of R. Hiyya in the Talmud has reference to no other passage than the one in the *Tosefta*, which has been quoted. It is well-known that our *Tosefta* is largely composed of the teachings or *baraitot* of R. Hiyya. The change of expression from "wine less than forty days old" to "wine from the press" is, of course, negligible since they are synonymous. It is strange that none of the commentators or codifiers has pointed out the identity of the *baraita* in the Talmud with the statement in the *Tosefta*. And yet there can be no question of their identity.

From the passage that has been quoted from the Talmud, it is clear that unfermented wine may be used for *kiddush lekatehillah* and this is emphasized by Raba's statement that one may recite the *kiddush* over juice freshly pressed from the grapes without waiting for fermentation to begin.

None of the commentators has explained how the Talmud derived the statement that the grade of wine sanctioned *bedi'abad* for the Temple service is sanctioned *lekatehillah* for the home service. It seems that the Talmud derives that from a redundancy in Rab's words. The usual expression for such a thought as Rab's would have been: "Wine fit for the altar is fit for *kiddush*". Such expressions are common in the Talmud. See, for example, *Niddah* 6:4: "A person fit to judge is fit to be a witness". From the circumlocution of Rab, the Talmud is led to suppose that he means that only wine unfit *bedi'abad* for the Temple is unfit for *kiddush*, but wine which is acceptable even *bedi'abad* for libation may be used *lekatehillah* for *kiddush*.

In the *Halakot Gedolot*, the earliest Jewish compendium of the Talmud, this passage from *Baba Batra* is re-stated with some changes. The statement of Raba as quoted there reads: "One may press out a cluster of grapes and pronounce the *kiddush* over the juice, since the juice of the grape is considered wine in connection with the laws of the Nazirite."[14] It is difficult to determine whether the part of the statement that is not found in the Talmud is an addition by the author of the *Halakot Gedolot*, or is taken from his text of the Talmud. The statement is repeated in the same form in *Sha'are Simhah* of R. Isaac ibn Ghayyat, I, p. 2, but he apparently took it from the *Halakot Gedolot*. The editor of the *Sha'are Simhah* objects to this proof that is based on the recognition of grape juice as wine in the case of the Nazirite because a Nazirite may not even drink vinegar. But this objection is not justified, since the prohibition of wine-vinegar for the Nazirite is based on the express words of the Bible, "he shall drink no vinegar of wine" (Numbers 6:3). On the other hand, since there is no express mention of grape juice among the drinks prohibited to the Nazirite, its prohibition by the Rabbis can only be justified on the ground that it is considered wine.

2. The Passage in *Pesahim* 108b - A passage which deals with the various grades of wine and which has troubled the commentators and codifiers is the *baraita* quoted in *Pesahim* 108b which states that the four cups of the Passover service may be "of either raw or mixed wine, new or old." The Orientals and Greeks usually drank wine mixed with water, in the proportion of three parts of water to one of wine. Such a preparation is called in Hebrew *Yayin Mazug*, mixed wine, while unmixed wine is called *Yayin Hai*, raw wine.

R. Samuel ben Meir (also called Rashbam from his initials; a grandson of Rashi who lived in France in the twelfth century), in his commentary on this passage, gives two interpretations. According to the first, new wine is preferable to old; according to the second, the old is preferable. *Tosafot* (ad loc.) accept the second view, basing their interpretation on a passage in *Megillah* 16b where we are told that Joseph sent his father old wine, which is good for aged men. But it is to be noted that the word "old" is not found in that passage in the better texts (see *Dikduke Soferim*, ad loc.).

The second interpretation of R. Samuel b. Meir, while it has the support of *Tosafot*, is open to a very serious objection. The Talmud does on rare occasions mention a simpler case last. But this cannot be true in the *baraita* under discussion. There is clearly a parallelism intended between the two parts of the baraita: "unmixed and mixed, fresh and old." Just as the minimum required for unmixed wine is the simpler case, so obviously is the use of fresh wine. If old wine is preferable to new, that should have been mentioned first just as the unmixed wine is mentioned first.

The *baraita* can best be understood in the light of a *mishnah* in *Menahot* 8:6. One may not use old wine for the libations according to Rabbi, but his colleagues sanction its use.

Maimonides, in his commentary on this passage, remarks that wine becomes somewhat spoiled after the first year, by developing an acid taste. This view of Maimonides, which would make old wine inferior to new, is contradicted by a passage in the *Sifra* (Leviticus 26:10, ed. Weiss, 111a) [on the verse] "Ye shall eat old store long-kept." This verse informs us that the older the food, the better it will be. One might suppose that this blessing of continual betterment with age would be limited to wine, which in the ordinary course of events *betters with age*. Therefore, [the verse adds] the word "long-kept" to imply that even such things as ordinarily deteriorate with age will improve because of this blessing. It is evident from this passage that the sages considered old wine superior to new. Further corroboration of this fact will be found in *'Abodah Zarah* 40b.

The first interpretation of R. Samuel b. Meir, which, like that of Maimonides, made new wine better than old, thus faces a contradiction in the passage of the *Sifra*, while the second, as we have seen, is hardly more tenable. The difficulty in the interpretation of the *baraita* in *Pesahim* disappears, however, in view of the interpretation of the *mishnah* of *Menahot* by the Talmud [ibid. 87a]. The Talmud explains that by "old wine" in that *mishnah* is meant wine more than a year old, which is unfit for use on the altar. It now becomes clear that while wine generally improves in quality for the first year, it may then begin to develop a pungent taste. From this point of view new wine, i.e., wine of less than a year's age, is superior to wine of more than one year's age, and so the *baraita* in *Pesahim* does well to mention the new wine first.

From this discussion it is evident that the *baraita* in *Pesahim* cannot be used to prove the superiority of fermented over unfermented wine, since it deals not at all with the difference between wine less than a year old and that more than a year old.

3. Passages Dealing with Intoxicating and Non-Intoxicating Wines - Besides these passages which deal with the legal status of fermented and unfermented wines in regard to some of the ceremonies, there are several other laws regarding which the Talmud discusses the distinction between intoxicating and non-intoxicating wines. Thus a priest having drunk a *rebi'it* (about a tenth of a pint) of wine may not enter the Temple. A judge may, in such a case, not render a decision. A young man cannot be convicted as a "rebellious son" in accordance with the law in Deuteronomy 21:18-21, unless he has proven himself intemperate by drinking a certain minimum of intoxicating wines and eating a minimum of meat that have been stolen. In order to deal comprehensively with the question of the various grades of wine in Jewish law, the passages bearing on these laws must be considered.

The *Tosefta* (*Keritot* 1:20), [ed. Zuckermandel, p. 562], in commenting on Leviticus 10:9, reads: "Who is considered a priest unfit to enter the sanctuary? One who has drunk a *rebi'it* of wine which was more than forty days old." The remainder of the passage of the *Tosefta* can only be understood by emending it in accordance with the text of the Talmud *Keritot* 13b. The following regulations then result:

(1) If he drank a *rebi'it* of fermented wine, he is unfit to enter the Temple. (2) If he drank a *rebi'it* of unfermented wine, he may enter the Temple. (3) If he drank more than a *rebi'it* of unfermented wine or if he drank very old wine - four or five years old - to the extent of more than a *rebi'it* and entered the Temple he is guilty. In the cases when the quantity mentioned is more than a

rebi'it, even mixed wine is prohibited. This now clarifies the opinion expressed by Maimonides (Laws of Things Unfit for the Altar 7:7) that wine after its second year is unfit for altar purposes. The commentators could not find the source for this statement. In *Menahot* [8:6], the passage referred to above, there is a difference of opinion between Rabbi and the other scholars only regarding the drinking of wine that is more than one year old. There is no distinction made there between wine less than three years old and wine more than three years old. The source for the statement of Maimonides is clearly the *Tosefta* which has just been quoted, which declares that wine four or five years old [has] the same status as unfermented wine. Since the *Mishnah* provides that one may not *lekatehillah* bring unfermented wine on the altar, that law applies also to very old wine. It appears too that Maimonides' reading of the *Tosefta* was "three or four years" instead of "four of five years" as in our texts.

4. The Passage in the Talmud of Jerusalem bearing on the Grades of Wine in regard to Religious Ceremonies - The only passage in the Talmud of Jerusalem bearing on the status of the various grades of wine in their relation to religious ceremonials occurs in Sotah 8:5, [fol. 22d]. The text of the printed editions has puzzled the commentators and it can only be understood if we reconstruct it with the help of the manuscript material supplied in the Yerushalmi Fragments.[15]

It then reads: "If he (the 'rebellious son') drank unfermented wine, what is the law? (According to the Talmud, the status of the wine with a pungent taste is the same as that of unfermented wine). We have a *baraita*: 'Wine with a pungent taste may be used for *erub* and *shittuf* (ceremonies for permitting carrying on the Sabbath under specified circumstances) and for saying grace after the meal, and to pronounce the marriage benedictions (according to the emendation suggested above, it is to be translated: "to sanctify the Sabbath") and for consoling mourners. It may be sold by a merchant as wine. If, however, one contracts to sell wine without defining the grade, one cannot compel the buyer to accept wine with a pungent taste. One who has drunk it may not decide cases of law or absolve vows or enter the Temple'. From this *baraita* we can only infer that wine with a pungent taste may not be used for libations, but whether a young man who drinks it may be convicted as a rebellious son, is undecided."

In the Babylonian Talmud (Sanhedrin 70a) the statement is made that a young man who had drunk unfermented wine may be adjudged a "rebellious son". But while the Babylonian rabbis were definite as to the law in the matter, the Palestinians were in doubt. The omission of any reference in the tannaitic source to the use of such wine for libations made it certain that it was not acceptable for that purpose. But the failure to mention the case of the "rebellious son" might be explained as due to the fact that the *baraita* does not deal with the prohibited uses of wine, witness its omission of any reference to the Nazirite.

From a purely logical point of view, too, it might be argued that while the wine may be acceptable for religious purposes, the only reason that the intemperate use of wine is considered a characteristic of the use of wine by a rebellious son is that it is habit-forming, and it is possible that wine with a pungent taste will not develop habitual use [to] the same degree as other wine.

Therefore, whether the emendation suggested above is accepted or not, the *baraita* definitely admits the use of wine with a pungent taste for religious ceremonies outside the Temple.

We have thus proven, on the basis of the main passages both of the Babylonian Talmud and that of Jerusalem, that unfermented wine may be used *lekatehillah* for *kiddush* and other religious ceremonies outside the Temple. In the Temple, its use is sanctioned only *bedi'abad*. Indeed, in no way is fermented wine to be given any preference over unfermented in the ceremonies outside the Temple. Raba summarizes the law well in the statement [Baba Batra 97b]: "One may press out the juice of grapes and immediately recite the *kiddush* over it."

This view is echoed in all the more important codes. It is found in geonic works such as *Seder R. 'Amram Gaon*, ed. Frumkin, II, p. 34;[16] *Sha'are Simhah* of Ibn Ghayyat, I, p. 2; and in the *Sefer Ha-'Ittim* of R. Judah b. Barzillai, (Spain, c. 1100), p. 204; *Mahzor Vitri*, p. 86; *Sefer Ha-Orah* by the pupils of Rashi, ed. Buber, Part I, p. 38; Asheri in his code to Baba Batra 97a; Tur Orah Hayyim by R. Jacob b. Asher (Spain, fourteenth century), par. 272 (beginning); and the Shulhan Aruk, Orah Hayyim, by R. Joseph Caro, 272:2. Since Isserles in his notes to the Shulhan Aruk makes no comment on this passage, it is to be presumed that he agrees with it. We therefore have the consensus of the opinion of all the codifers, early and late, to the fact that unfermented wine may be used for *kiddush* - and that implies the other ceremonies of Jewish ritual outside the Temple - on the same terms as fermented wine.

III. IS IT A MITZWAH MIN HA-MUBHAR TO USE FERMENTED WINE IN JEWISH RELIGIOUS CEREMONIES?

1. The View of the Author of the *Halakot Gedolot* - Having seen that unfermented wine may be used *laketehillah* for religious ceremonies outside the Temple, we must now turn to the study of the problem of whether it is not a better form of fulfilling those commandments to use fermented wine. As has been explained above, there are often details of Jewish ceremonial which, while not required for the proper fulfilment of a commandment, are nevertheless observed by more pious Jews as a *mitzwah min ha-mubhar*.

The author of the *Halakot Gedolot* (Laws of *Kiddush* and *Habdalah*, end) says: "If one has no wine, one may take grapes and press them out on Friday or the festival eve and in the night pronounce the *kiddush* over the juice. For Rabbah has said, etc. Where wine is difficult to procure, one may take dried grapes (raisins) and soak them in water and use the liquid for *kiddush*."[17]

It is to be noticed first that this author limits the application of Raba's rule, permitting one to recite the *kiddush* over juice immediately after being pressed from the grapes, to cases where one has no other wine; secondly, that the author limits the use of wine of raisins still further by permitting its use only in countries where wine is difficult to obtain; thirdly, that while the author refers to Raba's statement, and indeed quotes from *Baba Batra* 97a the entire passage which has been discussed above, he fails to quote the *baraita* of R. Hiyya which is included in that passage. These three facts present difficulties which must be explained in order to understand the views of the author on the use of the various kinds of wine in Jewish ceremonies.

2. The Reading of the Hildesheimer Edition of the *Halakot Gedolot* - The reading of the older version of the *Halakot Gedolot*, which has been cited, agrees with that quoted in Albarceloni's *Sefer Ha'Ittim*, p. [206]. In the Hildesheimer edition, which represents a different (French) version of the *Halakot Gedolot*, the use of the wine of raisins is permitted not only in countries where wine cannot be obtained but also in countries where grapes are procurable, provided the person has no wine of grapes or grapes available at the moment.[18]

3. Is the Restriction on the Use of Raisin Wine and [Freshly Pressed Grape Juice] Based on a Supposed Inferiority of Those Wines for Religious Uses? - The objection of the author of the *Halakot Gedolot* to the use of raisin wine is shared by other *Geonim*. R. Amram Gaon writes in his *Seder* (ed. Frumkin, II, p. 226):[19] "If one cannot find wine within a reasonable distance from his home, or if he is on board ship and cannot obtain any wine, he may obtain wine for the four Passover cups by soaking raisins in water. For the sages have taught [in *Baba Batra* 97b] that raisin wine ought not to

be used in the Temple service, but *bedi'abad* its use is sanctioned. Since it is sanctioned *bedi'abad* for the purpose of libation, it may be used *lekatehillah* for *Kiddush* and *Habdalah* [in a place where it is not possible to find wine]". Either from the *Seder R. Amram*, or some other geonic source maintaining the same principles, this statement is quoted by Ibn Ghayyat in his *Sha'are Simhah*, II, p. 99; in *Sha'are Teshubah*, no. 117; by Zedekiah b. Abraham 'Anaw (Italy, thirteenth century) in his *Shibbole Ha-Leket*, fol. 101a; by R. Abraham b. Nathan of Lunel (Toledo, twelfth century) in his *Manhig*, Laws of Passover, par. 92.[20] See also *Geonica*, II, New York 1909, p. 228.

The author of the *Manhig* (loc. cit.) criticizes the geonic objection to the use of raisin wine in these words: "I hold that since its use is sanctioned *bedi'abad* in the Temple service, it is acceptable *lekatehillah* for use in ceremonies outside the Temple even when other wine is procurable. [For when other wine is not obtainable, it may be used even in the Temple *lekatehillah*, and even when other wine is obtainable, if he brought raisin wine it is sanctioned *bedi'abad*]".

It is clear that the objections of the *Geonim* to the use of raisin wine is based not on any supposed inferiority of that wine for religious ceremonies outside the Temple, but on the apprehension that in its preparation too much water or raisins that are too dry might be used. For this reason they set down the law that raisin wine is not to be used wherever other wine or even raw grapes from which the juice may be pressed are procurable.

The great Spanish authorities, as well as those of France and Germany, did not accept this restriction of the *Geonim* on the use of raisin wine. The view of R. Abraham b. Nathan of Lunel, author of the *Manhig*, has already been quoted. Similarly, R. Isaac b. Sheshet Barfat in his responsa (no. 9) and his contemporary and countryman R. Simeon b. Zemah Duran (North Africa c. 1400) in his responsa (I, no. 57) severely criticized a rabbi for deciding against the use of raisin wine in a wine-producing country. Similarly, Albarceloni in his *Sefer Ha-Ittim* (p. 204) quotes R. Samuel ibn Nagdela (Spain, eleventh century) as having expressed dissatisfaction with [this] restriction. See also Duran's *Ma'amar Hamez*, fol. 34a, where he refers to the use of raisin wine in a wine-producing country such as Algiers.

While the views of the author of *Halakot Gedolot* restricting the use of raisin wine were shared by the other *Geonim*, his views restricting the use of fresh grape juice to such persons as had no other wine in their homes is shared by no other known authority. The pupils of Rashi quote the [passage from *Halakot Gedolot*] in the *Sefer Ha-Orah* [Part I, p. 38], but it is well-known that medieval writers often quote geonic statements with which they do not agree. R. Amram Gaon expressly quotes the Talmudic statement [*Baba Batra* 97b] that "a person may press out a cluster of grapes and pronounce the *kiddush* over the juice"and does not in any way qualify the permission.[21] R. Amram thus makes no distinction between unfermented wine and wine immediately pressed from the grapes. It seems that even the author of the *Halakot Gedolot* does not consider the one intrinsically inferior to the other. His objection to the practice of pressing out the juice of grapes on Friday for the *kiddush* of the oncoming Sabbath is that he apprehends that one may forget and press the grapes not on Friday but on the Sabbath. The question of whether grapes may be pressed on the Sabbath is discussed by R. Aaron of Lunel (Provence, thirteenth century) in his *Orhot Hayyim*, [Laws of the Sabbath, fol. 64a] and in the abstract of *Etz Hayyim* published in the Steinschneider Festschrift, p. 203.[22] See also the responsum of R. Hai Gaon (Pumbeditha, tenth century) in the commentary of R. Nissim on *Shabbat* (end)[23] and Rabiah, *Shabbat*, par. 330, [Vol. I, p. 370 ff.].

The views of the author of the *Halakot Gedolot* have now been explained. He omits the quotation of the *baraita* of R. Hiyya, although he doubtless had it in his text, because it was his purpose to explain only his own restrictions on the permission to use various grades of wine. As he had no restriction to offer against the use of unfermented wine, he omitted the mention of it. He objects to the use of raisin wine in countries where grapes or the wine of grapes [are] obtainable because he apprehends that raisin wine may not be prepared properly. He objects to the use of [freshly pressed grape juice] out of apprehension that that may lead to the violation of the Sabbath by having the grapes pressed on that day. He would therefore permit the use of [freshly pressed grape juice] on festivals since the apprehension does not apply to such days, in view of the fact that food may be prepared on them.

4. The View of Ibn Ghayyat and that of R. Jacob b. Asher - R. Isaac ibn Ghayyat in his *Sha'are Simhah*, [I, p. 2], infers from the objections of the author of the *Halakot Gedolot* to the use of raisin wine that the same restriction applies also to the other wines permitted in the Talmud for religious ceremonies outside the Temple, but qualified for the libation service only *bedi'abad*. He says that where wine of a superior grade can be obtained, its use is commendable. This is the source of the view of R. Jacob b. Asher (Spain, fourteenth century) in his *Tur, Orah Hayyim*, 272, that it is better to use wine of superior grade for *kiddush* than any wine which may have become soured or spoiled.

The care with which R. Jacob formulated his statement of the view of Ibn Ghayyat is noteworthy. He did not merely transcribe the words of that scholar, but changed them so that they might not imply any obligation to acquire wine of the first quality if one did not already possess it. He rather exhorted those possessing wines of different grades to use the better wines for *kiddush*. This is in conformity with the general rabbinical view that one ought not to be niggardly in the perfomance of a religious ceremony.

Moreover, it is noteworthy that both R. Jacob b. Asher in his *Tur* (loc. cit.), and R. Joseph Caro in his *Shulhan 'Aruk* (*Orah Hayyim*, 272) place unfermented wine in a category by itself and do not include it in the list of inferior grades. The kinds of wine to which they object are: the wine at the mouth of the barrel because it may be moldy; the wine at the bottom of the barrel, because it may be mixed with [dregs] and it is not permitted to pronounce the *kiddush* over [dregs]; black wine and white wine, because wine of red color is preferable; and wine which retains some of its flavor but has developed a somewhat acid taste.

It is thus seen that according to the views of the two most generally accepted Jewish codes, the *Tur* and the *Shulhan 'Aruk*, no [preference] whatever is to be given to fermented over unfermented wines. It is not even a *mitzvah min ha-mubhar* to use fermented wines.

IV. THE SOURCE OF THE ERRONEOUS OPINION THAT FERMENTED WINE IS PREFERABLE IN RELIGIOUS CEREMONIALS

1. The View of R. Abele Gumbiner - While it has been shown that for every religious purpose, save libations, unfermented wine is as acceptable as fermented, there still remains to be discussed the view of R. Abele Gumbiner (Poland, seventeenth century) in his commentary to the *Shulhan 'Aruk*, *Orah Hayyim* (272:2). He there states: "Although unfermented wine may be used for *kiddush*, it is [a *mitzvah*] to use fermented wine."The author refers to paragraph 600 of the book, where he quotes as authority for his view R. Moses Isserles in his commentary [*Darkei Moshe*] on the *Tur*, *Orah Hayyim*, 600. Isserles deals there not at all with the laws of *kiddush* but with those concerning the pronunciation of the benediction over the season (*sheheheyanu*) on the second night of *Rosh Ha-Shanah*. As is well known, this benediction forms a part of the *kiddush* of festival days and contains a prayer of thanks for having been permitted to live to celebrate the festival. [In Palestine,] it is recited only on the eve of the first day of the festivals. Since each festival is, in the lands outside of Palestine, observed for two days, the benediction is recited on both nights. But the two days of *Rosh ha-Shanah* are said in the Talmud to be considered as one long day. Some sages therefore objected to the recital of *sheheheyanu* on the second night of *Rosh ha-Shanah*. In order to be sure that one is not reciting an unnecessary

benediction, it was customary in Germany in the Middle Ages, and it is still the custom in many localities today, to recite the *sheheheyanu* over new wine on the second night of *Rosh ha-Shanah*. Since one would in any case recite that benediction over the new wine - one could satisfy the views of all the authorities by the use of new wine on that night.

Isserles, in commenting on this law, remarks that he read in a book of customs (*minhagim* - he does not specify which) that one who used new wine for *Sheheheyanu* should nevertheless use old wine for the *kiddush* itself. One would therefore on the second night of *Rosh ha-Shanah* need two cups for *kiddush*, one containing old wine for the general benedictions, and one containing new wine for the *sheheheyanu*.

As Isserles does not give the reason for the custom of having two cups of wine, R. Abele Gumbiner supposed that it was because fermented wine is preferable for *kiddush*.

With all due respect to this authority, it must be admitted that had he had before him the source quoted by Isserles he [would] certainly not have expressed this opinion, in view of the fact that it is not only contrary to the express law as laid down in the Talmud and codes, but also to the practice of the Ashkenazic Jews.

2. The Practice of the Maharil - The custom as described by Isserles is first found in the collection of customs by R. Jacob Molin, also called the Maharil from his initials (Germany, c. 1400). The Maharil is the greatest authority on the religious practice of Ashkenazic Jews. He says in his book (Laws of Rosh ha-Shanah): "There are some who decide that one should pronounce the entire *kiddush* on a cup of old wine rather than on new wine. The reason is that a benediction over new wine cannot include old wine, since we read in the Talmud of Jerusalem: '[If one is brought old wine in the middle of] a meal, he must recite a second benediction, although he [already] recited a benediction over new wine at the beginning of the meal'. Since old wine [deserves] a special benediction, it is [more important] and preferable for *kiddush*. When he reaches the benediction of *Sheheheyanu* he should take the cup of new wine in his hand."[24]

The passage cited from the Talmud of Jerusalem by the Maharil is not found in that Talmud in the form quoted, but there can be no doubt that this scholar had in mind the passage in *Berakot*, Chapter 6, [fol. 10d], which reads: "If one drinks new wine and thereafter old wine, one must recite a second benediction."[25]

The Maharil is quite correct in stating that the preference for old wine for *kiddush* is based entirely on the fact that since one might drink old wine during the meal, it is better to recite the *kiddush* over it in order not to pronounce an additional benediction. It is a general principle of rabbinic law that one should avoid the repetition of benedictions. But if one is not in the habit of drinking wine in the course of a meal, there is no objection to the use of unfermented wine for *kiddush*. See Rabiah, par. 152, I, p. 159 and *Shibbole ha-Leket*, [*Berakhot*, par. 144, fol. 57a].

This interpretation of the words of the Maharil receives full corroboration from a study of the rest of the passage. It continues: "Maharil once asked that unfermented wine be brought to the synagogue for *kiddush* on the second night of *Rosh ha-shanah*, and they pronounced the *kiddush* over that wine. Asked why the custom in the synagogue should differ from that at home (where one recites *kiddush* over fermented wine), Maharil replied that since in the synagogue it is customary for children to drink the wine, unfermented wine is preferable since children like it. At home, fermented wine ought to be used since older persons prefer that."

From this story it follows that in the opinion of the Maharil fermented wine is not to be preferred to unfermented except in cases where one might drink fermented wine in the course of the meal.

3. The Practice of R. Meir b. Baruch of Rothenberg - An examination of the book of customs which Isserles quotes as a basis for the requirement of two kinds of wine for *kiddush* on the second night of *Rosh ha-Shanah* will further show how baseless is R. Abele's interpretation of this custom. The book of customs to which Isserles refers is either that of R. Abraham Klausner (Austria, fourteenth century)[26] or that of his pupil, R. Isaac Tyrna.[27] In both of these books, the custom is stated as given in the Maharil. But [R. Abraham Klausner adds] as authority for the custom the following citation from R. Samson b. Zadok, a pupil of R. Meir b. Baruch of Rothenberg, who lived in Germany in the thirteenth century: "Unfermented wine [is good] for *kiddush* in accordance with the view of Raba, that a person may press out the juice of a cluster of grapes and pronounce the *kiddush* over it. That is the law, and such was the custom of R. Meir b. Baruch on the second night of *Rosh ha-Shanah*." This statement is found on page 5b and again on page 8b of Klausner's book.[28]

This quotation proves that R. Abele Gumbiner cannot be correct in his interpretation of the custom, for how can we assume that R. Meir b. Baruch, one of the greatest German rigorists, would use a less preferable wine for *kiddush*? Nor can it be said that he used unfermented wine when fermented wine was difficult to procure, since it is explicitly stated to have been his regular custom to use unfermented wine on the second night of *Rosh ha-Shanah*. Neither can it be said that he lived in a land where fermented wine was scarce; witness his own words (*Tashbez*, par. 301): "But [here all of the

Kingdoms are] full of wine." And further we know that he lived at first in Rothenburg, Bavaria, and later was held captive in the castle of Ensisheim, Alsace, both of which are districts very rich in wine. Finally, R. Samson b. Zadok, in recording his master's custom, would doubtless have added an explanation of it, if it were at all out of accord with the accepted law and usage.

R. Meir's custom of using a cup of unfermented wine instead of the two generally used for *kiddush* on the second night of *Rosh ha-Shanah* is easily explained. R. Meir b. Baruch was in the habit of fasting on *Rosh ha-Shanah* (*Hagahot Maimoniot*, Laws of Shofar, at the beginning; and responsa of R. Meir b. Baruch, ed. Bloch, no. 54), "but he would recite the *kiddush* because in his opinion the pronouncing of *kiddush* over wine is a biblical injunction." Since R. Meir fasted, the possibility of drinking fermented wine during the meal was excluded, and therefore he could use unfermented wine for *kiddush* without hesitation.[29]

(It should be noted that in our editions of the Tashbez, [par. 120], the description of R. Meir's custom has been abbreviated, and merely reads: "R. Meir was in the habit of refraining from drinking new wine [until the second night of] *Rosh ha-Shanah*, and then he would recite the *sheheheyanu* over it". From this statement one might suppose that R. Meir used two cups of wine, but the citation in the book of R. Abraham Klausner shows the above interpretation to be the correct one. It may be added that it is supported by the reading of the Ms. of the *Tashbez* in the library of the Jewish Theological Seminary of America.)[30]

4. The Practice of R. Shalom of Neustadt - Besides these great authorities, R. Meir, his pupil R. Samson b. Zadok, and the Maharil, who, as we have seen, used unfermented wine for *kiddush*, we must mention the usage of R. Shalom, the teacher of the Maharil, of Isserlein, and of most of the great German scholars of the first part of the fifteenth century. Of R. Shalom it is said by the Maharil: "R. Shalom [said]: one may use unfermented wine [*lekateillah*] for *kiddush* in accordance with the statement of Raba... and he, himself, used [to recite *kiddush* over] unfermented wine that was two weeks old, although fermented wine could be bought in the [city]".[31]

5. Another criticism of the view of R. Abele Gumbiner - R. Elijah Shapiro, in his commentary to the *Shulhan 'Aruk, Orah Hayyim*, writes, in criticism of the interpretation of R. Abele Gumbiner: "It seems to me that if one has in one's possession fermented wine [and he wants to drink from it, it takes precedence, which is not the case when he has no fermented wine, in which case he is not obligated to purchase it for *kiddush*"].

This view seems to agree with that of the Maharil, who declares the use of fermented wine for *kiddush* dependent on its intended use during the meal, but that intrinsically there is no reason why one should prefer to pronounce the *kiddush* over fermented wine.

Moreover, from the very fact that Isserles makes his comment about the use of two kinds of wine in discussing the laws of *Rosh ha-Shanah*, and not in discussing the laws of *kiddush*, it follows that in general he had no objection to the use of unfermented wine for *kiddush*. It is inconceivable that if he had had such an objection, he would have silently passed over the statements of R. Jacob b. Asher and of R. Joseph Caro sanctioning it.

The statements of R. Abele Gumbiner that fermented wine is to be preferred for *kiddush* thus stands refuted.

V. CONCLUSION

We thus arrive at the following decisions:

1. From the point of view of Jewish law and custom, there is no preference to be given to fermented wine over unfermented. Both are of equal standing. The author of the *Magen Abraham*, who alone among Jewish writers on the subject held a different view, was led to his opinion by a misunderstanding of the works of the earlier authorities.

2. Raisin wine may not be used for the temple service *lekatehillah* but its use is sanctioned *bedi'abad*. It may, however, be used for *kiddush* and other religious ceremonies outside the Temple *lekatehillah*. The *Geonim* restricted the use of raisin wine, but the great codifiers did not accept their view. The custom of using unfermented raisin wine was widespread in North Africa in the fourteenth century with the sanction of R. Isaac b. Sheshet Barfat and R. Simeon b. Zemah Duran. In our own time, it is prevalent in Lithuania.

3. As for the use of grape juice for *kiddush* and other religious ceremonies, that involves a discussion of the law regarding boiled wine. I have been authoritatively informed that grape juice is not heated to the boiling point, and moreover there is a possibility of its fermentation.[32] The Jewish codifiers differ in their views regarding boiled wine. The *Geonim* and the early Spanish scholars forbid its use for *kiddush*; the French and German scholars, followed by the later Spanish rabbis, like Nahmanides (thirteenth century) and Ibn Adret, his pupil, permit its use *lekatehillah*. The main question of interest here is the degree of boiling which renders wine unfit. This is mentioned neither by Maimonides nor by R. Joseph Caro in their codes. R. Jacob b. Asher (*Tur, Orah Hayyim*, 272) writes: "There are many views regarding boiled wine. R. Shemaiah wrote in the name of his master, Rashi, that the benediction for it is the same as that for water. And such is also the opinion of Ibn Ghayyat: 'If wine has been boiled even a little, and similarly if

even a little honey has been put into it, the benediction for it is the same as that for water'. R. Hai wrote: 'If one has put wine over the fire and it has boiled... one can no longer pronounce the *kiddush* over it...'".

On the basis of R. Jacob's words we might be led to suppose that Ibn Ghayyat's view differs from that of the *Geonim* whom he quotes, for it appears that while the *Geonim* prohibit the use of boiled wine, he prohibits the use of wine "boiled even a little". Fortunately, Ibn Ghayyat's book has been preserved and an examination of it [I, pp. 2-3] shows that the views of R. Hai and Ibn Ghayyat are identical. Doubtless R. Jacob had a corrupt copy of Ibn Ghayyat's work where the words "even a little" were inserted after the word "boiled".

Nahmanides, in his commentary on *'Abodah Zarah* 30, writes that wine is to be considered boiled only when its volume has decreased through the process. R. Joseph Caro, in *Yoreh De'ah* 123:3, decides that wine is not to be considered boiled unless it has been heated till it seethes. See also the notes of R. Elijah Gaon of Vilna to that passage. There can be no doubt that wine is not considered boiled in regard to the laws of *kiddush* unless it has been heated until it seethes.

4. As for the objection that has been raised against the use of unfermented wine for religious ceremonies on the grounds that it is against Jewish custom, the following must be remarked. There can be no doubt that in the past most of the wine used for religious purposes was fermented, since the process of preventing fermentation was unknown. But to base on such a fact the prohibition of the use of unfermented wine would be as unreasonable as to suppose that because only wax and tallow candles were used for lighting synagogues, the use of gas and electricity for that purpose is forbidden. It was well said by R. Samuel di-Medina (Responsa, *Yoreh De'ah*, no. 40) that no custom that has arisen from accidental association has any binding power. It is self-evident that the use of fermented wines hitherto for religious purposes was due to the natural fact that wine ferments within a short period. And in those countries where raisin wine, which ferments less readily, was used, most of the wine used for religious purposes was unfermented. (See R. Simeon b. Zemah Duran's *Ma'amar Hamez*, fol. 34a.) It is a known fact that in Lithuania, a country that has produced distinguished scholars, and where Jewish laws are very rigorously observed, the wine of raisins was regularly used for all religious purposes, in spite of the objections to its use raised by some of the *Geonim*. How much less objection can be raised to the use of unfermented wine, which, as we have seen, is declared by the scholars of all ages to possess the same status as fermented wine in regard to its use for religious purposes outside of the Temple.

1   This English version is much more than a translation. On the one hand, it adds sections missing from the Hebrew e.g. most of Section I about the use of wine in religious ceremonies is not found in the Hebrew version. On the other hand, the rest of the translation is a brief synopsis of the Hebrew responsum. I believe the English version was prepared by LG himself, because it is hard to believe that any of his students would have added to his responsum. However, it contains a few errors - see below, notes 18, 29, and 30.

2   D. Z. Hoffmann, *Die Erste Mischna und die Controversen der Tannaim*, Berlin 1882, pp. 8-9, 16-17 = *The First Mishna and the Controversies of the Tannaim*, trans. by Paul Forchheimer, New York 1977, pp. 9-11, 26-27.

3   The orginal says "modern times", but this merging took place in the Middle Ages and is even hinted at in the Talmud. See Adolph Büchler, *Studies in Jewish History*, London 1956, pp. 136-137; A. H. Freimann, *Seder Kiddushin V'nissuin*, Jerusalem 5705, pp. 17-18, 28-31; Ze'ev Falk, *Nissuin V'geirushin*, Jerusalem 1961, pp. 32-55; and Herman Pollack, *Proceedings of the Ninth World Congress of Jewish Studies*, Division C, Jerusalem 1986, pp. 47-53.

4   On the other hand, Rabbi Isaac of Vienna may have been quoting from memory and referred to chapter "כסמ" by mistake.

5   And see now *Siddur Rav Sa'adiah Gaon*, Jerusalem 5701, p. 97.

6   Regarding this custom, cf. below, Chapter V, No. 6, notes 5-6.

7   Regarding this passage, see the Hebrew version of this responsum, note 38.

8   In the Last edition, London, 5669 = ed. Yekutiel Cohen, Jerusalem 5749, pp. 65-70.

9   "Every commandment which they accepted upon themselves in joy such as circumcision" and Rashi adds: "that they make a feast (mishteh)".

10   The use of wine is mentioned there, but there is no reference to Rav Natronai and other *geonim*. Regarding this custom, see now *Halakhot Gedolot*, I, Jerusalem 5732, p. 214 in the critical apparatus and in note 30.

11   I.e., in the Warsaw edition, 5635.

12   Berlin 1848, fol. 7b. For a different version of this responsum, see R. Yitzhak ibn Giyyat, *Sha'arei Simhah*, II, Fuerth 5621, p. 65 to which LG refers in the Hebrew version of this responsum.

13   See OH 422:1.

14   See *Halakhot Gedolot* (note 10 above), p. 75.

15   Levi Ginzberg, *Seridei Hayerushalmi*, New York 1909, p. 215.

16   Which corresponds to the Goldschmidt edition, Jerusalem 5732, p. 67.

17   Loc. cit. (note 14 above) and cf. the Warsaw edition 5635, fol. 14c.

18   *Halakhot Gedolot*, Berlin 5648, p. 50. The word "French" should read "Spanish" since LG himself states in *Geonica*, I, New York 1909, pp. 103ff. that the Warsaw edition was the one which reached the Franco-German scholars while the Hildesheimer edition was the one which reached the Hispano-Provencal scholars.

19   Ed. Goldschmidt (note 16 above), p. 124.

20   Ed. Raphael, Jerusalem 5738, p. 503.

21   See above, note 16.

22   See now R. Ya'akov Hazzan of London, *Etz Hayyim*, ed. Brodie, I, Jerusalem 5722, p. 195.

23   Ed. Jerusalem 5735, pp. 222-225.

24   *Sefer Maharil*, ed. Shpitzer, Jerusalem 5749, p. 274.

25   LG here emends the passage from the Yerushalmi according to the reading of many of the *rishonim*. See the Hebrew version of this responsum, after note 7.

26   *Minhagei R. Avraham Klausner*, ed. Dissen, Jerusalem 5738, p. 19. LG used the Riva di Trento edition, 1559, fol. 5a.

27   *Minhagei R. Isaac Tyrna*, ed. Shpitzer, Jerusalem 5739, p. 100. LG apparently used the Warsaw edition, 5629, fol. 22a.

28   In the Riva di Trento edition (note 26 above) = ed. Dissen, p. 9 but see notes 7-8 ibid. for important variant readings.

29   In the Hebrew version, this sentence reads (before note 13): "Since he fasted on *Rosh Hashanah* and did not drink wine during the meal - either new or old - he did not refrain from making *kiddush* over new wine because of the *sheheheyanu* blessing". Regarding R. Meir's custom of fasting on *Rosh Hashanah*, see now Y. Gilat in: *Tarbiz* 52 (5743), pp. 13-15.

30   This last sentence is apparently an error. The Hebrew version (after note 14) says that the reading in the Tashbez manuscript is identical to that of the printed editions of the *Tashbez*.

31   *Sefer Maharil* (note 24 above), p. 203 and see now *Hilkhot Uminhagei Rabbeinu Shalom Mineustadt*, ed. Shpitzer, Jerusalem 5737, par. 106.

32   See the letters from the National Grape Juice Company and the Welch Grape Juice Company listed in the bibliography.

No. 17 The Use of a Radio on Shabbat and Yom Tov (not in OH)
Source: CJLS Box, "Shabbat" file

Question: I have just installed a radio set in my home and I am anxious to know what your attitude is, generally, towards the use of the radio on a *Shabbos* or *Yom Tov.*

Might I explain that my set works along the following lines. A plug is inserted in order to light the tubes or bulbs and thereby make the use of the set possible. After the general connection has been made by the insertion of the plug, the various stations are reached by the turning of a dial which in no way affects the lighted bulbs. In other words, unless the bulbs are lighted by the insertion of the plug, the set cannot be used at all, but the additional turning of the dial is required in order to tune in on the various stations.

I write the above details because I wonder whether you would make any distinction between the use of the radio, generally, on *Shabbos*, and its use if the plug were inserted and the bulbs thereby lighted before *Shabbos* began, or by a *Shabbos Goy.*

Answer (by Professor Ginzberg): The reason of the delay of my reply to your letter concerning the use of the radio on Sabbath and Holidays is entirely due to my ignorance of radio mechanics. Before replying to your letter, I wanted to make myself acquainted with the mechanism of the radio and it took me some time before I had the opportunity of doing so.

I see no objection to the use of the radio if the plug were inserted before Sabbath.[1] On the other hand, I do not think it proper to have the plug inserted by a Gentile on the Sabbath. The general rule is, that only work absolutely necessary is permitted to be performed by a Gentile for the use of a Jew on the Sabbath.[2]

---

1   In other words, if the radio is on, it is permissible to tune in to different stations.
2   See OH 276:2 in the Rema.

No. 18 The Use of the Organ in the Synagogue (OH 338:1-2)[1]
Source: CJLS Box, " Bet Knesset" file

Question: I am anxiously awaiting the reply of the Committee on Law to the query I sent you regarding the use of the organ at services.

Answer: In reply to your letter, I wish to inform you that I have consulted with Professor Ginzberg concerning this question. I wish to present his views with which I believe many members of the Committee will concur. First, it is a sign of liberalism not only to introduce innovations but also to show some respect for the opinions of others, even if they are not those which we cherish. Since there are many people who refuse to attend divine services where an organ is played, it would be unfair to deny them the privilege of attending services. Secondly, for the last 2000 years the use of the organ or any other instrumental music was unknown at divine services. Thirdly, it is only since the last 100 years, due to conscious imitation of Protestant services, that Reform Jews have introduced the use of the organ. In countries like Russia, where, the Greek Orthodox faith is predominant, the organ is entirely unknown and the Jews there have never thought of using an organ. Fourthly, in connection with divine services, vocal music was always allowed and encouraged, because it enables the individual to actively participate in the services; where instrumental music is used the worshippers are passive listeners only. Lastly, there is the difficulty of who should play the organ in a synagogue if it is introduced. It would be entirely out of the question to permit a non-Jew to play the organ because that would be contrary to the spirit of Jewish services to have a non-Jew participate in the services. It would not be possible to have a Jew play the organ, because that would be open desecration of the Sabbath.[2]

---

1   For LG's views on the organ, cf. above, Chapter I, No. 4. Also see below Chapter VII, No. 6 for another question on the subject. For other Conservative responsa on this subject, see David Golinkin, *An Index of Conservative Responsa and Practical Halakhic Studies 1917-1990*, New York, 1992, p. 62.
2   See OH 338:1-2.

No. 19 May Green Peas, String Beans and Tomatoes be Used on Passover? (OH 453:1)

Source: General Files, file 2 (1931-33)

May 5, 1932

Dear Rabbi Cohen:[1]

I am afraid that this letter will be a great disappointment to you. After a careful study of the case I came to the conclusion that the evidence is not strong enough to permit the husband to marry without giving his first wife a bill of divorce in accordance with Jewish law. The fact that once his wife attempted to serve meat without having it soaked and salted is not sufficient ground for grant[ing] him the privilege of a second marriage, especially as the husband is the only witness for the alleged fact.[2]

Though Passover has passed already, I wish to reply to your question with regard to the use of green peas and string beans on Passover. There is not the slightest reason why they should not be used, as by no stretch of the imagination could they be classified as belonging to [קטניות] which refers to dry peas or beans exclusively.[3] That there is not the slightest objection to the use of fresh tomatoes for Passover goes without saying. I assume that your local rabbi who prohibited their use shares his dislike for them with you. I don't use them not only on Passover, but on any other holiday neither.

Very sincerely yours,

LOUIS GINZBERG

Rabbi [Herman] M. Cohen[4]
799 Ashland Avenue
St. Paul, Minn.

---

1   See below, note 4.

2   For notes to this paragraph, see below, Chapter V, No. 9.

3   *Kitniyot* are legumes. LG is no doubt relying on *Eshel Avraham* to OH 453, subparagraph 2, which distinguishes between dried beans and fresh beans. Regarding *kitniyot* in general, see David Golinkin, "A Responsum Regarding the Use of *Kitniyot* on *Pesah*", *Responsa of the Va'ad Halakhah of the Rabbinical Assembly of Israel*, III:5748-49, Jerusalem 1989, pp. 35-56 (Hebrew) and the literature cited there.

4   The secretary typed *Harry* M. Cohen but this is a typographical error. Rabbi *Herman* M. Cohen (1888-1970) was ordained by the Seminary in 1913 and was rabbi of Temple of Aaron at the address listed in 1932-33 - see *PRA* 4 (1930-32), p. 384. Also see *Students' Annual* 3 (1916), p. 189, and *EJ*, XII, col. 38.

No. 20 May a Cracked Shofar be Repaired with Scotch Tape?
(OH 586:8-9)

Source: LGA, Box 1, "Harold J. Abrahams" file

October 25, 1951

Dear Dr. Abrahams:[1]

I am in receipt of your letter of October 7th, in which you propound the question of whether, according to Jewish lore, a cracked *Shofar* may be repaired by placing Scotch tape over it.

The matter you question has been discussed in the earliest Rabbinical sources, *Mishnah* and Talmud.[2] Unfortunately, however, the old texts permit of various interpretations and hence the variety of opinions among post-Talmudic authorities.[3] The generally accepted opinion is as follows: If the crack is lengthwise, no artificial pasting together of the crack is advisable; whereas, if the crack is in the width of the Shofar, it may used if repaired by closing it with Scotch tape or similar material.[4]

Very sincerely yours,

Louis Ginzberg

Dr. Harold J. Abrahams
330 West Johnson Street
Philadelphia, Pa.

---

1   Dr. Harold J. Abrahams seems to have been a chemistry teacher at Central High School in Philadelphia. See his article "The Use of Lye in Ancient Ritual", *The Jewish Forum* 31/6 (June, 1948), pp. 133-134, in which he explains how to plug up the holes in a *shofar* using *shofar* gratings and sodium hydroxide. There is a copy in his file in the LGA.

2   *Rosh Hashanah* 27a-b.

3   See *Tur*, OH 586 and *Bet Yosef*, ad. loc., as well as OH 586:8-9 with commentaries.

4   For more details, see OH 586:9.

No. 21 The Use of New Tunes in Place of Traditional Tunes (OH 619:1)

Source: CJLS Box, "Bet Knesset" file

Question: In order to stimulate Jewish enthusiasm amongst those who attend our Friday night services, we have decided to use the tune of the *Hatikvah* for the *Adoun Aulom*,[1] but insamuch as several members claim that the regular tune ought to be used for that purpose, I kindly beg to inquire from you whether we should continue using the *Hatikvah*.

Answer: There is no specific traditionally sanctioned melody for the *Adoun Aulom*. Various communities use different melodies and often the same community uses a number of melodies. There is, therefore, no objection from the religious viewpoint to the use of the *Hatikvah* tune for the *Adoun Aulom*.[2] (REPLY BY PROFESSOR LOUIS GINZBERG.)[3]

1 The questioner was probably a German Jew since they say "ou" instead of "o".

2 For resistance to changing traditional tunes, see the Rema to OH 619:1 which is based on the Maharil, ed. Shpitzer, Jerusalem 5749, pp. 339-340.

3 This note is capitalized in the original.

No. 22 Four Questions Regarding the Shofar (OH 623:6)
Source: LGA, Box 11, "Scruby" file

January 13, 1933

Dear Mr. Scruby:

I am in receipt of your letter of December 31 in which you propounded several questions concerning the use of the *Shofar* - trumpet is rather an inaccurate rendering of it - in the services of the Synagogue. I shall reply to them in the order that they are given in your letter:

1. In all Orthodox and Conservative Synagogues the sunset services of the Day of Atonement close with the blowing of the *Shofar*. The custom however, varies - some blow only one blast, some four.[1] There is documentary evidence to show that the ceremony was [observed] as early as a thousand years ago,[2] and I am inclined to assume that it goes back to even a much earlier age. We know from Josephus and Rabbinic sources that in Temple times, that is, before the destruction in the year 70, the outgoing of the Sabbath was announced from the Temple by the blast of the *Shofar*,[3] and one is quite safe in assuming that the Day of Atonement, the Sabbath of Sabbaths, was treated in the same way.[4]

2. The blast is not called the "Last Trumpet", an expression entirely unknown to the Jews. "The Shofar of the Messiah" is the usual phrase among the Jews for the last trumpet.[5]

3. The previous answer covers this question.[6]

4. Neither on New Year's Day, when the Shofar is sounded many a time, nor on the Day of Atonement is there a series of seven blasts. I do not know where in the *Jewish Encyclopedia* the statement quoted by you therefrom is found that on Fridays toward sunset seven blasts are given.[7] Such a statement would be entirely incorrect. In addition to the nine blasts sounded at every evening service in the Temple,[8] there were on Fridays six more, together fifteen, but not seven.[9]

Very sincerely yours,

LOUIS GINZBERG

Mr. John J. Scruby
1406 East 5th Street
Dayton, Ohio

1   One according to Rabbi Moshe Isserles; four according to Rabbi Yosef Karo - see OH 623:6

2   He is referring to a responsum of Rav Hai Gaon (d.1038) - see B.M Lewin, ed., *Otzar Hageonim*, VI, Jerusalem 5694, p. 42, par. 128.

3   Josephus, *The Jewish War*, IV, 9, 12, paragraph 582; *Shabbat* 114b according to the interpretation of Rabbeinu Hananel ad loc.; Maimonides, *Hilkhot Shabbat* 5:20; and Saul Lieberman, *Tosefta Ki-fshuta*, Moed, IV, New York 5722, pp. 897-898. In recent years, archaeologists have discovered part of the booth in which the *shofar* blower stood - see *Ketovot Mesaperot*, Jerusalem 1973[2], p. 165; and Meir Ben-Dov, *Hafirot Har Habayit*, Jerusalem 1982, pp. 93-96.

4   LG repeats the same hypothesis in his book, *An Unknown Jewish Sect*, New York 1976, p. 108, note 10: "It is probably to this trumpet signal at the end the Sabbath and the Day of Atonement that the Shofar-signal, still given at the end of the Day of Atonement, is to be traced".

5   See *Legends*, IV, Philadelphia 1936, p. 234; and VI, pp. 340-341, notes 112, 116.

6   The questions are, unfortunately, not in the LGA.

7   *JE*, XI, p. 304, states that *six* blasts were blown on Friday afternoon and refers to Shabbat 35b (see below).

8   He means *bein ha-arbayim* or late afternoon.

9   For the nine daily blasts in the late afternoon, see *Mishnah Sukkah* 5:5. For the six additional blasts on Friday afternoon, see ibid. as well as *Tosefta Sukkah* 4:11-12, ed. Lieberman, pp. 274-275, and *Shabbat* 35b.

IV. Responsa Related to Yoreh Deah

No. 1 "Jewish Sympathy for Animals" (YD 1ff.)   143

No. 2 "The Humaneness of *Shechita*" (YD 1ff.)   146

No. 3 Is Gelatin Kosher? (YD 87:10)   151

No. 4 Art in the Synagogue - 1923 (YD 141)   155

No. 5 Art in the Synagogue - 1927 (YD 141)   157

No. 6 May Jews Who Have Joined a Christian Science Church
       Be Members of a Synagogue? (YD 158:2 and HM 425:5)   164

No. 7 The Jewish Attitude Towards Spiritualism (YD 179:14)   165

No. 8 Must a Jewish Soldier in the United States Army
       Retain His Beard? (YD 181:10-11)   166

No. 9 What is Meant by the Expression "born in the
       Jewish faith"? (YD 268)   167

No. 10 The Conversion of a Gentile Woman Already Married
       to a Jew and Her Children (YD 268:6-7)   170

No. 11 Euthanasia (YD 339:1)   172

No. 12 The Burial of a Synagogue Member Who was also a
       Member of a Christian Science Church (YD 345:5 and 362:5)   175

No. 13 The Burial of Jews in a Separate Section of a Non-Jewish
       Cemetery and the Burial of an Intermarried Jew in
       a Jewish Cemetery (YD 345:5 and 362:5)   176

No. 14 Seven Questions Regarding Burial (YD 345:5 and 362:5)   178

No. 15 Autopsy (YD 349 and 357)   185

No. 16 Burial in a Mausoleum (YD 362:1)   189

No. 17 Reinterment in Costly Mausoleums (YD 362:1)   190

No. 18 Reinterment from a Mausoleum to a Cemetery (YD 362:1)   191

No. 19 Reinterment in a New Family Plot (YD 363:1)   193

No. 20 Reinterment in a New Family Plot (YD 363:1)   195

No. 21 Reinterment in a New Family Plot (YD 363:1)   197

No. 22 Reinterment in Order to Facilitate Easy Visitation
        (YD 363:1)   198

No. 23 May a Rabbi Who is a *Kohen* Officiate at Funerals?
        (YD 369ff.)   199

No. 24 May a *Kohen* Serve in the U.S. Army? (YD 369ff.)   200

No. 25 The Recital of *Kaddish* by a Son Who Bears a Grudge
        against His Father (YD 376:4)   201

No. 26 The Participation of Children in Mourning in Music
        Periods and School Assemblies (YD 391)   202

No. 1 "Jewish Sympathy for Animals" (YD 1 ff.)

Source: *The Nation* 83/2145, (August 9, 1906), p. 117 = *The New York Evening Post* (August 9, 1906) = *American Hebrew and Jewish Messenger* (August 17, 1906), p. 270
Secondary Reference: Cohen, p. 21, no. 17

Jewish Sympathy for Animals

To the Editor of *The Nation*:

Sir: Authorities go and authorities come, but authority abideth forever, was my involuntary exclamation when I read the brief notice in *The Nation* (No. 2142)[1] regarding the callous attitude of Judaism and Christianity toward the "little brothers" of men. The authority of Schopenhauer is invoked for the unqualified statement, that these two religious systems were oblivious to duty toward dumb creatures.[2] When a modern writer inclines to pick a flaw in the mentality of a medical predecessor, he charges him, as a rule, with blind adherence to authority.

The reproach is, that before the modern spirit of inquiry was abroad, all moot points were settled by merely quoting the dictum of some great man. Apparently we are no better off today, unless it be an advance to swear by Darwin rather than Moses, or have Kant crammed down our throats instead of St. Paul. For my part, I cannot call it other than blind adherence to authority, to rest satisfied with an *ex cathedra* statement by Schopenhauer, that Judaism has no regard for the feelings of the brute creation.

If, instead, the elementary method of consulting the Bible itself were adopted, we should find reason to wonder at the abundance of legal provisions, rather than their paucity. The humane institution of a day of rest embraces the beast of burden in its beneficence; the fourth commandment bids cessation from work on the Sabbath for the sake of one's cattle [Exodus 20:9]. A still more characteristic expression of feeling is the verse that forbids the muzzling of the ox while he is treading out the corn [Deuteronomy 25:4]. The Jewish law, however, goes further; it prohibits castration, and thereby imposed great sacrifices upon an agricultural community [Leviticus 22:24].[3] But the highest degree of tenderness and sympathy with brute life is implied in the Biblical injunctions that recognize and guard the relation of the mother animal to the offspring; a nest may not be robbed of the dam and the fledgling birds at once [Deuteronomy 22:6-7]; a cow or ewe and her young cannot be slaughtered for a sacrifice on the same day [Leviticus 22:28]; and three times the Mosaic law warns against seething the kid in its mother's milk [Exodus 23:19 and 34:26; Deuteronomy 14:21]. So much for the Biblical law. As for post-Biblical Judaism, if it knew no such institutions as Societies for the Prevention of Cruelty to Animals, the reason may be that they were made superfluous by the stringency of the law. The stranger desirous of sojourning among the Jews had to take upon himself a minimum of observance, and this minimum included the prohibition against rending a live animal and eating its flesh,[4] a demand so rigorous that the early Christians laid stress upon it (Acts xxi:25).[5] The rabbis would not permit animals to be tortured, even for the purpose of obtaining medical remedies.[6] Except as a measure of self-defence, the chase is unthinkable in the Jewish system. About a hundred years ago, a very wealthy Jew plied a celebrated rabbi, Ezekiel Landau of Prague [1713-93], with questions as to whether the prohibition against hunting could not be modified in some way. The rabbi gave reins to his astonishment that a Jew could desire to take the life of dumb creatures wantonly, and esteem it a pleasure at that.[7]

That the law was not a theory, but the practical and direct expression of the popular conscience, is demonstrated by legend and proverb. A pious husband and wife long remained childless. They begged a saint, who chanced their way, to pray for the removal of the curse from them. He answered: "If you will so place the watering trough that even the young chicks can quench their thirst, you will have cause for complaint no longer." And so it was; sterility had been their punishment for heedlessness in the treatment of the animals under their charge.[8]

And the whole case of Judaism, which has not been half-stated in the above, was pithily compressed into one sentence by the wisest of kings: "A righteous man regardeth the life of his beast" (Proverbs xii:12).

LOUIS GINZBERG

Jewish Theological Seminary of America, New York, August 6.

[We gladly give space to this interesting letter. Our note, however, while alluding to Schopenhauer, did not erect him into an authority nor was any attack made upon Jewish ethics. - Ed. Nation.][9]

---

1   83/2142 (July 19, 1906), p. 47: "The Society for the Prevention of Cruelty to Animals is asking in England for an Animal Sunday, after the fashion of Hospital Sunday. The hope is to secure public instruction in our duty to dumb creatures. The consideration now shown for the feelings of the lower animals is the result of long and slow moral progress. Schopenhauer bitterly

reproached both Judaism and Christianity for their shortcomings in this respect. It must be admitted that the earlier Christian ethics neglected the whole subject. A great gulf was supposed to separate the heaven-born soul of man and the blind instinct of the brute. But there has been improvement, however gradual...".

2   See Arthur Schopenhauer, *The Basis of Morality*, London 1903, p. 218, and idem, *The World as Will and Representation*, New York 1958, II, p. 645.

3   The verse is not entirely clear, but this is a widely accepted explanation. Also see *Shabbat* 110b-111a; *EH* 5:11-14; *EJ*, s.v. Castration; and Julius Preuss, *Biblical and Talmudic Medicine*, New York 1978, pp. 222-223.

4   He is referring to *ever min ha-hay*, one of the Seven Noahide Laws - see Genesis 9:4 as interpreted in *Sanhedrin* 56a, at bottom.

5   Also see Acts xv:20. Both verses prohibit "what has been strangled".

6   I was unable to locate the source of this statement. For responsa on this subject, see J. David Bleich, *Tradition* 22/1 (Spring, 1986), pp. 20-23.

7   See *Responsa Noda Beyehudah*, Second Series, *Yoreh Deah*, No. 10; *EJ*, s.v. Hunting; and David Novak, *Law and Theology in Judaism*, New York 1974, pp. 55-60.

8   The story is told about Rabbi Yitzhak Luria, the Ari (1534-72). See Elijah Schochet, *Animal Life in Jewish Tradition*, New York 1984, p. 247.

9   See above, note 1.

No. 2 "The Humaneness of Shechita" (YD 1ff.)

Source: *The American Hebrew and Jewish Messenger* 94/1 (Friday, October 31, 1913; Tishrei 30, 5674), pp. 5-6
Secondary References:
1. LGA, Box 11, "Stillman" file (a thank-you note from Dr. William Stillman, President of the American Humane Association, October 22, 1913)
2. Louis Ginzberg, *USAAR* 2 (1914), p. 30

The Humaneness of Shechita:
No Cruelty to Animals in Jewish Method, Says Prof. Louis Ginzberg

Prof. Louis Ginzberg, of the Jewish Theological Seminary, delivered the following address before the American Humane Association at its annual meeting recently held at Rochester, N.Y. He eloquently and with great erudition defended the Jewish method of *Shechita*.

It gives me great pleasure to extend to the American Humane Association greetings from the oldest association for the prevention of cruelty to animals in existence - the Jewish people. Speaking as a Jew and for the Jews, I may well point with pride to the fact that, more than three thousand years ago, our great Lawgiver, Moses, taught us our duties not only towards God and our fellow men, but also towards "the little brethren of men". The fourth commandment includes the beasts of burden in the humane institution of the Sabbath [Exodus 20:9]. A still more characteristic expression of feeling for animals is the biblical law that forbids the muzzling of the ox while treading out the grain [Deuteronomy 25:4]. But the highest degree of tenderness and sympathy with brute-life is implied in the biblical injunctions which recognize and guard the relation of the mother-animal to its offspring: a nest may not be robbed from the dam and the fledgling birds at one time [ibid., 22:6-7]. A cow or ewe or her young must not be slaughtered on the same day [Leviticus 22:28]. And three times the Mosaic law warns against seething a kid in the mother's milk [Exodus 23:19 and 34:26; Deuteronomy 14:21].

The humane attitude towards animals is apparent at all times in the Jewish law, from the Bible down to the emphatic Talmudic prohibition against cruelty to animals.[1] It is true, Judaism knows no such institutions as societies for the prevention of cruelty to animals. But the reason for it is that they were made superfluous by the stringency of the law. The rabbis would not even permit to have pain caused to animals for the purpose of obtaining medical remedies.[2] Except as a measure of self-defence, the chase is unthinkable to the Jewish mind.[3] The rabbis not only developed the laws against cruelty to animals, but also enjoined kindness to them. The principle doctrine of Judaism is described by an author, who lived about a century before the rise of Christianity, in the following words: "Keep the commands of the Lord; have compassion towards all, not towards men only, but also towards beasts".[4]

It is in this spirit that the rabbis taught that animals must first be fed before sitting down to a meal.[5] There is little to wonder therefore, at the following entry in the diary of a famous Jewish mystic of the sixteenth century which reads: "It is man's duty to love everybody whether man or animal".[6]

I hope that these few remarks on the attitude of the Jewish law towards the treatment of animals are not out of place in considering the question of the Jewish method of slaughtering called *Shechita*. Whether this divine commandment has its reason in the prevention of pain to the animals or not, nobody can tell. Obedience to the divine will is the first requisite of the Jewish religion, irrespective of whether we know the reason for it or not. But, as a working hypothesis, we readily assume that the law of *Shechita* had its reasons in the prevention of cruelty to animals. It may well be said, without hesitation, that those who are entitled on account of their theoretical and practical knowledge to speak authoritatively on this question are of the opinion that *Shechita* is one of the least painful forms of death. I have just now before me a book in which the opinions of no less than fifty professors of physiology, pathology and hygiene at the leading universities of Germany, France, England, Italy, Holland, Austria and Denmark and of three hundred veterinarians are recorded in favor of the Jewish method of slaughtering.[7] If among the authorities favoring *Shechita* are men like Du Bois-Reymond, Golz, Englemann, Hoppe-Seyler, Forster, Von Pettenkoffer, Lister, Verchow, Laborde, Richet, Chaveau, Dammann and many others who may be described as the fathers of modern medicine, physiology, pathology and veterinary art, it is difficult to understand how it is still possible to question the humaneness of the *Shechita*. It is true, in some parts of Germany the agitation against *Shechita* is still carried on, but, of course, everybody knows that the power behind this movement is not love for the animals but hatred against the Jews. The German Government, whom nobody would accuse of being biased in favor of the Jews, knowing the real source of agitation against *Shechita*, refused to comply with the wishes of the anti-Semitic agitators. The Director of the Military Equipment Bureau of the German Army, General von Gemmingen, declared at an open sitting of the Diet, that [at] the slaughter-houses of the government at Mainz, where the cattle for the use of the army are slaughtered, the Jewish method of killing is in vogue. He gave the following two reasons why the government preferred *Shechita*: First, because *Shechita* was declared the least painful method of slaughtering by the medical board appointed by the government to investigate the different forms of slaughtering, which counts among its members men like Virchow, Olshausen, von Bergmann, von Bardeleben [and] von Leyden to mention only a few. Secondly, because the soup prepared from the meat of cattle slaughtered according to the Jewish law contains less blood corpuscles than the soup prepared from the meat of cattle slaughtered differently. Yielding to the anti-Semitic outcry against *Shechita*, the government has discontinued the use of it, but not without declaring officially that it still adheres to the view that *Shechita*, even without stunning the animal before it, is not cruel.[8]

I mention these facts, because in a pamphlet lately published for the special benefit of the Humane Society of the United States, much space is given to disprove the statement made by the friends of *Shechita* that meat for the German army was from animals slaughtered according to the Jewish law.[9] The author might have saved himself a good deal of trouble if he would only have looked up the work of Dr. Hildesheimer on the *Shechita* question, where the facts are stated as they really are, and as given above by me.[10] This proves very plainly that the author of this pamphlet is not at all acquainted with the literature on the subject. For I have no reason to assume that he would have wilfully ignored the facts if he knew them. It seems that his only source of information about the *Shechita* question are a few anti-Semitic pamphlets of some obscure veterinarians and it not surprising, therefore, to find in it all the old junk which any man with scientific training would only look at askance. As a specimen of the entirely unscientific method used by the author in dealing with our question, I will only quote the following sentence from it: "I have watched this method till the assertion that it is the humane one compels me to offer a most positive denial and protest. It is difficult for me to understand how any man unprejudiced can watch this manner of slaughter without feeling that it is responsible for a vast amount of wholly unecessary suffering".[11]

Yes, I must confess that it is difficult to understand how any man unprejudiced can decide a question which requires a careful study of physiology, pathology, hygienics, and surgery simply by looking a few times at the act of slaughtering. The common adage: "Do not judge things by their appearance" ought to be a fair warning to this kind of sentimentalist.

The first argument against *Shechita* usually brought forward by people without sufficient knowledge of the subject is that the animal remains conscious for some time after both carotides and the other blood vessels of the neck have been divided simultaneously. As an answer to this fallacious argument, we have only to cite the opinions of the greatest authorities on physiology in modern times: Golz, Strassburg, Lister, London, Lundgreen, Stockholm, Laborde, Paris, Herzen, Lausonne, Mosse and Turin. All of these great authorities maintain that the animal becomes unconscious at the very moment the cut is performed. Of thirty leading physiologists of the world, not one would admit that it takes more than a few seconds after *Shechita* to cause loss of consciousness and sense of pain.[12]

The opponent of *Shechita* further points to the fact that sometimes the animal, after *Shechita* has been performed, kicks and plunges in its wild attempts to rise. Prof. Dammann, president of the Veterinary Academy of Hanover, the leading authority in Germany on veterinary medicine, writes: "Only one without any medical knowledge could maintain that the epileptoid convulsions after *Shechita* are to be taken as signs of consciousness. On the contrary, these epileptic movements are rather the best proof of the unconsciousness of the animal".[13]

Some scientists even maintain that this involuntary movement helps to make the meat more tender and to keep better.

The third objection sometimes raised against *Shechita* is that the laying down of the animal might cause it pain. But no lesser authorities than DuBois-Reymond, Dammann and Nissel declare that the laying down, if properly carried out, causes as little pain as the *Shechita* itself.[14] But nobody, to be sure, is more interested in the proper laying down of the animal than the Jews themselves, because if by any chance the animal should receive any injury, its meat would become unfit for food, according to the Jewish law. The mechanical arrangement used in Germany was declared painless by Dr. Budding in his testimony before the Admiralty Committee and recommended by him as successful even for wild cattle.

It is rather a curious coincidence that in this very same year, when the *Shechita* was legalized in Finland by the Czar and when the Medical Congress at Mala, Greece, adopted resolutions recommending the introduction of *Shechita* in Greece, when, further, the Court of Appeals at Halifax gave its opinion that *Shechita* is, at least, as humane as any other method of slaughtering in use, it is curious, I say, that we should have to defend it in the United States.

I have refrained from contrasting *Shechita* with other methods of slaughtering, although many a word might be said against some methods used now, which some would like to substitute for *Shechita*. I am not here to attack anybody, but to ward off attacks hurled unjustly against us. My remarks on *Shechita*, however, would be incomplete if they did not contain an answer to those who would like to tell us that *Shechita* is not at all a religious law with the Jews. To this presumptuous statement, I would only say that we Jews were for thousands of years the religious teachers of the world, and it shows lack of delicacy and real religious tolerance on the part of those who want to teach us our own religion. We are prepared to meet all arguments against *Shechita*, but refuse, as Jews and Americans, to debate the question whether we are entitled to believe as we see fit.

1   צער בעלי חיים. See *EJ*, s.v. Animals, Cruelty to; Noah Cohen, *Tsa'ar Ba'alei Hayim*, Washington. D.C. 1959, New York and Jerusalem, 1976²; and Elijah Schochet, *Animal Life in Jewish Tradition*, New York 1984, pp. 151-155.
2   See above, No. 1, note 6.
3   See ibid., note 7.
4   *The Testament of the Twelve Patriarchs*, Zebulun 5:1. My thanks to Dr. Hanan Eshel who steered me to this work.
5   *Berakhot* 40a = *Gittin* 62a, bottom.
6   I did not find this statement in *Sefer Gerushin*, Jerusalem 1962, a diary by R. Moshe Cordovero, but see a similar statement in his *Tomer Devorah*, Vilna 1911, Chapter 3, fol. 10a.
7   *Gutachten über das jüdische-rituelle Schlächtverfahren*, Berlin 1894.
8   This information is quoted by Hirsch Hildesheimer, *Neue Gutachten über das jüdisch-rituelle Schlächtverfahren*, Berlin 1909, in his unpaginated Forward.
9   I have not been able to locate this pamphlet.
10   See above, note 8.
11   See above, note 9.
12   See above, notes 7 and 8.
13   See above, note 7, pp. 28-31.
14   See above, notes 7 and 8.

No. 3 Is Gelatin Kosher? (YD 87:10)

Source: The entire correspondence is located in LGA, Box 10, "Rabino-witch" file, except for the letter of December 24, 1951, which is in Box 14, "Miscellaneous Letters" file.[1]

Background Reading:

1. Isaac Klein, *Responsa and Halakhic Studies*, New York 1975, pp. 59-74
2. David Sheinkopf, *Issues in Jewish Dietary Laws*, New York 1988, pp. 5-119.

I.M. Rabinowitch
M.D., C.M., D.Sc. (M&G)., F.R.C.P.(C)., F.A.C.P.

1020 Medical Arts Building
Sherbrooke & Guy Sts.
Montreal, 25
July 4th, 1949

Professor L. Ginsberg,
3080 Broadway,
New York, 27, N.Y.

Dear Professor Ginsberg,

I am addressing this letter to you at the suggestion of Rabbi Julius Berger, previously of Montreal and now of New Kensington, Pa.[2] It is with regard to an opinion which I had expressed about the ritual cleanliness of gelatin. The following are, briefly, the facts:

Early last year, one of my patients asked me whether gelatin is kosher. From my knowledge of its chemistry and manufacture, I stated that, unless the bones from which it is made are from a ritually clean animal, the animal has been ritually slaughtered, and the bones have been ritually cleaned, gelatin is *trefah*.

A short time after, the same patient brought to my attention a Responsum, in the Rabbinical publication *Hapardess*, between the late Rabbi Joseph Kanwitz and the great Rabbi Chaim Ozer Gradzinsky in which gelatin was pronounced kosher.[3] I, therefore, requested from the Editor of *Hapardess* a copy of this publication so as to enable me to study the reasons for the decision in detail, and, as the result of this study, it was clear to me that both Rabbi Konwitz and Rabbi Gradzinsky had been misinformed by someone about the manufacture of gelatin; that, in fact, that which Rabbi Gradzinsky feared might not be extracted completely from the bones and thus possibly reappear on heating and thus cause gelatin to be *trefah*, is that part of the bone which is the source, and the only source, of gelatin. I, therefore, addressed a letter to Rabbi Pardes, the Editor of *Hapardess* on April 11th, a copy of which please find enclosed.

As I had received no reply to the above letter, I addressed another on May 12th, a copy of which also, please, find enclosed.

Shortly after, I received a reply, but it was clear that Rabbi Pardes had confused junket (made with rennet) with gelatin.[4] I, therefore, again wrote to Rabbi Pardes, a copy of which letter is also enclosed, pointing out this fact, but, to-date, have received no reply.

Recently, during a conversation with Rabbi Berger, I showed Rabbi Berger my letters addressed to Rabbi Pardes. Rabbi Berger agreed completely with the opinion which I had expressed and suggested that I write to you for your opinion; hence this letter.

I am dear Professor Ginsberg,
Very respectfully yours,

I.M. Rabinowitch

~ ~ ~

Excerpt from reply of Prof. Ginzberg of August 12, 1949:
...The question of whether gelatin is ritually permissible has been often put to me and I am happy to say that my answer was in agreement with your opinion. Though not a chemist, I know enough of natural sciences to follow a problem in chemistry when it is properly explained to me. I was fortunate to have the assistance of my son-in-law, Dr. Bernard S. Gould, professor of bio-chemistry at Massachusetts Institute of Technology,[5] with whom I discussed the problem at length.

I am convinced that no rabbinical scholar who is in a position to comprehend a problem in chemistry would ever permit the use of gelatin. I did not read the opinions on this matter given in *Hapardess*, as I did not believe that the men discussing it are competent to decide a question of Jewish law which requires some knowledge of modern science. The late Rabbi Chaim Ozer Grodzinsky was well known to me personally; as a matter of fact, his wife was a close relation to me,[6] and I would certainly attach great weight to any decision by him on Jewish Law, but not in a case for which some knowledge of chemistry or physiology is necessary...

~ ~ ~

December 24, 1951
Dear Professor Rabinowitch:
I greatly appreciate your kindness and courtesy in sending me a copy of the letter which you addressed to Rabbi Samuel Baskin in regard to "Atlantic Gelatin".[7]
It is needless to say that I fully agree with you that there is no basis whatsoever for declaring gelatin *kasher*, but I doubt whether your very lucid explanation of the chemical processes will change the opinion of the two rabbis. Being an optimist by nature, I am inclined to assume that the position taken by the two rabbis on this matter is due exclusively to their ignorance of natural science. A less optimistic nature might explain their action in a different way, but I don't think it is worth discussing.
By the way, it is a queer coincidence that those two rabbis have based their opinion on two authorities to whom I happen to be related. In my first letter written to you, I mentioned the fact that Rabbi Chaim Ozer Grodzinsky was the husband of a cousin of mine; and I may add today that I am a direct descendant of Rabbi Moses Isserles, the greatest authority for Ashkenazic Jewry.[8] Yet with all due respect to this great man, I agree with you that he never would have expressed his view of dried stomach if he had lived today when the knowledge of chemistry is so much more advanced than that known to chemists of his day.

With kindest regards,
Very sincerely yours,

Louis Ginzberg

Professor I. M. Rabinowitch
1020 Medical Arts Building
Sherbrooke and Guy Streets
Montreal, Canada

1   Dr. Rabinowitch's lengthy enclosures have been omitted for the sake of brevity.
2   Rabbi Julius Berger (1893-1953) was ordained by the Seminary in 1927 and was rabbi of Shaare Zion in Montreal for many years. See *Students' Annual* 3 (1916), p. 201; *PRA* 5 (1933-38), p. 492; *PRA* 17 (1953), p. 272; and David Golinkin, ed., S. Gershon Levi, *Breaking New Ground: The Struggle for a Jewish Chaplaincy in Canada*, Montreal 1994, pp. 13-18, 24, and 35.
3   *Hapardess* 22/4 (January, 1948), pp. 19-21, which is slightly abbreviated in *Sefer Ahiezer*, III, Vilna 1939, No. 33, par. 5. The letter is from 1936. At that time Rabbi Konwitz was president of *Agudass Harabbonim* of the United States and Canada and Rabbi Grodzinski (1863-1940) was the Chief Rabbi of Vilna. Regarding Rabbi Konwitz (1872-1957), see Moshe

Sherman, *Orthodox Judaism in America: A Biographical Dictionary and Sourcebook*, Westport, Connecticut and London 1996, pp. 119-121.

4   Junket is a dessert made with rennet. Rabbi Shmuel Aaron Pardes (1887-1956) was the founder and longtime editor of *Hapardess* – see Sherman (above, note 3), pp. 161-162.

5   See *Keeper*, p. 263.

6   Leah Grodzinski was the daughter of R. Eliyahu Eliezer Shirwinter of Vilna and the granddaughter of R. Israel Lipkin Salanter (1810-83), the founder of the *Mussar* Movement. They were married on 9 Elul, 5643 (September 11, 1883). See Shemuel Rothstein, *Ahiezer*, Tel Aviv-Jerusalem 5706², p. 10; and Aharon Soresky, *Rabban Shel Yisrael*, Benei Berak 1980², pp. 20-21. For a vignette about R. Chaim Ozer and LG, see David Druck, *R. Levi Ginzberg*, New York 5694, p. 43 (Hebrew).

7   Dr. Rabinowitch was reacting to a pamphlet written by Rabbi Baskin and Rabbi Simon Winograd in which they declared Atlantic Gelatin kosher.

8   This is apparently a slight exaggeration. LG was a direct descendant of R. Samuel Judah Katzenellenbogen (12th generation) who was a second cousin of R. Moses Isserles. See Neil Rosenstein, *The Unbroken Chain*, I, revised edition, New York, London & Jerusalem 1990, the family tree before p. 1, p. 3, and pp. 216-217.

No. 4 Art in the Synagogue - 1923 (YD 141)

Source: "Current Aspects in Judaism", *USR* 3/2 (April, 1923), p. 2
Excerpt: *USAAR* 11 (1923), pp. 11-12

A question lately addressed to your committee reads: "Is it permitted according to Jewish Law and Tradition to have the Prophets of Israel presented on the stained glass windows of the Synagogue?" Another similar question was "whether it be permitted to place some statuary in front of the Synagogue".

An unqualified "no" was the answer to both of these questions. Your committee, without entering into a technical discussion of the law bearing upon these questions, remarked "that its decision is primarily based upon the fact that for thousands of years the absence of statuary and paintings from Jewish places of worship was their most characteristic feature".[1]

Now, these questions and many others of related nature require a definite statement as to the relation of art to religion according to [the] Jewish view. We are often told that the Jew, if he be of a real progressive religion, ought to endeavor to employ art in the service of religion and thus combine the Greek ideal, the religion of Beauty, with the Hebrew one, the religion of the True and Good.

Jewish history, when studied sympathetically, will, however, tell you that the endeavor after a simple form of worship discernible [at] the very beginning of the Synagogue was not a negative idea at all, and had nothing whatsoever to do with the rejection of beauty in any form.

It is not without interest to note that the same philosopher - Hegel - who coined the phrase, "Religion of Beauty", to describe the Greek ideal, has made the following penetrating remark: "It may", he said, "be specially noted that beautiful art can only belong to those religions in which the spiritual principle, though concrete and intrinsically free, is not yet absolute".[2] Or, to put it in less technical language, the fusion of religion with beauty was so fully achieved in Greece because the Greek spirit was possessed by the feeling of the immanence of the Divine and not its transcendence. Hence, as one of the leading philosophers of religion of our time has aptly remarked, as religion becomes more spiritual, the place of art in the cultus falls into the background.

It is, indeed, very humiliating for us Jews if we consider that the one truly great religious reform of modern times, that of the sixteenth century among the Christians, began with the removal of statuary and painting from the churches, while some of our brethren know of no better way of expressing their advanced ideas than by returning to forms of worship discarded by the Jews thousands of years ago as not being compatible with the spirituality of his religion. It would be a sad day for the Synagogue if it should fail to proclaim by external forms the inner truth that the only acceptable worship of God is of the heart, and that the intrusion of any material attraction is a degradation of this pure service. We must uphold the ideal that the best worship is to penetrate to that region where the things of sense cannot accompany us. Neither in life nor in worship should freedom be dependent upon mere material succor.

1   Nonetheless, since this responsum was written, dozens of ancient synagogues with mosaic floors portraying biblical figures and pagan gods (sic!) have been discovered - see, for example, the illustrations in Hershel Shanks, *Judaism in Stone*, Washington and New York 1979 [hereafter: Shanks] or Lee Levine, ed., *Ancient Synagogues Revealed*, Jerusalem 1981 [hereafter: Levine]. Regarding the pagan motifs, see Shanks, Chapter 11; and Bezalel Narkiss, in: Lee Levine, ed., *The Synagogue in Late Antiquity*, Philadelphia 1987, pp. 183-188. For art in medieval synagogues, see Shemuel Krauss, *Korot Batei Hatefilah B'yisrael*, New York 5715, pp. 297-301. But see below, No. 5, where LG mentions some of these discoveries and takes a more lenient approach.

2   I have not yet located the source of this quote.

No. 5 Art in the Synagogue - 1927 (YD 141)

Source: LGA, Box 9, "Marshall" file contains the question and the thank-you note. The responsum is in Box 17, "Questions and Answers" file. The letter to Robert Kohn is taken from Reznikoff.

Excerpts:
1. Herman Dicker, Of *Learning and Libraries: The Seminary Library at One Hundred*, New York 1988, pp. 42-43, 118
2. *Keeper*, pp. 231-235
3. Charles Reznikoff, ed., *Louis Marshall, Champion of Liberty: Selected Papers and Addresses*, II, Philadelphia 1957, p. 855

Guggenheimer, Untermyer & Marshall
120 Broadway, New York
Cable Address "Melpomene" New York

January 5, 1927

Dear Professor Ginzberg:

A question has arisen in connection with the construction of the new house of worship of Emanu-El Congregation[1] as to the limitations upon decorations imposed by the practices of traditional Judaism. There is a desire to establish memorial windows. Questions have also arisen as to carvings upon stone and wood. I have assumed that the "Lion of Judah" is an entirely permissible decoration, but that the representation of a human figure or of any other figures which may be suggestive of ancient idolatrous practices, or of certain symbols which have a non-Jewish connotation, is forbidden.

I would greatly appreciate your views upon this subject. It is our desire to avoid the use of any decoration which would offend the sensibilities of the most orthodox.

Very cordially yours,

Louis Marshall[2]

Prof. Louis Ginzberg,
531 West 123rd Street,
New York City

~   ~   ~

The biblical prohibition against fashioning of idols, especially that found in Exodus 20:3, was at an early time understood to include the making of all images of living things and for all purposes, for worship as well as for the sake of beauty. It is not without interest to note that Philo, the Jew most deeply imbued with Greek culture known to history, is the oldest authority for this sweeping prohibition. In his work *De Gigantibus* 13, he remarks: "Therefore, our lawgiver - Moses - excluded from our commonwealth the pleasing arts of fashioning human or animal likenesses because they falsify the truths and cause the souls of those who are easily misled to accept falsehood and sophism made acceptable to them by the charm of art".[3]

In these few words this great Jew and great philosopher sketched the close connection between Greek mythology and Greek art. Perfected human form is the Greek ideal of God, in art as well as in religion; the Jew idealized and expanded human virtues. To accept Greek art would have meant to him the exchange of his ideal of God for that of the pagan.

We are, therefore, not in the least surprised at the rigor with which the Jews of the first century of the common era applied the law against images. To mention only a few facts referred to by the Jewish historian, Josephus: The two great leaders of the Pharisees, Judas and Mattathias, died as martyrs at the stake by the hands of Herod for having torn down the golden eagle that he had erected over the great gate of the Temple, "contrary to the law that forbids to erect images or representations of any living creature" (Antiquities XVII, 6, 2).[4] A sedition of the Jews arose against Pontius Pilate when the Roman soldiers that were stationed in Jerusalem unfurled the standards upon which were Caesar's effigy, "whereas our law forbids us the very making of images" (Antiquities XVIII, 3, 1).[5] The first act of Josephus as Governor of Galilee during the revolution was to ask the Senate of Tiberias to demolish "that house which Herod, the Tetrarch, had built there and which has the figures of living creatures on it, although our laws have forbidden us to make any such figures" (Life 12).[6]

It is difficult to say how long the strict interpretation of the law against images continued to prevail among the Palestinian scholars, though one is quite safe in stating that the Tannaitic sources, the products of the Palestinian academies of the first two centuries, still maintain the old view and that even the Talmud of Jerusalem, compiled about the second half of the fourth century, hardly betrays any essential modification of the rigor of the law.[7] Attention must, however, be called to the fact that in the remains of ancient synagogues in Galilee, some of which were built in the second, but none later than in the fourth [century][8] (comp. Masterman, *Studies in Galilee* [Chicago, 1909] and Kohl and Watzinger, *Antike Synagogen in Galilaea*

[Leipzig, 1916]) were found representations of animals, eagles, lions, etc., not only in mosaic but also in plastic designs.[9] We meet with pictures of animals and other objects in mosaic also in the ruins of the recently discovered synagogue in Jericho - beginning of the fourth century[10] - and further in the famous ruins of the synagogue at Hammam-Lif, near Carthage, from about the same period.[11]

The question how to explain the discrepancy between theory and practice of the Palestinian Jews has not received a satisfactory answer. To maintain with some scholars that the people who erected the synagogues were ignorant of the law against images, or cared little for the interpretation thereof by the Rabbis,[12] amounts to explaining the past by the present, while true history endeavors to interpret the present by the past. The true answer is that with the gradual increasing influences of Babylonian Jewry not only upon the other parts of the Diaspora, but even on the Holy Land, the rigor of the law against images was greatly lessened. In Babylonia, a considerable part of the gentile population with whom the Jews came in contact were Zoroastrians and, like the Jews, abhorred the worship of images. The close connection between art and religion that the Palestinian Jew could not help notice among his gentile neighbors did not exist in Babylonia. Whatever art the Persians had developed in Babylonia or taken over from the Greeks was entirely divorced from religion and hence the quite liberal attitude taken by the Babylonian scholars towards the law against images. According to the Babylonian Talmud (main passage *Abodah Zarah* 42b-43b) this prohibition is restricted to:

1. Representations of the human form but only in relief, not otherwise.

2. Representation in relief of the four figures - as a unity - seen by the Prophet Ezekiel on the Divine Throne (Ezekiel 1:1 seq.)

3. Representation of sun, moon and stars, whether in relief or otherwise.

The historical reasons for these rulings of the Talmud may be said to be the following ones: Not only was the human form the most favored by the Greeks and other nations of antiquity for the representation of their gods, but the Jews had not yet forgotten their sufferings because of their refusal to pay the divine honors to the statues of the living or dead Caesars. The phenomenal development that Christianity took about the time of the rise of the Babylonian academies to importance could not but strengthen the aversion of the Jew against images of man. The fear that gnostic and syncretistic sects who often mistook symbol for reality, ideas for hypostases, might misinterpet the symbolic vision of the Prophet Ezekiel led the rabbis to prohibit the representation of the four figures in the Divine Throne. And finally, the old astral worship of the Semites was not yet quite dead among large numbers of the gentile inhabitants of Babylonia and Palestine and hence the unqualified prohibition against representation of the heavenly bodies.

The post-Talmudic authorities rarely changed Talmudic law, and as late a code as the *Shulhan Aruk*[13] has practically very little to add or to take away from the above-mentioned rules found in the Talmud. There arose, however, as early as the twelfth century the feeling that the highest ornament of the synagogue is its simplicity, and no less an authority than Maimonides, whom nobody would accuse of puritanical narrow-mindedness, was the great sponsor of simplicity.[14] Feeling, however, in contrast to law, is individual and one cannot say that for the last six centuries there has been complete uniformity in Israel with regard to ornamentation of the synagogue. On the whole, one may state that with very few exceptions, as for instance, the famous lions supporting the Ark of the synagogue at Ascoli, later removed to Pesaro (comp. Kaufmann in *Jewish Quarterly Review*, Old Series IX [1897], pp. 254-262) no designs in relief were used, the decorations of the synagogue being limited to mosaic, engraving or painting, and that representation of animals was restricted to lions. In accordance with this practice, I have frequently rendered the following decision:

1. No designs in bas relief are to be used.

2. Representations of animals to be limited to the lion.

3. That of the Heavenly Bodies to be excluded entirely.

4. The walls and windows of the synagogue should not contain any figure whatsoever.

It may not be out of place to call attention to the fact that the Christianization of art in the Middle Ages and at the time of the Renaissance could only discourage the artistically inclined Jews. The metamorphosis of Venus to the Madonna was obvious to the Jew, but he also was aware of the use the Church made of the old symbols of the Synagogue - the Lion of Judah meant to the former something entirely different from what the latter saw in it.[15] The Jew, therefore, preferred to have his place of worship without the graces of art than to have it filled with non-Jewish art.

May I, in conclusion, quote a few sentences that bear upon our subject from an address delivered by me about two years ago:[16] "We are often told that the Jew, if he be of a real progressive religion, ought to endeavor to employ art in the service of religion and thus combine the Greek ideal, the religion of Beauty, with the Hebrew one, the religion of the True and Good.

Jewish history, when studied sympathetically, will, however, tell you that the endeavor after a simple form of worship discernible [at] the very beginning of the Synagogue was not a negative idea at all, and had nothing whatsoever to do with the rejection of beauty in any form.

It is not without interest to note that the same philosopher - Hegel - who coined the phrase "Religion of Beauty" to describe the Greek ideal, has made the following penetrating remark: "It may," he said, "be specially noted that beautiful art can only belong to those religions in which the spiritual principle, though concrete and intrinsically free, is not yet absolute". Or, to put it in less technical language, the fusion of religion with beauty was so fully achieved in Greece because the Greek spirit was possessed by the feeling of the immanence of the Divine and not its transcendence. Hence, as one of the leading philosophers of religion of our time has aptly remarked, as religion becomes more spiritual, the place of art in the cultus falls into the background.

It is indeed very humiliating for us Jews if we consider that the one truly great religious reform of modern times, that of the sixteenth century among the Christians, began with the removal of statuary and painting from the churches, while some of our brethren know of no better way of expressing their advanced ideas than by returning to forms of worship discarded by the Jew thousands of years ago as not being compatible with the spirituality of his religion. It would be a sad day for the synagogue if it should fail to proclaim by external forms the inner truth that the only acceptable worship of God is of the heart, and that the intrusion of any material attraction is a degradation of this pure service. We must uphold the ideal that the best worship is to penetrate to that region where the things of sense cannot accompany us. Neither in life nor in worship should freedom be dependent upon mere material succor".

~   ~   ~

Guggenheimer, Untermyer & Marshall
120 Broadway, New York
Cable Address "Melpomene" New York

January 14, 1927

Dear Professor Ginzberg:

I am in receipt of yours of the 13th instant, enclosing your most illuminating opinion concerning the laws and regulations of traditional Judaism with regard to decorations in the Synagogue. We shall act in strict accord with it in the construction and decoration of the new Synagogue of Emanu-El Congregation.[17]

Thanking you for your promptness, I am,

Very cordially yours,

Louis Marshall

Prof. Louis Ginzberg
531 West 123rd Street
New York City

~   ~   ~

January 14, 1927

To Robert D. Kohn[18]

I am handing you a copy of the opinion which Prof. Louis Ginzberg of the Jewish Theological Seminary of America has prepared concerning the laws and regulations of traditional Judaism with regard to decorations in the Synagogue. It fully conforms with the results of my own investigation and will be accepted as a guide by our Board of Trustees in the solution of the questions which you have addressed to us. You will find it interesting, and particularly that portion which refers to the opinion of Maimonides that the highest ornament of the synagogue is its simplicity.

1   For an illustration of the building, see *EJ*, XII, col. 1108. The board decided to erect a new building in December, 1925 and the building was dedicated on January 10, 1930. See Rabbi Nathan Perilman, in: *Moral and Spiritual Foundations for the World of Tomorrow: The Centenary Series...Congregation Emanu-el*, New York 1945, pp. 221-223, 229-231.

2   Louis Marshall (1856-1929) was Chairman of the Executive Committee of the Seminary (1902-05) and Chairman of the Board of Directors (1905-29). See Nadell, pp. 266-267; and *EJ*, XI, cols. 1060-1062. Regarding his activities at Temple Emanu-el, see Reznikoff, pp. 831-859, and Perilman quoted above.

3   Philo, II, London and New York 1929, pp. 474-475.

4   Josephus, VIII, Cambridge, Mass. and London 1963, pp. 440-441.

5   Ibid., IX, 1965, pp. 42-47

6   Ibid., I, 1926, pp. 26-27.

7   For a different view, see Ephraim E. Urbach, *Israel Exploration Journal* 9 (1959), pp. 149-165, 229-245, who proves that the Palestinian *Amoraim* were more lenient that the *Tannaim*.

8   But many synagogues excavated after 1927 date from the fifth-sixth centuries.

9   See Shanks and Levine cited above in No. 4, note 1.

10   For an illustration, see Shanks, p. 40. For a description and literature, see Marilyn J.S. Chiat, *Handbook of Synagogue Architecture*, Chico, California 1982, pp. 253-255.

11   Also called Naro. For illustrations and brief descriptions, See Shanks, pp. 97-100; and Levine, p. 171.

12 For this approach, see Ludwig Blau, HUCA 3 (1926), pp. 175-190; and especially Erwin R. Goodenough, *Jewish Symbols in the Graeco-Roman Period*, 13 vols., Princeton 1953-1968 or the abridged version edited by Jacob Neusner, Princeton 1988.

13 YD 141.

14 He is apparently referring to the *Responsa of the Rambam*, ed. Blau, II, Jerusalem 1960, No. 215, pp. 379-380.

15 In Revelation 5:5 (and cf. 22:16), the Lion of Judah denotes Jesus the Messiah but the lion rarely appears in Christian art - see W. and G. Audsley, *Handbook of Christian Symbolism*, London 1865, p. 40; and Louis Brehier, *L'art Chrétien*, Paris 1928, pp. 220-221.

16 From here until the end is a quote from above, No. 4.

17 See the following letter.

18 Kohn, Butler, and Stein was the architectural firm engaged by the congregation - see Perilman (above, note 1), p. 222.

No. 6 May Jews Who Have Joined a Christian Science Church Be Members of a Synagogue? (YD 158:2 and HM 425:5)

Source: Rabbi Louis Epstein, "Report of the Committee on the Interpretation of Jewish Law", LGA, Box 17, "Committee on Interpretation of Jewish Law" file = *USAAR* 7-8 (1919-20), p. 90.

Following upon this as a precedent,[1] the Committee feels that congregations affiliated with the United Synagogue shall not tolerate in their membership persons connected with the Christian Science Church or its activities.

---

1   See below, No. 12, where the Committee ruled that a Jewish woman who was also a member of a Christian Science Church should be buried as an apostate.

No. 7 The Jewish Attitude Towards Spiritualism (YD 179:14)
Source: *Exponent* = LGA, Box 17, "Questions and Answers" file

At your last Convention, my friend, Rabbi Louis M. Epstein, reported to you the decision rendered by your Committee with regard to persons affiliated with the Christian Science Church.[1] This year, your Committee had to deal with the question of Spiritualism.[2] I put Spiritualism side by side with Christian Science because, different as they may otherwise be, they are the ugly symptoms of the same cause. A longing to pry into the mysteries of the grave is as much a sign of intellectual and spiritual decay as is the quest for a science that would supplant the physical law by a metaphysical one. The sphere of our human science is the visible world in which for a brief space between two eternities we labor and suffer, are glad and sorry, and do good and evil. Clouds and darkness hide from us the whence and whither of humanity. The mystery of generation and the mystery of death are inpenetrable to us. The Synagogue throughout the ages has sternly set her face against the practices which are best described in the Biblical phrase "asking questions from the dead" [Deuteronomy 18:11]. The God of Israel is the God of the living and not of the dead.[3]

---

1   See above, No. 6, and below, No. 12. For biographical details reagarding Rabbi Epstein, see below, Chapter VII, No. 11, note 1.

2   *The World Book Dictionary* (2 vols.; Chicago 1983) defines "spiritualism" as: "the belief that the spirits of the dead can hold communication with the living, especially through persons called mediums".

3   Yet, surprisingly enough, the Rema allows conversing with the spirits of the dead - see YD 179:14.

No. 8 Must a Jewish Soldier in the United States Army Retain His Beard? (YD 181:10-11)

Source: *Keeper*, p. 222
Secondary Reference: Address, p. 116

Shortly before my father's death, while the Korean War was under way, I involved him in another military problem which I called "The Case of the Bearded Soldier". General Schulz, President Eisenhower's Military Aide,[1] called me at Columbia to inquire whether it was true that Jews couldn't shave. He told me that the President had received a letter from a soldier who had been forcibly shaved by the Army and who was threatening to bring a suit against the Army. A reading of the file revealed that the case had been dragging along for months and it came to contain all sorts of opinions and letters, including one from the Adjutant General's Office to the soldier, quoting the Talmud and other Jewish works, signed Mary Quinn, 1st Lieutenant, WAC (!). The soldier contended that he was a member of a Hasidic sect in Brooklyn,[2] that he served as a part-time rabbi, that cutting his beard was against his religious beliefs, and that his future had been jeopardized by the Army's forcibly shaving him.

I sought my father's advice, and he took the position that the Army had the right to require the soldier to remove his beard (by cutting, not shaving),[3] and that there was no merit to the soldier's claim that he was a member of a sect, since Jewish law recognizes no sects. My father felt that if the soldier's position were upheld, and since the Army insisted that soldiers be clean shaven, a draft loophole might develop. My own recommendation, which was eventually accepted, was to avoid the issue by sending the soldier overseas to an out-of-the-way assignment and forward advice through the Chaplains' Corps that he was to be permitted to grow a beard.

---

1   Robert Schulz was one of Eisenhower's military aides for many years and was gradually promoted from Major to General. In 1953 he was still a Colonel - see Stephen Ambrose, *Eisenhower*, I, New York 1983, pp. 435, 481, 510; and II, New York 1984, pp. 611, 637.
2   According to Address, he was a Lubavitcher *hossid*.
3   See YD 181:10, that shaving with a scissors is permissible.

No. 9 What is Meant by the Expression "born in the Jewish faith"? (YD 268)
Source: LGA, Box 11, "Shubow" file

RABBI JOSEPH S. SHUBOW[1]
125 HOLLAND ROAD
(Corner Fisher Avenue)
BROOKLINE 46, MASS.
ASpinwall 7-7626

OFFICE
TEMPLE BNAI MOSHE
1845 COMMONWEALTH AVENUE
BRIGHTON 35, MASS.
ALgonquin 4-3620

January 21, 1953

Professor Louis Ginzberg
Jewish Theological Seminary
Broadway
New York, N.Y.

Dear Prof. Ginzberg:

It was a great joy and honor to see you recently at the meeting of the New Century Club. It was a thrill especially to hear the greatest scholar of our time, who thank God has attained four score years and will yet attain more, with the help of Heaven, speak so clearly, so wisely, so movingly. We were all entranced. It must have been a great joy for you to have had your highly distinguished son-in-law[2] preside at the exercises, and it was an inspiration to see Mrs. Ginzberg so buoyant and vibrant, so joyous and happy.

May I now come to you with an important problem. Some time ago an old Orthodox Jew, preparing to meet his Maker, wrote a will wherein he specifically stated that if any of his children married a person "not born in the Jewish faith" they would be cut off from his estate. Considerable litigation is taking place in this regard, and I have been asked to give an opinion in this connection. I naturally turned to one of the great masters of our time in order, if possible, to obtain a statement from you as to what is meant by the expression "born in the Jewish faith".[3] I have gone through a great deal of literature, both English and Hebrew, and I found a statement, quoting Juster, that in classical times there was a distinction made between a proselyte and one born in the Jewish faith.[4]

May I trouble you for a statement in this regard, and if possible a suggestion of passages that I might investigate?

Trusting that you will forgive my intrusion upon your scholarly and deservedly quiet life, I am as ever

Respectfully and cordially yours,

Rabbi Joseph S. Shubow

~   ~   ~

February 17, 1953

Dear Rabbi Shubow:

Because of my rather precarious state of health, I could not acknowledge your letter of January 21 any sooner. I surely appreciate the kind words you said about me in your letter, but, of course, at my age one becomes somewhat callous to compliments, especially if one does not deserve them.

With regard to your question in Jewish law, there is, of course, a definite distinction according to rabbinic law between one born in the Jewish faith and a proselyte converted to [the] Jewish faith. There are, for instance, certain functions which a proselyte could not perform while one born in the Jewish faith can.[5] Even with regard to marriage laws there is a distinction between these two classes. For instance, a *Kohen* can marry only a woman born in [the] Jewish faith but not a proselyte.[6] The main passages in the Talmud are to be found in *Yebamot* 101b end of page [-102a] and in *Kiddushin* 76b.

With kindest regards.

Very sincerely yours,

Louis Ginzberg

Rabbi Joseph S. Shubow
125 Holland Avenue
Brookline, Massachusetts

1   Rabbi Shubow was ordained by the Jewish Institute of Religion, joined the Rabbinical Assembly in 1951, and passed away in 1969. He was rabbi for many years in Brighton, Massachusetts. See *PRA* 15 (1951), p. 44; and 34 (1970), pp. 181-182. For another letter from Shubow to LG, see above, Chapter II, No. 4, note 2.

2   Dr. Bernard Gould - see *Keeper*, p. 263.

3   I do not understand why this needed clarification. The father clearly wanted his children to marry Jews by birth as opposed to non-Jews or converts.

4   The reference was probably to Jean Juster, *Les juifs dans l'empire romain*, I, Paris 1914, pp. 253-274.

5   A convert cannot be a king, cannot hold certain public offices, and cannot serve as a judge for *halitzah* or for capital crimes - see the two sources quoted by LG as well as *ET*, VI, cols. 266-269; and Rabbi Eliyahu Bakshi-Doron, *Torah Shebe'al Peh*, XX (5739), pp. 66-72.

6   *Mishnah Yevamot* 6:5 and EH 6:8.

No. 10 The Conversion of a Gentile Woman Already Married to a Jew and Her Children (YD 268:6-7)

Source: LGA, Box 3, "Birnbaum" file = BCA, Box 4, "Birnbaum" file = CJLS Box, "Nissuin and Gittin" file
Excerpt: *Keeper*, pp. 235-237

Taylor Farms
Oakland, Me.

Dear Doctor Birnbaum:

I am in receipt of your letter of 11th inst[ant] in which you ask my advice concerning the matter of conversion to Judaism. Following the maxim of our Rabbis, I shall reply "al rishon rishon".[1]

1. Married women can become converts to Judaism under the same conditions as unmarried ones. If one were to insist upon the strict Talmudic law, it would be the duty of the Rabbi to advise the Jew who had lived with a gentile woman to divorce her immediately upon her conversion.[2] No less authority, however, than Maimonides has decided a practical case against this Talmudic regulation,[3] notwithstanding the fact that in his code he has incorporated this Talmudic regulation.[4] In a case where there are children that were born by the gentile mother and one is quite sure that divorce would be out of the question, we may be guided by the decision of Maimonides. Another regulation mentioned in the Talmud with regard to the conversion of women is that no conjugal relation is permitted for ninety days after conversion.[5] Of course, we do not know what kind of people you have before you and whether advice of this nature would be listened to. You may, of course, explain to the husband that this abstinence is commanded as the first step in the Jewish life of holiness and discipline. If the woman is pregnant, the period of abstinence is not required.[6]

2. I strongly advise against hurrying a matter of this kind. You ought to have the opportunity of meeting the woman several times and talking to her concerning the step she is considering to take. She also ought to read some books on Judaism, as for instance, Morris Joseph, *Judaism as Creed and Life* [London 1903 and Lewis] Dembitz, *Home and Synagogue Ceremonies*, published by the Jewish Publication Society.[7] It may also be advisable to have her read selected chapters in Graetz's *History of the Jews*. In my opinion, at least three months' preparation ought to be insisted upon. I suggest three months because in that case we may expect the couple to comply with the three months' abstinence. It is true that Talmudic law insists on the abstinence *after* conversion but from a psychological point of view

abstinence before conversion, during the time of preparation, can more easily be expected.

3. The children need conversion and their conversion is the same as that of adults and the instruction is to be adopted to the mind of the child. Of course, for male children, the circumcision must precede the baptism.

There is very little to add to the method of conversion to that given in *Shulchan Aruch Yoreh Deah* 268. May I, however, remark that for the baptism she may use a loose bathing gown. To carry out literally the regulation of the *Shulchan Aruch* would be very awkward in our time. You need three learned men to witness the baptism, preferably rabbis, and, if unavailable, some laymen who have Jewish learning.[8]

May I call your attention [to the fact] that Jewish law does not recognize mixed marriages and hence the marriage ceremonies. *Kiddushin* as well as *chuppah* must be performed after conversion. The *Ketubah* is to contain [גיורתא] instead of [בתולתא] and a hundred zuz instead of two hundred.[9] It is customary to give a proselyte a Jewish name at the time of conversion and this name is to be used in the *Ketubah*. Her father's name is Abraham, the father of the Jewish nation.[10]

I expect to be back in New York by the end of next week and any communication addressed to me to my home address or to the Seminary will reach me without delay.

With best regards to Mrs. Birnbaum and yourself, I am,

Very sincerely yours,[11]

---

1   "About first things first."

2   *Mishnah Yevamot* 2:8.

3   *Responsa of the Rambam*, ed. Blau, II, Jerusalem 1960, No. 211.

4   *Hilkhot Gerushin* 10:14.

5   *Yevamot* 34b-35a, but there is some disagreement among the halakhic authorities as to when this rule applies - see *ET*, VI, cols. 29-30.

6   The period of abstinence was intended to establish paternity of any child she might bear. In this case, the child was clearly fathered by her Jewish spouse.

7   LG was clearly quoting from memory, since he was probably writing from his summer home in Maine. The book in question is called *Jewish Services in Synagogue and Home*, Philadelphia 1898.

8   See YD 268:2-3; *ET*, VI, cols. 437-440; and Rabbi Tuvia Friedman, *Responsa of the Va'ad Halacha of the Rabbinical Assembly of Israel*, III (5748-49), Jerusalem 5749, pp. 66-67.

9   Regarding the sum of money, see *Mishnah Ketubot* 1:2 and Rambam, *Hilkhot Ishut* 11:1.

10   See EH 129:20 and *Beit Yosef* to *Tur*, ibid.

11   The signature is, unfortunately, missing from all three copies of this responsum, but the style and the typewriter and the address - see above, Chapter II, No. 6, note 6 - all point to LG as the author.

No. 11 Euthanasia (YD 339:1)
Source: LGA, Box 4, "Ginsburg" file
Excerpt (almost complete): *Keeper*, pp. 239-241

January 8, 1936

Dear Doctor Ginsburg:[1]

Complying with your request, I shall put down in writing the statement I made to you orally with regard to the attitude of Jewish law and practice towards euthanasia.

The earliest Jewish authority who discusses this problem directly and explicitly is Rabbi Judah of Regensburg, Bavaria (died 1217), who, in his work *The Book of the Pious* no. 315 (ed. Berlin, p. 100), remarks as follows: "If one who suffers excruciating pain says to his fellowman, 'You see [that] I shall not live much longer, and as I cannot bear my pain any longer, I beg of you to kill me,' he (the one asked to do so) must not as much as touch him." The author, one of the most famous scholars and saints of the Middle Ages, quotes Bible and Talmud in support of his decision and is particularly interested in the correct explanation of the two cases of euthanasia mentioned in Scripture - one of the Judge Abimelech (Judges 9:54) and the other of King Saul, so graphically described in the opening chapter of the Second Book of Samuel. Rabbi Judah is not quite certain whether the arm-bearer of Abimelech was as wicked as his master and slew him in defiance of the law, or that the exigencies of war justified his death; the speedy dispatch of Abimelech ended his attack on the tower and thus saved hundreds of people from sure death. He has no doubt whatsoever that the Amalakite committed murder in slaying Saul at his own request after he had wounded himself fatally.[2] It is true Saul was justified in committing suicide (this is stated in as early a source as *Genesis Rabbah* 34:13); the honor of Israel required that its first King should not permit himself to be captured alive. But the Amalakite had no justification for hastening the King's death, and since shortening human life, even for a few moments, is punishable by death, he suffered by the hands of David the punishment he deserved.[3]

The correctness of the explanations given by our author for the justifiable suicide of Saul and for the [punishment by death] of the Amalakite is open to serious doubt and, as a matter of fact, there are several different explanations to be found in Rabbinic literature. I shall only mention the view of the famous philosopher and astronomer, Rabbi Levi Ben Gerson - usually called by the scholastics "Maestre Leo de Bagnols" - according to which David was solely motivated by his desire to uphold the newly established institution of monarchy in Israel (compare his commentary to II Samuel 1:14). Be that as it may, the author of the *Book of the Pious* nevertheless is quite correct in maintaining that from the point of view of Jewish law, saving from pain is no excuse neither for homicide nor suicide, and that, further[more], in evaluating human life, its duration is of no moment. The following few quotations from the authoritative sources of the *Mishnah*, Talmud and Codes will suffice to corroborate this view. "One must not close the eyes of a person in agony of death–to hasten the end and thus save pain–and one who touches or moves his body 'sheds blood'." Said Rabbi Meir (the most famous doctor of the law about the middle of the second century): "A person in agony of death is like a flickering candle, it extinguishes as soon as one touches it and, similarly, the closing of the eyes of a dying person is like pulling out the life from the body". This statement is found in all codes of Jewish law, from the *Mishnah* composed about 200 [c.e.] to the *Shulchan Aruch* composed about the middle of the sixteenth century (Compare *Mishnah Shabbat* 23:5 and Talmud ibid. 151b ; *Masseket Semahot* 1:4; Maimonides, *Ebel* 4:5 and *Shulchan Aruch Yoreh Deah* 339:1)

In this connection, reference should be made also to the statement found in Talmud *Sanhedrin* 78a that he who kills a person in agony of death is punished with death. This is an application of the general rule found in many old sources ([*Masseket*] *Semahot* 1:1 and parallel passages given on the margin) that according to Jewish Law a person is considered as living as long as there is some life left in him.

Very instructive is the story told in the Talmud *Abodah Zarah* 18a about the death of the martyr Rabbi Hananiah ben Teradion, a victim of the Hadrianic persecution [around the year] 140 c.e. Wrapped in the scroll of the law, he was placed on a pyre of green brush; fire was set to it and wet wool was placed on his chest to prolong the agonies of death. His disciples asked him to open his mouth wide that the fire might enter and thus put an end to his suffering, but his answer was: "it is best that He who has given the soul should also take it away; no man should destroy himself".

This story about the gruesome death of the Rabbi might be a legend, but it nevertheless expresses the Jewish view of the sacredness of human life. "Our life", remarks Maimonides (*Hilchot Rotzeach* 1:4), "belongs to the Giver of Life" - and nobody has any right to dispose thereof.

This does not mean, however, that according to the Jewish view a physician is not to try his utmost in alleviating pain. On the contrary, this is one of his main duties even if through certain pain-soothing medicine, the resistance of the patient might be weakened and finally cause his death.[4]

I hope that the material given above will be of some use to you in forming an opinion on the Jewish attitude to euthanasia.

Very sincerely yours,

LOUIS GINZBERG

Dr. Sol W. Ginsburg
17 East 96th Street
New York City

1   Dr. Sol Ginsburg, a psychiatrist, was LG's favorite nephew. See *Keeper*, p. 253, the passages cited in the Index and the fourth photograph after p. 214.
2   This is not explicitly stated in *Sefer Hassidim.*
3   See above, note 2.
4   For a similar opinion, see R. Eliezer Waldenberg, *Responsa Tzitz Eliezer*, XIII, Jerusalem 5742^2, No. 87.

No. 12 The Burial of a Synagogue Member Who was Also a Member of a Christian Science Church (YD 345:5 and 362:5)

Source: Rabbi Louis Epstein, "Report of the Committee on the Interpretation of Jewish Law", LGA, Box 17, "Committee on Interpretation of Jewish Law" file = *USAAR* 7-8 (1919-20), p. 90

Secondary Reference: a responsum on the same subject in CJLS box, "Kevurah" file[1]

A congregation affiliated with the United Synagogue had among its membership a woman who was also affiliated with a Christian Science Church and at her death the survivors applied for her burial [in] the congregation's cemetery. The congregation referred the matter to your Committee on the Interpretation of Jewish Law and the Chairman,[2] with the consent of the other members of the Committee, has decided, in view of Jewish law and as a matter of expediency to check a current evil, that the woman be given the burial rite prescribed by the Law for apostates.[3]

---

1 "May I add that at the convention of the United Synagogue 1921, the report of the Chairman...on this subject has been unanimously accepted and, as far as my knowledge goes, the congregations affiliated with the United Synagogue have acted in accordance with this decision". He may mean 1920, but for the same confusion see below No. 14, note 2. Indeed, LG did mention this ruling in passing in *Exponent* in 1921 but the major statement was made by Louis Epstein in 1920.

2 I.e., Louis Ginzberg.

3 It is unfortunate that they did not elaborate, because there is tremendous disagreement among halakhic authorities regarding this very topic. Some prescribe normal burial, some burial without shrouds and *tohorah*, and some forbid Jews to bury them at all - see *Massekhet Semahot* 2:8, ed. Higger, p. 106; Rambam, *Hilkhot Evel* 1:10; *Tur*, YD 345 with the *Beit Yosef* ad. loc.; YD 345:5; and Rabbi Yekutiel Greenwald, *Kol Bo Al Aveilut*, New York 1947, pp. 91, 191-194.

No. 13 The Burial of Jews in a Separate Section of a Non-Jewish Cemetery and the Burial of an Intermarried Jew in a Jewish Cemetery (YD 345:5 and 362:5)

Source: BCA, Box 4, "Cemetery, Benjamin, Samuel" file

CONGREGATION B'NAI ISRAEL
Duval and Jefferson Sts.
Jacksonville, Florida

January 2, 1927

Prof. Louis Ginzberg,
531 West 123rd St.,
New York, N.Y.

Dear Dr. Ginzberg:

Permit me to ask your opinion on a problem which exists in our congregation. Before my coming here this congregation deeded its cemetery to a Gentile cemetery association with a proviso that no bodies were to be buried [in] that particular portion without sanction from the cemetery committee of the congregation. Please let me know whether, under the circumstances, the cemetery can be considered a proper Jewish burial ground.

In connection with the same problem, permit me to ask if it is permissible to bury Jewish women who have intermarried and raised families in the Christian faith upon a Jewish cemetery.

I would appreciate an early reply to these questions and sincerely hope that you are well. With kindest personal regards, I am,

Respectfully yours,

SAMUEL BENJAMIN

~ ~ ~

January 7, 1927

Dear Rabbi Benjamin:

I hasten to reply to your letter of January 2nd in compliance with your request:

1. If the portion of the cemetery has been sold once, it cannot be used again as a Jewish cemetery even if no bodies have been buried there by

Gentiles. To make it a Jewish cemetery again, it shall have to be consecrated as such, and could be used as such provided that no Gentile bodies have been buried there.[1]

2. It is a well-established custom among the Jews not to bury in the cemetery proper anybody who has married out of the Jewish faith. In many congregations, they have, at the end of the cemetery, plots for the burial of persons who were born Jews but did not live a Jewish life.[2]

With kind regards, I am,
Very sincerely yours,

Chairman,
COMMITTEE ON INTERPRETATION OF JEWISH LAW

Dr. Samuel Benjamin,[3]
Cong. B'nai Israel,
Duval and Jefferson Streets,
Jacksonville, Fla.

---

1   In general, see Rabbi Yekutiel Greenwald, *Kol Bo al Aveilut*, New York 1947, p. 163 and the responsa listed in: David Golinkin, *An Index of Conservative Responsa and Practical Halakhic Studies: 1917-1990*, New York 1992, p. 50.

2   See below, No. 14, note 4.

3   Regarding Rabbi Benjamin, see Chapter VII, No. 3, note 3.

No. 14 Seven Questions Regarding Burial (YD 345:5 and 362:5)
Source: LGA, Box 9, "Neuman" file
Excerpt: *Keeper*, pp. 227-228

THE CONGREGATION MIKVEH ISRAEL
IN THE CITY OF PHILADELPHIA
November 14th, 1927
Abraham A. Neuman[1]
Rabbi
Broad and York Streets

Dear Professor Ginzberg:

I received the enclosed communication sometime ago and I had hoped that I would be able to discuss it with you in person. But I have been unable to arrange for a trip to New York, so I'm taking this means of seeking your advice before formulating my reply.

The letter is self-explanatory. For your further information, I wish merely to add that the Mount Sinai cemetery is the "fashionable" Jewish cemetery in Philadelphia, and is used, in the main, by the reformed congregations and those whose social aspirations extend also to the grave.

While the Association is in the control of those who have affiliated themselves with Reform Judaism, they want, in this respect, to adhere to Jewish law. In effect, it seems to me that they have, in some instances, gone beyond the requirements of Jewish law.

Their questions may be summarized in the following manner: (1) Is [a] Christian Scientist to be regarded as a Jew or as an apostate who has left the fold? (2) Is a member of the Ethical Culture Society in the same status? (3) If they are not regarded as Jews, may they be buried [in] a Jewish cemetery [in] their family lot? (4) Is it permissible for a non-Jewish spouse of a Jewish person to be buried [in] a Jewish cemetery? (5) If a non-Jewish spouse of a Jewish person attended Jewish services without having been formally converted to the Jewish faith, is that person to be regarded as a Jew in relation to burial? (6) Is it permitted to allow the burial of a Jewish person [in] a Jewish cemetery without the usual Jewish rite? (7) Is there any objection in law to the substitution of the Jewish rite by the reading of a poem or the funereal formula of the Masonic fraternity or the Elks or a similar Order?

As to question (1), it is apparent from their letter that they themselves regard a Christian Scientist as having left the fold. This is also my view. And I recall that you delivered an official opinion to the same affect at one of the sessions of the United Synagogue Convention. Was this opinion published? If so, when and where?[2] If it was not published, I would very much like to have your opinion stated again in an authoritative form, so that I could quote you to this effect.

Question (2) - This question is more difficult to answer categorically. As far as I know, the platform of the Ethical Culture Society does not necessarily require the abandonment of synagogue or church affiliation, this act being optional with the individual member, and depending on his own theological viewpoint, about which the Society is neutral. Doctor Felix Adler himself can be regarded as having definitely abandoned Judaism.[3] He has repeatedly read himself out of the fold, and this is no doubt true of many of his adherents, but a great many number of his followers, who attend the meetings of the Society regularly and who may have even joined the Society as members, have done so without the intention of abandoning Judaism. If pressed for their point of view, they would reply that they find the meetings of the Ethical Culture Society interesting and stimulating; that the practical work of the Society in education and social activities appeal[s] to them; that, if they absent themselves from the synagogue, it is not because they intended to read themselves out of Judaism, but purely [as] a matter of indifference or general neglect, an attitude which characterizes many men and women of the Jewish faith who have not linked themselves up definitely with the Ethical Culture movement.

It is my opinion that in regard to members of the Ethical Culture Society, only those are to be treated as having left the fold, who have so declared themselves in some form of public declaration. Mere membership in the Society should not be accepted as such a declaration.

Question (3) - In regard to this question, the authorities of the cemetery are apparently more strict than the requirements of Jewish law demand. Our Codes provide for the burial of apostates, suicides and criminals, etc. [in] the Jewish cemetery, in a special section near the fence.[4]

I feel, however, very strongly that the cemetery authorities are quite right in their practice, and that their evident desire to be severe in drawing the line against apostates is promoted by exigencies of the time. They want rabbinical support for this attitude, so that they should not appear arbitrary in their dealings with the lot-holders, and I wonder whether it is not permissible to do so in some official authoritative manner.

Question (4) - This I would answer definitely in the negative.

Question (5) - This I would also answer in the negative.

Question (6) - This question obviously would arise at the burial of a person who is an atheist or who is opposed to ceremonial religion. In such event the spirit of Jewish law, it seems to me, would rather be opposed to the reading of the customary burial prayer of *Zidduk Ha'din* and the *Kaddish*.[5] But it is a very serious question as to whether this ought to be tolerated when the non-reading of the religious service would be interpreted, not as a disapproval of the deceased by the Jewish people, but as a concession to the wishes and principles of the decedent.

Question (7) - The answer to this question of course depends on the reply to the preceding question. I shall be very grateful for your opinion on any or all of these questions, both as to law as well as to general policy.

Very sincerely yours,

Abraham Neuman

Professor Louis Ginzberg,
568 West 149th Street,
New York, N.Y.

~   ~   ~

October 4th, 1927

Rabbi A. A. Neuman
Congregation Mikveh Israel
Broad & York Sts.
Philadelphia, Pa.

My dear Rabbi:

We are addressing identical communications to several rabbis for the purpose of obtaining their authoritative interpretations of Jewish Law upon the question of interments in Jewish cemeteries.

This Association, which is a stock company, was organized in 1853 by a number of Jewish residents of Philadelphia and vicinity. It is not, nor has it been, affiliated with any particular Congregation. While it is non-congregational, it is not non-sectarian, its shareholders having been and being Jews and its officers and directors, likewise, Jews. Its purpose was, as expressed in the earliest printed copy of its Constitution which we have been able to find (dated 1863):

"To purchase and provide a proper and suitable place or Cemetery to be used for the interment of deceased human bodies; PROVIDED that they be the bodies of those only who, by birth or profession and public declaration, shall have been of the Jewish faith according to their laws prescribed". (Article 11)

The same Article, in the revised Constitutions of 1872, 1895 and 1901, provides as follows:

"The object of this Corporation shall be to purchase and provide a proper and suitable place for a Cemetery to be used only for the interment of deceased human bodies of those who by birth, profession or public declaration shall have been of the Jewish Faith, under such conditions, rules and regulations as the Association or Board of Officers may from time to time establish for the government of lotholders, burial of the dead and visitors to the Cemetery".

For your further information we desire to state that during more recent years it has been our practice to require a signed ORDER FOR INTERMENT to be furnished this office before issuing a PERMIT for burial.

We are enclosing a copy of the present form[6] which requires the signature of the lotholder or of one closely related to him or to the decedent to the following declaration, to wit: "I/we also certify that the decedent was by birth, profession or public declaration of the Jewish faith."

The name of the officiating rabbi is also required.

So far as is possible, we have by these means and pracautions endeavored to protect this Association against any violations of its Constitutional provisions governing interments in this Cemetery, at the same time conforming, we believe, with Jewish laws applying to the interment of the dead in a Jewish cemetery.

Confronted as we are, however, with possibilities of serious embarrass-ment both to the families of decedents and to ourselves, in these matters we are desirous of obtaining your viewpoint as rabbi, to assist us in formulating definite and precise regulations to govern us in our respective cases as they may present themselves.

What is the interpretation of Jewish law in the following illustrated cases?

In the event of the decease of the non-Jewish wife of a Jew, the latter a lotholder in this Cemetery, or of a non-Jewish husband of a Jewess, herself being a lotholder or the daughter of a lotholder, is it consistent with Jewish law to permit the interment of a non-Jewish spouse in a Jewish cemetery? Our Constitution provides that the decedent "shall have been by birth, profession or public declaration of the Jewish faith". Whenever it has come to our notice that the decedent had been confirmed in the Jewish faith,[7] it has been our custom to require either a copy of the Rabbi's confirmation certificate or the affidavit of one acquainted with the fact, before permission for burial has been granted.

Parenthetically, we might state that we have learned that in some instances the records of the Rabbi showing the confirmation of a non-Jew or Jewess have been regarded as personal or private records and they have not been recorded as records of the Congregation, hence they are not readily available for use or reference as referred to above.

If a non-Jewish spouse shall not have been confirmed in the Jewish faith but had been attending services in a synagogue, would that fact alone be evidence that he or she had by "public declaration" been of the Jewish faith and, as such, be entitled to interment in a Jewish cemetery? Or would it be necessary that he or she were registered members of a synagogue?

In the cases of those who, though born Jews, have become affiliated with the Christian Science Church, instances have presented themselves which require decision. One concrete illustration is presented as follows: A Jewish member of this community, himself a member of a synagogue and active in the direction of some of the affiliated bodies of the Federation of Jewish Charities, is married to one who was born of Jewish parents but who has actively identified with the Christian Science Church. He makes inquiry about the purchase of a burial lot in this Cemetery and asks whether, if he purchases same, his wife, born a Jewess but now a Christian Scientist, may be interred therein? He stated that in the event of her decease it was her express desire that a Christian Science reader is to officiate at her funeral.

While our Constitution provides [interment for] those who shall have been "by birth" of the Jewish faith, is it consistent with Jewish law, irrespective of our Constitution, to permit the interment of one who has consciously and deliberately identified herself with a religious body which is not only non-Jewish but inconsistent with Judaism?

In recent years, many other instances have arisen in which the children of Jewish parents have become Christian Scientists and who, nevertheless (their parents being lotholders in this Cemetery), may desire burial in Mt. Sinai Cemetery. What is the rabbinical attitude towards such burials as based upon Jewish law, coupled with the provisions of our Constitution regarding those who may have been by BIRTH born in the Jewish faith? May we also inquire about the status of those who, though by BIRTH of the Jewish faith, have become affiliated with the Ethical Culture Society?

Is it permissible, from a Jewish viewpoint, to have interments conducted without any religious services, by an individual layman reading a poem or a prose composition or simply making some impromptu or extemporaneous remarks, which in themselves are non-sectarian or by having the services conducted exclusively by the Masonic fraternity or lodge or by the Elks or any other secret Order. Or is it required by Jewish law that the *Kaddish* be read at the side of the grave, even though no other religious service be held? We have stated the above in some detail in order to acquaint you with the problems with which we are confronted and we shall most gratefully receive your helpful advice to assist us in determining what our position should be as the custodians of this sacred place of interment. We shall greatly appreciate your early reply,

Very truly yours,

Gordon A. Block
CHAIRMAN (for the Committee)

~   ~   ~

November 28, 1927
Dear Doctor Neuman:
Because of lack of time, I delayed my answer to your letter of November 14th, which required a good deal of thought as the matter is rather of importance. I shall now reply to the questions propounded by you in the order given. May I, however, call your attention to the fact that the conception of "consecrated ground" is entirely foreign to Jewish Law. The strict rule that nobody who has left the Jewish fold is to be buried in a Jewish cemetery is based upon the statement of the *Mishnah, Sanhedrin* 46a with regard to cemeteries for criminals. On the basis of the law referred to in the *Mishnah*, the Talmud draws the inference that the wicked and the just, the sinful and the pious, ought not to be buried in the same cemetery [ibid. 47a].

1) The Christian Science Church is undoubtedly a part of the general Christian communion, and any Jew who has become a member of this Church severs his connection with the Synagogue. In an address delivered before the annual convention of the United Synagogue several years ago, I strongly emphasized this fact. I have no copy of my address and doubt whether the United Synagogue has one.[8]

2) I fully agree with you that the Ethical Culture Society is neither a religious [nor] anti-religious society, and hence, membership in it could not be considered as a break with the Synagogue.

3) The answer to question three is contained in my general remarks at the beginning of the letter, according to which it is against Jewish Law and practice to bury a person who has left the Jewish fold [in] a Jewish cemetery.

4) and 5) There is, of course, only one answer to questions four and five, and that is, that one who has not been formally converted to the Jewish faith is not to be regarded as a Jew in relation to burial.

6) I would strongly advise against leaving out the customary burial prayer and *Kaddish* in case of one who is opposed to ceremonial religion, as it might be interpreted in a wrong light.

7) I would, however, not raise any strong objection to the reading of a poem or a prose composition, which in themselves are non-sectarian.[9]

With kindest regards to Mrs. Neuman and yourself, and the little fellow, I am

Very sincerely yours,

LOUIS GINZBERG

Doctor Abraham A. Neuman
3213 Diamond Street
Philadelphia, Pa.

1   Rabbi Abraham Neuman (1890-1970) was ordained by the Seminary in 1912 and earned a Doctor of Hebrew Letters there in 1914. He was on the faculty of Dropsie College (1913-66) and served as its President (1941-66). He also served as rabbi of B'nai Jeshurun and Mikveh Israel in Philadelphia (1919-43). See *EJ*, XII, cols. 1009-1010; and Nadell, pp. 198-199.

2   Rabbi Neuman may have been referring to LG's undated address listed in the Appendix, No. 9, p. 4, but he probably meant Rabbi Louis Epstein's "Report of the Committee on the Interpretation of Jewish Law" quoted above, Nos. 6 and 12.

3   Dr. Felix Adler (1851-1933) founded the Society for Ethical Culture in 1876. See EJ, II, col. 276.

4   This is not stated in "our codes." YD 345 states that one does not *mourn* for a suicide or an apostate while YD 362:5 says "that one does not bury a wicked person next to a righteous person". The common *custom* was to bury a suicide in a special section near the fence of the cemetery, at least eight cubits from the other graves (*Gilyon Maharsha* to YD 345:4; Sidney Goldstein, *Suicide in Rabbinic Literature*, Hoboken, New Jersey 1989, p. 60; Maurice Lamm, *The Jewish Way in Death and Mourning*, New York 1969, p. 219) while many rabbis refused to bury apostates in a Jewish cemetery *at all* (see Y. M. Tukechinsky, *Gesher Hahayyim*, Jerusalem 5720[2], pp. 274-275; and Lamm, p. 83).

5   He seems to think that omitting these prayers is a good way to express "disapproval of the deceased by the Jewish people".

6   This was not found in the LGA.

7   I.e., converted.

8   See above, note 2.

9   It is worth noting that Masonic rituals were sometimes included at Orthodox funerals in England ca. 1950 - see Louis Jacobs, *Helping with Inquiries: An Autobiography*, London 1989, pp. 90-91.

No. 15 Autopsy (YD 349 and ·357)

Source: LGA, Box 17, "Autopsy" file
Excerpt: *Keeper*, pp. 237-239
Comment: There is good reason to question whether this responsum was written by LG. It was typed on a different typewriter. It is single-spaced as opposed to all of his other responsa which are double-spaced; it contains many sources in parentheses; it uses different abbreviations; it contains a number of unclear, run-on sentences; and, lastly, the English style is quite different from LG's usual, clear style. Nonetheless, it is in the LGA, as a result of which Eli Ginzberg included it in his book. If it was not written by LG, it was probably written by a member of the Committee on Jewish Law in the 1930s. Rabbi Louis Epstein mentions a responsum on autopsy in *PRA* 6 (1939), p. 157, but that appears to have been a different responsum.

The motive of preventing disrespectful treatment of the dead is found in Tanaitic law (cf. *Bava Batra* [154a and] 155a). Greater consideration was given the body of a woman (cf. [*Mishnah*] *Moed Katan* 27a). The Talmud does not seek to prove the validity of the sentiment from the Bible, but justly feels it to be in keeping with the general Biblical attitude to the dead as well as with the general moral sense.

Disrespectful treatment of the dead consists in leaving the body unburied for any duration of time after the day of death ([*Mishnah*] *Sanhedrin* 46a), disturbing the body after interment,[1] and disfiguring the body (no Talmudic source).[2]

Disrespectful treatment of the dead is permitted under the following circumstances. Postponing interment is permitted if the preparations for burial require it ([*Mishnah*] *Sanhedrin* 46a), or for the sake of notifying relatives to come to the funeral (*Semahot*, Chapter 11) or to announce the death in neighboring towns (*Sanhedrin* 47a). Disturbing the body after interment is permitted if the grave is unsafe [*Hagahot Asheri* to *Moed Katan*, Chapter 3, par. 38] or for the sake of transferring the body to the family grave (*Yerushalmi Moed Katan* 2:4 [fol. 82b, bottom]) or to Palestine (*Beth Joseph* to *Tur*, *Yoreh Deah* 363). These cases represent one motive, giving the dead a better resting place or a better funeral or doing [them] some honor. The rule, therefore, is laid down that whatever is done for the sake of the dead does not constitute disrespect, even though the act in itself is a disrespectful one (cf. *Radbaz*, [Part 1], no. 484).

Certain exceptions are made for the sake of others. The grave may be opened and the body examined for the sake of testimony in the interest of others who bought property from the person during [his lifetime] (*Bava Batra* 154b)[3] and according to certain authorities for the sake of identifying the person in the interest of his wife [being permitted to remarry] (*Pithe Teshubah, Yoreh Deah* 363:7).

From the fact that the body may be examined *only* if it is needed for testimony to establish the validity of a deed which the person made out during life on the ground[s] that the purchaser has a claim on him (*Bava Batra* 154a-b)[4] and from the arguments adduced by those who oppose the ruling in the last case in the interest of a wife, it appears evident that the resistance offered to the opening of the grave and thus treating the body disrespectfully was so strong that no consideration outweighed it save the personal responsibility of the dead person.

These cases are sufficient to present the general limits within which Jews will permit or prohibit disrespectful treatment of the dead. The propositions that these cases yield are the following:

1. The prohibition against disrespectful treatment is authoritative.

2. It is permitted in all cases where the interest of the dead is involved, and

3. The interest of others are considered only if these interests constitute a legal or moral claim upon the dead person.

I do not think anyone will seriously doubt that an autopsy on the dead body is a disrespectful treatment of it, though there is no Talmudic authority for it. In the discussion of the subject (*Noda bi-Yehudah*, [Part 2], *Yoreh Deah*, no. 210; *Chatam Sofer, Yoreh Deah*, no. 336) all sides agree that it does constitute disrespectful treatment. Even the incisions necessary in connection with embalming are granted by early authorities (*Rashba*, Vol. 1, no. 369) to constitute disrespectful treatment,[5] and it is permitted only because it is in the interest of the dead person himself. *Hence the prohibition against autopsy is clear.*

Permission is sought (*Noda bi-Yehuda*, ibid.) on the grounds that autopsy is necessary in the interest of advancing medical science which involves the saving of human life. It is granted that whatever offers even a doubtful saving of human life is permitted, save idolatry, adultery, and murder. The argument is offered, however, that there must be a direct relation between autopsy and the saving of human life, i.e., when the autopsy performed on one person is expected to suggest a possible cure for another definite person who is inflicted with the same disease and for whom physicians seek a cure. Only, therefore, when there and then another person's life is to be saved by the autopsy of the dead person, may the autopsy be performed. The advancement of science in general does not constitute saving of life, else we would argue that medical students may violate the Sabbath in the study of their vocation.

This argument is not altogether conclusive in itself in view of the leniency of the law in all cases where danger to life is in question. To prevent danger, not only is the actual act of prevention permitted but as many links in the act as may be necessary to reach the final prevention [are permitted as well] (cf. *Orach Chayim* 328ff.). Possibly even the desecration of the Sabbath for the study of medicine would be permitted if the study of it could not be done without the desecration of the Sabbath. The distinction between an act that has direct bearing on the saving of a life and the one that has an indirect bearing is logical but not based on or supported by any Talmudic or Geonic authority.

Furthermore, the case discussed represents in the mind of the authorities an experiment for general scientific purposes. How about a disease that is very prevalent that may be treated as a general public danger? What shall we say of the present[-day] hospital where at all times there are many patients suffering from diseases for whose cure the autopsy is to be made? Is not that the case in the mind of the author[6] where the autopsy is sought for the sake of a definite patient? Is the law altered because the scientist has a further aim, extending beyond the immediate purpose? On what ground would that authority prohibit autopsy of a T.B. case where we have hospitals filled with patients suffering from the same disease?

I am convinced that the demand for autopsies in hospitals cannot be treated by Jewish law as merely in the interest of general scientific progress, but, conditions as they are, must be treated as cases where the lives of patients *there and then present* are to be saved. It is the regular case of פיקוח נפש [= saving of a life].

There may be another consideration for permitting autopsies, namely, the moral right which the hospital has to make certain demands from the patient [i.e.,] if it is a part of the moral code of the hospital that in return for treatment given to the patient by the hospital, the latter expects the advance of medical science and the patient's cooperation in that direction. If, for example, the hospital reserves the moral right - if not the legal right - to permit students to be present at an operation, contrary to the will of the patient, in the interest of the progress of medicine as part of the terms under which the patient is given hospital service; and if that interpretation of the agreement between the hospital and the patient can apply also to the treatment of the body after death - though this interpretation is not explicitly stated [and] though a court would not honor such an understanding of the rights of the hospital over the patient[7] - the law of the disrespectful treatment of the dead is suspended.

Rabbi Moses Sofer (*Chatam Sofer*, ibid.) adds another argument to strengthen the prohibition against autopsy in the fact that the remains of a person are איסורי הנאה, of the class of objects that may not be put to any use.[8] He agrees, though, that should the question of saving of life be involved, that objection would fall away. This argument is weak. Autopsy itself is not a "use" or an enjoyment of something. The use will come in when the knowledge gained by it is employed. When this is done, it will in all cases be a question of medicine for the sick and an attempt to save a human life. In the second place, the prohibition of איסורי הנאה falls on the one who uses the body, not on the family of the deceased. Could we enforce Jewish law, it might be the duty of the court to prevent the use of the Jewish dead, if we were to assume that it is prohibited. But without a court to enforce Jewish law, and [if] the use, if it be so termed, is made by gentiles or by Jews who do not ask the permission of Jewish law, against whom shall we pronounce the prohibition to make use of the dead body? Even if we grant that the use of the dead body for autopsy be permitted, there would be a prohibition against the heirs selling it for that purpose or deriving some other benefit from giving it to that purpose without monetary compensation. But if there is no gain to them, as [is evident in this case,] the prohibition can apply to no one within the jurisdiction of Jewish law.

I would draw the following conclusions from the above. In hospitals whose function is a double one, the cure of patients and the advance of medical science and if that duality of function is publicly known, an autopsy may be made on a body of a Jew who died from a certain disease, with the expectation that the autopsy may help to bring relief or to lessen the danger of other patients known to the physicians to be suffering from that or similar disease. The knowledge of one patient in existence within reach of the physicians is sufficient from the point of view of Jewish law. Under these conditions, the autopsy may be made against the will of the family, and the family is commanded by Law to permit autopsy in such instances. Unnecessary scarring, delay of the funeral, and leaving parts of the body unburied must be avoided.

---

1   The original refers to *Moed Katan* 13a, but that reference is incorrect. See, however, *Bava Batra* 154a and 155a mentioned above.

2   But see *Bava Batra* 154a and 155a mentioned above as well as *Hullin* 11b regarding *nivul hamet*.

3   This reference is surprising since the poskim derived therefrom that it is *forbidden* to examine the body. See Rambam, *Hilkhot Mekhira* 29:16; and YD 363:7.

4   See above, note 3.

5   The Rashba does not say this. He says: "it is permitted and there is no pain [to the deceased]...*and no disrespect*".

6   Perhaps he means the questioner in the *Noda bi-Yehudah*?

7   A sentence has been omitted for the sake of clarity.

8   Literally, "it is forbidden to derive any benefit from them". See *Avodah Zarah* 29b; and YD 349:1-2.

No. 16 Burial in a Mausoleum (YD 362:1)
Source: *USR* 2/2 (April, 1922), p. 4

What is Jewish Burial?

An interesting decision of the Committee on Interpretation of Jewish Law is disclosed in the following letter by Professor Louis Ginzberg, Chairman of the Committee, to Rabbi Abraham E. Halpern of St. Louis, Mo.:[1]

Dear Rabbi Halpern:

I hasten to reply to your letter of 5th inst[ant], with reference to the structure of a Sarcophagus Monument.

If I understand the enclosed statement of Mr. Rosenbloom, the structure is meant to be used as a place where the coffins containing the bodies are to be kept. If my assumption is correct, of course, it would not be permitted, as, according to Jewish Law, the coffin must be put into the ground and not into a structure.[2]

May I advise you to use your influence with your congregation to avoid as far as possible costly monuments and similar structures. Simplicity is the outstanding feature of Jewish Laws concerning the honor due to the dead, and it would be very regrettable if we should give this up.

Very sincerely yours,

LOUIS GINZBERG

1   Rabbi Abraham Halpern (1891-1961 or 1962) was ordained by the Seminary in 1917 and served for about forty years as rabbi of Bnai Amoona in St. Louis. See *Students' Annual* 3 (1916), p. 202; *PRA* 5 (1933-38), p. 496; 24 (1960), p. 335; and 26 (1962), p. 225; and *Conservative Judaism* 47/3 (Spring, 1995), pp. 65-67.

2   See YD 362:1 and the *Tur*, and *Bet Yosef*, ad loc.

No. 17 Reinterment in Costly Mausoleums (YD 362:1)[1]

Source: Rabbi Abraham Burstein, "The Decisions of Professor Louis Ginzberg", pp. 3-4, CJLS Box, "Bet Knesset" file = BCA, Box 4, "Burstein, Abraham" = LGA, Box 17 (p. 1 missing)
Excerpt: *Keeper*, pp. 226-227

There is one more common problem I would mention....Jews are everywhere aware of our prohibition against the moving of bodies after they have been properly interred. Yet scores of people write in, to obtain legal permission to take the remains of departed parents from their resting places into newer cemeteries and mausoleums. Often there seems to be no valid excuse for this type of desecration except possibly the sudden enrichment of the children and their consequent desire to place the bodies of their elders in graves more fashionable - if I may use the term in this connection - or in a more exclusive environment. We refuse to lend our sanction to such acts. Death, to the Jew, is the great leveler. The distinctions of life must not be carried into the earth. All Jews must be buried simply, in a plain coffin, without ornamentation, fine garments, or other displays of vanity in death. Rabbi Gamliel the Elder made a special decree to that effect, at a time when funerals had become more ornate than many joyous functions of the living.[2] To seek new burial grounds under the conditions advanced to our Committee is not a commendable attempt. Of course, there are legitimate exceptions. Bodies may be moved when the land containing them has been condemned for some public purpose - though even here we must interpose every possible exception - or when there is danger of their being washed out or otherwise desecrated, or when proper burial has not taken place in the first case, or for certain other limited reasons.[3] But to move the remains of parents solely to satisfy the new-grown vanity of their descendants is hardly an honor to the Jewish dead. The Jewish viewpoint is now, and always has been, that the money spent for costly mausoleums - which will only slightly outlast the lesser memorials of the dead in the passage of time - might better be employed in supporting schools and institutions for the cultural enrichment of mankind. The result of such expenditures will be lasting, for the impress on a living soul is transmitted forever, while inanimate stones only await the inevitable change that befalls all visible matter.

1   For more details about this interview and about Rabbi Burstein, see above, Chapter III,
No. 8, notes 1-2.
2   *Moed Katan* 27b.
3   See YD 363; and Rabbi Yekutiel Greenwald, *Kol Bo al Aveilut*, New York 1947, pp. 226-
249.

No. 18 Reinterment from a Mausoleum to a Cemetery (YD 362:1)

Source: BCA, Box 4, "Burial, Mausoleum" file

RABBI ABRAHAM E. KAPLAN[1]

5348 Cabanne Avenue

Saint Louis, Missouri

March 7th, 1927

Dear Doctor Ginzberg:

We have on our cemetery a Mausoleum which was built before I came to
St. Louis. There are two persons buried there for many years, a mother and a
child. The husband has been a member of my *Shule* for thirty years or more.
He has been a very disagreeable man and very hard to get along with.

Three years ago he resigned from the congregation. Today [he] came to
the Board meeting which had already adjourned and asked for permission to
remove those bodies to another cemetery. You can well understand this man
when I say that he brought a *Yoreh Deah* along with him ready to try and
prove the fact that it was permissible. I told him to bring the matter before
the cemetery Board at which meeting we would discuss the details and merits
of the case as there was a religious question involved.

He uses as an argument that there is water seeping into the vault and this
is the reason he wants to remove the bodies,[2] but to me this is merely an
excuse. I would like to have your ruling on this at once if possible so that I
may be better prepared to answer when the matter is presented to the
cemetery and *Shule* Boards.

My personal opinion is that he may not remove the bodies and certainly
not to another cemetery.

I shall appreciate your decision on this matter in detail.

With kindest personal regards to you and[3]

~   ~   ~

March 14, 1927

Rabbi Abraham E. Halpern
5348 Cabanne Avenue
St. Louis, Mo.

Dear Rabbi Halpern:

I am in receipt of your letter of March 7th, in which you ask my advice with regard to the removal of a body which has been placed in a mausoleum. From the strict point of the law, I am afraid that the trouble-maker has the better of you, since, according to Jewish law, the body has never been really buried,[4] and hence the prohibition against removing the body[5] does not apply.

Burial, as defined by Jewish law, means placing the body into the grave and not keeping it in a mausoleum.

Nevertheless, I am fairly convinced that this craving for removal of bodies which I have noticed in the last years is nothing but a certain kind of snobbery met with [among] our so-called better classes. It is often nothing but the desire to remove all vestige of old associations and if you have any means to prevent it, do it.

Sincerely yours,

1   This is an error. The questioner was Rabbi Abraham E. *Halpern* as is evident from LG's reply and from the St. Louis address. See above, No. 16, note 1, and there, too, the question concerned mausoleums.

2   See YD 363:1.

3   The end of the letter is cut off.

4   See YD 362:1 and the *Tur* and *Bet Yosef*, ad loc.

5   See above, note 2.

No. 19 Reinterment in a New Family Plot (YD 363:1)
Source: BCA, Box 4, "Disinterment" file

RABBI GOODMAN A. ROSE[1]

September 14, 1925

Professor Louis Ginzberg
Chairman, Committee on Interpretation of Jewish Law
521 West 123rd Street,
New York City, N.Y.

Dear Dr. Ginzberg:

Our Congregation has just purchased a farm which will be made into a Congregational Cemetery. It is planned to make it the most beautiful Jewish cemetery in Pittsburgh, and to devote a portion to family plots which will be sold among the membership families.

A member of our Congregation inquired whether it is permissible to disinter the bodies of his parents from one of the older cemeteries and to reinter them in his family plot in our cemetery.[2]

His motive is not one of congregational loyalty, but rather one of giving greater respect to his parents, as the older cemetery is located in a neighborhood difficult to approach and has been ordered in a manner distasteful to the modern man and woman. There is no space between graves, which are located so closely one upon the other that it is necessary to step over graves and stones to reach any one particular grave. The sensibilities of the children are hurt by the conditions of the cemetery and their visits to their parents' graves are made very distressing.

Is it permissible according to Jewish law to have the bodies removed to the more beautiful plot [in] the more beautiful cemetery?

Thanking you for your kind response, I am,
Very sincerely yours,

GOODMAN A. ROSE

~   ~   ~

October 20, 1925

Dear Rabbi Rose:

I am in receipt of your letter of September 14th in which you ask my opinion with regard to a case of disinterment.

The answer to this question could only be that under the circumstances described, Jewish Law would not permit disinterring the bodies. As long as the bodies are buried in the Jewish cemetery it would be against Jewish law to disturb them.[3]

I hope that you will succeed in convincing the member of your congregation who would like to have the bodies of his parents disinterred that the greatest respect that he could show to them is in not disturbing the dead.

Very sincerely yours,

LOUIS GINZBERG
Chairman, Committee on Interpretation of Jewish Law

Rabbi Goodman A. Rose,
5952 Phillips Avenue,
Pittsburgh, Pa.

---

1   Rabbi Goodman A. Rose was ordained by the Seminary in 1921 and served as rabbi of *Beth Shalom* in Pittsburgh from 1923 until his death on December 17, 1950. See *PRA* 15 (1951), p. 252.

2   For similar questions, see the next two responsa as well as below, Chapter VII, No. 2.

3   See YD 363:1; and Rabbi Yekutiel Greenwald, *Kol Bol al Aveilut*, New York 1947, pp. 235-237.

No. 20 Reinterment in a New Family Plot (YD 363:1)
Source: BCA, Box 4, "Burial, Exhumation" file

CONGREGATION BAITH ISRAEL ANSHEI EMES
Harrison Street near Court Street
Brooklyn, New York

March 27, 1927

Dear Doctor Ginzberg:

The enclosed letter explains itself.[1] I am very anxious to have your opinion in the matter. I thought that the principle of [ערב לאדם שיהא נח אצל אבותיו],[2] as well as the fact that this removal of the body is being done [לכבוד המת],[3] should be sufficient reasons for allowing to remove the body. However, I did not want to commit myself before hearing from you.

I shall greatly appreciate a prompt reply.

With kindest personal regards both to you and Mrs. Ginzberg, I am,

Yours very sincerely,

ISRAEL GOLDFARB[4]

Prof. Louis Ginzberg
568 West 149th Street,
New York, N.Y.

~   ~   ~

March 30, 1927

Dear Rabbi Goldfarb:

I am in receipt of your letter of March 27th in which you ask my advice as to whether it be permitted to remove a body for the purpose of having it placed in a [family plot][5] erected by the members of the family.

I find that the Lodge that refuses to give its permission of removal, acts in accordance with Jewish Law. If at the time of the burial there would have been in existence a family plot where several members of the family were buried, there might be a reason for having a member of the family buried in another plot removed to the family plot. As I understand, in this particular case, however, at the time of the burial of the body, no family plot did exist and it would be against Jewish Law, therefore, to have the body removed.

May I add, that I [have] had the opportunity to observe a new form of snobbery developing among us Jews to be separated in death as in life from the "common" people. There is an enourmous waste of money in erecting [family plots][6] which certainly could be spent [on] a much worthier cause. I think it is the duty of each rabbi to try his utmost to prevent this latest fashion which is contrary to Jewish Law and spirit alike.

Very sincerely yours,

LOUIS GINZBERG, Chairman
Committee on Interpretation of Jewish Law

Rabbi Israel Goldfarb,
360 Clinton Street,
Brooklyn, N.Y.

1   The letter is missing from the BCA. The question is repeated in LG's reply.
2   The Hebrew phrases are missing from the carbon copy in the BCA. I have added the missing phrases according to the context.
3   See above, note 2.
4   Rabbi Israel Goldfarb (1880-1966 or 1967) was ordained by the Seminary in 1902 and served as rabbi of Beth Israel Anshe Emet in Brooklyn for over sixty years. See *Student's Annual* 3 (1916), p. 191; and *PRA* 31 (1967), pp. 172-173.
5   LG says "mausoleum" twice, but he clearly means "family plot" because he himself explains that removal to a pre-existing family plot is permitted (see YD 363:1) whereas burial in a mausoleum is always prohibited (see YD 362:1 as well as above, Nos. 16 and 17). For similar questions, see Nos. 19 and 21, as well as Chapter VII, No. 2.
6   See above, note 5.

No. 21 Reinterment in a New Family Plot (YD 363:1)[1]
Source: General Files, Folder 3 (1934-1936)

328 Joralemon St.,
Belleville, N.J.
Dec. 14, 1936

Prof. Louis Ginzberg,
Jewish Theological Seminary of America,
Broadway and 122 St.,
New York City.

Dear Professor Ginzberg:
    I am taking the liberty of writing you for your opinion and suggestion in a matter that has been perplexing me in recent [days]. I have been referred to you by local Jewish authorities.
    I am a young man of the Jewish faith. Last May my father passed away. He was a member of a lodge which offers two graves, namely, for man and wife, and he was buried in one of these graves. At present, my mother, brothers and sisters are interested in purchasing a larger plot elsewhere for the entire family. I wanted to know if, according to our faith and law, we are permitted to remove the body from its present place so that the final resting place of the entire family may be together. I certainly would appreciate your impartial opinion in this matter.
    Thanking you very sincerely for this guidance, I am,

Very respectfully,

Maurice Schwartz

~ ~ ~

December 21, 1936

My Dear Mr. Schwartz:
    I am in receipt of your letter of December 14, in which you ask my opinion whether according to Jewish Law, it would be permitted to remove the body of your father from its present place to a family plot which your mother and members of her family are contemplating to purchase. My reply to this question is an emphatic no. Jewish sentiment and Law insist upon the principle "Let the dead rest in peace". I am sure that you could not show

your filial piety towards your deceased father in any more concrete manner than in respecting his resting place.[2]

Very truly yours,

LOUIS GINZBERG

Mr. Maurice Schwartz,
328 Joralemon Street,
Belleville, N.J.

---

1   For similar questions, see the previous two responsa as well as below, Chapter VII, No. 2.
2   See above, No. 19, note 3.

No. 22 Reinterment in Order to Facilitate Easy Visitation (YD 363:1)
Source: LGA, Box 3, "Drob" file

May 11, 1939

Dear Doctor Drob:[1]

I hate always to be of the *Nein Sagers*[2] but I fail to see how I could with good conscience permit the removal of the bodies. There is certainly no need for children visiting the graves of their parents to come in direct contact with the particular lot in which their parents are interred.[3] I still am of the opinion that we ought to discourage as much as possible any disturbance of the dead.

Very sincerely yours,

LOUIS GINZBERG

Doctor Max Drob
2323 Grand Concourse
New York City

---

1   Rabbi Max Drob (1887-1959) was ordained by the Seminary in 1911. At the time this *teshuvah* was written, he was the rabbi of Concourse Center of Israel in the Bronx (1930-47). See Nadell, pp. 72-73; and Sanford Drob, *Conservative Judaism* 39/3 (Spring, 1987), pp. 34-44.
2   Naysayers.
3   Perhaps the children were *Kohanim* and could not get near the graves because of ritual impurity (YD 369ff.).

No. 23 May a Rabbi Who is a Kohen Officiate at Funerals? (YD 369ff.)

Source: CJLS Box, "Bet Knesset" file = BCA, Box 5, "Miscellaneous Questions and Answers" file

Question: [Our] Rabbi, during the time he was here, attended to all funerals, and everything was running smoothly until one of our members met one of the members of the Rabbi's previous post who informed him that he [had observed the] regulations of a *Cohen*. This information has been brought up now before the officers of this congregation and we are in doubt as to what we shall do with our Rabbi hereafter. Some of our members think that he has committed a gross sin, and others think that this is only an ancient custom and one of the minor things of these times, as we are an Orthodox Conservative congregation.

Answer: (by Rabbi Samuel M. Cohen)[1] In answer to your letter, I have consulted Professor Louis Ginzberg, Chairman of our Committee on Interpretation [of] Jewish [Law], and he advises that in consideration of the extenuating circumstances it would be proper for your congregation to retain your rabbi, provided that he made his promise that in the future he would observe the laws of *Kehunah*.[2]

---

1 Rabbi Samuel Cohen (1886-1945) was the first director of the United Synagogue of America (1917-44). This responsum was probably written between 1923, when LG published his last Committee report, and September 1927, when the Committee was reorganized under the Chairmanship of Rabbi Julius Greenstone (*PRA* 3 [1929], p. 57). Regarding Cohen, see Nadell, pp. 61-62 and *Conservative Judaism* 47/3 (Spring, 1995), pp. 62-63.

2 It is worth noting that this issue was reopened a few years later and a responsum was written, enabling Rabbis who are *Kohanim* to officiate at funerals - see *PRA* 3 (1929), pp. 155-165.

No. 24 May a Kohen Serve in the U.S.Army? (YD 369ff.)

Source: *Keeper*, p. 222
Secondary Reference: Address, p. 116

During World War I, the Federal Government sought my father's opinion on the problem presented by a selectee who insisted that he should not be drafted because, since he was a member of a priestly family, he was forbidden by Jewish law to come into contact with the dead. Professor Ginzberg in this instance had a very brief opinion: he pointed out that Judas Maccabeus came from a priestly family![1]

---

1   See the *Al Hanissim* prayer (Jules Harlow, ed., *Siddur Sim Shalom*, New York 1985, p. 116) as well as *I Maccabees* 2:1 and Josephus, *Antiquities*, XII, 6, 1, par. 265. This statement of LG is quoted in a Conservative responsum on the same topic during World War II - see "Cohen as Chaplain and Soldier" in CJLS box, "Kevurah" file.

No. 25 The Recital of Kaddish by a Son Who Bears a Grudge against his Father (YD 376:4)

Source: LGA, Box 13[1]

June 25, 1951

My dear Mr. _____ :[1]

I am in receipt of your letter of June 13 and after considering the matter propounded by you, I wish to say the following: According to Jewish teachings there is no sin that is not wiped out by repentence.[2] In view of the fact, therefore, that your late father, shortly before his death confessed the wrong he had done to you, his sin was forgiven by the good Lord and hence should also be forgiven by you.

I fully understand the difficult position you find yourself in, but to forgive and forget is not only a religious command but also a very wise rule for one's conduct in life. It goes, of course, without saying that you ought to continue to recite the *Kaddish*. To refrain from doing so certainly would reflect unfavorably not only on the memory of your father but also upon yourself.

May I conclude my letter by quoting the following remark of our old sages. Commenting upon the Biblical story of Abraham's emigration to the Holy Land which is told in scripture immediately after [the story] regarding the death of his father,[3] they remark: "Abraham remained with his father as long as he lived but did not receive the Divine command to emigrate that people should not say: What kind of a son is he to depart from his old father",[4] and yet, according to Jewish tradition, the man whose name was Terah was not only an idol worshipper but [also] an idol maker.

Sincerely yours,

Louis Ginzberg

1   The name and address of the questioner have been omitted for obvious reasons.
2   See, e.g., *Rosh Hashanah* 17b: "Great is repentance for it cancels the evil decree passed on a person".
3   Genesis 11:32-12:1.
4   *Bereishit Rabbah* 39:7, eds. Theodor-Albeck, p. 369.

No. 26 The Participation of Children in Mourning in Music Periods and Assemblies (YD 391)

Source: LGA, Box 11, "Schlockow" file
Secondary References:
1. *Exponent* = Box 17, "Questions and Answers" file
2. *Keeper*, p. 223

OSWALD SCHLOCKOW   DEPARTMENT OF EDUCATION   MARY L. HOLM
Principal   CITY OF NEW YORK   STELLA SILBERBERG
                   THE JOHN D.WELLS SCHOOL   Assistant Principals
             PUBLIC SCHOOL NO. 50, BROOKLYN
       SOUTH THIRD STREET AND DRIGGS AVENUE
WATCHWORD 1920-1921   YEAR TEXT
DEMOCRACY

"The foundation of our government is, first, that every man shall govern himself."
Lyman Abbott

Brooklyn, November 24, 1920

President, Jewish Theological Seminary,
531 West 123rd Street,
New York City.

My dear President:

This school is situated in the heart of Williamsburg; our pupils are in large numbers the children of orthodox Jews. Dealing as we do with over 3000 pupils, it naturally happens that a considerable number always observe a period of mourning for parents or near relatives; on such occasions they invariably inform us they are not permitted to hear music. In deference to their wishes, we have, in the past, been permitting them to stay out of the auditorium where occasional songs are sung, and to omit the regular music periods. In this congested school it is frequently impossible to place them elsewhere and they, in consequence, loiter in basements where they play ball and enjoy themselves in conversation.

It has occurred to me to inquire of you as an authority in such matters whether these children may not passively sit with their colleagues in the auditorium and not participate in actual singing. If this can be done, it will greatly simplify our administrative problem and place the children under closer supervision. I shall deeply appreciate any advice you can give us.

Very truly,

Oswald Schlockow

~   ~   ~

December 22, 1920
Dear Sir:
Doctor Cyrus Adler, the Acting President of the Jewish Theological Seminary, referred to me your letter of November 24th.
In reply thereto I wish to say that if the assembly periods and music hours are parts of the regular curriculum of study, there is no harm in having the children attend. The only objection will arise if the main function of those assembly hours were amusement, which I do not take to be the case.[1]

Yours very truly,

LOUIS GINZBERG
Chairman of the Committee on the
Interpretation of Jewish Law

Mr. Oswald Schlockow, Principal   .
  The John D. Wells School
  Public School No. 50
    South 3d St. & Driggs Ave.
    Brooklyn, N. Y.

---

1   Regarding music during the twelve months of mourning, see Rabbi Yekutiel Greenwald, *Kol Bo al Aveilut*, New York 1947, pp. 361-362.

V. Responsa Related to Even Haezer

No. 1 Artificial Insemination by a Donor (EH 1 in *Birkei Yosef*)   207

No. 2 Marrying a Woman with the Same Name as One's Mother
(EH 2 in *Pithei Teshuvah*, par. 6)   214

No. 3 Should a Rabbi of Uncertain Priestly Status Continue
to Behave Like a *Kohen*? (EH 3)   215

No. 4 *Fellatio* (EH 23:1 and 25:2 and OH 240:4)   216

No. 5 Does a Couple that Eloped and Spent Several Hours
Together Require a *Get*? (EH 26 and 33)   217

No. 6 The History of the Marriage Ring (EH 27:1 and 31:2)   218

No. 7 Weddings on *Hol Hamoed Sukkot* (EH 64:6 and OH 546:1)   220

No. 8 Weddings on *Hol Hamoed Sukkot* for Soldiers Leaving for
Overseas (EH 64:6 and OH 546:1)   221

No. 9 Remarriage without a *Get* If the First Wife Was a
Transgressor (EH 115:1)   222

No. 10 A Protest against the Laxity with which Jewish Divorce is
Practiced (EH 119ff.)   223

No. 11 Giving a *Get* without Documentary Evidence of a Civil
Divorce (EH 119ff.)   224

No. 12 Is a Woman Divorced by a *Get* without a Civil Decree
Considered Divorced? (EH 119ff.)   225

No. 13 Agency Appointment for a Soldier Going Off to War
(EH 144:5)   226

No. 1 Artificial Insemination by a Donor (EH 1 in Birkei Yosef)

Source of the Brief Typed Responsum by an Anonymous Questioner: New Box
Source of LG's Handwritten Answer: New Box
Source of LG's Typed Answer: BCA, Box 5, "Nashim" file; the question from this version, without the answer, is also found in: LGA, Box 17, "Questions and Answers" file
Secondary References:
1. *PRA* 6 (1939), p. 157
2. *Bulletin of the Rabbinical Assembly* 2/4 (June, 1939), p. 5
3. Autobiographical Fragment, last unnumbered page
4. A letter from LG to Rabbi Theodore Friedman dated May 2, 1952, LGA, Box 4, "Theodore Friedman" file
5. *Keeper*, p. 241
6. Rabbi Herman Rosenwasser, "Eight Monographs Related to the Response of Rabbi Louis Ginzberg", New Box
7. Rabbi Alan Iser, "A Summary of Rabbi Louis Ginzberg's Responsum on Artificial Insemination", Summer, 1987, 11pp.
8. A letter from Eli Ginzberg dated October 5, 1993
Comment: This responsum is by far the most difficult surviving responsum authored by LG. It has also had the most colorful history. It was first mentioned in 1939 and then disappeared from sight. Towards the end of his life, LG mentions it in his Autobiographical Fragment. In 1952, Rabbi Friedman requested a copy from LG, only to be told that he had lent his only copy to Prof. Finkelstein. Years later, the handwritten version was discovered by LG's daughter, Sophie Gould, in Brookline, Massachusetts, when it fell out of a desk which had once belonged to her father. In 1984, at the suggestion of Prof. David Weiss Halivni, Eli Ginzberg gave the brief typed responsum and LG's handwritten reply to Rabbi Herman Rosenwasser, who transcribed LG's reply in longhand. The brief typed responsum and Rabbi Rosenwasser's transcription - but not LG's handwritten responsum - were later given to Rabbi David Novak, who gave them to Rabbi Alan Iser who wrote a paper about them in the summer of 1987. In 1991-92, Rabbi Iser was kind enough to give me copies of the brief responsum, the Rosenwasser transcription - which he took to be LG's handwriting - and his own paper. On September 30, 1992, I looked through the New Box which Eli Ginzberg had recently donated to the Seminary library and discovered LG's handwritten responsum, Rosenwasser's transcription, Rosenwasser's "monographs", and the brief typed responsum. Finally, on that same day, I discovered a 36-page *typed* version of LG's responsum in the Boaz Cohen archives at the Seminary.

The latter is clearly the "official" version prepared by LG himself. The title page attributes the responsum to לוי בן מרנו הרב יצחק זצ״ל לבית גינצבורג which is identical to the attribution used in his responsum on grape juice published in 1922 (above, Chapter III, No. 16) and almost identical to the attribution used in his *Commentary to the Palestinian Talmud* published in 1941. In addition, LG himself quotes the conclusion of his "36 page responsum on artificial insemination" in his Autobiographical Fragment which was later quoted in *Keeper*. He can only be referring to the typed version since his handwritten version does not contain 36 pages and since the paragraph in question is not found in the handwritten version. Therefore, LG's responsum printed in the Hebrew side of this volume was taken from the typed version of his responsum.

Lastly, we must explain the relationship between the brief typed responsum and LG's lengthy responsum on artificial insemination. Rabbi Rosenwasser and Rabbi Iser assumed, and I originally concurred, that both were written by LG himself for the simple reason that the detailed question which appears at the beginning of the brief responsum also appears at the beginning of LG's *handwritten* responsum. Yet this assumption raised a number of difficult problems. First of all, the question which appears in both versions contains a sentence which would have been appropriate for a rabbi writing to LG but totally inappropriate for LG himself. The sentence reads: "אמרתי לפנות אל עמודי ההוראה ולבקש דעת תורה בזה" [= "I decided to turn to the pillars of halakhic authority and request a Torah opinion from them"]. As explained in the Introduction to this volume, LG was the foremost talmudist of his generation *and he knew it*. He therefore could not have written such a sentence. Furthermore, there are a number of glaring differences between the two responsa. The style of the brief responsum is short and to the point while the style of LG's responsum is verbose and digressive and similar to his style in his responsum on grape juice and in his *Commentary to the Palestinian Talmud*. The brief responsum contains no hint as to its author while LG's handwritten responsum is signed by him and refers both to his uncle Rabbi Aryeh Leib Rashkes and to his ancestor the *Gaon* of Vilna. The author of the brief responsum relies heavily on *Hagigah* 14b-15a and on Rabbeinu Peretz and *Alpha Beta d'ven Sira* while LG ultimately rejects both sources. Most importantly, the author of the brief responsum *allows* artificial insemination by a donor providing that the couple divorce, undergo AID and remarry, while LG entirely *forbids* artificial insemination by a donor. Thus, we are confronted with the paradox of identical questions and contradictory answers apparently written by the same person.

The mystery was solved by the discovery of the *typed* version of LG's responsum which was, as shown above, the official version of his responsum. First of all, the brief responsum and LG's typed responsum were typed on different typewriters. More importantly, the typed version of LG's responsum begins with a *different* question than the handwritten version and that question solves all of the problems described above. It states: "I was asked by a rabbi about a woman who came before him...*And the rabbi who asked me replied at length* on the basis of the *aharonim* regarding a virgin who conceived in a bath [*Hagigah* 14b-15a], but since it has always been my practice to base myself on the words of the Talmud and the *rishonim*, I have avoided quoting his words and discussing them...". In other words, the rabbi who sent LG the original question included a brief responsum of his own! This frequently occurs in the responsa literature when a local rabbi sends a question to a higher authority. This explains the phrase quoted above from the *original* question: "I decided to turn to the pillars of halakhic authority and request a Torah opinion from them". That is exactly what LG supplied: a lengthy "Torah opinion". But in his original handwritten version, he simply copied the original question from the letter which he had received. When LG had his responsum typed, he rewrote the question because he realized that the style of the original question was misleading and inappropriate for his reply.

In light of all of the above, we have reproduced on the Hebrew side of this volume both the question and brief responsum by the anonymous rabbi and the typed version of LG's responsum. I have briefly summarized both responsa below, omitting most of the involved halakhic reasoning which would not interest the English reader. I have utilized Rabbi Iser's paper in preparing these summaries.

A Summary of a Responsum on Artificial Insemination by an Anonymous Rabbi

[*Question:*] I was asked by a doctor about a man who contracted an illness in his reproductive organs before marriage. His wife knew this before their marriage and said "even so I will marry him" because out of her great love for him she was willing to bear the loneliness of remaining childless for her entire life. But now she is in constant anguish because her desire for children increases from day to day and the doctors fear she will become insane from grief. Indeed, according to the doctors, there is a remedy in that doctors have invented a new invention - that it is possible to inject into her uterus the

sperm of another man without physical contact. The husband and wife have
agreed to this procedure because of their great love for each other. The
doctor asked if this procedure is permissible according to our Holy Torah in
light of the prohibition of a man having sexual relations with a married
woman. He further asked if one has to be careful to take the sperm from a
Jew or a non-Jew, from anyone or even from a person with whom she is
forbidden from having relations, and what will be the halakhic status of the
child? Since this a very serious matter both from the point of view of having
relations with a married woman and from the point of view of public policy
(*hanimuss ha-enoshi*), I decided to turn to the pillars of halakhic authority
and request a Torah opinion from them and especially since it is a practice
which will increase in the course of time and many childless Jews will turn to
this remedy and will turn to rabbis to ask whether it is permitted or
forbidden.

[*Answer:*] I shall only write a brief reply from what I think about this issue
based on the words of the Sages and on the medieval authorities. At first
glance, it would seem possible to learn the *halakhah* in this case from the case
of a pregnant virgin in *Hagigah* 14b-15a. The Talmud asks there whether she
may marry a High Priest who is only permitted to marry a virgin, and it
replies that it is permissible since she may have become pregnant from sperm
which was floating in a bath. If so, we might say that just as a woman who
conceives in a bath may marry a High Priest, so too a woman who conceives
by artificial insemination has not trangressed the prohibition of a man
having sexual relations with a married woman. And if you try to differentiate
between the laws of a High Priest and a married woman, we would reply that
the same restrictions apply to both.

Furthermore, *Mishneh L'melekh* to the Rambam (*Ishut* 15:4) quotes the
Glosses of Rabbeinu Peretz to the *Semak* that a woman does not become
forbidden to her husband if she absorbed another man's sperm in her uterus
without physical contact. He proves this from the case of Ben Sira whose
mother was a virgin who conceived in a bathtub from sperm left there by the
Prophet Jeremiah. This passage is also quoted by the *Ba"H* to *Yoreh Deah*
195; *Bet Shemuel* to *Even Haezer* 1, subparagraph 10; and the *Tashbetz*, Vol.
3, no. 263. Since these authorities rule that a married woman is not forbidden
to her husband if she conceives from sperm in a bathtub, so is the law in our
case as well.

"In the final analysis, in my humble opinion, it is proved by the Talmud
that conception without physical contact is not considered intercourse and
she is therefore permitted to her husband and that is the opinion of the
authorities cited above. But it would seem that this is forbidden before the

fact...because of the decree lest he inadvertently marry his own sister
[*Yevamot* 42a]...unless he lets the child know who his father is or unless the
sperm should specifically come from a non-Jew since paternity cannot be
transmitted by a non-Jew. But even if they take the sperm from a non-Jew, I
am hesitant to permit this before the fact because of lineage and because of
various misgivings. So there remains only one solution for this unfortunate
woman: She should be divorced from her husband, be injected by the doctors
with the sperm of a non-Jewish donor, and then be remarried by her Jewish
husband... because [even a divorced woman who has sex with another man]
is allowed to return to her first husband [*Mishnah Sotah* 18b]. Of course, this
solution is only feasible if the husband is an Israelite, [because a *kohen* may
not marry a divorcee]".

A Summary of a Responsum on Artificial Insemination by Prof. Louis Ginzberg

"*Question:* I was asked by a rabbi about a woman who came before him
with her question. Since her husband's reproductive organs became diseased
so that he will never father children, is it permissible to inject in her uterus
sperm from another man using a new invention invented by doctors in our
time which enables a woman to conceive from sperm injected into her uterus
without physical contact? And the rabbi who asked me replied at length on
the basis of the *aharonim* regarding a virgin who conceived in a bath
[*Hagigah* 14b-15a], but since it has always been my practice to base myself on
the words of the Talmud and the *rishonim*, I have avoided quoting his words
and discussing them. And this is my reply with the help of God, may He be
blessed."

Answer: Mishnah Yevamot 4:13, fol. 49a is the *locus classicus* for the laws
of *mamzerut*. At first glance, it would seem from that *mishnah* that, according
to all of the *Tannaim* cited there, a *mamzer* can only be the product of a
forbidden sexual relationship. But it could be that a child born of the sperm
and the egg of a man and a woman who are forbidden to each other is still a
mamzer because *conception*, not *intercourse*, causes *mamzerut*. Thus, for
example, when a gentile has relations with a Jewess, many sages consider the
child a *mamzer* even if the mother was unmarried (*Yevamot* 45a) even though
intercourse with a gentile who is not one of the seven nations of Canaan is
not forbidden by the Torah. Therefore, perforce, the cause of the *mamzerut* is
the seed itself and not the intercourse. Therefore, not only is there no
conclusive proof from this *mishnah* that there is no *mamzerut* without
forbidden intercourse, but on the contrary, according to the simple meaning,
this *mishnah* thinks that the sperm causes *mamzerut* and not intercourse. In

any case, the *mishnah* in *Yevamot* doesn't teach us anything conclusive about whether the child in our case is a *mamzer* or not.

The first to discuss our question was the *Mishneh L'melekh* to the Rambam (*Ishut* 15:4) who commented on the *Ba''h* to *Yoreh Deah* 195 who quotes the Glosses of Rabbeinu Peretz to the *Semak*. The Glosses say that a menstruating woman is allowed to lie on her husband's sheet because even is she conceives from some sperm on the sheet, there was no forbidden intercourse and the child is entirely kosher, but women are accustomed not to lie on the sheet of another man because, even though any offspring would be kosher, we are afraid lest they conceive and lest the child inadvertently marry his sister. This quotation is missing from our printed editions of the Glosses of Rabbeinu Peretz, but I did find it in two of the twelve manuscripts of the *Semak* which I checked at the library of the Jewish Theological Seminary.

The Glosses derived this ruling from a late midrash entitled *Alpha Beta d'ven Sira* which relates that Ben Sira was the offspring of Jeremiah the Prophet and his own daughter because some ruffians forced Jeremiah to "spill his seed" in a bath and his daughter then bathed there and conceived Ben Sira. But there are two different versions of a crucial sentence. The second version published in *Hatzofeh L'hokhmat Yisrael* 10 (1926), p. 253 says that Ben Sira's mother was embarrassed "that now people will say *that this child is a mamzer*", while the first edition published by Steinschneider, Berlin, 1858, fol. 17a reads: "She was embarrassed since people said *she had conceived from prostitution*". There is no question that the latter reading is correct because Jeremiah's daughter was unmarried and when an unmarried woman conceives, the child is not a *mamzer*. The point of the story is simply that she was blameless and conceived by accident and not by prostitution.

Yet, in any case, one cannot decide *halakhah* on the basis of this legend, for we have learned in the *Yerushalmi* (*Peah* 2:6, fol. 17a etc.): "One does not learn (or: rule) *halakhah* from *haggadot* [= legends or non-legal material]". If they said this about Talmudic *haggadot*, how much moreso is it true regarding a legend from *Alpha Beta d'ven Sira* which is a late work first quoted by the *Arukh* and which contains things "which the mind cannot endure" and which "do not find favor in the eyes of the sages". Indeed, the *Tashbetz* (Vol. 3, no. 263) hints that one should not believe this legend, and one should certainly not rule on a serious matter such as *mamzerut* on the basis of such a dubious source. Lastly, the *Nodah B'yehudah* (second edition, *Yoreh Deah*, no. 161) and Rav Hai Gaon (*Responsa of the Geonim*, ed. Harkavy, no. 9) have also ruled that one doesn't decide halakhic issues on the basis of *haggadot*.

Therefore, we must see what the Babylonian Talmud has to say on our subject because "we are dependent on its word". At first glance, there is an entire passage in the Talmud which is relevant to our subject. We have learned in *Hagigah* 14b-15a: "They asked Ben Zoma: May a High Priest marry a virgin who became pregnant? Do we take into account the opinion of Samuel who said: I can have repeated intercourse with a virgin without causing bleeding or is Samuel's case perhaps unusual? He replied: Samuel's case is unusual, but we do consider the possibility that she may have conceived in a bathtub".

This passage was interpreted by the *Geonim* and *Rishonim* in four different ways. Yet an in-depth analysis of the interpretations of Rashi and the Rosh, Tosafot, Rabbeinu Hananel and the *Geonim*, and the *Tashbetz* and Rambam reveal that this passage sheds little light on our problem. For Rashi and Tosafot, the Talmud wants to know whether such a pregnant virgin may marry a High Priest. According to the reading of Rabbeinu Hananel and the *Geonim*, the Talmud does not even mention a High Priest and merely wants to know whether such a virgin must follow the prescribed rites of purification upon giving birth. And according to the reading of the *Tashbetz*, the Talmud is asking whether she may marry a priest, not a High Priest. In any case, according to all four interpretations, the passage in *Hagigah* is not really interested in the halakhic status of the child, yet none of the interpretations of *Hagigah* imply that a child conceived in a bath is kosher.

"All of the above is sufficient to prove that we have not found a peg in the Talmud or in the *Rishonim* on which to hang a lenient ruling in this serious matter. On the contrary, even though there is no proof to forbid, there is support for one who says that, according to the opinion of the *rishonim*, a child who is born from sperm absorbed by his married mother without intercourse is a *mamzer*. And God forbid to rely in such a case of possible *mamzerut* on the legendary material in *Alpha Beta d'ven Sira*, a book filled with strange and surprising things which do not 'find favor in the eyes of the sages'. And if we find reliance on this legend in a few manuscripts of the Glosses of Rabbeinu Peretz, 'he did not sign those glosses' [= we do not know if Rabbeinu Peretz actually wrote those sections], the proof being that in the printed editions and most manuscripts of the Glosses this passage is missing. And it is superfluous to add how ugly this practice is from the point of view of ethics and purity to inject the sperm of another man into the uterus of a married woman. And it has already been said: 'And you shall be... a holy people to the Lord your God' [Deuteronomy 26:19]".

No. 2 Marrying a Woman with the Same Name as One's Mother (EH 2, in Pithei Teshuvah, par. 6)

Source: LGA, Box 8, "Lewis" file

January 13, 1947

Dear Mr. Lewis:[1]

If you believe that words of mine will have an influence upon your parents, tell them that the best thing to do is to forget all about the "names". You may assure them there is nothing in Jewish law prohibiting a man to marry a woman whose name is the same as the man's mother.[2]

As a matter of fact, one cannot even speak of an accepted custom in view of the fact that it is not widely spread, being limited to the Ashkenazim and not known at all to the Sephardic or Oriental Jews.

How about you calling your wife by some pet name, [or] at least to do so in the presence of your parents.

Very sincerely yours,

Louis Ginzberg

Albert L. Lewis, Esq.
540 West 123rd Street
New York, N.Y.

---

1   Rabbi Albert Lewis was ordained by the Seminary in 1948 and served as rabbi of Temple Beth Shalom of Haddon Heights (later: Cherry Hill), New Jersey, from 1948-1992. He was also President of the Rabbinical Assembly (1988-90). This letter is reprinted here with his permission.

2   He means "Jewish law" as opposed to a custom. The source of this custom is "The Testament of Rabbi Judah the Hassid" - see *Sefer Hassidim*, ed. Reuven Margaliot, Jerusalem 5717, pp. 4, 17-18; and Binyamin Adler, *Hanissuin K'hilkhatam*, Jerusalem, 5745[2], pp. 55-65.

No. 3 Should a Rabbi of Uncertain Priestly Status Continue to Behave Like a Kohen?[1] (EH 3)

Source: CJLS Box, "Bet Knesset" file = BCA, Box 5, "Miscellaneous Questions and Answers" file

Question: Our Rabbi claims that until he was twenty-four years of age he obeyed the rite of *Yisroel.* Then he claims that his father related a dream to him stating that his grandfather told him that he was a *Cohen* and he would like for his great-grandson to observe the laws of a *Cohen.* Without giving much thought to the matter, he started to be called up to the Torah as a *Cohen,* feeling that that is only a *Minhag,* although his father and his grandfather were never called up as a *Cohen.*[2]

Answer: Professor Ginzberg has asked me to respond to your interesting letter. Once a man has observed the laws of *Kehunah,* he may not go back without producing legally acceptable evidence to the effect that he is not a *Cohen.* It is not enough to show that [at] some time in the past he did not observe the laws. He must actually prove that he is not a *Cohen.* That is the Jewish law on the subject.[3]

---

1   This appears to be the question, judging from the answer.

2   This is permissible in our day according to the Rema in EH 3:1 and see ibid., 3:2, that a father can testify that his son is a *Kohen.* Regarding the influence of dreams on the *halakhah,* See Reuven Margaliot, *She'elot U'teshuvot Min Hashamayim,* Jerusalem 1957, pp. 6-13.

3   I do not know the source of this strict ruling. Granted, if a man was considered a *Kohen* for many years or if his ancestors had an established tradition (*hazakah*) of *Kehunah,* it is hard to undo the *hazakah* - see EH 3:7 and Pithei Teshuvah to EH 6, par. 1. In this case, however, he declared himself a *Kohen* without any hard proof and despite his family tradition, so why should he have to prove that he is not a *Kohen?*

No. 4 Fellatio (EH 23:1 and 25:2 and OH 240:4)
Source: LGA, Box 12, "Whitaker" file

February 16, 1950

Dear Mr. Whitaker:

Because of protracted and painful illness, I was unable to reply sooner to your letter of February 8th, and even today I will have to be very brief, as I find dictating rather difficult.

There is no reference neither in the early nor in the later Rabbinic literature to *fellatio*, though there can be no doubt that according to [the] Jewish view, it is strictly prohibited, since it culminates in ejaculation and any manipulation leading to ejaculation is considered by the Rabbis as a very grave moral and religious sin (comp. Babylonian Talmud, *Niddah* 13a and b and *Shulhan Arukh, Even Haezer* 23:1.[1] As to the beast and *fellatio*, _____ ,[2] there is a reference to it in Talmud *Nedarim* 20a and b and *Shulhan Arukh* [*Orah Haim*], 240.[3]

I am forwarding your letter to Doctor Lieberman[4] to enable him to give you his own opinion in the matter.

Sincerely yours,

Louis Ginzberg

Norman T. Whitaker, Esq.
Legal Researcher
776 North 26th Street
Philadelphia, Pa.

---

1 Nonetheless, some rabbis permitted unusual forms of intercourse (*Nedarim* 20b; *Tur* EH 25; EH 25:2 in the Rema; *ET*, XI, col. 136) even if they resulted in the spilling of semen.

2 The secretary left room for the handwritten Hebrew phrase which is missing from the carbon copy in LGA, but see the following note.

3 I do not know what "the beast and *fellatio*" means nor is there any reference to beasts in the sources cited. For the talmudic attitude towards sexual relations with a beast, see Louis Epstein, *Sex Laws and Customs in Judaism*, New York 1948, pp. 132-134; and Julius Preuss, *Biblical and Talmudic Medicine*, New York 1978, pp. 496-498.

4 Prof. Saul Lieberman (1898-1983), one of the foremost Talmudists of the twentieth century, taught at the Seminary from 1940 until 1980 and LG was instrumental in his appointment - see *EJ*, XI, cols. 218-220; *Keeper*, pp. 140-142; and Nadell, pp. 178-180.

No. 5 Does a Couple that Eloped and Spent Several Hours Together Require a Get? (EH 26 and 33)
Source: CJLS Box, "Nissuin and Gittin" file

Question: A couple eloped and had spent just several hours together. Would a *Get* be necessary?

Answer: With regard to the matter concerning a couple who had eloped and had spent just several hours together, long enough to be married,[1] Professor Ginzberg was of the opinion that if it is an established fact that the couple did not live together as man and wife,[1] that no *Get* would be necessary, and the [fact] that they had received a civil divorce instead of an annulment would not prejudice the matter.

---

1   These seem to be euphemisms for sexual relations, in which case LG seems to think that if they *did* have sexual relations, they would require a *get*. However, most modern authorities do *not* require a *get* after a couple has lived together or had a civil marriage - see, for example, Rabbi Pesach Schindler, *Responsa of the Va'ad Halakhah of the Rabbinical Assembly of Israel*, IV (5750-5752), Jerusalem 1992, pp. 81-90; and Rabbi Joel Roth, *PRA* 52 (1990), pp. 137-148.

No. 6 The History of the Marriage Ring (EH 27:1 and 31:2)

Source: LGA, Box 11, "Schauss" file

Secondary References: Hayyim Schauss, *The Lifetime of a Jew throughout the Ages of Jewish History*, New York 1950, pp. ix, 161, 317

March 3, 1947

Dear Mr. Schauss:[1]

The passage about the marriage ring is certainly a very difficult one.[2] Several explanations have been given but none of them [is] quite satisfactory. As I understand it, the difference between the Babylonian[s] and [the] Palestinian[s] is that the former considered any ring sent by the fiancé to his fiancée as a ring of betrothal, while the latter considered it simply a gift. This would mean that the marriage ring was in common use in Babylon and not in Palestine where a ring was looked upon as any other gift sent by an engaged couple.

As a matter of fact, the earliest reference we have to the marriage ring is a responsum by Hai *Gaon* who refers to the marriage ring used about 100 years before his time among the Jews of Eastern Iraq.[3] I have my serious doubts [as] to the generally accepted view that the marriage ring came from the Romans to the Jews. What [were] the Romans [doing] in Eastern Iraq?![4]

I want to call your attention to the following fact: according to the marriage ceremonies described by Saadia in his prayerbook,[5] the instrument of *Kiddushin* is the cup of wine in which a silver coin is placed - no reference whatsoever [is made] to the marriage ring. If I am not mistaken, this is the way the Yemenites perform today the *Kiddushin*.[6]

Do you know that there was a time when in Moslem countries the Jews were not permitted to wear any rings?[7] This perhaps would explain the fact that in some countries the marriage ring came in[to] disuse.

I consider the name _____ as corrupted - intentionally so - of _____ which is taken from the Greek.[8]

Kind regards.

Sincerely yours,

Louis Ginzberg

Hayyim Schauss, Esq.
2922 Barnes Avenue
Bronx 67, N.Y.

1   Hayyim Schauss (1884-1953), a prolific Yiddish writer, was also the author of two popular English books - *The Jewish Festivals*, Cincinnati 1938, and *The Lifetime of a Jew throughout the Ages of Jewish History*, New York 1950. He used to consult LG on a regular basis - see the Preface to each of his books. For a detailed biographical sketch, see Israel Elfenbein in *Hadoar* 36/16 (14 Adar I, 5717), p. 296.

2   LG is referring to one of the *hilukim* between *Eretz Yisrael* and Babylonia as quoted in *Sha'arei Tzedek*, Salonica 1792, fol. 19b: אנשי מזרח רואין אין ישראל ארץ ובני, קידושין טבעת" טבעת קידושין", and his explanation follows that reading. But all other versions have the *opposite* reading: "אנשי מזרח רואין אין טבעת קידושין, ובני ארץ ישראל רואין טבעת קידושין". See Mordechai Margaliot, ed., *Hahilukim Shebein Anshei Mizrah U'venei Eretz Yisrael*, Jerusalem 5698, pp. 83, 139-140; and B.M. Lewin, *Otzar Hilluf Minhagim*, Jerusalem 5702, pp. 52-54.

3   Idem, *Otzar Hageonim*, VIII, Ketubot, Jerusalem 5699, pp. 18-19, par. 60. The place mentioned is כוראסן.

4   Schauss, *The Lifetime of a Jew*, p. 317, note 192, adopted LG's view without specifically citing him. But, as explained above in note 1, the view LG rejects is based on the correct reading in *Hahilukim*, which connects the ring to Eretz Yisrael - see, for example, Israel Abrahams, *Jewish Life in the Middle Ages*, London 1896, p. 183 and note 2.

5   *Siddur Rav Sa'adiah Gaon*, Jerusalem 5701, p. 97.

6   For the Yemenite custom, see Ya'akov Sapir, *Even Sapir*, I, Lyck 1866, fol. 81b; and R. Yosef Kafah, *Halikhot Teiman*, Jerusalem 1969[3], p. 142. Also see LG's responsum on grape juice in the Hebrew section of this volume, note 37, and the recent discussion by Daniel Sperber in his *Minhagei Yisrael*, II, Jerusalem 1991, pp. 222-226.

7   I consulted with Prof. Menahem Ben-Sasson of the Hebrew University, an expert on Jews in the Islamic world, but he was unable to find any corroboration of this statement.

8   The Hebrew words are missing from the carbon copy in the LGA.

No. 7 Weddings on Hol Hamoed Sukkot (EH 64:6 and OH 546:1)
Source: LGA, Box 9, "Minkin" file

Western Union
Telegram

1924 Oct. 4 PM 7:27

ROCHESTER NY4
PROFESSOR LOUIS GINZBERG
568 WEST 149 ST NEW YORK NY

BIRMINGHAM ALABAMA BOY MARRIES ROCHESTER GIRL OCTOBER FIFTEENTH.[1] DATE INNOCENTLY CHOSEN BUT APPROVED BY REFORM RABBI COMING TO OFFICIATE. ARRANGEMENTS MADE. CHANGE IMPOSSIBLE. AM ASKED TO ASSIST IN CEREMONY. KNOW ORTHODOX STAND BUT WILL CONSERVATIVE JUDAISM TAKE A MORE LENIENT VIEW. WIRE BY WESTERN UNION IMMEDIATELY COLLECT. HOLIDAY GREETINGS TO FAMILY AND YOURSELF.

JACOB S. MINKIN[2]

Rp: cannot permit. LG.[3]

1   I have added periods for the sake of clarity. October 15, 1924 was the first day of *Hol Hamoed Sukkot* - see *EJ*, I, p. 111. According to *Mishnah Moed Katan* 1:7 and the *Shulhan Arukh*, it is forbidden to marry on *Hol Hamoed* "so as not to mix one joyous occasion with another".

2   Rabbi Jacob S. Minkin (1885-1962) was ordained by the Seminary in 1910. Between 1919 and 1929 he was rabbi of Temple Beth El in Rochester, New York - see Nadell, pp. 190-191. He appears in a photograph with LG in *Keeper* on the seventh page of photographs after p. 214. For his eulogy of LG, see the article listed in the Introduction, note 1.

3   This line is handwritten and must have been LG's instruction to his secretary.

No. 8 Weddings on Hol Hamoed Sukkot for Soldiers Leaving for Overseas (EH 64:6 and OH 546:1)[1]

Source: CJLS Box, "Nissuin and Gittin" file

Question: I've had a case recently involving the application of the principle of אין מערבין שמחה בשמחה[2] with regard to officiating at a wedding during *Hol Hamoed Sukkot*. Knowing what the law is in this matter,[3] I would like to know what the prevailing practice is among conservative rabbis, and, also, whether exceptions can be made in case of emergency. Personally I feel that in a case involving a man in the armed forces, if he was planning for some time to get married, and received a furlough that falls during *Hol Hamoed Sukkot*, and the wedding could not be performed at any other time, I would be lenient and officiate. If, however, there is a possibility of setting a date before or after the holiday, I would refuse to officiate.

In the case in question, I refused to officiate because there was a possibility of having the wedding between *Yom Kippur* and *Sukkot*. As it turned out, however, the wedding did take place during *Hol Hamoed Sukkot* and officiating were two Conservative rabbis. This, of course, put me in a very embarrassing position with regard to my congregation.

It seems to me that some guidance should be given to our men in meeting situations of [this] nature, for this is not the first time that this has occurred. I have had several cases where parties have come to me during *Sefirah*, asking me to officiate at weddings, and although I felt strongly inclined to be lenient because of the emergency nature of each case, I did not have the courage to buck up against an accepted practice or law.[4] If we could arrive at some consensus of opinion regarding such matters, it would be very helpful to all of us. And then, if anyone wishes to diverge from this opinion, he would, of course, do so on his own responsibility.

Answer: In reply to your letter relative to the performance of a marriage ceremony during the *Hol Ha-Moed* period, I wish to inform you that Professor Ginzburg had given permission to one of our alumni to perform a marriage ceremony on *Hol Ha-Moed* for a soldier who was leaving for overseas immediately after the Holiday. In such an emergency, you may follow the same precedent. The same rule would naturally apply to the period of *Sefirah*.[5]

---

1   This responsum is from 1946 or 1947 - see Boaz Cohen, *PRA* 11 (1947), p. 61.

2   "Not mixing one joyous occasion with another" - see above, No. 7, note 1.

3   Ibid.

4   Regarding marriages during *sefirah* (i.e., between *Pesach* and *Shavuot*), see OH 493;
David Feldman, *PRA* 26 (1962), pp. 201-224; and David Golinkin, *Conservative Judaism* 37/4
(Summer, 1984), pp. 59-60.
5   For lenient opinions regarding *sefirah*, see Binyamin Adler, *Hanissuin K'hilkhatam*,
Jerusalem 5745[2], p. 176.

No. 9 Remarriage without a Get If the First Wife Was a Transgressor (EH 115:1)

Source: General Files, File 2 (1931-33)

May 5, 1932

Dear Rabbi Cohen:[1]

I am afraid that this letter will be a great disappointment to you. After a careful study of the case I came to the conclusion that the evidence is not strong enough to permit the husband to marry without giving his first wife a bill of divorce in accordance with Jewish law. The fact that once his wife attempted to serve meat without having it soaked and salted[2] is not sufficient ground for granting him the privilege of a second marriage, especially as the husband is the only witness for the alleged fact.[3]

Though the Passover has passed already, I wish to reply to your question with regard to the use of green peas and string beans on Passover.[4] There is not the slightest reason why they should not be used as by no stretch of the imagination could they be classified as belonging to [קטניות] which refers to dry peas or beans exclusively. That there is not the slightest objection to the use of fresh tomatoes for Passover goes without saying. I assume that your local rabbi who prohibited their use shares his dislike for them with you. I don't use them not only on Passover, but on any other holiday neither.

Very sincerely yours,

LOUIS GINZBERG

Rabbi [Herman] M. Cohen[5]
799 Ashland Avenue
St. Paul, Minn.

1   See below, note 5.
2   See YD 69:1ff.
3   See EH 115:1.

4   For the notes to this paragraph, see Chapter III, No. 18.
5   The secretary typed *Harry* M. Cohen but that is a typographical error. Rabbi *Herman* M.
Cohen (1888-1970) was ordained by the Seminary in 1913 and was rabbi of Temple of Aaron at
the address listed in 1932-33 - see *PRA* 4 (1930-32), p. 384. Also see *Students' Annual* 3 (1916), p.
189; and *EJ*, XII, col. 38.

No. 10 A Protest against the Laxity with which Jewish Divorce is Practiced (EH 119ff.)

Source: Box 17, "Questions and Answers" file = *Exponent*
Excerpt: *Keeper*, pp. 224-225

...To turn home from the synagogue, you may be interested to hear that the Chairman of your Committee[1] came before the Court of Domestic Relations - not in his private capacity - but to give his opinion in a very complicated question of Jewish divorce law. I shall not enter into a discussion of the fine technicalities of the law involved in the case, but I cannot help mentioning the distressing effect it had upon me in bringing home to me in a very tangible form the laxity with which Jewish divorce law is practiced. Judaism never taught the indissolubility of marriage; of the Torah it is said: "Her ways are ways of pleasantness and all her paths are peace" [Proverbs 3:17]. Hence rather peace without union than union without peace.

But only one entirely ignorant of the spirit of Judaism as developed in the course of its glorious history could sanction such laxity in the domain of law as practiced by some of those who claim to hold the monopoly upon the true guardianship of Judaism.[2] It is time that the rabbis who are members of the United Synagogue call a halt to this disgraceful practice.

1   I.e., Louis Ginzberg.
2   He is apparently criticizing Orthodox rabbis who execute *gittin* in a sloppy fashion.

No. 11 Giving a Get without Documentary Evidence of a Civil Divorce (EH 119 ff.)

Source: LGA, Box 17, "Questions and Answers" file = *USR* 1/3 (July, 1921), p. 7

Excerpt: *Keeper*, pp. 224-225

The Get Question

The Association of Reform Rabbis in New York City and vicinity requested the United Synagogue to pass the following resolution: "RESOLVED that [under] no circumstance is any Rabbi to give a religious divorce (*GET*), unless he has documentary evidence that the civil marriage has been annulled or a divorce has been given to the parties concerned by a competent court of any State of the Union. Furthermore, that no rabbi is to undertake, in any way, to evade the law of the State by giving a Jewish divorce, whose complete validity, with permission of re-marriage, is necessarily dependent on the issue of a civil divorce".

This resolution was referred to the Committee on the Interpretation of Jewish Law, which has decided that while the United Synagogue is in full sympathy with any undertaking to suppress the abuse of the "*Get* Mills", still the form in which this resolution is worded is hardly acceptable, as this would make it impossible for a Rabbi to forward a *Get* to a country where Jewish divorce is recognized by the State.[1] It was therefore suggested to have the resolution somewhat modified to the effect that the Rabbis may be permitted to send a *Get* to those States [= countries] where it is recognized by the civil courts.

---

1   E.g., Austria and Russia at the beginning of this century - see *UJE*, III, p. 580.

No. 12 Is a Woman Divorced by a Get without a Civil Decree Considered Divorced? (EH 119ff.)

Source: LGA, Box 8, "Kugel" file
Excerpt (almost complete): *Keeper*, pp. 223-224

October 13, 1947

Dear Mr. Kugel:

I shall not fail to put down into writing the answer I gave you to your question concerning the Jewish law of divorce.

Marriages and divorces are, according to Jewish belief, religious institutions, and their validity is dependent exclusively on their being performed in accordance with Jewish law. People married according to the "law of Moses [and] Israel" can only be divorced by a Bill of Divorce known as a *Get*. Once the *Get* is properly executed, the husband and wife are free to marry whomever they wish. Of course, it is understood that a Jewish court would never perform a divorce as long as the law of the state in which [the couple] resides has not declared the couple divorced according to the state law. The validity of the *Get*, however, is not dependent upon civil law.

Whether, according to French law, the Rabbi of Paris who executed the divorce of the Polish woman residing in France acted in accordance with French law is a matter to be decided by French lawyers and not by me. As far as Jewish law is concerned, the divorce is valid.

May I add that, according to Jewish law, the woman claiming [to have] been divorced must prove her statement by reliable witnesses or by her former husband.[1]

Sincerely yours,

Louis Ginzberg

Joseph L. Kugel, Esq.
521 Fifth Avenue
New York 17, New York

---

1   See EH 152.

No. 13 Agency Appointment for a Soldier Going Off to War (EH 144:5)

Source: LGA, Box 17, "Rabbinical Assembly Material" file contains most of the material. Box 18, "Boaz Cohen" file contains the letters from July 17 and Nov. 24, 1942.

Secondary Literature:
1. *PRA* 8 (1941-44), pp. 143-144
2. *Bulletin of the Rabbinical Assembly* (April, 1951), p. 3
3. Isaac Klein, *A Guide to Jewish Religious Practice*, New York 1979, pp. 454-455, 457-460

Comment: On June 30, 1942, the Rabbinical Assembly of America, at its annual convention, adopted the proposal of the Committee on Jewish Law that a husband going off to war appoint the members of the Central Bet Din of the Rabbinical Assembly as his *shelihim* to execute a *get* should his whereabouts remain unknown for three years after the general demobilization of the Armed Forces of the United States. The *shetar* was prepared by Rabbi Boaz Cohen and circulated to all of the members of the Rabbinical Assembly in November, 1942. Rabbi Cohen repeatedly emphasized that the proposal was prepared under the guidance of LG. The Hebrew and English *shetarot* have been reprinted by Rabbi Klein. We are printing below a few of the letters which emphasize the halakhic role played by LG.

THE JEWISH THEOLOGICAL SEMINARY OF AMERICA
NORTHEAST CORNER, BROADWAY AND 122ND STREET
NEW YORK CITY

July 17, 1942

Dear Professor Ginzberg,

I was glad indeed to hear from you and to learn that you are well settled. I trust that the second batch of books reached you safely too....[1]

I am enclosing several papers concerning the *Agunah*. I would appreciate it if you could read them through and let me have your criticisms and approval before we send it to the printer. We have made some slight changes in the Hebrew מנוי שליחות.[2] We have omitted the clause pertaining to the civil decree but inserted it in the English.

I expect to join Doctor Gandz[3] at Fleischman's at the beginning of August and remain there for about two weeks.

Wishing you and Mrs. Ginzberg a pleasant and profitable summer, I am

Cordially yours,

Boaz Cohen[4]

Professor Louis Ginzberg
East Pond
Oakland, Maine[5]

~ ~ ~

THE RABBINICAL ASSEMBLY OF AMERICA
3080 BROADWAY
NEW YORK CITY

Louis M. Levitsky, President
    Newark, N.J.
Robert Gordis, Vice President
    Belle Harbor, N.Y.
Harry E. Schwartz, Treasurer
    Hempstead, N.Y.
Lewis B. Grossman, Rec. Sec'y
    Mt. Vernon, N.Y.
Maxwell M. Farber, Cor. Sec'y
    Philadelphia, Pa.

November 24, 1942

Dear Professor Ginzberg:

Under separate cover, we are sending you a copy of the *Shetar Minuy Shelihut*[6] with literature appertaining thereto, which is also being sent to all the alumni.

I wish to take this opportunity to thank you in the name of the Committee on Jewish Law for the great assistance which we have received from you in this undertaking. It goes without saying that we would not have been able to carry this proposal into effect without your sanction.

I have just learned that Sophie has given birth to a baby boy, and I wish to extend my heartiest congratulations to you, Mrs. Ginzberg and the family on this happy occasion.[7]

With kindest regards, I remain

Cordially yours,

Boaz Cohen, Chairman
Committee on Jewish Law

Professor Louis Ginzberg
514 W. 114 Street
New York City

1   LG used to spend every summer in Maine - see above, Chapter II, No. 6, note 6. Boaz Cohen had sent him a package of books from New York.
2   = agency appointment.
3   Dr. Solomon Gandz (1887-1954) was a noted expert on the Jewish calendar. See below, Chapter VI, Nos. 17-18; *EJ*, VII, col. 309; and *Keeper*, pp. 184, 317, 319.
4   Prof. Boaz Cohen (1899-1968) was one of the foremost halakhic authorities of the Conservative Movement. See above in the Introduction, note 119.
5   See above, note 1.
6   See above, note 2.
7   See *Keeper*, p. 263.

VI. Miscellaneous Responsa

No. 1 A Reply to Mr. Paranaitis Concerning the Blood Libel
at Kiev (1913)   231

No. 2 A Reply to Mr. Szacki (1919)   253

No. 3 The Jewish Attitude Towards the Crippled (1938)   263

No. 4 Why was the Palestinian Talmud Never Translated
into English? (1940)   265

No. 5 The Denial of Religious Services to an Unaffiliated
Jew (1940)   267

No. 6 Which Midrash Asks Why the Decalogue Does not
Mention God's Role as Creator of the Universe? (1943)   269

No. 7 Women on Synagogue Boards (1944)   270

No. 8 The Languages of the Jews in Ancient Times (1944)   272

No. 9 Ordination in Ancient Times (1946)   273

No. 10 Four Miscellaneous Questions (1947)   277

No. 11 The Legal Responsibility of a Married Woman (1948)   281

No. 12 Impeachment in Talmudic Literature (1949)   283

No. 13 The Inscription on a Parokhet (1949)   284

No. 14 Three Miscellaneous Questions (1950)   286

No. 15 Two Miscellaneous Questions (1951)   287

No. 16 The Numbers in Daniel (1951)   288

No. 17 The Civil Calendar Date of Yom Kippur in 1844 (1952) 289

No. 18 The Fixing of the Jewish Calendar (1952)   290

No. 19 The Renewal of the Sanhedrin (undated)   293

No. 1 A Reply to Mr. Paranaitis Concerning the Blood Libel at Kiev (1913)

Sources:
1. LGA, Box 9, "Marshall" - the two letters and the responsum
2. LGA, Box 16, in a separate file - the responsum without the letters
Excerpt: *Keeper*, pp. 216-218
Background Reading:
1. For Louis Marshall's efforts on behalf of Russian Jewry and Mendel Beiliss, see Charles Reznikoff, ed., *Louis Marshall Champion of Liberty: Selected Papers and Addresses*, II, Philadelphia 1957, p. 674.
2. For detailed accounts of the Beiliss trial, see Maurice Samuel, *Blood Accusation: The Strange History of the Beiliss Case*, New York 1966 (hereafter: Samuel); and Ezekiel Leikin, *The Beilis Transcripts: The Anti-Semitic Trial that Shook the World, Northvale*, N.J. 1993, esp. pp. 14-16, 39, 224-225.

47 East 72nd Street

Oct. 28,1913[1]

Dear Professor Ginzberg:

Among the testimony which is to be given by the prosecutor in the Beiliss case at Kiev, is that of a Roman Catholic monk Pranaitis,[2] of which I have received in strict confidence an advance copy.[3] It is possible that the Russian press agency may attempt to give it publicity, and for that reason we may find it desirable to establish its falsity. As you will see, stress is laid on alleged excerpts from the Talmud, from Maimonides, the *Zohar*, and various Chassidistic and Kabbalistic writings. No doubt you are familiar with the substance of this article, since it is a rehash from Eisenmonger[4] and other scoundrels of similar type. If you can, without devoting too much time, give me the benefit of your views and a sketch of such an answer as would impress the average reader, written in popular style, I would greatly appreciate it. You will, of course, recognize the importance of prompt action since this vile stuff may be given publicity shortly.

With best regards I am very truly yours,

Louis Marshall[5]

~ ~ ~

AUGUST DILLMANN, the famous oriental scholar and Professor of Hebrew at Berlin University,[6] once remarked: "I do not see any use in refuting the Blood-Accusation; those who spread it do not believe it, and the fanatic [mob][7] who believe it do not read the refutation, nor would it have any weight with them if they would read it". Undoubtedly this remark is correct. It is certainly a waste of time to attempt to prove the incredibility of an incredible thing. The Beiliss affair, however, throws so many interesting side-lights upon the political and cultural life of the biggest Empire of modern times, that it may be worthwhile to examine the expert opinion utilized by the Russian Government to prove the Blood-Accusation.

At the very beginning we consider it our duty to protest strongly against the charges hurled in the American and European press that the Russian Government is reviving medieval barbarism in the Twentieth Century. A superficial examination of the tactics of the Russian Government and that used in the first "practically applied" case of ritual murder will suffice to do away with this unjust outcry against medieval Russia.

The first case of ritual murder known to history is that of the year 1171, when Count Theobold of Chartres, France accused the Jews of Blois of having crucified a Christian boy.[8] This noble Count was by no means an enemy of the Jews, but his treasury happened to be at a very low ebb, and the blood accusation seemed to him to be the best way by which to refill it. Unfortunately for the Count, and still more so for the Jews of Blois, the fanatic mob preferred to take the life with the money, and fifty Jews[9] died at the stake after their guilt was proved by ordeal. Their accuser was set in a [tub] filled with holy water - of course not too much of this precious liquid was squandered - and as he did not sink, nobody could doubt any more his veracity. In view of these facts, who would now accuse the Russian Government of medieval barbarism! It certainly has no intentions whatsoever [of extorting] money from the Jews. Russian Jewry is too poor for such a purpose. All that the Government is trying to do is to discredit the Jews in the eyes of the world so that the cry of the Liberals for equal rights or at least for the amelioration of the condition of the Jews cease[s]. It is true, the fanatic masses may be carried away by the accusation, and murder Jewish men, violate Jewish women and maim Jewish children. But such outrage can be laid at the door of the Russian Government, as little as the noble Count of Chartres can be blamed for the fifty Jews burned at the stake in Blois. He certainly would have preferred the money of the Jews than their life. Enlightened Russia is far from approving medieval practices in establishing the truth [by an ordeal]. Instead of that, it adopts the modern ways of looking for "experts". And when they [could not] find among the hundred million and more inhabitants of European Russia an expert to please them, they did not spare either labor or expense till they found one in Asiatic Turkestan in the person of the Monk Paranaitis. The truth of the saying *"ex oriente lux"*[10] was again vindicated by this monk, who puts to shame all the great scholars of Europe and America. Their refutation of the Blood-Accusation is simply due to their ignorance, while the "learned monk" was able to find in the Jewish writings direct evidence for ritual murder. And now let us examine the "expert opinion" of the learned Paranaitis.

It is out of respect for the Russian Government that we speak of the opinion of Paranaitis. He is officially the authority upon which the prosecution [at Kiev] based the case of ritual murder. The truth of the matter, however, is that "the learned expert" never examined the sources to which he referred. What he did was to extract verbatim a considerable part of the writings of the notorious Rohling.[11] The great surprise of the Kiev court when the counsel for Beiliss showed that Paranaitis could not read the quotations from the Jewish writings given in his opinion[12] was entirely out of place. A superficial glance at this "expert opinion" should have told them that the author of it has never seen a copy of the Talmud or of the other Rabbinic books quoted by him, and that his Jewish learning consisted of nothing else than his ability to read Rohling. However, this pious monk need not worry about being accused of plagiarism by Rohling. The greatest authorities in the domain of Jewish literature among the Christians, men like Franz Delitzsch, de Lagarde, Noeldeke, Strack, Wunsche, and many other famous scholars, long ago proved Rohling's ignorance, mendacity and absolute lack of sense.[13] He certainly has now no desire to lay claim to all the absurdities and lies in the Paranaitis "opinion". But our sense of justice prompts us to apply the principle *"suum cuique"*,[14] even to a man like Rohling, and we therefore call attention to this most flagrant case of plagiarism committed by Paranaitis.

Following in the footsteps of his master Rohling, he commits in this "expert opinion" all the mistakes, distortion of facts and falsehoods known to us from Rohling's and other anti-semitic writings. Here are a few examples of this triad of ignorance, malice, and mendacity. Having the word of the poet in his mind, "Hates any man the thing he would not kill", Paranaitis starts to prove his thesis of the ritual murder by showing how deep the hatred of the Jews is against Christianity and its founder. The Jews blaspheme Jesus and deride the Christians in their daily prayers by praising God that he did not make Israel like the other nations, "who prostrate themselves before that which is vain and to no purpose, to a god that cannot save".[15] It is quite clear, says Paranaitis, that "the god that cannot save" is Jesus, the meaning of that name in Hebrew is "Savior" whom the Jews deride as a "god that cannot save". We do not know whether the order to which this monk belongs prohibits the reading of the Bible; we are rather inclined to assume it. Otherwise we would be at a loss to understand how one acquainted with the Bible would not recognize that the sentence quoted in the Jewish prayer is literally taken from Isaiah 30:7 and 45:20. Or does Paranaitis believe that this Prophet, living several centuries before the founder of Christianity, was one of the Jesus-blaspheming and Christian-cursing Jews! By the way, it is quite probable that the prayer under discussion dates from pre-Christian times, and at all events was composed at a time when the Persian rulers still styled themselves "Kings of Kings", wherefore God is described in this prayer as a "King of Kings of Kings".[16] Of course, we do not expect a Turkestan Monk to be at home in Jewish history and literature, but it is rather astonishing to find that he does not know either the New Testament or the history of his own Church.

The German-Russian Jews call Christmas *Nital* from the medieval Latin *Natale (Domini)*;[17] the French "Noel" is of the same origin. For Paranaitis, *Nital* expresses a blasphemy against Jesus![18] Is it thinkable that a priest should not know the Latin for Christmas? Of course we have to admit, we have no knowledge of the education of the Turkestan priesthood, and it is perhaps possible that Paranaitis does know Latin. More difficult is it, however, to assume that a priest, and be he even from Turkestan, does not know the New Testament. His remarks about *Am Haaretz* (ignoramus) in the Talmud prove plainly that he is not acquainted with the words of St. John (7:49) about "the people who knoweth not the law who are cursed". Only a thorough *Am Haaretz* (ignoramus) can translate *Am Haaretz* with Gentile, while it never describes anybody else but the ignorant and at the same time immoral element of the Jewish nation, or as St. John says, "the people who knoweth not the law". It is therefore of no purpose to discuss the statements quoted by Paranaitis from the Talmud concerning *Am Haaretz*,[19] as they have absolutely no bearing on the question before us, the relation of the Jew to the Gentile. The attitude of the Rabbis towards the ignorant and uncultured class of their own people was not a kind one, though their sayings touching upon this matter are entirely misunderstood by Paranaitis. But as said before, this has nothing to do with the question before us.

We are afraid, however, that we do some injustice to the pious monk. Ignorant as he certainly is, he may still know that *Nital* is not a Hebrew curse but the Latin for Christmas,[20] and further that the Rabbis in speaking of the *Am Haaretz* do refer to the ignorant Jew and not to the Gentile. But knowing all this and something beside, he nevertheless does not hesitate to tell deliberate lies. We have abundant proof that his mendacity is not inferior to his ignorance. The testimony of converted Jews against the Blood Accusation, says Paranaitis, is of very little weight, as these converts may have turned Christian for the sole purpose to be better able to defend Judaism and attack Christianity.[21] The monstrosity of this statement is obvious! Imagine Paulus Burgensis, a Primate of Spain, and one of the bitterest enemies of his former co-religionists;[22] Pfefferkorn, who after turning Christian, spent his life in denouncing the Jews and who nearly succeeded in having all Jewish books burned at the stake;[23] or Stahl, [who though] himself a Hebrew, [is] the spiritual father of modern anti-Semitism in Germany[24] - imagine them being described as fanatical Jews who accepted Christianity that under this cloak they may be able to defend the ritual murder, the existence of which was known to them!

But we are not interested in these mad fantasies of Paranaitis. We want only to call attention to his deliberate lies. To corroborate his statement about the duplicity and unreliability of Jewish converts, he quotes the following passage from the *Shulhan Aruch*, the Rabbinical code of law: "It is permitted to a Jew to deceive the Gentiles by telling them that he is one of them." Ergo, says Paranaitis, it is the teaching of Rabbinism that [it] is permissible to turn Christian if it is only a blind. Section and paragraph of the quoted code are given correctly, but the text reads as follows: "A Jew is *not* permitted to say that he is a Gentile, *not even to save his life by it*".[25] Ergo, the statement of Paranaitis, according to which Rabbinism permits the Jew to change his religion as a blind, is a deliberate lie.

One must not think, however, that the pious monk manufactures only quotations from Hebrew writers. With the very same ease, he quotes passages from the Church Fathers which either do not exist at all, or which read entirely differently. St. Agobardus, Bishop of Lyons, France in the beginning of the ninth century, is introduced as a witness for the ritual murder, and as source for this statement this Church Father's writings against the Jews, *De Insolentia Judaeorum* and *De Judaicis Superstisionibus* are given.[26] St. Agobardus was perhaps the bitterest opponent of Jews and Judaism among the Church Fathers. He accuses the Jews of many crimes - of trafficking [in] Christian slaves and of selling to the Christians unclean meat - but not one word is found in his writings which could even by a stretch of the wildest imagination be taken to refer to the Blood-Accusation.[27] Of course, Paranaitis is too ignorant to have manufactured this quotation himself. We doubt if he ever has seen the writings of Agobardus. He only copies Rohling, but not mentioning the fact of which he is certainly aware that Professor Weinreich, a famous Christian scholar and an acknowledged authority in the

Patristic literature,[28] declared under oath that Rohling lied when he quoted St. Agobardus as a witness for the ritual murder.

In view of these examples of ignorance and gross indifference to truth displayed by Paranaitis in his "expert opinion", we think it entirely unnecessary to enter into a further discussion with him on the legal status of the Gentiles according to Talmudic law. The whole question is for us of no purpose since the Talmud, with the exception of two passages where reference is made to the Christian celebration of Sunday, never mentions Christians.[29] Such eminent Christian Hebraists, as Delitzsch[30] and others, even reproach the Talmud for not having taken any notice of Christianity, and this, they claim, shows that the Rabbis had no understanding for the great historical importance of the [oldest] daughter-religion of Judaism. The Rabbis in post-Talmudic times decided that the Talmudic laws against the heathens do not apply to Christians and Mohammedans.[31] They could not [possibly hold any] different [opinion] in view of what is said in the Talmud concerning the "Proselyte at the Gate", who is equal before the law with the Jew.[32] Under this term, the Talmud understands the Gentile who observes the following seven laws which, according to the Rabbis, are incumbent upon all mankind, while the rest of the Mosaic laws were given to Israel only. These laws are:

1. Not to worship idols
2. Not to blaspheme the name of God
3. Not to commit incest or adultery
4. Not to murder
5. Not to rob or steal
6. Not to tear an animal's limbs while it is still alive, and eat the meat thereof
7. To establish Courts of Justice, that law and order may be maintained.

Any man who subscribes to these laws is to be regarded as our brother, and the Jews are obliged not only to protect him against any kind of injury, but also to support and maintain him, if necessary. According to the opinions of the Rabbis, the Biblical commandment "One Law and one manner shall be for you and for the stranger that sojourneth with you" [Numbers 15:16] refers to him. Accordingly, if even all the Christians were like our pious monk - which they fortunately are not - the Rabbis could not help but classify them as "Proselytes at the Gate" who are to be treated as our brethren.

The Rabbis maintained that the idol-worshippers who knew neither law nor morals were not to share the entire benefit of the Mosaic law. This view is shared by all Biblical scholars, Catholic as well as Protestant. They all are of the same opinion that the Biblical laws, as any other ancient system of law, primarily deal with the relation of members of the same nation to each other. And, if any reproach is due here, it is the Bible and not the Rabbis who deserve it. It is perhaps not out of place to quote the following words of Joseph Kohler, the greatest authority on comparative jurisprudence in Germany:[33]

The view that strangers are, more or less, not within the sphere of law, is common to all mankind; it is found in antiquity and continued till the Middle Ages; yea, till modern times.

It is, however, a diabolical lie to maintain that the Rabbis would permit to rob or slay a heathen. They strongly prohibit one as the other, except that no capital punishment is set on the murder of a heathen.[34] Yet, even this exception is not to be taken as expressing their view on the inferiority of the life of a heathen, but it is a natural consequence of the pronounced aversion of the Rabbis to capital punishment. "A court that once in seventy years sentenced a man to death is a murderous court" is a well known saying of the Rabbis.[35] If it were possible, they would have abolished capital punishment entirely, but the Bible does recognize this severe punishment as just, and the Rabbis never claimed the authority to abrogate the word of God.[36] They nevertheless developed a criminal code which practically makes capital punishment impossible. And as the Bible never mentions capital punishment in connection with the murder of a heathen, the Rabbis had no reason to extend a law that was extremely distasteful to them to new cases.

How the Rabbis thought about the value of human life, be it that of a Jew or of a heathen, is best illustrated by the following saying of the famous Rabbi, Ben Azzai, who lived in the beginning of the second century. The earlier teachers in Israel, Hillel and R. Akiba, had declared the Golden Rule as the greatest fundamental principle of Judaism.[37] Ben Azzai, however, remarked: "The basic principle of Judaism is given in the words of the Scriptures (Genesis 5:1): 'In the day that God created *man*, in the likeness of God made He him'".[38] Man, Hebrew or Gentile, Jew or Heathen, is [made in] the image of God, and is, as such, a sacred being. How does this teaching of the Rabbis compare with that of pagan philosophers when dealing with the barbarian or Medieval Christianity in treating unbelievers! Of course, "la guerre comme a la guerre!"[39] In times of intense national struggle, the humane teachings of Rabbinical Judaism were sometimes obscured; hatred and national animosity reigned supreme. A rabbi who had suffered greatly from the Romans, living during the Hadrianic persecutions when the Jewish nation and the Jewish religion were threatened with extinction, once remarked: "The best among the Gentiles deserve to be killed".[40] Certainly a harsh word, but by far less so than the utterances against the Roman Empire by the Church Fathers at that time. Yea, the hatred of Christians against Christians was at times as strong as that of the Jews against the Romans. Baldwin the First, who in the year 1204 became Emperor of Constantinople, writes to Pope Innocent the [Third]: "The Greek Christians call all Franks (i.e., the Crusaders from Middle and Western Europe) dogs, and consider it a pious act to shed their blood". Ergo,[41] the Greek Orthodox Church of today, preaches and teaches the murder of all Christians who do not belong to it!

Of course, it would be too much to expect any sense of humor from Paranaitis, and we therefore explained the anti-Roman saying of the rabbi as if it were meant literally. The truth of the matter, however, is that the words "the best among the Gentiles deserve to be killed" [are] only an emphatic way of expressing his intense dislike of the Romans, just as a modern man in a similar mood would explain, for instance: "the best among the Mexicans may go to ...". One needs only to see the context in which this statement occurs to be convinced of the correctness of this explanation. R. Simon says: "The best among physicians is destined for Gehenna; the best among women is a witch; the best among the Gentiles deserve to be killed; and the best of serpents to have his head crushed".[42] If taken literally, this rabbi would teach, not only the murder of Gentiles, but also that of his own mother and wife! Witchcraft is a capital offense according to Biblical law, and if all women, even the best among them, are witches, the consequence would be that the extermination of women would be a meritorious act!

For those who are acquainted with the style of the Talmud, this hyperbolic way of expression is not at all strange. For the benefit of the "learned priest", for whom the Talmud is undoubtedly a book with seven seals, we will quote a few sayings from it which will give him an idea of this peculiarity of style: "A scholar", says the Talmud, "on whose garment is found a stain, is guilty of death".[43] Jewish history is not an occult science. It is studied by many, but the most thorough-going research has failed to bring to light a case of a rabbi killed by his parishioners on account of his filthy attire! The sanitary rule to wash oneself in the morning is taught in Talmud as follows: "The unwashed hand that touches the eye should be cut off, the unwashed hand that touches the mouth should be cut off, the unwashed hand that touches the ear should be cut off".....[44] It is not known to us that the percentage of one-handed people among the Jews is larger than among the other nations!

But now, enough of the Talmud since, even according to Paranaitis, it only recommends the killing of Gentiles, but does not yet know the ritual murderer. This, as "the learned priest" tells us, or to be correct, his master Rohling, is found only in the *Cabala*, the mystic lore of the Jews. Great as his display of learning is in the domain of the Talmud, his knowledge of the *Cabala* is still greater. Here are a few examples of his Cabalistic knowledge:

In a poetical description of Paradise, in the Cabalistic book of the *Zohar*, we read:

In the fourth hall of Paradise are the mourners of Zion and Jerusalem, *as well as those killed by the idolatrous nations*. The Messiah weeps over them, but all the princes of the seed of David take hold of him and try to console him....The Messiah then ascends to Heaven, where he remains until the day of the New Moon, when he descends again. With him many lights descend, which light all the halls of Paradise and bring healing and splendor to all the martyrs and to those who suffer illness and pain with the Messiah, to atone by it the sins of Israel. The Messiah clothes himself with a purple mantle upon which the names of all the martyrs are recorded.....In the innermost [part] of the fourth hall of Paradise, are the ten great scholars, R. Akiba and his Colleagues.[45]

One must admit that only such ingenious scholars of the type of Rohling-Paranaitis can detect the ritual murder in this description of Paradise. By means of a critical emendation, "*those killed*" is changed to "*those who kill*", and "*the Christians*" are put in the place of "*the idolatrous nations*". Accordingly, does the *Cabala* provide a place of honor in Paradise for the murderers of Christians! Yet the Messiah seems to be a friend of the Christians, as he weeps over their fate [of having] been murdered by the Jews! What we do not understand is that the Messiah should have chosen the company of the murderers to weep over their victims. No less strange is that R. Akiba and his colleagues - the so-called ten martyrs, murdered by the Romans during the Hadrianic persecutions - should be made to share the same [division] in Paradise with those who killed Gentiles. Masters of the *Cabala*, as Rohling and Paranaitis are, they might have been able to explain all these difficulties. What a pity that the mystical description of Paradise in the *Zohar* is found also in other Rabbinic [writings] and in such a manner that no ingenuity is able to confuse the passive with the active form.[46] The purple mantle with the names of the martyrs inscribed upon it is also well known to Jewish legend,[47]and it must [therefore] be admitted that the *Zohar* speaks of Jewish *martyrs* and not of Jewish *murderers*.

We must confess that we do not understand the necessity for this great display of ingenuity on the part of Paranaitis. The ritual murder is, as he assures us, so frequently referred to in Jewish writings, and in such very plain language, that he ought to have disregarded all those passages where his thesis can be proved only by higher criticism (we were on the point of saying: higher nonsense). Do we need plainer words than those of the Cabalist who writes: "Take [the] life of [the] *Kelipot*, and the *Shechinah* will account it to you as if you would have brought incense".[48] Would anybody doubt that under *Kelipot* are meant the Christians, the murder of whom is plainly described as a sacrificial act! It is true, even one who has only a smattering of the *Cabala* knows that the *Kelipot*, "shells", stand for the material world which the Cabalists tell us is evil, and therefore man is admonished to combat the material. The changing of the material into the spiritual, or, to use the Cabalistic phraseology, "the killing of the shells", is the only purpose in life, according to the Cabalists; and not the killing of Gentiles, as Paranaitis would have it. But nobody expects "the Turkestan sage" to know anything about the terminology of the *Cabala*. And were it not for the fact that in another passage he betrays himself, we might have been inclined to ascribe his identification of the *Kelipot* with the Christians, to his ignorance rather than to his mendacity. But "liars must have good memories". Paranaitis first translates *Kelipot* by Christians, but later forgets himself and gives the correct translation.[49] Or are we to assume that Paranaitis had made use of two different sources, the *Kelipot*-Christians he took from his master Rohling, and the *Kelipot*-material world, he took from another, [a] reliable source!

The famous passage about "the blood of virgins", which made Rohling the laughing stock of all scholars, is not missing in Paranaitis' opinion.[50] He even has the effrontery to argue with Franz Delitzsch, who fiercely denounced Rohling for his mendacity, and tries to defend Rohling's translation of "*dam betulim*" by "blood of virgins". It may not be out of place to explain the Cabalistic passage where this expression occurs.

The four riddles which the wise king (Proverbs 30:18ff.) said that he could not solve, are explained by the Cabalist allegorically. The Cabalists maintain that creation was made possible only by the union of the divine masculine principle of love with the divine feminine principle of justice. The problem which Solomon confessed not to be able to solve is the mystery of the origin of the feminine principle, that of strict justice, or [to quote the Cabalists]: "It is in love that the secret of divine unity is found; it is love that unites the higher and lower stages, and that lifts everything to that stage where all must be one". Strict justice, or, to use the Cabalistic terminology, the origin of "*dam betulim*", "the divine feminine principle", is an indissoluble problem. By the way, the passage on "the blood of virgins" is taken from the works of the Cabalist Vital,[51] who describes as one of the conditions for the acquiring of the gift of the holy spirit "love all creatures, Jew or Gentile". It would be a very unusual way of love to have one's love murdered.

Luria, the master of Vital, was careful not to kill any living creature, not even an insect or worm,[52] and from the writings of this saint, Paranaitis quotes the statement that it is the duty of a Jew to kill the Gentiles as Moses killed the Egyptian.[53] Of course, Luria maintains just the opposite of that ascribed to him by Paranaitis. He says: "Moses brought upon himself a deadly sin by killing the Egyptian (Exodus 2:12) and he was exiled to a strange land and people to expiate for this". Luria expresses in a Cabalistic [manner] the very same thought we find in other Jewish writings, that human life is so precious, that to destroy it, be it even in the case of necessity, is something for which one will have to answer to his Creator. A [rabbinic] legend tells us of the following dialogue between God and Moses when the latter prayed to be allowed to cross the Jordan: "Was it I, perchance, that counselled thee to slay the Egyptian?" Moses: "Thou didst slay all the firstborn of Egypt, and shall I die on account of one single Egyptian that I slew?" God: "Art thou perchance my equal? I slay and restore to life, but canst thou perchance revive the dead?"[54]

Another legend about the slaying of the Egyptian is that the Egyptian had dishonored the wife of a Hebrew, and when he found out that his crime had come to the knowledge of the injured husband, he, being his taskmaster, goaded him with excessive vigor and dealt him blow after [blow] with intention to kill him. Moses happened [at] the place at which the much-abused and tortured Hebrew was at work. Full of wrath, Moses, whom the Holy Spirit had acquainted with the injury done to the Hebrew by the Egyptian, cried out to the latter, saying: "Not enough that thou hast dishonored this man's wife, thou aimest to kill him too?" Moses, however, still hesitated to take the law in his own hands. He did not know whether the evildoer might not be brought to repentance. He also considered that there would perhaps be some among the descendants to spring from the Egyptian for whose sake the wicked ancestor might rightfully lay claim to clemency. The Holy Spirit allayed all his doubts. He was made to see that not the slightest hope exists that good would come, whether from the malefactor himself, or from any of his offspring. Then Moses was willing to requite him for his evil deeds. Nevertheless, he first consulted the angels, to hear what they had to say, and they agreed that the Egyptian deserved death. And Moses acted according to their opinion. He pronounced the name of God, and the Egyptian was a corpse. So far, the legend.[55] It is in connection with the mode of slaying the Egyptian that Luria makes the remark which Paranaitis distorted in such a fashion as to contain the teaching of the killing of Gentiles. The Cabalists ask: why is it that while Balaam was slain with a *sword* (Numbers 31:8), the wicked Egyptian was slain *by the holy name of God*, and the answer of Luria is: "By the Holy Spirit, Moses knew that the soul of the Egyptian contained a holy spark, and to free this he used the holy name, while Balaam died by his own impure sword".[56]

The following is another illustration of the bloodthirsty teachings of the Cabalists.[57] The Biblical law concerning the firstling of an ass (Exodus 13:13) is explained by them allegorically. The ass is typical of the impure, the evil inclination; the lamb of the pure, the good inclination. Further, the ass, the stupid animal, stands symbolically for the *Am Haaretz*, the ignorant Jew - not Gentile! - who knoweth neither God nor His law; the lamb is the symbol of the true Israelite who obeys God and observes His law. The Biblical verse (ibid.): "and every firstling of an ass thou shalt redeem with a lamb, and if thou wilt not redeem it, then thou shalt break his neck", reads in the Cabalistic allegory: "Change the evil inclination into the good inclination, redeem the ass by the lamb; if thou wilt do it, even if thou art an ignoramus, thou wilt be redeemed from Exile when the lamb, i.e., true Israel, will be redeemed. But, if thou returneth not to God and remaineth stiff-necked, thou art among those who will be stricken from the Book of Life, concerning whom it is said (Exodus 32:33): 'whosoever hath sinned against me, him will I blot out of my book'". This is the Cabalistic passage which, according to Paranaitis-Rohling, teaches the Jew to break the necks of the Gentiles and blot them out of the Book of Life! We never before knew that the Jews are in the possession of the Book of Life. It is rather strange that they do not live forever.

More elaborate than this allegory is that which deals with the Jewish dietary laws, by means of which the *Cabala* teaches that the *Am Haaretz* (the ignorant and non-observant Jew) is doomed if he does not repent of his sins and does not return to God. Their only salvation, the *Zohar* says, is repentance and complete resignation to the will of God, saying: "I can neither open my mouth nor raise my head on account of my sense of guilt". If he confesses daily in this manner, and while declaring the unity of God - the recital of the *Shema* - makes up his mind to be ready to die the death of a martyr if necessary, then God will be with him and his doings.[58] By means of some changes of the text, Paranaitis-Rohling find in this allegory a special ritual prescribed for the murdering of Christians! The *Am Haaretz* is the Christian whose mouth must be closed while murdered. Paranaitis calls attention to the fact that the mouth of the boy found killed in Kiev was plugged and that thirteen wounds were found on the body. Of course, thirteen is the numerical value of the Hebrew "*Ehad*", "one" expressing the unity of God, to which reference is made in the allegory mentioned.[59] Is there anybody who still doubts that the Kiev boy was murdered by the Jews according to the ritual prescribed?

One more illustration of the Cabalistic learning of Paranaitis, and then we are acquainted with all his proofs of the ritual murder.[60] The *Cabala*, as it is well known, is mainly based upon the doctrine of the Ten *Sephirot*, emanations, the agencies by means of which the finite developed from the infinite. As the last *Sephirah* is the sum of all the other *Sephirot*, the Cabalist usually speaks of the Three Triads of the *Sephirot*. From another point of view, they also speak of the first triad in contrast to the six lower *Sephirot*, for which the term "*Tzon*", "the lamb", is used. Commenting upon the Biblical law concerning the Paschal lamb (Exodus 12:3ff.), the *Zohar* has the following remark: As the heavenly *Sephirot* consist of three triads which form a unit, so do the *Sephirot* of evil consist of three triads, forming a unit. Again, as the heavenly *Sephirot* consist of the first three and the last six, called "Lamb", so is it in the world of evil. It is the first triad in the world of evil to which the scriptures refer in the words: "the firstborn of Egypt...the firstborn of the captive...and all the firstborn of cattle" (Exodus 12:29). And it is the six lower *Sephirot*, called "lamb" which are united with the first three *Sephirot*, to which the Scripture refers by saying: "that they shall take to them every man a lamb [v. 3] and shall keep it until it is slaughtered [v. 6]". Bind the power of evil with the power of good, the lamb of the evil with the lamb of the good. Bind the evil that it be in your power until the time that you slaughter it and perform judgement on it; that time of which it [is] said "Who is it that cometh from Edom" (Isaiah 63:1) and again: "for the Lord hath a sacrifice in Bozrah" (ibid., 34:6). Again it is said: "And the Lord shall be king over all the earth; in that day there shall be one Lord and His name One" (Zechariah 14:9).[61]

The Cabalistic allegory is quite obvious. The slaughtering of the lamb stands for the complete victory of the principle of good over the principle of evil. This will take place in the promised Messianic time. But until that time, everyone is admonished to bind "the lamb", to retain power over evil. The very same allegory is found in the *Zohar* in another passage, which even Paranaitis could not distort. Considering the obscurity of the passage explained, we will readily overlook his failing to understand it. But unpardonable is his attempt to smuggle human sacrifices into this passage. When the convert, Pfefferkorn,[62] in the beginning of the sixteenth century, brought the charge that the Talmud and other rabbinic writings contain anti-Christian blasphemies, Jewish literature was saved from being exterminated by the great humanist, Reuchlin.[63] He insisted that the Rabbinical literature deserves to be saved if only on account of the *Cabala*, which furnishes the best weapon to Christianity, as its teachings agree with the teachings of the Church. To maintain the Christian character of the *Cabala* is childish and foolish, yet a pardonable error, but, to maintain that the *Cabala* teaches human sacrifice is a monstrous lie. The change of front in the anti-Semitic attacks upon Jewish literature from the time of Pfefferkorn to that of Paranaitis is not without interest to the historian. At a time when Christian scholars spoke of "Rabbi Talmud" and "Rabbi *Baba Metzia*" - the names of Treatises of the Talmud -[64] any converted rascal could tell his new co-religionists all kinds of monstrosities supposedly found in the Talmud without fear of being convicted of mendacity. In modern times, a very considerable part of prominent Christian scholars devote their studies to the Talmud, so it will no longer do to lie about the Talmud to the Christian world. All that men the type of Rohling-Paranaitis can do is to distort things; plain falsification, manufactured quotations from the Talmud would not be suffered any more by Christian scholars. Not so with the *Cabala*. The knowledge of this branch of Jewish literature is very rare today, even among Jewish scholars. To the Christian world, it is in a real sense of the word, "mystical lore", a great mystery to them. Now we know the reason why the *Cabala* is made the target by the modern school of liars and falsifiers. They think themselves safe from being detected, but their ignorance and mendacity is so obvious, that even those who are not experts in the *Cabala*, if they only understand how to read Hebrew, can very easily detect the falsehoods and lies of these libelers.

We dealt fully with the Cabalistic proof, not for any special regard we have for the *Cabala*, nor because any section of Jewry considers its teaching authoritative - the statement of Paranaitis to the contrary is a deliberate lie; the source quoted by him plainly states that the *Cabala* is *not* binding[65] - but for the sole reason that modern man is inclined to believe any monstrosity ascribed to mystics. Human blood played an important part in the beliefs of primitive people and left its traces in folklore of all modern nations, where it is employed for medical, superstitious, and criminal purposes. The only exception is the Jew, upon whom the discipline of a law practiced for thousands of years was not without effect. The prohibition against the use of blood brought it about that even Jewish folklore shows no trace of the use of blood.

The great aversion of the Jews [to] the use of blood seems to be known [even] to Paranaitis, who is not burdened by too much knowledge. To harmonize this well-known fact with his thesis of the use of Christian blood by Jews, he struck upon the ingenious idea that the law prohibits only the use of raw blood and not when it is cooked. We do not know whether any Jews reside in the Turkestan village from where Paranaitis hails, and for his benefit we will assume that he really believes the Jew to use the cooked blood of animals. We would, however, advise him to consult the Christian neighbors of the Jews, who would tell him that before cooking meat, [the Jew] must soak [it] in cold water for half an hour and then salt it for an hour to have the blood drained entirely. It is, however, permitted to the Jews to use animal blood for the food of Gentiles or animals, and it is this case that is mentioned in the *Mishnah* to which Paranaitis refers as his source for the statement that the Jews use blood when cooked.[66] "Where there is smoke, there is fire" is a pretty wise saying, but for Paranaitis it is the acme of historical truth. Notwithstanding many proofs Paranaitis found in rabbinical literature for the existence of ritual murder, he seems to doubt their convincing power and his last resource is therefore to prove the blood-accusation by the fact that such an accusation does and did exist. The learned monk did not notice that by subscribing to the scholastic principle according to which the universal acceptance of an idea was a certain proof of its truth, he became a worse calumniator of Christianity than any heathen ever was. For several centuries, the Greek and Roman world accused the Christians of the most abominable crimes which a diseased fantasy could invent, and compared with which the alleged ritual murder of the Jews loses its horror. Some backsliders of Christianity [in] the early centuries testified that the initiations into the Christians' mysteries took place in the following way:

A newborn infant entirely covered over with flour was presented like some mystic symbol of initiation to the knife of the proselyte, who unknowingly inflicted many a secret and mortal wound on the innocent victim of his error; that as soon as the cruel deed was perpetrated, the sectaries (i.e., the Christians) drank up the blood, greedily tore asunder the quivering members, and pledged themselves to eternal secrecy by a mutual consciousness of guilt. It was as confidently affirmed that this inhuman sacrifice was succeeded by a suitable entertainment, in which intemperance served as a provocative to brutal lust; [at] the appointed moment, the lights were suddenly extinguished, shame was banished, nature was forgotten and, as accident might direct, the darkness of the night was polluted by the incestuous commerce of sisters and brothers, of sons and of mothers.[67]

Since this and similar accusations against the Christians were generally considered to be true, it follows, according to Paranaitis, that they are true. But, says Paranaitis, the accusations against the Jews are supported by evidence. To examine the evidence of all the cases would require a good-sized book. We will therefore limit ourselves to a few of those cases cited by Paranaitis, where the guilt of the Jews was proven.

The evidence of Blois (1171) we had occasion to mention above. The accuser of the Jews was set in a [tub] containing holy water, and as he did not sink, the evidence was strong enough to have fifty Jews burned at the stake.[68] The best known case of blood accusation is that of Trent, where in the year 1475 some Jews admitted to have killed a Christian child.[69] Here is a brief extract from the letter written by Bishop Hinderbach of Trent to the Pope which gives the evidence in this case:

On 30th March, Samuel, the most respected of the incarcerated Trent Jews, was "tried" for the first time. At the conclusion, he was led back to prison "in order to recover". The following day he was stripped naked, bound hand and feet, and drawn up high by a rope, so that his limbs, drawn down by the weight of his body, were wrenched out of their sockets. As he protested his own and other Jews' innocence, he was quickly let drop in order that he might be pulled up again quickly. They then struck the tense-stretched rope on which he was hanging and made him "jump" several times more. A swoon prevented the continuation.

Torture was resumed on 3rd April with the repetition of all the tortures already applied. As he asseverated that he can pledge his word for the innocence both of himself and of all Jews, the rope was "vigorously moved" and he was made to "jump" twice from twice the height of his arms. Run up again, the poor wretch cried: "Where has your worship learnt that Christian blood has importance and use for us!" The jumping procedure was then twice repeated, each time twice or thrice the height of his arms, and as even this torture did not force any confession, he was left floating aloft for two-thirds of an hour till a swoon again overpowered his senses.

The fourth day of torture (7th April) began with a repetition of the previous grades of torture. As Samuel not only disputed any guilt but called out: "Were I to confess I had done any evil, I should be lying", they tied to his leg as he floated in the air, a piece of wood which wrenched his limbs yet further apart and substantially increased the pain. Next they took an iron pan filled with burning material on which sulfur was thrown and held it under his nose. In spite of the stinking sulfur gas, fatal to all breathing and feeling, and the pressure of interrogations, he abided by his denial of any guilt. Accordingly, they moved the rope several times and thereupon tied the piece of wood between the shin bones, whereby the weight became yet heavier and the pain greater, and let the poor wretch hang thus for a quarter of an hour. When the "jumping" process was now again repeated, Samuel's power of resistance was broken. He "confessed" that he and Tobias "put a pocket-handkerchief round the boy's neck and drew it tight so that the boy was strangled".

I could give pages and pages of similar matter, but they would offer very little variation: Jews tortured in the most diabolic way and all in "*magnum gloriam Dei*".[70] This is the evidence in history referred to by Paranaitis!

We have made the acquaintance of Paranaitis the philologian, the historian, the logician, and the jurist. He is a remarkably versatile genius, but his real greatness is in the domain of theology. The paramount question in all criminal cases is "cui boni".[71] Paranaitis says that the Jews hate Christianity and the Christians and that the Jews are permitted to kill Gentiles and further that their religion does not prohibit the use of human blood, but there is still an important question to answer. The Jews certainly paid very dearly for the killing of Christians. Quite often entire Jewish communities were wiped out on an account of a supposed murder of a Christian child committed by Jews. Why then did the Jews endanger their life to satisfy their hatred against Christians? Ought not the instinct of self-preservation have prevented them from committing such suicidal acts? The answer by Paranaitis reads: "The Rabbis are rather in doubt whether Jesus was not after all the promised Messiah" - the very same Rabbis who, according to Paranaitis, curse and blaspheme Jesus thrice a day! - "and therefore they use the blood of Jesus's followers to be saved".[72] A more ingenious theory of salvation is not known to us in the entire theological literature! Paranaitis certainly [carries off] the palm [in] theological acumen.

Greatness and modesty are often mated. Paranaitis is not only great but also modest. He says: "I do not know whether the Jews' writings contain anything about prayer and charity taking the place of sacrifice. But I do know that they do mention the possibility of sacrifice after the destruction of the Temple".[73] The inference is clear. Atonement is only possible by sacrifice, and the destruction of the Temple is not a hinderance. The ritual murder is therefore the sacrifice brought to atone for the sins of Israel. We admit that we cannot compete with Paranaitis's learning nor with his modesty. Our little knowledge of Rabbinic laws tells us, however, that a sacrifice in any other place but in the holy place in Jerusalem, is a deadly sin. It is true, a Rabbi living shortly after the destruction of the Temple did consider the question whether sacrifices might be brought in Jerusalem on the holy mountain without a Temple.[74] But a sacrifice outside Jerusalem, not to mention outside of the Holy Land, is quite inconceivable to the Rabbinic Jew. At the same time, we are in a position to allay his doubts in regards to the question whether Rabbinic Judaism knows any substitute for sacrifice or not. The Rabbis tells us that Rabbi Johanan Ben Zakai, the leader of the Pharisees at the time of the destruction of the Temple, at one time passed Jerusalem in the company of his pupil, Rabbi Joshua. At the site of the ruins of the Holy Place, Rabbi Joshua exclaimed: "Woe unto us that the place where the sins of Israel were expiated is now in ruins". "My son", answered Rabbi Johanan, "be comforted, we have something which takes the place of sacrifice, charity and lovingkindness, as the Scriptures (Hosea 6:6) say, 'I desire mercy and not sacrifice'".[75]

The wrong conception Paranaitis had concerning the importance of sacrifice is shared by not a few and it may not be out of place to quote the following words of the [midrash]:

They asked the Books of Wisdom: "What is the punishment of the sinner?" The Books of Wisdom answered: "Evil pursues sinners" (Proverbs 13:21). They asked the prophetical books: "What is the punishment to the sinner?" The prophetical books answered: "The soul that sinneth, it shall die" (Ezekiel 18:4). They asked the [Torah]: "What is the punishment of the sinner?" The [Torah] answered: "Let him bring a guilt offering, and it shall be forgiven unto him". They asked the Holy One, blessed be He: "What is the punishment of the sinner?" and the Holy One, blessed be He, answered: "Let him do repentance and it shall be forgiven unto him". [Therefore it is written:] "Good and upright is the Lord, therefore will he [lead] sinners in the right way'" (Psalms 25:8).[76]

We are at the end of the expert opinion of the ritual murder offered to the world by the Russian Government. It will be understood that we are not engaged in a refutation of this abominable lie. Our pride as Jews prohibits us from defending ourselves against accusations of cannibalism. We, the descendants of prophets and saints, wise and holy men, have no need to do it.

If the promoters of pogroms, of inhumanity equal to if not worse than cannibalism, want to excuse themselves in the eyes of the civilized world, let them. This is our candid advice, choose defenders other than Paranaitis. The atrocity and barbarism of the Russian Government had been known to the civilized world before now. Its stupidity is revealed by the manner in which it tried to use a half-witted [babbler] as its spokesman. Truth may be silenced for a time, but "Truth will spring out of the earth".[77]

~   ~   ~

GUGGENHEIMER, UNTERMYER & MARSHALL
NO. 37 WALL STREET, NEW YORK
CABLE ADDRESS "MELPOMENE" NEW YORK

December 6, 1913

Dear Doctor Ginzberg:

I am in receipt of your letter enclosing your very complete and interesting comments on the testimony of Paranaitis. It is exactly what I wanted and couched in popular style, and cannot fail to impress a reader of even ordinary intelligence. I am somewhat at a loss to know just exactly how, or when, I shall have it published, in view of the present status of the Beiliss case. It is quite probable that the Russian Government will take an appeal,[78] in which event it will be important to give this article an extensive circulation. I am conferring with a number of the members of the American Jewish Committee for the purpose of getting their views as to the procedure. In the meantime, I wish to express to you, on behalf of the Committee, our sincere thanks and appreciation of your presentation of the subject.

With best regards, I am,

Very truly yours,

Louis Marshall

DR. LOUIS GINZBERG
Care, Jewish Theological Seminary,
521 West 123rd St., New York

1   The Beiliss trial took place in Kiev from September 25 through October 28, 1913 - see *EJ*, IV, col. 400.

2   See ibid. and Samuel, pp. 87-88, 162, 212-216. LG calls him Paranaitis; most sources call him Pranaitis. Pranaitis was selected because he had previously published a book in Latin entitled *Christianus in Talmude Iudaeorum* in 1892 which was subsequently translated into German (Vienna 1894), Italian (Rome 1939), English (New York 1939 and reprints), and Spanish (Buenos Aires 1976). The English version bears the title *The Talmud Unmasked*. The JNUL in Jerusalem has copies of all of the versions; Samuel, pp. 87 and 285, saw only the English version.

3   The testimony itself is missing from the LGA but has apparently been preserved in German at the JNUL in Jerusalem under the title *Gutachten von Pranaitis* (call number: 22 V 1414; hereafter: Pranaitis). It is a 48-page mimeographed pamphlet in German which contains the "expert" testimony of Pranaitis given at a hearing in the criminal court of St. Petersburg between November 15-23, 1912. Louis Marshall probably sent LG a copy of this German pamphlet which contains almost all of the passages quoted by LG.

4   Johann Eisenmonger (1654-1704) was the author of *Entdecktes Judenthum (Judaism Unmasked)*, a 2,000-page diatribe against the Jews culled from over two hundred books. It appeared in Berlin in 1711 and in an English edition in 1732-33 - see *EJ*, VI, cols. 545-546. Pranaitis quotes him on pp. 17-18, 21, 23, 24.

5   For biographical details, see Chapter IV, No. 5, note 2. Marshall was writing here in his capacity as President of the American Jewish Committee (1912-1929).

6   1823-94. See *EJ*, VI, cols. 47-48.

7   Some of the bracketed words in this responsum were added by hand between the lines. Others were added by the editor of this volume.

8   Regarding this blood libel, see *EJ*, IV, col. 1113; A.M. Haberman, *Sefer Gezerot Ashkenaz V'tzarfat*, Jerusalem 1945, pp. 124-126, 133-144; and cf. below, note 68.

9   According to all of the Hebrew accounts published by Haberman, there were 31 or 32 victims.

10   "Light comes from the east".

11   August Rohling (1839-1931) was the antisemitic author of *Der Talmudjude* (1871), which was based on Eisenmonger (see above, note 4) - see *EJ*, XIV, col. 224.

12   See Samuel, pp. 214-216.

13   See above, note 11.

14   "To each his due".

15   Pranaitis, p. 12. This is a sentence from the *Aleinu* prayer which has been censored from most prayerbooks. It is found in Israeli prayerbooks, such as Shlomo Tal, ed., *Siddur Rinat Yisrael*, Jerusalem 1972, pp. 101, etc. For the history of this sentence and its interpretation, see Naphtali Wieder, *Sinai* 76 (5735), pp. 1-14.

16   The origins of the *Aleinu* are still shrouded in mystery. For recent discussions, see Jacob Neusner, *A History of the Jews in Babylonia*, II, Leiden 1966, pp. 163-166; Michael Swartz, JQR 77 (1986-87), pp. 179-190; and Meir Bar-Ilan, *Sitrei Tefilah V'heikhalot*, Ramat Gan 1987, pp. 32-37.

17   "Birth of the Lord".

18   Pranaitis, p. 13, but on p. 8 he translates it correctly!

19   Pranaitis, pp. 10-11, 14, 20, 22, 29.

20   See above, note 18.

21   I did not find this statement in Pranaitis.

22   Also known as Pablo de Santa Maria (ca. 1350-1435) - see *EJ*, XIII, cols. 3-4.

23 Johannes Pfefferkorn (1469-after 1521) - see ibid., cols. 355-357.
24 Friedrich Stahl (1802-1861) - see *EJ*, XV, cols. 325-326.
25 Pranaitis, pp. 2, 15-16. The source is YD 157:2. The emphasis is in the original.
26 I did not find this statement in Pranaitis.
27 Regarding St. Agobardus (799-840), see *EJ*, II, cols. 371-372 and, more recently, Reuven Bonfil, in: *Studies in Jewish Mysticism, Philosophy and Ethical Literature Presented to Isaiah Tishby*, Jerusalem 1986, pp. 327-348 (Hebrew).
28 Probably Otto Weinreich (b. 1886), who published widely in the field of classics and ancient religions.
29 *Avodah Zarah* 6a = 7b and *Ta'anit* 27b; and cf. the discussion in R. Travers Herford, *Christianity in Talmud and Midrash*, London 1903, pp. 171-173. Pranaitis, p. 14, quotes the first passage.
30 Franz Delitzsch (1813-90) - see *EJ*, V, cols. 1474-1475.
31 This is a generalization. For some of the opinions on the subject, see *EJ*, VII, cols. 412-414; Louis Jacobs, *A Tree of Life*, Oxford 1984, pp. 92-94 and the sources cited ibid. in note 12; and Jacob Katz, *Exclusiveness and Tolerance*, Oxford 1961. Also cf. above, Chapter III, No. 6, note 3 and No. 12, note 3.
32 See *ET*, s.v. *Ger Toshav*.
33 Josef Kohler (1849-1919). I have yet to locate the source of this quote.
34 See ET, s.v. *Gezel Goy* and s.v. *Goy*, col. 355ff.
35 Or "once in seven years" - see *Mishnah Makkot* 1:10.
36 This is not entirely accurate - see Shelomo Greenberg, in: *Hagut Ivrit B'amerika*, I, New York 5732, pp. 329-336; and Yitzhak Gilat, *Perakim B'hishtalshelut Hahalakhah*, Ramat Gan, 1992, pp. 191-204.
37 Hillel in *Shabbat* 31a and Rabbi Akiva in *Sifra* to Leviticus 19:18, ed. Weiss, fol. 89b.
38 *Sifra*, ibid.
39 An idiom, meaning: "one must take the rough with the smooth".
40 Pranaitis, pp. 16-19, discusses this passage at length. He quotes Rabbi Shimon bar Yohai in *Mekhilta Beshalah*, Chapter 1, eds. Horowitz-Rabin, p. 89, and later parallels such as *Massekhet Soferim* 15:7, ed. Higger, pp. 281-282 and Tosafot to *Avodah Zarah* 26b, s.v. *ve-lo moridin*.
41 In other words, according to Pranaitis's logic.
42 LG was obviously quoting from memory. The first phrase was said by R. Judah in *Mishnah Kiddushin* 4:14. The latter three phrases were said by R. Shimon and are found in *Massekhet Soferim* and in some of the parallels cited by Higger (above, note 40).
43 *Shabbat* 114a.
44 *Shabbat* 108a.
45 Pranaitis, pp. 22-23. The source is the *Zohar*, I, fols. 38b-39a. The italics were added by the editor.
46 I did not find any rabbinic parallels to this passage.
47 See *Midrash Tehillim* to 9:13, ed. Buber, p. 89 and *Yalkut Shimoni* to Psalms, par. 869. For medieval Ashkenazic parallels, see Yisrael Yuval in *Tziyon* 58 (5753), p. 36.
48 Pranaitis, p. 21, quoting Rabbi Yisrael Yaffe, *Sefer Or Yisrael*, Frankfurt on the Oder 1702, fol. 177b.
49 Pranaitis, p. 22: "Klipoth (Schalen)...", and again on p. 27.
50 Pranaitis, pp. 33ff.
51 *Sefer Halikutim*, fol. 156a, quoted by Pranaitis, p. 34.
52 Cf. above, Chapter IV, No. 1, note 8.

53   Pranaitis, p. 26, and cf. p. 28.
54   See *Legends*, III, p. 428, and the sources cited ibid., note 891.
55   See *Legends*, II, pp. 279-280, and the sources cited ibid., notes 73-74.
56   See above, note 53.
57   I did not find this passage in Pranaitis.
58   *Zohar*, II, fol. 119a.
59   Pranaitis, pp. 29-30.
60   Ibid., pp. 28-29.
61   *Zohar*, II, fol. 40b.
62   See above, note 23.
63   Johannes Reuchlin (1455-1522) - see *EJ*, XIV, cols. 108-111.
64   It is worth noting that Beiliss's defense attorneys proved Pranaitis's ignorance by asking him questions such as: "When did *Baba Bathra* live and what was her activity?" to which he replied: "I don't know". See Samuel, pp. 214-216.
65   See Pranaitis, p. 7, who quotes a number of sources.
66   See Pranaitis, p. 35, but no *mishnah* is quoted there.
67.   This is a quote from Octavius 9:5-6, by Minucius Felix, a third-century pagan apologist. See G.W. Clarke, ed., *The Octavius of Marcus Minucius Felix*, New York 1974, as quoted by Robert Wilken, *The Christians as the Romans Saw Them*, New Haven and London 1984, p. 19.
68   See above, notes 8-9. Ginzberg says "boat", but the original says "גיגית", i.e. a large vessel or tub. Regarding this type of trial by ordeal in the Middle Ages, see Henry Charles Leo, *The Ordeal*, Philadelphia 1973, pp. 72-88, and see ibid., p. 79 for the use of a tub.
69   Pranaitis, pp. 38, 45-46. Regarding this blood libel, see *JE*, XI, pp. 374-375; the illustration in *EJ*, III, cols. 97-98; the extensive bibliography which recently appeared in *PAAJR* 59 (1993), pp. 103-135; and Ronnie Po-Chia Hsia, *Trent 1475: Stories of a Ritual Murder Trial*, New Haven 1992.
70   "For the greater glory of God".
71   "Who stands to gain" or "who profits by it".
72   Pranaitis, p. 35.
73   Pranaitis, p. 31.
74   Rabbi Joshua in *Mishnah Eduyot* 8:6, quoted by Pranaitis, p. 31.
75   *Avot d'rabi Natan*, Version A, Chapter 4, ed. Schechter, fol. 11a.
76   *Pesikta d'rav Kahana, Shuvah*, ed. Mandelbaum, p. 355 and parallels.
77   Psalms 85:12.
78   This did not occur. For the aftermath of the trial, see Samuel, pp. 250ff.

No. 2: A Reply to Mr. Szacki (1919)

Source of Szacki's article and LG's reply: LGA, Box 12, "Szacki" file
Source of Louis Marshall's letter of thanks: LGA, Box 9, "Marshall" file
Comment: In 1919 one P. Szacki[1] published a 39-page pamphlet in Warsaw entitled *Dogmaty Ligi Naradow a Etyka Judaizmu* (JNUL call number: 22 V 14732). Louis Marshall obtained a typed English translation entitled *"The Dogmas of the League of Nations in Comparison with the Ethics of Judaism: Materials concerning the Jewish Problem*, gathered and arranged by P. Szacki, translated from the Polish language by K.L." [hereafter: Szacki] which he sent to LG. An incomplete copy, which ends on p. 27 (= p. 24 in the Polish original), is found in the LGA, Box 12. LG's reply is printed below along with a thank-you letter from Marshall. Space does not allow us to reprint the partial translation of Szacki's anti-Semitic tract.

Mr. P. Szacki
on the Ethics of Judaism*

(*The Dogmas of the League of Nations in Comparison with the Ethics of the Judaism: Materials concerning the Jewish Problem*, gathered and arranged by P. Szacki.)

Ernest Renan[2] once remarked: "If you scrutinize closely the enemies of Judaism, you will find them to be on the whole the enemies of the modern spirit, or, to quote the original: "Les ennemis du Judaisme, regardez-y de pres, vous verrez que ce sont en general des ennemis de l'esprit moderne". No wonder, therefore, that anti-Semitic literature bears the [earmarks] of a bygone age, of a time past when people, caring neither for fact or common sense, used to settle all questions by reference to authorities. A mere glance through Mr. Szacki's "Materials" suffices to convince anyone who is acquainted with the Talmud and Rabbinic literature that he plowed these ancient and well-worked heifers, the *Tela igna satanae*,[3] the *Abgezogener Schlangenbalg*,[4] *Entdecktes Judenthum*,[5] *Judenspiegel*,[6] and their venomous kindred which German anti-Semitism has bestowed upon a blessed humanity. One is indeed rather surprised that Mr. Szacki does not even once use the phrase "says Rabbi Talmud" as did the erudite Capucin Friar Henricus Seynenis.[7] But it seems that the authorities in whom our author trusts are exclusively German anti-Semites and in the Land of Kultur the anti-Semites knew that the Talmud was not a bearded Rabbi. We are grateful even for small gifts and gladly admit that Mr. Szacki or, to be correct, his

German masters ([of whom] he mentions only two by name - Wagner and Wahrmund,[8] but his materials consist of "silent quotations" from the books mentioned above) have advanced a little in Talmudic learning and know that the Talmud is the name of a book and not of a man. Yet how much more do he and his German masters know about it? Let us hear his delightful definition of the Talmud:

> The Jewish religion is based on the Old Testament, and on equally ancient commentaries to the above, preserved for ages as oral tradition, and known, after being registered, under the general name of the Talmud.[9]

I am not pedantic enough to quibble and ask how a commentary can be equally as ancient as a text it comments [upon]. Yet, granted there are commentaries equally as ancient as [their] texts, it is [certain] that whatever the Talmud may be, it is certainly not a commentary to the Hebrew Bible. Labels are devices for saving talkative persons the trouble of thinking, and nothing is easier but nothing is more dangerous than definitions. I shall therefore attempt a description rather than a definition of what the Talmud is.

The word Talmud means "teaching" and, true to the name, one may well say that the Talmud is the deposit of all knowledge that the Jew during the first five centuries of the common era thought worth teaching. One may well say of it: "Nihil humani ab ei alienum est".[10] The Talmud covers every domain of law, whether applying it to the State, the individual, or the family, whether civil or criminal. Its main portion, however, relates to all the sides and points of the religious ceremonial by which Jewish life both individual and social is regulated. And it is not mere conclusions as to what is valid in law which are set forth in the Talmud; the discussions are given. We see, as in the action of a drama, how the result is reached through the conflict of opinions and arguments pro and con. Learned men and schools of learning belonging to five centuries, the first five of the common era, take part in the discussion. The language of this jurisprudence and of its dialectic is sharply and finely cut, [but] in absolute contrast to clear and full exposition, it passes over into thought ciphers and thought abbreviations. But the Talmud is more than a book of laws. It aptly has been said that it is as if all the prose and the poetry, the science, the faith and speculation of the old world were, though only in faint reflections, bound up in it in _____.[11] The man of science will find in the Talmud much interesting material concerning medicine, astronomy, mathematics, botany and no less so will the student of poetry find there proverbs, parallels and legends. It is very characteristic [of] the authors of the Talmud that they have been reproached for wasting their time in the pursuit of medical and physical studies by the Church Father Jerome, the pupil of the Palestinian Rabbis of the 4th century under whose guidance he composed the translation of the Hebrew Bible into Latin known as the Vulgate.[12]

A poet by the grace of God, Heine, describes the non-legal part of the Talmud, the so-called *Haggadah*, as follows:

But the latter, the *Hagada*,
I should rather call a garden;
Yes, a garden, most fantastic,
Comparable to that other,

Which in days of yore was planted
In the town of Babylon,
Great Semiramis's garden,
That eighth wonder of the world.[13]

Having made it clear that the Talmud is neither a code of laws only, nor a mere book of morals only, it becomes self-evident that to state with authority the view of "the Talmud" on points of moral law and religion requires the mastery of the whole of it and that it would not do to quote passages from it without due consideration to the connections in which they are given. The devil not only quotes Scripture but moreso Talmud.

And now let us examine the quotations from the Talmud in Mr. Szacki's Materials:

A treatise of the Talmud called *Pesachim* even states that [the] "Talmud was created previous to the Universe. If it were not for Talmud, earth and heaven could not have existed'".[14]

No such statement is found either in the treatise referred to or in any other place [in] the Talmud. Following the advice of the Rabbis to "judge every man in the scale of merit",[15] I give Mr. Szacki the benefit of the doubt that he is merely the dupe of the German anti-Semites whom he trusted blindly. What the Talmud maintains in *Pesachim* 54a is that "the *Torah* was created before the world" and this, of course, is the way of the Rabbis to express the idea that the Word of God revealed - the Torah - emanated from divine wisdom which was the instrument of Creation. Any student of

Scriptures, the old and the new, is well acquainted with the theological doctrines of the previous existence of divine wisdom. An almost blasphemous statement of Szacki reads:

> According to [the] Jewish religion, notions of the idea of the deity appertain to one nation only, as Jehova is represented as a specially Jewish God, belonging exclusively to the selected nation and not to all humanity. The Jewish God is not the father of all men and the ideal of love, justice, and mercy, like the Christian God or even like Ahura-Mazda or Brahma, the Ancient Aryan gods. On the contrary, he is the God of vengeance down to the tenth generation, just and merciful only to his own people, but foe to all other nations, denying them human rights and commanding their extermination....[16]

Americans, Jews and Gentiles alike, who still see in the Bible the foundation of modern civilization, will take virulent attacks on the God of the patriarchs and the prophets at what they are worth, as the fantasies of a harebrained mind. We must, however, apologize to Mr. Szacki and admit that he is not responsible for this blasphemy. He only copied the words of Houston Stewart Chamberlain, the renegade Englishman who in his notorious book attempts to show that the other claimants for the title of "Chosen Race" have no claim to creative genius, and that no other race but the "Teutonic" has ever made any contribution worth considering.[17] I cannot refrain from stating in a few words the attitude of the Rabbis concerning the election of Israel.

The rabbis find the essence of Judaism expressed in Deuteronomy 6:4: "Hear, O Israel, the Lord is our God, the Lord is One". Commenting upon these words, they remarked: "He is our God [who makes] His name particularly attached to us, but He is also the one God of all mankind. He is our God in this world, He will be the only God in the world to come, as it is said: 'And the Lord shall be King over all the earth; on that day there shall be one Lord and His name One' (Zechariah 14:9). For in this world, the creatures, through the insinuation of the evil inclination, have divided themselves into various tongues, but in the world to come they will agree with one consent to call only on His name, as it is said: 'For them I will restore to the people a pure language, that they may all call upon the name of the Lord, to serve Him with one consent' (Zephaniah 3:9)"; comp. *Sifrei Devarim*, [*Piska* 31, end] and *Tanhuma Noah* 19. Thus the Rabbis [saw] in the doctrine [of] the election of Israel not any special privilege but the additional burden put upon it for spreading true religion through the world until the Kingdom of God will be established on earth.

Mr. Szacki is as ignorant concerning the Jewish view about the Messiah as he is about his doctrine of God. He writes: "The Jewish Messiah, quite differently, is a great conqueror, who will subdue all the nations of the world in order to make them slaves of the Jews and deprive them of their riches."[18]

On the most solemn days of the year, the New Year and the Day of Atonement, the Jew prays:

Now, therefore, O Lord our God, impose Thine awe upon all Thy works, and Thy dread upon all that Thou hast created, that all works may fear Thee and all creatures prostrate themselves before Thee, and they may all form a single band to do Thy will with a perfect heart, even as we know, O Lord our God, that dominion is Thine, strength is in Thy hand, and might in Thy right hand, and that Thy name is to be feared above all that Thou hast created.[19]

In his discussion [of] Talmudic law, Mr. Szacki starts with a sweeping statement:

The learned rabbis who had written these books, realized the necessity of certain perfections and reforms of Judaism, in order to provide the Jews with [an] advantage in their [struggle] for existence with other nations. The said reforms are contained in the following directions: 1. In the depreciation of the authority of the Old Testament owned by the Christians too, and at the same time augmenting the authority and faultlessness of the Talmud and Rabbins, its commentators and authors.[20]

This statement of his he supports by two quotations from the Talmud which he misunderstood or perverted. In [*Mishnah*] *Sanhedrin* 11:3 the law concerning the rebellious elder (comp. Deut. 17:8-13) is given. The Rabbis remark [there] that that law refers to a judge who rebelled against the authoritative interpretation of the Bible, but not one who disregarded a Biblical commandment. It is obvious that the Rabbis, far from depreciating the authority of the Bible, were actuated by the great desire to uphold it by having an authoritative body regulating it. In *Megillah* [21a], the text reads exactly [the] opposite [of] what Mr. Szacki maintains. The legend given there states that [during the forty days that Moses] spent on Mt. Sinai, he studied *the written Word* standing like an angel.[21]

Mr. Szacki has the audacity to maintain that *Goy* means "dirty, unclean",[22] whereas a beginner in Hebrew might have told him if he were anxious to know the truth that *Goy* is the Hebrew prototype of the word "Gentile". As a matter of fact, *Goy* is used several times in the Bible to describe any people including Israel, but later it was limited to the meaning of "Gentile".

For the correct understanding of Talmudic Law concerning the Gentile, one must bear in mind not only the fact that by "Gentile" the Talmud always understands a heathen (in the few passages where Christians are referred to they are always called *Minim*, Sectarians, comp. Herford, *Christianity in Talmud and Midrash* [London, 1903]), but also that it dates from the time when the Jews had their independent state. The *jus civile* of the Romans applied only to Roman citizens, whereas the *jus naturae* was the [law] for the *peregrini* or foreigners. Jewish civil law being very closely bound up with religious law could hardly be applied to Gentiles and a set of laws regulating the right of the *peregrini* have been formulated by the ancient Jewish jurists. After the loss of Jewish independence, the supreme law regulating Jewish jurisprudence was [that] "the law of the country is the only valid law".[23] The Jews continued in some countries to apply their own civil code, sometimes even criminal, but only as far as it was not contrary to the law of the country.

The *Shulchan Aruch* that may be described as a digest of Talmudic law for theoretical and practical purposes, has in many places incorporated Talmudic law and practice concerning the *peregrini* which at the time of the compilation of the digest, and still moreso today, have no practical application whatsoever.[24]

Mr. Szacki not only is unacquainted with the principles underlying Talmudic law but nearly always all his quotations from the *Shulchan Aruch* and other Rabbinic writings are perverted. In *Shulchan Aruch Hoshen Hamishpat* [348:2], we read: "Any Jew who steals or robs an article of the slightest value from a Jew or a Gentile transgresses the Biblical commandment 'Thou shalt not steal'". This passage it made to read by Szacki: "A Jew may rob a *Goy*"![25]

According to Rabbinic jurisprudence, he who finds and takes up lost goods acquires thereby a special ownership. But Mosaic law puts upon him the duty to seek out the true owner and to restore the lost things. These laws, according to the Rabbis, apply exclusively to Jews. A Jew was not obliged to return a lost article to a Gentile, but neither was a Gentile obliged to return a lost article to a Jew. The Talmud, however, maintains that a Jew should return the lost article to a Gentile if by doing so he would impress the outside world with the honesty of Israel or, to use the phrase of the Rabbis, "To sanctify the Holy Name". Thus the Rabbis far from doing any injustice to the *peregrini*, rather impose upon the Jew duties which he cannot expect the heathen to [reciprocate]. This Talmudic law is also found in the *Shulchan Aruch* but not as quoted by Szacki.[26]

According to Talmudic law, a witness who refuses to testify after an oath had been imposed upon him to do so, is guilty of a severe transgression of the law. However, if he refuses to testify *at the bidding of* a heathen authority, robbers, and publicans, he is not guilty. This statement reads in Mr. Szacki's Materials: "[He] who took an oath *in the presence of* the goys, the robbers and the customs house officers, is not responsible (*Tosefta Shebuoth* 2:14)".[27]

According to Jewish law, the testimony of one witness is not strong enough to decide a case. At the time when the Jews had their own jurisdiction, it was prohibited for a Jew to testify before a heathen court in case he was the only witness and this law holds good either if the testimony would be for or against the Jew.

This law in Mr. Szacki's Materials reads as follows:

> If a *goy* (Christian) wants a Jew to stand witness against a Jew at the Court of Law, and the Jew could give fair evidence - he is forbidden to do it, but if a Jew wants a Jew to be a witness in a similar case against a *goy*, he may do it (*Shulchan Aruch, Hoshen Hamishpat* 28:3-4).[28]

The bane of Jewish life during the Middle Ages were the informers. To protect themselves against spoliation of their property and extermination of their lives, the most stringent measures were taken by the Jews against the malignant growth of the informers to [the] extent that, if necessary, the informers should be delivered to the authorities and, if found guilty, executed. In the year 1280, King Pedro III of Aragon ordered the execution of a Jewish informer[29] and, similarly, King John I of Castile had the informer Joseph Picho executed on August 21, 1379.[30] Though, in general, the jurisdiction of Jewish criminal courts ceased [after] the destruction of the Jewish Commonwealth, in the case of informers the penalty remained in force because these miscreants endangered and threatened the existence of the Jewish people. [From] the fact that punishment of this kind [was] carried out by non-Jewish authorities, it is clear that the punishment meted out to them was well-deserved.

The *Shulchan Aruch* contains a number of regulations concerning the informers,[31] but none of these laws or regulations can be described as inhuman or cruel, if considered in the proper light.

The Mosaic law described specific marriage laws concerning the priests, the so-called descendants of Aaron. At the beginning of the common era, the priests became so exclusive that they would not enter into any marriage relations except with members of their own clan. Later, however, this stringency of law has been somewhat softened. The custom, however, remained that priests should only marry women whose parents have both been born of Jews. This regulation reads in Szacki's Materials: "According to the Talmud: 'every woman belonging to goys is a prostitute' (*Shulchan Aruch, Eben Haezer* 6:8)".[32]

I think that the above specimen of Szacki's learning and love of truth will suffice to give any unprejudiced reader a proper appreciation of the latest contribution to anti-Semitic literature.

~   ~   ~

GUGGENHEIMER, UNTERMYER & MARSHALL
120 BROADWAY, NEW YORK

CABLE ADDRESS "MELPOMENE" NEW YORK

December 13, 1919.

Dear Professor Ginzberg:

I am in receipt of yours of the 9th instant, and have received your comments on Szacki's infamous paper. I do not know whether Abrahams[33] showed you my letter on the subject, but it is quite interesting to know that both of us worked along parallel lines. The result is satisfactory in view of the fact that the offensive paragraph of the supplemental report of General Jadwin and Mr. Johnson was eliminated by them.[34]

I agree that the time has come when a treatise on the Gentile in the Talmud and *Shulchan Aruch* should be written. You may not know that Judge Sulzberger has recently prepared a course of lectures on a subject which includes the status of the stranger in Jewish life from the biblical standpoint.[35]

Thanking you for your prompt and efficient assistance, I am

Cordially yours,

Louis Marshall

PROF. LOUIS GINZBERG,
531 West 123rd Street,
New York City.

1   I have been unable to ascertain any facts about the author. He does not appear in the
National Union Catalog or in any of the Polish encylopedias that I checked.
2   Ernest Renan (1823-92) was a renowned French orientalist - see *EJ*, XIV, cols. 71-72.
Regarding his attitude toward the Jews, see Shmuel Almog, in: Shmuel Almog, ed., *Antisemitism
Through the Ages*, Oxford 1988, pp. 255-278.
3   I have been unable to learn anything further about this book.
4   See the previous note.
5   See above in this chapter, No. 1, note 4.
6   There are two anti-Semitic tracts by this name. The first, published in 1862, was written
by Wilhelm Marr (1818-1904) who coined the term "anti-Semite" in 1879 - see *EJ*, XI, col. 1015,
and Ya'akov Katz, *Sinat Yisrael*, Tel Aviv 1979, pp. 180-181. The second, which was reprinted
many times (the fourth and fifth editions are from 1883 and 1892 respectively) was written by a
renegade Jew named Aaron Briman who used the pen-name "Dr. Justus" - see *EJ*, XIV, col. 224.
7   I have been unable to learn anything further about this author.
8   Richard Wagner (1813-83) was a noted composer and anti-Semite - see *EJ*, XVI, cols.
240-241. Wahrmund is probably Adolf Wahrmund (1827-1913) who published a number of
books about the "Jewish Problem".
9   Szacki, p. 7.
10   "Nothing human is alien to him."
11   This word is illegible in the original.
12   He may be referring to the passage from St. Jerome quoted by Harry Friedenwald, *The
Jews and Medicine: Essays*, II, Baltimore 1944, p. 555.
13   These two stanzas are taken from Heine's "Jehuda ben Halevy" - see Louis Untermeyer,
Heinrich Heine: Paradox and Poet, II, New York 1937, pp. 372-373.
14   Szacki, p. 7. The second sentence, which is not discussed by LG, is taken from *Pesahim*
68b and parallels.
15   *Mishnah Avot* 1:6.
16   Szacki, pp. 7-8.
17   Houston Stewart Chamberlain (1855-1927) was the author of *Die Grundlagen des 19
Jahrhunderts* (1899) which became a major source of Nazi ideology - see *EJ*, V, col. 332.
18   Szacki, p. 8.
19   "ובכן תן פחדד", which can be found, e.g., in the *High Holiday Prayer Book*, ed., Morris
Silverman, Hartford, Conn. 1951, p. 11 and frequently.
20   Szacki, p. 10. The sources which follow appear in a note on the same page.

21   Szacki misquotes *Megillah* as follows: "*Jehova* himself in Heaven studies the *Talmud* standing, he has such respect for that book". In any case, *Megillah* 21a actually says that *God* asked Moses to stand next to Him when he gave Moses the *Torah*, but there is no mention there of Moses standing like an angel.

22   Szacki, p. 11 in a note.

23   "דינא דמלכותא דינא" - see *EJ*, VI, cols. 51-55; and *ET*, VII, cols. 295-308.

24   LG is reacting to Szacki, p. 20, who emphasized that the *Shulhan Arukh* "serves till the present day as a moral and legal code for the Jews".

25   Szacki, p. 11. But see the Rema to the passage quoted who takes a more lenient approach to deceiving a gentile.

26   HM 266:1 is quoted by Szacki on p. 11, but he quotes only the beginning, which is negative.

27   Szacki, p. 11 The passage is found in the *Tosefta*, ed. Zuckermandel, p. 448.

28   Szacki, pp. 11-12.

29   Pedro III was King of Aragon from 1276-85. Regarding this execution, see Yitzhak Baer, *A History of the Jews in Christian Spain*, I, Philadelphia 1966, pp. 168-170.

30   John I was King of Castile from 1379-90. Regarding this execution, see ibid., pp. 375-376.

31   Quoted by Szacki, p. 12.

32   Szacki, p. 27. The quotation is accurate, but Szacki failed to explain, and probably did not know, the context.

33   According to Robert Gordis, Joseph Abrahams was a "lifelong friend" of LG "who for many years was closely associated with our Seminary" - see *PRA* 8 (1941-44), p. 382. Indeed, he was Secretary of the Seminary for over forty years - see Cyrus Adler, *I Have Considered the Days*, Philadelphia 1941, pp. 281, 400-401. And see Abraham's article on "The Buildings of the Seminary", in: Cyrus Adler, ed., *The Jewish Theological Seminary: Semi-Centennial Volume*, New York 1939, pp. 65-72.

34   I have yet to discover any details about the individuals or the "report" mentioned.

35   Judge Mayer Sulzberger (1843-1923) was a good friend of both Marshall and LG - see *EJ*, XV, cols. 509-510; and *Keeper*, pp. 72-73 and Index.

No. 3 The Jewish Attitude Towards the Crippled (1938)
Source: LGA, Box 10, "Neustätter" file

THE JOHNS HOPKINS UNIVERSITY
INSTITUTE OF THE HISTORY OF MEDICINE
1900 EAST MONUMENT STREET
BALTIMORE, MD

Feb.15, 38

Prof. Dr. Ginsburg
Jewish Theological Seminary N.Y.
122 Str. and Bway

Dear Prof. Ginsburg,
Dr. Friedenwald[1] has advised me to apply to you in the following.
In his book *Civilization and the Cripple*, Frederick Watson [of] London says the words of the Levitican law "a broken-handed or a crooked-backed etc. shall not come near the altar" [Leviticus 21:19-20] served as a useful stick with which to beat the cripple.[2]
Now I am interested, in my studies on the history of orthopedics and the care of the crippled, how these words, which were meant to let no priest to be anything else but perfect, have been interpreted in the Talmud and other Jewish sources. They are, of course, apt to let a cripple appear as an inferior being, and Mummenhoff, e.g., says that in the care of the maimed the towns of the Middle-Ages often showed an absolute failure. The deaf and dumb, the blind, and the cripples of all kinds were left to themselves and therefore had to apply to private charity.[3]
I should appreciate it very much if you would be kind enough to let me have your opinion on the matter and would tell me where I could find material on the matter as well in regard to Jewish ideas on it and also of the Christian standpoint in historical times, and when the change of them in the line of modern humanitarian trends arose.
Looking forward to the favor of your reply.

Yours sincerely,

Dr. Otto Neustätter[4]

March 11, 1938

Dear Dr. Neustäetter:
I am in receipt of your letter of February 15th in which you ask me whether the Biblical Law concerning the unfitness of [priests] with a blemish for sacrificial purposes[5] was understood by the Talmud or other Rabbinical sources to convey the idea of the inferiority of the cripple. I wish to state that while a good deal of speculation is found in Rabbinic sources about the causes of human deformities, there is not the slightest attempt to consider the cripple inferior in any respect. The general tendency in Rabbinic sources is to consider deformity as a punishment for the sins committed by the parents, but not by the cripple himself.[6]

Sincerely yours,

LOUIS GINZBERG

Dr. Otto Neustäetter
The Johns Hopkins University
Institute of the History of Medicine
1900 East Monument Street
Baltimore, Maryland

1   Dr. Harry Friedenwald (1864-1950) of Baltimore was, in his time, the foremost authority on the Jews and medicine - see EJ, VII, col. 176.
2   Frederick Watson, *Civilization and the Cripple*, London 1930. The book is not available in Jerusalem; it is listed in the *National Union Catalog*, vol. 651, p. 2. It should be emphasized that the verses refer specifically to *priests* who are physically deformed.
3   Ernst Mummenhoff (1848-1931) published extensively on the history of Nuremberg. I do not know to which publication Dr. Neustätter is referring.
4   Dr. Otto Neustätter (b. 1870) was an opthamologist, an editor, and a prolific author who published numerous books and articles on medicine and the history of medicine. See the *National Union Catalog*, Vol. 411, p. 673; and S. Wininger, *Grosse judische National-Biographie*, IV, Czernowitz, after 1928, p. 528.
5   LG mistakenly wrote "animals with a blemish" but that is clearly not the question and he himself refers below to "*human* deformities".
6   I do not know to what sources he is referring. There are rabbinic sources which state that children are sometimes punished for the deeds of their parents, but usually, it is because they continue their wicked deeds - see Claude G. Montefiore and Herbert Loewe, *A Rabbinic Anthology*, New York 1974², pp. 553-555.

No. 4 Why was the Palestinian Talmud Never Translated into English? (1940)
Source: LGA, Box 11, "Starzenski" file

VICTOR STARZENSKI   BURNT HILLS   SARATOGA COUNTY N.Y.

January 10, 1940

Professor Ginsberg
Jewish Theological Seminary
133rd & Broadway
New York City
Dear Professor Ginsberg:
    The other day when I was in New York, I stopped in at the Hebrew Literature Department of the 42nd Street Library[1] to find out if the Palestinian Talmud [was] available. I learned that only one volume had been translated into English although a French translation is available.[2]
    I was told that the Babylonian Talmud was much more popular and that is the reason it has been translated. The librarian suggested I turn to you for further detail. I did not have the time to stop in to see you and I am therefore presuming on your good nature by writing to you.
    Why was the Palestinian Talmud never translated into English? Why is the Babylonian Talmud more popular?
    Are the quotations that appear in Maurice Harris' *Hebraic Literature* from the Palestinian or Babylonian version, or both?
    Am I correct in assuming that Dr. Harris is a competent authority?[3]

Very truly yours,

Victor Starzenski

~   ~   ~

January 15, 1940

Dear Mr. Starzenski,
    I am in receipt of your letter of January 10 and in reply to your questions contained therein, I wish to say as follows:

When the Palestinian Talmud was compiled about the middle of the 4th Century, great persecutions of the Jews took place, in consequence of which the leading academies in Palestine were closed and the scholars fled to Babylonia. Consequently, the Babylonian Talmud is in a certain sense the continuation of the Palestinian Talmud and hence of paramount influence upon the later development of Judaism. At the time of the rise of Jewish life in Europe, Palestine had long ceased to be the seat of Jewish culture, while Babylonia had taken its place. Thus it was the Babylonian Talmud that was studied in the schools of Spain, France and Germany.[4]

In modern times, quite naturally, the Babylonian Talmud was translated into modern languages because it was better known than the Palestinian one.

I never saw or heard of Maurice Harris's *Hebraic Literature* and am not in a position to judge the nature of this work. The author was a prominent preacher.[5]

Sincerely yours,

LOUIS GINZBERG

Mr. Victor Starzenski
Burnt Hills
Saratoga County, N.Y.

---

1   He is referring to the Jewish Division of the New York Public Library in Manhattan.

2   Moïse Schwab, *The Talmud of Jerusalem*, I, Berakhot, London 1886, and idem, *Le Talmud de Jerusalem*, 11 volumes, Paris 1932-33.

3   Rabbi Maurice Harris (1859-1930) was a Reform rabbi and prolific author who served at Temple Israel in Harlem for almost fifty years - see *UJE*, V, p. 219. His book, *Hebraic Literature: Translations from the Talmud, Midrashim and Kabbala*, was published in 1901 and reprinted in 1936 and 1939. Pages 1-231 consist of translations from the Babylonian Talmud.

4   For more details, see LG, *A Commentary on the Palestinian Talmud*, I, New York 1941, pp. xxxvi ff.

5   See above, note 3.

No. 5 The Denial of Religious Services to an Unaffiliated Jew (1940)

Source: LGA, Box 3, "Berman" file
Excerpt: *Keeper*, p. 235

TEMPLE ISAIAH ISRAEL
1100 Hyde Park Boulevard
CHICAGO   OFFICE OF THE TREASURER

February 19, 1940

Dear Dr. Ginzberg,

I have been delegated by the Rabbinical Association of Chicago to ask your kindness in helping us to understand what position Jewish tradition takes with respect to this question: Is it possible on the basis of Jewish tradition to justify a denial by a Rabbi of religious services such as burial, marriage, et cetera, to men and women who are not affiliated with congregations? This question is one that the laymen interested in the conduct of congregations have raised, largely motivated by the desire to secure additional support form the great mass of unaffiliated men and women in the community.

The Rabbis of our Association are eager to find what the position of Jewish tradition would be on this question and I have been given the privilege of putting this question to you. I do trust that you will provide us with a response which I will be able to submit to the Rabbinical Association at their next meeting, a fortnight away.

Thanking you for your kindness, I am

Respectfully yours,

Morton M. Berman[1]

Dr. Louis Ginzberg
3080 Broadway
New York City, New York

~   ~   ~

February 27, 1940

Dear Rabbi Berman:

I am in receipt of your letter of February 19 in which you ask me on behalf of the Rabbinical Association of Chicago to state the position of Jewish tradition with regard to the question whether a Rabbi be justified in refusing religious services to those who are not affiliated with a congregation. May I state briefly my view on this matter.

With very few exceptions, Jewish life up to recent times had as its center of gravity the community and not the congregation. One who did not belong to the community put himself - or was put by others - outside the Jewish fold. The ideal thing would be, of course, to have the synagogue in America take the place of the community of old. Economic as well as other reasons, however, have prevented so far the realization of this ideal plan. There are certainly thousands of Jews who do not belong to congregations because of their inability [to contribute] to them and at the same time would like[2] to be treated as beneficiaries of the synagogue. On the other hand, there are many more who are too indifferent to bother about anything Jewish as long as they are not forced to do so. It seems, therefore, to me that while the policy of a congregation should be in the direction of excluding "outsiders", a hard and fast rule would be dangerous.

Very sincerely yours,

LOUIS GINZBERG

Rabbi Morton M. Berman
Temple Isaiah Israel
1100 Hyde Park Boulevard
Chicago, Ill.

---

1   Rabbi Morton M. Berman (1899-1986) was a Reform rabbi who served as rabbi of Temple Isaiah Israel of Chicago from 1937-57 - see *EJ*, IV, col. 667.
2   I have emended "not like" to "like".

No. 6 Which Midrash Asks Why the Decalogue Does Not Mention God's Role as Creator of the Universe? (1943)

Source: LGA, Box 12, "Weisfeld" file

November 24, 1943

Dear Doctor Weisfeld:

I am in receipt of your letter of November 8 in which you ask me to locate for you the Midrashic comment upon the opening words of the Decalogue. May I say, as far as I know, the poet-philosopher, Rabbi Judah Halevy, was the first one to raise the question why the Decalogue speaks of God as one who "brought thee out of the land of Egypt" and not as one who created man. His comments on this point are found in the *Kuzari*, I, 25, and [in] Ibn Ezra in his commentary to Exodus 20:2.[1] The answer to [your] question, however, is not that.[2] You have mentioned in your letter the idea that creation without accompanying freedom would have been meaningless. This seems to me rather too sophisticated for the authors of the Midrash. The nearest to it is the remark found in [the] *Mekilta* (edited by Lauterbach, II, 237-238), that the law was revealed only after Israel had willingly taken upon themselves the Kingdom of God. Comp. also ibid., p. 230: "When they all stood before Mount Sinai to receive the Torah, they all made up their minds to accept the reign of God joyfully."

Very sincerely yours,

Louis Ginzberg

Doctor Israel H. Weisfeld
449 N. Lombard Avenue
Oak Park, Illinois

---

1   Also see the Ramban, in: *Kitvei Ramban*, ed. Chavel, I, Jerusalem 5723, p. 151; and R. Ya'akov Anatoli, *Malmad Hatalmidim*, Lyck 1866, fol. 66b-67a.

2   Dr. Weisfeld apparently made the suggestion that the Decalogue mentions the Exodus rather than Creation because the latter "without accompanying freedom would have been meaningless".

No. 7 Women on Synagogue Boards (1944)
Source: LGA, Box 3, "Coblenz" file
Shulhan Arukh: HM 7:4

January 20, 1944

Dear Rabbi Coblenz:[1]
I reverse the regular order by supplementing the oral lore by the written and the reason for this reversed order is that I have some inhibitions against telephoning.[2]
My suggestion made to you in regard to the election of women to the Board was mainly for the sake of peace. When you ask me however, the actual law on that point, I must confess that according to my opinion, there is not the slightest objection to having women on the board of a synagogue. The source of Maimonides[3] for declaring women disqualified from holding office is *Sifre Deuteronomy* par. 157, where he read in agreement with some of the manuscripts: "Hence, it said that women are not to be appointed ministers of the affairs of the community."[4] The Tosafists, who declare women eligible for judgeships,[5] undoubtedly do admit them to any other office, and it is more than likely that the Tosafists had another reading in the text of the *Sifre*. No less an authority than the *Gaon* of Vilna suggests a reading which takes away any basis for the opinion of Maimonides.[6] At all events, the *Shulhan Arukh* [*Hoshen Mishpat*], par. 7 only mentions the disqualification of women as judges, but not as any other administrators. I would even go one step further and maintain that Maimonides would have no objection to women on the boards of synagogues. What he had in mind was exclusively the administration of city or town affairs.[7]
I am rather interested in the problem and I would like to know what your congregation decides.
With kindest regards, I am

Very sincerely yours,

Louis Ginzberg

Rabbi Adolph Coblenz
Chizuk Amunah
Eutaw Place and Chauncey Ave.
Baltimore, Maryland

1   For his biography, see above, Chapter III, No. 9, note 13.
2   For LG's aversion to the telephone, see *Keeper*, p. 216.
3   *Hilkhot Melakhim* 1:4-5.
4   Ed. Finkelstein, pp. 208-209 and cf. the variant readings there.
5   Tosafot to *Bava Kama* 15a, s.v. *asher tassim*, according to *Birkei Yosef* to HM 7, subpar. 11.
6   In his commentary to *Sifrei*, ad loc.
7   The question of women in public office has been treated extensively in the responsa literature of the twentieth century. For a thorough discussion and extensive bibliography, see my responsum, in: David Golinkin, ed., *Responsa of the Va'ad Halakhah of the Rabbinical Assembly of Israel*, V (5752-5754), Jerusalem 1994, pp. 43-46, 56, 63-65 (Hebrew).

No. 8 The Languages of the Jews in Ancient Times (1944)
Source: LGA, Box 10, "Offermann" file

February 4, 1944

Dear Mr. Offermann:

I am in receipt of your letter of January 29 in which you propounded several questions. I shall try to answer them to the best of my knowledge.

1) Rabbinic sources contain references to communications made by the Sanhedrin in Jerusalem to the Diaspora Jews. The oldest communication of that nature is written in Aramaic and dates from about the middle of the first century of the common era.[1]

2) Hellenistic Jews used Greek in their religious services not only in the Diaspora but even in Palestine in those places where Hellenistic Jews settled in large numbers and had established their own communities.[2]

3) With the rise of Christianity, the authority of the *Septuagint* dwindled very considerably among the Jews because of the misuse made of this translation of the Bible by some Christians. With the beginning of the second century, the translation by Aquila became the standard one amongst Hellenistic Jews.[3]

4) The *Peshita* was made somewhere in Eastern Syria about the middle of the second century. Its author was undoubtedly a Jew, though later the *Peshita* became the Bible of the Syriac Christians.[4]

Very truly yours,

Louis Ginzberg

Mr. Klemis A. Offermann
5000 Walnut Ave., Rte. 1
Downers Grove, Illinois

---

1   It consists of three letters written by Rabban Gamliel the Elder - see *Tosefta Sanhedrin* 2:6, ed. Zuckermandel, pp. 416-417; *Yerushalmi Sanhedrin* 1:2, 18d; *Bavli Sanhedrin*, 11b.
2   For example, in Caesarea - see *Yerushalmi Sotah* 7:1, fol. 21b.
3   See *EJ*, II, col. 855; and Bleddyn J. Roberts, *The Old Testament Text and Versions*, Cardiff 1951, pp. 117-123.
4   For various opinions, see *EJ*, II, cols. 858-859.

No. 9 Ordination in Ancient Times (1946)
Source: LGA, Box 10, "Richardson" file

UNION THEOLOGICAL SEMINARY
BROADWAY AT 120TH STREET
NEW YORK 27, N.Y.

November 20, 46

Dear Dr. Ginzberg,
May I be so bold as to ask your expert opinion on another matter?[1] I am bewildered about the Talmudic evidences for ordination by laying on of hands.

1   Is there any good evidence that scholars (scribes?) ordained their pupils by laying on of hands? Is *Jerusalem Sanhedrin* [Chapter 1, fol.] 19a relevant in this connection - or any other passage?

2   I understand you interpret [*Mishnah*] *Sanhedrin* 4:4 as "filling a vacancy" and not as ordaining. Is this so?

3   Is there any evidence that the Great Sanhedrin or local Sanhedrins required any kind of ordination?

4   Could the Christian reference in *I Timothy* 4:14 presuppose a Jewish custom the Christians took over?

5   Does the tradition of the Elders of Numbers 11:16ff. (which appears in Christian ordination prayers, as Hippolytus, *Apostolic Tradition* 8:3)[2] imply anything about [the] laying on of hands? I have heard Maimonides interprets Numbers 11:16ff. in the light of Deuteronomy 34:9 (re. Moses laying his hands on Joshua).[3] But I gather reciting the candidate's name was substituted for laying on hands after 135 A.D. (so *Jewish Encyclopedia*).[4] It is all very confusing to one as ignorant of the Talmud as I. I should greatly value any help you could give me.

Yours sincerely,

Cyril Richardson

~   ~   ~

December 9, 1946

Dear Professor Richardson:

Returned to the city, I am now able to reply to your letter of November 20th in which you propounded a number of questions in regard to the ordination by laying on of hands. I shall discuss the different points in the order given by you.

1. The problem that intrigues you engaged the attention of the Babylonian Amoraim more than 1500 years ago. We read in *Sanhedrin* 13b: "R. Aha the son of Rabba asked R. Ashi: 'Does ordination take place by actually laying on of the hands [or merely by conferring a title?]'.[5] R. Ashi said: 'Ordination is performed by conferring the title Rabbi and the authorization to impose fines when necessary.'"

I quote in accordance with the reading of the text in our editions and manuscripts, as well as medieval authors. One author, however, Rabbi Judah Al Barceloni (about the beginning of the 11th century) in his work *Sefer Ha-Shetarot*, page 132, has the reading in the Talmud according to which R. Ashi's statement would read: "The ordination takes place *by laying on of the hand* and conferring the title Rabbi."[6] There can be, however, no doubt that this is a faulty reading as can be seen from the following discussion in the Talmud where the assumption is that ordination might take place in absentia.[7] It is quite evident that laying on of hands could not be performed in absentia.

2. In my *Commentary on the Palestinian Talmud*, Vol. III, page 178, I have proved, and I hope convincingly so, that the *Mishnah Sanhedrin* 4:4 speaks of filling a vacancy and has nothing to do with ordination. I could adduce a number of additional proofs for the correctness of my interpretation. I will, however, limit myself to one.

According to *Tosefta Sanhedrin* 7:1, the great Sanhedrin would send out delegates all through the country to appoint local judges. If it be true that ordination was by the laying on of hands, the candidates would have had to be sent up to Jerusalem for the act of ordination. It would therefore not do to assume with Bacher (the article on ordination in the *Jewish Encyclopedia* is entirely based upon Bacher's essay on the subject)[8] that in olden times ordination was by laying on of hands. As a matter of fact, I doubt altogether the existence of any form of ordination before the establishment of the academy at Jabneh.

The passage you refer to about Rabban Johanan Ben Zakkai[9] does not [prove the existence of] ordination [earlier] than that by this leader of the academy of Jabneh. It seems as if up to the destruction of the Temple in the year 70, appointment of judges was the function of the secular Jewish government and it was only after the Jews had completely lost political rights that the scholars of Jabneh attempted to take the place of the Jewish government now extinct. This will also explain why the title Rabbi was never used before 70.

3. Not only is there no evidence that the great Sanhedrin or local Sanhedrin required any kind of ordination but, as remarked under 2, the evidence is quite in the opposite direction, that it was introduced at Jabneh. It is true [that] the Babylonian Talmud, which later authors such as Maimonides follow, assumes that for certain juridical functions an ordained judge is required. But, there is no proof in older sources for it.

One must altogether be very careful in evaluating the statements of the Babylonian Talmud concerning ordination since this institution was considered to be a privilege of the authorities in Palestine, and what the Babylonian scholars have to say about it is either from hearsay or mere speculation. Palestinian sources who, by the way, never used the word "ordination" but "appointment"[10] do not permit any doubt that ordination was not by laying on of hands. The Palestinian Talmud refers in many places to ordination that actually took place in absentia which clearly demonstrates that a personal contact between the ordainers and the ordained was not considered necessary - comp. [*Yerushalmi*] *Bikkurim* III, 65d.

4. In the light of the remarks given above, it is very unlikely that *I Timothy* 4:14 presupposes a Jewish custom of ordination. As a matter of fact, if one were to translate into Hebrew this passage of the New Testament, it would read: [עם סמיכת ידי הזקנים][11] which would mean the laying on of hands by the elders *on the sacrifice*, in which sense it is used in the *Mishnah* and other Tannaitic sources.

5. Maimonides in his code (*Sanhedrin* 4:1) is very accurate, writing: "Our master Moses ordained Joshua by laying on of hands as he said - Numbers 27:23 - 'and he laid his hands upon him and gave him a charge', and also the 70 elders were ordained by Moses so that the *Shekinah* rested upon them." He does distinguish quite clearly between [the] ordination of Joshua [which] in accordance with Scripture was by laying on of hands, and that of the elders which was like any other ordained judge, not by laying on of hands.

It may be of interest to know that *Sifre Numbers* 140 paraphrases Numbers 27:18 as follows: Moses gave Joshua the opportunity to discuss problems [of] the law and decide practical questions of law as long as Moses [was] still alive so that when Moses died, his people should not say: [in] the lifetime of his master he had no authority to decide the law, and now he does so![12] It is quite evident that this Tannaitic source does not take literally the Biblical passages where Moses is [said] to have laid his hands on Joshua, but, as the Babylonian Talmud defines ordination, by receiving title and power to act as judge. Other Tannaitic sources, however (for instance *Sifre Zutta* on Numbers 27:18), take the Biblical verses literally.[13] In no Jewish source, however, is the laying on of hands mentioned in connection with the election of the 70 elders. I hope that these few remarks on ordination will be of some use to you.[14]

Very sincerely yours,

Louis Ginzberg

Professor Cyril Richardson
Union Theological Seminary
Broadway at 120th Street
New York 27, N.Y. nh

1   For some of Richardson's other questions to LG, see below Chapter VII, Nos. 13-14.
2   The standard edition is that of G. Dix, ed., *The Treatise on the Apostolic Tradition of St. Hippolytus of Rome*, Rome and New York 1937; it is not available at the JNUL.
3   See LG's answer below, paragraph 5.
4   All of the references in the question are taken from *JE*, IX, s.v. Ordination, pp. 428-430.
5   LG added the phrase which I have placed in brackets on the basis of the Munich manuscript quoted by *Dikdukei Soferim*, ad loc.
6   The italics were added by the editor. A similar reading is quoted by Raymond Martini in his *Pugio Fidei*, Lipsaea 1687 as quoted by S. Lieberman, *Sheki'in*, Jerusalem 1970², p. 77.
7   This possibility is raised by the Talmud (*Sanhedrin* 14a) and adopted in a modified form by Maimonides (*Hilkhot Sanhedrin* 4:6), but it is clear from all the actual stories quoted in the *Bavli* ibid. that the ordainer and the ordainee had to be in the same place.
8   *Monatsschrift für Geschichte und Wissenschaft des Judentums* 38 (1894), pp. 122-127.
9   *Yerushalmi Sanhedrin*, Chapter 1, fol. 19a.
10   *Semikha* in the *Bavli* is called *minui* in the *Yerushalmi*.
11   The Hebrew is missing from the carbon copy in the LGA; I have filled in the Hebrew translation of Franz Delitzsch. I fail, however, to understand LG's interpretation because, in context, the verse means that the elders laid their hands *on* Timothy and thereby transferred to ḥim "the gift" "by prophetic utterance". Thus, *I Timothy* is clearly referring to ordination by the laying on of hands.
12   *Sifre Numbers*, ed. Horowitz, p. 186.
13   Ibid., p. 321.
14   On the subject of ordination also see *Acts* 6:6, *II Timothy* 1:6, S. Safrai, in: Joseph Salmon, Menahem Stern & Moshe Zimmerman, eds., *Iyunim B'historiografia*, Jerusalem 1988, pp. 73-79, and all of the literature cited there.

No. 10 Four Miscellaneous Questions (1947)
Source: LGA, Box 3, "Joseph Berger" file[1]
Excerpt: *Keeper*, pp. 311-312

November 21, 1947

Dear Mr. Berger:

I fully share your interest in the Jewish version of the "Oedipus Legend" but not in your enthusiasm for psycho-analysis.[2] You see, I have a nephew who is a brilliant practitioner of psychoanalysis,[3] my son dabbles in it, my daughter reads about it, my wife speaks of it, and I am amused by it. To be serious, when I consider that in my own lifetime, or to be accurate, in that period of it that elapsed from my student days to now, only extending over slightly more than half a century, no less than a half dozen theories have been established and thrown over in explaining myth and legend, I cannot but be extremely skeptical about the latest of these theories, the psychoanalytical one. Not being a physician, it would be not only presumptuous on my part, but what is still worse, foolish, to express an opinion on the great importance of psychoanalysis for psychology and psychiatry. What I object to is the complete disregard for historical facts and literary forms, in which setting myth and legend came down to us, on the part of many of the ardent disciples of Freud. One must be particularly careful to consider the historical facts in dealing with Jewish legends. The People of the Book remained bookish even in their fancies, and I could find no better illustration for this than the cycle of legends connected with Joshua.

In your letter you state your great surprise at my neglecting to point out the parallelism between the Greek Oedipus myth as found in Sophocles and the Hebrew account of the Achan episode as narrated in the book of Joshua. My surprise at these, your remarks, is a still greater one than yours. One who finds in an episode where neither incest nor traces of the father-complex are indicated, affinity with the Oedipus myth, will also be able to play Hamlet without Hamlet! The Hebrews never went to war without asking an Oracle, as can be seen from many places in the Bible, comp. for instance Judges 20:18ff. and I Samuel 14:18.[4] There is, therefore, nothing unusual in the mentioning of the Oracle in the Achan episode.[5] Anyone who appreciates good literature cannot help but see the beauty of the dramatic presentation of the history of the great warrior, Joshua. He starts his career with the splendid victory at Jericho, to suffer defeat immediately after, but finally gaining the greatest victory of his life by making the sun stand still and thus helping him to defeat his enemies.[6] How one can find any parallelism between the Achan episode and the [Oedipus] story is more than puzzling to me.

With regard to the [late] legends concerning Joshua's parentage and marriage, the following is to be remarked. They are all based on the assumption derived from First Chronicles 7:27 - wrongly or correctly so - that Joshua left no sons. This must have given a good deal of trouble to the learned mind, as well as to the popular fancy, and hence the different solutions found in Jewish legends. Some maintained that Joshua died childless because of some sins he committed. Others, in a more kindly spirit, maintained that while he had no sons, he was the father of a daughter - or daughters - who became the ancestors of Prophets, High Priests, and even of kings; comp. *Legends*, VI, p. 95, note 526 and p. 171, note 12, and see also *Matthew* 1:5. The legend transmitted by Shapiro likewise tries to explain the childlessness of Joshua by making use of the Oedipus legend in its own way. As I have remarked in my notes, the swallowing up by a fish of the infant Joshua is very likely based on the name of his father, Nun [which means] fish.[7] As the story of Jonah was surely known to Jewish Legend, the swallowing up of Joshua is simply old material worked in a new tale.

There is no way of telling where Shapiro found the legend, and I have very little hope that at present anybody would be willing to undergo the trouble [of] examining the rather bulky transcripts of Shapiro. There can be, however, no doubt that it is not a very old source, as can be seen by the style and language, which indicate a rather late period.

Years ago I examined the legendary material in *Antar* and my impression was that it merely contains a mixture of Jewish, Christian, Persian and old Arabic elements in such a confusion that the different layers are very difficult to separate.[8]

Your question why the daughter is not expressly included in the list of prohibited relations as given in Leviticus [Chapter 18] has puzzled many a student of the Bible. The only answer I have is that it required no legislative pronouncement concerning such an unusual and abhorrent form of incest. I may quote in this connection the remarks made by the greatest authority on the institution of marriage. [Edward] Westermarck in *The History of Human Marriage*, II [London, 1921], p. 82, writes: "The most frequent of all exogamous rules are those which prohibit a son from marrying his mother and a father from marrying his daughter. These rules seem in fact to be universally prevalent in mankind." It is true, in the earliest code known to us, the *Code of Hammurapi*, incest with a daughter is punished relatively lightly by the penalty of banishment,[9] but this is due to the fact that according to this Code the *potestas patris*[10] over his children, especially over the female ones, is so great that even the greatest form of violence against them could not be punished by death. This explains also why according to this Code it is only the father who is punished and not the daughter, the assumption being that the daughter had no choice but to submit to the father. A good deal has been written in modern times about this problem, and for a long time the prevailing theory was that in Biblical Law you have a development from the metronymic to patronymic society. I have no doubt, however, that gradually scholars will see the fallacy in this theory, as it has been seen more than sixty years ago by my teacher and master, Theodore Noeldeke.[11] A promising sign is the recent publication by [Walter] Koshland, *Mother-Right and Biblical Judaism*, Jerusalem 1943.[12]

Because of poor health, I was unable to write sooner to you, and even today I am still not strong enough to write in full as I would have liked to do.

Very sincerely yours,

Louis Ginzberg

Joseph Berger, Esquire[13]
215 Dinwiddie Street
Pittsburgh, Penna.

1   For Berger's lengthy reply of December 18, 1947, see LGA, Box 14, "Miscellaneous Letters" file.
2   For LG's attitude to psychoanalysis, see *Keeper*, pp. 311-316.
3   Dr. Sol Ginsburg - see above, Chapter IV, No. 11, note 1.
4   And cf. I Samuel 23:9ff. and 30:7ff.
5   Joshua 7:13ff.
6   Joshua 6:2ff.; 7:2ff.; and 10:1ff.
7   LG, *Legends*, VI, p. 169, note 2, quotes a midrash quoted by Avraham ben Elijah of Vilna, *Rav Pe'alim*, Warsaw 1894, fol. 12a, in the name of R. Nathan Spira (1585-1633) author of *Megaleh Amukot*. According to that unknown midrash, Joshua executed his own father and nearly slept with his mother. Joseph Berger probably based his whole Oedipal theory on this one late midrash.
8   The Romance of Antar was written in Arabic between the eighth and twelfth centuries. See *Antar: A Bedoueen Romance*, translated by Terrick Hamilton, 4 volumes; London 1819-20; and *The Encyclopedia of Islam* (new edition), I, pp. 518-521.
9   Paragraph 154, in: James Pritchard, ed., *Ancient Near Eastern Texts*, Princeton, NJ 1969, p. 172.
10   "Power of the father".

11   For LG's close relationship with Noeldeke (1836-1930), see *Keeper*, pp. 45-56 and 269, and Address, p. 111.

12   There is a vast literature on this subject. See Roland de Vaux, *Ancient Israel*, I, New York 1965, pp. 19-20 and the bibliography on pp. xxvi-xxvii; Avigdor Aptowitzer, *Hamishpat Ha'ivri* (5687), pp. 9-23; and Chaim Tchernowitz, *Toledot Hahalakhah*, I, New York 1945, pp. 232-234.

13   In his reply, Joseph Berger states that he was a friend of Rabbi Zev Wolf Leiter of Pittsburgh. It is worth noting that in 1962, Berger corresponded with Boaz Cohen on the very same topic - see BCA, Box 7, "Berger, Joseph" file.

No. 11 The Legal Responsibility of a Married Woman (1948)

Source: LGA, Box 5, "Gross" file
Excerpt: *Keeper*, p. 318 (the answer only)

LAW OFFICES OF

JOSEPH GROSS

SUITE 703-4-5

MARKET STREET NATIONAL BANK BUILDING

Telephones   JUNIPER AND MARKET STREETS
LOcust 7-4760-4761   PHILADELPHIA

                                        November 24, 1948
Dr. Louis Ginsburg,
New York City.

Dear Dr. Ginsburg:
   Several years ago you were kind enough to reply to a question of mine regarding Talmudic Law. This encourages me to write you again in the hope of a similar favor.
   Under the Common Law, a woman who does wrong in the presence of her husband is presumed to be acting under his influence, and not responsible therefore. Is there anything similar to that in Talmudic Law?
   Thanking you again therefore, I remain,

                     Sincerely yours,

                     Joseph Gross[1]

                ~   ~   ~

                                        December 3, 1948
Dear Mr. Gross:
   I received your letter of November 24th in which you ask me whether there is anything in Talmudic law similar to the common law according to which a woman who does a wrong in the presence of her husband is presumed to be acting under his influence and not responsible therefore. The answer to this question is "no" for the simple reason that, according to

Jewish law, a person is responsible for his actions even if it could be proved that he acted under the influence of somebody else.[2]

Sincerely yours,

Louis Ginzberg

Mr. Joseph Gross
703 Market Street
National Bank Bldg.
Philadelphia, Pa.

---

1   For other questions by Gross, see the following responsum and see his question to Boaz Cohen, in: BCA, Box 10, "Gross" file.

2   See *Kiddushin* 42b and parallels: "אין שליח לדבר עבירה" - "there is no agency for an illegal act".

No. 12 Impeachment in Talmudic Literature (1949)
Source: LGA, Box 5, "Gross" file

Janaury 5, 1949

Dear Mr. Gross:

Let me first thank you for your kind congratulatory message on the occasion of my 75th birthday. I hope and pray that you shall celebrate many a happy birthday in old age, surrounded by friends.

The main passage bearing upon the problem of impeachment in Talmudic literature is found in the *Palestinian Talmud, Sanhedrin*, Chapter II, at the very beginning, [fol.19d]. The passage makes it, of course, quite clear that an ordinary priest cannot be demoted though he might be disqualified from performing priestly services because of transgressing the priestly laws.[1] On the other hand, it is the High Priest, who is a high official, about whom controversy in the *Palestinian Talmud* enters.[2]

Very sincerely yours,

Louis Ginzberg

Mr. Joseph Gross, Esq.[3]
703 Market St.
Nat. Bank Bldg.
Philadelphia 7, PA

---

1   LG was probably quoting from memory. This is nowhere stated in the *Yerushalmi* passage or in the parallel passage in *Yerushalmi Horayot*, Chapter 3, fol. 47a. It is, rather, stated in *Mishnah Bekhorot* 7:7 and OH 128:40-41.

2   The *Yerushalmi* states that he receives lashes, but is not demoted.

3   For other questions by him, see the previous responsum and note 1, ad loc.

No. 13 The Inscription on a Parokhet (1949)[1]

Source: LGA, Box 4, "Harry Friedman" file

January 31, 1949

Dr. Harry G. Friedman[2]
25 East 86th Street
New York City

Dear Dr. Friedman:

There is no doubt that the generous donor of the curtain was a Bohemian - I use it in the literal sense and not the applied. He came from or was called after the town of Kuttenplan.[3] I am therefore rather inclined to assume that the name Petschi is not Italian but Slavic. My knowledge of Slavic languages is rather weak, somewhat similar to the knowledge of Hebrew by some Reform rabbis, but I consider it quite possible that Petschi is a diminutive or caritative of Peter.[4]

As to the abbreviation under the two tablets, I am still in doubt whether it stands for _____ or, as it seems to me, _____.[5] In my student days, they used to tell of a professor who would often refer in his lectures to some source as: "See me on page 45." I think I am rather free of professional vanity, but I cannot help referring you to page 59, Volume VI, of the *Legends [of the Jews]*, where a number of sources are given for the statement that the tablets had been taken from "a sapphire quarry under the Throne of Glory".

With kind regards to you and Mrs. Friedman,

Very sincerely yours,

Louis Ginzberg

1   Despite repeated enquirees, the staff of the Jewish Museum in New York City were unable to locate the *parokhet* in question, but I am confident that it will eventually be found - see the following note.

2   Dr. Harry Friedman (1882-1965) donated 5,000 *objets d'art* to the Jewish Museum in New York City - see *EJ*, V, col. 311. He must have sent LG a transcription or a photo of a *parokhet* in his collection. It stands to reason that the original parokhet is now in the Jewish Museum collection. For the Ginzbergs' ties to Friedman, see Eli Ginzberg, in: *Conservative Judaism* 33/4 (Summer, 1980), p. 33.

3   The Polish name was Chodova Plana - see *EJ*, V, cols. 485-486.

4   Caritative means "charitable" and is apparently an error. In any case, it is more likely that the name Petschi was derived from the Bohemian town of Petschau, which was located not far from Kuttenplan. The Petschek family originated there and came to the United States after

1938 (*EJ*, XIII, cols. 347-348). Perhaps they brought the *parokhet* with them and sold it or gave it to Harry Friedman or the Jewish Museum. For a picture of the interior of the synagogues of Kuttenplan and Petschau see Alfred Grotte, *Deutsche, böhmische und polnische Synagogentypen*, Leipzig 1915, pp. 68 and 86. On the first page, there is a clear picture of the *parokhet* but it is different from the one described here; on the second, the ark is closed.

5   The Hebrew is, as usual, missing in the carbon copy in the LGA.

No. 14 Three Miscellaneous Questions (1950)

Source: LGA, Box 11, "Spiro" file

September 18, 1950

Dear Rabbi Spiro:

I greatly appreciate your kind wishes on the occasion of the New Year, and I reciprocate them, wishing you happiness and the fulfillment of all your wishes.

The little booklet *Tagin* is undoubtedly of very late origin, perhaps not [earlier] than the 11th Century. The fanciful chain of tradition beginning with Eli and closing with Nahum "the scribe" seems to me to be [nothing] but the invention of mere fantasy.[1] It is hardly likely that in such late a time as the 11th Century any Jew bothered about the Samaritans and their traditions.

The origin of the crowns over certain letters is still very obscure. I am rather inclined to assume that some of them are purely ornamental while others have the purpose of avoiding confusing similar letters of which the Hebrew alphabet has quite a number. *The Antiquities Ascribed to Philo* is undoubtedly a product of the first century of the common era, a time [when] a tangent between the Jews and the Samaritans was very strong.[2] Yet I cannot find any anti-Samaritan tendencies in this book. It is true, Shechem is rarely mentioned and sometimes even Shilo is substituted for it. This, however, may be due to the carelessness of the scribe who mistook the abbreviation [ש'] for [שילה].[3]

With kind regards, I am

Sincerely yours

Louis Ginzberg

Rabbi Abram Spiro[4]
Hotel Kimberly
74th Steet and Broadway
New York, N.Y.

---

1   *Sefer Tagin* was published by Beer Goldberg and Shneur Sachs, Paris 1866; by Shimon Hurwitz in *Mahzor Vitry*, Berlin 1889-97, pp. 674-683; and by Judah David Eisenstein, *Otzar Midrashim*, New York 1915, pp. 563-569. Regarding this book, see *JE*, IX, pp. 666-667.

2   Regarding this book, see *EJ*, XIII, cols. 408-409.

3   There are two blank spaces in the carbon copy in the LGA. I have added the appropriate Hebrew words - assuming LG thought that *Pseudo-Philo* was originally written in Hebrew.

4   Rabbi Spiro was not a member of the Rabbinical Assembly. Shortly after this correspondence, he published a series of articles on *Pseudo-Philo* in *PAAJR* 20-22 (1951-53), followed by his doctoral dissertation at Columbia University entitled, *Manners of Rewriting Biblical History from Chronicles to Pseudo-Philo*, New York 1953.

No. 15 Two Miscellaneous Questions (1951)
Source: LGA, Box 8, "Lechner" file

October 25, 1951

Dear Mr. Lechner:

I am in receipt of your letter of October 6th, in which you asked me if there be any Jewish writer who has mentioned the parents of Francis of Assisi. It may sound presumptuous, but I shall nevertheless not refrain from stating that there is no reference in Jewish sources to St. Francis.[1] As far as I know, Assisi, the birthplace of Francis, had no Jewish community.

One may also state with certainty that Maimonides never visited Italy; though he did a good deal of travelling, it was in Asia and Africa and not in Europe. I do not need to tell you how interesting it would be to establish the fact that St. Francis was a Jew.

Very truly yours,

Louis Ginzberg

Mr. Michael Lechner
Hickory Way
Springfield, Conn.

1   In general, see *EJ*, VII, cols. 47-48; *The New Encyclopaedia Britannica, Macropaedia*, VII, Chicago 1979[15], pp. 682-683; and Jeremy Cohen, *The Friars and the Jews*, Ithaca and London 1982.

No. 16 The Numbers in Daniel (1951)

Source: LGA, Box 4, "Froom" file

June 6, 1951

Dear Doctor Froom:[1]

Because of a severe attack of illness, I was unable to acknowledge sooner the receipt of your letter of April 16th, but I shall not wait any longer though I have very little information to give you on the subjects you are interested in.

Jewish writers in the 19th century have made, to my knowledge, no new attempt to expound or explain the mystic numbers of Daniel.[2] They follow either the rationalistic explanation which finds in this book nothing but allusions to the conditions in the Near East during the Maccabean Revolution, or adhere to the old traditional view according to which the book of Daniel contains prophecies about that which will happen shortly before the appearance of the Messiah sometime towards the end of 6000 A.M. I have, however, a vague recollection that some of the early Zionists are tempted to find in Daniel indications of what will happen in our day.[3]

If I locate some of these passages, I shall not fail to communicate them to you.

Very sincerely yours,

Louis Ginzberg

Dr. L.E. Froom
Theological Seminary
6830 Laurel Street, N.W.
Washington 12, D.C.

---

1. Leroy Edwin Froom was a special instructor (he did not have a Ph.D.) in the Department of Church History at the Seventh Day Adventist Theological Seminary in Washington, D.C. - see below Nos. 17-18. All three of these letters were written in connection with his *magnum opus, The Prophetic Faith of Our Fathers*, 4 volumes, Washington, D.C. 1950-54, which is a one of the standard works on Adventist literature.

   In a letter to Gershom Scholem dated September 27, 1955, found in Scholem's copy of Froom's book at the JNUL, Froom writes: "...I have many Jewish scholars among my personal friends. The late Dr. Louis Ginzberg of New York City, the great Talmudist...these are men whom I greatly respect and whose friendship I treasure".

2. Seventh Day Adventists, like the Millerites and other nineteenth-century Adventist groups, predicted the coming of the Millennial kingdom of Christ on the basis of verses in Daniel and

Revelations. See *The New Encyclopaedia Britannica, Macropaedia*, I, Chicago 1979[15], pp. 101-102; and Froom, *The Prophetic Faith*, IV, pp. 429-851.
3. See, e.g., Nahum Sokolow, *History of Zionism: 1600-1918*, II, London 1919, p. 167.

No. 17 The Civil Calendar Date of Yom Kippur in 1844 (1952)
Source: LGA, Box 4, "Froom" file

April 28th, 1952
Dear Dr. Froom:
I was delighted to see from your letter that you are "at the approximate close" of your work on *The Prophetic Faith of our Fathers*. I shall, of course, be very happy to be of aid whenever I shall be in a position to do so. At present my state of health is such that complete rest was ordered by my physicians.

As to your specific question, to find the civil equivalent of the Day of Atonement in the year 1844,[1] I would refer you to my friend, Dr. Solomon Gandz, who is undoubtedly the best authority on the Jewish calendar.[2] You may write him at 2716 Monterey Avenue, Atlantic City, New Jersey, or at the Dropsie College, York and Broad Streets, Philadelphia, Pennsylvania.

By the way, the Karaites fixed their calendar by the visibility of the new moon,[3] and I am afraid that it will be difficult to establish the exact date when the moon became visible on the 29th day after the first of Elul.

Very sincerely yours,

Louis Ginzberg

Dr. Leroy Edwin Froom[4]
7th Day Adventist Theological Seminary
6830 Laurel Street Northwest
Washington, D.C.

---

1 William Miller (1782-1849) was founder of the Millerites. He declared that Christ would come between March 21, 1843 and March 21, 1844. When that failed to happen, his followers set a second date, on October 22, 1844, which was the *Karaite Yom Kippur*. See Froom (above, No. 16, note 1), IV, pp. 784-826, and especially pp. 821-822. The *Jewish* Yom Kippur in 1844 fell on September 23rd.
2 Regarding Solomon Gandz, see above, Chapter V, No. 13, note 3.

3   See *EJ*, X, cols. 778-779.
4   For biographical details, see above, No. 16, note 1.

No. 18 The Fixing of the Jewish Calendar (1952)
Source: LGA, Box 4, "Froom" file
Excerpt: *Keeper*, p. 319 (the answer only)

Seventh-day Adventist
THEOLOGICAL SEMINARY
6830 Laurel Street., N.W., Washington 12, D.C.

DEPARTMENT OF CHURCH HISTORY
DEVELOPMENT OF PROPHETIC INTERPRETATION
LEROY EDWIN FROOM[1]

November 7, 1952

Dr. Louis Ginzberg
Jewish Theological Seminary of America
Broadway and 122nd Street
New York, New York

My dear Doctor Ginzberg:
Your past kindnesses embolden me to come to you again for help. This time it pertains not only to the position of the Karaite Jews on the calendar and the protest that arose over the change by the Rabbinical leaders and the substitution of a calendar one moon earlier, so far as the new year day was concerned, but I need the information concerning when the Rabbinical change came in. Was it under Hillel, [in] the latter part of the fourth century, in order to bring about uniformity in observance of the Jewish feasts, widely scattered as they were, without controlling word from Jerusalem, and thus the expedient of choosing a fixed historical point - the vernal equinox - which would bring about uniformity? I am not having too great success in getting the full facts.

Where can I get this information? Who are the experts? I need to get this in English, or at least in modern languages.

I shall be in New York City from about November 11 to 18 and will try to make contact with you by phone. I thought I should tell you in advance of my need, thus you might have some suggestion for me when I call.

Very sincerely yours,

L.E. Froom

~   ~   ~

November 24, 1952

Dear Dr. Froom,

I am in receipt of your letter of November 7 in re the fixed calendar introduced by the Jews.

You are quite right in assuming that it took place some time in the second half of the fourth century. Whether the later tradition ascribing it to the Patriach Hillel II is based on fact, I have my doubts.[2] The tendency toward fixation of the calendar was noticed several centuries before the time of Hillel. Nor is it quite correct to say that the final fixation was established in the fourth century. You undoubtedly know the controversy that arose among the Rabbanite Jews in the tenth century, which almost led to a split between Palestinian and Babylonian Jewry.[3] One might, however, state with some certainty that the persecution of the Jews by the Roman Emperors was a factor in the great calendar reform.

There is a good deal of literature on the history of the Jewish calendar, but almost exclusively in Hebrew. You may, however, find some material that would interest you in the book on the Jewish Calendar by Adolph Schwartz, the title of which is *Der Jüdischer Kalender*, Breslau, 1872. I mentioned to you the name of Dr. Solomon Gandz, professor at Dropsie College, whom I consider the best authority on the Jewish calendar.[4]

With all good wishes.

Very sincerely yours,

Louis Ginzberg

Dr. L.E. Froom
7th Day Adventist Theological Seminary
6830 Laurel Street, N.W.
Washington 12, D.C.

~   ~   ~

Seventh-day Adventist
THEOLOGICAL SEMINARY
6830 Laurel Street., N.W., Washington 12, D.C.

DEPARTMENT OF CHURCH HISTORY
DEVELOPMENT OF PROPHETIC INTERPRETATION
LEROY EDWIN FROOM

December 7, 1952
Dr. Louis Ginzberg
Jewish Theological Seminary of America
Broadway and 122nd Street
New York, New York

Dear Doctor Ginzberg:

This will thank you most sincerely for your response of November 24. Your paragraph is very clear and succinct concerning the final fixation of the calendar and dealing with the question of the fourth century preliminary developments and the later heavy discussion between the Palestinian and Babylonian segments of Jewry.

Thank you again for your kindness in bringing to my attention the item by Schwartz, which I will secure through the Library of Congress.

I am sorry that you have had illness in the form of arthritis,[5] and I sincerely trust that you are not enduring too much discomfort or pain.

The fourth volume of my *Prophetic Faith of Our Fathers* is now in the last stages of manuscript checking before it goes into the hands of the compositors. It has been a very long, exacting task, the production of these four sizeable volumes, running close to a thousand pages each.

With cordial regards, I remain

Very sincerely yours,

L.E. Froom

1   For biographical details, see above, No. 16, note 1.
2   For this tradition, see *EJ*, VIII, col. 486.
3   See *EJ*, IV, cols. 539-540, and the literature cited there.
4   See above, No. 17, note 2. For two recent studies on the fixation of the Jewish calendar, see Zvi Langerman, *Assufot* 1 (5747), pp. 159-168; and Rahamim Sar-Shalom, *Sinai* 102 (5748), pp. 26-51.
5   He probably means neuritis - see *Keeper*, pp. 305, 316, passim.

No. 19 The Renewal of the Sanhedrin (undated)[1]
Source: LGA, Box 1, "Kasovsky" file

הודות לידידי הנעלה, כבוד הרב י.ח. קוסובסקי, שבקשני למסור בשמו שלום
לפרופסור לוי גינזברג,[2] עלה בידי להתראות עם ענק המדע הזה. זה מזמן שלא היה
לי תענוג רוחני והנאה שכזו. פרופסור גינזברג יודע את כל המצב הרוחני בארץ,
ובפרט בעניני מדע ותרבות. נצלתי את ההזדמנות בהיותי עמו לשמוע את חות דעתו
על דבר הקמת הסנהדרין מחדש בארץ ישראל.
רושם אני בזה, כמה מהרשמים אשר נחקקו במוחי, מפאת אמיתותם וההגיוניות
שבהם.
פרופסור גינזברג הצהיר והביע את דעתו באמרו כי ימינו אנו אינם כלל וכלל
מתאימים לחידוש הסנהדרין. רבוי המפלגות והדעות בישראל הם בעוכרנו. לדעתו,
[ה]סנהדרין הוא מוסד אשר החלטותיו מוכרחות להתקבל באופן מוחלט בלי כל
פקפוקים על ידי העם כולו. והיות והמצב בימינו הוא:
   א. ישנם אנשים שרוצים באי-אלה היתרים או שינוי של מנהגים וכו' וחושבים
      להעזר על ידי הסנהדרין, להם דרוש ההיתר של המוסד העליון.
   ב. ומצד אחר ישנם מפלגות בישראל אשר שום דעת רוב לא תשכנע אותם לשנות או
      לבטל אפילו מנהג קל, ומכל שכן להתיר את האסור לפי דעתם ומנהגם.
   ג. חלק מהמפלגות השמאליות [כך!] אשר לדעתן הדת היא דבר של מה בכך,
      ודבר ששייך רק להעבר, הם מצידם מאמינים, כי אין צורך בהיתרים כלל וכלל ועל
      אחת כמה וכמה שלא צריכים לסנהדרין שיתירו את מה שכבר התירו לעצמם מזמן.
אין אפשרות לחשוב, שמוסד רוחני גבוה אחד יאחד את העם, וכי העם ישמע
לקולו. האיחוד צריך להשתרש מלמטה, מבתי הספר[3] ואחר כך דרך כל השלבים
להגיע לידי הסנהדרין. החינוך בכל עם זהו הדבר היסודי המאחד את העם, העושה
אותו לחטיבה אחת ואצלנו לעת עתה הענין הוא להפך, החינוך הוא המחלק את העם
לזרמיו ו"מנהיגיו" דואגים לכך שהחילוק והפיצול הזה גם יימשך, ולכן המציאו
פרדוקס של זרמים שונים בחינוך. כל זמן שזה קיים, פרופסור גינזברג מדגיש ואומר,
כל זמן שפרוד הלבבות בישראל כה גדול, אין הוא רואה אפשרות ואף שמץ של
אפשרות לתקומת הסנהדרין. אך הוא אומר כי יתכן והנוער הישראלי סוף כל סוף
יגיע לכלל מסקנה כי מפלגות כה רבות בארץ כה קטנה אינן מועילות לרעיונם הנעלה
אלא מזיקות לו, ובצורה איטית יתאחדו. הוא מקוה שגם התנאים האקונומיים,
הסוציולוגיים והכלכליים שיתפתחו במרוצת הימים ישפיעו וגם יעזרו מאד לאיחוד
העם, ואז בעוד תקופה של דור או שנים תהיה לנו אולי אפשרות לייסד הסנהדרין
שהעם כולו ישמע בקולה.[4]

1   This article may have been written ca. 1951, when Y.L. Maimon and others were advocating the renewal of the Sanhedrin in Israel. It was apparently a newspaper article written by an Israeli, a friend of Chayim Y. Kasovsky of Jerusalem, who was visiting in the United States.

2   Chayim Yehoshua Kasovsky (1873-1960) was the author of concordances to the *Mishnah, Tosefta, Targum Onkelos*, and *Bavli* - see *EJ*, X, col. 809. It is worth noting that LG gave him constant financial and moral support. The LGA contains their correspondence as well as numerous letters in which LG solicits funds for Kasovsky's projects. See in this regard *Keeper*, pp. 173-175 and 182.

3   For a similar stress on Jewish education, see above, Chapter II, No. 5.

4   For some of LG's other views on Zionism and the State of Israel, see *Keeper*, Chapter IX and pp. 322-326. Also see Eli Ginzberg, *The Eye of Illusion*, New Brunswick, NJ 1993, p. 25 (and cf. *Keeper*, p. 242), who says that LG wanted to assemble a Sanhedrin in Paris after World War One in order to ease the plight of the many *agunot* caused by the war.

VII. Questions to Which No Answers Have Been Found

No. 1 Dancing in the Synagogue Basement (1920)   297

No. 2 Reinterment for Various Reasons (1920)   298

No. 3 May a Synagogue be Sold to a Church? (1920 and 1921)   299

No. 4 May a Widow Marry Her Late Husband's Brother? (1921)   302

No. 5 A Reburial Ceremony for a Soldier Whose Body is Being Brought from Overseas (1921)   304

No. 6 May the Organ be Used in the Synagogue? (1921)   305

No. 7 Is There Any Way to Permit a *Halutzah* to Marry a *Cohen*? (1921)   306

No. 8 A Woman and a Non-Jew as Witnesses at a Wedding (1926)   307

No. 9 Shakespeare and the Talmud (1926)   309

No. 10 An Intermarried Woman as a Member of the Ladies Auxiliary (1927)   311

No. 11 Anaesthetizing Animals Before *Shehitah* (1928)   313

No. 12 The Use of Hog Intestine Casings for Surgical Gut   314

No. 13 Did the Guests Bring Their Own Food to *Chaburah* Meals? (1946)   316

No. 14 Did Jews Before the Year 70 C.E. Bless People by the Laying on of Hands? (1946)   317

No. 15 The *Tosafot* of *Arvei Pesahim* (1949)   318

No. 16 The Source of an Unusual Midrash (1949)   319

No. 1 Dancing in the Synagogue Basement (1920)
Source: LGA, Box 9, "Mendes" file[1]

Rev. Dr. H. Pereira Mendes[2]
99 Central Park West
New York City

February 16th, 1920

My dear Dr. Ginsburg:
    There are a few people who have asked for permission to dance in the basement of our Synagogue. I object on the score of such passages as from the Torah (ומקדשי תיראו)[3] and from the Codes (*Orah Hayyim* 151:1 and 2).
    Dr. Gaster (England), Rabbi Weil (Sephardic Congregation, Paris), Haham Palache (Amsterdam), Dr. Hertz (Chief Rabbi of England), and quite a few on this side of the Atlantic support me [in] my opposition.
    But I would like to have your views as to whether it is or is not contrary to the spirit of the Torah and Jewish Law, Talmudic, etc., to allow dancing in the basement of a Synagogue, more especially if said basement is used for Divine service on *Rosh Hashana* and *Kippur*.
    May I hear from you at your earl[iest] convenience?
    Believe me to be,

Faithfully yours,

H. Pereira Mendes

Jewish Theological Seminary,
    53[1] West 123rd St.,
        City.

---

1   The papers of Rev. Mendes are located in the Rare Book Room of the Seminary, at Shearith Israel Congregation in New York City, and at the home of his granddaughter, Mrs. Margo Mendes Oppenheimer, in Scarsdale, New York. LG's reply was not found at the Seminary or at Shearith Israel, and the third collection has yet to be sorted.
2   Rabbi Henry Pereira Mendes (1852-1937) was rabbi and *hazzan* at Shearith Israel Congregation in New York City from 1877 until his death. See *EJ*, XI, cols. 1343-1344 and *Tradition* 30/1 (Fall, 1995), pp. 68-73; and Moshe Sherman, *Orthodox Judaism in America: A Biographical Dictionary and Sourcebook*, Westport, Connecticut and London, 1996, pp. 150-152.
3   "You shall venerate My sanctuary" - Leviticus 19:30.

No. 2 Reinterment for Various Reasons (1920)

Source: LGA, Box 2, "Abramowitz" file

REV. DR. H. ABRAMOWITZ[1]
507 ARGYLE AVENUE
WESTMOUNT
QUE.

June 15th, 1920

Dear Professor Ginsberg:

I desire your opinion as Chairman of the United Synagogue Committee on the Interpretation of Jewish Law, on the following two matters:

1. A mother who had interred her son in our cemetery over a year ago now desires to move his remains to another part of the same cemetery for the reason that she desires to form a family plot to enable her in time to lie next to him, all the available space next to the present grave being now occupied. Her request is prompted by a mother's ardent love, and I would [ask] your opinion whether in Jewish Law it could be permitted.[2]

2. Children who buried their father in a part of the cemetery that had not been drained, and where a grave when opened shows water, desire to remove the remains of their father to a dry part of the cemetery.[3] Their reason being that when their mother's time should come, they cannot contemplate burying her alongside the father under those conditions. Their proposed action however cannot be called forming a family plot for the reason that after the father will have been removed, they will still leave behind a brother and sister who are buried alongside him.

I shall appreciate an early reply inasmuch as I should like to submit your opinion before I leave for the summer.

I hope you and your family are in the best of good health, and with cordial regards, I remain

Yours sincerely,

H. Abramowitz

---

1 Rabbi Herman Abramowitz (1880-1947) was ordained by the Seminary in 1902 and served as rabbi of Shaar Hashomayim in Montreal from 1903 until his death. See *EJ*, II, col. 169;

and Nadell, pp. 26-27. It is worth nothing that he wrote to LG even though he himself was a member of the Committee on the Interpretation of Jewish Law! See *USAAR* VI (1918), p. 6.

2   For responsa on this subject, see above, Chapter IV, Nos. 19-21.

3   This alone is sufficient justification for reinterment - see YD 363:1.

No. 3 May a Synagogue be Sold to a Church? (two questions; 1920 and 1921)[1]

Sources:

1. LGA, Box 3, "Benjamin" file
2. LGA, Box 2, "Baroway" file[2]

Cong. Anshe Emeth Beth Tefila
SAMUEL BENJAMIN, RABBI[3]
1212 E. 105TH STREET
CLEVELAND, O

Feb. 18, 1920

Professor Louis Ginzberg
   531 W. 123rd St.
      New York City

My honored and beloved master:

I trust that you are well and that I am not burdening you with the request I have to make.

My congregation is desirous of selling its old synagogue and a colored Baptist church wants to buy it. Is it lawful to sell the synagogue for a church? The circumstances are these. The present population of the locality where the synagogue is situated consists almost entirely of negroes and Italians. The building is a magnificent structure but is rapidly decaying for lack of attention. Our members are now living a long distance away from the old synagogue, have lost all interest in it, and are building a new one now. Once before they sold a house of worship to an individual with the restriction that it should not be sold for a church.[4] The restriction did not prove binding and the individual sold it at a huge profit to the Catholic Church. If we sell the synagogue now, we will be greatly aided in our work of establishing a much needed new *Shoul*. If we don't, it will become a dilapidated ruin and at best be used as a storehouse or junk yard. Please advise me what to do and kindly give me the references in Jewish law where this topic is considered.

I would also like your opinion on the question of permitting men and women [to sit] together at services.[5]

Thanking you for your kind interest and with the most fervent wishes for your good health I am

Respectfully yours,

Samuel Benjamin

~   ~   ~

Congregation Anshe Emeth
230 SOUTH BALCH STREET
AKRON, OHIO

Moses Baroway[6]
RABBI

April 11, 1921

Professor Louis Ginsberg,
   Chairman, Committee on Jewish Law,
      United Synagogue of America,
         531 West 123rd Street,
         New York City.

Dear Doctor Ginsberg:

May I trouble you with the following question:

Congregation Anshe Emeth now worships and conducts its school in a little wooden building, formerly a dwelling but later remodelled as far as possible for synagogal purposes. The building was intended to be used temporarily, and a new and elaborate synagogal structure was later to be erected on the same site.

At the present time, it is necessary to build a new synagogue in another part of the city. The congregation can sell its present little building to a Christian church for the sum of $15,000, which is needed very much for the fund towards the new building.

Will Jewish law permit such a sale - in the case of a building which is neither adequate nor of a permanent character? I shall be very grateful for your answer and for a list of the authorities, which I should like to read over and absorb myself.

Very sincerely,

Moses Baroway

P.S. Could I hear from you immediately, since the matter is exceedingly urgent and my own activity here hinges upon it.

---

1   See above, Chapter III, No. 12, for a complete responsum on this subject.

2   The reply was not found in the LGA or in the Baroway archives (Archive 14) in the Rare Book Room at the Seminary.

3   Rabbi Samuel Benjamin was born in Jerusalem in 1894 and ordained by the Seminary in 1919. He is last mentioned in the *PRA* in 1932 at a Tel-Aviv address. See *Students' Annual* 3 (1916), p. 201; *PRA* 4 (1930-32), p. 383; and *PRA* 5 (1933-38), p. 492.

4   For a similar suggestion by LG, see above, note 1.

5   For responsa on this subject, see above, Chapter III, Nos. 7-9.

6   Rabbi Moses Baroway (1894-1926) was ordained by the Seminary in 1919 and held pulpits in Akron, Ohio and Wilmington, Delaware. See a detailed eulogy by Frank Schechter, in: *PRA* 1 (1927), pp. 92-95. Also see *Between the Lines* (the JTS library bulletin) 4/1 (Spring, 1991), p. 2.

No. 4 May a Widow Marry Her Late Husband's Brother? (1921)
Source: LGA, Box 3, "Colish" file

RABBI NATHAN H. COLISH[1]
CONGREGATION ADAS ISRAEL
6TH AND EYE STREETS, N.W.
WASHINGTON, D.C.

45 New York Ave. N.W.,
Washington, D.C. March 22, 1921

Professor Louis Ginzberg,
Jewish Theological Seminary of America,
New York.
My dear Professor:
I wish to ask your advice in reference to the Jewish law or practice in the following case that was brought to me, to wit:
A certain man X, a *Kohen*, married a woman who was eligible in all matters but that she bore the same Jewish name as the mother of the groom (i.e., her mother-in-law), because of which the parents of the groom discountenanced the marriage.[2] Six months after the marriage, the husband X died through an accident. Seven years have passed since. In the meanwhile the brother of the deceased Y and the young widow have grown fond of each other and are desirous to marry. The father of the חתן Y objects to the marriage again, although the difficulty of identity of bride's and mother-in-law's names no longer exists as the latter has recently died. The rest of the family is very favorably disposed to the marriage but is willing to abide by the father's will if Jewish law or practice is in consonance with his desire. The question is: Is there any prohibition in Jewish law or custom against the marriage of this man, Y, and the widow?[3]
As the family is eager to obtain the decision as soon as possible, I would greatly appreciate an early reply.
Thanking you, I am with kind greetings to you and yours,

Faithfully yours,

Nathan H. Colish

1   Rabbi Nathan Colish (1895-1982) was ordained by the Seminary in 1920 and served congregations in Washington and New York before serving a lengthy tenure at Beth El in Houston, Texas (1929-62). See the detailed eulogy in *PRA* 44 (1982), pp. 150-151.

2   See above, Chapter V, No. 2 for a responsum on this very question.

3   There is, of course, a major halakhic obstacle to this marriage. In former times the brother could have married his late brother's widow (*yibum*), but Ashkenazic Jews no longer practice *yibum* so he would have had to perform *halitzah* and thereby pledge not to marry her - see *EJ*, XI, col. 127. It is surprising that Rabbi Colish was unaware of this basic law.

No. 5 A Reburial Ceremony for a Soldier Whose Body is Being Brought from Overseas (1921)
Source: LGA, Box 2, "Baroway" file[1]

Congregation Anshe Emeth
230 SOUTH BALCH STREET
AKRON, OHIO

Moses Baroway[2]
Rabbi

April 10, 1921

Dear Professor Ginsberg:
    As you know, the government is bringing over the bodies of soldiers who died in France and who were buried there. A member of my congregation has just told me that the body of his son will arrive soon and another burial ceremony will be conducted.
    Is there any special Jewish procedure? Quite candidly, the matter is quite a new one to me; and I want to ask you whether the ordinary burial ceremony is used or is there something else to be done.[3]

Very sincerely,

Moses Baroway

---

1   The reply was not found in the LGA or in the Baroway archives (Archive 14) in the Rare Book Room at the Seminary.
2   For biographical details, see above, No. 3, note 6.
3   In general, see YD 403 and Y.M. Tuckechinsky, *Gesher Hahayyim*, Jerusalem, 5720[2], pp. 280-282.

No. 6 May the Organ be Used in the Synagogue? (1921)[1]
Source: LGA, Box 8, "Langh" file

CONGREGATION ANSCHE EMES
GARY PLACE NEAR BROADWAY
CHICAGO
Member of the United Synagogue of America

PHILIP A. LANGH, RABBI[2]   *Office*
853 Newport Ave.   610 Ashland Block
Telephone Graceland 1222   Telephone Central 8432
                                                   8/22 - 1921

Dear Dr. Ginzberg,

Our congregation is purchasing the Reform Temple of our neighborhood. The temple contains an organ. This fact makes the organ question an issue in our congregation. There are some who want its use, at least during *Yom Tov*. They know my attitude very well.[3]

It will help to obtain from you, as Chairman of the Committee on Interpretation of Jewish Law, an authoritative responsum on the question of the use of the organ, which responsum I can then place before the congregation. a) What are the legal objections to the organ on Sabbaths and on other holydays? b) What other objections, if any, are there such as historic objections, present Jewish feeling, etc.?

Thanking you in advance, I am
Cordially yours,

Philip A. Langh

---

1. For LG's objections to the organ, see above, Chapter I, No. 4 and Chapter III, No. 18.
2. Rabbi Philip Langh (1893-1946 or 1947) was ordained by the Seminary in 1918. See *Students' Annual* 3 (1916), p. 203; and *PRA* 11 (1947), p. 372.
3. It is clear from what follows that Rabbi Langh was opposed.

No. 7 Is There Any Way to Permit a Halutzah to Marry a Cohen? (1921)

Source: LGA, Box 6, "Hershman" file

CONGREGATION

A.M. HERSHMAN, RABBI[1]   SHAAREY ZEDEK   TELEPHONE GLENDALE 5197
                                  OF DETROIT

WILLIS AVENUE AT BRUSH STREET

AFFILIATED WITH

THE UNITED SYNAGOGUE OF AMERICA

Sep. 7, 1921

Professor Louis Ginsburg
531-535 W. 123rd Street
New York, N.Y.

Dear Doctor Ginsburg:

Can you find a היתר for a חלוצה to marry a כהן?[2] I should add that the young lady I refer to, had given birth to a normal child; but the child lived only twelve days.[3]

The father of the young lady is a respectable and respected member of the Community. He is distressed about the whole affair. I promised him that I would communicate with you. An early answer would be highly appreciated.

Respectfully yours,

A.M. Hershman

1   Rabbi Abraham M. Hershman (1880-1959) was ordained by the Seminary in 1906 and was rabbi at Shaarey Zedek in Detroit from 1907 until 1946. He wrote *Rabbi Isaac ben Sheshet Perfet and his Times*, New York 1943 and other scholarly works. See *EJ*, VIII, col. 395; and *PRA* 23 (1959), pp. 101-104. It is worth nothing that he wrote to LG even though he himself was a member of the Committee on the Interpretation of Jewish Law! See *USAAR* VI (1918), p. 6.

2   For the prohibition, see EH 6:1.

3   If the child died before the father, the mother was still required to undergo *halitzah* - see EH 156:1ff.

No. 8 A Woman and a Non-Jew as Witnesses at a Wedding (1926)

Source: LGA, Box 3, "Bienenfeld" file

TEMPLE ADATH YESHURUN
CORNER SOUTH CROUSE AVENUE AND HARRISON STREET
SYRACUSE, NEW YORK

May 17, 1926

Professor Louis Ginsberg
531 W. 123rd St.
New York City

Dear Dr. Ginsberg:

A member of my congregation asked me if I could officiate at a wedding with my wife and a non-Jewess as witnesses. I told him I could not, and when pressed for a reason explained that one of the prime requisites of a wedding ceremony is competent witnesses, and such witnesses would not be competent in Jewish law.[1] He then showed me a marriage certificate issued by one of my colleagues in a nearby city, a Seminary man, where only such witnesses had been present and where no *Kasuba*[2] had been given. He told me that his question had been rhetorical and that he had asked me merely to have me confirm his opinion, and then asked me that matters being as they were, what my comment was and what should be done. Naturally, I told him I could not comment on the methods of a colleague, a graduate of my Seminary, but stated that I would refer the matter to the Chairman of the Committee on the Interpretation of Jewish Law.

May I have your opinion for purposes of record, on the case as to the validity of that marriage. And may I also have your quite informal and friendly advice as to what method to pursue in this specific case.

Mrs. Bienenfeld and I think we are going to our camp sometime very soon for a visit of just a day or two. I wish we could induce you and Mrs. Ginsberg, or either one of you, to spend some time with us now in Syracuse, and possibly visit the Fourth Lake territory. The weather here is delightful, ideal, I might say. We enjoy running around in our car and manage to have quite an enjoyable time.

With Yom-Tov greetings[3] to you and Mrs. Ginsberg and the children, I am,

Cordially,

Jesse Bienenfeld[4]

914 Ackerman Ave.

AFFILIATED WITH THE UNITED SYNAGOGUE OF AMERICA

---

1   For women see HM 35:14; for non-Jews, see ibid. 34:19.
2   I.e., *Ketubah* or marriage contract.
3   *Shavuot* fell on May 19th in 1926.
4   Rabbi Jesse Bienenfeld (1891-1944 or 1945) was ordained by the Seminary in 1919. See *Students' Annual* 3 (1916), p. 201; and *PRA* 9 (1945), p. 226.

No. 9 Shakespeare and the Talmud (1926)
Source: LGA, Box 10, "Raisin" file

JEWISH WELFARE BOARD
UNITED STATES ARMY AND NAVY
COOPERATING WITH AND UNDER THE SUPERVISION OF
WAR DEPARTMENT COMMISSION ON TRAINING CAMP ACTIVITIES

Charleston, S.C. 10/28/26

Prof. L. Ginzberg
Jewish Theological Seminary
New York City

Dear Professor:

In reading Shakespeare, I came across several remarks and situations which suggested similar instances in the Talmud. Not having the necessary reference books with me, will you kindly give me the sources which parallel them? I need not tell you I'll [not] be כפוי טובה.[1]

1) In the *Merchant of Venice*, the story of the three chests[2] reminds me of something like it in the Midrash. There is also a story [there] of three laborers who worked on three trees and one of them was paid 200 *dinarim*, while the others received only one.[3] In the New Testament there is also something similar to it.[4]

2) In *Coriolanus* there is the fable of the members of the body who mutinied against the belly.[5] I once translated it from the Talmud but cannot recall whence I took it.[6]

3) In *Measure for Measure*[7] and again in *All's Well that Ends Well*,[8] there is a situation where a husband, without intending it, possesses his own wife.[9] I know there is something to that effect about a certain *Tanna*[10] and also about Jesse who before the birth of David: כעס על אשתו ואמר לנערה לבוא אליו בלילה ולשכב עמו. והנערה מסרה סימניה לאשתו והוא שכב עמה והוליד את דוד.[11]

You may also know about other parallels to Shakespeare which I will greatly appreciate.

Thanking you in advance and with best wishes, I am,

Cordially yours,

Jacob S. Raisin[12]

1   I.e., "ungrateful".
2   Act II, Scene vii.
3   The source is *Devarim Rabbah* 6:2. The wages there are one, one-half, and 200.
4   He is probably referring to *Matthew* 20:1-16.
5   Act I, Scene i.
6   There is no close rabbinic parallel to the parable in Shakespeare. *Genesis Rabbah* 100:7, eds. Theodor-Albeck, p. 1290 contains an argument between the stomach and the mouth. In another frequently cited midrash about the parts of the body, the tongue emerges victorious. See *Midrash Tehillim* 39:2, ed. Buber, p. 255; *Yalkut Shimoni* to Psalm 34, par. 721; *Yalkut Hamekhiri* to Psalms 39:2, ed. Buber, p. 234; *Yalkut Hamekhiri* to Proverbs, Chap. 18, ed. Grunhut, fol. 3a; *Derashot ibn Shu'ib*, Shelah Lekha, ed. Cracow, fols. 65d-66a; and *Orhot Zaddikim*, end of *Sha'ar Leshon Hara*, ed. Seymour Cohen, pp. 442-444.
      For ancient parallels to this motif, see Emanuel Ben Gurion, *Shevilei Ha'aggadah*, Jerusalem 1949, pp. 79 and 109-110, who refers to the parable of Agrippa Menenius quoted by Livy, II, xxxii, 8-12, translated by B.O. Foster, I, London and Cambridge, Mass. 1967, pp. 322-325 (and cf. the references there) and to *I Corinthians* 12:14-26 and who quotes an Indian parallel. (My thanks to Prof. Ya'akov Elboim of The Hebrew University who supplied me with most of these references.) Finally, it should be added that Shakespeare's parable is actually based on the story in Livy - see *The Tragedy of Coriolanus*, ed. John Dover Wilson, Cambridge 1964, pp. xi-xvi.
7   Act III, Scene i; Act IV, Scene i; and Act V, Scene i.
8   Act IV, Scene ii and Act V, Scene iii.
9   I.e., sleeps with his own wife.
10   Not a *Tanna*, but rather the *Amora* Hiyya bar Ashi - see *Kiddushin* 81b (top).
11   This is a paraphrase quoted from memory. The midrash is found in *Yalkut Hamekhiri* to Psalms, Chapter 118, p. 214. For parallels, see *Legends*, VI, p. 246, note 11.
12   Rabbi Jacob Raisin (1878-1946) was ordained by Hebrew Union College in 1900 and was rabbi of Beth Elohim in Charleston, South Carolina from 1915-44. See *UJE*, IX, p. 68 and *EJ*, XIII, col. 1525.

No. 10 An Intermarried Woman as a Member of the Ladies Auxiliary (1927)

Source: LGA, Box 12, "Vaniewsky" file

CONGREGATION SONS OF ISRAEL
(CONSERVATIVE)
EDSALL BOULEVARD AND BROAD AVENUE
PALISADES PARK, NEW JERSEY

EDGEWATER, N.J.

ENGLEWOOD, N.J.

FORT LEE, N.J.

LEONIA, N.J.

MORSEMERE, N.J.

PALISADE, N.J.

PALISADES PARK, N.J.

RIDGEFIELD, N.J.

——

December 8, 1927

I.S. RAVETCH, Rabbi[1]

300 ELM PLACE

LEONIA, N.J.

United Synagogue,[2]
    531 West 123rd St.,
        New York City.

Gentlemen:

Kindly take the following matter into consideration as we are looking forward to your decision; our Rabbi refused to act in the matter and referred same to you.

A Jewish woman, whose husband is a *Goy*, has asked admission into the Ladies Auxiliary of our Temple. Are we permitted to accept her under these circumstances or not?

We hope that you will give this matter your immediate attention and let us know your decision.[3]

Very truly yours,

CONGREGATION SONS OF ISRAEL

I. Vaniewsky, President

1   Rabbi Isadore Shalom Ravetch was born in Chudnow, Russia in 1899 and was ordained by The Jewish Institute of Religion in New York in 1934. Nonetheless, he was already the rabbi at Sons of Israel in Palisades Park, New Jersey from 1927-29. See *Who's Who in American Jewry*, III:1938-39, New York 1938, p. 840.

2   This question was addressed to the United Synagogue, but was apparently forwarded to LG even though at the date in question LG was no longer head of the Law Committee which had been reorganized in September, 1927.

3   LG's reply is quoted in a question addressed to the Committee on Jewish Law regarding burial of a non-Jew: "I recall a decision by Dr. Ginzberg where a Jewish woman who was married to a non-Jew was not even entitled to be admitted to the sisterhood of the congregation because by her marriage she had renounced the Jewish faith." (CJLS Box, "Kevurah" file)

No. 11 Anaesthetizing Animals Before Shehitah (1928)
Source: LGA, Box 9, "Moore" file

3 Divinity Avenue
Cambridge, Mass.

May 23, 1928

Professor Louis Ginzberg
Jewish Theological Seminary
531-535 West 123rd Street
New York City

Dear Professor Ginzberg:

I have a note this morning from Rabbi Epstein[1] which gives me a little concern. Two or three weeks ago a surgeon in the U.S. Marine Hospital in Chelsea sent me some questions about the permissibility in Jewish law of anaesthetizing animals to be slaughtered in the Jewish mode, by the use of ether or carbon monoxide. I knew nothing about it and, having just been reading Epstein's *Jewish Marriage Contract*,[2] I asked him.[3] He replied that he was going to New York and expecting to see you and would inquire of you. He writes me today that he has seen you and asked you to write to me about it.

I should be conscience-striken if I thought that I was thus even indirectly adding another straw to the burden which is already enough to break a camel's back. That is why I did not inquire of you in the first instance. Please do not take any time to look the matter up or to write to me. If you have any colleague or assistant in the library on whom you could put it off, I should not mind; but don't treat it as an additional obligation for yourself.

Sincerely yours,

George F. Moore[4]

---

1 Rabbi Louis Epstein (1887-1949), Prof. Ginzberg's pupil and friend, was rabbi in Brookline, Massachusetts from 1925-47. See *Keeper*, p. 293 and Index; Seminary Family, p. 124; *EJ*, VI, col. 834; and Nadell, pp. 80-81.
2 *The Jewish Marriage Contract*, New York 1927.
3 Brookline is not far from Harvard, where Moore taught.

4   George Foot Moore (1851-1931) was a good friend of LG - see *Keeper*, pp. 269, 283-284. The LGA contains a thick file of correspondence between them written while Moore was working on his *magnum opus, Judaism in the First Centuries of the Christian Era*, Cambridge, Massachusetts 1927-30. See Moore's Preface, p. x, and his Preface to the Notes, p. v.

No. 12 The Use of Hog Intestine Casings for Surgical Gut[1]
Source: General Files, File 10 (July-December, 1942)

C O P Y
Johnson & Johnson

New Brunswick, N.J.
August 31, 1942

Dr. Louis J. Finkelstein[2]
Jewish Theological Seminary
3080 Broadway
New York, N.Y.

Dear Sir:
Through his brother, one of my associates, Rabbi Irving Ganz of Johnstown,[3] has suggested that you may be able to advise us on a question that might concern the Jewish community.

As you may know, we are one of the important manufacturers of surgical gut for sutures and ligatures. These strings are commonly made from split sheep intestines which are then spun, dried and polished for surgical use. A recent survey by our military authorities indicates that the available supply of sheep gut will be inadequate to supply Army, Navy, Lease-lend, and Good Neighbor demands, added to our usual civilian requirements. Serious consideration is, therefore, being given to the possibility of using hog intestine casings for surgical gut, as they have been used for tennis and other sport purposes.

It is our impression that the pork taboo of your law would not apply to such an emergency use of hog intestines for surgical purposes, but in any event we should welcome a statement from you and any associates you may choose to consult on the present or probable reaction of the Jewish community to such material.

Sincerely yours,

Herbert L. Davis

~ ~ ~

September 1, 1942

Dear Professor Ginzberg:
I received a letter, a copy of which I am enclosing, from Johnson and Johnson, manufacturers of medical materials. What do you think I should say to them?[4]
With warmest regards to yourself and to Mrs. Ginzberg,

Affectionately, as ever,

Louis Finkelstein

Professor Louis Ginzberg
East Pond
Oakland, Maine[5]

1   Despite extensive searches of both archives and microfilm file storage at Ethicon Inc., a Johnson & Johnson company, the reply to this letter was not located (a letter from Thomas Eagan, Product Director, October 15, 1992).
2   Dr. Louis Finkelstein (1895-1991) was President (1940-51) and later Chancellor (1951-72) of the Jewish Theological Seminary. He was also one of LG's favorite disciples. See *EJ*, VI, cols. 1293-1295; *Keeper*, pp. 137-139; Nadell, pp. 83-87; and *PRA* 9 (1945), pp. 196-198.
3   Rabbi Irving Ganz was ordained by the Seminary in 1938 and died in 1969 or 1970. See *PRA* 5 (1933-38), p. 494, and *PRA* 34 (1970), pp. 172-173.
4   This is probably permissible, since pig is only forbidden to be *eaten* - Rambam, *Hilkhot Ma'akhalot Assurot*, Chapter 2ff.; *Sefer Hahinukh*, ed. Chavel, no. 159; and especially Avraham Steinberg, *Entziklopedia Hilkhatit Refuit*, II, Jerusalem 1991, col. 212, end of note 49.
5   For other responsa written in Maine, see above, Chapter II, No. 6, note 6.

No. 13 Did Guests Bring Their Own Food to Chaburah Meals? (1946)

Source: LGA, Box 10, "Richardson" file

UNION THEOLOGICAL SEMINARY
BROADWAY AT 120TH STREET
NEW YORK 27, N.Y.

19 September, 1946

Dear Dr. Ginzberg:

May I trouble you with a question which has been haunting me? Is there any evidence that at a *Chaburah* meal (in the first century A.D.) the guests brought their donations, and these were placed on a side-board as they entered the house?

The question is interesting as indicating the Jewish origin of the Christian "offertory" in the Liturgy.[1]

The existence of these *Chaburoth* is difficult to discover, for me not versed in the Talmud.[2] Perhaps even apart from that vexed question, there is some evidence of "picnic" meals in Judaism.

I should be deeply grateful to you for any help you could give me - I hope it will not put you to too much trouble.

Yours very Truly,

(Prof.) Cyril C. Richardson[3]

---

1 The "offertory" is the Christian rite in which each member of the congregation presents bread, wine, and water to the priest celebrating the Mass. For the history and variations of this custom, see *New Catholic Encyclopedia*, X, New York 1967, pp. 649-651.

2 See *EJ*, VII, cols. 1489-1492, for the terms *haver* and *haverim*. To the best of my knowledge, there is no similarity between a *havurah* meal and the offertory. A more likely parallel would be the Jewish practice of people bringing their animal and non-animal offerings for sacrifice on the altar.

3 For other questions from Richardson, see the following question as well as above, Chapter VI, No. 9.

No. 14 Did Jews Before the Year 70 C.E. Bless People by the Laying On of Hands? (1946)

Source: LGA, Box 10, "Richardson" file

UNION THEOLOGICAL SEMINARY

BROADWAY AT 120TH STREET

NEW YORK 27, N.Y.

Dec. 12.46

Dear Dr. Ginzberg:

You were very generous to write me such a helpful letter on this question of ordination, and I am, indeed, much beholden to you. Please accept my deep thanks for the care and time you spent in looking up the relevant passages.[1]

One further point occurs to me, but I hesitate to ask even a further favour of you. I have been wondering if there is any evidence in Judaism before 70 [C.E.] of *blessing persons by laying on of hands*.[2] This would, I suppose, differ from the Aaronitic lifting up of the hands in blessing.[3]

I suppose there must be some custom on which Rabbi Johanan ben Zakkai was dependent for his innovation in the academy of Jabneh.[4] And, so far as Christian history goes, the laying on of hands in *Acts* 6:6 and 13:1-3 needs some explanation in Jewish customs.

Perhaps, at your leisure, you could offer a suggestion or two along these lines; otherwise we seem very much in the dark about this question.

Sincerely,

Cyril Richardson

1   See above, Chapter VI, No. 9. And cf. the previous question in this chapter which was also asked by Richardson.

2   See Genesis 48:14-20.

3   Leviticus 9:22.

4   See Yerushalmi Sanhedrin Chapter 1, fol. 19a, which was discussed above, Chapter VI, No. 9.

No. 15 The Tosafot of Arvei Pesahim (1949)
Source: LGA, Box 10, "Rabinowitz" file

Sept. 2, 1949

Prof. Louis Ginzberg
3080 Broadway N.Y.C.

Dear Prof. Ginzberg:

I am puzzled about a little תוספות of ערבי פסחים, fol. 117b, ד״ה למען
תזכור. What midrash does the text refer to?[1] What is the meaning of the
acrostic and how is it all derived from בפרך?[2] It seems to me that the Tosafot
of this chapter differ from the rest of this tractate and seem to be a late
version by a pupil of R. Jehiel whom he mentions a number of times [as]:מורי
רבינו יחיאל. Perhaps the compiler of these "supplements" is a colleague or
even a disciple of R. Meir of Rothenburg whom he mentions in this little
portion ושמעתי מהר״ימ.[3]

I did not wish to disturb you as I understand that you are not in very
good health, but this question has been troubling me for a while. I hope you
excuse my presumption.

If I may be permitted to insert a personal note, I have been very ill last
winter for almost a half year and I despaired of my life after a serious
operation. Thank the all-merciful, I am well-recovered.

God grant you many years in health and strength, for we all need you.

Respectfully yours,

Elias N. Rabinowitz[4]

---

1   This is apparently the only source for this midrash - see Rabbi M.M. Kasher, *Torah
Sheleimah*, VIII, New York 5714, p. 31, par. 140.

2   The word is found in Exodus 1:13-14. The midrash says that פר״ך in אתב״ש gematria
equals וג״ל, which hints at the 39 labors forbidden on *Shabbat*. In other words, since the
Egyptians forced us to do 39 types of labor, we remember our redemption from Egypt by
abstaining from those 39 types of labor on *Shabbat*.

3   Regarding the *Tosafot* to *Arvei Pesahim*, see Ephraim E. Urbach, *Ba'alei Hatosafot*,
Jerusalem 1980⁴, pp. 608-609.

4   Rabbi Elias Rabinowitz (1883-1959 or 1960) was ordained by the Seminary in 1908 and
worked as an educator. His *magnum opus* was *Midrash Hagadol* to Leviticus, New York 1932.
See *Students' Annual* 3 (1916), p. 194, and *PRA* 24 (1960), p. 254.

No. 16 The Source of an Unusual Midrash (1949)
Source: LGA, Box 10, "Richman" file

P.O. Box 1825
Trenton, N.J.
Sept. 20, 1949

Professor Louis Ginzberg
Jewish Theological Seminary
Broadway and 123rd Street
New York, New York

Dear Dr. Ginzberg:

I will appreciate it very much if you will be good enough to refer me to the source of the story about the Sage who roused the interest of his students by stating that a certain woman gave birth to 600,000 children. Was it Rabbi Akiba or Rabbi Judah Ha-Nasi?[1]

Unfortunately my books are in storage and I have no easy access to them to make the search myself. I regret the encroachment upon your valuable time. For your convenience, I enclose [a] stamped and addressed envelope.

Respectfully yours,

Jacob Richman[2]

---

1   It was Rabbi Judah Ha-nasi in *Shir Hashirim Rabbah* to 1:15, ed. Vilna, fol. 13a.
2   I have yet to locate any biograhical details about Jacob Richman.

Appendix and Indices

The Reports of the Committee on the Interpretation
    of Jewish Law, 1917-1926   323

Index of Sources   325

Index of Subjects   338

Index of Names   346

Index of Places   351

Appendix

The Reports of the Committee on the Interpretation
of Jewish Law, 1917-1926

1. 1917: *USAAR*, V:1917, New York 1918, pp. 43-51 (LG recommends formation of a committee with five members; includes discussion)

2. June 16, 1918: *USAAR*, VI:1918, New York 1919, pp. 23-24 = Prof. Louis Ginzberg, *The United Synagogue of America*, New York [1919?], pp. 16-17 (announces formation of the committee; according to *USAAR*, VI, p. 6, the members of the committee were: Prof. Louis Ginzberg, Chairman; Rabbi Herman Abramowitz; Rabbi Louis Epstein; Rabbi Abraham Hershman; and Prof. Alexander Marx. The same names are listed in *USAAR*, VII-VIII, p. 6)

3. February 2, 1920: *USAAR*, VII-VIII:1919-20, New York 1920, pp. 90-91 = Box 17, "Questions and Answers" file = CJLS Box, "Kevurah" file = BCA, Box 4, "Burstein, Abraham" file [p. 1 missing] (in absence of LG, Report read by Louis Epstein)

4. [February?], 1921: *The Jewish Exponent* 72/21 (February 18, 1921), pp. 1, 9 = Box 17, "Questions and Answers" file = CJLS Box, "Bet Knesset" file = BCA, Box 3, "Ginzberg L., Report of the Committee" file

5. July, 1921: *USR* 1/3 (July, 1921), pp. 7-8 = BCA, Box 3, "Ginzberg, Louis, Responsa" file

6. January 24, 1922: *USR* 2/2 (April, 1922), pp. 3-4

7. February, 1923: *USR* 3/2 (April, 1923), pp. 2-3 (abbreviated in *USAAR* 11 [1923], pp. 11-12); and 3/3 (July, 1923), p. 10

8. 1926(?): Rabbi Abraham Burstein, "The Decisions of Professor Louis Ginzberg", Box 17 (p. 1 missing) = CJLS box, "Bet Knesset" file = BCA, Box 4, "Burstein, Abraham" file

9. Undated: BCA, Box 4, "Birnbaum" file (stapled to above, Chapter IV, No. 10)

Index of Sources

Bible

Genesis 5:1	237
Genesis 9:4	144
Genesis 11:32-12:1	201
Genesis 17:7	צז
Genesis 48:14-20	317
Exodus 1:13-14	318
Exodus 2:12	241
Exodus 12:3ff.	243
Exodus 12:29	243
Exodus 13:13	242
Exodus 20:2	269
Exodus 20:3	158
Exodus 20:9	143, 146
Exodus 23:19	144, 146
Exodus 29:40	112
Exodus 30:34-35	81
Exodus 32:33	242
Exodus 34:26	144, 146
Leviticus 2:11	עד
Leviticus 9:22	317
Leviticus 10:9	120
Leviticus 12:2	קיט
Leviticus 18	278-279
Leviticus 18:22	קג, קז
Leviticus 19:14	קטז
Leviticus 19:30	297
Leviticus 21:7	קיא, קיג
Leviticus 21:13	קח, קיא
Leviticus 21:14	קיא, קיג, קיח
Leviticus 21:19-20	263
Leviticus 22:12	צה
Leviticus 22:24	143
Leviticus 22:28	143, 146
Leviticus 26:10	כג

Numbers 6:3	מט, 118
Numbers 11:16ff.	273
Numbers 15:16	236
Numbers 19:2	קיד-קטו
Numbers 27:18	275
Numbers 27:23	275
Numbers 28:7	נא, 112
Numbers 28:14	112
Numbers 28:19-20	לג
Numbers 31:8	242
Deut. 6:4	256
Deut. 7:6	עז
Deut. 14:21	144, 146
Deut. 17:8-13	257
Deut. 17:11	42
Deut. 18:11	165
Deut. 20:6	כה
Deut. 21:18-21	120
Deut. 22:6-7	143, 146
Deut. 23:2-4	פו
Deut. 23:3	פח
Deut. 25:4	143, 146
Deut. 26:19	קכו, 213
Deut. 33:4	91
Deut. 34:9	273
Joshua 6:2ff.	277
Joshua 7:2ff.	277
Joshua 7:13ff.	277-278
Joshua 10:1ff.	277-278
Judges 9:54	172
Judges 17:6	42
Judges 20:18ff.	277
I Samuel 14:18	277
Isaiah 2:4	54-57
Isaiah 28:7	עז
Isaiah 29:23	עז

Isaiah 30:7	234	**New Testament and Church Fathers**	
Isaiah 34:6	243	Mathew 1:5	278
Isaiah 43:2	56-57	Mathew 20:1-16	310
Isaiah 45:20	234	Mathew 26:27	112
Isaiah 54:13	44	John 7:49	234
Isaiah 63:1	243	Acts 6:6	276, 317
Jeremiah 31:33	54, 56	Acts 13:1-3	317
Ezekiel 1:1	159	Acts 21:25	144
Ezekiel 18:4	248	Acts 25:20	144
Ezekiel 27:18	לח	I Timothy 4:14	273, 275
Ezekiel 44:22	קטו	II Timothy 1:6	276
Hosea 6:6	248	Revelation 5:5	163
Zephaniah 3:9	256	Hippolytus,	
Zechariah 8:19	97	Apostolic Tradition 8:3	273
Zechariah 14:9	243, 256		
Malachi 1:8	נה-ס, עד	**Philo**	
Psalms 25:8	248	De Gigantibus 13	158
Psalms 85:12	249	On the Contemplative	
Proverbs 3:17	223	Life 32-33	86, 88, 92
Proverbs 12:12	144		
Proverbs 13:16	נט	**Josephus**,	
Proverbs 13:21	248	War IV, 9, 12, par. 582	139
Proverbs 23:31	לה-לז	Antiquities	
Proverbs 30:18ff.	240	XII, 6, 1, par. 265	200
Job 8:7	43	XVII, 6, 2, par. 151	158
Job 12:11	נו	XVIII, 3, 1, par. 55-56	158
Job 24:13	נט	Life, 12	158
Daniel 6:11	79		
Nehemiah 8	46	**Mishnah**	
I Chronicles 7:27	278	Berakhot 4:5	79
		Peah 3:6	צב
Ancient Near Eastern Texts		Demai 1:4	כז
Code of Hammurabi,		Shevi'it 9:5	צב
par. 154	278-279	Shevi'it 9:9	צב
		Terumot 1:1	44-45
Apocrypha		Terumot 3:1	מה
Testament of the Twelve Patriarchs,		Terumot 8:7	נה
Zebulun 5:1	147	Hallah 1:8	כז
Jubilees 49:6	112	Hallah 1:9	צב
I Maccabees 2:1	200	Hallah 3:1	צב

Bikkurim 2:1	צב	Makkot 2:6	צב
		Eduyot 6:1	יח ,117
Shabbat 23:5	173	Eduyot 8:6	248
Eruvin 3:1	כז	Avodah Zarah 1:9	105-106
Eruvin 7:1	פז	Avot 1:6	255
Pesahim 4:4 = 53b	ס	Avot 2:5	44
Yoma 8:8	צב	Horayot 2:2	פז
Sukkah 3:6	לד		
Sukkah 4:10 (end)	נה, עד	Menahot 8:2 = 85a	לג
Sukkah 5:5	139	Menahot 8:6	119, 121
Betzah 1:2	פז		כד, לה
Rosh Hashanah 1:4	פז	Menahot 8:7 = 86b-87a	לב
Rosh Hashanah 4:9		Hullin 1:4-6	כ
(and parallels)	67	Hullin 1:7	לט
Megillah 3:2	105	Bekhorot 7:7	283
Moed Katan 1:7	220, 221	Tamid 7:4	65
Moed Katan 3:8 = 27a	185		
		Oholot 5:6	פז
Yevamot 2:8	170	Niddah 1:3	צב
Yevamot 4:13 = 49a	פה-צב ,211	Niddah 6:4	כ ,118
Yevamot 6:5	168		
Ketubot 1:2	171		
Ketubot 1:9 = 13a	פא, צח, קא,	**Tannaitic Midrash**	
	קט, קי, קטז, קיז	Mekhilta, eds. Horowitz-Rabin	
Ketubot 3:1	צב	p. 89	238
Ketubot 3:2	צב	Mekhilta, ed. Lauterbach, II	
Sotah 2:6 = 18b	פג ,211	p. 230	269
Sotah 7:1	91	p. 237-238	269
Kiddushin 4:14	238		
		Sifra, ed. Weiss	
Bava Kamma 4:4	צב	Leviticus 12:2, 57d	קכא
Bava Batra 6:3	נ	Leviticus 19:18, 89b	237
Sanhedrin 1:4	צב	Leviticus 21:7, 94c	קיא, קיד
Sanhedrin 4:4	273-274	Leviticus 26:10, 111a	כב-כג ,119
Sanhedrin 6:5 = 46a	183, 185		
Sanhedrin 11:3	257	Sifrei Bemidbar, ed. Horowitz	
Sanhedrin 11:4-5	צב	piska 23, p. 27	מח, נ
Sanhedrin 11:6	צב	piska 140, p. 186	275
Makkot 1:10	237	piska 143, p. 190	מח-נ

Sifrei Zutta ed. Horowitz
Numbers 6:3 (a suggested
reading)   מט
Numbers 27:18, p. 321   276

Sifrei Devarim, ed. Finkelstein
piska 31, p.54   256
piska 154, p. 207   42
piska 157, pp. 208-209   270
piska 171, p. 218   צ
piska 195, p. 235   כה
piska 248, p. 276   פו, צ

Midrash Tannaim, p. 120   כה

Tosefta
Tosefta, ed. Lieberman
Berakhot 3:22, , p. 360   79
Sukkah 4:11-12, pp. 274-275   139
Bava Batra 6:7, p. 148   לב
Bava Batra 6:10, p. 149   לא-לב, מו

Tosefta, ed. Zuckermandel
Sanhedrin 2:6, pp. 416-417   272
Sanhedrin 7:1, p. 425   274
Shevuot 2:14, p. 448   259
Menahot 9:9, p. 526   לד, לו, לט,
מא, מד, מו, מז,
מח, נ, נא, נה
Menahot 9:12, p. 526   117
כ, סז, סח, ע, עא, עג, עד
Keritot 1:20, p. 562   120-121,
מט-נ, סז

Yerushalmi
Berakhot 3:1, 6a   115, ל
Berakhot 5, 9b, end   עו
Berakhot 6, 10d   127,
טו, כג, כד

Peah 2:6, fol. 17a   צט, 212
Bikkurim 1:3, 63d, bottom   גג
Bikkurim 3:3, 65d   275
Shabbat 7:3, 10a   גג
Pesahim 8:8, 36b   116
Pesahim 10:1, 37c   סא, עב
Yoma 4:5, 41d   לז-לח, עד-עה
Megillah 4:4 (as quoted by
rishonim)   לא
Moed Katan 2:4, 82b   185

Yevamot 4:15, 6b, end   פו-צ
Sotah 7:1, 21b   272
Sotah 8:5, 22d   113-115, 121,
כד-לב, מו, נ, סז
Ketubot 1:3, 25b   קח-קט
Nedarim 7:1, 40b   יד
Gittin 3, 45b   כז
Nazir 6:2, 55a   כא

Sanhedrin 1, 19a   273-274, 317
Sanhedrin 2:1, 19d   283
Sanhedrin 6:11, 23d   116
Horayot 3, 47a   283

Bavli
Berakhot 3a (and parallels)   68
Berakhot 4b   67
Berakhot 16b-17a   68
Berakhot 30a   79
Berakhot 35b, end   נו
Berakhot 40a   147
Berakhot 40b   סט
Berakhot 43b   יט
Berakhot 48a   כז
Berakhot 48b   כח

Shabbat 24a   68
Shabbat 24b   66
Shabbat 31a   237

Shabbat 35b	139
Shabbat 75a	יט
Shabbat 108a	238-239
Shabbat 110b-111a	145
Shabbat 114a	238
Shabbat 114b	139
Shabbat 130a	115
Shabbat 151b	173
Eruvin 29a	כז
Pesahim 54a	255-256
Pesahim 68b	255
Pesahim 108b	119-120, כב-כד, לה, לז
Rosh Hashanah 17b	201
Rosh Hashanah 27a-b	137
Yoma 29a	צ
Yoma 47a	מג
Yoma 69a-b	96
Yoma 76b	יד
Sukkah 27a	עה
Sukkah 36a	לו
Sukkah 49b (and parallels)	נא
Sukkah 50a	נה
Ta'anit 27b	236
Megillah 13b	צח-צט
Megillah 16b	119, טז
Megillah 21a	257
Megillah 25a	צ
Megillah 29a	92
Moed Katan 27a	ל
Moed Katan 27b	190
Hagigah 14b-15a	208-211, 213, פ, פא, צט-קכו
Yevamot 9a	קיט
Yevamot 11b	פג
Yevamot 12-13	קט
Yevamot 22a	צז, קכו
Yevamot 34b-35a	170
Yevamot 42a	211, פב, צז
Yevamot 44b	צה
Yevamot 45a	211, צג, צט
Yevamot 49a	פז ואילך
Yevamot 55a-b	עט, פ, צו
Yevamot 56b	קיג
Yevamot 59a	קג, קו-קז
Yevamot 62a	צז
Yevamot 68a	צה
Yevamot 76a	פ
Yevamot 83b	קג, קז
Yevamot 84b	קיא-קיב, קיד, קטו
Yevamot 92a	פט, צ
Yevamot 101b-102a	168
Ketubot 8b	115, ל
Ketubot 10a	קו
Ketubot 10b	קכב
Ketubot 14a	קא, קב, קכב-קכג
Ketubot 15a	קא, קב, קה
Ketubot 29b	פח, צ, צא
Ketubot 30a	פט
Nedarim 20a-b	216
Nazir 38b	כא
Nazir 59b	קט
Sotah 40b-41a	96
Sotah 43b	כה
Gittin 3b	נא
Gittin 62a, bottom	147
Kiddushin 9a	קיד
Kiddushin 9b	קז
Kiddushin 36a-b	קיב
Kiddushin 42b	281-282
Kiddushin 68a	צ
Kiddushin 76b	168
Kiddushin 78b	קטו
Kiddushin 81a	88
Kiddushin 81b, top	309
Bava Metziah 59a-b	41-42

Bava Batra 20b	נג	Bekhorot 17a	מו-מז
Bava Batra 91b	כב-כג	Bekhorot 30	נח
Bava Batra 95b	לא-לב, מב, סט	Keritot 6a (and parallels)	81
Bava Batra 95-96	מז	Keritot 6b	לז-לח
Bava Batra 97a-b	116-119, 122-125,	Keritot 7b	קכא
	יד, יח-כב, כז, לב-נא, סב,	Keritot 13b	120,
	סג, סז, סח, ע, עא, עג, עד		לב, מט, נ, סז
Bava Batra 154a	185, 186		
Bava Batra 154b	186	Niddah 13a-b	216
Bava Batra 155a	185, 186	Niddah 19a	לה
Sanhedrin 13b	274	Niddah 40a	קכא
Sanhedrin 14a	274	Niddah 64b	קו, קח
Sanhedrin 17b	צב		
Sanhedrin 29a	קכא	**Minor Tractates** (Higger editions)	
Sanhedrin 47a	183, 185	Kallah 1, pp. 170, 172	115
Sanhedrin 56a, bottom	144	Semahot 1:1, pp. 97-98	173
Sanhedrin 69a	קח	Semahot 1:4, p. 98	173
Sanhedrin 70a	121-122,	Semahot 2:8, p. 106	175
	יח, כה-כו, ל, סז	Semahot 11:1, p. 186	185
Sanhedrin 73b	קז, קח	Semahot 14:14, p. 209	115,
Sanhedrin 74b	צח		ל, לא
Sanhedrin 78a	173	Soferim 15:17, pp. 281-282	238
Sanhedrin 82b	99	Soferim 19:9, pp. 334-335	115,
Avodah Zarah 6a = 7b	236		כט, לא
Avodah Zarah 18a	173		
Avodah Zarah 23a	קיד	**Aggadic Midrash**	
Avodah Zarah 29b	188	Alpha Beta d'ven Sira, ed. Yassif,	
Avodah Zarah 40b	119, כג	p. 199	208, 212-213
Avodah Zarah 42b-43b	159		פ, צז-ק, קכו
		Avot d'rabi Natan, ed. Schechter,	
Zevahim 64a	נג	A, Chapter 4, 11a	248
Zevahim 119b	צ	Bereishit Rabbah,	
Menahot 85b-86a	לג	ed. Theodor-Albeck,	
Menahot 86b-87a	לח-לט ,נ, נג, סז,	34:13, p. 324	172
	סח, ע	39:7, p. 369	201
Menahot 87a	120,	41:8, p. 414	44
	לג, ס	100:7, p. 1290	310
Hullin 11b	188	Devarim Rabbah 6:2	309
Hullin 60b	נט	Kohelet Rabbah, ed. Vilna,	
Hullin 69b	צ	9:15, 25c	68

Lekah Tov to Deut. 23:2   פו
Midrash Hagadol, ed. Rabinowitz,
Numbers, p. 77   מט
Midrash Tehillim, ed. Buber,
9:13, p. 89   240
39:2, p. 255   310
Pesikta d'rav Kahana, ed.
Mandelbaum, p. 355   248
Pirkei d'rabi Eliezer, ed. Luria,
11a-b   68
31a   כח
Shir Hashirim Rabbah, ed. Vilna,
1:15, 13a   319
Tanhuma Noah, par. 19   256
Vayikra Rabbah, ed. Margaliot,
9:2, pp. 175-176   ס
13:5, p. 290   צח
Yalkut Hamekhiri, ed. Buber,
Psalm 118, p. 214   309
Yalkut Shimoni to Psalms,
par. 869   240

Zohar
I, 38b-39a   239
II, 40b   243
II, 119a   242

Geonim
Geonica,
II, p. 26   מד, מח
II, p. 121   כב
II, p. 228   סג
Hahilukim Shebein Anshei Mizrah
U'venei Eretz Yisrael, ed. Margaliot,
no. 19, p. 81   נא, עא
no. 25, p. 83   218
no. 28, p. 83   כח
Halakhot Gedolot, ed. Berlin,
p. 50   סג, .123ff

Halakhot Gedolot, ed. Jerusalem,
I, p. 75   .118, 123ff,
                                 יט, כא, לט-מ
I, pp. 76-77   נה
I, p. 214   115
II, p. 222   ל
Halakhot Gedolot, ed. Warsaw,
14c   לט-מ, סב-סז
Hemdah Genuzah, no. 35   מד
Otzar Hageonim,
VI, p. 42, par. 128   139
VIII, pp. 18-19, par. 60   218
Responsa of the Geonim, ed.
Harkavy, no. 9   212-213, צט
Responsa of the Geonim, ed. Lyck,
no. 25   קה, קכ
Seder Rav Amram, ed.Goldschmidt,
p. 67   122, 125,
                                 יט, סד-סה, עד
p. 124   123, סג
Sha'arei Tzedek, Salonica 1792,
19b   218-219
She'iltot, no. 54 = ed. Mirsky,
no. 60   לד, נב-נג
Siddur Rav Sa'adia,
p. 13   67
pp. 32-34   67
p. 97   114, 218, כח-כט
Toratan Shel Rishonim, II, p. 51
                                 כב, סה

Rishonim and Aharonim
Abraham Ibn Ezra
to Exodus 20:2   269
Abudraham Hashalem, ed. Kreuzer,
p. 126   לח
Arukh s.v. ilyaston   נד
Arukh s.v. parish   צט
Arukh s.v. talmud   צא
Eitz Hayyim, I, p. 195   כב, סה

Elyah Rabbah to OH 272 129, יח
Hagahot Asheri to Moed Katan,
  Chapter 3, par. 38 185
Hagahot Rabbeinu Peretz to Semak
  (mss. only) 208, 210, 212, 213
  פ-פג, צה-צז, קד, קכו
Hilkhot Uminhagei R. Shalom
  Mineustadt, par. 106 129, יז-יח
Kaftor Vaferah, Chap. 10, ed.
  Luncz, p. 165 לד
Kuzari, I, 25 269
Ma'amar Hametz, 33d-34d 124, 131
  מג, סד, סח, עב, עז
Ma'aseh Rav, par. 95 נז
Magen Avot, ed. Last, pp. 30-32 כט
Mahzor Vitry,
  p. 46 81
  p. 79 לח
  p. 86 עד
Meiri to Sanhedrin, ed. Sofer,
  p. 274 קז
Minhagei R. Avraham Klausner,
  ed. Dissen
  p. 9 128,
  טז, כא
  p. 19 128, טז
Minhagei R. Isaac Tyrna,
  ed. Shpitzer,
  p. 13 68
  p. 100 128, טז
Mordechai to Bava Batra 97b,
  ed. Vilna, 91b לג
Nimmukei Yosef to Bava Batra
  97b, ed. Vilna, 47b מב
Orhot Hayyim, I, 64a כא-כב, לג, סה
Or Zarua,
  I, par. 162 מה
  I, par. 752 113, כח
Ra'avan to Yevamot, par. 44, end
  צד-צה

Ra'aviyah,
  I, p. 77, par. 98 כט
  I, p. 106, par. 123, סא
  I, p. 125, par. 135 עג
  I, p. 159, par. 152 טו
  I, p. 370, par. 330 כב, סה
  II, p. 52ff., par. 423 סא
Rabbeinu Gershom
  Bava Batra 97b לו, מב, מח, נד, ע-עא
  Menahot 86b נד
Rabbeinu Hananel to Hagigah
  14b-15a קב, קה, קיט-קכב, קכה
Ralbag to II Samuel 1:14 172-173
Rambam
  Mishnah Menahot 8:6 כג, לו,
  לח, נג-נד, ס, עג
  Mishnah Menahot 8:7 לג
  Mishnah Terumot 8:7 נה
Ramban
  Deut. 32:26 לח
  Avodah Zarah 30 131, עב-עג
  Bava Batra 97b לד, לה-לו
  Bava Batra 98a כד
  Yevamot 49a פט, צ
  Milhamot to Yevamot,
  Chap. 6 צד
  Torat Ha'adam, ed. Chavel,
  p. 204 ל
Ran
  on the Rif to Pesahim 108b,
  ed. Vilna, 22b מ-מא
  Ketubot, Chapter 3, end קז
  Shabbat, end, ed. Jerusalem,
  pp. 222-225 סה
Rash Mishantz to Sifra Emor,
  ed. Jerusalem, 97b קיד, קטז
Rashba to Nedarim 90b קיא
Rashi
  Betzah 21a כז
  Hagigah 14b-15a ק-קד, קכד-קכה

Menahot 86b נד
Menahot 87a כד
Shabbat 151a ק, קד
Zevahim 68b נח
Rid
    Berakhot 53b כז
Sefer Hamakhria, par. 3,
    beginning כז
Rif to Pesahim 108b, ed. Vilna,
    22b מד-מה, סד
Ritba
    on the Rif to Nedarim 90b,
    ed. Vilna, 27a קיב, קטז
    Yevamot 56b צד
    Yevamot 92a פט
Rosh
    Ketubot, Chapter 1, par. 16
    114, כח
    Ketubot, Chapter 3, end קז
    Kiddushin, Chapter 1, par. 41
    115
    Shabbat, Chapter 23, par. 9 ק
Sefer Ha'eshkol, III, p. 102 נח-נט
Sefer Ha'ittim,
    p. 203 מג
    p. 204 124,
    סג, סד
    p. 206 123,
    לה, לט, מב, סג
    p. 207-208 מד-מה
Sefer Ha'ittur, Matzah Umaror,
    p. 264 עב
Sefer Hamanhig, ed. Rephael,
    p. 151 כ
    p. 503 124, סג-סד
Sefer Ha'orah, I, p. 38 124-125, סד
Sefer Hapardess, ed. Ehrenreich,
    pp. 57-58 סא, עב
    p. 65 מא, מד
Sefer Harokeah, par. 352 כט

Sefer Hashetarot of R. Judah
    Albarceloni, p. 132 274
Sefer Hassidim, ed. Berlin, par. 315,
    p. 100 172-173
Sefer Hassidim, ed. Margaliot,
    pp. 4, 17-18 214
Sefer Maharil, ed. Shpitzer,
    p. 203 129, יח
    p. 274 127-128, טו-יח
    pp. 339-340 138
Sefer Mitzvot Gadol, Negative
    Commandments, no. 315 נח
Sha'arei Simhah,
    I, p. 2 118, 125-126, 130-131
    כא, לד, לז, לט, מב,
    מד-מה, נו, נז-נח,
    סד, סו, עב, עג
    I, p. 3 סא, סט, עא
    I, p. 4 סט, עג
    I, p. 117 נט
    II, p. 51 ל
    II, p. 65 לא
    II, p. 98 כד
    II, p. 99 סג
Shitah Mekubezet,
    Bava Batra 97b מד ואילך
    Bava Kamma 115b נה
    Ketubot 14b-15a קכג
    Nedarim 90b קיא
Tal Torah, Yerushalmi, 29a קח
Tashbetz,
    par. 120 129, יו
    par. 301 128-129, יו
Tosafot
    Bava Batra 18a, s.v. lo yiftah
    נג, עג
    Bava Batra 96a, s.v. habodek
    סט
    Bava Kama 15a, s.v. asher 270
    Bava Metziah 30b, s.v. ha קיג

Hagigah 14b, s.v. betulah
קד-קיט, קכה
Ketubot 3b, s.v. v'lidrosh צד
Ketubot 6b, s.v. rov קה
Ketubot 14b-15a קא, קה
Menahot 87a, s.v. helistyon נד,
סג, עא
Nedarim 90b קיא-קיב
Pesahim 108b, s.v. ehad
hadash טז, כג
Pesahim 117b, s.v. l'ma'an 318
Yevamot 5a, s.v. v'akkatei קיג
Yevamot 16b, s.v. kasavar צג, צד
Yevamot 56b, s.v. mai צד
Yevamot 59b, s.v. ela קז
Tosfot Yom Tov to Bekhorot 5:5
קי
Turei Even to Hagigah 15a צז
Yad Malachi, par. 144 קטו

Mishneh Torah
Avodah Zarah 9:4 (uncensored
editions only) 84
Tefillah 11:3 101
Tefillah 11:17 105
Berakhot 4:8 כג
Shabbat 5:20 139
Shabbat 29 מא, סט
Shabbat 29:14 מח, נה-נו
Shabbat 29:17 מו-מז, נא
Shofar, beginning, in Hagahot
Maimoniyot 129, יז
Ta'aniyot 5:7 כו
Ishut 3:24 114, כח
Ishut 11:1 171
Ishut 15 in Bnai Ahuvah פ, צו, קי,
קיח-קיט
Ishut 15:4 in Mishneh L'melekh
210, 212,
פ, צה-צז, קו

Gerushin 10:14 170
Na'arah Betulah 8:5 קז
Issurei Bi'ah 1:10 עט
Issurei Bi'ah 3:6 קז
Issurei Bi'ah 3:15 עט
Issurei Bi'ah 12:1-2 צג
Issurei Bi'ah 15:1 צג
Issurei Bi'ah 15:2 צא
Issurei Bi'ah 15:3 צג-צד, קכב
Issurei Bi'ah 17:13 in Mishneh
L'melekh צה, קו
Issurei Bi'ah 17:13 in Sha'ar
Hamelekh קו
Issurei Bi'ah 18:2 in Mishneh
L'melekh צד-צה
Issurei Bi'ah 19:11 קיב
Ma'akhalot Assurot,
Chapter 2ff. 315
Ma'akhalot Assurot 11:9 in
Lehem Mishneh מח
Nazir 5:9 מט
Bi'at Hamikdash 1:1 מט
Issurei Mizbe'ah 2:10 נח
Issurei Mizbe'ah 6 מא, עג
Issurei Mizbe'ah 6 in
Kesef Mishneh ע
Issurei Mizbe'ah 6 in
Lehem Mishneh מח
Issurei Mizbe'ah 6:3 לג
Issurei Mizbe'ah 6:9 לח, נב-ס
Issurei Mizbe'ah 6:9 in Lehem
Mishneh נב
Issurei Mizbe'ah 6:10 מו, נה-נו
Issurei Mizbe'ah 7:6 נב
Issurei Mizbe'ah 7:7 121,
לה, נ
Ma'aseh Hakorbanot 13, end,
in Lehem Mishneh עה
Hovel Umazik 4:1 in Migdal Oz נה
Rotze'ah 1:4 173

Rotze'ah 11:14   נה
Sanhedrin 4:1   275
Sanhedrin 4:6   276
Sanhedrin 24:7   59, 61
Mamrim 7:4   כו
Evel 1:10   175
Evel 4:5   173
Evel 13:7   לא
Melakhim 1:4-5   270

Tur
Tur OH 153   105
Tur OH 204 in Ba''h   סט
Tur OH 272   122, 125-126, 130,
     יח, כא, לז, מה, נו,
     סא, סו-סז, עא, עב
Tur OH 272 in Bet Yosef   נב
Tur OH 272 in Darkei Moshe   יד-טו
Tur OH 272 in Perishah   כ
Tur OH 586   137
Tur OH 600 in Darkei Moshe
     126-127

Tur YD 116   נה
Tur YD 195 in Ba''h   210, 212,
     פ, צה
Tur YD 305   115
Tur YD 345   175
Tur YD 363 in Bet Yosef   185
Tur YD 378   ל

Tur EH 62   כח

Shulhan Arukh
OH 2:6   76-77
OH 53:25   75-76
OH 75:1-3   89
OH 91:3   76-77
OH 94:2   78-80
OH 101:4   91

OH 128:40-41   283
OH 135:1 in Mishnah Berurah,
     par.1   84
OH 150:5   78-80, 101-102
OH 150 in Bei'ur Hagra   101
OH 151:1-2   103-104, 297
OH 153   105-106
OH 154:12 in Magen Avraham   נח
OH 182 in Bei'ur Hagra   כז
OH 240:4   216
OH 261:4   109
OH 272:1   סט
OH 272:2   110-133
OH 272:2 in Magen Avraham
     126-130,
     יד-יח, סו-סז
OH 272:3   לג, לט-מ
OH 272 in Bei'ur Hagra   לג, נו
OH 272 in Peri Megadim   עד-עה
OH 272 in Taz   סט
OH 276:2   134
OH 328ff.   187
OH 338:1-2   135
OH 422:1   116
OH 453:1   136
OH 453 in Eshel Avraham   136
OH 493   221
OH 546:1   220-222
OH 586:8-9   137
OH 600 in Magen Avraham   סו-סז
OH 619:1   138
OH 623:6   139

YD 1ff.   143-150
YD 69:1ff.   222
YD 87:10   151-154
YD 104:2 in the commentaries   נח
YD 116   נז
YD 123:3   131, עג
YD 141   155-163

YD 151:10	105-106	EH 64:6	220-222
YD 157:2	235	EH 115:1	222-223
YD 158:2	164	EH 129:20	171
YD 179:14	165	EH 152	225
YD 181:10-11	166	EH 156:1ff.	306
YD 268	167-169		
YD 268:2-3	171	HM 7:4	270
YD 268:6-7	170-171	HM 7 in Birkei Yosef	271
YD 305	115	HM 28:3-4	259
YD 339:1	172-174	HM 34:19	307
YD 345:5	175-184	HM 35:14	307
YD 349	185-189	HM 266:1	259
YD 357	185-189	HM 348:2	258
YD 362:1	189-192	HM 425:5	164
YD 362:5	175-184		
YD 363:1	190, 191, 193-198, 298	**Responsa**	
YD 363:7 in Pithei Teshuvah	186	Hakham Zvi, no. 140	נד-נה ,מג-מד
YD 369ff.	198-200	Hatam Sofer, YD, no. 336	186, 188
YD 376:4	201	Hatam Sofer, EH, no. 143	קח
YD 391	202-203	Mabit, no. 252	מג
YD 403	304	Maharil, ed. Satz, no. 138, p. 235	יח
		Maharit, II, no. 2	מג
EH 1 in Birkei Yosef	207-213	Maharam, ed. Lvov, no. 125	נט
EH 1 in Bet Shemuel	210,	Maharam, ed. Bloch, no. 54	129
	צז ,פ	Noda Biyehudah,	
EH 1 in Helkat Mehokek	צז	I, EH, no. 70	קיג
EH 2 in Pithei Teshuvah	214	II, OH, no. 118	קיג
EH 3	215	II, YD, no.10	144
EH 5:11-14	145	II, YD, no. 161	212, צט
EH 6:1	306	II, YD, no. 210	186-187
EH 6:8	168, 260	II, EH, no. 12	קיג
EH 6:17	קכג	Radbaz, I, no. 484	185
EH 10:1	פג	Rambam, ed. Blau,	
EH 23:1	216	II, no. 178	65
EH 25:2	216	II, no. 211	170
EH 26	217	II, no. 215	160
EH 27:1	218-219	Rashba,	
EH 31:2	218-219	I, no. 369	186
EH 33	217	I, no. 1231	צד
EH 34 in Bei'ur Hagra	כח	Ribash, no. 9	124, סד

R. Samuel di-Medina, YD, no. 40

131, עו

Sefer Hayashar, p. 82   ל

Tashbatz,

    I, no. 57   124,

לו, סד

I, no. 85   לח

III, no. 263   210, 212

פ, צט, ק-קא,

קב, קכא-קכו

Index of Subjects

adon olam 69, 138
agency appointment for a soldier
  going off to war 226-228
aggadah 255
Agudass Harabonim 27, 58, 59, 61
agunah 226-228, 294
aleinu 233-234
al hanissim 68, 200
All's Well that Ends Well 309
American Academy for Jewish
  Research 19, 20
American Humane Association
  146-150
American Jewish Committee 249
am ha'aretz 234, 242-243
Amidah 66-68
anaesthetizing animals before
  shehitah 313-314
animals, Christian attitude
  towards 143
animals, Jewish attitude
  towards 143-150
Antar 278
anti-semitism 147-148, 231-262
Antiquities Ascribed to Philo 286
apostates 32, 164, 175, 178-184, 235
Arabic 17-18, גג-גד
Aramaic 272
areiv l'adam sheyehe nah eitzel
  avotav 195
aron kodesh 84
art in Christianity 155-156, 159,
  160-161
art in the synagogue 32, 155-163
artificial insemination 213-207,
  עט-קכו
Ashkenazim 214
autopsy 185-189

ba'al moom 263-264
Babylonians 218
beard 166
Beiliss Case 231-252
Berlin University 232
bet midrash 103-104
bimah 101-102
blessing people by laying on
  of hands 317
blood, Jewish aversion to
  use of 244-245
blood libel of Blois 232, 246
blood libel of Kiev 231-252
blood libel of Trent 246-247
B'raita d'rabi Yishmael 66
Brandeis University 4
burial, delayed 185
burial, of apostates 175, 178-184
burial, of intermarried Jew
  in Jewish cemetery 176-177
burial, of Jew in non-Jewish
  cemetery 176-177
burial, of Jew without usual
  funeral rites 178-184
burial, of non-Jewish spouse
  in Jewish cemetery 178-184
burial, postponement of 185
burial, simple 189
burial, using rites of Masons
  or Elks 178-184

Cabala 15, 239-244
Cabala, use of by anti-semites 244
calendar 289-292
cantor 75-76
capital punishment 237
Catholicism 84
Central Bet Din 226

chaburah meals 316
chemistry 152-153
children punished for sins of
  parents 264
choir, mixed 96
chosen people concept 69, 256-257
Christian attitude towards
  animals 143
Christian hatred of other
  Christians 238
Christian Scientists 164, 165, 175,
  178-184
Christianity 10, 84, 105, 233ff., 236
Christianity, art in 155-156, 159,
  160-161
Christianity, in eyes of
  Romans 245-246
Christmas (*Nital*) 234
church, direction of prayer 79
church, mixed pews in the 86
circumcision 115
civil divorce 33, 217, 223-225
Committee on Jewish Law 26,
  226-228
Committee on the Interpretation
  of Jewish Law 25-27, 41-44, 46-47,
  52, 76, 86, 103, 107, 109, 155-156, 164,
  175-177, 189, 194, 196, 199, 203, 223,
  224, 298, 305, 307, 323
Committee on the Prayer Book 52
Common Law 281
Conservative Judaism/synagogues
  22-27, 33, 94, 139, 199, 220, 221
consolation of mourners 115-116
construction of synagogue on
  Shabbat 32, 108
conversion 103, 168, 170-171
Coriolanus 309-310
Court of Domestic Relations 223
crippled 264-263

crowns on certain Hebrew
  letters 286
customs 131, עי
dances in the synagogue
  basement 32, 297
Daniel, the mystical numbers in 288
dead, disrespectful treatment 185-186
Dead Sea Scrolls 22
Decalogue, why no mention of
  God as Creator 269
denial of religious services to
  unaffiliated Jews 32, 267-268
*Die Haggada bei den
  Kirchenvätern* 3-4, 21
Diet (the German parliament)
  147-148
dina d'malkhuta dina 258
direction of synagogue 32, 78-80
disinterment 186
divorce 211, 217, 223-228
divorce, civil 33, 217, 223-225
divorce, grounds for 136, 222
dreams, influence on the
  halakhah 215
Dropsie College 289, 291

education as a source of unity
  in Israel 293
ein keloheinu 68
ein me'arvin simhah b'simhah 221
ein shaliah lidvar aveirah 281-282
ejaculation 216
el adon 67
elohay netzor 68
elopement 217
erusin and *nissuin* 113, כח-ל
Ethical Culture Society 178-184
euthanasia 172-174

fasting on *Rosh Hashanah* יז
fellatio 216
Festival Prayer Book 53-55
fixing of the Jewish calendar 290-292
Fleischman's (hotel) 226
Frankfurter Zeitung 16
funeral, may rabbi who is
   kohen officiate 199
funeral practices 32, 189-198, 298-299

gelatin 151-154
gentiles 237, 258-260
Geonica 1, 21,
   כ, לד, מד, סג
ger toshav 236
get 33, 217, 222-228
Ginzei Schechter 1, 21, 66-67
God as Creator, why no
   mention in Decalogue 269
"*goy*" 258-259
grape juice for *kiddush* 110-133, יג-עז
Greek 218, 272
Greek ideal of beauty 155, 158,
   160-161

hakhel 96
halakhah kidvarav in the Mishnah צב
halakhic authority, lack of
   in the United States 25-26, 42-47
hallanat hamet 185
hallel 68
halutzah, marriage to a *kohen* 306
handicapped 263-264
Hapardess 151-154
Harvard University 16, 20
Hatikvah 138
havdalah 113
hayshinan in the Talmud ק-קא
headcovering for men 76-77, 91, 96
Hebrew Union College 18-19

Hebrew University 20
herem 59, 61
hezkat kohen 215
HIAS 101
hillul hashem עה
hog intestine casings for
   surgical gut 314-315
hol hamoed, marriage on 220-222
holeh l'faneinu 186-187
homoioteleuton קד
hospitals 187-188
hossid 166
human life, value of 237
Humane Society of the United
   States 148
hunting 144, 146-147

informers 259
impeachment of a *kohen gadol* 283
intermarriage 32, 167-171, 176-177,
   311-312
intermarried woman in the
   Sisterhood 311-312
issurei hana'ah 188

Jewish Encyclopedia 18, 19, 65, 76,
   139, 273, 274
Jewish Institute of Religion 4, 20
Jewish Museum 284
Jewish Theological Seminary 19, 23,
   307
Johns Hopkins University 263-264
Johnson and Johnson 314-315
junket 152

kaddish 68-69, 180, 183, 184, 201
kaddish d'rabbanan 67
karaites 289, 290, נט
karet צא-צב
kashrut, gelatin 151-154

kedushah	68
kelal yisrael	47
kelipot	239
ketubah	307
kevod hamet	195
kibbud av va'em	201
kibla	79
kiddush	66, 110-133, יג-ע
kiddush hashem	258-259
kiddushin, using cup of wine with a coin inside	218, כ-כט
kitniyot on *Pesah*	136, 222
kohen, marriage to a convert	168
kohen, marriage to a divorcee	211, גפ
kohen, marriage to a *halutzah*	306
kohen, may only marry a woman with two Jewish parents	260
kohen gadol, impeachment of	283
Korean War	33, 166
lamb, as metaphor for the Jewish people	242
lamb, as term for the six lower *sephirot*	243
languages of Jews in ancient times	272
late Friday evening services	109
laying on of hands to bless people	317
law committees	25-27
League of Nations	253
Lebush	11
legal responsibility of married woman	281-282
Legends of the Jews	1, 14, 20-21, 278, 284
"Lion of Judah"	157, 160
liturgy	51-71, 81-83

liturgy, changes in	27-28, 51-53, 58-63, 69, 82
liturgy, *musaf*	52-53, 68
liturgy, notes on the *siddur*	65-71
liturgy, sacrifices	52-53
Lubavitcher *hossid*	166
magen avot	66
Mahzor Vitry	68
Maimonides, did he visit Italy	287
Major Trends in Jewish Mysticism	20
mamzerut	211-212
mar'it ayin	29, 75, 108
marriage during *sefirah*	221
marriage of daughter to father	278-279
marriage of a *kohen* to a *halutzah*	306
marriage on *hol hamoed*	220-222
marriage ring	218-219
marriage to woman with same name as one's mother	214, 302
married woman, legal responsibility of	281-282
Massachusetts Institute of Technology	82, 152
mausolea	189-192
Measure for Measure	309
mehitzah	85-100, 300
Merchant of Venice	309
Messiah	239, 257, 288
metronymic society	279
Metropolitan Opera House	75-76
Mexicans	238
midrash re. woman who gave birth to 600,000 children	319
minim	258
minuy	275
minuy shelihut	226-228
mitat bet din	צא-בצ
mixed pews	85-100, 300

mizmor shir l'yom hashabbat   65
Mount Sinai Cemetery,
    Philadelphia   178-184
mourning, music assemblies
    during   202-203
Muslims   236
mussar movement/*yeshiveh*   3, 7, 9

neilah   10-11, 29, 75-76
New Century Club   167
New York Public Library   265
new tunes in the synagogue   138
Nital (Christmas)   234
nivul hamet   185-186
Noahide laws   236
non-Jew as witness   307

Oedipus myth   277-278
offertory   316
opera   75-76
ordination   273-276
organ in the synagogue   32, 47, 96,
                             135, 305
"Orthodox Conservative
    Congregation"   199
Orthodox position/rabbis   220, 223

Palestinian Talmud, importance
    to Maimonides and
    Rabbeinu Nissim   כט
Palestinian Talmud, quoted by
    rishonim but missing from
    our editions   כט, סא-סב
Palestinian Talmud, why never
    translated into English   265-266
Palestinians   218
Paradise   239
parokhet   284-285
patronymic society   279

Peirushim V'hidushim
    Bayerushalmi 1, 6, 12, 21, 68, 208, 274
peregrini (= foreigners)   258-259
Pesah, green peas on   136, 222
Pesah, *kitniyot* on   136, 222
Pesah, string beans on   136, 222
Pesah, tomatoes on   136, 222
Peshitta   272
pesukei d'zimra   67
Philo   86, 88, 92
pidyon haben   115
pikuah nefesh   187
pittum haketoret   81-83, לז-לח
"Prayer for Divine Aid"   56-57
"Prayer for the Government"   54-55
Prohibition   111
Pseudo-Philo   286
psychoanalysis   277

questioners   24-25

rabbi of uncertain priestly status 215
rabbi who is *kohen* at funerals   199
Rabbinical Assembly   26, 69, 111,
                             226-228
Rabbinical Association of
    Chicago   267-268
rabbis, ignorant   33, 167-169, 302-303
rabbis, transgressors 33, 199, 221, 307
radio on *Shabbat*   134
Reform Judaism/rabbis/Temples
                          25, 47, 94, 135,
                          157-163, 178, 220,
                          224, 284, 305
reinterment   185, 190-198, 298-299, 304
rennet   152
repentance   201
responsa, non-Hebrew   24, 26
returning a lost article   258-259
ring   218-219

Roman Emperors 291
Romans 218, 238
Rosh Hashanah 297
Rosh Hashanah, fasting on כ׳
Russian government 232ff., 248-249

Sa'adia-Ben Meir controversy 291
Sabbath and Festival
    Prayerbook 27-28, 54-55, 64-71
Sabbath Prayer Book 27, 58-63
sacrifices after the
    Destruction 247-248
safek kohen 215
safek pikuah nefesh 186
sale of synagogue 32, 105-107, 299-301
Samaritans 286
Sanhedrin 273-275
Sanhedrin, renewal of the 293-294
Sefer Tagin 286
sefer Torah 84
"Sefer Yerushalmi" כט, סא-סב
sefirah, weddings during 221
semikhah 273-276
Seminary professors and
    halakhah 22-24
Sepharadim 214
sephardic custom 101-102
sephirot 243
Septuagint 272
Seridei Yerushalmi 1, 21, כה
service for reinterment 304
Seventh Day Adventist
    Theological Seminary 288-292
Seventh Day Adventists 288-292
Sha'agat Aryeh 11
Shabbat 10, 29, 108, 109, 110ff., 134
Shabbat, driving on 47
Shabbat, late Friday evening
    services 109

Shabbat, radio on 134
Shabbat, thirty-nine types of
    forbidden labor 318
Shabbes Goy 134
Shakespeare 309-310
sheheheyanu on Rosh
    Hashanah 126-130, כ׳
shehitah, anaesthetizing
    animals before 313-314
shehitah, defense of 146-150
shetar minuy shelihut 226-228
Shir Hakavod 67
shlom bayit 90, 94-99, 270
shofar, at end of Yom Kippur 139
shofar, repair of cracked 137
shofar, seven blasts of 139
Shulhan Arukh 258
siddur, notes on the 65-71
Sisterhood, intermarried
    woman in the 311-312
Society for the Advancement
    of Judaism 59, 61
Society for the Prevention of
    Cruelty to Animals 144, 146
soldiers 84, 166
spirit of law 29-30, 75, 108
spiritualism 165
Students Scholars and Saints 6
surgical gut from hog
    intestine casings 314-315
sympathy for animals 143-150
synagogue, art in the 32, 155-163
synagogue, bimah 101-102
synagogue, construction on
    Shabbat 32, 108
synagogue, dances in the 32, 297
synagogue, direction of 32, 78-80
synagogue, membership of
    Christian Scientists in 164
synagogue, new tunes in the 138

synagogue, sale of   32, 105-107,
                                   299-301
synagogue, use of lower floor for
    bet midrash and social hall
                                   103-104
synagogue, women on
    board of   270-271
synagogues, ancient 80, 88, 92, 158-159
Syriac   272

tagin   286
tallit   96
Talmud   254-255, 265-266
Talmud, authority of   30-31
Talmud, use of by anti-semites 244,
                            253ff., 257ff.
Tanna d'vei Eliyahu Rabbah   66-67
Temple Emanuel   157-162
Temple prostitution in the
    Ancient Near East   91, 96
tenan before a *beraita*   כ, סט
The Nation   143-145
Therapeutae   86, 88, 92
thirty-nine types of forbidden
    labor on *Shabbat*   318
Torah reading   68, 84
torture   246-247
Tosafot to *Arvei Pesahim*,
    who wrote the   318
trial by ordeal   232, 246
tum'at kohen   199
tza'ar ba'alei hayyim   143-150

unaffiliated Jews   32, 267-268
Union Theological Seminary
                            273-276, 316-317
United States Army   84, 166, 200,
                            221, 226, 304,
                                   314-315

United Synagogue   25-26, 51-53, 69,
                         95, 164, 175, 183,
                         223, 224, 298, 305,
                              306, 308, 311
United Synagogue Recorder   26
unity in Israel through
    education   293
University of Chicago   15

Volstead Act   111
Vulgate   255

weddings during *sefirah*   221
weddings on *hol hamoed*   220-222
weddings, woman and non-Jew
    as witnesses   307
wine, at circumcision   115
wine, at house of mourning 115-116,
                                   לא-ל
wine, at *pidyon haben*   115
wine, boiled   130-131,
                              ס-סב, עב-עג, עה
wine, for *erusin* and *nissuin* 113, כח-ל
wine, for *kiddush*   110-133,
                                   יג-עז
wine, *ilyaston*   לח-מ, נד, ע-עא
wine, *kossess*   מד-מח, סט
wine, *mazug*   מח ואילך
wine, *meguleh*   נה-נח, עד
wine, old   יד ואילך
wine, on *Pesah*   112
wine, on *Rosh Hashanah*   126-130
wine, raisin   130-131,
                         מב-מד, סב-סז, עא, עו-עז
wine, *shel martef*   מ-מב, ע
wine, *shel shemarim*   מג-מד
wine, with honey   עד-עה
witchcraft   238
witnesses, woman and
    non-Jew as   307

woman who gave birth to
600,000 children,
source of midrash — 319
women and public office — 270-271
women as judges — 270-271
women as witnesses — 307
women in the Ancient Near East 91
women in the synagogue — 32, 85-100,
270-271, 300
women on synagogue
boards — 270-271
"Women's Court" in the
Second Temple — 92 ,96
World War I — 33, 200, 294, 304

World War II — 33, 84, 226-228,
314-315
ya'aleh v'yavoh — 68
yekum purkan — 67
yibbum — 302-303
Yom Kippur — 96, 221, 289, 297
Yom Tov — 307
Yom Tov, organ on — 305

zidduk hadin — 180
Zionism and the Book of
Daniel — 288
Zoroastrians — 159

Index of Names

Abel, R. Zalmen 13-14
Abraham 201
R. Abraham, brother of the
Gaon of Vilna 5, 6, יא
Abrahams, Harold 137
Abrahams, Joseph 260
Abramowitz, R. Herman 298, 323
Achan 277-278
Adler, Dr. Cyrus 78-80, 203
Adler, Dr. Felix 179
Agobardus of Lyons,
France 235-236
Aquila 272
Aronson, Raphael 16
Aronson, R. David 16
Avimelech 172

Balaam 242
Baldwin the First 238
Baroway, R. Moses 300-301, 304
Baskin, R. Samuel 153
Benjamin, R. Samuel 176-177, 299-300
Ben Sira 210, 212
Berger, Joseph 277-280
Berger, R. Julius 151
Berman, R. Morton 267-268
Bienenfeld, R. Jesse 307-308
Birnbaum, Dr. 170-171
Blaser, R. Itzile 9
Block, Gordon A. 183
Bosniak, R. Jacob 101-102
Budding, Dr. 149
Burstein, R. Abraham 88-89, 108,
190, 323

Chamberlain, Houston Stewart 256
Coblenz, R. Adolph 95, 99, 270

Cohen, Prof. Boaz 20, 23, 29, 84,
105, 208, 226-228
Cohen, R. Herman M. 136, 222
Cohen, R. Samuel 199
Colish, R. Nathan 302-303
Cordovero, R. Moshe 147

Dammann, Prof. 147, 149
Darwin, Charles 143
David, King 309
de Lagarde, Paul Anton 233
Delitzsch, Franz 233, 236, 240
Dembitz, Lewis 170
Diesendruck, Prof. Zvi 14
Dillman, August 232
Drob, R. Max 198

Ehrlich, Arnold 19
Einstein, Prof. Albert 16
Eisenhower, President Dwight D. 166
Eisenmonger, Johann 231
Elijah of Vilna, the Gaon R.
5-6, 30, 101, 270
כז, לג, נו, נז, סט, עג
Enelow, R. Hyman 19
Epstein, R. Louis 164, 165, 175, 185,
313, 323

Farber, R. Maxwell 227
Fassett, Fred 18
Finkelstein, Prof. Louis 10, 22, 207,
314-315
Finkelstein, Nathan 85-87
Fischer, Prof. Kuno 15
Fisher, Irving 76
Fleischer, Milton 90-98
Foster, R. Solomon 78
(St.) Francis of Assisi 287

Frankel, R. Zechariah 39
Friedenwald, Dr. Harry 263
Friedlander, Prof. Israel 19
Friedman, Dr. Harry 284-285
Friedman, R. Theodore 207
Froom, Leroy Edwin 288-292

Gandz, Dr. Solomon 19, 226, 289, 291
Ganz, R. Irving 314-315
Gaster, Dr. Moses 297
Gershfield, Prof. Edward 23
Ginsberg, Prof. H.L. 19
Ginsburg, Dr. Sol 172-174, 277
Ginzberg, Adelle 75, 82, 167, 195, 227, 277, 307, 315
Ginzberg, Prof. Eli 6, 12, 13, 15, 28, 31, 34, 64-65, 82, 85, 166, 185, 207, 277
Ginzberg, R. Isaac Elias 5, 7-9, 11, 208
Ginzberg, Louis:
  ancestry 4-6, 32
  apologetics against
    anti-semites 32, 231-262
  bar mitzvah 2-3, 14
  biographical data from
    his responsa 31-32
  education 2-4
  genius 13-18, 32, 287
  halakhic approach 27-31, 39-47, 98, 99, 109, 152-153, 209, 212-213, 214, סב, פה, צט-ק, קכו
  health 3, 13, 31, 82, 96, 99, 168, 216, 279, 289, 292, 318
  historical data from
    his responsa 32-33
  languages, love of 16-18
  mathematics, love of 15-16

  modesty 4-5, 168
  piety 9-13, 19
  pious upbringing 6-9
  responsa 22-34
  semikhah 3
  sense of humor 31, 277, 284
  telephone, aversion to 270
Ginzberg, Sophie 65, 82, 207, 227, 277
Ginzberg, Zippe Jaffe 5, 9
Goldfarb, R. Israel 195-196
Gordis, R. Robert 64, 227
Gordon, R. Eliezer 14
Gottlieb, Albert 78-80
Gould, Prof. Bernard S. 82, 152, 167
Gould, Sophie Ginzberg
  see Ginzberg, Sophie
Graetz, Dr. Heinrich 39, 170
Greenstone, R. Julius 199
Grodzinski, R. Chaim Ozer 151-153
Grodzinski, Leah 152
Gross, Joseph 281-283
Grossman, R. Lewis 227

Halivni, Prof. David Weiss 207
Halpern, R. Abraham 189, 191-192
Hamlet 277
Hananiah ben Teradion 173
Harris, R. Maurice 265-266
Hegel, Georg Wilhelm
  Friedrich 155, 161
Heine, Heinrich 255
Heinemann, Dr. 15
Herford, Robert Travers 258
Herod 158
Hershman, R. Abraham 306, 323
Hertz, R. Joseph 297
Heschel, Prof. Abraham
  Joshua 19, 101-102
Higger, Dr. Michael 23
Hildesheimer, R. Hirsch 148

Hillel II 290-291
(Bishop) Hinderbach of Trent 246
Hoffmann, R. David Zvi 112

(Pope) Innocent the Third 238
Iser, R. Alan 207-209
Isserles, R. Moshe 153
R. Izel of Slonim 44-45

Jadwin, General 260
Jeremiah 210, 212
Jerome, St. 255
Jesse 309
Jesus 233-234, 247
(King) John I of Castile 259
Johnson, Mr. 260
Joseph, R. Morris 170
Joshua 273, 275, 277-278
Judah Maccabee 200
Judas 158
Juster, Jean 168

Kant Immanuel 143
Kaplan, Prof. Mordecai 12, 27, 58-63
Kasovsky, R. Hayyim
  Yehoshua 19, 293, פ
Kaufmann, Dr. David 160
Klein, R. Isaac 226
Kleinman, R. Philip 103-104
Kohl, H. 158-159
Kohler, Joseph 237
Kohn, R. Jacob 53
Kohn, Robert D. 162
Kohut, George A. 20
Konwitz, R. Joseph 151
Koshland, Walter 279
Kugel, Joseph 225

Langh, R. Philip 305
Lasker, R. Arnold 81-83

Lechner, Michael 287
Lehman, Judge Irving 16
Levinthal, R. Israel 75-76, 94
Levitsky, R. Louis 227
Lewin, R. B. M. 19
Lewis, R. Albert 214
Lieberman, Prof. Saul 14, 19, 22, 27, 58-63, 216
Luria, R. Yitzhak 144, 241-242

Maimonides 287
Marcus, Prof. Ralph 15, 19
Marshall, Louis 157-162, 231, 249, 253, 260-261
Marx, Prof. Àlexander 27, 52-53, 58-63, 64, 323
Masterman 158
Mattathias 158
R. Meir of Rothenburg 318
Mendes, Rev. Dr. Henry Pereira 297
Miller, William 289
Minicius Felix 245-246
Minkin, R. Jacob 220
Moore, Prof. George Foot 313-314
Moses 143, 158, 241-242, 273, 275
Mummenhoff, Ernst 263

Neuman, R. Abraham A. 178-184
Neustatter, Dr. Otto 263-264
Noeldeke, Prof. Theodor 3, 17, 31, 233, 279
Novak, Prof. David 207

Offerman, Klemis 272

Palache, R. 297
Paranaitas, Monk Justin 231-252
Pardes, R. Shmuel Aaron 152
Paul, St. 143
Paulus Burgensis 235

(King) Pedro III of Aragon 259
Petschi 284
Pfefferkorn, Johannes 235, 244
Picho, Joseph 259
Pontius Pilate 158

Quinn, First Lt. Mary 166

Rabinowitch, Dr. I.M. 151-154
Rabinowitz, R. Elias 318
Rabinowitz, Prof. Mayer 24
Raisin, R. Jacob 309-310
Rashkes, R. Aryeh Leib 3, 9,
יג, צד
Ravetch, R. Isadore Shalom 311
Renan, Ernest 253
Reuchlin, Johannes 244
Richardson, Prof. Cyril 273-276,
316-317
Richman, Jacob 319
Rohling, August 233, 235-236, 239,
240, 243, 244
Rose, R. Goodman 193-194
Rosenbloom, Mr. 189
Rosenwasser, R. Herman 207-208
Rosinger, R. Samuel 78
Roth, Prof. Joel 24

Sachar, Prof. Abram 4
Salanter, R. Israel 7, 9, 154
Samuel of Trent 246-247
Saul, King 172
Schauss, Hayyim 218-219
Schechter, Prof. Solomon 19
Schlockow, Oswald 202-203
Scholem, Prof. Gershom 20, 288
Schopenhauer, Arthur 143-144
Schorsch, Prof. Ismar 22-23, 34
Schreiber, R. Abraham 19
Schulz, General Robert 166

Schwartz, Dr. Adolph 291
Schwartz, R. Harry 227
Schwartz, Maurice 197
Scruby, John 139
Seynenis, Henricus 253
Shakespeare, William 309-310
Shirwinter, R. Eliyahu Eliezer 154
Shubow, R. Joseph 56-57, 167-169
Siegel, Prof. Seymour 23
Silverman, R. Morris 27-28, 64-71,
108
Sonderling, R. Jacob 85
Sophocles 277
Spiegel, Prof. Shalom 19
Spinoza, Baruch 15
Spira, R. Nathan 278
Spiro, R. Abraham 286-287
Stahl, Friedrich 235
Starzenski, Victor 265-266
Stillman, Dr. William 146
Strack, Prof. Hermann 233
Sulzberger, Judge Mayer 260
Szacki, P. 253-262
Szold, Henrietta 11

Terah 201
(Count) Theobold of Chartres 232
Tobias of Trent 247
Tucker, Cantor Richard 29, 75-76

Vaniewsky, I. 312
Vittal, R. Hayyim 241
von Gemmingen, General 147-148

Wagner, Richard 254
Wahrmund, Adolph 254
Watson, Frederick 263
Watzinger, C. 158-159
Weil, R. 297
Weinreich, Prof. Otto 235-236

Weinstein, Joseph	90, 97	Wolfson, Prof. Harry	19
Weisfeld, Dr. Israel	269	Wunsche, August Karl	233
Weiss, R. Isaac Hirsch	12		
Westermarck, Edward	278	R. Yechiel (of Porto, Italy)	5
Whitaker, Norman	216	R. Yehiel (of Paris)	318
Winograd, R. Simon	154		
Wise, R. Isaac Mayer	18-19	(Rav) Zutra bar Tuvya	ט׳
Wise, R. Stephen S.	4	Zwerin, Kenneth Carlton	77

Index of Places

Akron, Ohio   300-301, 304
Amsterdam   6, 9, 11, 15, 101
Ascoli, Italy   160
Atlantic City, New Jersey   289
Austria   224

Babylonia   159
Bad Homburg, Germany   9
Baltimore, Maryland   28, 90-100,
                             263-264, 270
Basel, Switzerland   10
Beaumont, Texas   78
Belle Harbor, New York   227
Belleville, New Jersey   197-198
Berkeley, California   77
Berlin, Germany   3, 15, 232
Birmingham, Alabama   220
Blois, France   232, 246
Breslau, Germany   23
Brighton, Massachusetts   167
Bronx, New York   218
Brookline, Massachusetts   167-168,
                                207, 313
Brooklyn, New York   75-76, 85-87,
                             94, 102, 166,
                        195-196, 202-203

Caesarea   272
Cambridge, Massachusetts   82, 313
Charleston, South Carolina   309
Chartres, France   232
Chelsea, Massachusetts   313
Chicago, Illinois   79, 267-268, 305
Cincinnati, Ohio   18
Cleveland, Ohio   299-300
Constantinople   238
Copenhagen, Denmark   10

Dayton, Ohio   139
Detroit, Michigan   306
Downers Grove, Illinois   272

Ensisheim, Alsace   יז

Finland   149
Flint, Michigan   81-83
France   225, 304
Frankfurt am Main,
  Germany   3, 6, 16, 17

Galilee   88, 158-159
Germany   147-149
Gorodetz, Russia   101-102
Greece   149

Halifax   149
Hammam Lif, Tunisia   159
Hanover, Germany   149
Hartford, Connecticut   64, 69
Havran, Syria   לח
Heidelberg, Germany   3, 15
Helbon, Syria   לח
Hempstead, New York   227

Jacksonville, Florida   176-177
Jericho   159, 277
Johnstown, Pennsylvania   314

Kiev, Ukraine   231, 233, 243
Klin (near Moscow)   2, 7
Kovno, Lithuania   2, 5, 9
Kuttenplan, Bohemia   284

Leonia, New Jersey   311
Lithuania   2-4, 6, 9, 130, 131,
                                  עא, עו

Lyons, France   235   Porto, Italy   5

Mainz, Germany   147-148   Rochester, New York   146, 220
Milan, Italy   10   Rothenburg, Germany   ‎רי
Montreal, Quebec, Canada   151-154   Russia   224
Moscow, Russia   13
Mount Vernon, New York   227   Saratoga County, New York   265-266
                                            Shechem   286
Neustadt (on the Lithuanian-   Shilo   286
    German border)   2, 7, 12   Shnipishok (a suburb of Vilna)   3
Newark, New Jersey   78, 227   Slobodka (a suburb of Kovno)   3, 9
New Brunswick, New Jersey   314   Springfield, Connecticut   287
New Kensington, Pennsylvania   151   St. Louis, Missouri   189, 191-192
New York, New York   18, 20, 23, 58,   St. Paul, Minnesota   103-104, 136, 222
                    78, 86, 144, 157,   Strassburg, Alsace, Germany 3, 10, 17
                171, 174, 178, 198,   Syracuse, New York   307-308
                214, 224, 225, 249,
                260, 284, 286, 291,   Telz, Lithuania   2-3, 7, 14
                        297, 313   Tiberias   158
                                            Trent, Italy   246-247
Oakland, Maine   65, 170-171, 227, 315   Trenton, New Jersey   319
Oak Park, Illinois   272
Oslo, Norway   10, 17   Vilna, Lithuania   3, 17, 101

Palisades Park, New Jersey   311   Warsaw, Poland   253
Paris, France   225, 294   Washington, D.C.   288-292, 302-303
Pesaro, Italy   160   Westmount, Quebec, Canada   298
Petschau, Bohemia   284   Williamsburg, Brooklyn,
Philadelphia, Pennsylvania   78-80,   New York   202-203
                137, 178-184, 216,
                227, 281-283, 289   Yavneh   274-275
Pittsburg, Pennsylvania   193-194, 279
Plunge, Lithuania   8   Zamut, Lithuania   ‎עו

HEBREW SECTION

שמיקל בספק ספיקא אפילו בשמא, אבל לרבן גמליאל אין כאן מקום לשאלה שהוא מכשיר לכתחילה ברוב פסולין.

[יד. פסק הלכה]

והנה די בכל אלה הדברים הנאמרים למעלה להוכיח להמעיין שלא מצינו לא בתלמוד ולא אצל הראשונים יתד לפסוק עליו היתר בדבר חמור זה. ואדרבא, אף על פי שאין ראיה לדבר לאסור, יש סמך למי שאומר שלדעת הראשונים ולד שנולד מזרע שקלטתו אמו בלא קירוב בשר אם היא אשת איש הוא ממזר. וחס ושלום לסמוך בחשש ממזרות על דברי אגדה שבספר אלפא ביתא דבן סירא, ספר מלא דברים זרים ותמוהים שאין דעת חכמים נוחה מהם. ואם מצינו באי-אלו כתבי יד של הגהות הסמ״ק דרבינו פרץ סמך על הגדה זו ״לאו מר קא חתים עלה״,[33] והראיה שבספרים וברוב כתבי יד של הגהות הסמ״ק לא נמצאה הגהה זו. ומהנותר להוסיף כמה מכוער הדבר מנקודת מבט המוסר והטהרה להכניס ברחם אשת איש זרע מאיש אחר, וכבר נאמר והיית ״עם קדוש לה׳ אלקיך״ [דברים כ״ו:י״ט].

---

33   כלומר, ״מר לא חתום עליו״ — זאת מליצה על פי יבמות כ״ב ע״א.

בתולה — למה לא נאמין לה שבאמבטי עיברה אחרי שסוף כל סוף נתעברה **בדרך** שאינו רגיל או על ידי בעילת הטיה או באמבטי?

ב) לדעת התוספות שאין אשה נפסלת לכהן גדול על ידי בעילת איש כל זמן **שבתוליה** קיימים, צריך לפרש שצדדי הספק הם אי שכיחא דשמואל נאמנת לומר לכשר נבעלתי בהטיה, ואפילו לר' יהושע שאומר "לא מפיה אנו חיין" נאמנת כשבאה לשאול על עצמה, שאינה חשודה לישב בעבירה כל ימיה, וכאן, כשכבר נשאה כהן גדול, השאלה היא אם רשאי לקיימה, ואי לא שכיחא אינה נאמנת, שאנו אומרין שהיא והוא טועים בדבר לחשוב אותה עדיין בתולה ואפילו לרבן גמליאל אסורה. והתשובה היא "דשמואל לא שכיחא" וכשאומרת עדיין אני בתולה שבא עלי איש והיטה אסורה, שאפשר שהיא טועה. ואולם באומרת באמבטי עיברתי מותרת, שאי אפשר לטעות, ואין כאן מחלוקת בין רבן גמליאל ור' יהושע, שבשבאה לשאול על עצמה ר' יהושע מודה לרבן גמליאל שאין אנו חושדין אותה לשקר.

ג) רבינו חננאל על פי קבלה הגאונים מפרש, על פי גירסתם שלא גרסו "לכהן גדול", שהשאלה היא לעניין טומאת לידה וקרבנה והיא בבתולה שלא הרגישה שבא עליה איש ונמצאת מעוברת ועדיין בתולה היא שנבדקה. והספק הוא אם בא עליה איש בהטיה כשהיתה ישנה והיא טמאה לידה וחייבת בקרבן או שעיברה באמבטי ואין יולדת על פי הזרעת זרע שלא על פי דרך כל הארץ מטמאת לידה, והתשובה "דשמואל ליתא", ולא איפשיטא אם חיישינן שמא באמבטי עיברה ולכן טמאה מספק, שאפשר שלא נבדקה יפה.

ד) הרב בעל התשב"ץ גורס : "בתולה שעיברה מהו לכהן" והשאלה היא לרבן גמליאל ברוב פסולין אם מותרת לינשא לכתחילה שיש כאן ברי שלה שאומרת באמבטי עיברתי, וספק ספיקא להתיר, ספק עיברה באמבטי ספק בא עליה כשר, ולר' יהושע שמיקל בספק ספיקא אפילו בשמא, השאלה היא גם כשהיא אינה אומרת ברי באמבטי עיברתי אלא שאומרת עדיין אני בתולה ואפשר בא עלי איש בהטיה או נתעברתי באמבטי. ולשניהם עיקר הספק הוא אם עיבור באמבטי הוא ספק שראוי להצטרף או כיוון דשמואל שכיחא אין אנו מתחשבין כלל עם אפשרות רחוקה כעיבור באמבטי. והתשובה, בין לרבן גמליאל בין לר' יהושע, "דשמואל לא שכיחא" ולכן מותרת מטעם ספק ספיקא, שהספק שמא באמבטי עיברה הוא ספק שיש להתחשב עמו אחרי שגם "דשמואל לא שכיחא", ואם כן עיבור שלה הוא שלא כדרך הרגיל ואפשר שעיברה באמבטי. וכפי מה שהעירונו למעלה נראה שגם הרמב"ם גרס כגירסת התשב"ץ אלא שפירש שכל המשא ומתן הוא אליבא דר' יהושע

לומר שהוולד שנולד מזרע איש שאסור לאמו ואף שלא בא עליה ממזר הוא
וכמו שביארנו למעלה.

[יב. גירסת הרמב״ם בחגיגה י״ד-ט״ו ופירושה]

ובקשר עם פירוש הסוגיא על פי גירסת התשב״ץ אמרנו להעיר על השמטת
הרמב״ם שלא הביא הלכה זו של בתולה לכהן גדול לא לאסור ולא להתיר
וקשה לומר שטעם ההשמטה הוא משום שהדבר לא שכיח. ואולם אם נאמר
שגירסת הרמב״ם היא כגירסת התשב״ץ לא קשה מידי שהוא פירש שהשאלה
ששאלו את בן זומא היא רק אליבא דר׳ יהושע, שאילו לרבן גמליאל שהלכה
כמותו אין כאן מקום לא לשאלה ולא לתשובה שאם טוענת ברי בוודאי
מהימנא. והיה נראה לי דוחק להרמב״ם לאמור שהשאלה היא ברוב פסולין
או לכתחילה, שדעתו שמה שאמרו בכתובות שם לחלק אלה החילוקים, לא
אמרו כן אלא שבימי האמוראים הנהיגו להחמיר ברוב פסולין או לכתחילה
אבל רבן גמליאל מכשיר לכתחילה וברוב פסולין, כמו שמראים דבריו
במשנה, ולכן אי אפשר לומר ששאלו את בן זומא על דעתו של רבן גמליאל
אלא רק על דעתו של ר׳ יהושע, והרמב״ם שפוסק כרבן גמליאל לנכון השמיט
תשובת בן זומא.

[יג. סיכום ארבעת הפירושים לחגיגה י״ד-ט״ו]

והנני חוזר בסוף דברי על הד׳ פירושים שנאמרו לראשונים על הסוגיא
דבתולה שעיברה:

א) לדעת רש״י והרא״ש אשה שנבעלה לאיש, ואף שבתוליה קיימים,
אסורה לכהן גדול משום בעולה ורק בשקלטה זרע באמבטי כשרה היא, שהרי
לא נגע בה איש. ולפי דעתם צריך לומר שהשאלה שישאלו את בן זומא״ היא
אליבא דרבן גמליאל, שהלכה כמותו ב״ראוה מדברה״ ו״שהיתה מעוברת״,
שנאמנת לומר לכשר נבעלתי, שאפשר לומר שעיברו באמבטי הוא מיעוט דלא
שכיחא ולכן אף שאנו מאמינין לה שעדיין בתולה היא אנו אומרין בא עליה
איש והיטה והיא פסולה לכהן גדול. ותשובת בן זומא על השאלה היא כשרה
משום שבעולה בהטיה גם כן לא שכיחא, ואם כן אחרי שנאמנת לומר שהיא
בתולה — או לפירוש השני של רש״י שכבר נישאה לכהן גדול ומצאה

ואומר שגם בשמא כשרה ואם כן כשנבדקה, עיין בר״ח ובתוספות, יש כאן
ספק ספיקא להתיר, שמא לא נבעלה לאיש כלל אלא קלטה זרע באמבטי
והיא כשרה, וגם אם היה הזרע של פסול, ואם תאמר שנבעלה לאיש אפשר
שהיה כשר והיא כשרה לר׳ יהושע לא לבד בשטוענת ברי, או לכשר נבעלתי או
באמבטי עיברתי, אלא גם בשמא ובשאינה יודעת אם נבעלה ישנה או באמבטי
כמו שפירשנו לדעת הגאונים והרי״ח. ואולם רק אי דשמואל לא שכיחא יש
לסמוך על הספק שמא באמבטי עיברה, שאף שבוודאי גם זה לא שכיחא הרי
היא בתולה לפנינו שכבר נבדקה, וכיון שזה וזה לא שכיחא אפשר [לצרף]
הספק שמא באמבטי עיברה לספק שמא לכשר נבעלתי, אבל אי דשמואל
שכיח הספק באמבטי עיברה הוא כל כך רחוק שאין מצטרף לספק ספיקא.
ותשובת בן זומא, דשמואל לא שכיחא, והספק באמבטי עיברה הוא ראוי
להצטרף והיא מותרת לכהן מטעם ספק ספיקא, ובין אם נגרוס כגירסת
הספרים אחר ״דשמואל לא שכיחא״ [את] המאמר ״וחייישינן שמא באמבטי
עיברה״, בין אם לא נגרוס המאמר הזה, וכבר ראינו למעלה שהתשבי״ץ לא
גריס ליה, הכל עולה לדבר אחד : שכיון דשמואל לא שכיחא, מצטרף הספק
״שמא באמבטי עיברה״ להספק שמא לכשר נבעלה וכשרה. וצדדי הספק
אליבא דרבן גמליאל הם בשטוענת ברי, או שנבעלה לכשר או שבאמבטי
עיברה אלא שהוא ברוב פסולין שלכתחילה לא תינשא — ולדעת קצת
מהראשונים גם ברוב כשרים לכתחילה לא תינשא וצריך ב׳ רובי, עיין [שלחן
ערוך] אבן העזר [ו׳:י״ז] ובשטמ״ק כתובות י״ד, ב וט״ו, א — והשאלה היא
אם כשנבדקה ונמצאה בתולה שיש כאן עוד ספק להצטרף, שמא באמבטי
עיברה, אפשר שגם לכתחילה תינשא ואולם רק אם דשמואל לא שכיחא, דאי
בעילה בהטיה שכיחא ספק זה של עיבור באמבטי אינו ראוי להצטרף כמו
שפירשנו למעלה אליבא דר׳ יהושע. והתשובה ״דשמואל לא שכיחא״, ולכן
הספק השני של אמבטי ראוי להצטרף והיא מותרת גם ברוב פסולין לינשא
לכתחילה משום ספק ספיקא, ספק לכשר נבעלה וספק באמבטי נתעברה.
ובכתובות י״ד, א, אמרו שבספק ספיקא ר׳ יהושע הוא המקיל ורבן גמליאל
הוא המחמיר, אבל לא אמרו אלא שלרבן גמליאל יקיל ליה, שמא אפילו
בספק ספיקא נמי פסול, והכא בברי גם רבן גמליאל מודה שתינשא לכתחילה
ברוב פסולין משום ספק ספיקא. והדבר שקול אם לפי פירוש זה היא לבדה
כשרה או גם ולדה, שכיון שאנו מאמינין לה כשאומרת באמבטי נתעברתי
ולא נפגמה בבעילת איסור גם ולדה כשר, ויש פנים לכאן ולכאן. ואולם אין זה
עניין להשאלה שלפנינו, שבממזרות הפסול אינו תלוי בפגימת האשה ואפשר

שפלט באמבטי. ואשת איש שנתעברה באמבטי מזרע אחר הוולד ממזר, ובפנויה הולך אחרי הפגום אם הוא ישראל, ובעכו״ם הוולד כשר לפי מה שקיימא לן ״עכו״ם ועבד הבא על בת ישראל הוולד כשר״.[32]

ומה שלא פירשו הגאונים כרש״י ותוספות ששאלו את בן זומא לעניין כשרות בתולה לכהן גדול, אפשר שהיה קשה בעיניהם לפרש ששאלו אותו הלכתא למשיחא כאשר העירונו למעלה, או שלפי דעתם אין כאן מקום לשאלה, שבתולה שנתעברה לכהן גדול תלוי במחלוקת רבן גמליאל ור׳ יהושע בהיתה מעוברת אם נאמנת או לא, ונראה להם דוחק לאמור שיש כאן חששא שמא היא טועה בדבר כמו שפירשנו לדעת התוספות, או שמא במיעוט שאינו מצוי כבעילת הטיה אינה נאמנת כמו שפירשנו לדעת רש״י. ולפי פירוש הגאונים ור״ח אין השאלה אם היא נאמנת או לא אלא אשה שאומרת אני מרגישה בעצמי שמעוברת אני ואף שעדיין בתולה אני ונבדקה — על בדיקה זו עיין כתובות י׳, ב — ומצאו כדבריה ויש כאן ב׳ אפשריות: או שבא עליה איש כשהיתה ישנה והיתה, והיא טמאה לידה, או שעיברה באמבטי, ואיננה טמאה לידה. ולגירסת הגאונים תשובת בן זומא היא, דשמואל לית ליה, ואולם לא איפשיטא אם האפשרות השניה ראויה להתחשב עמה וטמאה מספק משום דאמרינן שמא לא נבדקה יפה יפה. ולגירסת הגאונים היה אפשר לומר שהתתשובה ״דשמואל ליתא״ היא תשובה שלימה שכיוון שאין אנו חוששין לדשמואל והיא עדיין בתולה בודאי באמבטי נתעברה. אלא שר״ח אומר בפירוש ״ולא איפשיטא״, וכן הגאונים כפי מה שראינו למעלה מדברים על עיבור באמבטי כעל דבר המוטל בספק, ועל כרחך שגם הם מפרשים דברי הגמרא כמו שפירש ר״ח שעל השאלה הראשונה השיב בן זומא, דשמואל לית ליה, ועל השניה לא השיב משום שלא היה בידו משנה ברורה.

[יא. גירסת התשב״ץ בחגיגה י״ד-ט״ו ופירושה]

ועתה לא נשאר לנו אלה אלה לפרש הסוגיא על פי גירסת התשב״ץ [חלק] ג׳, [סימן] רס״ג שהבאנו למעלה והיא: ״בתולה שעיברה מהו לכהן״, מה שקשה לתקן ״לכהן גדול״ שכן נאמר שם פעמיים ״לכהן״ ובתרי זימנא לא טעי אינשי לכתוב ״כהן״ במקום ״כהן גדול״. ובאמת אין מן הצורך לשבש הספרים, שכן השאלה ״מהו לכהן״ יש לה מקום בין לרבן גמליאל בין לרבי יהושע. וכבר אמרו בכתובות י״ד, א, שבתרי ספיקי ר׳ יהושע הוא המיקל

שלפנינו שהיו לפניו גם ראו ולא שהרב כותב מפורש "ולא איפשיטא" ואם כן
"וחיישינן שמא באמבטי עיברה" בגירסתו [שייך] להשאלה ולא כפי גירסתנו
להתשובה, שהוא וכל אלה שנזכרו למעלה לא גרסו "וחיישינן שמא" וכו'
בתשובת בן זומא, שלפי גירסת ב' כתבי יד לא השיב בן זומא כלל על ב'
השאלות ששאלוהו.

וראוי להעיר בקשר עם זה על דברי התשב"ץ [חלק] ג', [סימן] רס"ג וזה
לשונו: "שאלו את בן זומא [בתולה שעיברה] מהו להתירה לכהן דשמא נבעלה
או חיישינן שמא באמבטי עיברה, [פירוש] שהאיש פלט [שכבת זרע] בתוך
אמבטי והיא רחצה בו ונכנס ברחמה ונתעברה ומותרת לכהן והיקשו: והאמר
שמואל כל [שכבת זרע] שאינו יורה כחץ אינו מזריע ותירצו: ה"נ מעיקרא
יורה כחץ הוה" וכו'. וקשה להפריד בתשובת הרב הזה בין דברי הגמרא
ופירושו עליהם — עיין על זה לקמן — ואולם ברור הוא שגם הוא גורס
"שמא באמבטי עיברה" בשאלה ולא בתשובה ולכן הוא מטיל ספק אם עיבור
באמבטי אפשר. וקרוב הדבר שגירסתו [זהה לגירסת כתב היד], שבן זומא לא
השיב שום תשובה לא על השאלה "מי חיישינן לדשמואל" ולא על השאלה
"שמא באמבטי עיברה". והיה אפשר לומר שגם ר"ח לא גרס "דשמואל לא
חיישינן" או "ליתא" כגירסת רב האי. ואולם אחרי שרוב גירסאות שלו הן על
פי קבלת הגאונים יותר נראה לומר שקיצר בלשונו ועל קיצורו מרמז במילה
"כו'" אחר "עיברה" שהוא כמו "וכו'", ואף שבדפוס השמיטו הקווים מעל
"כו'" ובמקומו הוסיפו "וכו'" אחר "שכיחא" וכבר העירונו למעלה שתיקון זה
אינו אלא קלקול ועל הוספות כעין אלו אמרו [סנהדרין כ"ט ע"א] "כל
המוסיף גורע".

ומפירוש הגאונים ור"ח מפורש יוצא שכל המשא ומתן בסוגיא זו אין
ענייני כלל אצל כשרות האשה או ולדה בשעיברה באמבטי, ואף שאין ספק
שאין אשת איש נאסרת על ידי קליטת זרע באמבטי מאיש אחר, אלא
שהשאלה בתלמוד היא רק לענין טומאת לידה וקרבנה שי"אשה כי תזריע",
כדרך כל הארץ אמרה תורה ולא בדרך משונה כזו, וקרוב לזה אמרו בספרא
ראש תזריע [מהד' וייס, נ"ז ע"ד] ובתלמוד כריתות ז', ב, ונדה מ', א, "עד
שתלד ממקום שמזרעת".[31] ולפי זה אין לנו מכאן שום ראיה להתיר ולד אשת
איש שעיברתו באמבטי מזרע איש אחר, ואדרבא ממה שנדחקו הגאונים
לפרש הסוגיא לעניין טומאת לידה ולא פירשו בבתולה ארוסה ולעניין
ממזרות — עיין דברינו למעלה — מוכח קצת שלא הטילו ספק בדבר שלעניין
כשרות הוולד אין הפרש בין שהולידו אביו כדרך כל הארץ או על ידי זרע

---

31 רל"ג מצטט מכריתות; הסגנון במקורות האחרים שונה.

והנה כאשר גירסא זו משונה הרבה מגירסת הספרים שלנו אמרתי להעיר
על כל השינויים החשובים שביניהן. המילים "ולכהן גדול" שלפנינו בספרים
אחר "מהו" ליתא לא בשני כ"י של התלמוד לא בהגדות התלמוד ובעין יעקב
הוצאה ראשונה ולא בתשובת רב האי גאון בשו"ת הגאונים ליק, סימן כ"ה,
כפי מה שכבר העיר בעל דקדוקי סופרים במקומו. ואנו רואים שגם רבינו
חננאל לא גרס לה וכן ליתא בהוצאה ראשונה של מסכת חגיגה פיזארו קודם
ר"יפ. ומדברי ר"ח אנו למדים שאין זו השמטת סופרים שאינן דוקנים, שהרי
הרב מפרש השאלה לענין טומאת לידה ועל כרחך שהוא והגאונים לא גרסו
"ולכהן גדול". וממה שכתב הרב "ולא איפשיטא" מוכח שלא צדק בעל דקדוקי
סופרים באמרו שבטעות נשמט על ידי הסופרים המאמר מן "א"יל דשמואל"
עד "באמבטי עיברה" שחסר בשני כתבי יד ובהגדות התלמוד שכבר אנו
רואים שגם ר"ח לא גרס המאמר הזה ולכן הוא אומר "ולא איפשיטא".

ותמה אני על בעל דקדוקי סופרים איך בא לידי טעות זו אחרי שהוא
בעצמו העיר על תשובת רב האי גאון שאומרת : "אותה שכבת זרע כיון
שמעיקרא יורה כחץ... **אפשר** שהיא מתעברת ממנה כדאמרינן התם : "שאלו
את בן זומא... א"יל דשמואל ליתא איני והאמר שמואל [כל שכבת זרע שאינו
יורה כחץ אינה מזרעת', הא נמי] מעיקרא יורה כחץ", ולפי גירסת הספרים
שלנו איך כתב הגאון בלשון ספק "**אפשר** שהיא מתעברת" והלא בפירוש אמר
בן זומא : "וחיישינן — לקולא, עיין למעלה — שמא באמבטי עיברה", ואם
כן לפי דברי בן זומא ודאי גמור שאשה יכולה להתעבר באמבטי! ואין לפרש
"אפשר" בדברי רב האי במשמע "יכולה", שאם כן היתה כוונת הגאון, היה
אומר : "אפשר לה להתעבר" ולא "אפשר שהוא", שאין לו מובן אחר אלא
שהדבר בספק אם יש לו מציאות או לא והספק הוא משום שבן זומא לא
השיב תשובה חלוטה בזה. ומלבד זה מוכח שגירסת הגאון היתה כגירסת ר"ח
וכ"יי ושאר ראשונים שלא גרסו בסוף הסוגיא "וחיישינן שמא באמבטי
עיברה", שהרי הוא מביא כל הסוגיא שלפנינו עד הסוף חוץ מהמאמר
"וחיישינן שמא" וכו' ועל כרחך שלא גרס לו, שלולא כן לא היה נמנע
מלהביאו, שהמאמר הזה הוא אותו הדבר ממש שהגאון נושא ונותן בו אם
אפשר לאשה להתעבר מבלי קירוב בשר. ולכן אין ספק שלפי גירסת רב האי,
רבינו חננאל, הגדות התלמוד, עין יעקב ושני כתבי יד, לא השיב בן זומא אלא
"דשמואל ליתא" — לפנינו "לא שכיח" — ועל החשש השני, "שמא באמבטי
עיברה" לא השיב כלום שלא היה בידו תשובה ברורה על זה. ומגיהי ספרים
עתידים ליתן את הדין שהוסיפו בדברי ר"ח "וכו'" אחר "שכיחא" כדי
להשוות גירסתו עם גירסת הספרים [כאילו] שר"ח קיצר דברי הגמרא

מפסול, אלא שדחה ראיה זו שאפשר שמיירי כאן בשאין פסול כלל.[27] וכמה
מן הדוחק לאמור כן! ולפי דברינו כל המשא ומתן הוא אם היא כשרה ולא
דנו על הולד כלל שאפשר שהיא כשרה והוולד פסול, ולפי דעתו היה לו להרב
לאמור שמיירי שאמרה נכנסתי לאמבטי וג׳ חדשים אחר כן הרגשתי בעצמי
שאני מעוברת ויודעת אני שהאיש שקדמני באמבטי היה זה כשר וממנו נתעברתי
ולכן הוולד כשר. ולמעלה העירונו על דברי הגמרא ביבמות ט׳, א [ואילד],
שנשאו ונתנו בקושיא ״וליתני ט״ז״[28] שאם נאמר שאשה שעיברה באמבטי
מערוה שחייבים עליה כרת שהוולד כשר שאין הוולד מתייחס אחר אביו כלל,
אבל לפי מה שראינו אפשר לומר שלדעת התלמוד הוולד ממזר ולכן הקושיא
״וליתני ט״ז״ מעיקרא לא קשיא, שכבר אמרו שם בכשרים קא מיירי,
בפסולים לא קא מיירי.[29]

[י. גירסת רבינו חננאל, רב האי והתשב״ץ בחגיגה י״ד-ט״ז ופירושה]

אחרי שביארנו שבין לפי פירושו של רש״י ובין לפי פירושם של בעלי
התוספות על דברי הגמרא בחגיגה אין ראיה משם שוולד שעיברתו אמו
באמבטי כשר גם אם קלטה זרע מפסול או אם היא אשת איש, נבוא לפירושו
של רבינו חננאל על סוגיא זו, וכבר ידוע שדבריו דברי קבלה מן הגאונים. וזה
לשונו שם : ״בתולה שעיברה מהו, מי חיישינן לדשמואל דאמר יכול אני לבעול
כמה בתולות — כך גרסו הראשונים וכן בכ״י, ולא ״בעילות״ כאשר הוא
לפנינו בספרים, עיין דקדוקי סופרים — בלא דם או דלמא הא דשמואל לא
שכיחא וחיישינן שמא באמבטי עיברה וכו׳. פירוש — לגאונים — אשה הרה
שנבדקה ונמצאת בתולה מי אמרינן מביאה נתעברה כשמואל והריני קורא
בה ׳אשה כי תזריע וילדה זכר וטמאה [ויקרא י״ב:ב׳] וחייבת
[קרבן] לידה או דלמא אימור באמבטי של מרחץ נתעברה... וזה מעשה ניסים
ואינה טמאה לידה — ״וכן אינה [מביאה] קרבן״ אלא שקיצר ואפשר שצ״ל
״ואינה חייבת קרבן לידה״ שהסופרים דילגו על מה שבין ״לידה״ ל״לידה״ —
שאין אני קורא בה ׳אשה כי תזריע׳ ... ולא איפשיטא״.[30]

---

27   ראה בני אהובה הנ״ל (לעיל, הערה 10).

28   שנו במשנה ביבמות דף ב׳ ע״א : ״חמש עשרה נשים פוטרות צרותיהן... מן החליצה״
וכו׳, והגמרא שואלת : ״וליתני ט״ז״, זאת אומרת שישנו שש עשרה נשים במשנה במקום חמש
עשרה.

29   זהו ציטוט חפשי של הסוגיא ביבמות — עיין שם.

30   ראה לעיל, הערה 17.

והשאלה היא בין לרבן גמליאל בין לר' יהושע, שעד כאן לא אמר רבן גמליאל
בהיתה מעוברת שהיא נאמנת באומרת ברי שנבעלה מכשר משום ששם הספק
הוא אם היא משקרת או לא וברי ושמא ברי עדיף ואנו מאמינין לברי שלה,
אבל כאן שהספק הוא אם עדיין היא בתולה ואפשר שהיא טועה וחושבת
שהיטה ולא היטה ואפילו אם כבר נישאה לכהן גדול והוא אומר שמצאה
בתולה אפשר שגם הוא טועה. ועד כאן לא אמר ר' יהושע "לא מפיה אנו חיין"
אלא כשבאה לשאול על הוולד שכיוון שהיא אינה עוברת עבירה בידים אלא
שגורמת לכהן ולוולדה עבירה ו"לפני עור" "לפני עור" קל הוא בעיני הבריות, אבל כאן
שהשאלה היא אם בעלה הכהן הגדול רשאי לקיימה אפשר שר' יהושע מודה
לרבן גמליאל שאין אנו מחזיקין אותה למשקרת שאין בת ישראל חשודה
לישב בעבירה כל ימיה שכבר למדנו שאשה מוזהרת על ידי איש באיסורי
ביאה של כהונה. ותשובת בן זומא על השאלה הזאת היא "דשמואל לא
שכיח", ואם אומרת שעדיין בתולה אני משום שבא עלי איש בהטיה אנו
אומרים שטועה היא בדבר ולכן אסורה לכהן גדול וגם אם כבר נישאה לו,
שאפשר שגם הוא שאומר שמצאה בתולה טועה אבל "חיישינן שמא באמבטי
עיברה", שאם אומרת שנתעברה באמבטי ואולם עוד בתולה היא נאמנת, ואף
שגם זה לא שכיח מכל מקום אין כאן מקום לטעות. ולרבן גמליאל ברי שלה
מועיל בכעין זה ור' יהושע מודה לו על פי הטעם שנאמר למעלה שכיוון
שהשאלה היא על האשה ולא על וולדה מאמינין לה ואינה חשודה לשקר
ולישב עם בעלה כל ימיה בעבירה.

ולפי זה אין בסוגיא זו אפילו רמז קל לנידון דידן, שכל המשא ומתן אינו
אלא לענין איסור בעולה לכהן גדול שבה נאמר "והוא אשה בבתוליה יקח"
וכל זמן שבתוליה קיימין מותרת בין בשבא עליה איש בהטיה ולא נשרו
בתוליה בין כשנתעברה באמבטי, ולא שמענו כאן שום דבר על מעמד הוולד
שנולד מקליטת זרע באמבטי. ואדרבא, קצה ראיה מכאן שהוולד של אשה
שעיברתו באמבטי פסול. שאם לא כן לפי נוסח הרגיל של התלמוד היה לו
לאמר: "לדשמואל לא חיישינן וחיישינן שמא באמבטי עיברה **ולא מיבעיא
שהיא כשרה אלא גם ולדה כשר**". שהרי הדבר ברור שבאופן הראשון ולדה
פסול, שביאה בהטיה שמה ביאה לכל הדברים חוץ מלאסור בעולה לכהן גדול
ואם בא אליה פסול בהטיה פסלה לאם ולבת. ומזה אנו למדים שאין נפקא
מינה כלל לענין הוולד אם חיישינן לדשמואל או לשמא באמבטי עיברה
שבשניהם הוולד כשר אם בא מזרע כשר, ופסול אם בא מזרע פסול.

והרב בעל בני אהובה פרק ט"ו מהלכות אישות פלפל להוכיח שאם קלטה
זרע באמבטי מפסול שהוולד כשר שאם לא כן מנא ידעה דאפשר שקלטה

דנין אלא על פי תנאי המעשה שבא לפנינו ולא על פי תולדותיו. ואולם אין
צורך להאריך בזה אחרי שגם התוספות לא כתבו שכן הוא באמת אלא שלכן
שאלו שאלה זו את בן זומא, גם אם הלכה כר' יהושע בהיתה מעוברת, משום
שהיה אפשר לחלק כן.

ואם ישאל השואל איך אפשר לפרש דברי התוספות כמו שפירשנו,
שהחילוק בין המשנה דכתובות להסוגיא שלפנינו ששם היא באה לשאול על
ולדה וכאן על עצמה, והרי ברישא דמתניתין שם נשאו ונתנו ב"ראוה מדברת"
וגם בהאומר ר' יהושע "לא מפיה אנו חיין" ואף שבודאי עליה אנו דנין?
והתשובה על זה שב"ראוה מדברת" יש טעם לאסור מה שאין כשהיתה
מעוברת ובבתולה שעיברה שבשנבעלה לרצונה — עיין כתובות י"ג, א — וזו
היא "ראוה מדברת" אבדה חזקת צידקות שלה ולכן אינה נאמנת לר' יהושע,
אבל בהיתה מעוברת ובבתולה שעיברה יש לה חזקת צידקות שאפשר
שנתאנסה, וגם לפי האמור שם בכתובות "מאי מדברת... נסתרה" אבדה
חזקת צידקות שלה על ידי סתירה. ולפי זה נעמוד על דברי התוספות
שלכאורה קשה למה היקשו מסיפא דמתניתין דכתובות "היתה מעוברת" ולא
מרישא "ראוה מדברת", ואין לומר משום שבתולה שנתעברה דומה יותר
ל"היתה מעוברת" מל"ראוה מדברת", שבאמת הדמיון הזה הוא רק חיצוני
[ואילו] לפי טיבם של הדברים הדמיון שבין בתולה שנתעברה ל"ראוה
מדברת" יותר קרוב שבשניהם השאלה היא על האשה ואילו ב"היתה
מעוברת" השאלה היא על הולד. ואולם לפי מה שביארנו, בדיוק גדול היקשו
מסיפא דמתניתין, שמרישא "ראוה מדברת" לא קשיא כלל שבה יש טעם גדול
שלא להאמינה משום שאבדה חזקת צידקות שלה, אבל מסיפא שהוא דומה
ממש לבתולה שעיברה שבשניהם אפשר לומר שנתאנסה ולא איבדה חזקת
צידקות שלה שפיר היקשו דבמשנה שלר' יהושע אינה נאמנה ובבתולה
שעיברה משמע ששאלו שאפילו לר' יהושע שתהי נאמנת, ועל הקושיא מסיפא
דמתניתין על סוגיית הגמרא השיבו שבמשנה השאלה היא על הולד ולכן
אינה נאמנת ובגמרא השאלה על עצמה ואינה חשודה שתהי כל ימיה בעבירה
עם בעלה.

[ט. פירוש הסוגיא לפי תוספות]

ונשוב עתה לפירוש הסוגיא ד"בתולה שעיברה" על פי דעתן של בעלי
התוספות כפי מה שביארנו דבריהם והיא שהשאלה ששאלו את בן זומא היא
אם בתולה שעיברה והיא אומרת שבא עליה כשר בהטיה כשרה לכהן גדול.

ואשר לכוונת דברי התוספות, לא שהן מחלקים בין שאר איסורי כהונה
שלא נצטוו עליה הנשים למצוות עשה ד״בתולה יקח״ שגם האשה מוזהרת
עליה, מה שאי אפשר לאמור כלל כפי מה שהוכחנו למעלה, אלא שלפי
פירושינו בדברי התוספות קושייתם היתה שלר׳ יהושע אין כאן מקום לשאלה
שאפילו אם היא נאמנת שעדיין בתולה היא הרי אפשר שבא עליה פסול
בהטיה ופסולה לכהן, ועל זה תירצו שאפשר לומר שכאן ששאלו בתולה לכהן
גדול והשאלה היא על עצמה ולא על הוולד (לפי פירוש שני של רש״י כבר
נשאה כהן גדול ומצאה בתולה) נאמנת, שאינה חשודה שתעבור על לא תעשה
שבתורה, ואילו בכתובות, ששם השאלה היא מה טיבו של עובר זה והחשש
שמא היא אינה רוצה כלל להינשא לכהן והיא משקרת כדי להכשיר ולדה
ואיסור של ״לפני עור״ [ויקרא י״ט:י״ד] קל בעיניה, ולכן ר׳ יהושע מחמיר
ואומר ״לא מפיה אנו חיין״. וכאשר לפי פירוש הר״ש משאנץ [על תורת כהנים
הנ״ל], על הדרשה ״לא יקחו״ מלמד שהאשה מוזהרת על ידי האיש״ יש
מקום לבעל דין לחלוק ולומר שלא הוזהרה האשה אלא במקום שנאמר בו
״יקחו״ לשון רבים, ולא באלמנה ובעולה לכהן גדול שנאמר בהם ״יקח״,
ואפילו לפירוש רש״י אפשר לומר שאלמנה לכהן גדול שלא הוכפלה אזהרתה
לא נצטוו עליה נשים, לכן הדגישו התוספות ואמרו ״דכתיב ׳כי יקח איש
אשה׳ קרי ביה ׳יַקַּח׳״, שבכל איסורי כהונה נאמר הלשון ״יקח״ או ״יקחו״
ולכן הכל שווים בזה שהאשה מוזהרת בהם שקרי ביה ״יקח״ או ״יקחו״.
וחילוק זה של בעלי התוספות אפשר רק לפי מי שאומר בכתובות י״ג, א, וכן
היא ההלכה, שלדברי המכשיר מכשיר בה ובבתה ולכן אפשר לחלק שכאן
שהיא באה לשאול על עצמה נאמנת ושם שאפשר שלא תינשא לכהן כלל אלא
שרוצה להכשיר ולדה אינה נאמנת. ואולם לדברי האומר שם שגם מי
שמכשיר בה פוסל בבתה, בודאי אין לחלק בין המשנה דכתובות להסוגיא
דחגיגה שבשניהם השאלה היא רק על עצמה.

וסברא קרובה לסברת התוספות כאן לפי פירושינו בדבריהם נמצאת גם כן
אצל הריטב״א סוף נדרים [צ׳ ע״ב] בעניין אשת כהן שאמרה טמאה אני לך
שכתב: ש״היא לא באה מתחילה ליאסר בתרומה אלא לאסור עצמה
לבעלה — עיין פירוש דבריו למעלה — אומדן דעתא דמוכח הוא דקא
משקרא דכי היכי דלא מהימנא לגבי בעלה לא מהימנא נמי לגבי נפשה
לאתסורי בתרומה״, והיא היא סברת התוספות כאן אלא שכאן נהפוך העניין,
שאנו אומרין כיון שבאה לשאול על עצמה אומדן דעתא שלא משקרא ולכן גם
ולדה מותר ובכתובות אנו אומרים שכיוון שאפשר שבאה לשאול על ולדה
היא משקרת ואינה נאמנת גם על עצמה. ויש הרבה דוגמאות לזה שאין אנו

אדומה]י [במדבר י״ט:ב׳], בני ישראל יקחו ואין הנכרים יקחו״, ופירושו כמו שפירש רש״י שם: ״׳ייקחו׳ — ימכרו קרי ביה ׳ויקיחו׳״. ואולם התוספות הביאו דרשה של ״ייקחו״, ״ייקיחו״ מקידושין משום שגם שם נדרשה לעניין אישות כ״לא יקחו״, ״ייקיחו״ שבאיסורי כהונה, ואף ששם לא עמדה לה דרשה זו במסקנא ובעבודה זרה לר׳ אליעזר היא דרשה גמורה, ועוד שבקידושין נאמר בגמרא בפירוש ״קרי ביה יקח״ מה שלא נמצא בעבודה זרה.

וראיתי להרב יד מלאכי סימן קמ״ד שנתקשה בדברי התוספות [בחגיגה], שבגמרא יבמות [פ״ד ע״ב] למדו אזהרה לנשים מ״לא יקח״, ״לא יקיחו״, זאת אומרת מריבויא דקרא כמו שפירש רש״י שם, והתוספות דורשים ״לא יקחו, לא יקיחו״, ולפי מה שכתבנו לא שהתוספות דורשים דרשה לעצמן נגד מה שדרשו בגמרא אלא שכך הם מפרשים דרשת הגמרא, ולא כפירוש רש״י ולא כפירוש הר״ש משאנץ שהבאנו למעלה שפירושיהם קשים להעמיד. וקרוב לאמור שבספרים שלנו נשמט מאמר שלם בתוספות על ידי דילוג סופרים שההתחלות השוות גרמו לו וכך צריך להיות: ״ושמא כאן שאף היא בכלל האיסור [**כדכתיב** לא יקחו לא יקח קרי לא יקחו יקח כמו שרצו לומר באשה נקנית שמשום] **דכתיב** כי יקח איש אשה קרי בית יקח״. והסופרים דילגו מן ״דכתיב״ הראשון ל״דכתיב״ השני. ואולם אין הכרח להגיה כן, שאפשר שהתוספות רמזו בקיצור על הדרשה בקידושין.

ובדפוסים החדשים, מדפוס אמסטרדם תמ״ו ולהלן, שינו דברי התוספות מבלי להשאיר זכר לדבריהם המקוריים והשמיטו המאמר ״דכתיב כי יקח איש אשה קרי בית יקח״, ומדפוס זה עד דפוס אמסטרדם קי״ג ולא עד בכלל, הציגו בהסגר ״אלמנה וגרושה לא יקחו כי אם״ (בוודאי כיוונו ליחזקאל מ״ד, כ״ב, אלא שלא העתיקו הפסוק הזה בדיוק ששם כתוב ״ואלמנה וגרושה לא יקחו להם לנשים כי אם בתולות״ וכו׳). ומהוצאת אמסטרדם קי״ג עד הדפוסים שבזמננו, הציגו בהסגר ״והוא אשה בבתוליה יקח״, אלא שבהוצאה הגדולה של ראם הוסיפו על הגליון הפסוק מיחזקאל. וכל אלה ״התיקונים״ אינם אלא שיבושים, שאין עולה על הדעת שהתוספות יביאו הפסוק מיחזקאל שנאמר באלמנה (לכהן גדול לפי קבלת חז״ל, עיין קדושין ע״ח, ב) וגרושה מה שאין עניינם כלל אצל סוגיא זו שבחגיגה שבה נשאו ונתנו בבעולה לכהן גדול. ואם באנו להגיה אין לנו אלא ההגהה שהצעתי למעלה שעל ידי דילוג סופרים חסר כאן מאמר שלם בתוספות או שקיצרו בדבריהם. ואולם איך שיהיה ברור שרמזו להדרשה ״ִיקַח יַקַח״ שבקידושין וכן דרשו גבי איסורי כהונה ״ִייקחו יקיחו״ ו״ִייקח יַקַח״.

שהתוספות מפרשים הדרשה ביבמות פ"ד, ב, ובספרא [על ויקרא] כ"א, ז,
"ולא יקחו" מלמד שהאשה מוזהרת על ידי האיש", שדרשו "לא יקחו" כמו
"לא יַקחו", והוסיפו בתוספות לאמור שכן "לא יקחו" בפסוק יי"ד באיסור
בעולה לכהן גדול אנו דורשין "לא יַקחו". ורש"י והמאירי שם ביבמות [פי"ד
ע"ב] פירשו שמריבויא דקרא למדו דרשה זו שכן בפסוק יי"ד בויקרא כ"א
נאמר "לא יקחו". ולפנינו בספרים "לא יקחו, לא יקחו מלמד שהאשה
מוזהרת" וכו' ועל פי גירסא   זו בודאי יפה פירשו רש"י והמאירי, אלא
שקשה מניין שאשה מוזהרת באלמנה לכהן גדול שלא נאמר בה אלא פעם
אחת "לא יקחו"? והר"ש משאנץ בפירושו על הספרא אינו גורס "לא יקחו, לא
יקחו" כמו שהוא לפנינו בתלמוד ובכי"י מינכען וכאשר הוא גם
לפנינו בספרא אלא: "לא יקחו מלמד" וכו'[26] וכן היא גירסת רי"ד במקומו
[ביבמות] וגירסת הרשב"א סוף נדרים, והר"ש מפרש שדורש "יקחו" לשון
רבים שכולל האיש והאשה. ואולם פירוש זה קשה עוד יותר מפירושו של
רש"י, שאם כן אלמנה לכהן גדול ובעולה לכהן גדול שנאמר בהן לשון יחיד
"לא יקח", מניין שאשה מוזהרת? ובודאי קשה לחלק באיסורי כהונה בין
איסור זונה וחללה וגרושה לבין איסור אלמנה ובעולה לכהן גדול. וכל אלה
הקושיות כלא היו אם נפרש הדרשה "לא יקחו מלמד" וכו' כמו שפירשו
התוספות ש"יקחו" וי"יקח" קרינן בהו יַקיחו וַיַקח ולכן בכל איסורי כהונה
האשה מוזהרת על ידי האיש.

ואחר כל אלה הדברים נבוא לבאר דברי התוספות שבחגיגה, שכבר ראינו
שאי אפשר לייחס להם הדעה הזרה שרק בעשה ד"יבתולה יקח" האשה
מוזהרת ולא בשאר איסורי כהונה, שמעולם לא עלה על דעת אדם לאמור כן
ואלו שנינתלו באילן גדול, ר' אליעזר בעל ספר יראים, להעמיד חילוק זה
נכשלו בגירסא מוטעית של הספרים. ובראשונה צריך אני להעיר **שבכל**
ההוצאות העתיקות — שאין כולם לפניי — מן ההוצאה הראשונה
שבפיזארו, נדפס קודם ר"פ, עד הוצאת [בנבנשתי] תי"ד-תי"ה ועד בכלל,
הגירסא בתוספות [בחגיגה יי"ד ע"ב] היא "כדכתיב 'כי יקח איש אישה' קרי
ביה 'כי יַקּח'" וכיוונו למה שאמרו בקידושין ט', א, על הפסוק "'כי יקח איש
אשה', קרי ביה 'כי יַקּח'". ואף שבמסקנא נדחתה דרשה זו לא נמענו מלהביא
דברי הגמרא בקידושין כעין סמך לפירושם שהאזהרה לנשים באיסורי ביאה
שבכהונה דרשו משום שנאמר בהם "יקחו" וי"יקח", קרי בהון יקיחו ויקח.
ובעבודה זרה סוף כ"ג, א, דרשו דרשה כזו על הפסוק "'ויקחו אליך [פרה

26   תורת כהנים, ירושלים תשי"ט, צ"ז ע"ב, ד"ה לא יקחו.

ולא כתבתי כל זאת אלא להוציא מדעתו של הרב בעל נודע ביהודה
שבכמה מקומות בתשובותיו (מהדורא א', אבן העזר, [סימן] ע'; מהדורה
תניינא, אבן העזר, [סימן] י"ב; ועיין גם כן בתשובה לבן המחבר במהדורה
תניינא, אורח חיים, [סימן] קי"ח)   חוות דעתו שהעיקר כה"ר אליעזר שלא
אמרו "לא יקחו" להזהיר אשה על ידי איש אלא במה שכתוב שם בפרשה
דאמור, גרושה זונה וחללה, ולא בלאו דטומאה, וכאשר הר' אליעזר פוסק
כלישנא בתרא ביבמות נ"ו, ב, ש"באונס לא קרינא בה זונה" באשת כהן
שנאנסה אינה אסורה משום זונה אלא משום טומאה ועליה לא הוזהרו נשים
כלל. ודבריו תמוהין, שבתוספות נדרים [הנ"ל] נאמר בפירוש "דלא מצינו **זונה**
שהיא אסורה לכהן" והוא אומר שלכן אשת כהן שנאנסה איננה מוזהרת
משום שבאונס **איננה זונה** אלא אסורה רק משום טומאה. ועוד ששם ביבמות
[נ"ו ע"ב] אמרו בפירוש שללישנא בתרא, שלפי פירושו של הרב בעל נודע
ביהודה בדברי ר' אליעזר הרב הזה פוסק כלשון זה: "הכל היו בכלל 'אחרי
אשר הוטמאה'... דאשת כהן כדקיימא קיימא", ואם כן באיסור טומאה אין
צריך כלל לרבות שהנשים הוזהרו על ידי אנשים מ"לא יקחו", שהרי באיסור
זה של טומאה לא נאמר בו "בני אהרן" למעט בנות אהרן, אלא כבכל איסורי
תורה הנשים שוות לאנשים. ואין ספק שלולא היו לפני הרב בעל נודע ביהודה
דברי הרשב"א, הריטב"א והשטמ"ק לא היה דוחק את עצמו להוציא דברי ר'
אליעזר מידי פשוטן וליחס לו דעה זרה שהיא נגד השכל הישר כפי מה
שראינו למעלה. ואולם גם אם נקבל דעתו של בעל נודע ביהודה אי אפשר
לומר שהתוספות בחגיגה [י"ד ע"ב] כיוונו לדעה זו של ר' אליעזר בנדרים
שבכל איסורי כהונה האשה מוזהרת חוץ מאיסור טומאה, שאם כן ב"ראוה
מדברת" מפני מה אינה נאמנת לר' יהושע והרי היא זונה ודאית שנבעלה
ברצון, ולפי סברת התוספות במקום שהיא עוברת היא נאמנת.

ודברי תורה עניים במקום אחר ועשירים במקום אחר שביבמות ה', א,
בד"ה ואכתי ובבבא מציעא ל', ב, בד"ה הא, כתבו התוספות בפירוש: "כיוון
שהאלמנה עשתה איסור כמו הכהן דאקרי ביה הא לא יקח לא יַקחו" (ביבמות
"לא יקחו" וי"לא תקחי" וצריך להיות "יקחו" במקום "תקחי", ואולם הסדר
הוא הנכון כמו שהוא ביבמות שכן הם כתובים בתורה, ויקרא כ"א, ז, "אשה
זונה וחללה לא יקחו" ואחר כך בפסוק י"ד "אלמנה וגרושה וכו' לא יקח";
ובהוצאות בומברג בבבא מציעא טעות הדפוס, "לא יקיפו" במקום "לא
יקחו"), ואם כן דבריהם ברור מללו **שבכל** איסורי כהונה האשה מוזהרת ולא
כמו שכתבו האחרונים בפירוש דבריהם   שרק במצוות עשה "והוא אשה
בבתוליה יקח" האשה מוזהרת ולא בשאר איסורי כהונה. ואין ספק

מעיני ר' אליעזר מאמר הגמרא שביבמות, אלא שעליו סמך סברתו שהאשה אינה עוברת אלא כשהאיש עובר ולכן באשת כהן שאומרת לבעלה נאנסתי והוא אינו מאמינה, כיון שהוא אינו עובר, שהרי אינו חייב להאמין לה, גם היא אינה עוברת ואף שהיא בעצמה יודעת שהיא אסורה לו. ודעתו של הרב יסודה בסברא ישרה, שאיסורי כהונה נאמרו לאנשים ולא לנשים, שהרי לא הוזהרו כשרות לינשא לפסולים כמו שאמרו שם ביבמות [פ"ד ע"ב], אלא שאשה פסולה אסורה להינשא לכהן כשר, שהרי היא הגורמת בעבירה זו, ואם הוא אינו עובר גם היא איננה עוברת.

ובריטב"א שם בנדרים [על הרי"ף, דפ' וילנא כ"ז ע"א, ד"ה והשתא] מובאת דעה זו סתם אלא שיש שם ליקוי בדפוס וכך צריך לומר: "והשתא דאמרינן דכי לא מהימן לה לא מיסתרא ליה לדידיה נמי ליכא איסורא ולא מיבעיא באשת כהן שנאנסה שלא הוזהרה — זאת אומרת אם אין מאמין לה — דמשתריא לכהן פסול, שלא [הוזהרה] לינשא **לפסולי** כהונה — כך צ"ל ולא כאשר הוא בדפוס "לינשא "לינשא לכהונה"] ובני אהרן הוא שהוזהרו בכך כדאיתא בקידושין" וכו'. ודבריו הם דברי ר' אליעזר [ממיץ] כפי מה שמובאים ברשב"א, אלא שהוסיף הריטב"א ואסבר לן, [ש]כיוון שכשרות מותרות לינשא לפסולים אנו למדים מזה שאינה עוברת אלא אם כן הוא עובר, וכמו שביארנו למעלה. והרמז לקידושין הוא למה שאמרו שם ל"ו, א' וב', שבנות אהרן נמעטו מהגשות, קמיצות, הקטרות ושאר עבודות הכהנים משום שנאמר "בני אהרן" ולא בנות אהרן. ואולם לא נאמר שם ולא במקום אחר שלכן לא הוזהרו כשרות לינשא לפסולים משום שנאמר בראש [פרשת] אמור "בני אהרן", ודרשה כעין זו לא נמצאת אלא ברמב"ם ב[הלכות] איסורי ביאה י"ט, יא, ואפשר שכך היה לפניהם בספרא ראש אמור. וכאשר כלל גדול בתורה [ש]אין דבריו של אחד במקום שניים, אין להטיל ספק בדבר שדברי התוספות שלפנינו [בנדרים צ' ע"ב] נשתבשו וצריך לתקנם על פי מה שמובא בשם ר' אליעזר [ממיץ] ברשב"א וסתם בריטב"א, וכך צריך לומר: "ותירץ הרב רבי אליעזר דלא מצינו זונה שהיא אסורה לכהן — זאת אומרת מצד עצמה ולא משום שגורמת עבירה לכהן — דודאי הוא מוזהר עליה אבל היא אינה מוזהרת עליו הילכך גם לדבריה אינה אסורה בו דקאמר פרק יש מותרות [יבמות פ"ד ע"ב] דכל היכא דאיהו מוזהר איהי מוזהרת — וכן הוא אינו מוזהר שאינה מאמינה הילכך גם היא אינה אסורה בו — אבל קשה דאמר בגמרא דאוכלת בתרומה" וכו'. ולפנינו בספרים הוסיפו "וקשה" קודם "דקאמר" [וגם הוסיפו] "ועוד" אבל אין ספק שיד הסופרים במעל הזה.

היא בכלל האיסור כדכתיב [ויקרא כ״א:י״ג] ״והוא אשה בבתוליה יקח׳ —
קרי ביה יַקִיח׳ נאמנתי״. ולכאורה דבריהם אלו מראים שלא על איסור זונה
הם דנים כאן, כפי מה שפירשנו, אלא על איסור עשה ד״בתולה יקח׳״, שאם
בא עליה אדם בהטיה אסורה לכהן גדול, היפך ממה שכתבנו למעלה בפירוש
דעתן של בעלי התוספות. ואולם דברי התוספות קשים גם לפי הבנת
האחרונים בדבריהם, וכבר העירו הרב בעל טורי אבן במקומו ור׳ עקיבא
אייגר בתוספותיו למשנה סוף פרק ד׳ דיבמות שדברי התוספות סותרים
מאמר שלא נמצא עליו חולק בתלמוד יבמות פ״ד, ב, ומקורו בתורת כהנים
ראש [פרשת] אמור שדרשו שם: ״״לא יקחו׳, ׳לא יקחו׳ [ויקרא כ״א:ז׳] מלמד
שהאשה מוזהרת על ידי האיש״,[24] ופירושו שבכל איסורי כהונה אף שבנות
אהרן הכשרות לא הוזהרו לינשא לפסולין מכל מקום הפסולות אסורות
להינשא לכהנים כשרים, ואין חילוק בין מצוות עשה דהיא ״אשה בבתוליה
יקח׳ ללא תעשה ״אלמנה וגרושה [וחללה זונה את אלה] לא יקח׳ [ויקרא
כ״א:י״ד], שבכולן האשה הפסולה עוברת אם נישאה לכהן כשר. וגם אם
נניח, והנחה כעין זו כמעט אינה עולה על הדעת כלל, שנעלמו מהתוספות
בחגיגה דברי הגמרא והספרא, הלא מתוך הסברא עצמה של בעלי התוספות
מוכח שכן הוא, שאם אנו דורשין ״׳והוא אשה בבתוליה יקח׳ קרי ביה יַקִיח׳
(כך צריך לומר וכן בהוצאה ראשונה בומברג ר״פ, ואולם בהוצאת פיזארו
שלפני זה ובשאר ההוצאות נשתבש לי״יקיח׳) למה לא נדרוש גם כן ״לא
יקחו׳ שבשאר איסורי כהונה, ״קרי ביה יַקחו׳״, והוא שהאשה מוזהרת על
ידי האיש?

והרב ר׳ עקיבא אייגר במקום הנ״ל ובהגהותיו לחגיגה העיר על דברי ר׳
אליעזר [ממיץ] — הוא בעל ספר יראים — בתוספות נדרים צ׳, ב, דלא מצינו
זונה שהיא אסורה להינשא לכהן, ועל פי זה הוא מפרש דברי התוספות
בחגיגה שדעתם כדעת בעל ספר יראים אלא שחידשו שהמצוות עשה
ד״בתולה יקח׳ שאני מלא תעשה דאיסורי כהונה — ואף שלא תעשה חמור
ממצוות עשה — שבזו גם היא מוזהרת. ואולם אין ספק שדברי ר׳ אליעזר
[ממיץ] נשתבשו בתוספות שלפנינו והם מובאים כהוגן ברשב״א שם,
בחידושיו לנדרים [ד״ה חזרון] ובשטמ״ק שם [ד״ה מתני׳] בלשון זה:
״ותירץ הר׳ אליעזר דזונה לא מוזהרת מכהן אלא כל היכא דאיהו מוזהר
וכדאמר ביבמות — פ״ד, ב — כל היכי דאיהו מוזהר איהי מוזהרת דילא
יקחו׳ כתיבי״[25] — עיין לקמן פירוש דרשה זו. ולפי זה לא בלבד שלא נעלם

24 תורת כהנים, פרשת אמור, מהד׳ וייס, צ״ד ע״ג.
25 רל״ג העתיק מהרשב״א; בשטמ״ק הסגנון שונה במקצת.

(עיין בתוספות יום טוב בכורות ה׳, ה׳, מה שהעיר אם הכלל הזה **הוא** רק
בדרבנן או גם בדאורייתא וכאן הוא ספק איסור תורה), ולכן היא נאמנת כאן,
מה שאין כן במשנה דכתובות [י״ג, א׳] ב״יראה מדברת״ שאומר ר׳ יהושע לא
מפיה אנו חיין. ואדרבא, אם יש כאן קושיא, היא אליבא דרבן גמליאל שלפי
דעתו שנאמנת בברי שלה ב״יראוה מדברת״ ומכל שכן כאן בדעבידא לגלויי
ולמה הוצרכו לשאול שאלה כזו? וכבר העירונו למעלה מה שיש להשיב על
קושיא זה.

והרב בעל בני אהובה [להלכות] אישות ט״ו, א, באמת כתב לתרץ קושיית
התוספות על רש״י בדרך זו וזהו לשונו: ״וא״כ השאלה היא אי לסמוך על פיה
כיון דמעוברת היא ובזו מילתא דעבידא לגלויי לא משקרת ובזה לא קשה כלל
מהך פלוגתא דר׳ יהושע ורבן גמליאל גבי ׳ראוה מעוברת׳ — צ״ל הייתה או
מדברת — דשם אי אפשר להתברר [סבירא ליה] לר׳ יהושע ׳לא מפיה אנו
חיין׳, מה שאין כן כאן דיכול הדבר להתברר ולא משקרת ואתי שפיר וברור
ופשוט הוא״.[23] ובמחילה מכבוד תורתו, ברור ופשוט שלא ירד לסוף דעתן של
בעלי התוספות וכשנעמיק בדבריהם נראה שמה שהיקשו יפה היקשו. שעל פי
דעתן שביררנו למעלה שבעילה שבעילה בהטיה בעילה גמורה היא לכל דבר חוץ
[מ]לענין בעולה לכהן גדול שכיוון שבתוליה קיימין מותרת היא לו, קושייתם
היא שלר׳ יהושע גם אם נאמין לה שהיא בתולה, זאת אומרת שעוד בתוליה
קיימין משום דמלתא דעבידא לגלויי היא, מכל מקום אסורה היא לכהן גדול
ואפילו לכהן הדיוט שהרי הוא אומר ״לא מפיה אנו חיין״ וחיישינן שמא
נבעלה לפסול ואם בא עליה פסול נפסלה ואסורה לכהן גדול ואף שבא עליה
בהטיה ועדיין בתולה היא. וביותר יש לתמוה על הרב הגדול הזה שהיקשה
על התוספות אותה קושיא קושיא עצמה שהיקשו הם על רש״י, ונדחק לתרץ שמיירי
במקום דליכא פסולים כלל, ודבריו דברי נביאות ולא עוד אלא שכבר אמרו
אין אפוטרופוס לעריות. ולפי מה שכתבנו הכל עולה לנכון, שקושיית
התוספות היא שלר׳ יהושע אף שאנו מאמינין לה שהיא בתולה הרי היא
בחזקת בעולה לפסול ונפסלה. וראה עד כמה דקדקו רבותינו בעלי התוספות
בלשונם שאחר שהביאו מהמשנה דכתובות דברי ר׳ יהושע ״לא מפיה אנו
חיין״ הוסיפו ״וכו׳״, שעיקר קושייתם הוא מסוף דבריו שם במשנה שאמר
שהיא ״בחזקת בעולה לנתין ולממזר״ והיא פסולה לכהן ולתרומה.

ואל השלישי אני בא, לחלק השלישי שבתוספות [בחגיגה י״ד ע״ב] והוא
תירוצם שגם לר׳ יהושע יש כאן מקום לשאלה זו שכתבו: ״ושמא כאן שאף

---

23   ראה בני אהובה הנ״ל (לעיל, הערה 10), מ״ז ראש ע״ג.

שלא נשרו בתוליה, שאף שלפעמים רחוקות מוליד אין בו כוח ליגע בסימנים. ומהירושלמי כאן סתירה למה שכתב הר"ן שם שאחרי שאמרו ביבמות [דף] י"ב-י"ג ש"בנים הרי הם כסימנים", קטן שהוליד גדול הוא. וכאן בירושלמי אמרו שקטן זה שהוליד עוד קטן הוא ולכן אשה זו שנתעברה ממנו היו בתוליה קיימין משום שקטן שאין יכול ליגע בסימנים. ונראה שלדעת הירושלמי לא אמרו "בנים הרי הם כסימנים" אלא באשה ולא באיש, ואף שאפשר לדחוק ולומר שעל כרחך לא כתב הר"ן שקטן שמוליד גדול הוא אלא בשילדה אשה ממנו ולא כשנתעברה בלבד וכאן בירושלמי לא אמרו אלא מעשה ש"יעיברה" ולא ש"יילדה". ולפי זה הקושיא קטן אינו מוליד מעיקרא לא קשיא שלא אמרו אלא שאינו מוליד ולא שאין אשה מתעברת ממנו.

אחר שביארנו עיקר דעת התוספות [בחגיגה י"ד ע"ב] והוא שבעולה לכהן גדול שונה משאר איסורי ביאה שכל זמן שבתוליה קיימין מותרת לו ואף אם בא עליה איש ביאה גמורה אלא שהיטה, נבוא לבאר יתר דברי התוספות שנדחקו בהם האחרונים מבלי שעלתה בידם להעמידם. בראשונה היקשו שבמשנה כתובות י"ג, א נחלקו רבן גמליאל ור' יהושע בהיתה מעוברת אם נאמנת לומר לכשר נבעלתי, והכא [בחגיגה] משמע דקבעי אליבא דכולי עלמא, אפילו לר' יהושע שאומר שם שאינה נאמנת. ומשמעות זו יצאה להם ממה שלא אמרו [בחגיגה] "בתולה שעיברה **לרבן גמליאל** מהו לכהן גדול". בהוצאה ראשונה של התלמוד כולו, בומברג שנת ר"פ, הגירסא "מהו **לר"ג**", ואולם אין ספק שזו טעות הדפוס שנתחלפו לו להמדפיס ר' בכ' וצריך להיות "**לכ"ג**" = "לכהן גדול" כאשר הוא כבר לנכון בהוצאה השניה ובכל ההוצאות שלאחריה — שהרי בן זומא היה תלמידו של ר' יהושע כפי מה שמוכח מנזיר נ"ט, ב, שאמרו שדברי ר' יהושע במשנה שם הם "לחדד בה את התלמידים", זאת אומרת לחדד תלמידו בן זומא שנשא ונתן עמו בהלכה השנויה שם. וכן בסוגיא שלפנינו בחגיגה [ט"ו ע"א] סיפרו על בן זומא שכל כך היה שקוע בלימודו שלא עמד מלפני ר' יהושע רבו, ואם כן בודאי אינו מן הנימוס לשאול שאלה לחכם שאין לה מקום כלל לדעת רבו מבלי לרמז שהשאלה היא על פי דעת החולקים על רבו, ולא עוד אלא שאין דרכן של חכמים לשאול שאלות שתשובתן גלויה, והיה להם להשואלים את בן זומא להשיב לעצמם [ש]ברי שהתשובה שלו תהיה כדעת רבו ר' יהושע שאומר "לא מפיה אנו חיין". ואולם אף שההנחה של בעלי התוספות, שהסוגיא בחגיגה היא אליבא דכולי עלמא, היא ישרה ונכונה ולחינם נתקשה בה הרב בעל טורי אבן, קושייתם על רש"י איננה מובנת כלל, שהרי דבריו ברור מללו שלכן חשבו שאפשר שהיא נאמנת משום דמילתא דעבידא לגלויי לא משקרי אינשי

בהשרת בתולים, ואיך שיהיה כבר ראינו שקושיית השער המלך על התוספות
לא קשה כלל.

ומה שקשה לכאורה על מה שכתבנו בביאור דברי התוספות הוא
שבירושלמי כתובות א', ג [כ״ה ע״ב] אמרו: "קטן פחות מבן תשע [שנים]...
ביאתו ביאה אבל אין בו כח ליגע בסימנים" ולפי זה כמו שביאת קטן לא
שמה ביאה משום שאין נוגע בסימנים, הדין נותן שכל ביאה ואפילו ביאת
גדול שאין נוגע בסימנים, לא שמה ביאה. ואילו לפי דברינו בפירוש דברי
התוספות, הם מחלקים בין איסור בעולה לכהן גדול שבו נאמר "והוא אשה
בבתוליה יקח" [ויקרא כ״א: י״ג] וכל זמן שבתוליה קיימים אינה אסורה לו
לשאר איסורי ביאה שאינה תלויה כלל בהשרת בתולים. ואולם בלא דברינו
דברי הירושלמי צריכים ביאור שאם ביאת קטן ביאה היא אלא שאינו נוגע
בסימנים למה [אין] ביאתו ביאה בבעולה שכבר נשרו בתוליה, ועוד מה ענין
השרת בתולים לביאה וכי איש ש״ירב גובריה" [נדה ס״ד ע״ב] ויכול לבעול
כמה בעילות בלי שישיר בתולים אינו חייב כשבא על נערה המאורסה בתולה?
ועל כרחך שכוונת דברי הירושלמי היא שקטן כיוון שאינו "יכול" ליגע
בסימנים ביאתו לא שמה ביאה, אבל גדול ש״יכול" ליגע בסימנים ביאתו
ביאה ואף אם לא נגע חוץ מאיסור בעולה לכהן גדול שכל זמן שבתוליה
קיימין איננה אסורה לו וכמו שביארנו למעלה. ובודאי דברי הירושלמי הם
רק לדעת האומר — והלכה כדבריהם — שהעראה היא [הכנסת] העטרה
[שמשירה את] הבתולים כמו שאמרו בסנהדרין ע״ג, ב, ולכן כל ביאה שחייבין
עליה היא ביאה ש״יכול" ליגע בסימנים, אבל לדעת האומר העראה היא
נשיקת אבר שאין השרת בתולין על ידה כמו שאמרו שם [בסנהדרין], אי
אפשר לאמור שלכן אין ביאת קטן ביאה משום שאין יכול ליגע בסימנים,
שהלא כל הערה שחייב עליה אי אפשר ליגע בסימנים. ושם בירושלמי הביאו
ראיה למה שאמרו ביאת קטן ביאתו ביאה אבל אין בו כח ליגע בסימנים
ממעשה שעיברה אשה מביאת קטן ובתוליה קיימין.

ודברי הירושלמי פשוטים כפי מה שביארנו. ולא ידעתי מה דחקו להרב
בעל חתם סופר אהע״ז [סימן] קמ״ג להעמיס כוונה זרה בדבריו ומה שהיקשה
הרב ר' מאיר אריק בספרו טל תורה,²² שהרי בפירוש אמרו בסנהדרין ס״ט,
א, שקטן אינו מוליד, לא קשיא כלל שכבר כתבו הראשונים, הר״ן והמאירי,
שם בחדושיהם שלפעמים רחוקות קטן מוליד אלא שלא חששו חכמים
למיעוטא דמיעוטא כזו, ובירושלמי הביאו מעשה שנתעברה אשה מקטן אלא

---

²² ר' מאיר אריק, טל תורה, וינה תרפ״א, הגהות ירושלמי, דף כ״ט ע״א.

אלא משום אלמנה ועל כרחך שכהן גדול אסור בבעולה על ידי הטיה. ולפי מה שביארנו בפירוש דברי התוספות לא קשיא כלל מה שהיקשה הרב בעל שער המלך, שהרי לפי דעת התוספות אשה שאמרה בתולה אני שבא עלי איש בהטיה אינה נאמנת ולא משום שאנו אומרין שהיא משקרת אלא משום דשמואל לא שכיחא אנו אומרין שהיא טועה בדבר, ולא עוד אלא שאם נשאה כהן גדול ואמר שמצא לה בתולים אסורה לו שחוששין שמא הוא טועה. ואם כן שפיר קא מקשי בגמרא [ביבמות הנ"ל] אלמנה לכהן גדול "תיפוק ליה משום דהויא לה בעולה", שגם אם הוא אומר שבא עליה והיטה אנו אומרין שטעה [ולא] היטה והיא אסורה לו משום בעילת עצמו. ומלבד זה אפשר לומר [שעד כאן] לא כתבו התוספות בחגיגה [י"ד ע"ב] שאם חיישינן לשמואל מהימנא ומותרת אלא למאן דאמר (שם ביבמות אמרו שתלויה במחלוקת ר' מאיר ור' אלעזר) נבעלה שלא כדרכה אינה פסולה לכהונה וכל שכן שאיננה בעולה לכהן גדול וכן נבעלה בהטיה כשירה שהרי לא נשרו בתוליה, ואולם למאן דאמר נבעלה שלא כדרכה פסולה, כל שכן שנבעלה בהטיה שפסולה לכהן גדול. ולכן שם ביבמות שהיקשו על רב שאמר "נבעלה שלא כדרכה פסולה" שפיר היקשו, תיפוק ליה משום אלמנה שלדעת רב אין חילוק בין נשרו בתוליה או לא. ואולם גם אם נאמר לחלק בין ביאה שלא כדרכה לבעולה בלי נשירת בתולים, שכיוון שהקישה התורה "משכבי אשה" להדדי ביאה שלא כדרכה היא בעילה גמורה לכל דבר,[21] אבל אין בעילה בלי נשירת בתולים עושה בעולה לכהן גדול, לא קשיא כלל על התוספות בחגיגה, שאפשר שהם סוברים כרש"י (עיין תוספות יבמות נ"ט, ב, [באמצע] ד"ה אלא) והרמב"ם [הלכות] נערה בתולה ח', ה' דאין משלם קנס עד גמר ביאה שיש השרת בתולים, ואם כן כשבעל והיטה אין משלם קנס ולכן לא אמרו שאלמנה לכהן גדול מיירי בשבעל והיטה שבכעין זה אינו משלם קנס כלל. אלא שלפי זה קשה מה שהיקשו הראשונים — הרא"ש והר"ן סוף פרק ג' דכתובות והמאירי לסנהדרין [מהד' סופר] עמוד 274 — על הרמב"ם ממה שאמרו בקידושין ט', ב, "באו עליה י' אנשים ועדיין היא בתולה" שהכל מודים לעניין קנס דכולהו משלמי ומשמע שגם אם נאמר שאין קנס בהעראה יש קנס בשהיטה שעל זה אמרו שעדיין היא בתולה, עיין ברמב"ם [הלכות] איסורי ביאה ג', ו'. ומכל מקום אפשר שלדעת התוספות דבר זה תלוי במחלוקת, שרבן גמליאל בקידושין שם סובר שמשלם קנס גם בלי השרת בתולים וסתמא דגמרא בסנהדרין ע"ג, ב, סובר שאין משלם קנס אלא על גמר ביאה

סתם אין כאן מקום לשאלה זו דמאי נפקא מינה אם היטה או לא היטה? אם
ברי לה שהבועל כשר נאמנת לרבן גמליאל, ולהתוספות בשבאה לשאול על
עצמה נאמנת גם לר' יהושע, ואם אינה יודעת פסולה, שאפשר שהבועל היה
פסול ונפסלה ואף אם היטה, אלא שבכהן גדול אסורה גם בשברי לה שהיה
כשר אם נבעלה בעילה גמורה בלי הטיה.

וגם לפירוש שני שברש"י שם שמיירי כאן בשכבר נשאה הכהן הגדול ומצא
לה בתולים, אם אמרינן דשמואל לא שכיחא אסורה לו, שאנו אומרים שהוא
טעה לחשוב שהיא עדיין בתולה ובאמת כבר נשרו בתוליה וכמו שאמרו
בכתובות י', א, "אסבוהו כופרי", שקל הוא לטעות בדבר זה. ולפי פירוש זה
תשובתו של בן זומא היא "דשמואל לא שכיחא" ולכן אם היא אומרת "בא
עלי כשר והיטה" אסורה לכהן גדול שטוען היא ואולם חיישינן שמא באמבטי
עיברה, שאם אומרת לא בא עלי איש ונתעברתי באמבטי נאמנת כיון שטוענת
ברי. ולפי פירוש זה עולה יפה מה שאמרו "דשמואל לא שכיחא וחיישינן שמא
באמבטי עיברה". והמאמר הזה לכאורה מתמיה וכי עיבור באמבטי שהוא לפי
דברי רבינו חננאל שהבאתי למעלה "מעשה ניסים" שכיח יותר מבעילה
בהטיה שאסרו בנדה ס"ד, ב, שלאדם "יבעל כח" הוא דבר קל?! ולפי מה
שכתבנו בביאור דברי התוספות לא קשיא מידי, שכוונת הגמרא היא שכיוון
דשמואל לא שכיח — ברוב אנשים — אנו אומרים בעל והיטה והיא טועה
באומרה שעדיין בתולה היא, אבל חיישינן שמא באמבטי עיברה, שאף שהוא
דבר שלא שכיח אי אפשר לטעות בו, ולכן כשאומרת "נתעברתי באמבטי שלא
בא עלי איש" נאמנת, שיפה הברי שלה להכשירה ולהתירה לכהן גדול.

וראיתי להרב בעל משנה למלך והרב שער המלך[20] בחידושיהם להלכות
אישות ט"ו [הלכה ד'] ואיסורי ביאה י"ז [הלכה י"ג] שהאריכו להוכיח שכהן
גדול אסור באשה שנבעלה על ידי הטיה, והוא נגד מה שכתבנו בפירוש דברי
התוספות דאי חיישינן לדשמואל היא מותרת לכהן גדול. ואין כאן המקום
להאריך בדבריהם, שגם אם נסכים למה שהעלו שלדעת רש"י והרא"ש
"בעולה" היא אשה שנבעלה גם בלי השרת בתולים, בכעין זה נאמר "גברא
אגברא קרמית", שברור הוא שדעת התוספות אינה כן אלא ש"בעולה"
משמעה נבעלה בהשרת בתולים ואם היטה הרי זו כשירה. ולא באתי כאן
אלא להשיב על דברי הרב שער המלך שסתר דעת התוספות מדברי הגמרא
ביבמות נ"ט, א, שהקשו: אלמנה לכהן גדול "תיפוק ליה [משום דהויא לה]
בעולה" ולא תירצו שבא עליה בהטיה ועדיין בתולה היא ואין אסור עליה

20   ר' יצחק בר' משה נוניס-בילמונטי, ספר שער המלך, להלכות איסורי ביאה י"ז:י"ג,
חלק ב', ברין תקס"ב, דף קט"ז ע"ב - קי"ח ע"ב.

אלא שבאמת אין כאן מקום להגהות שברור שהתוספות הלכו בפירוש
דברי הגמרא בדרך אחרת ממה שהלך בה רש״י משום שהיה קשה להם על
פירושו של רש״י ב׳ קושיות אלו: הקושיא הראשונה היא זו שכבר העירונו
עליה למעלה, שלמה שאלו בכהן גדול דוקא ולא בכהן הדיוט והלא לפי
המסקנה בכתובות ט״ו, א (ועיין שם בתוספות בד״ה דלמא [ובדף י״ד ע״ב]
בד״ה כמאן) צריכים לכתחילה תרי רובי שלולא כן חיישינן דילמא אזלא
איהי לגביה. ואם כן גם לפי מה שפסקו שם י״ד, ב, [ש]הלכה כרבן גמליאל
ברוב אחד אסורה להינשא גם בשאומרת ברי אם חיישינן לדשמואל, ואם
דשמואל לא שכיחא ובאמבטי עיברה מותרת לכתחילה, ואם כן למה לא
שאלו ״בתולה שעיברה מהו לכהן״, מי חיישינן לדשמואל ואסורה לכתחילה
ברוב אחד או דשמואל לא שכיחא וחיישינן שמא באמבטי עיברה ומותרת
לכתחילה? ולמעלה כתבנו שלפי פירושי רש״י צריך לומר שהיה ספק להם אם
בעיין, זה שהוא מיעוט שאינו מצוי, נאמנת לרבן גמליאל או לא, ולכן לא היו
יכולים לשאול שאלה זו בכהן סתם שבזה נאמנת משום מיגו דאי בעיא אמרה
לכשר נבעלתי שנאמנת לרבן גמליאל, ואולם התוספות לא נחה דעתם בזה
שהרי עדיין יש מקום לשאלה זו בכהן סתם ובדאיכא רק רוב אחד אם מותרת
להינשא לכתחילה. ועוד היה קשה להם על פירוש רש״י לשון הגמרא ״מי
חיישינן לדשמואל״ זאת אומרת ואסורה או ״דשמואל לא שכיחא״, והיא
מותרת. ולשון זה תמוה מאוד שלא הזכירו בשאלה כלל שמא באמבטי עיברה
והלא רק על הנחה זו נוסד כל ההיתר, ובוודאי אין הנחה זו פשוטה כל כך עד
שלא הוצרכו לזוכרה. וכבר הבאתי למעלה בשם רבינו חננאל שהוא קורא
לעיבור באמבטי ״מעשה ניסים״,[19] ואיך לא רמזו בשאלה על אפשרות עיבור
באמבטי? והגאונים בשו״ת ליק [סימן] כ״ה והתוספות בכתובות ו׳, ב, בד״ה
״רובי״ ועוד אחרים — עיין דקדוקי סופרים במקומו [בחגיגה] — גורסים ״או
דלמא (ויש שגורסים ״שמא״ — עיין שם בדקדוקי סופרים ובתשב״ץ במקום
הנ״ל) באמבטי עיברה״, אבל התוספות בחגיגה גרסו כגירסת הספרים שלנו
והיה קשה להם למה לא נזכרה בשאלה האפשרות שבאמבטי עיברה. ולכן
פירשו ש״חיישינן לדשמואל״ פירושו חיישינן לקולא כמו שפירש רש״י
״חיישינן״ בקשר עם באמבטי עיברה והשאלה היא לפי זה דוקא בכהן גדול
שנאמר בו ״[אשה] בבתוליה יקח״, וכל זמן שלא נשרו בתוליה היא מותרת,
ואם לא שכיחא דשמואל והיא אומרת שהיא עדיין בתולה אינה נאמנת
שטועה היא וחושבת שהיטה ובאמת לא היטה ואסורה לכהן גדול. ובכהן

---

19   ראה לעיל, הערה 17.

למעלה שגם הרב בעל הגהות הסמ"ק לא נסתייע מהסוגיא דחגיגה משום שמשם אין ראיה כלל.

[ח. שיטת תוספות בחגיגה י"ד-ט"ו]

ועתה נבוא לפירוש השני על "בתולה שעיברה" וכו' והוא פירוש התוספות שם שדבריהם קשים מאוד וכבר נתקשו בהם הרבה מהאחרונים: עיין משנה למלך ובני אהובה במקומות הנ"ל, תוספות ר' עקיבא אייגר למשנה סוף פ"ד דיבמות וטורי אבן במקומו [בחגיגה]. ולכן מוכרח אני להרחיב הדברים מעט. וזה לשון התוספות [בחגיגה י"ד ע"ב], בד"ה בתולה שעיברה מהו לכהן גדול: "ופי' רש"י שהיא אומרת בתולה אני ואי שכיחא דשמואל מהימנא וקשה להר"י דהא פרק קמא דכתובות תנן: היתה מעוברת מה טיבו של עובר זה מאיש פלוני וכהן הוא וכו' ר' יהושע אמר לא מפיה אנו חיין וכו' והכא משמע דקבעיא אליבא דכוליה עלמא".

ובראשונה צריך להעיר שהמאמר "שהיא אומרת בתולה אני ואי שכיחא דשמואל מהימנא", היא הרצאה במילים אחרות לדברי רש"י "והיא אומרת שימצאו לה בתולים" ולא שהיה לפניהם נוסחא אחרת ברש"י. ומה שקשה הוא למה נדחקו התוספות להוציא הדברים מידי פשוטן ולפרש שאם דשמואל שכיחא מהימנא, זאת אומרת וכשרה לכהן גדול, ולא פירשו כפשוטן שאם דשמואל שכיחא היא אסורה ואם דשמואל לא שכיחא היא מותרת. וכפי מה שראינו למעלה מוכח מרש"י שבת [קנ"א ע"א] שזו היא דעתו ולא עוד אלא שפירושן של התוספות בדברי רש"י אי אפשר להעמידו כלל, שבוודאי אם בא עליה איש בהטיה הרי זו אסורה, שביאה כעין זו היא ביאה לכל דבר, ואי נתעברה באמבטי היא מותרת שלא היה כאן ביאת איש. וכבר הרגיש בזרות דברי התוספות הרב ב"ח בהגהותיו [בחגיגה] והגיה דברי התוספות, ותמיהה גדולה על כל אלה האחרונים שנזכרו למעלה שנעלמו מהם דברי הב"ח, כדי להסכים עם פירוש רש"י בשבת. ואולם מאן יוכל להחויה כאילין מליא [= מי יוכל לספר כדברים האלה], שלא הניח דבר וחצי דבר בדברי התוספות שלא הגיה ואם בא באנו להגיה יותר קל הוא לאמור שבראש דברי התוספות היה כתוב: "ואי שכיחא **דשמואל** לא מהימנא, ואי לא שכיחא **דשמואל** מהימנא" והסופרים דילגו על מה שבין "דשמואל" הראשון ל"דשמואל" השני ודילוג כעין זה רגיל ומצוי כל כך עד שמהנותר להביא ראיות לטעויות סופרים שמסוג זה.

היא שכיוון שגם הטיה היא לא שכיחא תולין שבאמבטי עיברה כמו שהיא
אומרת, בין לרבן גמליאל שאומר בהיתה מעוברת נאמנת לומר לכשר נבעלתי
בין לר׳ יהושע שבאה לשאול על עצמה כמו שכתבו התוספות שם ויתבארו
דבריהם לקמן. ועתה אין להקשות למה לא שאלו ״בתולה שעיברה מהו
לכהן״ ושאלו דווקא ״מהו לכהן **גדול**״ שבכהן הדיוט הרי לרבן גמליאל גם
אשה מעוברת נאמנת לומר לכשר נבעלתי, שבודקת ומונה, ואם כן אין כאן
מקום כלל לשאלה זו, שבודאי היא נאמנת לומר בתולה אני ונתעברתי
באמבטי במיגו [ד]לכשר נבעלתי, ואולם בכהן גדול אין כאן מיגו שגם אם
נבעלה לכשר פסולה לו משום בעולה, והשאלה היא אם ברי שלה בכעין זה גם
כן מהני או שהמיעוט שאינו מצוי כעיבור באמבטי אין מתחשבין עמו כלל
ואפילו כשאומרת ברי. ולפי דעת התוספות שבאה לשאול על עצמה גם ר׳
יהושע מודה לרבן גמליאל, ואם כן גם אליבא דר׳ יהושע השאלה דווקא בכהן
גדול. ורש״י, או שסובר כדעת התוספות בזה או שמפרש שהשאלה ששאלו את
בן זומא היא אליבא דהלכתא, דקיימא לן כרבן גמליאל, ואליבא דר׳ יהושע
אין שאלה לא בכהן גדול ולא בכהן הדיוט שלא מפיה אנו חיין.

והנה לפי מה שביארנו, פירוש הסוגיא דחגיגה על דעתו של רש״י אין
עניינה כלל לנידון שלנו, שלא אמרו אלא שאשה שעדיין בתולה שלא בא עליה
אדם ואפילו אם היא מעוברת על ידי קליטת זרע באמבטי כשרה לכהן גדול,
שהרי במצוה זו הקפידה התורה שתהי בתולה והרי היא בתולה. ואם אמרו
ביבמות נ״ט, א, ״נבעלה שלא כדרכה פסולה״, הטעם הוא משום ש״משכבי
אשה״ כתיב, וכיון שנבעלה כדרכה פסולה, גם נבעלה שלא כדרכה פסולה.[18]
אבל בממזרות, שאפשר שהקפידה התורה שלא ייכנס זרע לרחם אשה
שאסורה לו, גם בשנתעברה באמבטי הולד ממזר באיסורי עריות ופסול
בפסולי כהונה. ואדרבא, לפי פירוש רש״י נראה יותר שיש ממזרות ופסול
בולד שאמו נתעברה באמבטי ולכן לא שאלו [על] בתולה ארוסה שעיברה
והארוס אומר שאינו ממנו אם הוולד ממזר אם לא. ויש כאן מקום לשאלה
כזו, בין לרבן גמליאל שאפשר שבמיעוט שאינו מצוי כעיבור באמבטי אינה
נאמנת ואפילו באומרת ברי, בין לר׳ יהושע שאומר שלא מפיה אנו חיין
בשודאי נבעלה ואולם כשהספק אם נבעלה כל אפשר שמודה — עיין דברינו
למעלה — ואולם לא [נשאלה] שאלה כזאת משום שלעניין ממזרות ופסול אין
הדבר תלוי כלל בביאה אלה בהזרעת הזרע. ואולם איך שיהיה, אף שאין לנו
ראיה ברורה לאסור מסוגיא זו, אין בה אפילו רמז קטן להתיר וולד אשה
שנתעברה באמבטי מקרוב או אשת איש מאיש שאינו בעלה, וכבר ראינו

---

18 ראה ויקרא י״ח:כ״ב כפי שהוא נדרש ביבמות פ״ג ע״ב.

זומא חי אחרי החרבן, והרי לר׳ יהושע החשש ב״ראוה מדברת״ הוא משום שחיישינן שמא נבעלה לפסול ונפסלה ואם כן יש כאן מקום לשאול בתולה שעיברה מהו לכהן, [ש]אם חיישינן לדשמואל אפשר שבא עליה פסול ונפסלה ואף שאין ספק שהיא בתולה, או דשמואל לא שכיחא ואם היא בתולה בוודאי נתעברה באמבטי וכשרה. ובאמת בתשב״ץ במקום הנ״ל [חלק ג׳, סימן רס״ג] הגירסא ״לכהן״ ולא ל״כהן גדול״ אבל לרש״י והרא״ש שגרסו ״לכהן גדול״ השאלה במקומה עומדת, למה שאלו בכהן גדול ולא ב״כהן״ סתם? ומלבד זה קשה לומר שהשאלה ששאלו [את] בן זומא היא לא אליבא דהלכתא, שהרי קיימא לן כרבן גמליאל, ולפי דעת התוספות בחגיגה בבתולה שעיברה גם ר׳ יהושע מודה לרבן גמליאל — עיין פירוש דבריהם לקמן — ואם כן גם אם נגרוס ״לכהן״ כגירסת התשב״ץ הקושיא במקומה עומדת, שלרבן גמליאל אין כאן שום שאלה שבוודאי נאמנת היא בטוענת ברי. גם אין לומר שמיירי כשהאשה אומרת: ״הריני מעוברת ואולם יודעת אני שלא בא עלי אדם כשהייתי ערה וכן אני יודעת שעדיין בתולה אני ואולם אפשר שבא עלי אדם כשהייתי ישנה ולא הרגשתי בו או שנתעברתי באמבטי״, שאם כן הדרא קושיא לדוכתה למה לא שאלו בכהן סתם, שכאן שהיא אינה אומרת ברי גם רבן גמליאל מודה שהיא ובתה [פסולות] ואם חיישינן לדשמואל אפשר שבא עליה פסול כשהיתה ישנה.

ומה שנראה לי בזה הוא שעל כרחך לא אמר רבן גמליאל, ולדברי התוספות בשבאה לשאול על עצמה ר׳ יהושע מודה לו, שנאמנת לומר לכשר נבעלתי ובדיעבד גם ברוב פסולין, עיין כתובות י״ד, א, ושם ט״ו, א, ובדברי הראשונים שם, אלא כשהספק הוא אם נבעלה לכשר או לפסול שסוף כל סוף מיעוט כשרים הוא מיעוט המצוי. אבל אפשרות עיבור באמבטי רחוקה כל כך שאפשר שאף רבן גמליאל מודה שאין מתחשבין עימה כלל. אלא אנו אומרים בא עליה איש והיטה ולכן עדיין בתולה היא, וזהו ששאלו את בן זומא ״בתולה שעיברה מהו לכהן גדול״, ותשובת בן זומא היא: ״דשמואל לא שכיח״. ואם כן אחרי שמוכרחים אנו להודות שאשה זו שנתעברה בדרך שאינו רגיל, או על ידי בעילת הטיה או על ידי קליטת זרע באמבטי, וכאשר היא טוענת ברי שלא בא עליה איש אין אנו מאמינים לה. וברור [ש]כשאמרו ״דשמואל לא שכיח וחיישינן שמא באמבטי עיברה״ לא כיוונו לומר שקליטת זרע באמבטי היא שכיחה שבוודאי לא כן הוא כידוע לכל אדם, ורבינו חננאל שם בפירושו מתאר דבר זה כ״מעשה ניסים״[17] (ומה שמסופר שם על בתולה שהקשתה לילד מוזכר גם בתשב״ץ בנוסח אחר קצת). אלא שכוונת הגמרא

במקום הנ״ל שכתב: "בתולה שעיברה מהו להתירה לכהן — עיין לקמן על הגירסא "לכהן" במקום "לכהן גדול" שלפנינו [בחגיגה] — דשמא נבעלה — זאת אומרת ופסולה — או חיישינן שמא באמבטי עיברה... ומותרת לכהן".

וצריכים אנו פירוש לפירוש זה של רש״י שלכאורה קשה להבין, שהרי בוודאי מיירי הכי כשהיא אומרת שלא נבעלה לשום אדם, שאם לא כן כשמודה שבא עליה בהטיה אין כאן מקום לשאלה, שברור שפסולה לכהן גדול, ואם כן נחזי אנן אליבא דמאן נשאלה השאלה. אם אליבא דרבן גמליאל במשנה פרק א׳ דכתובות [דף] י״ג, א, שאומר היתה מעוברת ואמרה עובר זה של כהן נאמנת משום שאומרת "ברי" כמו שפירשו שם י״ד, א, למה לא תהי נאמנת באומרת לא נבעלתי לאדם אלא נתעברתי באמבטי? ואם אמרו שלא הכשיר רבן גמליאל אלא בדאיכא תרי רובי (שם ט״ו, א — עיין בשטמ״ק הפירושים השונים של הראשונים על זה), לא אמרו כן אלא כשהספק הוא אם נבעלה לפסול או לכשר וצריך תרי רובי נגד הפסולים, אבל כאן שהספק הוא אם נבעלה בהטיה או קלטה זרע באמבטי ואולם אנו מאמינין לה שהיא עדיין בתולה משום שאינה משקרת במילתא דעבידא לגלויי, או לפירוש שני של רש״י שבא עליה כהן גדול ומצאה בתולה — עיין לקמן על זה — ואין כאן שום ספק שהיא עדיין בתולה, ואם כן למה לא נאמין ל״ברי" שלה שאומרת לא נבעלתי אלא נתעברתי באמבטי — מה תרי רובי שייך כאן?

ואפילו לדעת התוספות שם י״ד, ב, בד״ה כמאן, שגם לרבן גמליאל אינה נאמנת בטענת ברי אלא בשיש לה מיגו, קשה שהרי גם הם מודים דהיכא דלא ראינו שנאנסה נאמנת בלא מיגו, דאשה בודקת ומונה. וביותר קשה שאלת התלמוד לדעת ר׳ יוסף אבן מיגאש ושאר ראשונים, עיי״ש בשטמ״ק, שהם אומרים שלרבן גמליאל נאמנה בטוענת ברי גם בלי מיגו ואם כן תהי נאמנת לומר באמבטי נתעברתי ואף שאין לה מיגו. וכן יש כאן קושיא אם נאמר שהשאלה היא אליבא דר׳ יהושע שאומר שם במשנה [דף י״ג ע״א] "לא מפיה אנו חיין", שהיה אפשר לומר ששאלו אליבא דר׳ יהושע אם [הוא] מודה כאן, שאחרי שאנו מאמינין לה שהיא בתולה משום דמילתא דעבידא לגלויי היא, או שכבר בא עליה כהן גדול ומצאה בתולה, והספק הוא אם בא עליה איש בהטיה או שנתעברה באמבטי והדבר שקול והיא אומרת ברי נאמנת, שעל כרחך לא אמר שאינה נאמנת אלא בשברי שנבעלה לאיש והספק הוא אם נבעלה לכשר או לפסול וכאשר רובא דעלמא פסולים סובר שלא מפיה אנו חיין. ואולם כאן שאפשר שלא בא עליה איש כלל אומר [ר׳ יהושע] שנאמנת. ואולם הקושיא אליבא דר׳ יהושע היא שאם כן למה לא שאלו בתולה שעיברה מהו **לכהן**, ולמה דווקא **בכהן גדול** שהוא הלכתא למשיחא, שבן

בתו, שלא בלבד שקשה להורות מן ההגדות עוד הדבר מוטל בספק אם לפי
ההגדה זו בן סירא היה ממזר או לא, נבוא אל העיון ונראה מה יאמר
התלמוד, שמפיו אנו חיין, בדבר זה. והנה המעיין בהגהות סמ״ק כאשר הן
בכ״יי ובב״יח יראה שבעל ההגהות לא היה לו איזה ראיה לדבריו מדברי
התלמוד, שלולא כן בוודאי לא היה נמנע מלהביאה במקום לאמור ״כי הלא
בן סירא כשר היה״, מה שלא נמצא בתלמוד. ואיך אפשר לומר שכיוון לומר
שוולד כזה הרי הוא כשר לגמרי, כי בוודאי בן בתו של אותו צדיק היה כשר
לגמרי, [אבל] מהתלמוד עצמו אפשר שיש להוכיח שאינו ממזר אבל לא כשר
לגמרי. ואיך שיהיה לכאורה סוגיא שלמה היא לפנינו בחגיגה י״ד, ב, וגוי גבי
״בתולה שעיברה מהו לכהן גדול״, שוולד שנולד מעיבור באמבטי בתר אימיה
שדיין ליה והוא כשר אם היא כשרה, שאינו מתייחס אחר אביו כלל.
והאחרונים הרב בעל משנה למלך והרב בעל בני אהונה כבר העירו על הסוגיא
בחגיגה אלא שלדעתי לא יצאו ידי צרכן בהעמקת הסוגיא החמורה והנני
לפרשה כיד ה' הטובה עלי.

״שאלו את בן זומא: בתולה שעיברה מהו לכהן גדול? מי חייישינן
לדשמואל דאמר שמואל: יכול אני לבעול כמה בעילות בלי דם או דילמא
דשמואל לא שכיחא? אמר להו: דשמואל לא שכיח וחיישינן שמא באמבטי
עיברה.״ והנה לפי גירסת רש״י, התוספות ורוב הספרים שלנו — אבל לא
כולן, עיין לקמן — השאלה היא, שגם אם נאמין לדבריה שעדיין בתולה מכל
מקום אפשר שפסולה היא לכהן גדול שאפשר שבא עליה איש בהטיה וכבר
נפסלה לכהן גדול או דשמואל לא שכיחא ואם היא עדיין בתולה אין לך דרך
אחרת אלא שנתעברה באמבטי וכשרה לכהן גדול. והתשובה [היא] ״דשמואל
לא שכיח״, ולכן כשרה שבאמבטי נתעברה. ואין ספק שכך פירש רש״י, ואף
שדבריו בחגיגה אינם [מוכרחים] כאשר נראה לקמן בפירוש דברי התוספות,
הרי מוכח כן ממה שכתב בשבת קנ״א, א, שלפעמים ״חיישינן״ הוא לקולא
[כדאמרינן] ״חיישינן שמא באמבטי עיברה״ (והרבה מקומות כיוצא בו
״חיישינן״ לקולא — עיין תוספות קדושין נ', ב, בד״ה הכי גרסינן וכללי
התלמוד למרן הרב בית יוסף ק', ב, הוצאת ליוורנא).[16] והרואה יראה שלפי
דעת רש״י ״חיישינן לדשמואל״ הוא חיישינן לחומרא ״וחיישינן שמא
באמבטי עיברה״ הוא לקולא כמו שפירשנו ולכן הבא חיישינן השני לראיה
שיש חיישינן לקולא. ומדברי הרא״ש שם בשבת [פרק כ״ג, סימן ט'] ובגיטין
[פרק] ד', [סימן] ל״א מוכח שגם הוא פירש כרש״י וכן מראים דברי התשב״ץ

---

16   ראה כללי הגמרא של ר' יוסף קארו המודפס כחלק של ספר הליכות עולם לר' ישועה
     הלוי, ורשה תרמ״ג (ודפוסי צילום), דף נ״ח ע״ד.

בענין בנה של אסתר היה אפשר להשיב שרב הוא שאומר שהיה בנה של אסתר והוא שסובר שם ביבמות [מ"ה ע"א] שנכרי הבא על בת ישראל הולד כשר, ואולם הגירסא "[משמיה] דרב" ליתא בכ"י מדוייקים ואצל הראשונים [במגילה].[14]

[ו. אין מורין הלכה מאלפא ביתא דבן סירא]

ואיך שיהיה אי אפשר להורות הוראה מהגדה זו, שלא בלבד כפי מה שראינו אפשר לומר שבאמת בנה של בת ירמיה היה ממזר, הלא כבר אמרו בירושלמי פאה ב', ו' [י"ז ע"א] וחגיגה סוף פ"א [ע"ו ע"ד] "אין למדין" או כמו שהוא במקום השני "אין מורין מן ההגדות". ואם בהגדות של זמן התלמוד אמרו כך, קל וחומר בן של קל וחומר בהגדה זו שנמצאת רק באלפא ביתא דבן סירא שהוא ספר מאוחר — הראשון שמביאו הוא בעל הערוך כפי מה שהעירותי במקום אחר[15] — והוא ספר שיש בו כמה דברים שאין הדעת סובלתן ושאין רוח חכמים נוחה מהם. והרב ר' שמעון בר' צמח בשו"ת שלו [חלק] ג', [סימן] רס"ג כתב על הגדה זו: "**ואם נאמין לספרים חיצוניים** מצינו בספר בן סירא — התואר "ספרים חיצוניים" שנותן לספר זה איננו שם הכבוד — כי אמו נתעברה משכבת זרע [של ירמיה] באמבטי" וכו'. וכדרכו של חכם שאינו מאמין לכל דבר, הוא מרמז שאין להאמין בהגדות כאלה, ובודאי שאי אפשר להורות בענין חמור כממזרות על סמך [מקור] קל כזה. וגדול האחרונים הרב בעל נודע ביהודה, מהדורה תניינא, יורה דעה, [סימן] קס"א חיזק במסמרים דברי הירושלמי שאין להורות מן ההגדות, וחכם עדיף מנביא, שכך מצינו להגאונים שכתבו כן בפירוש, עיין לדוגמא תשובת רב האי גאון בשו"ת הגאונים הוצאת הרכבי סימן ט' שכתב: "והגדה אין סומכין עליה".

[ז. חגיגה י"ד ע"ב-ט"ו ע"א ושיטתו של רש"י על אתר]

אחרי שראינו שקשה לסמוך לדבר חמור כזה על ההגדה שבספר אלפא ביתא דבן סירא, שבן סירא זה נולד מזרע שפלט ירמיה באמבטי ושקלטתו

---

14   עיין בהערה הקודמת.

15   הכוונה למאמרו ב-*Jewish Encyclopedia*, כרך ב', 1902, עמ' 678-681, ושם הוא מפנה לערוך השלם הנ"ל (לעיל, הערה 5), חלק ששי, עמ' 450, ערך "פרישי".

שילדתו אמו היתה מתביישת כלומ׳ עכשיו יאמרו **שזה הילד ממזר הוא,** מיד
פתח פיו אותו הולד ואמר: אמי, אמי מפני מה את מתביישת״ וכו׳. אבל
בהוצאה ראשונה י״ז, א׳ הגירסא: ״היתה מתביישת שהיו אומרים **מזנות
ילדה״.**[12] והחילוק שבין ב׳ הגירסאות הוא שלפי הגירסא הראשונה בא בן
סירא לבשר את אמו שלא תתבייש שמא הוא ממזר, אחרי שנתעברה באמבטי
ואיננו ממזר, ולהגירסא השניה הודיעה שלא היה עיבורו בזנות. ואין ספק
שהגירסא השניה היא העיקרית שהרי בתו של ירמיה פנויה היתה כפי מה
שמסופר שם ופנויה שנתעברה אין בנה ממזר אפילו לר׳ יהושע בכתובות י״ג,
א, שאמר ״לא מפיה אנו חיין״, אלא שהיא ובתה פסולות לכהונה, ולרבן
גמליאל שהלכה כמותו כשרה אפילו לכהונה. ועיקרה של הגדה זו להשמיענו
שבתו של ירמיה לא פעלה און ואם ירננו עליה שנתעברה גם היא תשיב
שנתעברה באונס ולא זנתה.

ואולם לפי הגירסא הראשונה כבר באתה ההגדה להוציא מדעת אלו
שחשבו שנכדו של ירמיה היה ממזר ומאותו צדיק עצמו שממנו נתעברה בתו
ואמרה שכיון שנתעברה באמבטי לא היה ממזר. והבקי בדרכי ההגדה ידע
שזה ״חידוש״ של אחרונים שההגדה העממית איננה מתחשבת בדברים
כאלה. וכבר מצינו במגילה י״ג, ב, שדריוש היה בן אסתר מאחשורוש[13] ולא
חששו כלל להוציא לעז על אותה נביאה שהיה לה בן ממזר לפי דעת
האומרים — עיין למעלה — שנכרי הבא על בת ישראל אפילו פנויה הולד
ממזר ומכל שכן אשת איש, שלפי ההגדה אסתר היתה אשתו של מרדכי, עיין
שם, משום שהרי אנוסה היתה וכמו שאמרו בסנהדרין ע״ד, ב, ״אסתר קרקע
עולם״ ואם כן אין בה זה פגם; וכן אפילו נאמר שבן סירא היה ממזר אין בזה
פגם לירמיה. ואולי אפשר שגם לפי הגירסא א׳ ״ממזר״ כאן אינו במובן
הטכני אלא כפי הרגיל בספרים האחרונים משמעו בן שנולד בזנות, ולכן גם
לפי גירסא זו אפשר לומר שבן סירא אמר לאמו [ש]אם יחרפוך בני אדם שיש
לך בן הנולד בזנות וזונה מופקרת את, אמרי להם שנולדתי מן הזרע שקלטת
באמבטי ואין שום תרעומת עליך שהרי אנוסה [היית]. ועל הראיה ממגילה

12　והשוה למהד׳ יסיף, עמ׳ 199, וברור משם ששתי הגירסאות השונות נבעו משתי
מהדורות שונות של הסיפור.

13　רל״ג כנראה ציטט מהזכרון ולכן טעה. במגילה י״ג ע״ב נאמר: ״אמר רבה בר לימא
משמיה דרב: שהיתה עומדת מחיקו של אחשורוש וטובלת ויושבת בחיקו של מרדכי״, אבל
אין שם זכר לדריוש. מצד שני, נאמר בויקרא רבה י״ד:ה׳, מהד׳ מרגליות, עמ׳ ר״ג = אסתר
רבה ח׳:ג, וילנא י״ג ע״ד: ״אמר ר׳ יהודה בר־סימון: **דריוש האחרון בנה שלאסתר** היה
טהור מאמו **וטמא מאביו״.** רל״ג כנראה מיזג את שתי המסורות והסיק שרב אמר (ראה
בהמשך כאן) ״שדריוש היה בן אסתר מאחשורוש״.

של האב. והרב בעל משנה למלך מדייק מדברי רבינו פרץ בהגהותיו שהוא בנו
לכל דבר שהרי הוא אומר ד״יקפדינן אהבחנה גזרה שמא ישא אחותו מאביו״,
[ואכן] כך היא הגירסא בב״ח ובכתב יד של הגהות הסמ״יק שזכרתי למעלה,
אבל בכ״יי אדלער הנ״יל נאמר: ״אלא כדי להבחין של מי יהיה הולד״, וכיוון
למה שאמרו ביבמות מ״ב, א, ״דאמר קרא ׳להיות לך לאלהים ולזרעך
אחריך׳ [בראשית י״יז:ז׳] להבחין בין זרעו של ראשון לזרעו של שני״. ועיקר
ההקפדה הוא שלא יתייחס אחר בעל אמו על ידי זה הרבה תקלות אפשר
לבוא שיפטור אמו מיבום וחליצה כשימות בעלה ולא שיתייחס אחר אביו.
ולפי זה אין להקשות מה שהיקשה בבני אהובה במקום הנ״יל למה לא אמרו
ביבמות כ״ב, שמאמר במשנה ״מי שיש לו בן מכל מקום פוטר״ בא לרבות
בשנולד על ידי אמבטי דכעין זה לא הוי בנו כלל ואין מיוחס אחריו.

וכן לא קשיא מה שהיקשה בטורי אבן חגיגה ט״ו, א, על מה שאמרו
ביבמות י, א, ״באחותה דהתירא קמיירי, דאיסורא לא קמיירי״, והא משכחת
לה אם נופלת ליבום בהיתר בנה וכגון שנתעברה כלתה מחמיה באמבטי
ומת בעלה ונפלה ליבום לפני בנה שהוא אחי בעלה מן האב, שבן שנולד
באמבטי אינו בנו כלל ואין הוא אחי בעלה מן האב. גם מה שצידדו לאמור
הרב בעל חלקת מחוקק [לאבן העזר סימן] א׳, [סעיף קטן] ח׳ ושם בבית
שמואל א׳, [סעיף קטן] י׳ שעל ידי זה קיים אביו מצוות פרו ורבו, ליתא
לפי גירסת כ״יי הסמ״יק, שאם אינו מתייחס אחריו אינו מקיים בו מצוות פרו
ורבו וכמו שאמרו ביבמות ס״יב, א, ״הכל מודים בעבד שאין לו חייס״.

[ה. אלפא ביתא דבן סירא]

אחרי שביארנו דעתו של רבינו פרץ בהגהות סמ״יק צריכים אנו לעמוד על
טעמו. והמעיין בדבריו יראה שלא הוציא דבר זה לא מן התלמוד ולא מתוך
הסברא אלא מן ההגדה שבן סירא היה בן בתו של ירמיה שנתעברה באמבטי
מזרע של אותו צדיק שאנסוהו פריצי הדור להוציא זרע באמבטי ואחר כך
באתה בתו ורחצה בה וקלטה זרע אביה. ההגדה הזאת נמצאת לפנינו באלפא
ביתא ב׳ של בן סירא שנדפס בברלין תרי״ח ובהוצאה שניה על פי כ״יי בהצופה
לחכמת ישראל שנה י׳ [תרפ״יו, עמ׳ 281-250].[11] והנה בעיקרה ההגדה שווה
בב׳ הנוסחאות ואולם ראוי לשים לב שבהוצאה שניה עמוד 253 נאמר: ״וכיוון

---

11 וראה עכשו המהדורה המדעית של עלי יסיף בתוך ספרו סיפורי בן סירא בימי
הביניים, ירושלים תשמ״יה, עמ׳ 301-195.

ומצאתי תאמין,[9] שבדקתי בי"ב כתבי יד של הסמ"ק ובאחד מהם (כ"י אדלער סימן 2052, נכתב בפריס שנת ק"י, אבל ההגהות הן בכ"י אחר מאוחר קצת מכ"י הסמ"ק עצמו) מצאתי אותה ההגהה שמובאת בב"ח והיא הגהה לסימן רצ"ד של הסמ"ק קרוב לסוף הספר. וכן מצאתי הגהה זו בכ"י של הגהות הסמ"ק [ב]סימן פ"יא. וב' כתבי יד אלו הם בספריה של בית מדרש הרבנים שבאמריקא.

ותמוהים לי דברי הרב בעל בני אהובה פרק ט"ו מהלכות אישות שכתב: "ולי נראה דאין משם — הגהות הסמ"ק — ראיה כלל דלא הזהירה התורה בנדה רק מבלי לבעול אותה, אבל להיות הרה ממנו על ידי סדין או אמבטי אנה והיכא אסרה התורה כיון דהוא בעלה מה שאין כן באיש אחר, 'שכבת זרע' כתיב והרי בא למעט שכבת זרע מאחר'".[10] ודבריו תמוהים שהרב בעל משנה למלך מביא כל אותה ההגהה בלשונה ממש כמו שמובאת בב"ח ובה נאמר מפורש כמו שהעירונו למעלה שרק משום הבחנה אין הנשים שוכבות על סדין של איש אחר ואף **שהיולד שנולד מטיפה שעל הסדין כשר**, ואיך הוא משיג על המשנה למלך ואומר לחלק בין נדה לאשת איש שהגהות הסמ"ק לא נאמרו באשת איש אלא בנדה ובהגהות נאמר נמי להיפך! גם מה שכתב שבאשת איש נאמר שכבת זרע למעט שכבת זרע מאחר תמוה הוא, שלפי דבריו אשה שקלטה שכבת זרע מאיש שאינו בעלה תהי חייבת מיתה, ולא עוד אלא גם האיש חייב מיתה אם הוא משליך זרע לרחם אשת איש בלי ביאה. וממקום שבאו לדרוש בגמרא יבמות נ"ה, ב, להיפך ואמרו ש"שכבת זרע" בא למעט משמש מת והרי במשמש מת אפשר שיבוא זרעו לרחם האשה, ומכל מקום אמרו שפטור. ואפילו למאן דאמר משמש מת חייב, לא משום ש"שכבת זרע" כתיב שבודאי למאן דאמר שחייב חייב בהעראה לבד מבלי שכבת זרע, אלא משום שביאה כזו היא ביאה גמורה והוא דורש שכבת זרע **למעט** משמש מת, לא **לרבות** כמו שחשב הרב בעל בני אהובה. ואילו באנו לדון בדברים כאלה על פי סברא יש מקום לדון להיפך, שבנדה שהאשה בטומאתה גזרה התורה שלא תתעבר אפילו על ידי סדין או אמבטי שדם טומאתה יזיק להעובר, אבל באשת איש אפשר לומר שרק על הביאה אסרה תורה ולא שלא תתעבר.

ואיך שיהיה, צדק הרב בעל משנה למלך, שלפי דעת הגהות סמ"ק אשת איש שנתעברה באמבטי ולדה כשר, ואפשר לומר שאף אם קלטה זרע מקרוב שאסור לה, הוולד כשר כיון שלא נזרע כדרך כל הארץ והוא בנה של האם ולא

9 זאת מליצה על פי הפתגם במגילה ו' ע"ב.

10 ר' יהונתן אייבשיץ, בני אהובה, פראג תקע"ט, דף מ"ז ע"ב.

איסורי ביאה יי"ח, ב נעלמו כל מה שכתבו בזה הראשונים הנ"ל!) שאשת
ישראל שנאנסה אף שהיא אסורה לכהן אינו לוקה עליה לא משום זונה ולא
משום טומאה אלא שפסולה לכהונה ולתרומה משום שנבעלה לפסול לה
וכתיב "ובת כהן כי תהיה לאיש זר היא בתרומת הקדשים לא תאכל" [ויקרא
כ"ב:י"ב] ולמדנו מפסוק זה שם [ביבמות] ס"ח, א, "כיון שנבעלה לפסול לה
פסלה". ואולם לדעת הראב"ן, ואפשר שששאר הראשונים מודים לו בזה,
שיש חילוק בין פסול זונה וטומאה לפסול זה, שבזונה וטומאה נפגמה האשה
ולכן גם וולדה פסול לכהונה, אבל מהפסוק "כי תהיה לאיש זר" וכו' אנו
לומדים רק שהיא אסורה בתרומה ולהינשא לכהן מבלי שנפגמה על ידי כך
ולכן ולדה כשר. ויצא לו החילוק הזה ממה שכללה התורה איסור תרומה
לבת כהן שנישאה לזר ואיסור אשה שנבעלה לפסול בפסוק אחד וכשם
שהנשואה לזר לא נפגמה שהרי היא שבה לבית אביה כשמת בעלה בלי זרע,
כך נבעלה לפסול לא נפגמה אלא שאסורה בתרומה ולהינשא לכהן. ולפי זה
יפה כתב שאף שעכו"ם ועבד הבא על בת ישראל נשואה הוולד כשר אפילו
לכהונה, זה דוקא באונס שלא נפגמה ואי אפשר להשוותה עם אלמנה לכהן
גדול – עיין יבמות מ"ד, ב – שכן זו נפגמה ואסורה בלאו, אבל באשת איש
ברצון שהיא אסורה בלאו דזונה ובלאו דטומאה שפיר ילפינן מאלמנה לכהן
גדול ולדה פסול לכהונה. הארכתי קצת בפירוש דברי הראב"ן כדי שלא ליתן
מקום לטעות ולאמור שלדעת הראב"ן ממזרות תלויה באיסור הביאה
שממנה בא הוולד.

[ד. הגהות רבינו פרץ לספר מצוות קטן]

והנה כבר ראינו שהמשנה ביבמות מלמדתנו דבר ברור בנידון שלפנינו
אם אשת איש שקלטה זרע מאיש מבלי שבא עליה ולדה ממזר או לא.
והראשון שנשא ונתן בזה הוא הרב בעל משנה למלך, [להלכות] אישות ט"ו, ד,
שהעיר על דברי הב"ח יו"ד [סימן] קצ"ה שמביא בשם הגהות סמ"ק לרבינו
פרץ שאין קפידא לנדה לשכב על סדין בעלה שאף אם תתעבר משכבת זרע
שעל הסדין הרי לא היתה כאן ביאת איסור והוולד כשר לגמרי, אבל נהגו
הנשים שלא לשכב על סדין של איש אחר שאף שהוולד כשר "קפדין אהבחנה
גזירה שמא ישא אחותו מאביו". ועיין גם כן מה שכתב בזה הרב בעל משנה
למלך פרק י"ז, י"ג מהלכות איסורי ביאה. ובראשונה אמרתי להעיר
שבהגהות סמ"ק שלפנינו לא נמצא מה שמביא הב"ח משם, ואולם יגעתי

כשר,[6] לא משום שאיסור ביאה שבו אינו חמור כל כך כאיסורי ביאה של
עריות ושאר חייבי לאווין — לר׳ עקיבא — לגרום ממזרות אלא שרחמנא
אפקריה; לזרעיה והוולד הוא וולד האם ולא וולד האב. ותדע לך שכן הוא
שהרי עבד (ולדעת כל הפוסקים חוץ מרבינו תם בכתובות ג׳, ב, בד״ה
״ולדרוש״ גם בנכרי כן) שבא על בת ישראל נשואה, הוא והיא נהרגין משום
אשת איש, שהרי עבד כאשה ושניהם כאיש לענין עונשין ומכל מקום הוולד
כשר ואף שנולד מביאה שחייב עליה מיתת בית דין. ועל כרחך שהוא כמו
שכתבנו, ועיין תוספות יבמות ט״ז, ב, בד״ה ״קסבר״ מה שנדחקו בזה.
היוצא מזה שלא בלבד שאין לנו ראיה מוכרחת ממשנתינו שאין ממזרות בלי
ביאת איסור, אלא שאדרבא שלפי פשוטן של דברים נראה שדעתה שלא
הביאה גרמה ממזרות אלא הזרע שנקלט ברחם אשה שאסורה לאיש שממנו
בא הזרע.

[ג. פירוש דברי הראב״ן ליבמות, סוף סימן מ״ד]

ואמרתי להעיר כאן על דברי הראב״ן יבמות [סוף] סימן מ״ד שכתב:
״הילכך עכו״ם ועבד הבא על בת ישראל בין פנויה בין אשת איש הוולד כשר
[והני מילי] באונס אבל ברצון לא [באשת איש] אבל פנויה אפילו ברצון״.[7]
וכבר העיר העיר דודי הרב הגאון ר׳ אריה ליב ראשקעס ז״ל בפירושו ״אבן לשם
בדביר״ על הראב״ן שלא נתכוון הראב״ן לאמור שהוולד ממזר באשת איש
ברצון אלא שהוא פסול לכהונה.[8] ודעת הראב״ן היא כדעת הרבה מהראשונים
(רמב״ן במלחמות יבמות פרק ו׳; תוספות חד מקמאי [בש״ס וילנא] והמאירי
שם נ״ו, ב; הרשב״א בתשובותיו חלק א׳ אלף רל״א, ורמז על דעה זו
הריטב״א שם בחידושיו [לדף נ״ו ע״ב] אבל חולק עליה; ובדפוס נשתבשו
דברי הריטב״א ובד״ה דאמרי צ״ל **ולא** נראים הדברים דאפילו״ וכו׳
עד סוף הדיבור ושם צ״ל, ״ולא אמרו אלא באשה ולא כשהיא תחת בעלה דהיא כשרה
דכיון דשריא לבעלה שריא אפילו לכהונה וכן פי׳ בתוספות״, וכיוון לדברי
התוספות [נ״ו ע״ב] בד״ה ״מאי״, שרק באשת איש יש לחלק בין אונס לרצון
לענין פסולי כהונה ולא בשאר עריות. ומעיני הרב משנה למלך [הלכות

---

6   ראה רמב״ם, הלכות איסורי ביאה ט״ו:ג׳.

7   הוא מצטט ממהדורת דודו ר׳ אריה ליב ראשקעס, ספר ראב״ן, חלק שלישי, ירושלים
תרפ״ה, ט״ו ע״ד.

8   ראה ההערה הקודמת. על ר׳ אריה ליב ראשקעס, ראה מה שכתבתי לעיל ב״תשובה
בדבר יינות הכשרים״, הערה 1.

ב

[האם הביאה גורמת ממזרות או הזרע שנקלט ברחם?]

הרחבנו הדברים בביאור המשנה הזאת שעיקר הלכות ממזרות שקוע בה,
ועתה נבוא להשאלה שלפנינו. ולכאורה דברי המשנה מראים שאין לך ממזר
אלא מי שנולד מביאה אסורה ולא נחלקו ר' עקיבא ושמעון התימני ור'
יהושע אלא בגדר האיסור של הביאה, שלר' עקיבא גם איסור לאו עושה
ממזרות, ולר' יהושע רק איסור מיתת בית דין ולשמעון התימני, שהלכה
כדבריו, אין לך ממזר אלא מביאה שאסורה בכרת. ואולם אי אפשר להוציא
הלכה פסוקה מדברי המשנה שאפשר שכוונתה לאמור שכל שנולד מזרע
איש באשה שאסורים זו בזו, לכל חד כדאית ליה — איסור לאו או כרת או
מיתת בית דין — הוולד ממזר שלא הביאה היא הגורמת את הממזרות אלא
קליטת זרע האיש ברחם האשה האסורה לו. והדעת נותנת שכן הוא, שהרי
אין ספק בדבר שאיש ואשה שנאנסו שניהם והן באיסור כרת זו על זו שהוולד
שנולד מביאה זו ממזר וכמו שאמרו בהרבה מקומות בתלמוד ומובא להלכה
ברמב"ם פרק ט"ו, [הלכה] א מהלכות [איסורי ביאה] ואף שאין כאן ביאת
איסור במובנה הממשי שהרי אונס רחמנא פטריה, הוולד ממזר משום שנוצר
מזרע איש ברחם אשה שאסורה עליו בכרת. ולא נעלם ממני שיש לחלק בין
ולד שנולד מביאת איסור באונס שהרי יש כאן ביאה, ובין הנולד מקליטת
זרע ברחם אשה שלא בביאה כלל. אבל לא נראה לחלק כן, שכיון שאפשר
לאשה להתעבר באמבטי בלי ביאה למה נאמר שהביאה היא הגורמת את
הממזרות והלא לא היא שגרמה יצירת הוולד אלא שכבת הזרע [ש]במעי
האשה. וראיה גדולה לזה מנכרי שבא על בת ישראל, שלדעת הרבה תנאים
ואמוראים הוולד ממזר ואפילו מפנויה וכמו שאמרו בפירוש ביבמות מ"ה, א.
וכבר ידוע שביאת נכרי [שאינו] משבעת עממין אין אסורה מן התורה כלל
וביחוד אם בא שלא לשם אישות, עיין יבמות ט"ז, ב, בתוספות בד"ה קסבר
ורמב"ם [הלכות] איסורי ביאה י"ב, א' וב', ועל כרחך שגורם הממזרות הוא
הזרע הפסול. ולכן נכרי שבא על בת ישראל הוולד ממזר שנולד מזרע פסול
שנכנס ברחם אשה כשרה ואף שהביאה לא היתה באיסור. והלכה זו אינה
נגד התנאים ר' עקיבא ר' יהושע ושמעון התימני שאמרו במשנה שאין לך
ממזר אלא באיסורי ביאה שהם דיברו מוולד של ישראל שבא מזרע כשר ורק
כשנכנס לרחם אשה האסורה לו נעשה פסול, אבל זרע של גוי הוא זרע פסול
גם בלי איסור ביאה. ואף שקיימא לן גוי ועבד הבא על בת ישראל הוולד

שלא נמצא בשום מקום אחר שכל כרת הוא בידי שמים, שכאן "כרתי" הוא
מקביל ל"מיתה" ו"בידי שמים" ל"בית דין". ואולם בכתובות ג', א' לא דייקה
המשנה כל כך להתאים הביטויים ואמרה : "אף על פי שהן בהכרת אין בהן
מיתת בית דין". ואשר לביטוי "מיתת בית דין", צריך להעיר שסתם מיתה
במשנה היא מיתה בידי שמים, עיין לדוגמא שביעית ט', ט' ; חלה א', ט' וג',
א' ; בכורים ב', א' ; יומא ח', ח' ועוד בהרבה מקומות, חוץ אם נאמרה מיתה
בקשר עם שאר בעלי חיים בתורת עונש שסתמה מיתה בידי אדם שהרי אין
להן מיתה בידי שמים, עיין ב"ק ד', ד' וגו'. אבל בקשר עם בני אדם לא
נמצאה מיתה סתם אלא מיתת בית דין או מיתה בידי אדם, עיין סנהדרין
י"א, ד' וה' ; מכות ב', ו' ; כתובות ג', ב' חוץ מבמקומות שאי אפשר לטעות
שמיתה היא מיתה בידי אדם כמו סנהדרין א', ד' "כמיתת בעלים כך מיתת
השור" שבא על זה, מיתת השור, ולמד על זה, מיתת בעלים שהיא מיתת בית דין
וכן שם י"א, ו' "לאותה המיתה" שאין מיתה מיוחדת אלא בידי אדם.

ובסוף דברינו על המשנה ראינו להעיר שהיא אחת מהמשניות המועטות
שמסדר המשנה פסק ההלכה, והביטוי "הלכה כדבריו" נמצא עוד רק בשני
מקומות אחרים בכל הש"ס : בפאה ג', ו' ובשביעית ט', ה'. וכשנתעמק בדברי
המשנה נראה שיש שיש טעם לפסק הלכה באלה המשניות, שבכולן משמיענו מסדר
המשנה חידוש גדול. במשנה שלפנינו נחלקו גדולי הדור ר' יהושע ור' עקיבא
עם תלמידים שמעון התימני שהיה דן לפניהם [בקרקע] כמו שאמרו בסנהדרין
[דף] י"ז, ב, ומכל מקום הלכה כדבריו ולא כרבותיו. וכן בפאה נחלק ר' יהושע
בן בתירא עם אבות המשנה ר' אליעזר, ר' יהושע, ר' טרפון ור' עקיבא וחידוש
גדול השמיענו מסדר המשנה שמכל מקום הלכה כר' יהושע בן בתירא.
ובשביעית נאמר "הלכה כדבריו" במחלוקת רבן גמליאל עם חבריו ר' אליעזר
ור' יהושע ואין כאן חידוש כלל שההלכה כמותו ולכן נראה עיקר כגירסת
כתבי יד והירושלמי, עיין דקדוקי סופרים [לשביעית, עמי 31, אות ו'], שלא
גרסו שם "והלכה כדבריו". ובנדה א', ג' הדבר מוטל בספק אם "אבל הלכה
כרבי אליעזר" פירושו כמו שפירש דודי וזקני הגר"א ז"ל שהם דברי מסדר
המשנה או כמו שפירשו אחרים שר' יהושע בעצמו אמר, שאף שאני לא
שמעתי אלא בתולה הלכה כר' אליעזר. ואיך שנפרש משנה זו, יש בה חידוש
גדול שהלכה כר' אליעזר ששמותי הוא ולא עוד אלא שאפילו ר' יהושע פוסק
כמוהו, עיין שם בתוספות חדשים.

אלא למעט שלא אמר ר עקיבא דבריו בפסולי כהונה, ולא מצינו מי שאומר שאין ר' עקיבא עושה ממזר אלא מחייבי לאווין דשאר רק התנא דברייתא ביבמות צ"ב, א.

ומה שהיקשה בשיירי קרבן שם על הרמב"ם שלפי פירושו במשנה שאלת הירושלמי "הרי נדה" אין לה תשובה שאי אפשר לתרץ כמו שאמרו בירושלמי "שאין כתיב בה שאר בשר" שהרי לפי פירוש הרמב"ם ר' עקיבא עושה ממזר מכל חייבי לאווין ואפילו שאינן שאר, לא קשיא כלל, שמה שאמרו "שנייא היא הנדה שאין בה שאר בשר" (כך הגירסא הנכונה בערוך ערך "תלמודי"[5] ולא כמו שהיא לפנינו, "שאין כתיב בה", שברובן של עריות לא "כתיב" בהן שאר בשר) פירושו שאין איסור נדה איסור אישות כמו שאר איסורי ביאה, לא לבד איסורי ערוה שאישות גרמה האיסור שבהם אלא גם כל שאר איסורי ביאה שעיקרם הוא איסור אישות, ובייחוד לדעת הרמב"ם [הלכות] איסורי ביאה ט"ו, ב "שאין לך בכל חייבי לאווין מי שלוקה על בעילה בלא קידושין" מה שאין כן בנדה שהרי נדה אסורה לבעלה. ומשום שבמשנתינו השתמשו בלשון "שאר בשר" השתמשו בו גם בגמרא ואולם במשמע אחר קצת, שבמשנה משמעו קירבה ובגמרא איסור אישות. ותדע שכן הוא, שגם אם לא נפרש כפירוש הרמב"ם, הקושיא "והרי נדה" במקומה עומדת לר' סימאי שאמר [בכתובות כ"ט ע"ב] "מן הכל עושה ר' עקיבא ממזרין" ולר' ישבב שאמר "בואו ונצווח על עקיבא בן יוסף שהוא אומר כל שאין לו ביאה בישראל הולד ממזר". והיעלה על הדעת לאמור שלפי דעתן של אלה התנאים ר' עקיבא עושה ממזר מנדה או שהירושלמי לא ידע דבריהם של אלה התנאים כלל — ועל כרחך שהוא כמו שביארנו שהתשובה "שאין בה שאר בשר" פירושה שאין אסורה איסור אישות.

אחרי שהרחבנו דברינו לפרש החלק הראשון שבמשנתינו זו [ביבמות ד':י"ג] נעיר בקצרה על שאר הדברים שבה, ונאמר שמסדר המשנה סידר מחלוקת של ג' התנאים בגדרה של ממזרות לא לפי סדר דורותן, ר' יהושע, ר' עקיבא, ושמעון התימני אלא שנה בראשונה דעתו של ר' עקיבא המחמיר היותר גדול בהלכה זו שאומר "כל שאר בשר שהוא בלא יבא", ואחר כך דעתו של שמעון התימני המקיל קצת וסובר שאין ממזר אלא מחייבי כריתות ובסוף נישנו דברי ר' יהושע המקיל היותר גדול שאומר "כל שחייבין עליו מיתת בית דין". ומשום שבדברי ר' יהושע נזכר הביטוי "מיתת בית דין" השתמש מסדר המשנה בדברי שמעון [התימני] בביטוי "כרת בידי שמים"

5   הערוך השלם בעריכת ח"י קאהוט, חלק שמיני, מהד' ב', וינה תרפ"ו, עמ' 233, ערך "תלמודי".

שלר׳ עקיבא אין ממזר אלא מחייבי לאווין דשאר **בניגוד** לתנא דמתניתין שסובר שלר׳ עקיבא יש ממזר מכל חייבי לאווין של פסולי קהל. ובכ״יי מינכן הגירסא [בדף צ״ב ע״א] ״האי תנא כהך תנא **דר׳ ישמעאל** ור׳ עקיבא הוא דאמר״ וכו׳, ופירושו שכך שנה תנא דר׳ ישמעאל דברי ר׳ עקיבא בניגוד למשנתינו, שלפי דעתה יש ממזר גם מחייבי לאווין שאינן של שאר.

ועל הזרות שיש בזה שתנא דר׳ ישמעאל שנה דברי ר׳ עקיבא, עיין דומה לזה זבחים קי״ט, ב, וחולין ס״ט, ב [ויומא כ״ט, א] — ועל הגירסא ביומא עיין דקדוקי סופרים [שם] הערה כ׳: ״תנא דבי ר׳ ישמעאל ור׳ שמעון אומר״ וכו׳.[4] וכאן ושם הכוונה מדרשו של ר׳ ישמעאל שנו דברי ר׳ עקיבא ודברי ר׳ שמעון בנוסח אחר ממה ששנו אותם בבתי מדרשות של ר׳ עקיבא ור׳ שמעון. ויש סמך לגירסא זו שבכ״יי מינכן, שבסיפרי דברים [פיסקא] רמ״ח [עמ׳ 276] כמו שהבאנו למעלה אמרו בפירוש דברי ר׳ עקיבא: ״מה אשת אב מיוחד **שאר בשר** שהוא בלא יבא, כך כל **שאר בשר** שהוא בלא יבא״, ולפי ברייתא זו אין ר׳ עקיבא עושה ממזר אלא משאר וזו היא תנא דבי ר׳ ישמעאל ששנה דברי ר׳ עקיבא בנוסח זה. וכבר ידוע שבכמה מקומות מביא התלמוד דברי תנא דבי ר׳ ישמעאל על דברים והם לפנינו בסיפרי דברים — עיין לדוגמא מגילה כ״ה, א, ״תנא דבי ר׳ ישמעאלי״, והוא בסיפרי דברים [פיסקא] קע״א [עמ׳ 218] — ואף שבעיקרו חלק ההלכה של ספרי דברים הוא מבית מדרשו של ר׳ עקיבא.

ומה שהכריח להרמב״ם לפרש המשנה שלא כדברי הסיפרי הוא משום שבירושלמי על משנתינו [ו׳ סע״ב] מובאת אותה הדרשה שבסיפרי בלשון זה: ״מה אשת אביו מיוחדת שהיא בלא יבא״ וכו׳, ואין ספק שלפי הירושלמי אמר ר׳ עקיבא דבריו ב״כל שהוא בלא יבא״ והרמב״ם פירש המשנה כהירושלמי. וכבר ראינו למעלה מה שיש מן הדוחק לפרש המשנה על פי דעת הסיפרי, שנצטרך לומר או שרישא כהאי תנא וסיפא כאידך תנא, או שמחזיר גרושתו וסוטה הן לאווין דשאר. ותמוהים לי דברי הרמב״ן בחידושיו ליבמות שכתב: ״ובמס׳ קדושין ס״ח, א, וכתובות כ״ט, ב, נמי לא משכחינן דמרבי שאר חייבי לאווין אלא ר׳ סימאי״. והמעיין שם יראה שנהפוך הדבר שממה שאמרו שם, ״ולר׳ עקיבא דאמר אין קדושין תופסין בחייבי לאווין״ וכו׳ עד ״כר׳ סימאי״ מוכח שבלא שבלא דברי ר׳ סימאי היינו אומרין שיש ממזר גם מפסולי כהונה והוא משום שסתמא דמתניתין אומרת ״כל שהוא בלא יבא״ וכפירוש הרמב״ם שיש ממזר מחייבי לאווין שאינן של שאר ור׳ סימאי לא לרבות בא

---

4   בזבחים, חולין ויומא מדובר במקרה ש״תנא דבי ר׳ ישמעאל כר׳ שמעון בר יוחיי״.

הרחבתי קצת בפירוש דברי הירושלמי להוציא מידי דעתן של האחרונים
שלא בלבד שלא ראו שפירושו של הרמב״ם למשנתינו הוא הוא פירוש
הירושלמי עליה אלא שהקשו עליה ממקום שהוציא פירושו. ולדוגמא הרב
בעל שיירי קרבן ״מוכיח״ שלא כפירושו של הרמב״ם ממה שהקשו
בירושלמי ״והרי אלמנה לכהן גדול״ ואם כן ההנחה היא שמשנתינו שלא כר׳
ישבב, שר׳ עקיבא עושה ממזר מחייבי לאווין דכהונה וזה נגד מה שכתב
הרמב״ם שלר׳ עקיבא כל שאין לו ביאה בקהל הולד ממזר ואפילו מחייבי
לאווין דכהונה. ודבריו תמוהין שאילו כיוון הרמב״ם לדברי ר׳ ישבב היה
אומר כל שאין לו ״ביאה **בישראל**״ ולא ביאה ב**קהל**, ועל כרחך שדעתו [של
הרמב״ם] שמשנתינו כר׳ סימאי שאין ממזר אלא ממי שאין לו ביאה בקהל,
זאת אומרת מחייבי לאווין אפילו שאינן של שאר, אבל **חוץ** מחייבי לאווין
דכהונה. ובכוונה שינה הרמב״ם ״ביאה **בישראל**״ לביאה ב**קהל** — גם במקור
הערבי המאמר מן ״כל״ עד ״לאווין״ הוא בעברית — להדגיש שהוא מדבר על
פסולי קהל ולא על פסולי כהונה. ואילו ״כל שאין לו ביאה בישראל״ משמעו
הבבלי משמעו גם פסולי כהונה, ולא עוד אלא שיש שאמרו שם בכתובות [ל׳
ע״א] שנכלל בזה גם חייבי עשה, מה שאי אפשר כלל להעמיס בדברי המשנה
שאומרת ״שהוא בלא יבא״ ופירושו בלאו.

האמנם, בפירוש אמרו ביבמות צ״ב, א, ״האי תנא הך תנא דר׳ עקיבא הוא
דאמר מחייבי לאווין דשאר הוי ממזר מחייבי לאווין גרידי לא הוי ממזר״,
ופירושו, האי תנא דברייתא כתנא דמשנתינו שאין ממזר לר׳ עקיבא אלא
מחייבי לאווין דשאר כמו שפירש רש״י שם. והגאון ר׳ עקיבא אייגר בתוספות
במקום הנ״ל [על יבמות ד׳:י״ג] תמה על הרמב״ם מדברי הגמרא אלו. אבל
הרב הזה לא ראה שרש״י פירש לפי גירסת הספרים שלנו, אבל יש לנו שם
גירסאות שונות שעל פיהן ממקום שהקשה על הרמב״ם ראיה לדבריו.
הריטב״א גורס [ביבמות צ״ב ע״א] ״האי תנא דר׳ עקיבא הוא דאמר״ וכו׳,
ופירושו לפי גירסא זו, שהתנא של הברייתא המובאת שם הוא שסובר שלר׳
עקיבא אין ממזר אלא מחייבי לאווין דשאר, ומכאן ראיה לפירוש הרמב״ם
שלתנא דמתניתין יש ממזר גם משאר חייבי לאווין, שלולא כן לא היו נמנעין
מלאמר ״והאי תנא דברייתא כתנא דמתניתין, איזהו ממזר״ וכו׳ שכן דרך
התלמוד לסייע הברייתא מהמשנה. והרמב״ן מביא דברי הגמרא אלו
בחידושיו לדף מ״ט, א, בלשון קרוב לנוסח הריטב״א: ״האי תנא תנא דר׳
עקיבא הוא דאמר״, וגם לפי גירסא זו צריך לפרש כאשר פירשנו לפי גירסת
הריטב״א. ואפילו לפי גירסת רש״י והספרים אפשר לפרש כן: ״האי תנא הך
תנא דר׳ עקיבא הוא דאמר״ וכו׳, שתנא של ברייתא זו הוא התנא שאומר

הרמב״ם, וכאשר ידוע דרכו של רבינו הגדול לסמוך הרבה על תלמודה של
ארץ ישראל אין לתמוה אם במקום זה, שאין הכרע מהבבלי, נגרר אחרי
הירושלמי. וזה לשון הירושלמי: ״[התיבון] הרי אלמנה לכהן גדול? שנייא
היא שפירש בה חללי״. והשאלה והתשובה הן על דברי ר׳ יוסי בר חנינא
שפירש טעמו של ר׳ עקיבא: ״מה אשת אב מיוחדת שהיא בלא יבא [הולד
ממזר] אף כל שהוא בלא יבא [הולד ממזר]״. ואם נפרש המשנה כמו שפירש
רש״י, דברי הירושלמי תמוהים שהרי בפירוש אמר ר׳ עקיבא במשנתינו, ״כל
שאר בשר״ ואם כן מה הקושי מאלמנה לכהן גדול שאין [בה] לאו דשאר?
ואין לומר שהקושיא היא על ר׳ יוסי בר חנינא, שבטעם שנתן לדברי ר׳ עקיבא
לא נזכר כלל הטיב המיוחד של אשת אב שהיא שאר — עיין על זה לקמן
— שאם כן הרי לא תירץ כלום, שבשלמא פסולי כהונה נאמר בהם חלל,
״חילולין הוא עושה ואין עושה ממזרין״ כלשון בבלי כתובות כ״ט, ב, אבל
פסולי קהל למה אין עושה ממזרין? ועל כרחך שלדעת הירושלמי פירוש
המשנה הוא כמו שפירש הרמב״ם ששנתה כאן ב׳ אבות של ממזרות, א׳) כל
שאר בשר, זאת אומרת כל איסורי ביאה משום קירבה, ב׳) וכל שהוא ב״לא
יבא״, זאת אומרת איסורי לאוין שאינן דשאר וזו אף זו קתני. ומשום שר׳
עקיבא למד ממזר מאשת אב לא כלל כל חייבי לאוין ביחד אלא שנה
בראשונה לאוין דשאר ואחר כך שאר לאוין. ולפי זה יפה היקשו בירושלמי
שאם בכל חייבי לאוין עושה ר׳ עקיבא ממזר למה חייבי לאוין דכהונה אין
עושין ממזרין, והשיבו שחלל עושה [אבל] לא ממזר וכמו שאמר ר׳ סימאי
בתלמוד שלנו כתובות כ״ט, ב, ״חילולין הוא עושה״ וכו׳. ושם בבבלי הביאו
דברי ר׳ ישבב שאמר ״בואו ונצווח על עקיבא בן יוסף שהיה אומר, כל שאין
לו ביאה בישראל הולד ממזר״. ופירשו אותם בשתי דרכים: הדרך האי שלר׳
ישבב ר׳ עקיבא עושה ממזרין גם מחייבי לאוין דכהונה אבל לא מחייבי
עשה כמצרי ואדומי; והדרך הב׳ שגם באלו עושה ממזרין חוץ מבעולה לכהן
גדול. ואולם בירושלמי לא נזכר, לא כאן ביבמות ולא במקום אחר, מי שיאמר
שיש ממזר מחייבי לאוין דכהונה, והיה הדבר כל כך פשוט בעניניהם ששאלו,
״והרי אלמנה לכהן גדול״. ולא שדברי ר׳ ישבב לא היו ידועים לאמוראי ארץ
ישראל אלא שפירשו ״בישראל״ ישראל ממש בניגוד לכהן, ואין בינו לר׳
סימאי אלא חילוק לשון בלבד שזה שנה משנתו של ר׳ עקיבא בלשון ״מן הכל
היה עושה ר׳ עקיבא ממזרין חוץ מאלמנה לכהן גדול״ וזה שנאה בלשון ״כל
שאין לו ביאה ב**ישראל** הולד ממזר״ והמבטא ״כל שאין לו ביאה בישראל״
מתאים למבטא שהשתמש בו ר׳ עקיבא במשנתינו ובספרי במקום הנ״ל, ״כל
שהוא בלא יבא״ ושניהם מושפעים מלשון הכתוב ״לא יבא ממזר בקהל״ וכו׳
[דברים כ״ג:ג׳].

ביאה בקהל הולד ממזר ואפילו הוא מחייבי לאווין". ולדעתי צריך לומר
שהשיין בי"שהוא" כמו יי"ו והרבה כיוצא בזה במשנה. עיין לדוגמא ערובין ז',
י"א "שאין מערבין" וכו' וכבר שם הראי"ש שי"שאין מערבין" היא
מילתא באנפי נפשה. ובביצה א', ב' פירשו כל המפרשים שי"שאפר הכירה"
וכו' הוא כמו "ואפר הכירה" וכן בראש השנה א', ד', "שבהן השלוחין
יוצאין", אין נתינת טעם למה שקדם לו אלא כמו "ובהן השלוחין יוצאין". וכן
בהוריות ב', ב' אין צריך להפירוש הדחוק של [הברטנורא] ופשוטן של דברים
הוא כמו שפירש בעל תוספות יום טוב, שבי"שאין בית דין" וכו' מתחילה
הלכה שאין לה שום יחס עם ההלכה שלפניה. ובאהלות ה', ו' אי אפשר
למצוא איזה קשר בין ההלכה "סרידה שאין לה גפיים" עם זו שלאחריה,
"שאין הכלים מצילים" וכו', ועל כרחך שמתחיל כאן דבר חדש וכן [בפרה] ה',
ה' כפי מה שהעירו מפרשי המשנה "שאין מצילים מיד כלי חרס" הוא כמו
"ואין מצילים".

ומדברי הגמרא [ביבמות] מ"ט, א', אין הכרע לא לפירושו של רש"י ולא
לפירושו של הרמב"ם ואף שהגאון ר' עקיבא אייגר בתוספותיו על המשנה
העיר: "ואדרבה על הרמב"ם בפירוש יש לעיין דלא משמע כן מסוגיא דהכא
דאמרינן עלה דמתני' מאי טעמא דר' עקיבא אלמא מהני וכו' ולר' סימאי וכו'
משמע להדיא דלמתני' דהכא דוקא בשאר הוי ממזר". לא ידעתי "מאי
משמע" — שלפירוש הרמב"ם הגמרא מפרש טעמו של ר' עקיבא בין לדעתן
של חכמים דר' סימאי שלא אמר ר' עקיבא דבריו אלא בלאווין דשאר, בין לר'
סימאי שמן הכל היה ר' עקיבא עושה ממזר חוץ מאלמנה לכהן גדול, ובין לר'
ישבב שהיה ר' עקיבא עושה ממזר אפילו מחייבי לאווין דכהונה. ואולם
המשנה שלפנינו לפי פירושה של הרמב"ם היא על פי דעתו של ר' סימאי
בפירוש דברי ר' עקיבא. וברור שהרמב"ם בא לפרש המשנה כמו שפירש
משום שלפירוש רש"י צ"ל שהמשנה הקודמת למשנה זו, "המחזיר גרושתו"
וכו', חולקת ואומרת שר' עקיבא סובר שיש ממזר גם מחייבי לאווין שאינן
של שאר. ואולם בכעין זה לא היה נמנע התלמוד מלומר תרי תנאי אליבא דר'
עקיבא: רישא, המשנה "המחזיר גרושתו" כו', כר' סימאי, וסיפא, "איזהו
ממזר", כרבנן דר' סימאי, כמו שהעיר כבר הרמב"ן, אלא שהוא הולך בדעתו
של ר' תם שם בתוספות שמחזיר גרושתו הוא לאו דשאר וכן סוטה וכמה מן
הדוחק לאמר שאלו לאווין דשאר, ולפי פירושו של הרמב"ם אין צורך בכל
אלה הדיחוקים.

אמנם אף שאמרנו שאין מדברי הגמרא הכרע לא לפירושו של רש"י ולא
לפירושו של הרמב"ם, אין ספק כלל שהירושלמי פירש המשנה כמו שפירש

עם פצוע דכא וכרות שפכה שאינו מוליד, ועם עמוני ומואבי שאין לאווין דשאר?[2] ולמה לא אמר "שהוא בלאו", לשון מצוי ורגיל הרבה במשנה, בברייתא ובשני התלמודים, או "שהוא בלא תעשה" שנמצא גם כן פעמים הרבה במשנה — בא רק בניגוד למצוות עשה ובמקום אחד לבד בניגוד לשבות, עיין קונקורדנצייא של הרב קאסאבבסקי [למשנה] ערך "לא" עמוד אלף כ"ח — ובמקורי התנאים והאמוראים.

ובלקח טוב דברים כ"ג, ב, ובחידושי הרא"ה לכתובות כ"ט, ב, מובאת המשנה שלפנינו בלשון זה: "איזהו ממזר כל שאר בשר בלא יבא". ולפי גירסא זו דברי המשנה פשוטים ונכוחים שהתשובה על השאלה "איזהו ממזר" היא, "כל שאר בשר בלא יבא", זאת אומרת ב"לא יבא ממזר" [דברים שם], ומי"כל" הוציאו שלפי דעתו של ר' עקיבא יש ממזר מחייבי לאווין דשאר. ואולם אין ספק שגירסת הספרים שהיא גם כן גירסת כתי"י מינכען וקמברדגיא וגירסת הראשונים, רש"י, רמב"ם, רי"ד והמאירי היא העיקרית שבספרי דברים [פיסקא רמ"ח [מהד' פינקלשטיין, עמ' 276] אמרו בפירוש דברי ר' עקיבא: "מה אשת אב מיוחדת שהיא שאר בשר שהוא בלא יבא והולד ממזר, כך כל שאר בשר שהוא בלא יבא הולד ממזר". וכאן אי אפשר לפרש "בלא יבא" בדרך אחרת אלא "שהוא בלאו" ואמרו שכשם שאשת אב — אנוסת אביו — שהוא בלאו הולד ממזר כך כל שאר בשר שהוא בלאו הולד ממזר. ודרשה זו של הספרי מובאת בסגנון אחר קצת — עיין לקמן על החילוף לשונות שבין הספרי והירושלמי — בירושלמי על משנתינו בשם ר' יוסי בר' חנינא[3] וגם שם נאמר, "מה אשת אב מיוחדת שהיא בלא יבא ו[ה]הולד ממזר, אף כל שהוא בלא יבא הולד ממזר", ופירוש "בלא יבא" הוא "בלאו" כמו שמוכיחים דבריו. ונראה שר' עקיבא השתמש בלשון נופל על לשון ומשום שאיסור ממזרות נאמר בתורה בלשון "לא יבא" שנה במשנתו "כל שהוא בלא יבא", זאת אומרת ולד שנולד מביאה אסורה אסור לבא בקהל.

והנה אף שכל הראשונים שווים בפירוש המבטא "שהוא בלא יבא" שאינו אלא "שהוא בלאו", נחלקו רש"י והרמב"ם בביאור הלכה זו שרש"י וההולכים בשיטתו, הרי"ד, הרמב"ן, המאירי והריטב"א פירשו שר' עקיבא דמשנתינו סובר שאין ממזר אלא מלאווין דשאר ולא משאר לאווין, אבל הרמב"ם בפירוש המשנה, ונגרר אחריו הרב בעל נמוקי יוסף כתב: "שיעור דברי ר"ע כל שאר בשר שהוא **וכל** בלא יבא לפי שעיקר דעתו כל שאין לו

2　ראה דברים כ"ג:ב:ד'-ד'.

3　ירושלמי יבמות ד': ט"ו, ו' סע"ב.

תשובה

בהלכות אישות[1]
מאת
לוי בן מורנו הרב יצחק זצ"ל לבית גינצבורג

שאלה

נשאלתי מרב אחד על אודות אשה שבאה לפניו בשאלתה, היות שבעלה
שנחלו כלי הזרע שלו לעולם לא יוליד, אם מותר להכניס ברחמה זרע מאיש
אחר על ידי ההמצאה החדשה שהמציאו הרופאים בימינו המאפשרת לאשה
שתזריע הזרע הנכנס לרחמה מבלי קירוב בשר. והרב השואל האריך בחכמתו
לפלפל בדברי האחרונים בענין בתולה שעיברה באמבטי, ואולם באשר כן
דרכי מעולם לייסד דברי על דברי התלמוד והראשונים נמנעתי מלהביא דבריו
ולישא וליתן בהם. וזאת תשובתי בעזר השם יתברך.

א

[משנה יבמות ד':י"ג]

תמן תנינן, יבמות סוף פ"ד, מ"ט, א: "איזהו ממזר כל שאר בשר שהוא
בלא יבא דברי ר' עקיבא, שמעון התימני אומר: כל שחייבים עליו כרת בידי
שמים והלכה כדבריו. ורבי יהושע אומר: כל שחייבין עליו מיתת בית דין".
ובראשונה צריך לפרש הלשון, "שהוא בלא יבא", שהשתמש בו ר' עקיבא
שהוא קשה קצת, שלפי פירוש הראשונים רש"י, רי"ד, המאירי, ושאר
ראשונים ואחרונים, הוא כמו "שהוא בלאו". ויש כאן מקום לשאול למה
השתמש בלשון זה שלא נמצא בתורה אלא ביחס עם ממזר שעליו אנו דנין,

1   לנוסחיה וגלגוליה של תשובה זו, ראה הסבר מפורט בחלק הלועזי של ספר זה, פרק
ה', סימן א'. אנו מדפיסים כאן את הנוסח הארוך של התשובה שנדפס במכונת כתיבה בשנות
השלושים. על מנת להקל על הקורא, המרנו את הכתיב   החסר שבאותו נוסח לכתיב מלא,
פתרנו את רוב ראשי התיבות, הוספנו פיסוק וכותרות משנה וחילקנו סעיפים ארוכים
לסעיפים קצרים יותר.

מי הוא אביו או שיהיה הזרע דווקא מאינו יהודי כדי שלא יהיה לילד שום אחווה מצד האב. ואפילו לקחו הזרע מאינו יהודי לבי [נוקפני] להתיר לכתחילה משום יוחסין ומשום חששות שונות. אלא שנשאר רק עצה אחת לאשה האומללה הזו: שתתגרש מבעלה ותמסור את עצמה לרופאים שיזרקו ברחמה זרע של אינו יהודי ואחר כך יחזיר הבעל את גרושתו, דאז ליכא שום חששא, דאפילו זינתה מותרת לחזור לבעלה הראשון.[6] ומובן מאליו שזה אפשר להיות דווקא בבעל ישראל אבל לא אם הבעל הוא כהן דאז אסורה לחזור לו.

---

6   ראה משנה בסוטה י״ח ע״ב: ברייתא ביבמות י״א ע״ב; ושלחן ערוך אבן העזר י׳:א׳.

כשרים אצלה! שנית, מאין תדע האשה אם הזרע הוא של כשר או של פסול אם נתעברה באמבטי, ואם כן לפי מסקנת הגמרא לא שייך כלל האי פלוגתא אי מפיה אנו חיין או לאו. שלישית, לא יכולתי להבין פירוש סוגיא זו דבן זומא. אין ספק שבעלי התוספות היתה להם גירסא אחרת בדברי רש״י ממה שנמצא בספרים שלפנינו והיקשו מה שהיקשו, אבל מעולם לא עלה על דעת רש״י לפרש דהאיבעיא היא אם נאמנת על מה שאמרה או לאו. ואם הם עוד מחזיקים בפירוש זה, אין זה כי אם שנגררו אחרי גירסא משובשת שברש״י ואחרי גירסא משובשת זו נמשך גם בעל בני אהובה ובנה בנין על יסוד רעוע. ואנא אמינא דלעולם לא עלה על הדעת של מסדרי הגמרא דאי חיישינן לדשמואל תהא מותרת לכהן גדול כנראה מהתוספות וכדברי בני אהובה, אלא אדרבא אי חיישינן לשמואל תהא אסורה לכהן גדול דאז [היא] בעולה בלי ספק, דהא אפילו נבעלה [בהוראה] או נבעלה שלא כדרכה שלא [היתה] הסרת בתולים פסולה לכהונה וכל שכן [אם] נבעלה בהטיה אפילו אי לא היתה מעוברת. וזו היא ממש האיבעיא אי חיישינן לשמואל [והיא] בעולה או לא חיישינן לשמואל אלא חיישינן שבאמבטי עיברה ולא [היא] בעולה. ופשיט בן זומא דלא חיישינן לשמואל אלא לשמא באמבטי עיברה, ואין בנידון זה שום שאלה בדבר נאמנות אם היא בתולה או בעולה דהרי היא בתולה לפניך, אלא בדבר הספק אם היא נבעלה מאיש או לאו, ובספק זה אפשר שבין [לרבן גמליאל] ובין לר׳ יהושע לא סמכינן אדיבורא אלא סמכינן אחזקה או אאומדנא, או שנבעלה או שנתעברה באמבטי, ופשיט דחיישינן שמא באמבטי עיברה משום שזה יותר שכיח או משום שיש לה לבתולה חז[קת] כשרות וסמכינן אחזקה זו להחליט שבאמבטי עיברה. ועל פי ביאור זה בפשט הגמרא תמצא שהרבה מקושיות התוספות נתבטלות פה ובמקומות אחרים מתבטלות, אבל זה אין ענין לנו עכשיו, אבל ממילא מתבטל כל הדיוק של הבעל בני אהובה בין ראייתו דמעוברת באמבטי מותרת לבעלה ובין קושייתו לבטל זו הראיה, ודוק.

סוף דבר לעניות דעתי דממשמעות הגמרא מוכחת דעיבור בלי קירוב בשר לא הוי בעילה ואם כן מותרת לבעלה וכן דעת הפוסקים שהבאתי. אבל לכתחילה היה נראה שאסור לעשות תרופה שתתעבר בלי קירוב בשר, כמו שאסור לאשה לשכב על סדין של איש אחר, משום גזירה שמא ישא אחותו מאביו[5] כדהביא הגהות ר׳ פרץ, אלא אם כן יודיעו לילד מזה העיבור

4   כתוב ״ר״א״ אבל הכוונה כנראה לרבן גמליאל כי הוא בר פלוגתיה של ר׳ יהושע בכתובות י״ג ע״א.

5   יבמות מ״ב ע״א.

לשכב על הסדין של בעלה משום דאפילו תתעבר לא יהיה בזה איסור נידה. אבל איברא [שאפילו אם] לא אמר הר״ר פרץ בפירוש שאשה שנתעברה באמבטי מאיש אחר אינה נאסרת על בעלה, הייתי אומר נגד הרב בעל בני אהובה במחילת כבודו שאפשר ואפשר לדון דין זה ממה שהתיר איסור נידה בנתעברה באמבטי, ואיני רואה שום חילוק בין אשת איש ובין נידה, [שכל זמן] שלא נחשב לבעילה לגבי נידה לא נחשב נמי לגבי אשת איש ומי יאמר דהתורה [הקפידה] אקירוב בשר דוקא לגבי נידה ולא לגבי אשת איש?

אכן הרב בעל בני אהובה מודה בסוף דבריו לדברי הפוסקים הנ״ל דלא נאסרה אשה על בעלה כשנתעברה באמבטי מאיש אחר וחפץ להביא ראיה מהגמרא הנ״ל [בחגיגה] מהא דבן זומא ואחר כך דחה ראייתו, וזה לשונו: ״איברא ממקומו נלמד דבמסכתא חגיגה דף י״ד ע״ד אהא דשאלו את בן זומא ׳בתולה שעיברה מהו לכהן גדול׳ כתבו התוספות דהך אבעיא הוא אף לר׳ יהושע דסבר ליה בפרק קמא דכתובות [דף י״ג ע״א] לכהן גדול בראוה מעוברת דלא מפיה אנו חיין ופשיט בן זומא שם דמותרת לכהן גדול דבאמבטי עיברה. וקשה כיון דנפשט האיבעיא גם לר׳ יהושע דלמא מפסול היה השכבת זרע והיא פסולה לכהן וכל שכן לכהן גדול ולא תהא אלא מעוברת לר׳ יהושע דלא מפיה אנו חיין. אלא ודאי דבאמבטי אף דהיה לה שכבת זרע מפסול אין אשה נפסלת בכך דאין כאן בעילה והוא הדין לבעלה הישראל. אך בלאו הכי צריכין אנו לדייק בדברי התוספות דכתבו דהך שאלה ׳בתולה שעיברה׳ קאי אף לר׳ יהושע והשאלה היתה אי איתא לדשמואל דיכול לבעול על ידי הטיה וא עדיין היא בתולה מותרת לכהן גדול. דהא אף אם איתא לדשמואל מה בכך, מכל מקום היכא תהא מותרת לכהן גדול דלמא מפסול נתעברה ופסולה לכהונה וכל שכן לכהן גדול. דהא השתא לא הוי סלקא דעתך עדיין דמיירי באמבטי ואפילו ברוב כשרים פוסל ר׳ יהושע וע״כ צריך לומר דהאיבעיא הוי במקום דליכא פסולין כלל עד שלא יפול בו הספק אי כשר או לפסול נבעלה, רק הספק אי בתולה או בעולה היא. אם כן לפי זה השתא נמי דאמר דשמא באמבטי עיברה אין כאן ראיה דלא נאסרה בלא בעילה דיש לומר נמי דמיירי במקום דאין לחוש לפסולי״. עד כאן לשון הבני אהובה.

ולעניות דעתי ערבוביא קא חזינא הכא: ראשית, מה ראה להוכיח דבאופן שבאמבטי נתעברה אינה נאסרת על בעלה מהאי חששא דר׳ יהושע דשמא מפסול נתעברה יותר מעיקר הדבר דמעוברת מותרת לכהן גדול? ואפילו נאמין לה שמכשר נתעברה באמבטי, ממה נפשך: אי הוי בעילה הרי כולי עלמא הוי פסולים אצלה לגבי כהן גדול, ואי לא הוי בעילה הרי הפסולים גם כן הם

לחוד, אף על פי שלא נזכר בגמרא ואינו מוכח מהכתוב, אפשר שגם [על] זרע לחוד קרינן גילוי ערוה או בעילה או שכיבה.

ולכאורה היה אפשר ללמוד דין זה מדין בתולה מעוברת לכהן גדול (חגיגה י״ד ע״ב) מהא דשאלו [לבן זומא] ״בתולה שנתעברה מהו לכהן גדול״ ואמר להו מותרת ״חיישינן שמא באמבטי נתעברה״ ואם כן, לגבי אשת איש נמי זרע לחוד לא הוי בעילת איסור. [ואם תאמר] שיש לחלק ולומר דשאני כהן גדול דהתורה [הקפידה] על בתולים והכא הרי היא בתולה לפנינו, אבל באשת איש התורה [הקפידה] על תערובת הזרע והרי יש כאן תערובת? זה ליתא דלא מצינו שום חשש בעילה שיהא פוסל לגבי אשת איש ולא יהא פוסל לגבי כהן גדול, הרי [הוראה] פוסלת בשניהם ושלא כדרכה נמי פוסלת בשניהם, ואליבא דרב הונא נשים המסוללות זו בזו נפסלו מן הכהונה (יבמות ע״ו ע״א) ולגבי אשת איש הוי רק פריצותא בעלמא (יבמות נ״ה ע״ב). ואם כן לא מסתבר לומר דזרע לחוד בלי קירוב בשר הוי בעילה לגבי אשת איש ולא הוי בעילה לגבי כהן גדול.

והרב בעל משנה למלך בפרק ט״ו מהלכות אישות הלכה ד' הביא דברי הגהות רבינו פרץ על הסמ״ק דאשה אינה נאסרת על בעלה על ידי בליעת זרע ברחמה מאיש אחר בלי קירוב בשר, וראייתו מבן סירא שנולד מאמו בתולה שנתעברה באמבטי מירמיהו הנביא והובא גם כן בב״ח יורה דעה, [סימן] קצ״ה; ובבית שמואל לאבן העזר, [סימן] א', ס״ק י'; ובתשב״ץ חלק ג', [סימן] רס״ג. ואף על פי דלכאורה הוכחה זו אינה מכרעת דאפילו בשכבת זרע ממש לא פסלינן הילד הנולד מפנויה ״ואפילו לרבי אלעזר דאמר פנוי הבא על הפנויה שלא לשם אישות עשאה זונה״ [יבמות ע״א ע״א ומקבילות] היינו דוקא לפוסלה מן הכהונה אבל לא לאוסרה לבוא בקהל, וכל שכן דלא פסלינן את הוולד. אף על פי כן מצטרפים התשב״ץ והר״ר פרץ והב״ח ומשנה למלך לפסוק להלכה דאשת איש לא נאסרה לבעלה כשנתעברה באמבטי מאיש אחר והוא הדין בנידון דידן.

והרב בעל ספר בני אהובה בהגהותיו על הרמב״ם [הלכות] אישות פרק ט״ו הלכה ד' השיג על המשנה למלך ושם בפי בעל המשנה למלך דברים שלא אמרם.[3] המשנה למלך הביא רק דעת הר״ר פרץ דאפילו אשת איש שנתעברה באמבטי מאיש אחר אינה נאסרת על בעלה, ודבר זה הביא הר״ר פרץ מדעת עצמו ומסברא ומהוכחה ממעשה דבן סירא ולא השתמש המשנה למלך בראיה שהביא בעל בני אהובה מהא דפסק הר״ר פרץ דאשה נידה מותרת

---

3   ר' יהונתן אייבשיץ, ספר בני אהובה, פראג תקע״ט, דף מ״ז ע״א.

[תשובה בעניין הזרעה מלאכותית שנשלחה לרל״ג על ידי רב אלמוני שביקש את חוות דעתו][1]

נשאלתי מרופא אחד אודות אשה אחת שנישאה לאיש וקודם הנישואין נולד בו חולי בביצים עד שנסתמו הנקבים ואינו מזריע. והאשה ידעה מזה קודם הנישואין ואמרה ״אף על פי כן״, מפני שחשבה בלבה שמרוב אהבתה לבחור זה תסבול הגלמוד[יות] להישאר בלי בנים כל ימי חייה. ועכשיו היא בצער בלי הפסק משום שתשוקתה לבנים מתרבה מיום ליום והרופאים חוששין לסכנה שתשתגע מרוב הצער. אכן לפי דעת הרופאים יש לה תרופה בזה שהמציאו הרופאים המצאה חדשה שאפשר לזרוק ברחמה זרע של איש אחר בלי אבר המזריע ובלי קירוב בשר של איזה זכר. והאיש והאשה מסכימים לזה מרוב האהבה שיש ביניהם. ושאל הרופא אם זה מותר על פי דין תורתנו הקדושה משום חשש אשת איש. ועוד שאל אם צריך לדקדק שהזרע יהיה מיהודי או מאינו יהודי, מאיניש דעלמא או אפילו ממי שביאתו עליה בכרת, ומה יהיה משפט הוולד אם כשר או פסול? ומפני שהוא דבר חמור מאד בין לעניין איסור אשת איש ובין לעניין הנימוס האנושי ותלויין בו חששות רבות אמרתי לפנות אל עמודי ההוראה ולבקש דעת תורה בזה, ובפרט כשהוא עניין יתרבה במשך הזמן כי המצאה זו בחכמת הרפואה היא עוד צעירה וכשתתגדל ותעשה פרי יהיו רבים מבני ישראל אשר הם חשוכי בנים פונים לתרופה זו, ויפנו גם כן אל הרבנים בשאלה אם מותר או אסור ומה נאמר להו?

וארשום פה רק קיצור דברים ממה שנראה לי בזה העניין מתוך דברי חז״ל והפוסקים. ראשית מצד הסברא הייתי אומר כיוון דלא [הקפידה] התורה [על] שכבת זרע רק בשפחה חרופה [ואילו בשאר המקרים] אפילו [הערא]ה לבד מחייבת (יבמות נ״ה ע״א-ע״ב),[2] שמע מינה דעיקר חיוב באשת איש תלוי בקירוב בשר ולא בזרע וכל היכא דליכא קירוב בשר לא מחייב [על] זרע לחוד. אבל לאידך גיסא אין סברא זו לבדה מוכרחת שהתורה אסרה או קירוב בשר לבד בלי זרע או זרע לבד בלי קירוב בשר ומהכלל הנ״ל דאיסור אשת איש חל [על] קירוב בשר לחוד אי אפשר למידק שאינו חל [על] זרע

---

1   להסבר מפורט על גלגוליה של תשובה זו, ראה החלק הלועזי של ספר זה, פרק ה', סימן א'.

2   והשוה לרמב״ם, הלכות איסורי ביאה א':י'; ג':ט״ו.

יין צמוקים, רוב יינם לא היה ממין המשכר, כמו שכתב בפירוש הרב בעל
התשב"ץ בספרו מאמר חמץ ל"יד, א'.

סוף דבר הכל שקלתי בכף מאזנים של התורה ולא מצאתי אפילו פקפוק
קל בהיתר משקה של מהול ענבים לכל המצות הנסדרות על הכוס. ובטוח
אני שכל גדולי התורה יסכימו לדברי ויזהירו את העם לבלי לכת אחרי אלה
אשר "ביין שגו ובשכר תעו" [ישעיהו כ"ח:ז'] ואת קדוש ישראל יעריצו ושם
ישראל יקדישו[98] להתרחק מן הכיעור ומן הדומה לו, "כי עם קדוש אתה לה'
אלהיך" [דברים ז':ו' ועוד].

---

98 על פי ישעיהו כ"ט:כ"ג.

והנה שמעתי רבים אומרים אמת ונכון הדבר שמצד הדין יין חדש ויין
ישן שווין ואין מעלה להשני על הראשון כלום, אבל כבר נהגו בכל תפוצות
ישראל לסדר המצוות על כוס של יין ישן, ומנהג אבותינו תורה היא. אף אני
אומר, מנהג אבותינו תורה היא, וכשם שאין אדם יכול לעמוד על דברי
תורה אלא אם כן הוא חכם ומבין, כך אין אדם יכול לעמוד על המנהג, אם
אין לו לב חכם להבין ולהשכיל ולהבדיל בין מנהג למנהג, ואם אין בינה,
הבדלה מניין?[96] בודאי אין ספק הוא שבדורות שלפנינו, רוב היינות — של
מצוה ושל רשות — שעלו על השלחן היו יין ישן, שלא היו בקיאים אז איך
להעציר תסיסת היין ואחר ארבעים יום כבר נתגבר בו כח האלקאהאלי
והיה למשקה משכר, ורק אלו שלא היו קונים מן השוק לפעמים היה להם
יין חדש, ואלו באמת אמרו קידוש עליו כמו שראינו למעלה. אבל טפשות
גדולה היא לאמר כיון שבדורות הראשונים לא היה יין חדש מצוי לכן גם
אנו בדורותינו מחויבים שלא לשנות המנהג ואף שרוב היין הנמכר בשוק
הוא עתה יין חדש, רצוני לאמר יין [שנעצרה] תסיסתו ונפסד כוחו
האלקאהאלי. והיעלה על לב איש לאמר שכיון שבדורות שלפנינו הדליקו
בבתי כנסיות נרות של חלב ושל שעוה, אין לשנות המנהג ואסור להדליק שם
נר של גאס ועלעקטריק? בוא וראה יין של צמוקים שיש בו כמה חששות
ופקפוקים כמו שראינו למעלה בכל זאת נהגו בכל תפוצות ישראל לקדש עליו,
ועד היום בליטא ובזאמוט,[97] מדינות מלאות חכמים וצדיקים מדקדקים
במצוות, יין צמוקים הוא היין של מצה, וקל וחומר שיין ענבים ואף שהוא
חדש, שלא פקפק אדם על הכשרו ואין בו שום חשש שטוב ונכון לקדש עליו.
וכבר כתב הרשד"ם בתשובותיו, יורה דעה, סימן מ' שבכל מקום שאמרו
"מנהג" צריך שבכוונת המכוון קבלו עליהם כן ודעתם היה לנהוג כן לעולם,
לא שנהגו כן במקרה או מסיבת מה — באופן זה איננו מנהג שנהגו. והכל
יודעים שהסיבה שעד כה היו מקדשים על יין ישן היתה משום שיין חדש לא
היה מצוי ולא משום חשיבותו של יין ישן. ובאלה המדינות שנהגו לקדש על

---

96 זאת מליצה מתוחכמת על פי ירושלמי ברכות פרק ה', ט' סע"ב: כשם שברכת "אתה
חונן" מאפשרת אמירת ההבדלה במוצאי שבת, כך בינה מאפשרת הבדלה בין מנהג למנהג.
97 הכוונה למחוז זאמוט צפונה מווילנא, אחד מאחד-עשר המחוזות של ליטא במאה
הי"ז-הי"ח. ראה המפה באנציקלופדיה העברית, כ"א, עמ' 767; אני מודה לידידי ד"ר אלחנן
ריינר שהפנה אותי למפה זאת. הוא אף הוסיף שהשתמשו בליטא ביין צימוקים מטעמים
כלכליים. מכיוון שלא גידלו שם ענבים היו צריכים לייבא יין מהונגריה וכדומה ולכן היה זול
יותר להשתמש ביין צימוקים.

אמרה 'כי **כל** שאור וכל דבש'' וכו'.[93] ומזה ש''כל'' לרבות אפילו אין נותן
טעם או פחות ממשים, שקורטוב של דבש ב''שלש מאות וששים ושמונה
מנים'' בודאי אין נותן טעם והוא פחות מאלף, ועל כרחך שהאיסור של דבש
ושל שאור אפילו בכל שהוא, ואף שאפשר שאין לוקה עליו; עיין לחם משנה
סוף פרק י''ג מהלכות מעשה הקרבנות.

והנה אלו הט''ו יינות שמנינו בפרוטרוט יש מהם שכשרים לכתחילה וגם
מצוה מן המובחר אינה להדר אחרי יינות אחרים, כאשר כתבנו לעיל, אבל
אלו היינות שנתקלקלו קצת בטעם וריח ואף שכשרים לכתחילה מצוה מן
המובחר שלא לקדש עליהם אלא לברור יין שאינו מקולקל כלל כי לפעמים
קלקול קטן גורם לקלקול גדול. ועל יין חדש שאין בו שום פגם מקדשין
לכתחילה ואף שיש לו יין אחר.

והנני חוזר בשרות האחרונות של מאמרי זה על תשובת השאלה, אם
טוב ונכון לקדש על המשקה מהול ענבים, הנקרא במדינתנו גרייפ-יוס,[94]
והוא נעשה מתירוש שמחממין אותו עד שכח האלקאהאלי שבו נפסד ואינו
משכר לעולם. וכבר ראינו שלא נחלק אדם על ההלכה הפסוקה שבתלמוד
שמקדשין על יין מגתו לכתחילה, ודברי הרב בעל מגן אברהם שאומר
שמצוה מן המובחר להדר אחר יין ישן דחויים מכל וכל. אבל גם הרב הזה
בודאי היה מודה שטוב יותר לקדש על יין חדש מלהיות גורם חילול השם
וחילול האומה, והכל יודעים את נזקי האומה שגרם המסחר ביין מצוה.
ומלבד זה כל שבחו של יין ישן הוא רק במדינות שיין ישן עולה על השלחן
ויש מקום לאמר שמצוה היא להדר אחר יין משובח וטוב כשם שאמרו
[בסוכה כ''ז ע''א] ''כמה פרפראות אתה ממשיך לכבוד עצמך ואין אתה
ממשיך פרפרת אחת לכבוד קונך''. אבל במדינתנו שכמעט אי אפשר, ואסור
על פי חוק המדינה לקנות דברים המשכרים, מה סברא יש כאן לאמר שמצוה
מן המובחר לרדוף אחרי יין ישן המשכר? וכדי שלא יאמרו [הדקדקנים] הרי
זה בא להתיר יין מבושל שנחלקו בו רבותינו הראשונים, לא אמנע מלהודיע
ברבים כי המשקה ''מהול ענבים'' אינו יין מבושל שאינם מחממין אותו עד
כדי רתיחה,[95] ופחות מזה אינו נקרא יין מבושל כמו שבארנו לעיל עמוד עב-
עג.

93 ברייתא זאת נאמרת כל יום ב''סדר הקרבנות'' בסוף ברכות השחר והיא נמצאת
בשינויים בירושלמי יומא ד':ה', מ''א ע''ד.
94 כלומר, מיץ ענבים.
95 רל''ג בירר את הפרט הזה אצל שני בתי חרושת למיץ ענבים — ראה שני המכתבים
הרשומים בביבליוגרפיה של הנוסח האנגלי של תשובה זו, פרק ג', סימן ט''ז.

ובאמת סריחת היין הרבה פעמים אינה באה על ידי אי-נקיות החבית אלא מריח הרע הנשאר בעץ החבית.

יד) יין מגולה. גילוי הוא אחד מן הדברים שפוסלים יין ומים למזבח כמו שאמרו בסוכה במשנה ובגמרא סוף פרק ד' ובתוספתא מנחות פרק ט' ובבבא בתרא צ"ז, ב'. ובמקום האחרון הוסיפו שגם שלר' נחמיה יין מגולה שהעבירו במסננת מותר להדיוט ואין בו משום סכנה, מכל מקום למזבח אסור משום "הקריבהו נא לפחתך", וכן לקידוש. והנה אף שכל הראשונים הביאו דין זה של יין מגולה שאסור, יש מקום לאמר שבזמנינו אנו ובארצות אלו שאין איש מקפיד על גילוי אפשר שמקדשין עליו ובפרט בדאי-אפשר ביין אחר, עיין מה שכתבתי לעיל [עמ' נה ואילך] בענין זה. ודע שדברי רב עמרם גאון בסדורו שכתב בסוף מעריב של שבת "ולאפוקי נמי מגולה דילמא נפיל ביה מידי",[92] אי אפשר להסיעם לכוונה אחרת ולאמר שכיוון לתת טעם למה מגולה אסור גם במקום שאין חוששין לארס של נחש והטעם הוא שאפשר שנפל בו דבר מאוס. [אלא] אין ספק ש"מידי" משמעו כאן ארס של נחש. וכבר נדע עד כמה היו רבותינו הראשונים זהירים שלא להוציא דבר רע מפיהם ומפי עטם ובמקום ארס של נחש כתב "מידי". ובמחזור ויטרי עמ' 86 מובא מאמר זה של סדור רב עמרם כמו שהוא לפנינו, והמוציא לאור לא העיר [על] מקורו.

טו) יין שיש בו דבש. דין זה לא נזכר בתלמוד אבל הגאונים וחכמי ספרד ומערב פירשו שאין יוצא מן הכלל שכללו בגמרא דבבא בתרא, שכל שאסור בדיעבד למזבח פסול גם כן לקידוש, וכיון שאם נתן דבש של יין של נסכים פסול מן התורה ש"כל שאור וכל דבש לא תקטירו" [ויקרא ב': י"א] פוסל גם כן יין לקידוש. עיין תשובת רב האי גאון [שהבאתי] בסעיף י"א והמקומות שרמזתי לעיל בהמשא ומתן על יין מבושל. וראיתי להרב בעל פרי מגדים שכתב בחלק משבצות זהב של ספרו בסימן רע"ב וזה לשונו: "ובפרק כ"ט מהלכות שבת הלכה י"ד כתב [הרמב"ם] ינתערב [בן] טיפת דבש או שאור [אפילו כטיפת החרדל] בחבית גדולה אין מקדשין עליו' וכו' וכעת איני יודע מנלן דאפילו כל שהוא בחבית גדולה דכי 'כל' [בפסוק 'כל שאור וכל דבש'] לרבות ערובו בשיש בו טעם או פחות משישים? וצריך עיון כעת". ונוראות נפלאתי על הרב הגדול הזה שנעלם ממנו מאמר שבודאי היה רגיל לאמרו בכל יום והוא המאמר בברייתא דקטורת: "אילו היה נותן בה קורטוב של דבש אין אדם יכול לעמוד מפני ריחה. ולמה אין מערבין בה דבש? מפני שהתורה

האור, והר״ן בע״ז שם מצדד לאמר שדא ודא אחת היא, אבל אין דברי הרמב״ן נראים כן. וביורה דעה קכ״ג, ג׳ גבי יין נסך פסקו הטור והשלחן ערוך כדברי הגאונים שבשול של יין פירושו עד שהרתיח, ועיין שם מה שהעיר דודי זקני הגר״יא ז״ל. ולפי זה אין לפקפק בדבר שבשול של יין לקידוש משמעו עד כדי שירתיח.

יב) יין מעושן. במשנה [מנחות] סוף פרק כל קרבנות אמרו יין מעושן שוה ליין מבושל ופסול גם בדיעבד למזבח. וכבר הארכתי לעיל לבאר שיטות הראשונים מה הוא מעושן, ולא באתי אלא להעיר על דברי ר׳ יצחק בן גיאת בשערי שמחה, חלק א׳, עמ׳ ג׳ שמביא דעת ״יש אומרים״ שענבים שנתעשנו פסולים והוא חולק עליה, שלא אמרו יין מעושן ומבושל פסול אלא שהיין בעצמו נתעשן ונתבשל, אבל עישון הענבים הוא צימוקם ומקדשים אפילו לכתחילה על יין צמוקים. ולפי דרכנו למדנו מדבריו שענבים שנתבשלו כשרים גם לדעת האוסרים יין מבושל לקידוש, ולא מצאתי דין זה מפורש במקום אחר. ויין מעושן לקידוש לא נזכר אצל הפוסקים הראשונים חוץ מהראבי״ה שכתב בברכות סימן קל״ה, [חלק א׳, עמ׳ 125], ש״יכשר לברכה ולקידוש״. וברור שהרב בשיטתו — עיין לעיל עמ׳ סא-סב — עומד שגם מבושל כשר לקידוש ואם כן מעושן גם כן כשר, אבל לדעת האומרים שיין מבושל פסול לקידוש גם מעושן פסול, ואין ספק שכך היא דעתו של ר׳ יצחק ו׳ גיאת כמו שמוכח מדבריו שרמזתי עליהם לעיל. והמוציא לאור [של] ספר ראבי״ה לא ירד לסוף דעתו של הרב. ומדברי הראבי״ה תשובה לדעת ר׳ עקיבא איגר שבהגהותיו על אורח חיים [סימן] רע״ב העיר, שלדעת התוספות בבבא בתרא י״ח, א׳ — עיין לעיל עמ׳ נג-נד מה שכתבתי בענין זה — מעושן פסול לקידוש. והננו אנו רואים שהראבי״ה אף שדעתו כדעת התוספות שעשן מחליש היין, מכל מקום סובר שכשר לקידוש, שלא אמרו שמעושן ומבושל פסול אלא למזבח.

יג) יין שריחו רע. בין היינות הפסולים למזבח נשנה בתוספתא דמנחות פרק ט׳ ובבבא בתרא צ״ז, ב׳ גם יין שריחו רע. ובבבא בתרא אמרו שפסול גם בדיעבד לקידוש. וכבר הבאתי לעיל דעת הרמב״ם בפירוש המשנה שלו על המשנה דמנחות פרק ט׳, שמעושן הוא יין שריח רע שבחבית נקלט בו, אבל חזר בו הרב בספר היד שלו בפרק ו׳ מ[הלכות] אסורי מזבח ופירש מעושן כמו שפירשו כל הראשונים, והוא יין שהושם בעשן כדי לחממו והוא כעין בישול. ובשערי שמחה, חלק א׳, עמ׳ ד׳ כתב וזה לשונו: ״ומאי ריח רע? כגון משקה סרוחי״, וזה נוח יותר ממה שפירש הרשב״ם בבבא בתרא [ד״ה אלא למעוטי שריחו רע] שכתב: ״שהסריח קצת דמונח משום דמונח בכלי מאוס״.

יא) יין מבושל פסול גם בדיעבד למזבח כמו שמפורש במשנה [מנחות]
סוף פרק כל קרבנות, ומבושל לקידוש נחלקו בו רבותינו הראשונים. הגאונים
וחכמי ספרד הראשונים אוסרים מבושל לקידוש, וחכמי צרפת ואשכנז ונלוו
עליהם חכמי ספרד האחרונים כהרמב"ן, הרשב"א בתשובותיו והתשב"ץ
במאמר חמץ ל"ד, ד' מתירים אפילו לכתחילה, עיין המקומות בספרי
הראשונים שהעירותי עליהם למעלה. ולא באתי להעיר כאן אלא על שיעור
בשולו שלא נזכר לא ברמב"ם ולא בשלחן ערוך. ובטור [סימן] רע"ב כתב וזה
לשונו: "ועל יין מבושל רבו הדעות, הרב ר' שמעיה כתב בשם רבינו שלמה
— הוא רש"י, עיין פרדס ט"ז, א'[91] והוא מיסודו של ר' שמעיה תלמידו של
רש"י — שמברכין עליו שהכל. וכן כתב הרב ר' יצחק ו' גיאת, יין שנתבשל
אפילו מעט וכן מעט וכן נתן לתוכו מעט דבש מברכין עליו שהכל. וכך כתב ר' האי:
וכיון שנתן האור תחתיו והרתיח אין בו משום גלוי ולא משום יין נסך ואין
אומרים עליו קידוש היום ואינו נראה לבעל העטור — עיין דבריו בעשרת
הדברות, מצה ומרור, עמ' 264 — דלא גרע מקונדיטון דאיתא בירושלמי —
פסחים פרק י', [א', ל"ז ע"ג] עיין מה שכתבתי לעיל בעמ' סא-סב — שיוצאין
בו בפסח ידי ד' כוסות". ולולא לא היה מונח לפנינו ספרו של ר' יצחק ו' גיאת
כי אז היינו סוברים שהוא חולק על הגאונים בשיעור בישולו של יין, שהם
סוברים שלא נקרא יין מבושל אלא אם נתבשל עד כדי שהרתיח ולדעתו
אפילו נתבשל מעט. אבל באמת לא כן הוא, וזה לשון ר' יצחק ו' גיאת בשערי
שמחה, חלק א', עמ' ב'-ג': "ואמר מר רב האי צמוקין שנתערב אפילו דבר
מועט מן הדבש וכו' או שנתבשל וכו' אין מברכין עליו בורא פרי הגפן וכו' ואמר
מר רב האי דייקו הגאונים הראשונים יין מבושל כיון שנותן תחתיו אור וחם
עד כדי [שירתיח] — צ"ל כדי שירתיח כמו שהוא בטור, בפרדס ובעשרת
הדברות — אין בו משום גילוי" וכו'. והרואה יראה שהר' ו' גיאת אינו אומר
כלל דבר מדעתו, אלא מביא להלכה דברי רב האי גאון ובודאי הגאון לא
יסתור דברי עצמו. ועל כרחך שנוסחא מוטעת היתה לפני הטור ובמקום "או
שנתבשל" היה לפניו "או שנתבשל מעט", והיא אשגרא דלישנא ממה שקדם
לזה "שנתערב אפילו דבר מועט מן הדבש". [מאידך, יתכן] ש"מעט" פירושו
מיד שהרתיח והתחיל והתבשל מעט, ובא להשמיענו שלא נאמר שבשול
שנאמר כאן הוא כמו בשול תבשיל בשבת, שמשמעו יותר מכדי רתיחה אלא
שמיד שהרתיח פסול למזבח, משום שנשתנה מברייתו ואף שלא נתבשל כל
צרכו. והרמב"ן בע"ז דף ל' כתב שבשול של יין משמעו שנחסר ממדתו על ידי

הוא מתוק מברייתו ורק יין שנמתק על ידי [הפסד] כוחו אינו מביא לכתחילה למזבח וכן משמע מדברי הרשב"ם והרמ"ה שהבאתי. וליש אומרים שהובא דעתם בערוך בערכו, אלייסטון הוא יין שנשחר מראהו מן השמש והוא כעין יין כושי שדברנו עליו מלמעלה סימן ד'. והרמב"ם אף שהביא ב[הלכות] איסורי מזבח ההלכה שמתוק פסול בדיעבד למזבח, השמיט דין זה בהלכות שבת פרק כ"ט לגבי קידוש. ואפשר שהרב מפרש מתוק, יין ששם בו דבש להמתיקו, וכבר חיווה דעתו בהלכות שבת שיין כעין זה פסול גם לקידוש.

ט) יין צמוקים. יין זה הוא מן היינות שאינו מביא לכתחילה למזבח אבל בדיעבד כשר, ולקידוש כשר לכתחילה. וצריך אני להעיר מה שנעלם מכל וכל מהאחרונים שהגאונים ועמהם חכמי ספרד נראים כמחולקים עם בעלי התוספות בפירוש צמוקים. הגאונים וחכמי ספרד — עיין לדוגמא הלכות גדולות סוף הלכות קידוש והבדלה, הרי"ף בערבי פסחים וספר העתים עמ' 206 — פירשו שצמוקים הם ענבים שנתייבשו בגפניהם, אבל בתוספות במנחות פ"ז, א' בראש העמוד דעתם שצמוקים הם ענבים שנתייבשו בשמש אחר תלישתם. ויין ענבים שנתייבשו בגפניהם הוא אלייסטון. ולכאורה נראה שלדעת הגאונים יין ענבים שנתייבשו אחר תלישתם, והוא מה שנקרא אצלינו יין צמוקים, פסול גם בדיעבד למזבח וכן לקידוש, אבל עיין דברי ר' יצחק אבן גיאת בשערי שמחה, חלק א', עמי ג' וטור [סימן] רע"ב וצע"ג. ומה שנוגע ליין שיוצא מהצמוקים אחר שרייתם במים, הכל מודים שלקידוש כשר לכתחילה, אבל למזבח נראה כדעת האומרים שיין צמוקים לא הותר בדיעבד למזבח אלא ביין היוצא מהצמוקים על ידי דריכה, ולא על ידי שרייה שהרי יין מזוג פסול הוא למזבח, כמו שכתבתי לעיל. והגאונים החמירו ביין צמוקים ואמרו שלא יקדש עליהם אלא בדלא אפשר ביין אחר — או שאין לו או שאין יין מצוי, עיין לעיל — אבל גדולי הפוסקים לא קיבלו חומרא זו והתירו יין לצמוקים גם בשיין אחר מצוי. וכן נהגו בימי הריב"ש והתשב"ץ בארצות המערב, ובדורותינו המנהג הפשוט בליטא לקדש על יין צמוקים.

י) יין מזוג. בין אלו היינות שהם פסולים ואפילו בדיעבד, מנו התוספתא דמנחות והברייתא בבבא בתרא צ"ז, ב' גם יין מזוג. ולעיל הארכתי להוכיח שדבר זה במחלוקת שנויה ותלוי אם דורשים "שכר" ולא מזוג, או לא, ושדעת הרמב"ם שיין מזוג כשר אפילו לכתחילה למזבח וכן היא דעת ר' גרשום בפירושו לבבא בתרא. אבל הכל מודים שיין מזוג כשר לכתחילה לקידוש, אלא שמנהג ארץ ישראל לברך על יין חי, עיין חלוף מנהגים, סימן יי"ט[90] וגם זה נעלם מהאחרונים.

90 ראה לעיל, הערה 64.

יחיד בדבר זה ושדבריו הם דברי ר' שרירא גאון, ר' יצחק אבן גיאת, הרמב"ם ור' מאיר הלוי. ובודאי כל אלו הגדולים לא טעו בדבר פשוט, וכוונתם שטעם היין נוטה לחמיצות, ולא שהוא חומץ גמור, ויין שנוטה לחמיצות אפשר שיהי לו ריח יין.

ז) יין מרתף והוא יין הנמכר בחנות וסתמו קוסס, אבל לפעמים הוא גרוע ממנו שאפשר שנתחמץ לגמרי. ובתוספתא דמנחות פרק ט' וכן בבבא בתרא צ"ז, ב' אמרו שיין מרתף לא יביא לכתחילה למזבח אבל לקידוש כשר גם לכתחילה. והרבה מהראשונים דעתם שיין מרתף פגום הוא למזבח גם אם קוסס כשר בדיעבד, שלפעמים הוא גרוע ממנו כמו שכתבתי. והנראה שדעת הרמב"ם היא שיין מרתף כשר לכתחילה למזבח.

ח) יין אלייסטון כשר בדיעבד למזבח, ולקידוש גם לכתחילה — ראה משנה, תוספתא, וגמרא [מנחות] סוף פרק כל קרבנות ובבא בתרא צ"ז, ב'. והרבה פירושים נאמרו ביין אלייסטון. הרמב"ם ובעל הלכות גדולות פירשו שהוא יין שנתחמם בשמש ודומה למבושל, וכיון שאינו מבושל לגמרי כשר הוא בדיעבד גם למזבח. ולדעת רש"י, ונמשכו אחריו חכמי צרפת ואשכנז, הוא יין שנתחממו ענביו בשמש ועל ידי כך נמחק, ומתיקותו היא גריעותו שמתיקתו ממש פסול גם בדיעבד. והחילוק בין מתוק לאלייסטון הוא כמו שאמרו שם בגמרא שמתיקו שפסול, הוא יין שמתיקותו באה מחמת עצמו ומתיקות אלייסטון היא מהשמש. והרשב"ם בבבא בתרא שכתב "אלייסטון יין מתוק וחלש מאוד" וכן ר' מאיר הלוי שכתב יין "מתוק וקל" השמיטו התנאי העיקרי, שמתיקותו אינה מעצמותו של היין ונגררו אחריהם הטור והשולחן ערוך. ודעת ר' גרשום בפירושו למנחות שהחילוק בין אלייסטון למתוק שאלייסטון הוא מין יין שמתוק מטבעו כיין המוסקאט שאצלנו ולכן בדיעבד כשר גם למזבח, אבל יין שנמתק על ידי שנתבשלו ענביו בחמה או בחום יוונר מדאי פסול גם בדיעבד שנשתנה מברייתו. וגרסת הספרים [העתיקים] במנחות [פ"ז ע"א] "חוליא דפירי לא מאיס, חוליא דשמשא מאיס" מסייעת לפירוש ר' גרשום. ובדפוסים החדשים הגיהו "חוליא דשמשא לא מאיס, חוליא דפירי מאיס", והוא על פי פירוש רש"י, עיין דברי הכסף משנה ל[הלכות] איסורי מזבח פרק ו' ודקדוקי סופרים במקומו. ואפשר שגם רש"י מודה שאם מין היין ממין שמתוק מטבעו כיין המוסקאט כשר גם לכתחילה ולמזבח, ומתוק שפסול הוא יין ממין שאינו מתוק מטבעו ונמתק על ידי שנפסד כוחו. ועיין בפירוש ר' גרשום לבבא בתרא שכתב: "ליסטון — ירוק שהפיג טעמו ונפק מצורתו". וכבר כתבתי שהפירוש אלייסטון ירוק אי אפשר לקיימו כלל, מכל מקום נראה מזה שלדעת הרב יין מתוק אינו פגום כלל אם

חווריין שהוא יין לבן מענבים שחורים. והתשובה בגמרא שם "אל תרא יין כי
יתאדם", שאין חילוק מאיזה מראה הענבים, שאם היין לבן אינו מביא
לכתחילה למזבח.

ה) יין שריחו חמוץ וטעמו יין — הוא הנקרא קוסס בגמרא — כשר
למזבח בדיעבד ולקידוש גם לכתחילה לדעת הפוסקים. וכבר הוכחתי לעיל
שלדעת התוספתא והירושלמי קוסס פסול גם בדיעבד למזבח משום
שנשתנה ריחו ושינוי ריח פוסל ביין נסכים. ולפי דעת רבינו יונה כפי אשר
מובא בשמו בשיטה מקובצת לבבא בתרא קוסס פסול בדיעבד בין למזבח
בין לקידוש, אבל לא מצינו לו חבר שקוסס יהי פסול לקידוש, ולא גם אחד
מהפוסקים שמביא דעתו. ויש שאמרו שקוסס הוא שאמרו עליו בגמרא שיין
שריחו רע פסול לקידוש, אבל נחלק עליהם רבינו ר' יצחק בן גיאת בשערי
שמחה חלק א', עמ' ג' וכו'.

ו) יין שריחו יין וטעמו חומץ פסול גם לקידוש וקל וחומר לנסכים. דין
זה מביא הרב בעל המפה [באו"ח רע"ב: א'] מהטור, ותימה גדול שלא אחד
מהאחרונים ראה שדברי הטור לקוחים מהרמב"ם פרק כ"ט מהלכות שבת.
והרב במגיד משנה שם העיר שמקור הרמב"ם הוא הרי"ף בערבי פסחים, וזה
שלא בדיוק, שהרי"ף לא הזכיר כלל ריחו יין וטעמו חומץ שפסול אלא ריחו
חומץ וטעמו יין שכשר. והרמב"ם סמך על תשובת הגאון ר' שרירא המובאת
בשערי שמחה, חלק א', עמ' ד'.

וזה לשון רבינו בן גיאת: "אבל יין שהקרים לדברי הכל אינו יין 'דתנן
(הוא כמו דתניא, עיין מה שכתבתי לעיל עמ' כ' על ברייתות שהובאו בלשון
דתנן) על הפת שעפשה ועל היין שהקרים' וכו' [ברכות מ' ע"ב] והכי אמר מר
רב שרירא: ריחיה חמרא וטעמיה חלא היינו יין שהקרים ואומר שהכל".
והאחרונים שלא ראו דברי הגאונים נשתבשו הרבה בזה. עיין בית חדש, אורח
חיים, סימן ר"ד וטורי זהב ראש סימן [רע"ב], ובפרט דברי הט"ז שם תמוהים
שהעיר על דברי רב חסדא בבבא בתרא צ"ה [ע"ב], והלא לרב חסדא יין שריחו
חומץ מברכין עליו שהכל ואין הלכה כמותו. ומדברי ר' שרירא גאון נראה
שהגאונים מפרשים דברי הגמרא שם "בפורצמא דמיזדבן אקרנתא", שהוא
משקה שריחו יין וטעמו חומץ, וכן פירש שם רבינו מאיר הלוי ביד רמה וזה
לשונו: "בפרצופא — כך היא גרסת הספרדים — דטעמיה חלא וכו' דכי אמר
רב יהודה היכא דריחיה חלא וטעמיה חמרא אבל בטעמיה חלא — וריחו
חמרא, כך צריך להוסיף — לא קאמרי". ודודי זקני הגרי"א זצ"ל השיג על
הטור והעיר, שיין שריחו חמרא וטעמיה חלא הוא דבר שאי אפשר כמו
שכתבו התוספות בבבא בתרא צ"ו, א' בראש העמוד. והנה ראינו שהטור אינו

נחלקו ר' יוסי וחבריו שהיין שמנסך על המזבח צריך שלא יהו בו קמחין ומר
אמר חדא ומר אמר חדא ולא פליגי. החכמים אומרים שלכתחילה אין לוקחין
יין שבפי החבית שמא נתערבו בו קמחין ובדיעבד כשר שזה חששא בעלמא,
אבל אם בודאי נתערבו בו קמחין פסול גם בדיעבד וזה מה שאמר ר' יוסי יין
שעלה בו קמחין פסול. ואפשר גם כן שאלו החכמים דעתם שר' יוסי פוסל יין
שבא מחבית שיש בו קמחין וחכמים מכשירין כל זמן שהיין שנתנסך אין בו
קמחין. ולפי זה יין שבפי החבית מותר לכתחילה לקידוש, אבל יין שיש בו
קמחין פסול וצריך לסננו.

ג) יין שבשולי החבית כשר בדיעבד למזבח ולקידוש גם לכתחילה, שם
במשנה דמנחות ובבבא בתרא. ובודאי שמרים עצמם פסולים גם בדיעבד בין
למזבח בין לקידוש, ולא נזכר דין זה בפירוש ש״יזיל קרי בי רב הוא״.[89]
ומזה ראיה למה שכתבתי בסעיף הקודם בפירוש המשנה דמנחות, שיין
שבפי החבית ובשוליה נשנו כאחד, וכשם שהשמרים בעצמם פסולים כן
הקמחין.

ד) יין שנשתנה מראהו, כיין כושי [שהוא] שחור, ויין בורק [שהוא] לבן,
כשר בדיעבד למזבח ולקידוש גם לכתחילה — תוספתא מנחות שם ובבא
בתרא שם. ויין שהוא לבן ביותר, חמר חווריין, אמרו שפסול גם בדיעבד
ורבותינו הראשונים נחלקו בפירוש דברי הגמרא על חמר חווריין. הרמב״ן
ורבינו ר' מאיר הלוי פירשו שיין לבן — להרמב״ן גם אינו לבן ביותר — פסול
בדיעבד גם לקידוש ורוב הראשונים פירשו שפסול רק למזבח. עיין על זה
באריכה במאמר חמץ להתשב״יץ ל״ג, ד' ול״יד, א'. ושם במאמר חמץ ל״יד, א'
[נפלה] טעות סופר וצריך לאמר רשב״ים במקום רמב״ים, שהרמב״ים אינו
מביא כלל אלו ההלכות על יינות שנשתנו מראיהן. וכבר הארכתי לבאר דעת
הרמב״ים שהיא גם כן דעת הרי״יף, שעד כאן לא אמרו שלכתחילה יין כושי
וכדומה אינו מביא למזבח אלא בשיטת ר' יהודה שמקפיד על מראה יין,
[אבל] לחכמים שהלכה כמותם כל המראות כשרות ביין ואפילו לכתחילה.
וצריך אני להעיר שהגמרא וכן הראשונים סתמו דבריהם ולא חילקו בין יין
לבן היוצא מענבים שחורים או לבנים, וכבר ידוע שיש יין לבן מענבים
שחורים ויש יין אדום מענבים לבנים. ואפשר ששאלת הגמרא [על] חמר
חווריין היא על יין שיוצא מענבים שחורים ויש יין אדום מענבים לבנים.
ואפשר ששאלת הגמרא [על] חמר חווריין היא על יין שיוצא מענבים שחורים,
וזהו החילוק בין יין בורק שהוא יין של ענבים לבנים ומראהו לבן, וחמר

---

89 ״ילך קרא בבית הרב הוא״ — כלומר, דבר זה כה פשוט שכל מי שלמד תורה שבכתב
בבית הרב יודע שאין הדין כן — ראה סנהדרין ל״יג ע״ב ועוד.

אברהם שמצוה מן המובחר לקדש על יין ישן. וכבר כתבנו בראש מאמר זה שמעולם לא עלה על דעת בעל המנהגים לאמר שיין ישן מצוה מן המובחר, והנה זכינו עתה מדברי הטור בעצמם שאין מצוה מן המובחר ביין ישן. ולא הרגיש הרב בעל מגן אברהם שלפי פירושו בדברי בעל המנהגים, הרב הזה חולק על הטור, ותמיה אני על מפרשי המגן אברהם המחצית השקל והפרי מגדים שלא ראו הקושיא הזאת שיש בדברי הרב. ובסיום מאמרנו אמרנו לסדר בקיצור כל אלו דיני יינות אשר דיברנו עליהם למעלה ועוד נוסיף עליהם דינים אחדים אשר לא נגענו בהם במשך מאמרנו.[88]

[סיכום כללי ופסק הלכה]

א) יין מגתו ונקרא גם תירוש ויין חדש כשר בדיעבד למזבח, ולקידוש גם לכתחילה, אבל אינו חייב בששתה רביעית מיין זה ונכנס למקדש, ואם שתה יתר מרביעית חייב, ואין נעשה בן סורר ומורה עליו, ומותר לשתותו בערב תשעה באב בשלשת הימים הראשונים לתסיסתו. המקורות לדינים אלו הם: תוספתא מנחות פרק ט'; בבא בתרא צ"ז, א'; סנהדרין ע', א'; תוספתא כריתות פרק א' ובגמרא כריתות י"ג, ב'; וירושלמי פרק ח' דסוטה. ולענין קידוש ושאר מצוות כארבע כוסות וכדומיהן הכל מודים שלכתחילה כאן משמעו שהרשות ביד אדם לקדש על יין מגתו גם כשיש לו יין אחר בתוך ביתו, ואפילו מצוה מן המובחר אינה לקדש על יין ישן. והרב בעל מגן אברהם שפסק שמצוה מן המובחר לקדש על יין ישן לא ירד לסוף דעתם של הראשונים בדבר זה. רק בסוחט אדם אשכול, דעת בעל הלכות גדולות שאין לקדש עליו אלא בשאין לו מין אחר, וחומרא זו משום חששא דשבת שמא יסחוט בשבת. ולא נמצא לו חבר בדעה זו. ולפי המנהג שמובא במהרי"ל אין לקדש על יין חדש אם בדעתו לשתות יין ישן בתוך הסעודה כדי שברכת יין ישן יפטור גם יין חדש, ואם יקדש על יין חדש יצרוך לברך עוד פעם על יין ישן.

ב) יין שיש בו קמחין, מחלוקת חכמים ור' יוסי ברבי יהודה בסוף פרק כל קרבנות [מנחות פ"ו ע"ב-פ"ז ע"א] אם פסול למזבח, ולפי הכלל "יחיד ורבים הלכה כרבים" כשר למזבח בדיעבד ולקידוש לכתחילה. מכל מקום יש מהראשונים שאמרו שפסול כן לקידוש. ונראה שאלו החכמים דעתם שלא

88   רוב המקורות המובאים כאן נידונו כבר לעיל ולכן לרוב לא חזרנו על מראי המקומות שנרשמו לעיל.

ומחומרה זו של בעל הלכות גדולות ביין צמוקים, למד רבינו יצחק בן
גיאת בשערי שמחה, חלק א', עמי ב', שגם בשאר יינות שכשרים לכתחילה
לדינא דגמרא, כקוסס שהוא קרוב להחמיץ לגמרי, או הלייסטון שמתחיל
להחמיץ (או כפי הגהתי לעיל שמרתיח במעצרתא), היכא דאפשר להביא יין
טוב ולקדש עליו, הוא קודם ומצוה מן המובחר. ודברי הרב הזה הן המקור
למה שכתב הטור בסימן רעיב שבכל היינות שיש לחוש שמא נתקלקלו
לגמרי, כיין מרתף שאינו יודע אם לא נתחמץ וכדומיהן, "מצוה מן המובחר
לברור מן היין טוב לקדש עליו". וראה עד כמה דקדק הטור בדבריו שלא
העתיק דברי ר' יצחק בן גיאת בן כצורתן ולא כתב שכל היכא דאפשר יקדש
רק על יין טוב, אבל כתב "מצוה מן המובחר לברור", והוא שאדם שיש לו
יינות טובים לא יברר הרע שבהם למצוה, והטוב לשתיית רשות, ולא
שמחויב אדם לקנות יינות משובחים לקידוש, שהרי אמרו בגמרא שכל אלו
היינות כשרים לכתחילה ואפילו שאינם משובחים. וראה גם כן איך דקדקו
הטור והשלחן ערוך בסדור דבריהם, שמתחילה הביאו הדין דמקדשין על יין
מגתו, וזה לבדו יבוא, ואחר כך כללו כאחת אלו היינות שנתקלקלו קצת,
ויש לחוש שנתקלקלו לגמרי, ואף שמצד הדין אין מקום לחששא זו, מצוה
מן המובחר לקדש על יין שברור לו שהוא טוב. והיינות ממין זה הם: יין
שבפי החבית שאפשר שהיין כולו קמחין — עיין להלן עמי סז-סח; יין
שבשולי החבית מפני שסמוך לשמרים, ועל שמרים עצמם בודאי אין יכול
לקדש שאינו ראוי לשתייה כלל; יין שחור, שאבד מראה יין לגמרי ומצוה
שיהי בו כעין מראה יין; וכן יין בורק — רק בטור — שהוא לבן לגמרי
ואין בו מראה יין כלום; ויין שריחו חומץ וטעמו יין שיש לחוש שמא
נתחמץ לגמרי. וכבר ראה הרב בעל מגן אברהם[87] שיין מגתו הוא מין בפני
עצמו ולא עליו אמר הטור שמצוה לברור יין טוב, שאינו יין מגתו, אבל
בשאר היינות שמענו למעלה דעת הטור שמצוה מן המובחר לקדש על יין
טוב יש לו. ואף שהרב בעל מגן אברהם לא אמר זה בפירוש, מכללא
אתמר, שאם לא כן למה לו להביא ממרחק לחמו ממנהג שמובא בדרכי
משה, שמצוה מן המובחר לקדש על יין ישן — עיין ראשית מאמרי — הלא
במקומו הטור והשלחן ערוך אומרים בפירוש שמצוה לברור יין טוב. ומזה
מוכח שגם לדעת המגן אברהם יין מגתו נקרא יין טוב, והאחרון לא בא
להוציא אלא יין שנתקלקל קצת בטעמו, בריח או במראה. אבל אם כן הוא,
קשה באמת למה לא כלל הטור יין מגתו בהנך, אם צדק הרב בעל מגן

---

87 לאו"ח סימן רע"ב, ס"ק ג' ולסימן תי"ר, ס"ק א'.

לקדושי עליה, דאמר רבה סוחט אדם אשכול וכו' וכן הלכה'".[82] וברור לכל מי
שיש לו עינים לראות שי"שפיר דמי" אי אפשר לפרש במשמע אחר אלא שטוב
ונכון לעשות כן ואפילו מצוה מן המובחר הוא, בין שיש לו יין אחר בין שאין
לו. ור' עמרם אינו מחלק בין יין מגתו סתם לסוחט אדם, ובאמת אין שום
חילוק ביניהם לדעת בה"ג שלא הותר לסחוט בשבת עצמה, ואם כן מאי נפקא
מינה אם סוחט בערב שבת או בחמישי בשבת? והבה"ג שאמר שלא יקדש על
סחיטת ענבים אלא בשאין לו יין, ומשמעו גם יין מגתו, משום חשש אסור
שבת החמיר כדי שלא יבוא אדם לסחוט בשבת, מה שלדעתו אסור גמור הוא,
וחשש לזה משום שיש מתירין לסחוט גם בשבת עצמה, עיין ארחות חיים,
הלכות שבת, ס"ד ע"א, ובקצור ספר עץ חיים הנדפס בספר היובל להחכם
משה שטיינשניידער, עמ' 206.[83] וכבר נחלקו הגאונים והראשונים בענין סוחט
אדם אשכול של ענבים לקדרה, עיין תשובת ר' האי גאון בסוף ספר חדושי
הרי"ן על שבת,[84] ובתורתן של ראשונים ב', נ"א וגומ',[85] ורמז לתשובה זו
הרי"ף לשבת דף קמ"ד,[86] ועיין גם כן ספר ראבי"ה, שבת, סימן שי"ל, [חלק
א', עמ' 370 ואילך] ועיין מה שהעירותי לעיל עמוד כא-כב.

ועל פי מה שכתבנו הרווחנו להשיב תשובה ברורה על הג' קושיות
שמצאנו בדברי בעל הלכות גדולות. והתשובה היא שגם הוא מודה שמצד
הדין כל אלו היינות שאמרו בהם בגמרא שמקדשין עליהם לכתחילה, הרי
הם שווים לײנות המובחרים והמשובחים, אבל בשביל חשש איסור שבת
החמיר באשכול של ענבים שלא לסחטו לקידוש אם יש לו יין אחר, וכן
החמיר ביין צמוקים שלא לקדש עליו בדשכיחא חמרא, כי לאו כולי עלמא
דינא גמירא ואפשר שהצמוקים נתייבשו עד שאין בהם לחלוחית או שהמים
רבים עליהם עד שאין בהם טעם יין כלל. וביין מגתו גם בעל הלכות גדולות
מודה שמקדש עליהם לכתחילה ואף בשיש לו יין אחר שאין בזה שום חשש
לא חשש שבת או חשש אחר, ולכן לא העתיק הגאון דברי הגמרא על יין
מגתו, שלא בא אלא להשמיענו החידוש שיש באלו היינות, שאף שלדינא
דגמרא מקדש עליהן לכתחילה, מכל מקום מצד חומרא לא יקדש עליהם
בשיש לו יין אחר אבל ביין מגתו לא עלה על דעתו להחמיר.

82 ראה לעיל, הערה 19.

83 ראה לעיל, הערה 28.

84 במהד' ירושלים תשל"ה, בעמ' רכ"ב-רכ"ה.

85 ראה לעיל, הערה 29.

86 בדפי וילנא, ס"א ע"א.

אומר כיון דלקרבן אם הביא כשר בדיעבד אבל לכתחילה לא, אנן אפילו
לכתחילה ואף במקום שאיפשר למצוה (צריך לאמר למצוא) אחר, דאי בדלא
איפשר אף לקרבן כשר להביא לכתחילה, ואף במקום שאיפשר למצוא יין אם
הביא כשר לקרבן״.[80] וברור שהגאונים לא מדינא אמרו שיין צמוקים אינו
מקדש עליו רק בדלא איפשר, אלא שהחמירו משום שבצמוקים יש לחוש לתקלה,
שאם הצמוקים יבשים לגמרי או שמוסיף עליהם מים הרבה יותר
מדאי אין מקדש עליו (עיין שערי שמחה, חלק א׳, עמ׳ ב׳ ורי״ף, ערבי
פסחים[81] מה שהביאו בשם הגאונים בדינים אלו) לכן ראו הם שלא להקל
ולקדש עליו אלא בשאין לו יין אחר ואפילו אשכול של ענבים לסחיטה.

ודע שחומרא זו של הגאונים שלא לקדש על יין צמוקים אלא בשאין לו
יין אחר או בדלא אפשר לא נתקבלה אצל גדולי הפוסקים, חכמי ספרד,
צרפת ואשכנז כדמוכח מהרי״ף, הרמב״ם והטור שסתמו דבריהם וכתבו
שמקדשין על יין צמוקים לכתחילה. וכבר ראינו למעלה שבעל המנהיג השיג
על דעת הגאונים בזה, וכן הריב״ש בתשובותיו סימן ט׳, והתשב״ץ, חלק א׳,
סימן נ״ז גערו בחכם אחד שרצה להחמיר שלא לקדש על יין צמוקים, וכפי
שנראה מדברי התשב״ץ שם מוכח שהיה במקום דחמרא שכיחא ומכל
מקום לא חששו לדעת בעל הלכות גדולות לחומרא. ועיין גם כן בספר
העתים עמ׳ 204 שהרב ר׳ שמואל הנגיד לא נחה דעתו מחומרא זו וייחסה
לחד מדרבנן ואף שבודאי לא היה נעלם ממנו שהיא נמצאת אצל הגאונים.
ועיין גם כן דברי בעל התשב״ץ בספרו מאמר חמץ, לי״ד, א׳ שכתב: ״ויין של
צמוקים הנהוג בארצות האלה״, וכבר נדע שהרב חי במקום שהיין מצוי
לרוב ומכל מקום נהגו שם לקדש על יין צמוקים, וכן הכפיל דעתו שם בדף
לי״ד, ג׳.

ובסוחט אדם אשכול, בעל הלכות גדולות כמעט יחיד הוא בדבר בדעתו
שלא יקדש עליו אלא במקום שאין לו, ולא מצאתי לו חבר אלא שבעל ספר
האורה, עמ׳ 38 העתיק דברי בה״ג כצורתן — המוציא לאור ה[חכם] בובער
לא העיר על מקורו של ספר האורה — וכבר ידענו שבכמה מקומות העתיקו
הראשונים דברי הגאונים גם אם הם הסכימו לדעתם. ורב עמרם גאון ואף
שהסכים לדעת בה״ג לענין יין צמוקים כמו שכתבנו למעלה, מפורש יוצא
מתוך דבריו, במעריב של שבת, שמתיר סחיטת ענבים בכל אופן שיהיה, אם
יש לו יין אחר או לא, עיין שם שכתב וזה לשונו: ״אבל יין מגתו שפיר דמי

80 וראה עתה מהד׳ רפאל, ירושלים תשל״ח, עמ׳ תק״ג.
81 ראה לעיל, הערה 56.

להשיג יין של ענבים ולא של צמוקים. ושלש שאלות לנו על דברי בעל הלכות
גדולות: א) למה לא הזכיר הגאון הדין של יין מגתו אחר שהעתיק כמעט כל
הסוגיא דבבא בתרא, ודין יין זה נזכר שם בראשונה? ב) מניין לו שביש לו יין
אחר בתוך ביתו לא יקדש על סחיטת ענבים, והרי "סוחט אדם" משמע
לכתחילה גמור, שאין בין יין זה ליין אחר ולא כלום? ג) מניין לו החילוק בין
סחיטת אשכול ליין צמוקים, שזה האחרון לא התיר אלא בדלא שכיח ליה
חמרא ואין זה לכתחילה אלא בדיעבד, והגאון בעצמו מביא דברי הגמרא שיין
צמוקים מביא בדיעבד גם למזבח ולקידוש גם לכתחילה? וקודם שנבאר דברי
בעל הלכות גדולות עלינו להעיר על שינויי נוסחאות בגרסתם. הרב בעל ספר
העתים, עמ' 206 מביא דברי בעל הלכות גדולות כמו שהם לפנינו בנוסחא
הישנה[76] (ושם עמ' 204 קצת שלא בדיוק: בדלא אפשר, וכוונתו בשאין לו)
אבל בנוסחא החדשה של ספר הלכות גדולות, עמוד נ' הגרסא[77]: "והיכא
דלית ליה חמרא ולא קיטופא דעינבי מיתי עינבי יבישתא דיבשין בגופנייהו
(וזהו שלא כדברי התוספות דמנחות פ"ז, ע"א שהבאתי לעיל שצימוקים הם
ענבים שנתייבשו בשמש אחר תלישתן, ולהתוספות יין אלייסטון הוא מענבים
שנתייבשו בגפניהם) ותרי להו במיא ועצר להו" וכו'. וחילוק גדול לדינא בין
שתי נוסחאות אלו, שלפי הנוסחא השניה מקדש על יין צמוקים גם בדשכיח
חמרא אלא בשיש לו יין או אשכול ענבים מקדש עליהם, ולנוסחא הראשונה
לא יקדש על יין צמוקים אלא בדלא שכיח חמרא. והחומרא בייין צמוקים
מובאת בהרבה מקומות בספרי הגאונים, עיין לדוגמא בסדור רב עמרם גאון,
סדר הגדה, שכתב: "ואם אינו מוצא יין בכמה פרסאות או שהיה בספינה ואין
תקנה כל עיקר להביא יין, ישרה צמוקים במים ויעשה ארבעה כוסות, שכך
שנו חכמים [בב"ב צ"ז ע"ב] יין צמוקין לא יביא לקרבן ואם הביא כשר, וכיון
דלקרבן אם הביא כשר, לקידוש ולהבדלה כשר במקום שאי אפשר"[78].
ומסדורו של רב עמרם או [מקובץ] תשובות הגאונים הובאה תשובה זו אצל
כמה מהראשונים, עיין שערי שמחה, חלק ב', עמ' צ"ט; שערי תשובה, סימן
קי"ז; שבלי הלקט, דף קי"א, א'; המנהיג, הלכות פסח, סימן צ"ב. ועיין גם כן
שאלות ותשובות מן הגניזה, עמ' 228 בסוף העמוד[79] שהיא התשובה
המיוחסת לרב נטרונאי גאון בהלכות פסוקות מן הגאונים, סימן קס"ה,
ובחמדה גנוזה [סימן] ל"ה נתייחסה לר' צמח גאון. והנה הרב בעל המנהיג
הנ"ל השיג על דעת הגאונים שהחמירו ביין צמוקים וכתב, וזה לשונו: "ואני

77 כלומר, בדפי ברלין תרמ"ח.
78 במהד' גולדשמידט (לעיל, הערה 19), עמי קכ"ד.
79 הכוונה לגאוניקה (לעיל, הערה 24), חלק ב', עמי 228.

שהראבי"ה השתמש כאן ב"ספר ירושלמיי", והוא פירוש ישן על הירושלמי שהיה לפני חכמי אשכנז הראשונים, ולא בירושלמי עצמו.[75]

ג. [האם היינות שמקדשים עליהם לכתחילה שווים בכל דבר ליינות משובחים?]

אחר שעלה בידינו לפרש כיד ה' הטובה עלינו הסוגיות שבש"ס בבלי וירושלמי הנוגעות לדיני יינות פסולים וכשרים ולברר דעות הראשונים נוחי נפש בהלכות אלו, נבוא לעיין בדבר אחד עיקרי אשר עד כה לא נגענו בו אלא במקצת. השאלה אשר עד כה לא השבנו עליה תשובה ברורה היא, אם אלו היינות שאמרו מקדשין עליהם לכתחילה שווים בכל דבר ליינות משובחים וטובים, והרי אלו כמו אלו, או שמצוה מן המובחר לברור לו יין טוב ומשובח אם יש לו, ורק בשאין לו אלא מן אלו היינות מקדש עליהם לכתחילה ואינו מחויב לרדוף אחרי יינות משובחים. והנה בראשית מאמרי כבר הבאתי שבמה שבה שנוגע לייn מגתו, על פי שלושה עדים יקום דבר, שלושה גדולי ישראל, ר' מאיר מרוטנברג, ר' שלום מניישטאדט ותלמידו המהרי"ל שהם היו מקדשים על יין חדש ואף שהיה להם בביתם יין ישן או במקום שהיה קל להם להשיג מין יין ישן. רק במקום שיין ישן עלה על השולחן, דעת המהרי"ל לקדש עליו משום שברכתו כוללת גם יין חדש, אבל אין ברכת יין חדש מוציאה יין ישן. ואף ששלושה אלו כדאים המה לסמוך עליהם אפילו שלא בשעת הדחק, לא כך היא דרכה של תורה להורות הלכה על פי ספרי מנהגים במקום שיש לנו יתדות נאמנים בדברי הראשונים.

ונפתח בגדולים. הלכות גדולות סוף קידוש וההבדלה וזה לשונו: "ואי לית ליה חמרא מייתי עינבי ועצר להדן במעלי שבתא ומעלי יומא טבא ולאורתא מקדש עליה ד'אמר רבה סוחט אדם אשכול של ענבים ואומר עליו קידוש היום' [בבא בתרא צ"ז ע"ב] הואיל וגבי נזיר קרוא יין וכו' (עיין לעיל על הראיה מנזיר) והיכא דלא שכיח חמרא מייתי ענבי יבישתא דכמישן בגופנייהו ותארי להו במיא וכו' דתניא [שם] ייין כושיי'" וכו'.[76] והנה בעל הלכות גדולות מחלק בין סוחט אדם ליין צמוקים, שבראשון אף דשכיח חמרא אין מחויב להשתדל להשיגו, אלא בשיש לו יין בתוך ביתו לא יקדש על סחיטת ענבים, ועל יין צמוקים אינו מקדש אלא במקום דלא שכיח חמר, בדשכיח ישתדל

ועוקר ממקומו מתוק שנשנה עם מעושן ומבושל הפסולים ומעבירו
לאלייסטון הכשר בדיעבד, ולא מצינו כזה בכל הש"ס, ועל כרחך שכוונתו
שלא נזכרו במשנה כלל יינות הפסולים בדיעבד. ולרש"י שפירש "כרוך ותני"
לחומרא, שכולם פסולים, בודאי מוכרחים אנו לאמר שלרבינא אין חילוק בין
רישא לסיפא ולא כלום, שכל היינות, אלייסטון, מתוק, מעושן ומבושל
פסולים. וברור שהתתוספות לא נחלקו על רש"י במה שאמר שראש וסוף
המשנה דין אחד להם, אלא שלדעתם כאשר הוכיחו מהסוגיא דבבא בתרא,
הצד השוה שבהן שכולם כשרים, רצוני לאמר בין אלייסטון ומתוק בין מעושן
ומבושל. היוצא לנו מזה שגם להתוספות אין יין פסול נזכר במשנה לדעת
רבינא שאמר "כרוך ותני", ולכן לא אמרו בבבא בתרא "לֹמעוטי מבושל" כדי
לקיים דברי רב גם על דעתו של אמורא זה. ועיין מה שכתב הרמב"ן בחדושיו
לבבא בתרא על הקושיא מפני מה לא אמרו "לֹמעוטי מעושן", ולא העיר
שהתהירוץ שתירץ על קושיא זו יתרץ גם כן הקושיא למה לא אמר לֹמעוטי
מבושל.

ובדין של מבושל לקידוש נחלקו בו רבותינו הראשונים, עיין טור ובית
יוסף סימן רע"ב ולא באתי כאן אלא להעיר על מקומות שונים בדברי
הגאונים וראשוני הראשונים שלא היו ידועים לפוסקים בדורות האחרונים.
ר' האי גאון בשערי שמחה, חלק א', עמ' ג' ; תשובה של גאונים במעשה
הגאונים, עמ' 77; שערי תשובה סימן ד' — והיא להרי"ף וכן כל י"ב
התשובות הראשונות בקובץ זה הן להרי"ף; הלכות פסוקות מן הגאונים,
סימן י"ז ; פרדס ט"ז, א';[74] עטור, מצה ומרור, קל"ב, ד' ; אור זרוע חלק
א', סימן קס"ב — בשם ר' האיי גאון ושאר הגאונים, ובשם ספר בשר על
גבי גחלים שאין מקדשין על [יין] מבושל; ספר המכריע, סימן כ"ד; ראבי"ה
סימן תכ"ג, [חלק ב', עמ' 52 ואילך] — ועיין המקומות שהעיר עליהם החכם
המוציא לאור במקומו. ובספר ראבי"ה מכריע כדעת חכמי צרפת ואשכנז נגד
דעת הגאונים ורוב חכמי ספרד הראשונים שיין מבושל כשר וזה לשונו : "אבל
[יין] במבושל יש בו טעם יין, ולא סמכינן אירושלמי דמבושל מברך שהכל,
אלא אגמרא דידן". והרב הזה מביא גם בסימן קכ"ג, [חלק א', עמ' 106]:
"ירושלמי, יין מבושל מברך עליו שהכל נהיה בדברו". ולפנינו בירושלמי לא
נמצא מאמר כעין זה, ואדרבא הראשונים שהתירו יין מבושל מביאים ראיה
לדבריהם מהירושלמי דפסחים פרק י', א', [ל"ז ע"ג] שאמרו שם בפירוש
"יוצאין ביין מבושל." והמוציא לאור ספר ראבי"ה כיוון לאמת באמרו

---

74 במהד' קושטנדינא תקס"ב = מהד' עהרענרייך, בודאפעשט תרפ"ד, עמ' נ"ז-נ"ח.

לפתחד״ שייך בשאר תשמישי בית הכנסת, חוץ משמן להדליק בו שאסר הגאון כדי להוציא מלבן של צדוקים. ובתלמוד ובמדרש לא מצינו הדלקת נרות בבתי כנסיות ובתי מדרשות, אלא בזמן שנהנה מן האור ולא ביום, עיין פסחים נ״ג, ב׳ במשנה, בתוספתא, בבבלי ובירושלמי, ויקרא רבה ט׳, ב׳ ובמקומות שהעיר עליהם ר׳ דוד לוריא שם בחדושיו.

[יין מבושל]

וכאשר הזכרתי פעמים אחדות במאמרי זה ההלכה של יין מבושל שפסול בדיעבד למזבח, ולכמה מהראשונים גם לקידוש, לא אמנע מלהעיר על דבר אחד, שכפי הנראה העלימו עיניהם ממנו רבותינו הראשונים והאחרונים. כבר ידוע שהרבה מהראשונים כהתוספות והרמב״ן בחדושיהם לבבא בתרא צ״ז, א׳ רצו להוכיח ממה שלא אמרו בגמרא ״למעוטי מבושל״ שיין מבושל כשר לקידוש ואף שלמזבח פסול גם בדיעבד. והנה כבר הבאתי לעיל דברי הרמב״ם בפירוש המשנה למנחות סוף פרק כל קרבנות ובספר היד פרק ו׳ מהלכות אסורי מזבח [הלכה ט׳] שאיליסטון הוא כעין מבושל, אלא משום שאינו מבושל לגמרי כשר בדיעבד גם למזבח. ולפי דעת הרב, המשא ומתן בגמרא דמנחות פ״ז, א׳ על הקושיא שיש בין ראש המשנה לסופה היא, למה איליסטון כשר בדיעבד ומבושל פסול גם בדיעבד, וכן תירוצו של רבינא ״כרוך ותני״, פירושו שאין בין איליסטון ולמבושל, ששניהם כשרים. ואם כן לא אדע מה היה קשה להם לרבותינו הראשונים בהסוגיא דבבא בתרא דלעיל, שפשוט שהגמרא לא אמרה, למעוטי מבושל, משום שלרבינא שסובר ״כרוך ותני״ — עיין שם בתוספות שהוכיחו שפירושו ששינו שניהם לקולא, וכן פירש הרמב״ן בחדושיו לבבא בתרא — גם יין מבושל כשר בדיעבד שאין בינו לאיליסטון ולא כלום. ואחר שאמרו בגמרא שאי אפשר למעט איליסטון משום שכשר בדיעבד, וכל שכשר בדיעבד למזבח כשר לקידוש גם לכתחילה, לא היו יכולין לאמר למעוטי מבושל, שמבושל כאיליסטון. ואין מן הצורך להביא ראיות שאין מדרך הגמרא לאוקמי דברי אמורא בפלוגתא, וביחוד היה קשה להם לאמר שרבינא חולק על רב, שהיה נחשב כתנא, ולכן שתקו ממבושל לגמרי. אבל לא לבד לדעת הרמב״ם אלא גם לדעת אלו החולקים עליו, ר׳ גרשום, רש״י ותוספות (ודברי רש״י במשנה אפשר לפרש על פי הרמב״ם) נראה שרבינא באמרו שם [במנחות] ״כרוך ותני״ כיוון לאמר שכל אלו היינות הפגומים הנזכרים במשנה במדרגה אחת, והיא שאינו מביא אותם לכתחילה אבל אם הביא כשר, שאם לא כן רבינא, סכינא חריפא מפסקא לה למשנה,

רק כל זמן שלא נתבטל שדבר שאסור באכילה אסור לגבוה או גם אחר
שנתבטל ומותר לאכילה ומכל מקום אסור משום מיאוס. והמעיין באשכול
יראה, שאף שהמחבר לא הסכים לדעת הגאון וסובר שעכבר שנפל לשמן הוא
נותן טעם לפגם, מכל מקום מודה שלא ידליק בשמן זה בבית הכנסת שמאוס
ואף שהשמן אינו אסור. ולפי זה אין ראיה מדברי הגאון לדעת רש"י
והרמב"ם שגם בדברים האסורים להדיוט מצד הדין אמרינן "הקריבהו נא"
וכו', שבשמן שנפל בו עכבר אסור מטעם מיאוס. ומלבד זה ממקומו הוא
מוכרח, שהרי מדליקין בבית הכנסת בנר של חלב ואף שאסור באכילה, ועל
כרחך דשאני דבר שאסור ואינו נמאס מדבר הנמאס ואף שאינו אסור.

ודע שבתלמוד לא מצינו האיסור משום "הקריבהו נא לפחתך" אלא
לענין מזבח וקידוש אבל לא לענין תשמישי בית הכנסת. ולי אין ספק
שהגאון שאסר להדליק בבית הכנסת שמן שנפל בו עכבר לא אמר זה אלא
להוציא מלבן של צדוקים, אלה הקראים, שהיו מונים את[71] חכמינו וטוענים
עליהם שהם עושים את החול קודש ועורכים נרות בבית הכנסת כעריכת
הנרות בבית המקדש. עיין לדוגמא דברי הקראי יהודה הדסי בספר אשכול
הכופר שלו נ"א סוף הדף ונ"ב, א' וזה לשונו: "וראוי להדר ולייקר אותם —
בתי כנסיות — בקדושה ובטהרה לכבדה. אבל להקטיר קטורת בם (בימי
הגאונים היו מביאים מוגמרות לבית הכנסת ומעשנין לפני ספר תורה ביום
טוב האחרון של חג, עיין שערי שמחה, חלק א', עמ' קי"ז ושו"ת מהרי"ק,
שורש ט') או להעריך נרות ועשישות ולפידים בזה הזמן... אינו ראוי [ל]עשות
כן ולחשוב כזאת לה', יען כי כל אלה וכמותם למקדש ה' היו ראויים ולא בזה
הזמן לבית לבית ועד ובמושביך". פירוש עלתי[72] יען כי המקום זר והעבודה היא זרה
והמקריב נכרי וזר, והשמן (שמדליקים בו בבית הכנסת) מטונף ומטומא מכל
שרץ וערבוב כל טומאה ומעש[ה] ידי אכזר, ובלא צווי ה' מונזר, איך יקובל
לאלהים וירצה לפני בגבורה נאזר". והניגוד "למורדי אורי"[73] הוא המקור
למנהג שנתפשט בכל ישראל להדליק נרות בבית הכנסת בעת התפלה וגם
בתפלת השחר, ואף "דשרגא בטיהרא מאי מהני" [חולין ס' ע"ב] יש בזה כבוד
שמים.

ועיין בתשובות מהרי"ם מרוטנברג סימן קכ"ה, דפוס לבוב, מה שכתב
להתיר הדלקת נרות בבית הכנסת ביום טוב שחרית, ואף שאין מדליקין נר
של בטלה. ולפי פירושי בדברי הגאון, צ"ע אם האיסור משום "הקריבהו נא

---

71   אולי צ"ל "מוחים נגד" או "מורים עלי" וצ"ע.

72   אולי צ"ל "פרוש אולתי" על פי משלי י"ג:ט"ז.

73   על פי איוב כ"ד:י"ג.

בסימן רע"ב שנראה שהרגיש כעין זה, ואף שבימיו הספר שערי שמחה עוד לא
ראה אור הדפוס, ואילו ראהו היה מוצא סיוע לדבריו.

ואמרתי להעיר שהכלל שהדבר שהדיוט אין משתמש בו אסור לגבוה לא
מצינו בתלמוד אלא בדבר שהוא מאוס ופגום כמגולה, אבל לא הדבר
שאסור להדיוט מצד הדין, ומכל מקום גדולי הראשונים לא חילקו ביניהם.
עיין רמב"ם פי"ב, [הלכה] י' מאסורי מזבח שכתב ש"בהמה שנולד בה אחת מן
הטריפות האוסרות אותה באכילה אסורה" לגבוה משום "הקריבהו נא
לפחתך", ולא העירו מפרשי הרמב"ם שכן כתב גם כן רש"י בזבחים ס"ח, ב'
בדיבור המתחיל שנסמית עינה — שם השיגו התוספות עליו — ושם ע"ד, ב',
בדיבור המתחיל נפולה. וקרוב אני לשער שהיה לפני ראשונים דבר זה באיזה
מקור ישן, שקשה להאמין שהרמב"ם ורש"י ימציאו סברה חדשה בסגנון
אחד. ועיין גם כן ספר מצוות גדול, לא תעשה, סימן שט"ו שכתב, וזה לשונו:
"ויש ארבע חלאים אם נמצא אחד מהם בבהמה אין מקריבין אותה לפי
שאינה מן המובחר וכו' ג. אם נפגמו חיטים הפנימיות, ד. אם נגממו (במשנה
פרק מומין אלו דף מ"ה) בהמה שנולד בה אחת מן הטרפיות האוסרין אותה
באכילה אסורה לגבי מזבח הרי הוא אומר 'הקריבהו נא לפחתך הירצך או
הישא פניך' (שם דף לי) ואף על פי שאינה ראויה לקרבן אין פודין אותה" וכו'.
ולכאורה נראה שהרב בעל ספר מצות גדול היה לפניו בגמרא דבכורות דף לי
הטעם לאסור טריפות בקרבנות משום "הקריבהו נא" וכו'. אבל באמת אלו
המראי מקומות — שהוסיף ר' מתתיהו בר' שלמה בהוצאה משנת שי"ז
וממנה בכל שאר ההוצאות ובההוצאות שלפני זו לא נמצאו — שלא במקומן
הן. המראה מקום למשנה פי' מומין הוא לנפגמו חיטים, והמראה מקום
לבכורות ל' הוא להלכה אין פודין אותה,[69] אבל הטעם לאסור טרפות בקרבן
מצא הסמ"ג בספר היד של הרמב"ם כאשר הובא לעיל.

ועיין גם כן תשובת הגאון המובאת באשכול, חלק ג', עמי 102; ברא"ש
פרק גיד הנשה סימן ל"ה; ובר"ן שם בסוף הפרק[70] — ושם חסר מאמר
שלם וצריך להשלימו מהנוסחא שבאשכול — על שמן שנפל בו עכבר שפסק
הגאון שאסור להדליק בו בבית הכנסת משום "הקריבהו נא לפחתך". וכבר
נחלקו האחרונים בפירוש דברי הגאון, עיין ט"ז וש"ך ליורה דעה [סימן]
ק"ד, [סעיף] ב' ומגן אברהם לאורח חיים [סימן] קנ"ד, [סעיף] י"ב, [ס"ק י"ט]
ופרי מגדים ליורה דעה ואורח חיים, אם כוונת הגאון שאסור לבית הכנסת

---

69 תיקון זה צ"ע כי בדפי ויניציאה ש"י הציון לבכורות דף לי אכן מופיע מול ההלכה
"אין פודין אותה".

70 בדפי וילנא, ל"יו ע"יב למעלה, סוף ד"יה גרסי' בגמי.

מגולה טועם בו טעם יין. ונראה שקושיית הגמרא היא על סגנון לשונו של
מאמר רב, שכך היה לו לאמר: קידש על יין מגולה לא יצא ידי חובתו, ואילו
מדבריו משמע שאינו מקפיד על שתיית יין מגולה, ולכן אמרו שרב כר׳ נחמיה
ומגולה שבא לפסול לקידוש הוא מגולה שמותר לשתות שהעבירו במסננת.
אבל הרמב״ם כלל מגולה בין שאר יינות הפסולים וכתב, לא נאמר היין
הראוי לנסך על גבי מזבח אלא שהוציא יין שריחו רע או מגולה או מבושל,
ובודאי שאין להקשות מגולה תיפוק ליה משום סכנה, שבא להודיענו שאם לא
חשש לסכנה וקידש עליו אינו יוצא.

ודע שהגאונים וגדולי הפוסקים שבדורות שלאחריהם כהריי״ף והרמב״ם
שהביאו דין של יין מגולה לקידוש, אוסרים גם לשתיית רשות כידוע,
אבל חכמי צרפת ואשכנז שאמרו שבזמננו ובארצות אלו אין מגולה נוהג
(עיין יורה דעה [סימן] קט״ז) קט״ז והמקומות שהעיר עליהם דודי זקני הגרי״א ז״ל
בבאורו לשלחן ערוך, ואף שהוא בעצמו היה מחמיר גדול בכל אלו הדברים
שאסרום בתלמוד משום סכנה, עיין מעשה רב סימן צ״ה ובינת אדם סימן
ס״ג) באמת טעמא בעי למה מגולה אסור לקידוש. והנה המקור הראשון
שנמצא בו שאף במקום שבני אדם אין חוששין למגולה אין מקדשין עליו, הוא
הספר שערי שמחה לר׳ יצחק בן גיאת כאשר הבאתי דבריו לעיל וממנו העתיק
הטור ואחריו הרב בשלחן ערוך, אלא שזה האחרון נגרר אחר הרמב״ם ולא
הזכיר אפילו סננו במסננת, שלדעת הרמב״ם שפוסק כחכמים אין חילוק בין
סננו ללא סננו כאשר העירותי לעיל. ובשערי שמחה בשם הר׳ שמואל הנגיד
הטעם לאסור הוא שגם בימי הגמרא לא היו מקדשין עליו ואף בשסננו
במסננת משום ״הקריבהו נא לפחתך״, ואם כן גם אלו שאין חוששין לסכנת
מגולה מכל מקום לא יקדשו עליו משום ״הקריבהו״ וכו׳. ואם קבלה היא
נקבל, ואם לדין יש תשובה. בימי התלמוד שהיו חוששין לגילוי היה הדבר
מאוס ומגונה להשתמש במגולה לצורך גבוה כיין נסכים וקידוש גם אחרי
שסננו במסננת משום ״הקריבהו״, דבודאי לא היו נותנין לפני מלכים ושרים
משקה שאפשר שמעט מן ארס הנחש נשאר בו, אבל בדורותינו שאין מקפידין
כלל על גילוי, מאי ״הקריבהו נא״ שייך והכל יודעים שמשקאות כאלו עולים
על שלחן מלכים? וכשנעיין בדברי הנגיד נראה בפירוש שלא אמר אלא לימיו
שאז עוד היו מתי מספר שהקפידו על מגולה, ואף שהרוב לא הקפידו, ולכן
משום ״הקריבהו״ אין מקדשין עליו, ומשום שאין זה משקה העולה על שלחן
אנשים מפונקים המקפידים על מגולה. אבל בדורותינו שגם מיעוטא דמיעוטא
ליתא שחוששין על מגולה, אפשר שמקדשין עליו. ועיין בדברי המגן אברהם

שאמרו בגמרא ואף על פי שהעבירו במסננת, משום שלשיטתו שפוסק
כחכמים העברת מסננת אינה מוציאה מידי גילוי. והטור באורח חיים
[סימן] רע״ב מביא דין מגולה גבי קידוש, והקשו האחרונים עליו, עיין פרישה
במקומו וטורי זהב יורה דעה [סימן] קט״ז, שהוא סותר דברי עצמו, שביורה
דעה פוסק שלא כר׳ נחמיה [ואם כן] דין גילוי הוא מיותר כמו שאמרו
בגמרא ״אי למעוטי מגולה סכנה היא״. והיטב ראה הפרישה שהטור מביא זה
שגם לדידן שאיננו חוששין לגלוי מכל מקום מגולה פסול לקידוש משום
מאוס, ודברי הפרישה הם הם דברי ר׳ שמואל הלוי, והוא ר׳ שמואל הנגיד,
המובאים בשערי שמחה חלק א׳, עמ׳ ב׳, ספר שהשתמש בו הרבה רבינו
הטור. וכך הן שנויים שם: ״ואמר מר רב שמואל הלוי והשתא דלא קפדי
רובא דאינשי ולא חיישינן לארס נחש אף על פי דלא שפייה במסננת אומר
עליו בורא פרי הגפן, אלא שאין מקדשין עליו קידוש היום משום הקריבהו נא
לפחתך״. ואף שמצד דין גילוי לדעת הטור אין לחלק בין העבירו במסננת או
לא, הזכיר ואפילו העבירו במסננת, לתת טעם לאסור מגולה לקידוש בזמן
הזה, שהוא משום ״הקריבהו נא לפחתך״, כיון שגם בשאין לחוש לסכנה —
להסוברים כר׳ נחמיה — בזמן התלמוד היו נמנעים מלקדש עליו; עיין דברי
דודי זקני הגר״א ז״ל בבאורו על אורח חיים רע״ב.

והנה תמיה אני על האחרונים שקושייתם קשה יותר על הרמב״ם,
שבהלכות שבת פרק כ״ט [הלכה י״ד] הביא דין מגולה לקידוש ואף שלדעתו
מגולה אסור משום סכנה. והנה מה שהביא דין מגולה באסורי מזבח פרק ו׳
[הלכה י׳] לא קשה כלום שבא להשמיענו שאם קידש יין מגולה לוקה מכת
מרדות משום שקידש יין בעל מום, אבל הקושיא למה הביא דין מגולה לגבי
קידוש במקומה עומדת. ומה שנראה לי בישוב קושיא זו, הוא שלכאורה
קושיית הגמרא ״אי למעוטי מגולה סכנה היא״ קשה להבינה, שהרי ההלכה
שמגולה פסול לקידוש צריכה להאמר, שאם לא חש על גילוי ושתה יין מגולה
לקידוש אין יוצא ידי קידוש. ואל תשיבני כיון שאסור משום סכנה אין
מברכין עליו בורא פרי הגפן ושום ברכה, שכן אמרו שהשותה שמן זית כמו
שהוא אינו מברך עליה כלל משום ד״אזוקי מזיק ליה״, ברכות ל״ה, ב׳
[בסוף], וקל וחומר שהשותה דבר שיש בו סכנה שאין מברך עליו, וכיון דאין
מברכין עליו בורא פרי הגפן בודאי אין מקדשין עליו. אבל באמת אין הנדון
דומה לראייה. שמן כמות שהוא אין בני אדם שותין אותו שטעמו לא ינעם
לחיך ולא עוד אלא שהוא מזיק להשותה אותו ולכן אין מברכין עליו, אבל
האוכל ושותה דברים שיש בהם סכנה בודאי מברכים עליהם הברכות
שראויות להם. שהרי ״חיך אוכל יטעם״ [איוב י״ב:י״א] ובודאי השותה יין

היקשו כלום על רש״י שהרי צריך לאמר יין צמוקים כשר ואף שמים רבים בו,
ויין הליסטון הוא יין של ענבים שאינם שורים אותם במים.

הסוג האחרון — על שמרים עיין לעיל — ממין יינות שפסולים למזבח
הוא מגולה. והנה משנה שלמה היא בסוכה סוף פרק ד׳ ״שהיין והמים
המגולין פסולין לגבי המזבח״ וכן בתוספתא מנחות פרק ט׳: ״מגולה... הרי
זה מום למזבח״. ובמעביר במסננת אם יש בו משום גילוי או לא נחלקו בו
חכמים ור׳ נחמיה במשנה דתרומות פרק ח׳, ז׳, אבל גם לר׳ נחמיה פסול
למזבח משום ״הקריבהו נא לפחתך״, סוכה נ׳, א׳, ועל פי זה אמרו בסוגיא
שלפנינו [בבבא בתרא] שרב בא למעט ביין מגולה שהעבירו במסננת. והנה אם
הלכה כר׳ נחמיה או כרבנן נחלקו בו רבותינו הראשונים. הרמב״ם בפירוש
המשנה לתרומות ובספר היד, פרק י״א, י״ד מהלכות רוצח פוסק כחכמים וכן
דעת הטור, יורה דעה סימן קט״ז, וכתב עליו הרב בבית יוסף [בד״ה משקין],
וידוע שההלכה כתנא קמא. ודברי הרב [יוסף קארו] תמוהין, שבאמת כמעט
לא מצינו חבר להרמב״ם בדבר זה, שכל הפוסקים פסקו כר׳ נחמיה, עיין
לדוגמא הלכות גדולות סוף הלכות קידוש והבדלה;[65] רב עמרם בסדורו סוף
ערבית של שבת;[66] הרי״ף בערבי פסחים[67] (ובעבודה זרה ל׳ מביא מחלוקת
חכמים ור׳ נחמיה בלי הכרעה);[68] ר׳ יצחק בן גיאת בשערי שמחה, חלק א׳,
עמ׳ ב׳; הרב בעל ספר העתים עמ׳ 204, 206; ור׳ יונה בשיטה מקובצת לבבא
בתרא צ״ז, ב׳. וכל אלו הראשונים הביאו דברי הגמרא שם שרב בא להוציא
יין מגולה ואף שהעבירו במסננת כר׳ נחמיה. וטעם אלו הפוסקים שפסקו כר׳
נחמיה הוא שקבלה בידי הראשונים (עיין מגדל עוז, [הלכות] חובל פרק ד׳, א׳)
שההלכה כאיבעית אימא, וכיון שאמרו בסוגיא שלפנינו, איבעית אימא וכו׳
כר׳ נחמיה, מוכח שלדעת התלמוד ההלכה כר׳ נחמיה. ועיין גם כן בשיטה
מקובצת לבבא בתרא קמא קט״ו, ב׳ שמביא דברי הר׳ מאיר הלוי שכתב: ״וקיימא
לן כר׳ נחמיה דסוגיין בעלמא כוותיה״, וברור שכיוון להסוגיא דבבא בתרא
כאשר ראה לנכון בעל ספר עתים לבינה בפירושו על ספר העתים במקום
הנ״ל. ועיין גם כן תוספות אנשי שם לתרומות הנ״ל, ודבריו נעלמו מעיני בעל
ספר עתים לבינה.

והנה הרמב״ם בפרק כ״ט מהלכות שבת ובפרק ו׳ מהלכות אסורי מזבח
מביא ההלכה שמגולה פסול בין למזבח בין לקידוש, אבל לא הזכיר מה

65   במהד׳ ירושלים (לעיל, הערה 18), עמ׳ 76-77.
66   ראה לעיל, הערה 19.
67   ראה לעיל, הערה 56.
68   בדפי וילנא, י׳ ע״ב.

שגם בלשון המשנה מעושן הוא כמו מעופש, וכפי מה שראינו זה אינו והעיקר
כמו שמפרש בספר היד שמעושן הוא כעין בישול. וצריך עיון שבהלכות שבת
לא זכר הרב שמעושן פסול לקידוש, והרי הוא פוסל מבושל ולפי דעתו מעושן
ומבושל שוים הם. וכן לא זכרו הטור והשלחן ערוך דין מעושן, ואף ששניהם
הביאו דעת הפוסלים מבושל. ולדעת הרמב"ם אליוסטין הוא גם כעין מבושל,
אלא שמשום שאינו מבושל לגמרי כשר בדיעבד למזבח ולקידוש גם לכתחילה.

וכבר הבאתי לעיל פירוש הרב בפירוש המשניות שלו על אליוסטין
[במנחות ח':ו'] וכאשר בתרגום העברי מספרו זה הלשון מקולקל, אמרתי
להביאו מכתב יד לשונו הערבי ולתרגמו. וזה לשון הערבי: "אליוסטן משמס
אעני אנה יגעל פי אלגראר ללשמס חתי יטיב כמתל מא יפעיל פי מצר, ואסם
אלשמס באליונאניה קאל בעץ אלשארחין אליוסטן". וזה תרגומו:
"אליוסטן — בערבי — משומש, רצונו לאמר שנותנים אותו — את היין
— בכדים (לא בבדים כאשר הוא בהוצאה הראשונה של פירוש המשנה) נגד
השמש עד שיטיב — טעמו — כמו שהם עושים במצרים; ושם השמש ביונית
הוא אליוסטן, לפי אשר יאמרו קצת מפרשים". והרב או ששמע וטעה או
שהמפרשים שקדמוהו כבר טעו והחליפו איליוס, שמש ביונית, באליוסטון
שמשמעו ביונית דבר שזרח עליו השמש הרבה. והמתרגם פירוש המשנה
לעברית טעה עוד ביותר וחשב כי "אלי" בראש התיבה הזאת הוא כמו "אל"
בערבית (= ה' בעברית קודם השם) וכתב יוסטן. וראיתי דבר זר מאד בפירוש
ר' גרשום לבבא בתרא צ"ז, ב' שכתב: "ליסטון ירוק שהפיג טעמו ונפק
מצורתו". וברור שהרב דרש סמוכים, וכאשר בברייתא שם נזכרו שני מיני
יינות שמראיהם שונים, יין כושי והוא שחור, בורק והוא לבן ולכן פירש
שאליסטון הוא ירוק! ועיין בערוך ערך אליוסטון שהביא דעת "יש אומרים"
שפירשו אילוסטון "יין שחור שיש בו טעם שמש", ואולי שנתחלף כאן טעם
במראה, וכיוונו לאמר שמראה היין כאילו שזפתו השמש, וזה אפשר, אבל
ירוק אי אפשר להעמידו כלל. ובפירוש ר' גרשום למנחות פ"ו, ב' מביא שני
פירושים לאליסטון: "יין מתוק הרבה, ל"א מתוק שנקדחו ענבים בחמה".
וברש"י שם בנדפס: "הלסטון שנתבשלו הענבים בחמה יותר מדאי" וזה
מסכים לפירוש התוספות שם פ"ז, א' בראש הדף, אבל ברש"י כתב יד הנדפס
בש"ס ווילנא הגרסא "יין מתוק מחמת השמש שהיו תולין את הענבים
להשמש", ועל זה השיגו התוספות שם, דאם כן מה בין יין אליוסטון ליין
צמוקים, שהצמוקים הם ענבים שנתיבשו בשמש. ומדברי התוספות ראיה
לדברי החכם צבי שהבאתי לעיל שיין צמוקים שכשר למזבח בדיעבד הוא יין
הנעשה מצמוקים שנדרכו ביקב ולא מאותם שנישרו במים, שאם לא כן לא

השאלתות עיקר הקושיא הוא מיין צמוקים שנעשה מן ענבים שכבר נתייבשו,
ואם כן הוא נשתנה מברייתו ומכל מקום כשר ואף שכלל גדול הוא שיין
נסכים שנשתנה פסול, ודברי פי חכם חן. ולפי דבריו נבין למה הביא הרמב"ם
ב[הלכות] אסורי מזבח שיין צמוקים כשר בדיעבד, אחר שכבר שנה בהלכות
שבת שיין שכשר לכתחילה לקידוש כשר בדיעבד למזבח, ויין צמוקים כשר
לקידוש לכתחילה. והתשובה על זה שהיינו אומרים שיין צמוקים פסול גם
בדיעבד למזבח ולא משום שנפגם אלא משום שנשתנה, ואין לך שינוי שפוסל
לקידוש, ויין מבושל פסול לקידוש לא משום שנשתנה אלא משום שנפסד
טעמו, ולכן הכפיל הרב ההלכה דיין צמוקים. וכן הכפיל ההלכה של יין
מגולה, שלולא כן היינו אומרים שלקידוש פסול משום סכנה אבל לניסוך
כשר. ומה שהביא הרב באסורי מזבח יין מבושל ואף שכבר הזכירו בהלכות
שבת, כדי לשנות כאחד השלשה יינות שפגומם מטעם אחד: מעושן, מבושל
והליסטון, שהוא לדעת הרב יין שהוחם בשמש וכולם משום בישול.

ודע שבפירוש המשנה [למנחות ח':ו'] פירש הרב "מעושן" בדרך אחרת
ממה שפירש בספר היד שלו, וכך לשונו בכתב יד הערבי של פירוש המשנה
הנמצא בבית אוצר הספרים של בית המדרש לרבנים בנויארק: "מעושן
הוא — בערבית — אלמדכן (מעושן-מעופש), רצונו לאמר שאם הכלי היה כלי
שיש לו ריח רע, היין מתעפש וזה נקרא מעושן". ובתרגום עברי של פירוש
המשנה שבדפוס הלשון מקולקל וכך כתוב שם: "מעושן רצונו לאמר שאם
היה לכלי ריח אותו היין היה בו הבל והוא הנקרא מעושן"; והבל הביא גם
הוא. ולפירוש זה מעושן הוא יין שריחו רע שאמרו עליו בבבא בתרא שפסול
גם לקידוש. אבל חזר בו הרב שבודאי הפירוש הזה אינו על דרך האמת, שלא
בלבד שמצאנו בכמה מקומות ענבים ופירות מעושנים שאי אפשר לפרש שם
בדרך הרב, אלא מעושן ממש, שמעלה עשן עליהם כדי לבשלם מעט (עיין
לדוגמא ירושלמי בכורים א', סוף הלכה ג', [ס"ג סוף ע"ד] "ענבים
מאובקותי" — כך צ"ל — "ומעושנות אין מביאין" וכן בירושלמי שבת
פרק ז', הלכה ג', דף י', א'). הרי לפנינו גמרא מפורשת בזבחים ס"ד, א': "[כל
העולים למזבח:] מאי טעמא? אמר רבי יוחנן: נסכים שמא יתעשנו" ושם אי
אפשר לפרשו בדרך אחרת ממה שפירש רש"י בו: "יתעשנו, כשיקיף את
המערכה בעשן המערכה וקיימא לן [במנחות פ"ו ע"ב] יין מעושן פסול". ועיין
גם כן בבא בתרא כ', ב': "האי דידן אפילו קוטרא דשרגא נמי קשיא ליה"
ופירושו שאפילו עשן נר של נר מחליש חריפות היין, ועיין שם בתוספות י"ח,
[ד"ה לא יפתח] ובשיטה מקובצת במקומו. ונראה שהרמב"ם בפירוש המשנה
נגרר אחר לשון ערבית, ובערבית "מדכן" משמעו שתיים, מעושן ומעופש וחשב

[משנה תורה, הלכות אסורי מזבח, ו':ט']

כתב הרב: "ואלו הן היינות הפסולין לגבי המזבח, המתוק והמעושן
והמבושל באש או בשמש או שנשתנה טעמו בבישול, אבל יין שמחממין
אותו בשמש ולא נתנה בו טעם בישול, וכן יין צמוקין ויין מגתו שלא שהה
ארבעים יום וכו' כל אלו היינות לא יביא לכתחילה ואם הביא כשר. יין
שנתגלה פסול לגבי מזבח" וכו'. וכתב על זה הרב בעל לחם משנה: "קשה לי
למה לא הזכיר רבינו ז"ל מה שאמרו בפרק המוכר פירות [בבא בתרא צ"ז
ע"ב] 'יין כושי בודק (לפנינו בורק עיין לעיל) הליסטון של מרתף של צמוקים
לא יביא ואם הביא כשר' ולא הזכיר מכל אלו אלא הליסטון לחוד ושתק מכל
השאר? גם שם 'קוסס מזוג מגולה ושל שמרים ושריחו רע לא יביא ואם הביא
פסול' ולא הזכיר מכל אלו אלא מגולה". והנה היה לו להקשות למה לא הביא
הרב חמר חיווריין, שאמרו שם פסול בדיעבד ולדעת הרמב"ן — עיין לעיל —
פסול גם לקידוש, ולדברי הכל למזבח. וכבר העיר על השמטות אלו הרב בית
יוסף באורח חיים [סימן] רע"ב, [ד"ה גרסינן].

ולפי מה שכתבנו לעיל כל ההשמטות שהשמיט הרמב"ם בצדק העלים
עיין מהם. יין כושי, בורק, והוא לבן, וחמר חיווריין אינן מן המובחרין
לדעת ר' יהודה שמקפיד על מראה יין, אבל לחכמים שהלכה כמותם, מראה
יין אינו מעכב כלל וכשרים אפילו לכתחילה, וכן מזוג, פסול הוא רק לדעת
יחיד ולא לדעת אלו החכמים שהלכה כמותם, וכבר אמרתי לעיל שהרב בעל
לחם משנה שכח דברי עצמו שכבר ראה הוא כי הרמב"ם פוסק שמזוג כשר.
והשמיט הרמב"ם 'של מרתף' שהוא סובר שרק להאומר שקוסס פסול
בדיעבד, ספק קוסס אינו מביא לכתחילה, אבל אם קוסס כשר בדיעבד ספק
קוסס והוא יין של מרתף כשר גם לכתחילה. וקוסס עצמו כשר, ושל
שמרים שיש מהן שכשר ויש מהן שפסול, וכן יין שריחו רע שפסול, הביא
הרב בהלכות שבת פרק כ"ט לענין קידוש. ולא חש להכפיל כל אלו ואף
שהכפיל ושנה באסורי מזבח יין צמוקים — ותימה על הרב בעל לחם משנה
שהעלים עיניו מדברי הרב במקומו! — ויין מגולה שכבר שנה אותם
בהלכות קידוש. ועל שמרים עיין גם כן דברי הרמב"ם בפי"ז, ו' מהלכות
אסורי מזבח. ובשאלתות [סימן] נ"ד, גרסת ר' אחאי בהסוגיא דבבא בתרא
צ"ז, ב' כך היא: "סימן כבלמ"יי" — על הסימן עיין גם כן בדקדוקי סופרים
במקומו, ובפירוש ר' גרשום ושם הסימן צריך תיקון — "יין כושי, יין בודק,
יין אליוסטון, יין של מרתף, יין של צמוקים, והא תני ר' חייא יין של צמוקים
לא יביא ואם הביא כשר". ויפה העיר שם הרב בעל העמק שאלה שלפי גרסת

בעל מום (עיין חלוף מנהגים סימן [יי"ט][64] שעוד בימי הגאונים לא בירכו בארץ
ישראל ברכת המזון אלא על יין חי) והקשו על זה ואמרו "עלויי עלייה", וכיון
שהמזוג משביחו וההלכה ששכר מידי דמשכר, יין מזוג כשר לכתחילה
למזבח. ועל ידי זה נבין גם כן החלוק לעניין יין מגתו, שכשר בדיעבד למזבח,
ורק לכתחילה אינו מביא — ובודאי זה רק מדרבנן, שבדברי תורה אין לנו
לכתחילה ובדיעבד, עיין גיטין ג', ב', ומצוה ועיכוב הוא דבר אחר לגמרי, ואין
כאן מקומו להאריך בכלל זה — ואילו בביאת מקדש, שתה יין מגתו פטור.
והחילוק הזה נוסד על ההצעה ששכר הוא דבר המשכר, ולכן בביאת מקדש
ששעורו ברביעית צריך שיהיה בן ארבעים יום ולא מזוג שיין מגתו או מזוג
אינו משכר, אבל נסכים שאין לך בהם פחות מרביעית ההין, הרבה יותר
מרביעית, גם מדרבנן מביא יין מגתו ומזוג, שבמדה גדולה כעין זו גם אלו
יינות משכרים.

ודע ששכר שכתוב בנסכים [בבמדבר כ"ח:ז'] ושלמדו ממנו בספרי "חי
ולא מזוגי", נדרש בתלמוד ובמדרש לעניין אחר, עיין סוכה מ"ט, ב'; ירושלמי
שם, סוף פרק ד'; פסיקתא דרב כהנא, [מהד' בובר], נ"ז, ב'; פסיקתא רבתי,
[מהד' איש שלום], פ', א'; תנחומא ובמדבר רבה על הפסוק "נסך שכר".
וצריך אני להעיר שאפשר שלדעת האומרים שכר חי ולא מזוג, יין מגתו פסול
גם בדיעבד, שהרי גם הוא אינו משכר וכמו שראינו, ואף שמשכר ביותר
מרביעית, הלא גם מזוג משכר בששתה הרבה, ואין שום חילוק ביניהם. אמנם
בתוספתא פרק ט' דמנחות, [מהד' צוקרמנדל, עמ' 526] אמרו שיין מגתו כשר
בדיעבד ומזוג פסול גם בדיעבד, אבל כבר ידוע שהתוספתא שלפנינו לא מיד
אחת יצאה, ואפשר שאלו ההלכות הסותרות זו את זו הן לחכמים שונים
שנחלקו בדרשה של שכר. ומה שיש לפקפק בדברינו דשכר ולא מזוג הוא
מחלוקת תנאים, והרמב"ם פוסק שכר אפילו מזוג, הוא שהרמב"ם בפרק כ"ט
מהלכות שבת [הלכה יי"ז] פוסק שמקדשין לכתחילה על מזוג ולכאורה אם
מזוג כשר גם למזבח לכתחילה, מה בא להשמיענו? אבל אין זו קושיא כל כך
שהרי כבר ראינו שבארץ ישראל דקדקו על יין חי גם לברכת המזון, [ולכן] בא
הרב להוציא מדעה זו, ואדרבה ממה שלא אמר הרב בפירוש ב[הלכות] אסורי
מזבח פרק ו' שמזוג אינו מביא לכתחילה מוכח כמו שכתבתי. וכאשר כמה
הלכתא גברתא יש ללמוד מדברי הרב בפרק ו' מהלכות אסורי מזבח על יינות
הפסולין, אמרתי לבארם.

64 מהד' מרגליות, ירושלים תרצ"ח, עמ' 81.

"כל ששתה רביעית יין בן ארבעים יום וכו', שתה מגתו, שתה פחות מרביעית
פטור, יתר מרביעית , בן ארבע בן חמש שנים חייב, בין שמזגו ושתאו וכו'
חייב". וכך הוא פירוש התוספתא: הלכה א') שתה רביעית בן ארבעים יום
חייב; הלכה ב') שתה — רביעית — יין מגתו פטור וכן אם שתה פחות
מרביעית יין בן ארבעים יום פטור; הלכה ג') שתה יין מגתו יתר מרביעית וכן
אם שתה יין מיושן — בן ארבע בן חמש שנים — יתר מרביעית חייב, ובאלו
שהוא חייב רק בשתה יתר מרביעית חייב גם על מזוג, אבל בששתה רביעית
יין בן ארבעים יום פטור אם הוא מזוג, והן הן הדברים שנאמרו בגמרא: "הא
ביותר מכדי רביעית", שבשתה יותר מרביעית חייב גם על מזוג. ולפי דרכנו
למדנו גם כן המקור לדברי הרמב"ם ז', ז' מהלכות אסורי מזבח שפוסק
שמביא יין "מאחר ארבעים יום לדריכתו עד שתי שנים או יתר מעט". ונושאי
כלי הרב לא מצאו מקור לזה, שבמנחות פ"ו ע"ב במשנה ובגמרא וכן שם
בתוספתא פו ק ט' נחלקו רבי וחכמים ביין ישן והוא יין אחר י"ב חודש שלרבי
לא יביא לכתחילה ולחכמים גם לכתחילה, אבל לא מצינו שום חילוק בין יין
ישן שכשר לכתחילה ובין יין מיושן, יותר משלש שנים, שאינו מביא
לכתחילה. והנה ברור שהמקור לדבריו הוא התוספתא בכריתות שמשוה יין
מגיתו ליין של בן ארבע בן חמש שנים, שעל שניהם אינו חייב בשלא שתה
יותר מרביעית משום שהם קלים, וכיון שאמרו שלדברי הכל יין מגתו אינו
מביא למזבח לכתחילה, יין מיושן גם כן לא יביא לכתחילה. ונראה שהרב גרס
"בן שלש בן ארבע" במקום "בן ארבע בן חמש" וכן מוכח מהמשנה בבבא
בתרא ו', ג' שמיושן הוא בן שלש שנים. אבל בודאי אי אפשר לומר
שהתוספתא בכריתות היא אליבא דרבי שאומר יין ישן לא יביא, שהרי לרבי
שם אמרו בגמרא ובתוספתא שגם יתר מי"ב חודש לא יביא ועל כרחך
שהברייתא כחכמים דרבי. ומתוספתא זו הוכיח הרמב"ם גם כן שיין ישן
נפגם טעמו ולא ריחו — עיין מה שכתבתי לעיל בזה — ובנכנס למקדש טעם
עיקר ולא ריחו, ולכן גם בששתה קוסס שריחו חומץ אסור להכנס, עיין דברי
הירושלמי דסוטה פרק ח' שהבאתי לעיל.

היוצא לנו מכל זה שתנא קמא ור' אלעזר שהלכה כמותו — עיין שם
בגמרא [בכריתות י"ג ע"ב] — סוברים ששכר מידי דמשכר הוא, והוא רביעית
בן ארבעים יום חי או יותר מרביעית ואפילו יין מגיתו ומזוג. ולפי זה הדרשה
בספרי ששכר הוא חי היא דעת יחיד, והרמב"ם פוסק כהרבים ששכר כל מידי
דמשכר, והברייתא בבבא בתרא [צ"ז ע"ב] שפוסל מזוג גם בדיעבד למזבח
היא דעת יחיד. ומתחילה חשבו בעלי התלמוד [בבבא בתרא] לאמר שיין מזוג
פסול למזבח גם בלי הדרשה מן שכר, משום שהמים פוגמים את היין ונעשה

העיון נראה שזה אם מזוג כשר למזבח הוא מחלוקת תנאים, והרמב״ם הכריע
מהגמרא שההלכה כמאן דמכשיר, והנני לפרש דברי.

כבר ראינו שלפי הספרי דרשינן מ״שכר״, חי ולא מזוג, אבל הרמב״ם
בפרק ה׳, ט׳ מהלכות נזיר כתב ״ולא דבר שנתערב בו היין והוא השכר״,
ולדבריו שכר הוא ההפך מיין חי, והוא דבר אחר שנתערב בו היין. ולפנינו
בתלמוד בבלי וירושלמי ושארי מקורות לא נמצאה דרשה זו, אבל נאמן
עלינו רבינו הגדול שכך מצא באיזה מקום ותמך יסודו עליה. ואולי שכך
גרס בספרי זוטא בנשא על הפסוק ״מיין ושכר״ וכו׳ [במדבר ו׳:ג׳], ויש ראיה
להשערה זו, שבכתב יד ממדרש הגדול על פסוק זה מובא בראשונה הדרשה
שיש לפנינו בספרי, ״חי אתה מנסך״ וגומ׳ ואחר כך נמצא מאמר נוסף וזה
לשונו: ״דבר אחר ׳מיין ושכר׳ שכר זה האמור כאן הוא שכר של תערובת
היין״.[63] ודעתי נוטה שהמאמר הזה לא העתיק בעל מדרש הגדול מספר היד,
שאין זה לשון הרמב״ם כצורתו, אלא שהוא מספרי זוטא, אשר היה לפני בעל
מדרש הגדול כנודע, והספרי זוטא הוא המקור לדברי הרמב״ם בהלכות
נזירות.

אבל גם בלי זה, מוכח ממקומות אחרים בתלמוד ובתוספתא שלא כל
התנאים דרשו ״חי ולא מזוג״. וזה יוצא לנו ממה שאמרו בכריתות י״ג, ב׳
שכהן ששתה רביעית אינו חייב אלא אחי אבל יותר מרביעית אפילו מזוג,
ואלו ההלכות למדו שם בגמרא משכר, שאינו חייב אלא במה שיש בו לשכר,
רביעית מזוג אינו משכר, יותר מרביעית אפילו מזוג משכר. והנה דברי
הגמרא שם, ״הא ברביעית הא ביותר מכדי רביעית״, אפשר לפרש שיותר
מרביעית מזוג באזהרה ולא במיתה, והיא דעת הראב״ד בהשגותיו, [הלכות]
ביאת מקדש, א׳, א׳, אבל הרמב״ם שם פוסק שביותר מרביעית מזוג הוא
חייב ופוסל עבודה. ודברי רבינו מפורשים בתוספתא כריתות פ״א, כי, אלא
שלפנינו שם טעות סופר הבולטת לעינים ורבנו היתה לפניו הגרסא כתקונה.
וזה לשון התוספתא [מהד׳ צוקרמנדל, עמ׳ 562]: ״איזהו שתוי יין? כל ששתה
רביעית יין בן ארבעים יום הימנו למעלה, שתה מגתו יתר **מרביעית** פטור,
שתה **פחות מרביעית**, בן ארבע בן חמש שנים חייב בין שמזגו ושתאו ובין
ששתאו חצאין חייב״. והמאמר ״יתר מרביעית״ עד ״בן חמש שנים״ אין לו
שום הבנה, ואם נשווה לו דברי התוספתא עם הברייתא ודברי הגמרא
בכריתות יצא לנו שהגרסא העיקרית, והיא שהיתה לפני הרמב״ם, כך היא:

---

63   וראה עתה מדרש הגדול לספר במדבר, מהד׳ צ״מ רבינוביץ, ירושלים תשכ״ז, עמ׳ ע״ז.

שמאוס[61] — יש לו מקום בדברי הגאונים. עיין בהלכות גדולות סוף הלכות
קידוש [והבדלה] שבמקום אשר לפנינו בגמרא, כיון דאם הביא כשר אנן אפילו
לכתחילה נמי, הוא גורס או מפרש דאם הביא כשר מברכינן עליה בורא פרי
הגפן, וכן בשאלות ותשובות מן הגניזה עמ' 26 בראש העמוד,[62] וכאשר בסוגיא
שלפנינו כל המשא ומתן הוא אם מקדשין על יין שאינו מביא לכתחילה, מוכח
שברכה וקידוש שוים, ואם מברכין עליו בורא פרי הגפן גם מקדשים עליו.

הסוג השני ממין יינות שפסולים למזבח הוא "מזוג" שלפי הברייתא
בבבלי בבא בתרא צ"ז, ב' ותוספתא מנחות פרק ט' פסול גם בדיעבד
למזבח. והנה הרמב"ם בפרק ו' מהלכות אסורי מזבח לא הזכיר שמזוג
פסול למזבח, והרב בעל לחם משנה במקומו שהעיר על קושיא זו, נראה
ששכח דברי עצמו, שבפירושו ל[הלכות] מאכלות אסורות י"א, ט' כתב בעצמו
שהרמב"ם סובר שמזוג כשר למזבח, משום שהוא מפרש דברי הגמרא בבבא
בתרא "אי למעוטי מזוג עלויי עלייה" לענין מזבח ולא רק לענין קידוש. וחכם
עדיף מנביא מביא שעכשיו שזכינו לפירוש רבינו גרשום — רצוני לאמר לפירוש
תלמידיו, ולא שהוא בעצמו כתבו — נראה שגם הוא פירש כן דברי הגמרא
[בבבא בתרא], וזה לשונו: "ואמאי אינו רשאי לנסך על גבי המזבח". ובודאי
פירוש זה מוכרח לדעת הרמב"ם, שבפרק כ"ט מהלכות שבת [הלכה י"ד]
מביא דעת חכמי המערב ומסכים עמהם, שאם ערב דבש אפילו כל שהוא
פסול לקידוש, ומזה שהכלל שיין פסול למזבח בדיעבד פסול גם לקידוש, בין
שהפסול מחמת פגימת היין, בין שהוא משום דבר אחר כדבש שפוסל בקרבן
מגזירת הכתוב. ולפי זה אם מזוג פסול למזבח פסול גם כן לקידוש, ואם כן
מה זה שהקשו "עלויי עלייה", והרי אם הוסיף דבש ביין נסכים גם כן
משביחו, ולענין קטורת אמרו "אילו נתן בה קורטוב של דבש אין אדם יכול
לעמוד בה מפני ריחה", ומכל מקום פסול מגזירת הכתוב ולכן פסול גם כן
לקידוש. ועל כרחך שפירוש מאמר הגמרא הוא כר' גרשום, שלא זו בלבד
שמזוג כשר לקידוש אלא אפילו למזבח, שעל ידי המזוג הוא משביחו וכשר
לכתחילה, וכוונת הגמרא שסמא מכאן — מהתוספתא דמנחות — מזוג שאין
טעם לפסלו. ואי קשיא הא קשיא: הא אמרו בפירוש בשני מקומות בספרי,
בנשא פיסקא כ"ג, [עמ' 27] ובפנחס פיסקא קמ"ג, [עמ' 190] "הסך נסך שכר
לה', חי אתה מנסך ואי אתה מנסך מזוג", ואם כן איך אפשר לאמר
שלהמסקנא בגמרא דבבא בתרא מזוג כשר אפילו לכתחילה למזבח? ואחר

61 בבבא בתרא צ"ז ע"ב, ד"ה למעוטי מאי.
62 ראה לעיל, הערה 57.

לא מצינו בגמרא דקוסס כשר בדיעבד למזבח, ואדרבא ממה שלא הקשו מהברייתא שבתוספתא מנחות פרק ט', שנאמר שם שקוסס "הרי זה בעל מום למזבח", על ר' יוחנן שקוסס מברכין עליו בורא פרי הגפן, נראה שלדעת הגמרא גם לר' יוחנן קוסס פסול בדיעבד למזבח, ואין דרכו של הרמב"ם לדחות דברים שמפורשים בגמרא.

ועתה נחזור לפרש המאמר שבגמרא דבבא בתרא "פלוגתא דר' יוחנן ור' יהושע בן לוי" שנילאו המפרשים לפרשו, ונאמר שעיקר הגרסא שם "פלוגתא דר' שמעון בן אלעזר ורבנן", או וחבריו, וכיוונו להמחלוקת שבין התוספתא דבבא בתרא והתוספתא דמנחות, כמו שכתבנו לעיל. ושאלת הגמרא פשוטה היא, שלא רצו לאמר שרב בא לפסול יין קוסס לקידוש, שזה תלוי במחלוקת ר' שמעון וחכמים, שלר' שמעון שמכשיר קוסס בדיעבד למזבח הרי הוא כשר לכתחילה לקידוש, ואמרו פלוגתא דר' שמעון וחכמים, והאם נאמר שרב לאו דברי הכל הוא? וכבר שגורה הרבה בפי הגמרא השאלה "נימא כתנאי אמרה לשמעתיה". וגרסת הספרים "ר' יהושע בן לוי ור' יוחנן" נשתבשה על ידי הסופרים שהיה נכתב בראשי תבות רשב"ל[60] (=ר' שמעון בן אלעזר) ורבנן, ופתרו הראשי תבות וקראו ר' יהושע בן לוי משום שלעיל ב[דף] צ"ה וצ"ו נחלקו ר' יהושע בן לוי ור' יוחנן ביין קוסס לענין ברכה. וראיה להשערה זו, שבכתב יד רומי (עיין דקדוקי סופרים) הגרסא "ר"י וריב"ל ורב יהודה ורב חסדא", והשלשה שמות האחרונים הם במקום ורבנן. ועיין גם כן בפירוש ר' גרשום, שכפי הנראה גרס "רב יהודה ורב חסדא", וכל אלו השינויים באו על ידי שהיה כתוב "ורבנן", והכוונה ל"חכמים" של ר' שמעון בן אלעזר, אבל הסופרים שלא ידעו ממחלוקת ר' שמעון ורבנן קראו בשמות אלו החכמים על פי הסוגיא דלעיל.

ודע שמה שכתבתי שלהרמב"ם קוסס פסול בדיעבד למזבח, [אינו] סותר דבריו בהלכות שבת פרק כ"ט [הלכה י"ז] שקוסס כשר לכתחילה לקידוש, שהכלל "שכל שפסול בדיעבד למזבח, פסול גם כן לקידוש", יש לו [הרבה יוצאים מן הכלל]. אמנם דעת הרמב"ם שם נוטה לדעת חכמי מערב שיין שיש בתוכו דבש כל שהוא פסול לקידוש וכן פוסל יין מבושל לקידוש, ואם כן אינו מחלק אם פסול יין נסכים הוא משום שהיין נפגם או משום דבר אחר (עיין לקמן על זה). בכל זאת אפשר שמחלק בין פסול של יין עצמו ובין פסול של ריח היין; וצריך עיון. ועוד צריך אני להעיר שהכלל שכלל הרשב"ם שכל שמברכין עליו בורא פרי הגפן מקדשין עליו — חוץ מיין

הראשונה שהשבתי על הפירוש הראשון של ר' יונה היא גם כן תשובה על
פירושו השני, שבודאי לשון הגמרא אינה סובלת לפירוש זה, ועוד שתשובה
אחרת בצדו, שאם נסכים להצעתו, שפשיטא שדבר שאין מברכין עליו בורא
פרי הגפן אין מקדשין עליו, אם כן מזה שאמר רב אין מקדשין על קוסס,
אנו למדים שסובר שמברכין עליו בורא פרי הגפן כר' יוחנן, ואין כאן קושיא
למה לא אמר בפירוש שמברכין בורא פרי הגפן על קוסס אבל אין מקדשין
עליו, שהרי בא זה ולימד על זה.

והנה כבר הבאתי לעיל הירושלמי דסוטה פרק ח' [הלכה ה', כ"ב ע"ד]
שקוסס יין גמור הוא לכל הדברים ומכל מקום פסול הוא ואפילו בדיעבד
למזבח, והוא בשיטת התוספתא דמנחות פרק ט', שהובאה בסוגיא שלפנינו
בבבלי. ולעומת זאת בתוספתא דבבא בתרא פרק ו' [מהד' ליברמן, עמ' 149]
אומר ר' שמעון בן אלעזר שאם הביא קוסס על המזבח כשר בדיעבד. ובודאי
ר' יהושע בן לוי שסובר שאין מברכין בורא פרי הגפן על קוסס אינו כר' שמעון
בן אלעזר, אבל ר' יוחנן אפשר שדבריו כדברי הכל שיש טעם לפסול קוסס
למזבח, ואף שיין גמור הוא לכל דבר. וכאשר נעלם דבר זה מכל אלו שנשאו
ונתנו בסוגיא זו אמרתי להרחיב הדבר ולבארו.

תמן בבכורות י"ז א' אמרו: "זבח ונסכים מה זבח שלא נשתנה אבל
נסכים שלא נשתנו", ובסוף הסוגיא שם: "זה נשתנה ריחו וזה לא נשתנה
ריחו". והיוצא מזה שנשתנה ריחו — ומכל שכן טעמו — פסול למזבח מן
התורה ומעולם לא נחלק אדם על זה ולכן הדלה הגפן על גבי תאנה יינו
פסול לנסכים. אבל זה רק בשנשתנה על ידי אדם, ובשנשתנה מאליו בזה
נחלקו ר' שמעון בן אלעזר וחכמים; ר' שמעון סובר שזה לא נקרא שינוי
ולכן אף שבקוסס בודאי ריח היין נשתנה לגמרי שהרי ריחו חומץ כשר
בדיעבד, וחכמים סוברים שגם שינוי מאליו הוא שינוי, ולכן קוסס פסול
בדיעבד, ואף שלכל הדברים קוסס הוא כיין גמור, שריחו חלא וטעמיה
חמרא, למזבח פסול משום שנשתנה. ואפשר גם כן שחכמים ור' שמעון
מחולקים בעיקר הדין אם שינוי ריח הוא שינוי יין, שר' שמעון סובר
שמזבח ונסכים אנו למדים שאם נשתנה טעם היין — על ידי בישול
וכדומה — וחכמים סוברים ששינוי הריח הוא שינוי יין, ולפי פירוש זה
הרמב"ם שפסק בפרק ו' מהלכות איסורי מזבח [הלכה י'] שאם "הדלה גפן על
גבי תאנה יינה פסול לנסכים מפני שנשתנה ריחו", לא הוצרך להביא שקוסס
פסול למזבח שקוסס הוא יין שנשתנה ריחו. וזה נראה יותר, שקשה לאמר
שהרמב"ם סמך כאן על מה שהביא בפרק כ"ט מהלכות שבת [הלכה י"ז] גבי
קידוש שקוסס כשר לכתחילה, ואם כן גם למזבח כשר בדיעבד, שהרי באמת

סופר תוסס במקום קוסס והמוציא לאור לא הרגיש בדבר והדפיס פעמיים תוסס במקום קוסס — ספר העתים עמ' 208-207, וטור אורח חיים [סימן רע"ב) לר' יוחנן שקוסס מברכין עליו בורא פרי הגפן גם כן מקדשין עליו, שריחו חומץ וטעמו יין נחשב כיין גמור לכל דבר. אבל לדעת ר' יונה שם אין מקדשין על הקוסס ואף שמברכין עליו בורא פרי הגפן. ולכל הדעות שאלת הגמרא "פלוגתא דר' יוחנן ור' יהושע בן לוי" היא תמוהה. לפירוש הרשב"ם השאלה היא למה לא אמר רב קוסס מברכין עליו בורא פרי הגפן ואנא ידענא דמקדשין עליו. ובודאי אין זו שאלה כלל, שאדרבא דברי רב מראים באצבע שיין קידוש צריך להיות משובח, ויש יינות שאף שמברכים עליהם בורא פרי הגפן מכל מקום אין מקדשין עליהם. ותדע שכך הוא, שהרי הוצרכו להביא ברייתות להוכיח שיין מגתו ומשוליה ומפיה כשרים לכתחילה לקידוש, ולא שאלו איך אומר רב שאין מקדשין עליהם כיון שמברכים עליהם בורא פרי הגפן. ועל כרחך שברכת היין וקידוש על היין הם שני דברים נפרדים, שיש יינות שטעמם כיין גמור ומכל מקום פסולים למזבח ולקידוש משום שאינם משובחים. ובאור זרוע, חלק א', סימן קס"ב הוכיח מדברי הרשב"ם בראש הסוגיא שיש יינות שמברכים עליהם בורא פרי הגפן אבל אין מקדשין עליהם. ומתרומה אין ראיה כלל, כיון שקוסס תרומה גמורה היא לא רצו חכמים לפסלה כדי שלא יטעה ויתרום מן החיוב על הפטור, ואף שבתורם קישות ונמצאת מרה אמרו תרומה ויחזור ויתרום (עיין תרומות פ"ג מי"א), הרי יין קוסס רוב בני אדם שותין אותו והוא היין הנמכר בחנות ולמה יקנסוהו, אבל למזבח ולקידוש אמרו שאינו מן המובחר.

וכפי הנראה, רבינו יונה הרגיש שפירוש הרשב"ם קשה להעמידו ולכן נטה מפירוש זה ומפרש הגמרא בשתי דרכים אלו. הדרך האחת היא שכיון שלר' יהושע בן לוי אין מברכין עליו בורא פרי הגפן בודאי אין הכל מודים שאין מקדשין עליו, ואם כן מאי קא משמע לן רב? ופירוש זה של ר' יונה תמוה עוד יותר מפירוש הרשב"ם, שמלבד שלשון הגמרא "פלוגתא דר' יוחנן ור' יהושע בן לוי" אינה סובלתו כלל, שכך היה לו לאמר "מאי קא משמע לן פשיטא", לא מצינו בכל הש"ס שיקשו על מאמר אמורא "פשיטא" הא כבר נאמר מאמורא אחר, ואטו מאן דלא ידע לדברי ר' יהושע בן לוי, לאו גברא רבא הוא, שיקשו למה ליה לרב להשמיענו הלכה שאנו יכולין ללמוד מדברי ר' יהושע בן לוי? גם הפירוש השני של ר' יונה אינו נוח כלל. הפירוש הזה הוא, ששאלת הגמרא היא אם רב סובר כר' יהושע בן לוי, פשיטא שאין מקדשין כיון שאין מברכין עליו בורא פרי הגפן, ואי כר' יוחנן היה לו לרב לאמר, יין קוסס מברכין עליו בפה"ג אבל אין מקדשין עליו. והתשובה

טועין, בלי שום ראיה כלל. ובאמת כל אלו הגאונים והראשונים לא נשאו ונתנו כלל ביין צמוקים למזבח, אלא העתיקו דברי הגמרא שלמזבח כשר בדיעבד, ולקידוש גם לכתחילה, ופירשו שלקידוש משמעו ששורה הצמוקים במים, אבל למזבח בשדרך את הצמוקים, והאי כדאיתא והאי כדאיתא, וזה מוכרח מדין של שמרים שפירשו, שהוא בשנתן מים על השמרים, ואילו של שמרים למזבח פירושו שדרך את השמרים וכמו שכתבתי לעיל. וראיתי להעיר שהרי"ף בערבי פסחים שמביא בשם רבוותא החילוק בין צמוקים שיש בהן לחלוחית קודם ששורה אותן לצמוקים שנתיבשו לגמרי[56] כיוון להגאונים רב פלטוי, רב צמח ורב האי אשר דבריהם מובאים בשערי שמחה לר' יצחק גיאת, חלק א', עמ' ב'. ועיין גם כן תשובת הגאון בחמדה גנוזה סימן ל"ה, ספר העתים עמ' 207 ושאלות ותשובות מן הגניזה עמ' 26.[57]

המין האחרון של יינות שדברו עליהם בגמרא דבבא בתרא הוא "יין קוסס, מזוג, מגולה, ושל שמרים ושריחו רע" ועליהם אמרו שם: "דתניא בכולן לא יביא ואם הביא פסול". ולפנינו בתוספתא מנחות פרק ט' בהוצאת הדפוס חסרה ברייתא זו, אבל ישנה לנכון בכתב יד ווינע של התוספתא וכן בפרדס יי"ז, ב' אלא שבפרדס חסר "קוסס".[58] וכך היא שנויה [במהד' צוקרמנדל, עמ' 526]: "שמן השרוי והשלוק והמבושל של שמרים ושל ריח רע הרי זה בעל מום למזבח. הקוסס והמזוג" — צ"ל והמזוג בו' ולא בי', שלשון התוספתא הוא עברית ולא ארמית — "והמגולה ושל שמרים ושל ריח רע הרי זה בעל מום למזבח". [ובתוספתא] הנדפסת דילגו הסופרים ההלכה שבין שני המאמרים אשר סופם שוה והוא המאמר "של שמרים ושל ריח רע הרי זה בעל מום למזבח" ולא ראו שבראשונה מדבר מהלכות שמן ובשנייה מהלכות יין. וכאשר דיני יינות אלו לענין מזבח נישנו, קיצרו רבותינו הראשונים בפירושם, והנני לבאר כל אחד ואחד.

הראשון הוא קוסס ואמרו על זה בגמרא [בבא בתרא צ"ז ע"יב]: "אי למעוטי קוסס, פלוגתא דר' יוחנן ור' יהושע בן לוי", וכבר נדחקו הראשונים לבאר קושיית הגמרא ועיין ברשב"ם ובשיטה מקובצת בשם עליות של רבינו יונה. ויש חילוק גדול גם לדינא בין השלשה פירושים שנאמרו בדבר זה. לפירוש הרשב"ם, והסכימו עמו כמה מהראשונים, (עיין לדוגמא רי"ף הנ"ל בערבי פסחים,[59] ר' יצחק בן גיאת בשערי שמחה חלק א', עמ' ג' — ושם טעות

56 לדף קי"ח ע"ב, דפי ווילנא כ"ב ע"ב.
57 הכוונה לגאוניקה (לעיל, הערה 24), חלק ב', עמ' 26.
58 ראה לעיל, הערה 20.
59 ראה לעיל, הערה 56.

שכשר בדיעבד למזבח הוא שוה בכל ליין צמוקים שכשר לכתחילה לשאר
מצות. ומה שמביאנו לידי ספק זה הוא שמזוג פסול גם בדיעבד למזבח
— עיין לקמן — ואם כן איך אפשר לאמר שאם שרו צמוקים במים המשקה
הזה כשר למזבח ואם נתנו מים ביין ענבים פוסלים אותו לגמרי, "יציבא
בארעא וגיורא בשמי שמיא"![55] הראשון שהעיר על זה הוא הרב המבי"ט
בתשובותיו סימן רנ"ב, שמביא בשם ר"ד (ראשי תיבות, ר' דוראן, הוא הרב
בעל התשב"ץ) בספרו אגרת חמץ, בכתב יד (ועתה כבר נדפס בספר יבין
שמועה ונקרא שם מאמר חמץ, עיין שם ל"ד, א'-ב') שהצמוקים מהפכים
המים שנשרו בהם ליין, ואין זה יין מזוג אלא יין חי. ועיין גם כן תשובות
בנו של המבי"ט, הרב מהרי"ט חלק ב', סימן ב' שקילס לדברי אביו שהביא
ראיה לדעה זו, ולפנינו במאמר חמץ מביא מבית התשב"ץ בעצמו ראיה זו, מזה
שיין צמוקים כשר בדיעבד למזבח ואף שמזוג פסול, ועל כרחך שהמים
שנשרו בהם הצמוקים אינם נחשבים למים כלל. ויפה השיב הרב בעל הכם
צבי בתשובותיו סימן ק"מ, שמהגמרא אין ראיה כלל לדעת התשב"ץ,
שאפשר לומר שיין של צמוקים שכשר בדיעבד למזבח הוא יין שנעשה
מצמוקים לא על ידי שרייה במים אלא על ידי מעצרת ואין בהם מים כלל,
אבל יין צמוקים שנעשה משריית הצמוקים במים בודאי פסול גם בדיעבד
משום מזוג.

וראיה גדולה לדעת החכם צבי ממה שאמרו בסוגיא שלפנינו שיי"של
שמרים" פסול גם בדיעבד. והנה אין ספק שיין של שמרים כאן משמעו,
שדרך השמרים עד שיצא כל הלחלוחית שבהם ולא שנתן מים עליהם, שאם
לא כן מה בין של שמרים למזוג, וכי שמרי ענבים טובים יותר מהענבים
עצמם, אתמהה! אבל במה שנוגע ליין שמרים של קידוש בודאי משמעו
שנתן מים על השמרים כמו שאמרו כאן: "אי דרמא תלתא ואתא ארבעה
חמרא מעליא הוא". אף אנו נאמר שיין צמוקים של מזבח הוא יין שנעשה
על ידי דריכת הצמוקים, ויין צמוקים של קידוש פירושו יין שנעשה על ידי
שריית הצמוקים ביין. ולא ידעתי מה היה לו להמחבר ספר עתים לבינה על
[ספר] העתים שהשיג בעמוד 203 מספרו [הערה קי"ב] על החכם צבי וכתב:
"ובמחילת כבודו אישתמטתי' כל דברי הגאונים הבה"ג והפסוקות ורב האי
ז"ל וזולתן דמפורש שמפרשי גם כן כהבנת המבי"ט". ובודאי עליו לבקש
מחילה מהרב החכם צבי, שעשה אותו לטועה בדבר שאין תנוקות של בית רבן

55 מליצה על פי יומא מ"ז ע"א ומקבילות שפירושה: "האזרח בארץ והגר בשמי
השמים?!" כלומר, זהו ההיפך מן הסדר הראוי, וגם כאן היתכן שצמוקים שרויים כשרים
למזבח ואילו יין מזוג פסול?!

שקוסס כשר בדיעבד (עיין לקמן מה שכתבתי בזה) לצורך גבוה החמירו, ואמרו שלכתחילה גם בסתם [של] מרתף ידקדק שלא יקח אלא יין שברור לו שאינו קוסס. ולא זו בלבד אמרו, אלא כמה וכמה חומרות נאמרו בדברים אלו, ביין ושמן של מזבח, שידקדק עד אשר שידו מגעת שיהיו מן המובחר. ואל תטעה בדברי הרשב"ם לייחס לו מה שלא עלתה על דעתו כלל לאמור, והוא שלר' יוחנן יין מרתף כשר לכתחילה. ודברי הרב ברור מללו, שבא לתרץ הקושיא שאפשר להקשות על ר' יהושע בן לוי שאומר שקוסס פסול בדיעבד, אם כן למה יין מרתף כשר בדיעבד? והתשובה על זה: הני מילי קוסס ודאי, אבל הכא מי יימר דהוא קוסס, והוא כאשר בארתי לעיל שאינו ספק גמור, שאם לא כן ספק דאורייתא לחומרא, אלא חששא בעלמא ובדיעבד כשר. ולר' יוחנן שיין קוסס כשר בדיעבד אין כאן קושיא כלל ולא הוצרך הרב לפלפל ולתרץ הברייתא אליביה, שהדבר פשוט שהיא מעלה בקדש.

ובפירוש ר' גרשום [בב"ב צ"ז ע"ב] כתב וזה לשונו: "של מרתף, אותו יין הנמכר בחנות שאינו כל כך יפה". והנה בודאי יש כאן טעות סופר שהרי שם צ"ה, ב' וצ"ו, א' אמרו בפירוש שיין הנמכר בחנות הוא יין קוסס, ואם כן יין מרתף הוא מין אחר. והרב בעצמו בפירושו על הסוגיא שלפנינו כתב וזה לשונו: "יין קוסס, הא פליגי רב יהודה ורב חסדא לעיל, דפליגי ביין הנמכר בחנות דהיינו קוסס". אבל בעיקר הדבר פירושו [של ר' גרשום] טוב ויפה, שיין מרתף הוא יין שאינו כל כך יפה, והוא שכל זמן שלא נבדק יפה אפשר שהוא קוסס או נפסד טעמו ולכן לכתחילה, בין לר' יהושע בן לוי, בין לר' יוחנן לא יקח אותו. ועיין גם כן בנימוקי יוסף בסוגיא שלפנינו שכתב: "של מרתף, סתם מרתף יש בו [יין] גרוע",[54] ובודאי בכוונה לא העתיק דברי הרשב"ם כצורתן שלא ליתן מקום לטעות לאמר שלר' יוחנן שאומר שקוסס כשר בדיעבד, של מרתף כשר לכתחילה. היוצא ממה שכתבנו הוא שכל הראשונים מודים שיין מרתף אינו מביא לכתחילה למזבח, ולכן הראשונים, הלכות גדולות סוף קידוש והבדלה, הרי"ף, ר' יצחק אבן גיאת בשערי שמחה חלק א', עמ' ב', בעל ספר העתים עמ' 206 ועוד ועוד הביאו להלכה שניהם, יין מרתף ויין קוסס, שלמזבח אינו מביאם לכתחילה ולקידוש כשרים לכתחילה. והשמטת דין של יין מרתף למזבח בספר היד צריך תלמוד, עיין לקמן עמוד מו-מז.

מכל אלו היינות הנזכרים לעיל, "יין צמוקים" הוא הסוג האחד אשר הראשונים האריכו דבריהם עליו להגבילו ולהתחימו, באיזה אופן יוכשר לקידוש ולארבע כוסות אבל שתקו להודיע דעתם אם יין צמוקים שאמר

שבקוסס סובר כהטור, ותירץ הרי"ן שמשום שהתלמוד שונה יין של מרתף ושל צמוקים כאחת לא נמנע הרי"ף להביאם כסדר זה ואף דמילתא שאינה צריכה היא. ותירוצו על הרי"ף הוא תירוץ הבית יוסף על הטור. ולכאורה יש סימוכים לתירוץ זה ממה שלא הביא הרמב"ם בהלכות שבת פרק כ"ט גבי יין קידוש הדין של יין מרתף והוא משום שכיון שפסק שיין קוסס כשר לכתחילה לא היה נצרך לאמר שספק קוסס כשר. וכן לא הביא הרב ב[הלכות] אסורי מזבח פרק ו' בהלכות יין נסכים הך דיין מרתף, משום שעד כאן לא אמרו בברייתא דבבא בתרא שיין מרתף אינו מביא לכתחלה, אלא למאן דאמר יין קוסס פסול בדיעבד ולכן יין מרתף, שהוא ספק יין קוסס, אינו מביא לכתחילה, אבל למאן דאמר יין קוסס כשר בדיעבד, ספק קוסס כשר גם לכתחילה. ומה שלא הביא הרב ב[הלכות] אסורי מזבח הדין דיין קוסס הוא משום שסמך על מה שכתב בהלכות שבת לענין קידוש שכשר לכתחלה, ומיניה שלנסכים אינו מביא לכתחילה. וראיה לזה דיין מרתף כשר גם לכתחלה ולמזבח למאן דסובר שקוסס כשר בדיעבד, היא ממה שבתוספתא דמנחות פרק ט', [מהד' צוקרמנדל, עמ' 526] לא נזכר יין מרתף עם שאר היינות שאינו מביא לכתחלה, משום שתוספתא זו היא בשיטת ר' יוחנן שקוסס כשר בדיעבד ולכן יין מרתף כשר לכתחילה, והברייתא בבבא בתרא היא בשיטת ר' יהושע בן לוי שקוסס פסול גם בדיעבד, ויין מרתף [שהוא] ספק קוסס אינו מביא לכתחלה. אבל לאחר העיון ראיתי שכל זה ליתא שלא בלבד שכפי שנראה לקמן יש פנים לדבר שדעת הרמב"ם היא שקוסס פסול בדיעבד למזבח, אלא שנוסח הדפוס של התוספתא בודאי מוטעה, והעיקר כגרסת כתב יד וויין והיא גם כן גרסת רש"י בפרדס יי"ז, בי'[53] שמסכימה להברייתא דבבא בתרא, ושנה "יין מרתף" בהך יינות שאין מביא לכתחילה. וזה מוכרח, שהרי כך לשון התוספתא: "הקוסס והמזיג וכו' הרי זה בעל מום למזבח, יין אליסטון וכו' לא יביא ואם הביא הביא כשר", ועל כרחך שבטעות נשמט בדפוס "יין מרתף", שהרי לפי התוספתא קוסס פסול גם בדיעבד.

וכשנדקדק היטב נראה שמעולם לא עלה על דעתם של הרי"ן והבית יוסף לאמר שלמאן שאמר קוסס כשר בדיעבד למזבח, של מרתף כשר גם לכתחילה, שמהסוגיא שלפנינו מוכח שלא כסברא זו, שהרי לא הקשו בגמרא על ר' יוחנן מהך ברייתא דיין מרתף, ועל כרחך או שר' יוחנן מסמא יין מרתף מהברייתא, או שאומר שתנאים נחלקו בדבר זה, ולא מצינו בכל הש"ס שהתלמוד יעבור בשתיקה על דבר כזה. והדבר פשוט שגם לר' יוחנן

חילוק בין מתוק על ידי שמש, והוא אלייסטון, למתוק מעיקרו. והרב נגרר אחר הטור [שם] שגם הוא כתב אלייסטון מתוק, וזה אפשר לפרש מתוק על ידי שמש שאלייסטון משמעו הודאי הוא שזרח השמש הרבה עליו, אבל בעל השלחן ערוך השמיט אלייסטון וכתב מתוק סתם, וסתם מתוק בודאי הוא מתוק מעיקרו. וצריך להעיר גם כן שמדברי השלחן ערוך ובעל המפה נראה שמבושל מובחר מאלייסטון, לדעת האומרים שיין מבושל כשר לקידוש, ובודאי דעה זו אי אפשר לקיימה לדעת הרמב"ם שכל עיקר החסרון של אלייסטון הוא שמבושל קצת, והיא נכונה רק לדעת האומרים שאלייסטון הוא משום מתוק, וזה שייך גם כן ביין קידוש, אבל מבושל פסול רק לענין נסכים, משום שנשתנה ואף שלא נגרע טעמו ושינוי מטבעו אינו מפסיד ביין קידוש כלל. ועיין לקמן פרק אחרון, סעיף ח'.

הרבה פירושים נאמרו באלייסטון כמו שראינו, אבל יין של מרתף לא פירשוהו הראשונים כלל חוץ מהמהרשב"ם [בבבא בתרא] שכתב שיין סתם במרתף קרוב להיות קוסֶ. ודומה לזה פירוש ר' גרשום, עיין לקמן. והרב בעל העמק שאלה [לשאלתות], סימן נ"ד, אות [ו'] חשב להשיג על פירוש הרשב"ם שהרי מום ביין פסול מן התורה, ואם כן ספק מום פסול, שספיקא דאורייתא לחומרא. ולא ירד לסוף דעתו של הרשב"ם, שלא אמר הרב מעולם שיין מרתף הוא ספק קוסס, אלא שיש לחוש שהוא אפשר שהוא של קוסס ובכמה דברים חששו חכמים ואף שהספק רחוק. ומהמשנה דמנחות ומסוגיתנו בבבא בתרא מוכח שכן הוא, שהרי שמרים בודאי פסולים למזבח, עיין [להלן] פרק אחרון סעיף ג', ומכל מקום אמרו שבדיעבד מפיה ומשוליה כשר ולא אמרינן ספק שמרים הוא ספיקא דאורייתא. והכל יודעים שהחששא של שמרים בשולי החבית יש לה יסוד יותר חזק מהחששא דקוסס ביין של מרתף. והרב בעל העמק שאלה נשתבש בנוסחא מוטעת של הלכות שבנוסחא א' [הנ"ל]. הפירוש "דרתח במעצרתיה" כתוב אחר "של מרתף" וחשב הרב שזה פירוש של מרתף, ולא שאל את עצמו, מה ענין מרתף ליקב, אתמהה! וכבר כתבתי לעיל שבנוסחא ב' של הלכות גדולות "רתח במעצרתא" הוא פירוש ל"אלייסטון" וכן פירש הרמב"ם, ולכן אין לזוז מפירוש הרשב"ם שיין של מרתף הוא משום חששא דקוסס. והרב הבית יוסף הקשה על הטור שכיון שהוא פוסק שקוסס — והוא יין שריחו חומץ וטעמו יין — כשר, למה לו לאמר שיין של מרתף כשר שאינו אלא ספק קוסס? ונעלם ממנו שכבר הקשה כן הרי"ן על הרי"ף בערבי פסחים[52] שגם הוא הביא דין יין של מרתף ואף

---

52 לדף ק"ח ע"ב, דפי וילנא כ"ב ע"ב ד"ה גרסינן.

שם בתוספות בדיבור המתחיל כרוך. אבל תירוץ רב אשי "חוליא דשמשא לא
מאיס חוליא דפירא מאיס" — או להיפך עיין חילופי גרסאות בדקדוקי
סופרים ובפירוש ר' גרשום — קשה להבין דמה ענין מתיקות היין ליין
מבושל! ונראה שגרסת הרמב"ם היתה משונה מגרסתנו, וראיה לזה שגם הר'
יצחק אבן גיאת לא היה לפניו בגמרא "חוליא דפירא" וכו'. וזה אני לומד
ממה שכתב הרב בשערי שמחה, חלק א', עמ' ב': "הליסטון יין טוב שמתחיל
להחמיץ ורוב טעמו יין וריחו יין". וכבר הרגיש המוציא לאור של ספר זה
שפירושו הוא נגד דברי הגמרא במנחות שאליסטון הוא מתוק, אבל קירב את
הרחוקים בזרוע, ואין מן הצורך להשיב על דבריו. ומתחילה חשבתי
"שמתחיל להחמיץ" משמעו שמתחיל לתסוס ולקבל הטעם העז שביין, וכבר
מצינו במשנה חולין א', ז' "התמד עד שלא החמיץ" ופירושו שעוד לא קלט
טעם היין מהחרצנים, ובלשון אנגלית פערמענטעד (fermented), ומפרש ר'
יצחק שאליסטון הוא יין מתוק שעוד לא החמיץ כראוי, פירוש שעוד טעמו
מתוק וקל. אבל חוזר אני בי שאם כן אליסטון הוא יין מגתו, וזה נגד דברי
הגמרא בבבא בתרא צ"ז והתוספתא במנחות פרק ט' שיין מגתו ואליסטון
הם שני מיני יינות. ועיין גם כן בהלכות גדולות סוף קידוש והבדלה, נוסחא
ב': "יין בורק יין כושי יין אליסטון כדרתיח במערצתיה ושל מרתף ושל
צמוקין" וכו'.[50] ולפי פירוש זה אליסטון הוא יין שנתחמם הרבה עד שרתח,
בזמן שהיין במערצת, וכמעט שאין בין פירוש זה לפירוש הרמב"ם ולא כלום.
אמנם בהלכות גדולות נוסחא א'[51] וכן בספר העתים עמ' 206, המלות "דרתח
במערצרתיה" הן אחרי "של מרתף" כאילו הן פירוש של מרתף אבל אין ספק
שזו טעות סופר והעיקר כמו שהוא בנוסחא ב', [ועיין] על זה פירוש הרמב"ם
לאליסטון, ועיין מה שכתבתי לקמן בפירוש של מרתף. ולכן חוכך אני לאמר
שטעות סופר [נפלה] בשערי שמחה וצריך לאמר "שמרתיח במערצי" במקום
"שמתחיל להחמיץ". וגם אם לא נקבל השערה זו ברור שאלה שלושה עמודי
ההוראה, בעל הלכות גדולות, הרמב"ם, והרי"ץ אבן גיאת לא גרסו בגמרא
דמנחות "חוליא דשמשא" וכו', ואף שאי אפשר לאמר מה שהיתה גרסתם שם.

והנה לפי נוסחתנו, שהיא נוסחת רש"י וחכמי צרפת ואשכנז, מתוק
מטבעו פסול למזבח ומתוק על ידי שמש אין מביאין ואם הביא כשר. וקשה
שגם אחד מהפוסקים לא הביא שמתוק פסול לקידוש, לפי הכלל שכל שאינו
ראוי למזבח כל פסול גם לקידוש. וביותר קשה על הרב בעל השלחן ערוך
[באורח חיים רע"ב:ג'] שכתב "מקדשין על יין מתוק" ולא הזכיר כלל כל שום

50   הוא מצטט מדפי ברלין תרמ"ח. ראה את שה"ג במהד' ירושלים הנ"ל (לעיל, הערה 18).

51   כלומר, דפי ווארשא תרלי"ה, יו"ד סוף ע"ג.

והטעות בסדורי הספרדים באה על ידי הסופרים שהפרידו המלה לשתיים וכתבו חוור יין — וכן הוא בכתב יד בבבא בתרא, עיין דקדוקי סופרים במקומו — ואלה אשר באו אחריהם קראו חוור יין וכאשר "חמר חוור יין עתיקי" היא קריאה בלתי אפשרית כלל השמיטו "יין". וכבר נשתבש על ידי הקריאה המשובשת שבסדורי הספרדים הרב אבודרהים בספרו (ובא לציון) שכתב: "חמר חור, יין שאינו לבן מכל וכל ולא אדום".[49] אבל שאר גדולי הספרדים כהרמב"ן בפירושו לתורה [דברים] ל"ב, כ"ו ובן דורו הצעיר של הרב אבודרהים התשב"ץ חלק א', סימן פ"ה כתבו לנכון חוורין, וכאשר נראה מהסוגיא שלפנינו [בבבא בתרא] חמר חוורין הוא יין שלבן ביותר. וטעו גם כן האומרים שחמר חוורין הוא יין הבא מחורן במזרח ארץ ישראל, שלא בלבד שמהסוגיא שלפנינו מוכרח שחמר חוורין הוא יין לבן (ובמחזור ויטרי עמ' 79 בברייתא דפטום הקטורת הגרסא "יין לבן ישן" במקום "חורין עתיקי") אלא שעל פי חוקי לשון ארמי שם התואר מחורן הוא חורניא או חורנינא ולא חורין, ולכן במשנה ובגמרא אשה מחורן [מכונה] חורנית ולא חוריינית. וביחזקאל כ"ז, י"ח נזכר "יין חלבון" ופירש רש"י "יין לבן מבושל", ונראה שרש"י חשב כי חלבון הוא מן חלב = לבן, ולפי זה "חמר חוורין" הוא כמו "יין חלבון", אבל יפה ראה הרד"ק שחלבון שבמקרא הוא שם מקום ועד היום הכפר חלבון אצל דמשק הוא מקום שמגדלים בו יין הרבה.

הסוג השני ממין השלישי של היינות הכשרים בדיעבד למזבח ולכתחילה לקידוש הוא "אליסטון", של מרתף, ושל צמוקים" והם יינות שנשתנו טעמם מיין רגיל. והרבה פירושים נאמרו באלייסטון — אליאוס, "שמש" ביונית, ומזה אלייסטון יין שזרח עליו השמש הרבה, עיין בערוך ערך אלייסטון ובפירוש המשנה להרמב"ם מנחות סוף פרק ט' שלא בדיוק קצת — עיין לקמן. ובטעם חסרונו, רש"י, ר' גרשום, רש"י והתוספות מפרשים שהוא יין מתוק אלא שנחלקו איך ממתיקין אותו (בפירוש ר' גרשום צריך לאמר שנקדחו במקום שנקרחו!) — עיין במנחות פ"ו, ב' ופי"ז, א'. אבל לדעת הרמב"ם בפירוש המשנה שם ובספר היד, [הלכות] אסורי מזבח פרק ו', ט' חסרונו הוא משום שמחממין **היין** — לא **הענבים** כמו שפירשו הראשונים שהזכרתי — בשמש והוא קרוב למבושל אלא שמבושל ממש פסול גם בדיעבד וזה רק לכתחילה. ולפירוש הרמב"ם הקושיא בגמרא [במנחות פ"ז ע"א] מרישא לסיפא, אינה ממתוק לאלייסטון אלא ממבושל לאלייסטון, ולרבינא שתרץ "כרוך ותני" או ששניהם פסולים בדיעבד או ששניהם כשרים בדיעבד, עיין

49   אבודרהם השלם, מהד' שמואל קרויזר, ירושלים תשכ"ג, עמ' קכ"ו.

צריך שיהא בהן מראה יין. וקרוב לאמר שהם מפרשים המחלוקת בין
החכמים ורבי ביין ישן למזבח כמו שפירש רש״י וכפשוטם של דברים
בתוספתא דמנחות, שחכמים סוברים שחכמים סוברים יין שנשתנה מראהו כשר גם לכתחילה
למזבח ורבי אומר לא יביא, וחכמים של ר׳ יהודה בברייתא דפסחים בשיטת
רבי, והברייתא דיין כושי הוא גם כן כרבי וחכמים של ר׳ יהודה, ופסקו
כמותם שסוגיא דשמעתא בבבא בתרא בשיטתם. והשאלה ״חמר חיוורייו
מהו״ היא גם כן אליבא דחכמים של ר׳ יהודה משום שנשתנה לגמרי כמו
שכתבו התוספות, והתשובה ״אל תרא יין״ וכו׳ היא גם כן אליבא דחכמים
ואינה שוה ממש לדברי רבא בפסחים ק״ח ע״ב, שיין לבן ביותר גרוע
משנשתנה מראהו. והרשב״ם מפרש השאלה של חמר חיוורייו שלנסכים
נשאלה (ברמב״ן יש כאן טעות סופר וצ״ל ״מה שדחק הרב ר׳ שמואל״ ולא
״הרב רש״י״), והשואל לא ידע הברייתא דיין בורק, ואפשר שלא ידע גם כן
הברייתא דפסחים או דעתו שבנסכים חכמים מודים לר׳ יהודה. ומהתוספות
[בבבא בתרא] נראה גם כן שהם מפרשים שלנסכים נשאלה השאלה אלא שהם
מחלקים ביין לבן קצת, והוא בורק, לחיוורייו שהוא לבן ביותר. וצריך עיון
גדול בדברי הטור [או״ח סימן] רע״ב שכתב ״בורק פי׳ לבן **ביותר**״ והוא הפך
ממש מדברי התוספות ולא מצאתי לאחד מהראשונים שפירש בורק לבן
ביותר. ואפשר שהטור הוציא זה מדברי הרמב״ן שכתב שצריך לגרוס בודק
דלא תקשי אחמר חיוורייו, ואם כן בורק הוא כמו חיוורייו וזה האחרון הוא
יין שהוא לבן ביותר. אבל מדברי הרמב״ן אין ראיה כלל, שלא נראה לו לחלק
בין לבן קצת או לבן ביותר ולכן גרס בודק במקום בורק, ולא משום שסובר
שבורק הוא לבן ביותר. והרב ר׳ יצחק בן גיאת בשערי שמחה שנשתמש בו
הטור בהרבה מקומות כתב בחלק א׳, עמי ב׳: ״בורק לבן״, והרשב״ם
במקומו: ״לבן ורע״, וביד רמה להר׳ מאיר הלוי, ״יין בורק[48] שנשתנו מראיו״,
ואף אחד אין בהם שכתב ״לבן ביותר״. וראיתי להעיר שהיד רמה מפרש
השאלה חמר חיוורייו שלקידוש נשאלה, ונראה שדעתו נוטה לדעת הרמב״ן
שאף בדיעבד פסול. ועיין בפרק האחרון ממאמר זה סעיף ד׳.

ודע שעל ידי הסוגיא שלפנינו נעמוד גם כן על עיקר הגרסא בברייתא
דפטום הקטורת. בכריתות ו׳, ב׳ ובירושלמי יומא ד׳, ה׳, [מ״א ע״ד] וכן
בסדורי האשכנזים הגרסא ״חוורין״ (אין בין חיוורייו, חוורין, חוריאו,
חיווריאו ולא כלום שכולם צריכים להקרא חֲוַוְרָיָן, והוא על משקל עבריין מן
עבר וכן חוורין מן חוור, לבן בלשון ארמי) אבל בסדורי הספרדים ״חורי״.

48 אבל בדפ׳ וווארשא תרמ״ז, הנפוץ היום: בודק.

חמר חיווריין מהו, והרי מחלוקת ר' יהודה וחכמים היא בפסחים? ועל ידי
קושיא זו הוכרח הרב לאמר שיין שנשתנה מראהו פסול בדיעבד גם לנסכים
ולקידוש, וכושי שאני כמו שאמרו בסוכה ל"ו, א' לענין אתרוג, ובמקום בורק
הוא גורס בודק. ותמיה אני על רבינו שלא הביא תוספתא מפורשת במנחות
ט', ט': "ושנשתנה מראיו לא יביא ואם הביא כשר", ועל כרחך שיש מי
שסובר שאין שינוי מראה פוסל בדיעבד ביין, ולא כדבריו שלא נחלקו חכמים
ור' יהודה כלל בענין זה, ושר' יהודה מפרש דברי התנא קמא. וכבר אמרתי
לעיל שהרמב"ן יחיד בדעה זו ושכל רבותיו וחבריו ותלמידיו נחלקו עליו.
ולדעתם יש לפרש שהשאלה חמר חיווריין היא רק אליבא דר' יהודה שאומר
שבד' כוסות צריך שיהא בהן מראה יין וכל שכן שפסול למזבח, ובכל זאת
אפשר שזה דוקא ביין שהיה מראהו טוב ונפסד אבל חמר חיווריין שכך הוא
טבעו מודה שכשר וזהו טעמו ביין כושי ובורק. ובאה התשובה על זה, "אל
תרא יין כי יתאדם", שיין לבן ואף שכך הוא מטבעו פסול לר' יהודה ולא
הכשיר אלא ביין כושי ובורק מפני שמראיהן מראה יין ואף שאינן מן המובחר
כמו שכתבתי.

והתוספתא שיין שנשתנה מראהו אין מביא למזבח לכתחילה ואם הביא
כשר, אפשר לפרשה בב' דרכים. לפירוש רש"י במנחות פ"ז, א' שטעמו של
רבי שיין ישן לא יביא משום שנפסד מראהו, התוספתא הזאת היא אליבא
דרבי, ולפי סגנון לשונה נראה שכן היא סוף דברי רבי שם. ולהרמב"ם שיין
ישן לא יביא משום שנפסד טעמו, "נשתנה מראהו" כאן משמעו שנשתנה
קצת לשחור ולבן, וכמו שאמרו שיין כושי ובורק מתחלתו כשר בדיעבד לר'
יהודה, כך אם נשתנו [למראה] כאילו כשרים בדיעבד לר' יהודה ולחכמים גם
לכתחילה. וצריך אני להעיר שאף שהרמב"ם והרמב"ן מחולקים בעיקר הדין
אם שינוי מראה פוסל ביין, שלהרמב"ם גם למזבח כשר ולכתחילה,
ולהרמב"ן לקידוש גם לדיעבד פסול ובדיעבד, אבל שניהם מפרשים המשנה דמנחות
יין ישן לא יבוא בדרך אחת והוא, כמו שכתב הרמב"ם בפירוש המשנה (עיין
לעיל) שזה מטעם שנפסד טעמו. ובזה תסור ההשגה שהשיג התשב"ץ, חלק א',
סימן נ"ז על הרמב"ן, שאיך אפשר לומר כמו שסובר הרב ששינוי מראה פסול
לקידוש גם בדיעבד, אם יין ישן ואף שנשתנה מראהו כשר בדיעבד גם למזבח?
ולפירוש הרמב"ם קושיא זו ליתא, שאין פגמא של יין ישן משום שינוי מראה
שלו כמו שפירש רש"י אלא משום שינוי טעמו. ובפירוש המיוחס לרבנו גרשום
[לבבא בתרא] מפרש השאלה חמר חיווריין מהו בין לנסכים בין לקידוש והוא
בשיטת בעל הלכות גדולות ושאר ראשונים שהבאתי לעיל, שהביאו ההלכה
דיין כושי ויין בורק לענין קידוש ואף שלא הביאו דעת ר' יהודה שד' כוסות

והנה בתחילה אבאר הסוג הראשון מהמין השלישי, אלו היינות שמשונים במראיהם, והם יין כושי ובורק. השאלתות, בעל הלכות גדולות, ר' יצחק בן גיאת, ספר העתים עמ' 206 ושאר הראשונים שאחריהם הביאו להלכה הברייתא שיין כושי ובורק כשרים לכתחילה לקידוש, אבל הרי"ף, הרמב"ם והרא"ש השמיטוה. והרמב"ם לא בלבד שלא זכרה בהלכות שבת לענין קידוש אלא אפילו בהלכות אסורי מזבח פרק ז' שסידר שם יינות כשרים ופסולים שתק מלהביא ב' יינות אלו וכבר תמהו רבים עליו, אבל לא העירו שהרמב"ם הלך כדרכו בדעת הרי"ף וגם הוא עבר עליהם בשתיקה.

והנה כבר הבאתי לעיל הברייתא דפסחים ק"ח, ב' ופרשתיה שחכמים ור' יהודה חלוקים ביין שנשתנה מראהו, כיין ישן שאבדה אדימותו, שחכמים מתירים אפילו לכתחילה בין למזבח בין לקידוש ור' יהודה פוסל גם בדיעבד לקידוש וקל וחומר למזבח, וקרובה מחלוקתם למחלוקת חכמים ורבי בסוף פרק כל קרבנות ביין ישן,[47] אלא שר' יהודה מחמיר עוד יותר מרבי. ולפי זה הברייתא דיין כושי היא כרבי שנשתנה מראהו כשר בדיעבד למזבח, ולכן השמיטוה הרי"ף והולכים בדרכו שהם פסקו כחכמים שיין ואף שנשתנה מראהו כשר לכתחילה למזבח ואין צריך לאמר שכשר לקידוש.

אמנם כבר כתבתי לעיל שהרמב"ם בפירוש המשנה, ועיין גם כן בספר היד, אסורי מזבח, ז', ז' שכתב "יין ישן מכמה שנים הרי זה כשר והוא שלא יפסיד טעמו", מפרש מחלוקת חכמים ורבי ביין ישן משום שלרבי יין ישן מפסיד טעמו. ולדבריו היה אפשר להעמיד הברייתא דיין כושי כחכמים של ר' יהודה, שגם הם סוברים שלמזבח יין שנשתנה מראהו אינו מביא לכתחילה ורק בד' כוסות אמרו שמותר לכתחילה, על פי הכלל "כיון ד'אם הביא כשר' אנן אפילו לכתחילה". והתשובה על זה, שהרמב"ם מדייק מסוף הסוגיא שלנו שפתר רבא השאלה "יחמר חיווריין מהו" ואמר "אל תרא יין כי יתאדם", ופסוק זה הביא רבא בעצמו בפסחים ק"ח ע"ב לפרש טעמו של ר' יהודה שבד' כוסות צריך שיהי בהן מראה יין, ומזה הוציא הרב שכל הסוגיא כאן היא אליבא דר' יהודה.

והחילוק בין חמר חיווריין ליין כושי ובורק הוא, שיין כושי והוא יין שמראהו שחור, מראהו מראה יין, ששחור אדום הוא אלא שלקה, כמו שאמרו בנדה י"ט, א', ובורק הוא שנתלבן קצת כמו שכתבו התוספות [בבבא בתרא], אבל חמר חיווריין פסול הוא גם בדיעבד למזבח וכן לקידוש. ועיין ברמב"ן בפירושו על בבא בתרא במקומו שהקשה: מה שאלה היא זו

"מנחתם ונסכיהם", מה שפוסל בזה פוסל בזה, ועיין מה שהעירותי לקמן
בעמ' סז-סח בסעיף ב' של הפרק האחרון ממאמר זה.

המין השלישי של יינות שאינם כשרים לכתחילה למזבח אבל כשרים
לקידוש הוא יין כושי, בורק, הליסטון, של מרתף ושל צמוקים שאמרו
עליהם בגמרא: "והא תניא בכולן לא יביא ואם הביא כשר". גם כאן לא
העירו האחרונים שהברייתא ישנה לפנינו בתוספתא מנחות פרק ט, ט,
[מהד' צוקרמנדל, עמ' 526] ובמסורת הש"ס נסמן מנחות פ"ו ושם במשנה לא
נזכר רק הליסטון, ולא שאר יינות המנויים בגמרא. ואלו היינות ממין
השלישי הן אלו שמראיהם או טעמם משונה מיין הרגיל. יין כושי הוא יין
שנשתנה מראהו והוא שחור ככושי כמו "אתרוג הכושי" במשנה סוכה פרק ג',
ו' (ואם אתרוג כזה כשר, הוא חילוף מנהגים בין בני ארץ ישראל ובני בבל,
עיין כפתור ופרח, פרק י', מהד' לונץ, עמ' קס"ה). ודומה לו בורק שהוא יין
שמראהו נוטה ללבן כמו שפירשו כמעט כל הראשונים ובתוכם הגאונים שכל
דבריהם דברי קבלה. עיין הלכות גדולות, הל' קידוש והבדלה בשתי
הנוסחאות; ר' יצחק אבן גיאת, שערי שמחה, חלק א', עמ' ב'; בעלי התוספות
[ד"ה חמר] ור' מאיר הלוי ביד רמה בפירושיהם לבבא בתרא צ"ז ע"ב, שכולם
גרסו בורק ב"ריש" וכן הגרסא בתוספתא מנחות פרק ט' הנ"ל בדפוס ובכתב
יד. ותימה גדול על הרב ר' שמואל אביגדור שבפירושו על התוספתא הגיה
בוהק במקום **בורק**.[44] ואצל הראשונים לא נמצא כלל הגרסא **בודק** חוץ
מבערוך שבערך "ברק" מביא דעת יש אומרים שגורסים: "**בודק** שהוא קשה
ובודק את כל הגוף", והסכים לפירוש זה הרמב"ן בחידושיו לבבא בתרא כדי
לקיים דעתו שלבן פסול לקידוש ובדעה זו הוא יחיד ונחלקו עליו כל
הראשונים. ובשאלתות, סימן נ"ד לפנינו הגרסא **בודק**, אבל קרוב לודאי שיד
הסופרים במעל הזה שלא ידעו בורק מהו זה וכתבו בודק במקום בורק.[45]
וידוע לכל הרגיל בשאלתות ובהלכות גדולות שלרוב גרסותיהם שוות
שמחבריהם היו בני דור אחד ובני ארץ אחת (עיין מה שכתבתי בספרי בלשון
אנגלית געאניקא, חלק א', עמ' 97 וגומר) וכאשר גרסת הלכות גדולות היא
בורק, בודאי בודק בשאלתות הוא טעות סופר.[46]

44 במנחת בכורים, דפי וילנא, דפי ע"ד: "ויהבוהק גרסינן לבן" אבל בפירושו השני על
אתר — מצפה שמואל — הוא גורס "ויהבורק" וצ"ע.
45 לפנינו בדפוסי השאלתות כתוב רק "יין בודק".
46 ואכן חכם מנביא וברוב כתבי היד של השאלתות כתוב "בורק" וכדומה. ראה
מהד' ש"ק מירסקי, שאילתא ס', כרך ג', ירושלים תשכ"ד, עמ' קמ"ו בשה"ג וגם בפירושים
על אתר.

שלא נאמר במשנה "ואם הביא פסול" כאשר נאמר שם במבושל ומעושן, דייק ר' חייא [בבבא בתרא] שמפיה ומשוליה כשר בדיעבד למזבח, ומיניה לכתחילה לקידוש. והנה מסתימת לשון המשנה והגמרא הדבר בספק אם יין שיש לו קמחין בודאי, פסול בדיעבד למזבח ולכן גם לקידוש או שגם יין זה כשר בדיעבד למזבח ולקידוש לכתחילה. ובהגהות מרדכי בסוגיא שלפנינו נמצא כתוב [בדפי וילנא, צ"א ע"ב]: "יין שיש לו קמחין כיון דפסול לנסכים כדמוכח במנחות פרק כל קרבנות אין אומרים עליו קידוש היום". ובמשנה דמנחות שם: "ר' יוסי בר' יהודה אומר: שיש בו קמחין פסול" ולזה רמזה ההגהה שבמרדכי. ובארחות חיים, חלק א', ס"ד ע"א, מובאת דעה זו בשם תוספות אבל בתוספות שלפנינו ליתא. והרב בשלחן ערוך סימן רע"ב השמיט דעה זו ואף שבספרו בית יוסף רמז על הארחות חיים, אבל בעל המפה מביאה [בסעיף ג'] בשם יש אומרים. ותמיה אני על האחרונים שלא העירו שהרמב"ם בפירוש המשנה שלו כתב בפירוש "ואין הלכה כר' יוסי ברבי יהודה" וכן בספר היד שלו לא הזכיר שיין שיש בו קמחים פסול, ונראה קרוב לודאי שמפני טעם זה לא חש לה הרב להביאה בשלחן ערוך.

ולא זכיתי לרדת לסוף דעתו של רבינו הגדול דודי זקני הגר"א ז"ל שבבאורו לאורח חיים כתב, וזה לשונו: "ור' יוחנן בעי שם (במנחות פ"ז) אליביה". והמעיין שם יראה, ששאלת ר' יוחנן "הקדיש יין פסול מהו שילקה" אין עניינה כלל למחלוקת חכמים ור' יוסי [בר' יהודה] אלא שאלה כללית, אם מקדיש יין שפסול למזבח, מבושל, מעושן, גלוי, נעבד אם לוקה כשמקדיש בעל מום למזבח, ולר' יוסי [בר' יהודה] השאלה הזאת גם כן במקדיש יין שעלו בו קמחין. והרמב"ם אף שפוסק שלא כר' יוסי [בר' יהודה] מביא בספר היד, אסורי מזבח, פרק ו', ג' דברי ר' יוחנן. ולא בלבד שהשאלה הזאת היא גם אליבא דחכמים אלא שהיא כוללת גם כן פסולי שמן ולבונה, עיין שם במנחות פ"ה, ב' ופי"ז, א'. ולעניין יין, סידרה הגמרא שאלה זו אחר דברי ר' יוסי [בר' יהודה] משום שתנא זה הזכיר הפסוק "תמימים יהיו לכם" שגם ביינות מום פוסל, אבל בודאי לא נחלקו עליו חבריו בזה שהרי גם הם אומרים שיש יינות שהם בעלי מום למזבח, אלא שנחלקו אם קמחין מום הוא או לא. והמפרשים לא פירשו איך למד ר' יוסי [בר' יהודה] מהפסוק "תמימים יהיו לכם ומנחתם" שקמחין פוסלין ביין, שהרי הכל מודים שיש מומים שפוסלים היין אלא שחכמים סוברים שקמחין אין בו מום. ונראה שהדרשה של ר' יוסי [בר' יהודה] היא מיוסדת על מה שאמרו שם במשנה פ"ה, א' שבמנחה אם העלה אבק פסול ור' יוסי [בר' יהודה] סובר שקמחין של יין הוא כמו אבק של סולת וכשם שאבק פוסל במנחה כן קמחין פוסלין ביין וזהו מה שאמר

הגיעו" ועל פי התוספתא הזאת הגיה בעל קרבן העדה את הירושלמי. ולשוא
שיבש הנוסחא שלנו שהיא בודאי העיקרית, שלפי הגהתו הירושלמי סותר
[את עצמו] בתוך כדי דיבור. בראשונה הוא אומר "ונמכר בחנות לשם יין",
ומזה דוקא בחנות שסתם יין חנות גרוע — עיין לעיל — אבל שלא בחנות לא,
ומסיים "והמוכר לחבירו יין סתם ונמצא קוסס הגיעו" והוא שלא בחנות,
אתמהה! ותימה על הרב בעל קרבן העדה שהגיה הירושלמי כדי להעמידו על
פי דעת יחיד, ולא ראה שבתוספתא שם [בהלכה ז'] חכמים חולקים על ר'
שמעון בן אלעזר ואומרים "חבית של יין" — לא אמר לא "זה" ולא
"למקפה" אלא סתם, עיין בבא בתרא צ"ה, ב' מחלוקת אמוראים בזה —
"אני מוכר לך, נותן לו יין יפה" ור' שמעון בן אלעזר חולק על זה ואומר
"המוכר יין לחברו", רצונו לאמר שמכר לו חבית יין סתם, "הגיעו". ולפי זה
הירושלמי דסוטה בשיטת חכמים הוא ולכן אמרו, שאף שבחנות יין קוסס
נמכר לשם יין, במוכר לחבירו יין סתם נותן לו יין יפה ולא קוסס. ופירוש זה
מוכרח שבסוף הסוגיא בירושלמי אמרו "לית לך אלא שהוא אסור על גבי
המזבח", ו"אסור" בודאי משמעו שפסול גם בדיעבד, ומזה שהירושלמי
בשיטת חכמים עומד, שלר' שמעון יין קוסס אם ניסכו על המזבח יצא כמו
שאומר שם בתוספתא, ועיין מה שכתבתי לקמן על קוסס למזבח.

המאמר האחרון בברייתא דסוטה ירושלמית הוא: "ואסור בהורייה
ובהיתר נדרים ועל ביאת המקדש". גם בפירוש מאמר זה לא דקדקו בו
כהוגן מפרשי הירושלמי. הרב בעל פני משה הראה מקום על הסוגיא
בכריתות [י"ג ע"ב] שיין מגתו הרי הוא באזהרה בביאת מקדש (עיין לקמן מה
שכתבתי בזה), ולא ראה שהברייתא דירושלמי מדברת מקוסס ולא מיין חדש,
ואף שברוב הדברים שוים הם, בכל זאת בהך דביאת מקדש חילוק גדול בין
שני מינים אלו. יין מגתו ברביעית הוא רק באזהרה משום שאינו משכר
ואימעט משכר, אבל קוסס משכר ואם הוא כיין בודאי אינו רק באזהרה אלא
אפילו במיתה.

[סוגיית בבא בתרא צ"ז ע"ב ופירושה]

אחר שבארנו הסוגיא בירושלמי על יין מגתו ויין קוסס נחזור להסוגיא
בתלמוד שלנו בבבא בתרא צ"ז. המין הראשון של יינות שכשר גם לכתחילה
לקידוש ובדיעבד למזבח הוא יין מגתו והמין השני הוא יין מפי ומשולי
החבית. ועל המין האחרון אמרו במשנה דמנחות סוף פרק ט', פ"ו, ב' - פ"ז,
א': "אינו מביא מפיה מפני הקמחים ולא משוליה מפני השמרים", ומזה

וכו׳ ומובא ברמב״ם [הלכות] אבל יי״ג, ז׳. ומשום שבימיו כבר היו מנהגים
שונים לא כתב שמברין ביין, אלא שבמקומות שנהגו כן, לא ישקו בזכוכית
לבנה שלא לבייש את העניים שאין יינותיהם טובים.

והנה אף שאין ספק שהמנהג הישן היה להבריא ביין כמו שמוכח
מהמקומות שרמזתי עליהם, בכל זאת כבר אמרתי שבברייתא דסוטה
ירושלמית לא כיוונו לסעודת הבראה אלא לברכה האמורה על הכוס בבית
האבל. ודברי הירושלמי אין להם פירוש אחר, אלא על פי מה שמובא
מירושלמי מגילה ד׳, ד׳ (ולפנינו ליתא, והחכם המחבר ספר אהבת ציון
וירושלים לא העיר על זה) בשערי שמחה לר׳ יצחק אבן גיאת, חלק ב׳, עמ׳
סי״ה וזה לשונו: ״והתם״ — בירושלמי דמגילה — ״נמי, ברכת אבלים שהן
אומרים בביה״כ, תנחומי אבלים מה שהן אומרין בשורה״. ושם מביא הרב
שתי תשובות מהגאונים רב נטרונאי ורב פלטוי שעוד בימיהם היה המנהג
בכמה מקומות (בארץ ישראל?) כשחוזרין מן הקבר עם האבל **לברך על
הכוס** ״ברוך אתה יי״י דיין הרחמים וכו׳ ברוך מנחם לב אבלים וזו היא
כניסתן באבילות״. וכשחזרו מן הקבר עמדו בשורה כידוע, ולכן בירושלמי
במקום הנ״ל אמרו מה שהן אומרים בשורה [וקראו ל]הן ״תנחומי אבלים״
על שם שביכרו הברכה ״ברוך מנחם לב אבלים״, וכאשר ברכה זו טעונה כוס
אמרו בירושלמי דסוטה שמותר לאומרה על יין קוסס. ואפשר גם כן שבמקום
בביה״כ (= בית הכנסת) בירושלמי הנ״ל צריך לאמר בביה״א (= בית
האבל). ועיין במסכת סופרים פרק יי״ט, ט׳, [מהד׳ היגער, עמ׳ 334-335] על
ברכת אבלים בבית האבל שהיו אומרים על הכוס, ושמחות סוף פרק יי״ד
״המברך בבית האבל אינו מברך [ברכה] רביעית [של ברכת המזון]״, אבל אם
לזה כיוון הירושלמי דסוטה היה אומר **״ומברכין** בו את האבל״ ולא **״ומנחמין**
בו את האבל״, ולכן העיקר כמו שכתבתי.[43]

ונשאר עוד אצלנו לפרש סוף הברייתא דירושלמי. המאמר ״ונמכר בחנות
לשם יין״ הוא מקביל למה שאמרו בבבלי בבא בתרא צ״ה, ב׳ ״יין הנמכר
בחנותו״ וזהו יין קוסס כמו שאמר שם רב חסדא ״גבי חמרא דאקרים״ —
[שהוא] יין קוסס [לפין] הרשב״ם — ״למה ליי. אבל מה שנאמר בירושלמי
״והמוכר לחבירו יין סתם לא מכר לו יין קוסס״ לא נמצא לו דבר מקביל
בפירוש בתלמוד שלנו. ובתוספתא בבא בתרא פרק ו׳, י׳, [מהד׳ ליברמן, עמ׳
149] שנינו: ״ר׳ שמעון בן אלעזר אומר המוכר יין לחבירו ונמצא קוסס

---

43   על ניחום אבלים ביין ראה רל״ג בעצמו, פירושים וחדושים (לעיל, הערה 38), חלק
שני, עמ׳ 63-80 וכן אחד מתלמידיו המובהקים, הרב טוביה פרידמן, באר טוביה, ירושלים
תשנ״ב, עמ׳ כ״ד-כ״ה.

אבל רבינו תם בספר הישר שלו, [חלק התשובות,] הוצאת מקיצי נרדמים, עמוד 82 דעתו כדעת הרמב"ם, שאין כוס ארוסין מדינא דגמרא, וזה לשונו שם: "ואע"ג דלא מצינו כוס בתלמוד אלא אמרינן בריך שית, יש לנו לתפוס דרך הישרה הואיל ונהגו כוס ורב יהודאי הנהיגו". וכיון הרב לבה"ג ראש הלכות כתובות שכתב: "ברכת חתנים מאי מברך, בורא פרי הגפן, שהכל ברא לכבודו" וכו'.[40] ובודאי מכאן אין מוכח כלל שבעל הלכות גדולות הנהיג כך, אלא שכבר היה המנהג הזה נהוג בימיו, ודברי רבינו תם שלא בדיוק קצת שכך היה לו לאמר: וכבר מצינו המנהג הזה בהלכות גדולות של ר' יהודאי.[41]

ודע שמסֵדר הדברים בברייתא דירושלמי מוכח שלא כפירוש המפרשים שפירשו ש"מנחמין בו את האבל" משמעו לעשר כוסות שהיו משקין את האבל כמו שאמרו בכתובות ח', ב' ובסוף שמחות, שכל אלו שנזכרו קודם זה, "מברכין, מזמנין, מקדשין" ענינים מצוות האמורות על הכוס וכן בודאי משמעו של תנחום אבלים. והרב בעל שיירי קרבן במקומו כתב: "מכאן משמע דניחום האבלים דוקא ביין וכן הדין כדאמרינן ע', א', — סנהדרין ושכח לסמן את המקום — 'לא נברא יין אלא לנחם אבלים' אך לא ראיתי דבר זה מבואר בפוסקים". [ותימה] ששכח הרב שכבר הביאו הפוסקים המאמר מאבל רבתי (ולפנינו ליתא!): "מקום שנהגו לנחם אבלים בבצים ועדשים מאכילים, מקום שנהגו בבשר ויין מאכילין". עיין שערי שמחה לר' יצחק אבן גיאת, חלק ב', עמ' נ"א, ומשם ברמב"ן תורת האדם, אחוי הקרע, ס"י, ד' (והוא מביא בשם ר' יצחק אבן גיאת "תניא באבל" ושתי מלות אלו אינן לפנינו בשערי שמחה!),[42] וטור יורה דעה, [סימן] שע"ח. וכבר נראה מירושלמי ברכות ג', א', [ו' ע"א] שגם בימי האמוראים היו המנהגים שונים, ויש מקומות שהיו מברים ביין ויש בעדשים ובצים כמו שנהגו עתה, ומפני הקלקול שהיו שותין ומשתכרין נתבטל המנהג להבריא ביין. ועל השכרות בבית האבל עיין שם בירושלמי ובבבלי כתובות ח', ב', ובשמחות בסוף המסכת, ועיין גם כן מועד קטן כ"ז, א' "בראשונה היו משקין בבית האבל"

40   במהד' ירושלים, חלק ב', ירושלים תש"ס, עמ' 222 וראה דיון וספרות שם בעמ' 224, הערה 11.

41   רל"ג דבק כאן בשיטתו שרב יהודאי חיבר את ספר הלכות גדולות (לעיל, הערה 24), חלק א', עמ' 95 ואילך. לדעות אחרות ראה לדוגמא שמחה אסף, תקופת הגאונים וספרותה, ירושלים תשט"ו, עמ' קס"ז-קע"א; עזריאל הילדסהיימר במבוא להלכות גדולות, חלק א', ירושלים תשל"ב, עמ' כ"ח-מ"א; ונחמן דנציג, מבוא לספר הלכות פסוקות עם תשלום הלכות פסוקות, ניו יורק וירושלים תשנ"ג, עמ' 175-180.

42   אינני יודע איזו מהדורה עמדה בפני רל"ג. ראה עכשיו ח"ד שעוועל, כתבי רמב"ן, חלק ב', ירושלים תשכ"ד, עמ' ר"יד.

בהדין כסא ובמה דאית ביה״, והמנהג הזה היה נהוג עד זמנינו אצל אחינו
בני ישראל שבסינגאלי כפי אשר נראה מסדר התפלה שלהם הנדפס
באמסטרדם שנת תקכ״ט, דף מ״ה, ב׳.[37] אבל קשה לאמר שכבר בימי
תלמוד ארץ ישראל נתפשט המנהג לקדש בכוס של ארוסין. גם קשה העלמת
עין של הראשונים מהירושלמי, שהרמב״ם שסובר שאין ברכת ארוסין
צריכה כוס מדינא פוסק שלא כהירושלמי ורבינו נסים שמחלק בין ברכת
ארוסין לנשואין כאשר כתבתי לעיל גם כן אינו מסכים לדעת הירושלמי,
וכבר נדע שלא מצינו בין הראשונים כרבינו נסים והרמב״ם אשר דברי
הירושלמי שגורים בפיהם תמיד. ולכן נראה לי שעיקר הגרסא בירושלמי
היא ״ומקדשין בו״ – או עליו – ומשמעו כפשוטו שמקדש על יין קוסס
בשבתות ובימים טובים כאשר אמרו בגמרא שלנו. והמלות ״את הכלה״
הוסיפו הסופרים אשר דרשו סמוכים, וכאשר מיד אחר זה נאמר ״ומנחמין
בו את האבל״ חשבו ש״מקדשין״ פירושו מקדשין את הכלה.

וראיתי להעיר שהראשונים מביאים מירושלמי מאמר שנזכר בו כוס של
ארוסין ונשואין אבל לפנינו ליתא. וזה לשון הרוקח סימן שנ״ב: ״ירושלמי
בכיצד מברכין על היין פרי הגפן, מה נשתנה יין הואיל ועסקיו מרובין, ממנו
לקידוש ולהבדלה, ממנו לארוסין ולחופה, כיוצא בו פת ממנו לחלה
ולמצה״. גם הראבי״ה סימן צ״ח, [חלק א׳, עמ׳ 77] מביא מאמר זה
מירושלמי בשינויים קטנים, אבל צדק החכם המוציא לאור ספר ראבי״ה
שהעיר שמקור מאמר זה הוא ״ספר ירושלמי״ – קובץ פירושים על
הירושלמי – שהיה להם להראשונים ולפעמים קיצרו שמו וקראוהו
״ירושלמי״.[38] ולא מצינו ברכות ארוסין ונשואין על הכוס לא בבבלי ולא
בירושלמי, והמקור היותר עתיק שמזכיר מנהג זה הוא מסכת סופרים פרק
י״ט, ט, [מהד׳ היגער, עמ׳ 335-334] שנתחבר בימי הגאונים, ועיין גם כן במגן
אבות להרב המאירי, עמוד ל׳ עד ל״ב שכפי הנראה לא הטיל ספק בדבר,
שבזמן התלמוד היו אומרין ברכות ארוסין ונשואין על הכוס.[39]

37   והשוה לדברי רל״ג בחלק הלועזי של ספר זה, פרק ה׳, סימן ו׳, הערות 5-6.

38   על ״ספר ירושלמי״ זה יש ספרות עניפה. ראה רל״ג בעצמו, פירושים וחדושים
בירושלמי, חלק ראשון, נויארק תשי״א, עמ׳ כ״ח, קי״ד-קי״ה; אפטוביצר המובא ע״י רל״ג
בפנים; ולאחרונה דניאל שפרבר, סידרא ג (תשמ״ז), עמ׳ 83-81 והספרות שם בהערה 1; .T
Kwasman, *Untersuchung zu Einbandfragmenten und ihre Beziehung zum Palastinischen*
Talmud, Heidelberg 1986; וכן יעקב זוסמן, ״שרידי ירושלמי – כתי״י אשכנזי״, קובץ על
יד, סדרה חדשה ספר י״ב (כב), תשנ״ד, עמ׳ 1-120.

39   במהד׳ לאסט, לונדון תרנ״ט = מהד׳ יקותיאל כהן, ירושלים תשמ״ט, עמ׳ ס״ה-ע׳.

מהראשונים כפי הנראה לא גרסו כלל "יין" בברכות מ"ח, ב', עיין שם ברא"ש
ובטור אורח חיים [סימן] קצ"ז, ובכ"י הנדפס בספר בית נתן "יין" ליתא.
ורבינו ישעיה נוסחא מוטעית נזדמנה לפניו בביצה כ"א, א' שגורס "ומזמנין
עליה ומברכין [עליה]", ולכן הוכרח לדחוק את עצמו ולפרשה בדרך שפירש,
אבל כל הראשונים וכן בספרים שלנו הנדפסים ואלה אשר בכתב יד הגרסא
שם "מברכין ומזמנין" וכן במשנה דחלה ובמשנה דדמאי.

והמאמר "ומקדשין בו" — בכתב יד של שרידי ירושלמי "ומארשים בו
את הכלה" — אי אפשר לפרשו בדרך אחרת אלא שלדעת הירושלמי ברכת
ארוסין צריכה כוס מדינא ולא כמו שכתב הרמב"ם סוף פרק שלישי
מהלכות אישות: "ונהגו העם להסדיר ברכה זו" — של ארוסין — "על כוס
של יין". ועיין באור זרוע, חלק א', סוף סימן תשנ"ב שכתב: "וכמו שבע
ברכות דחתן וכלה שתקנו על הכוס כדאיתא בירושלמי דסוטה דפ' כשם".
ולפנינו בפרק "כשם", והוא הפרק החמישי של מסכת סוטה, לא נזכר דבר
מענין זה. וברור שאישתבש ספרא וכתבו "כשם" במקום "משים" = משוח
מלחמה, והרב בעל אור זרוע כיוון להבריית בפרק משוח מלחמה שאנו
עסוקין בה.[35] והרב לא העתיק דברי הירושלמי כצורתן שלא הוזכר שם כלל
ברכת נשואין אלא ברכת ארוסין, אבל אם ברכת ארוסין צריכה כוס קל
וחומר ברכת נשואין. עיין דברי רבינו נסים בראש לכתובות דף ח' [פרק א',
סימן ט"ז] ובטור אבן העזר [סימן] ס"ב ודברי האחרונים, בית שמואל
במקומו וביאור הגר"א לאבן העזר [סימן] ל"ד שכתבו שכוס עיקרו בחופה
ולא בארוסין.

וחוכך אני לאמר שגרסת הספרים "ומקדשין בו את הכלה", ואף שכפי
שראינו היתה כבר לפני הרב בעל אור זרוע, גרסא מוטעית היא, והרבה
טעמים לי להשערה זו. הלשון "מקדשין בו את הכלה" הוא חדש לגמרי
ומעולם לא שמענו אלא "ברכת חתנים" ולא ברכת כלות, ואף שמצינו
"מברך לכלה" בפרקי דרבי אליעזר, סוף פרק י"ב. ועוד מה זה "מקדשין בו
את הכלה"? האם מקדש בכוס של יין, הרי הוא מקדש בכסף או בשטר
ומברך ברכת ארוסין על הכוס! (אבל עיין חילוף מנהגים, סימן כ"ח:
"מקדשין את החתן בשבע ברכות".) אמנם בסדר ברכות ארוסין לרבינו
סעדיה גאון כפי אשר נעתק מכתב יד בסדור רב עמרם הוצאת פרומקין,
חלק ב', דף קצ"ו, א'[36] נמצא שאחר ברכת ארוסין אומר החתן לכלה:
"אריסת לי ומקודשת לי אנתי פלוניתא בת פלוני לדילי אנא פלוני בר פלוני

---

35   מאידך, יתכן שבעל אור זרוע ציטט מהזכרון והפנה לפרק "כשם" בטעות.

36   וראה עתה סידור רב סעדיה גאון, ירושלים תשי"א, עמי צ"ז.

בו". והנה משנה שלמה שנינו ראש פרק ג' של עירובין, "בכל מערבין ומשתתפין חוץ מן המים ומן המלח", ולפי זה לכאורה קשה גם אם נאמר שקוסס אינו כיין מערבין ומשתתפין בו, שלא יהא אלא חומץ, הלא אמרו בעירובין כ"ט, א' שמערבין בו.[33] ונראה שכיוונו כאן בירושלמי לשיעור יין קוסס, שהוא כיין ממש דיין שיעורו לעירוב שתי רביעיות, וחומץ כדי לטבל בו, עיין שם בגמרא דעירובין. ומה שאמרו [בירושלמי] "ומברכין עליו" פשוט שכיוונו לברכת בורא פרי הגפן שנחלקו בה בתלמודנו ר' יהושע בן לוי ור' יוחנן ושאר אמוראים, עיין בבא בתרא צ"ה, ה', ב'; צ"ו, א'; וצ"ז, ב'. ועיין גם כן ירושלמי גיטין סוף פרק ג' [מ"ה ע"ב] שפירשו מחלוקת ר' יהושע בן לוי ור' יוחנן בדרך אחר, ולפי דעת הירושלמי הכל מודים שקוסס יין גמור "בשנמצאו חומץ דהא". ועיין מה שהעירותי לקמן על זה. וממה שאמרו [בברייתא] "ומזמנין עליו" מוכח שלדעת הירושלמי ברכת המזון צריכה כוס בשלשה וכבר נחלקו בזה רבותינו הראשונים, עיין המקומות שרמז עליהם דודי זקני הגר"א ז"ל בבאירו לאורח חיים קפ"ב, ותמיהה גדולה שלא העיר על הירושלמי דסוטה.

ודע שסגנון לשון ברייתא זו שבירושלמי קרוב מאד לסגנון של המשניות דמאי א', ד' וחלה א', ח' שבשבתיהן אמרו "מערבין, משתתפין, מברכין ומזמנין" כמו שהוא בירושלמי. וכבר נחלקו רבותינו הראשונים בהך דמברכין בחלה א', ח' שרש"י, ביצה כ"א, א' פירש "מברכין ברכת המוציא", אבל רבינו ישעיה הראשון מפרש "מברכין ברכת המזון", עיין ספר המכריע שלו, [ריש] סימן ג'. ומהירושלמי שלפנינו מוכרח כפירוש רש"י, שבברייתא זו אי אפשר לפרש "מברכין" בדרך אחרת אלא מברכין בורא פרי הגפן, וזה מקביל לברכת המוציא במשנה דחלה, וכן "מזמנין" בירושלמי אי אפשר לפרשו בדרך אחרת אלא שמסדר ברכת המזון עליו וזה כפירוש רש"י [בביצה] על "מזמנין" דחלה שהוא מברכין עליה ברכת המזון. ולדעת ר' ישעיה במקום הנ"ל "מזמנין" במשנה [חלה] פירושו, שמצטרף לזמון, והוא על פי דעת הרי"ף והגאונים שלא אמרו אפילו אחד אכל ירק מצטרף [ברכות מ"ח ע"א] אלא לעשרה אבל לשלשה פת דוקא.[34] והנה במה שנוגע לדברי המשנה [חלה] בודאי יש להם פנים לכאן ולכאן, אבל הירושלמי אי אפשר לפרש בדרך זו, שהרי בכל מקום ששתיית כוס מצרפת לאו דוקא כוס של יין אלא כל משקה כמו שכתב ר' ישעיה בעצמו בפסקיו על ברכות נ"ג, ב'. והרבה

33 כלומר, בחומץ.

34 ראה ברכות מ"ח ראש ע"א; אוצר הגאונים שם, הפירושים, עמ' 82, סימן רל"א; והרי"ף על אתר, דפי וילנא, דף ל"ה ע"ב.

בשאר [עניינים] יין קוסס — וכן יין מגתו השוה לו — הוא יין גמור. ומכל מקום פקפקו ואמרו "וההן בן סורר ומורה צריכה" שאפשר, שאף [ש]אלו היינות הם יינות גמורים לכל דבר, אינו נעשה בן סורר ומורה על ידי שתייתם, משום שאינו חייב אלא על שתיית יין שממשיך לזוללות ושכרות וכמו שאמרו שם בבבלי : "הכא משום אימשוכי הוא ובכל שהוא לא מימשיך".

ועיין ברמב"ם, ממרים פרק ז', ד' שכתב "או שתה יין מגתו פטור", ולא הוצרך הרב לפרש מהו "יין מגתו" שבכל מקום משמעו יין פחות ממ' יום, בין למזבח בין לקידוש, בין לביאת מקדש בין לבן סורר ומורה. ובבבלי סנהדרין במקום הנ"ל אמרו "ויין [נמי] עד ארבעים יום [לא מימשיך]",[32] ואין זו שאלה כמו שצידד הרדב"ז בפירושו על הרמב"ם אלא מאמר פשוט כמו שכתב רבינו מאיר הלוי בספרו יד רמה במקומו. אבל בהלכות תעניות ה', ז' גבי תשעה באב באר הרב דבריו בפירוש וכתב : "אבל שותה הוא יין מגתו שיש לו שלשה ימים או פחות", ששם האיסור משום שמחה ויין שאינו בן שלשה ימים אינו משמח. ודברי הרב בעל לחם משנה בפירושו על ממרים במקום הנ"ל אינם מדויקים, שבאמת לא היה שום צורך לרבינו לאמר שיין מגתו הוא עד בן ארבעים יום כמו שבארתי. ואי קשיא הא קשיא למה פסק רבינו שנעשה בן סורר ומורה באוכל בשר מלוח פחות משלשה יום ואילו בגמרא אמרו "הכא משום אימשוכי הוא ובכל שהוא לא מימשיך", וכבר נתקשה בזה הרדב"ז. ונראה שהרמב"ם מפרש כל הסוגיא שם לענין יין מגתו ולא לענין בשר, ושאלת הגמרא "הכא מאי", אם גם כאן יין מגתו פירושו בן שלשה ימים או שיין מגתו כמו יין מגתו בקידוש ובנסכים. והתשובה על זה, "התם" גבי תשעה באב האיסור לשתות יין הוא "משום שמחה כל זמן שהוא **שלשה ימים**" — כך גרס הרב במקום "כשלמים" שלפנינו שהוא אשגרא מהך דלעיל — "נמי אית ביה שמחה הכא משום אימשוכי הוא ובכל שהוא" — בײן שהוא קל — "לא מימשיך, וײן" — המושך לבו של אדם לשכרות — "הוא בן ארבעים יום". ודע שהרמב"ם לא הביא כלל מה דינו של קוסס בבן סורר ומורה, וטעמו אחרי שפסק שײן מגתו אינו נעשה עליו בן סורר ומורה שאינו ממשיך, לא הוצרך להכפיל הדברים ולהזכיר כל אלו היינות הדומין לײן מגתו שאף שײנות גמורות הם אינו חייב עליהם.

ונחזור לבאר הברייתא דירושלמי [סוטה] שנשנו בה הדברים שײן קוסס נחשב בהם לײן גמור. ראשית דברי הברייתא היא : "מערבין [בן] ומשתתפין

הירושלמי: "יכול הנוטע ארבעה אילני מאכל או חמשה אילני סרק יהא חוזר? תלמוד לומר 'כרם' [דברים כ"ב: ו'], מה כרם מיוחד שהוא של חמש גפנים, יצא זה שאינו של חמש גפנים. **שהיין** מגיתו קוסס מערבין בו ומשתתפין בו ומברכין עליו ומזמנין בו את הכלה ומקדשין בו את האבל ונמכר בחנות לשם יין, והמוכר לחבירו יין סתם לא מכר לו יין קוסס. ואסור בהורייה ובהיתר נדרים ועל ביאת המקדש לית לך אלא שהוא אסור על גבי המזבח והן בן סורר ומורה צריכה".

והנה ראשית דברי הירושלמי היא הברייתא בספרי דברים פיסקא קצ"ה, [מהד' פינקלשטין, עמ' 235] ומקצתה גם כן במדרש תנאים עמ' 120 והובאה גם כן בבבלי סוטה מ"ג, ב'. וברור שכשמש ש"שאינו של חמש גפנים" היא סוף הברייתא ואחר כך מתחיל ענין חדש לגמרי כאשר יפה ראו המפרשים, אבל לא ראו שעל ידי חסירת אות אחת נשתבש כל הסוגיא, ולכן לא יכלו לעמוד על מובנה. ובראשונה אעיר שבכתב יד של הירושלמי שהוצאתי לאור בעזר השם בספרי שרידי הירושלמי [עמ' 215] הגרסא: "**שתין** – יין בין השורות – **שתין** – יין בין השורות – קוסס, תני יין קוסס מערב[ין עלי[ו]" וכו'. ועל ידי שתיהן, גרסת הדפוס וגרסת כתב היד, נוכל להחליט בלי שום ספק שצריך לאמר: "**שתה יין** מגתו, **שתה יין** קוסס". ובדפוס או בכתב יד שנדפסה ממנו ההוצאה הראשונה של הירושלמי נשמט הת' ובמקום "שתה יין" נכתב בטעות "שהיין" במלה אחת, ובכתב יד של שרידי הירושלמי נשמט הה' בהמלה "שתה" – ה' ות' בכתבי יד עתיקים, עלולים להתחלף על ידי שווי תמונתם – ובמקום "שתה יין" כתבו "שתין", ואחר כך הוסיפו הסופרים "ייין" בין השורות. ו"שתה יין מגתו, שתה יין קוסס" היא שאלת הגמרא, [כלומר]: מה הדין בשתה יינות אלו אם הם נחשבים כיין גמור או לא. ועיקר הסוגיא הוא בבן סורר ומורה והשאלה היא, אם הוא נעשה בן סורר ומורה בשתה יינות אלו. וכבר ידוע דרך הירושלמי לישא וליתן בהלכות בדרך אגב, ועל ידי שבמשנה דסוטה שם ובתלמוד שעל המשנה הגדירו מה הוא כרם, שנו גם כן ההלכות בהגדרתו של יין.

ובבבלי סנהדרין ע', א' נשנה במקומו במשנה: "מאימתי חייב? [משיאכל תרטימר בשר] וישתה חצי לוג יין [האיטלקי]", ואמרו שם בגמרא: "שתה יין מגתו אין נעשה בן סורר ומורה", ומאי דפשיטא להו לחכמי בבל מספקא להו לאמוראי ארץ ישראל. וכאשר יין מגתו ויין קוסס שוים הם – עיין לקמן – הביאו ברייתא (לפנינו בדפוס חסר 'תני' אבל ישנו לנכון בשרידי ירושלמי שלי) שיין קוסס כשר לכל דבר מצוה, ומזה הוציאו "לית לך אלא שהוא אסור על גבי המזבח", ולפנינו יתבאר אם אסור לכתחילה או גם בדיעבד, אבל

לי"אחד חי ואחד מזוג" ובמאמר זה, חי הוא הפשוט, שיש בו רביעית יין שלם ובמזוג רק חלק אחד הוא של יין והשאר מים וכמו שאמרו שם בגמרא, ועל כרחך שגם בסיפא "אחד חדש ואחד ישן", חדש הוא הפשוט. אבל לפי דברנו שחדש כאן משמעו יין של שנה זו אחר שעברו עליו ארבעים יום וישן הוא יותר משנה, דברי הברייתא ברורים שכיוונו למשנה סוף פרק ח' דמנחות שבנסכים מצוה לכתחילה ביין של שנה זו — אחר שעברו עליו ארבעים יום — ואמרו שכאן בארבע כוסות "אחד חדש", רצונו לאמר, אחד יין של שנה זו שהוא מצוה מן המובחר בנסכים, "ואחד ישן" יין של שנה שעברה, שאין מביאין אותו לכתחילה למזבח, שוין. ועיין שערי שמחה חלק ב', עמ' צ"ח שנראה שפירש כעין זה אבל הסופרים שיבשו לשון המחבר. ועל ידי פירוש זה הרווחנו לפרש גם כן דברי ר' יהודה הסתומים [בפסחים הנ"ל], שלפי פשוטו הוא חולק על התנא קמא כמו שפירשו כל הראשונים, עיין רשב"ם ועיין לקמן שהוכחתי שהרי"ף והרמב"ם והגאונים פסקו שלא כר' יהודה, חוץ מהרמב"ן שבפירושו לבבא בתרא [צ"ח, א'] צידד לאמר שר' יהודה מפרש ואינו חולק, אבל גם לפירושו, קשה מה מצא ר' יהודה בדברי החכמים שהוצרך לפרש ולאמר שאם אין ביין טעם ומראה פסול. בשלמא בטעם אפשר לאמר שבא להוציא מזוג יותר מדאי שאבד היין טעמו, אבל מראה מאן דכר שמיה! ולפי מה שכתבנו הכל עולה יפה, ור' יהודה חולק או מפרש, שיין ישן שאבד מראהו פסול לארבע כוסות, כמו שאינו מביא אותו לכתחילה למזבח, וכמו שאמרו שם במנחות [ח':ו'], שיין יותר משנה אין מביאין למזבח משום שאדמימות שבו נפסדה עיין ברש"י שם פ"ז, א' בדבור המתחיל היינו טעמא, וזה לשונו: "שאין מביא ישן דכתיב 'אל תרא יין כי יתאדם' דלא הוה חשיב יין אלא אדום, ושנה ראשונה יש בו עיקר אדמומית טפי [לא]". וצריך אני להעיר שלא מצינו בתלמוד "יין חדש" במובן תירוש או יין הבא מגתו, ואף ששיגור מבטא זה בפי רבותינו חכמי צרפת ואשכנז כאשר הבאתי דבריהם בראשית מאמרי זה, ונראה שגם בירושלמי ברכות סוף פרק ו', "יין חדש" וכו', כיוונו ליין של שנה זו ויין של שנה שעברה.

[סוגיית הירושלמי, סוטה ח':ה', כ"ב ע"ד ופירושה]

אחר שבררנו דעת התלמוד בבלי על יין הבא מגתו, או תירוש, או יין חדש, כאשר נקרא שמו בפי רבותינו הפוסקים ומפרשי התלמוד, אמרתי לבאר גם כן דברי הירושלמי בסוטה פרק ח', ה', [כ"ב ע"ד] והוא המקום האחד בירושלמי שנזכר בו יין מגתו ושארי יינות הדומין לו, וזה לשון

לעיל [צ״א סוף ע״ב] אלא ששם הגרסא ״דברים שדרכם ליישנן״ במקום ״יין שדרכו לכך״. ומדברי הספרא קושיא גדולה על הרמב״ם, שבפירוש המשניות, סוף פרק ח׳ של מנחות כתב: ״ואין מביאין יין ישן והוא שכלו י״ב חדש לפי שהוא חם ומתחדש בו מרירות״ וסומך זה למה שנאמר ״אל תרא יין כי יתאדם״ [משלי כ״ג: ל״א]. ומלבד הדוחק הגדול שבפירושו שהגמרא מביאה ראיה מן מראהו של יין לטעמו, דבריו סותרים דברי הספרא הנ״ל שיין ישן יפה מחברו. ועיין גם כן עבודה זרה מ׳, ב׳ בסוף הפרק המעשה על יין תפוחים של שבעים שנה שנתרפא ר׳ יוסי מחליו על ידי שתייתו ואמר [רבי] ״ברוך המקום שמסר עולמו לשומרים״. וגם זה מוכיח שיין ישן משביח ולא כפירוש ראשון שברשב״ם הנ״ל והרמב״ם הנ״ל. ואולי שאלו הראשונים גרסו בירושלמי ברכות סוף פרק ו׳, [י׳ ע״ד] כגרסת הספרים ״יין ישן ויין חדש צריך לברך״, ומזה הוכיחו שלדעת תלמוד ארץ ישראל יין חדש יפה מחבירו ולכן צריך לברך עליו אחר שכבר ברך על הישן. אבל דעת הרמב״ם, [הלכות] ברכות ד׳, ח׳ היא ששינוי יין צריך ברכה אפילו היין השני גרוע מהראשון, וחוץ מזה כבר כתבתי לעיל[31] שכמעט כל הראשונים גרסו ״יין חדש ויין ישן צריך לברך״, וברור שזו היא הגרסא העיקרית; והכל יודעים שהיין מוסיף כח על ידי יושן. והנה לדעת הרמב״ם והפירוש הראשון ברשב״ם בהך ״יין חדש ויין ישן״ שבפסחים לא כיוונו ליין הבא מגתו — קודם מ׳ יום — וליין אחר מ׳ יום, שהכל מודים שיין אחר מ׳ יום משובח מיין הבא מגתו, ולכן זה האחרון אינו מביא לכתחילה על גבי מזבח וכן לשאר דברים, במקום [שהקפידה] התורה על יין המשכר כגון בבן סורר ומורה ובבא אל המקדש, יין מגתו לא נקרא יין — עיין לקמן. ובודאי שבפסחים משמען כמשמע חדש וישן שבתורה, ויקרא כ״ו, י׳ והוא יין של שנה זו ויין של שנה שעברה. אבל גם לדעת התוספות [בפסחים ק״ח ע״ב ד״ה אחד חדש] שיין ישן יפה משל חדש צריך לפרש, שלא ליין הבא מגתו וליין של מ׳ יום כיוונו כאן, אלא ליין של שנה זו ושל שנה שעברה.

והשתא דאתין להכא נעמוד על כוונת הברייתא [בפסחים הנ״ל] שנתקשו בה רבותינו הראשונים. וכבר ראינו שהפירוש הראשון שברשב״ם — והוא גם כן פירוש הרמב״ם — שיין חדש טוב מיין ישן אי אפשר לקיימו מכל אלו הקושיות שהקשינו לעיל, אבל גם פירוש התוספות קשה, שאף שאמת שלפעמים — אבל רק לפעמים רחוקות — נקט שאינו פשוט קודם כמו שכתבו התוספות, אבל בברייתא זו ״אחד חדש ואחד ישן״ הוא מקביל

דהוא הדין בשבת בתוך האוכל דמשקה הבא על האוכל כאוכל דמי ומקדשין עליו קידוש היום" וכן היא דעת בעל ספר עץ חיים (אשר יצא לאור בספר היובל להחכם משה שטיינשניידער עמוד 206),[28] וקצת תימה שהטור והשלחן ערוך הביאו ההלכה דסוחט אדם בלי לפרשה. ועל סחיטת אשכול של ענבים לקדרה עיין מחלוקת הגאונים בתורתן של ראשונים ב', נ"א וכו';[29] שאלות ותשובות מן הגניזה קכ"א;[30] וספר ראבי"ה, סימן ש"ל, [חלק א', עמי 370 ואילך] והמקומות שהעיר עליהם המוציא לאור. והנה אם נאמר שסוחט אדם משמיענו בערב שבת, באמת אין חילוק כלל בין יין מגתו לסוחט אדם, שאם סוחט בערב שבת ומקדש עליו אחר שעה בשבת הרי מקדש על יין מגתו. ומתחילה חשבתי שמשמיענו מותר לסחוט בשבת עצמה, לפי הראשונים שמתירין, או שמותר לסחוט סמוך לשבת מבלי חשש שיעשה כן בשבת, לדעת האוסרים. אבל הך דנזיר "סוחט אדם" וכו' שהבאתי לעיל מוכיח שסוחט אדם הוא רק הפלגת ההיתר של יין מגתו, שכשר ואפילו הוא רק בן שעה.

[סוגיית פסחים ק"ח ע"ב ופירושה]

ומלבד המשא ומתן על יין מגתו לקידוש שבסוגיא זו דבבא בתרא, יש להעיר גם כן על מה שאמרו בברייתא דפסחים ק"ח ב' לענין ארבע כוסות של פסח, ואחד מהן כוס של קידוש: "אחד חי ואחד מזוג, אחד חדש ואחד ישן, רבי יהודה אומר צריך שיהא בו טעם ומראה יין". ורבותינו הראשונים נחלקו בפירוש "אחד חדש ואחד ישן", שיש שאמרו שיש ישן גרוע מחדש ויש שפירשו להיפך, עיין שם ברשב"ם ובתוספות. והנה בעלי התוספות הוכיחו מהאי דמגילה ט"ז, ב' שיין ישן טוב מיין חדש, וכבר העירותי לעיל עמ' טז שבכתבי יד ובדפוסים עתיקים ליתא שם "ישן". ועוד הביאו ראיה ממאמר הגדה שבבבא בתרא סוף צ"א "כל מילי עתיקא מעליא", ואין למדין מן הכללות. ופלא שלא העירו על הספרא בחוקותי, פסוק "ואכלתם ישן", [מהד' וייס, קי"א ע"א], שאמרו שם: "מלמד שכל המתישן יפה מחברו, נושן אין לי אלא יין שדרכו לכך", ושנוייה ברייתא זו גם בגמרא שלפנינו בבבא בתרא

---

28 וראה עכשיו ר' יעקב חזן מלונדרץ, עץ חיים, מהד' י' ברודי, חלק א', ירושלים תשכ"ב, עמי קצ"ה.

29 כלומר, ח"מ הורוויץ, בית נכות ההלכות או תורתן של ראשונים, חלק ב', פראנקפורט על נהר מיין תרמ"ב, עמי 51 ואילך.

30 הכוונה לגאוניקה (לעיל, הערה 24), חלק ב', עמי 121.

עמוד סט. ועל ידי גרסת בעל המנהיג נעמוד גם כן על דברי הטור בסימן רע״ב שכתב: ״ויתנן סוחט אדם אשכול״ וכו׳ והרב בעל בית יוסף העיר שזה טעות סופר שאין זה לא משנה ולא ברייתא אלא מאמר רבא או רבה — עיין דקדוקי סופרים במקומו וגרסת הראשונים שנזכרו למעלה, ובמנהגים לר׳ אברהם קלויזנר בדף ה׳ ע״ב הגרסא רבא ובדף ח׳ ע״ב רבה!²⁵ — והרב בעל בית חדש חשב להציל ולא הציל. וברור שהטור גרס כגרסת בעל המנהיג ״ויתנן יין מגתו״, ובהביאו דברי הגמרא אחז לשון קצרה וכתב ״ויתנן **וכו׳**²⁶ סוחט אדם״ והסופרים השמיטו ״וכו׳״. וצריך אני להעיר שבדקתי בשני כתבי יד של הטור הנמצאים בבית אוצר הספרים של בית מדרשנו וכן בההוצאה ראשונה (נדפס בפייביא דישקו בשנת רל״ה) ובשאר ההוצאות הישנות ובכולם הגרסא ״ויתנן סוחט״ וכו׳ כמו שהוא לפנינו, חוץ מהוצאת ש״ה (קושטא) ששם הגרסא ״רבה״ במקום ״ותנן״, ואין ספק שתקון סופרים הוא, וגרסת הטור היא ״ויתנן וכו׳ סוחט״.

והביאו ראיה בגמרא שיין מגתו כשר לכתחילה לקידוש ממאמרו של רבא, או רבה: ״סוחט אדם אשכול של ענבים ואומר עליו קידוש היום״. ובהלכות גדולות, קדוש והבדלה בסופו, בב׳ הנוסחאות נמצאת אחר מאמר זה הוספה זו: ״הואיל וגבי נזיר יין קרוי יין דכתיב ׳מכל אשר יעשה מגפן היין׳״.²⁷ וקשה להחליט אם ההוספה הזאת היא לבעל ההלכות גדולות או שכך גרס הגאון בגמרא, והראיה מנזיר מובאת גם כן בשערי שמחה חלק א׳, עמ׳ ב׳, ומחברו רבינו יצחק אבן גיאת בודאי השתמש בהלכות גדולות. ובהערותיו לספר זה [הערה י״א] מובאת קושיית חכם אחד על דברי הבה״ג, הא בנזיר אף בחומץ יין אסור מה שאין כן בקידוש. וקושייתו מעיקרא ליתא, שכוונת בה״ג — או דברי הגמרא — היא שבנזיר אשכול של ענבים מפיק ליה מקרא דיין ואילו חומץ מחומץ יין, ועל כרחך שסתם יין, מוציא חומץ ומביא אשכול, ולכן גם בקידוש על היין, מביא אשכול ומוציא חומץ. ועיין בנזיר ל״ח, ב׳ ״סחט אשכול של ענבים ושתה״ וכו׳ ולמאמר זה כיוון בה״ג, ועיין גם כן ירושלמי נזיר פרק ו׳, הלכה ב׳ [נ״ה ע״א] ״סחטו לשם יין״ וכו׳.

והך ד״סוחט אדם״ [בבא בתרא] לא איתפרש בגמרא אם סוחט אפילו בשבת וביו״ט עצמם או שסוחט סמוך לשבת קודם שקידש היום. וכבר נחלקו בזה הראשונים, עיין בה״ג במקום הנ״ל שאוסר לסחוט בשבת עצמה, אבל בארחות חיים, דין היין הראוי לקדש בו, דף ס״ד, א׳ כתב: ״ויש אומרים

25 במהד׳ דיסין (לעיל, הערה 10), עמ׳ ט׳ הגירסא היא ״רבא״.

26 ההדגשה נוספה על ידי העורך.

27 ראה לעיל, הערה 18.

ודייקו בגמרא על מאמרו של רב ואמרו: "למעוטי מאי? אילימא למעוטי
יין מגתו והא תאני ר' חייא יין מגתו לא יביא ואם הביא הוא כשר וכיון דאם
הביא כשר אנן אפילו לכתחילה נמי". ומפרשי התלמוד לא בררו דיוק זה
של הגמרא, מניין יצא להם שכל היינות שכשרים בדיעבד למזבח כשרים
אפילו לכתחילה לקידוש. ונראה שהיתה קשה להם אריכות לשונו של מאמר
זה, שכך היה לו לרב לאמר: "כל הכשר למזבח — או לנסכים — כשר
לקידוש" וסגנון כזה מצוי הרבה בפי התנאים, עיין לדוגמא נדה, פרק ו',
משנה ד': "כל הכשר לדון כשר להעיד". ומסגנונו הארוך של רב דייקו שרק
יין שאינו ראוי כלל, רצונו לאמר, יין שפסול גם בדיעבד למזבח, פסול גם
לקידוש, אבל אם ראוי ואף שאינו מן המובחר כשר לקידוש גם לכתחילה.
ולו היה רב שונה משנתו בדרך קצרה "כל הכשר למזבח" וכו' היינו אומרים
שאין מקדשין אלא על יין שכשר לכתחילה למזבח, שכשר, לכתחילה משמע,
עיין משנה חולין פרק א', ד', ה', ו', ולכן דייק רב בלשונו ואמר "יין
הראוי", שאם היין ראוי למזבח ואף שאינו מובחר לכתחילה, מקדשין עליו
לכתחילה. ותמיה אני תמיהה גדולה על הרב בעל הפרישה לטור אורח חיים
רע"ב שכתב: "אין מקדשין אלא על היין הראוי לנסך על גבי המזבח
למעוטי כו'. פירוש דוקא למעוטי הני דקחשיב אתא האי כללא, אבל לא
למדין מכלל זה למעט כל דבר שאין מנסכין על גבי המזבח, דהא מסיק
רבינו [=הטור] בסמוך דיין של צמוקים ויין מבושל מקדשין עליו". ודבריו
תמוהין דאדרבא, מסגנונו של כלל זה, "יין הראוי", אנו למדין שיין של
צמוקים כשר לקידוש משום שראוי גם למזבח, ואף שלכתחילה לא יביא וכלל
זה דוקא, למעוטי רק אלו שפסולים ואינם ראויים כלל למזבח, כיין שריחו רע
ומגולה, אבל לא יין מגתו ויין צמוקים וכדומיהן שכשרין בדיעבד גם למזבח.
וזה שיין מגתו כשר בדיעבד למזבח, הביאו בגמרא מברייתא דר' חייא
ונראה קרוב לודאי שכיוונו להתוספתא מנחות פרק ט', י"ב, [מהד'
צוקרמנדל, עמ' 526] וכך היא שנויה שם: "אין מביאין יין פחות מארבעים
יום ואם הביא הביא מגתו כשר". וכבר ידוע שרוב מניה ובניינה של התוספתא היא
ממשנת ר' חייא, ולא מצאתי לאחד מהראשונים או מהאחרונים שהעיר
שהברייתא בבבלי היא היא התוספתא. ודע שבמנהיג, שבת, סימן כ"א גורס
"ותנן יין מגתו לא יביא" וכו' במקום "והא תני ר' חייא" שבגרסתנו,[23] ואין
זה טעות סופר שבכמה מקומות מצינו "ותנן" במקום "ותניא" כמו שהעירותי
בספרי שאלות ותשובות הגאונים מן הגניזה, עמוד ק"ץ[24] ועיין גם כן לקמן

23   מהד' רפאל, חלק א', ירושלים תשל"ח, עמ' קנ"א.
24   הכוונה לגאוניקה, חלק ב', ניו יורק 1909, עמ' 190.

ב. [סוגיית בבא בתרא צ"ז ע"א-ע"ב ופירושה]

עיקרן של הלכות על יינות כשרים ופסולים הוא בסוגיא דבבא בתרא
צ"ז, א' וב'. ואמרתי לפרשה ולהעיר מה שיש לי לדרוש בה ובדברי
הראשונים שנשאו ונתנו בה.

"אמר רב זוטרא בר טוביה בשם רב: אין אומרים קידוש היום אלא על
יין הראוי לינסך על גבי מזבח"[17]. ומאמר זה הביאוהו להלכה כמעט כל
הראשונים ולא באתי להזכיר אלא אלו שגרסתם משונה מעט מגרסתנו:
עיין הלכות גדולות נוסחה חדשה, עמ' נ"א[18]; סדר ר' עמרם [חלק ב', י"ז,
א'-ב']‏[19]; רי"ף לפסחים, פרק אחרון, סימן תשע"ט; ספר העתים עמי 204;
פרדס י"ז, ב'‏[20]; מחזור ויטרי עמ' 86; ספר הישר שמ"ז[21]; ספר ראבי"ה סימן
תכ"ג, חלק ב', עמ' 53; אור זרוע, חלק א', סימן קס"ב; ורא"ש בבבא בתרא
במקומו.

(יש מאלו שלא גרסו "בשם רב" ויש שגורסין "מר זוטרא" במקום "רב
זוטרא". ואלה החלופי נוסחאות נמצאו גם בשאר מקומות בש"ס, שלפנינו
בדפוס "רב זוטרא בר טוביה בשם רב", ויש שגורסין "מר זוטרא" ויש שלא
גרסו "בשם רב". עיין לדוגמא שבת ע"ה, א' שהרבה מהראשונים, רש"י,
רי"ף ורא"ש גורסים "מר זוטרא", ובברכות מ"ג, ב' בכ"י מינכען ליתא
"בשם רב", ועיין דברי רש"י לשבת במקום הנ"ל שכתב: "הני תלת
שמעתתא שמעינהו מר זוטרא מרב כי הדדי וגרסינהו". ותמיה אני על הרב
בעל סדר הדורות בערך "רב זוטרא בר טוביה" שאחר שהביא הוא בעצמו
דברי רש"י אלו מביא גם כן המעשה מבבא בתרא קנ"א, א' על אמו של רב
זוטרא בר טוביה שנשאה רב זביד וגרשה בימי רב ביבי בר אביי ורב הונא
בריה דרב יהושע. ולא הרגיש שאי אפשר שאמו של תלמיד רב היתה עוד
בחיים בימי האמוראים האחרונים, וברור שרב זוטרא בר טוביה בן חורגו
של רב זביד הוא איש אחר ששמו כשם תלמידו של רב).[22]

---

17   הגירסא בדפוס ווילנא שונה במקצת — עיי"ש.

18   כלומר במהד' ברלין תרמ"ח = מהד' ירושלים, חלק א', ירושלים תשל"ב, עמ' 75.

19   כלומר במהד' פרומקין = מהד' גולדשמידט, ירושלים תשל"ב, עמ' ס"ז. במקור כתוב
     "כ"ו, ב'" ואיני יודע למה הכוונה.

20   במהד' קושטנדינה תקס"ב = מהד' עהרענרייך, בודאפעשט תרפ"ד, עמ' ס"ה.

21   במהד' ווינה תקע"א = מהד' שלזינגר, ירושלים תשל"ד, סימן תכ"ח.

22   זהו מאמר מוסגר; הסוגריים נוספו על ידי העורך.

הלכות שבת: "אמר מהרי"ש: רשאין לקדש לכתחילה על יין חדש מגתו כדתנן: 'סוחט אדם אשכול של ענבים ואומר עליו קידוש היום' **וכן הוא בעצמו היה מקדש על הנבצר תוך שבועיים גם אם מוכרים יין ישן בעיר".[15]** ובודאי אין חילוק בין יין של שבועיים או של ב' ימים, שלפי ההלכה יין מגתו הוא יין עד מ' יום כמו שמבואר בהרבה מקומות במשנה ובתלמוד (עיין לדוגמא עדויות פרק ו', א'; סנהדרין ע', א') אלא שכך היה המעשה שהרב הזה בחר ביין הנבצר תוך שבועיים שלא היה לא קל ולא חזק יותר מדאי. ואמרתי להעיר שהרב ר' שלום אף שלא היה "הוגה בטורים כולי האי" כפי עדות המהרי"ל (בתשובותיו, תשובת הגדר)[16] מכל מקום נגרר אחריו וכתב כמו שכתב הטור בסימן רע"ב "**דתנן** סוחט אדם" וכו', ואף שאין זה משנה אלא מאמרו של אמורא עיין בבא בתרא צ"ז, ב'. ועל הגרסא בדברי הטור עיין מה שכתבתי לקמן עמוד כא.

וחכם עדיף מנביא הוא הרב בעל אליהו רבא על אורח חיים, שבסימן רע"ב השיג על המגן אברהם ואף שלא ראה דברי הראשונים שהבאתי לעיל, מתוך הסברא הסכים לדעתם, וזה לשונו: "בסימן ת"ר נראה לי דמיירי כשיש לו ישן ורוצה לשתות ממנו הוא מוקדם מה שאין כן כשאין לו [יין] ישן אין מחויב" — רצונו לומר גם משום חיבוב מצוה אין עליו חיוב — "לקנות משום קידוש". וכבר ראינו שדעה זו קרובה היא לדעת המהרי"ל ושאר גדולי עולם שמורין כן, אלא שהם אמרו שרק מטעם ברכה יש ליין ישן קדימה על יין חדש כשרוצה לשתות משניהם. ודע שגם מדברי הדרכי משה עצמם מוכח שדעתו כדעת מהרי"ל, שאילו היה חולק עליו וסובר כדעת המגן אברהם שבכל אופן שיהיה מצוה מן המובחר לקדש על יין ישן, בודאי לא היה נמנע מלהעיר על זה בסימן רע"ב בהלכות קידוש ולא בהלכות ראש השנה, וביחוד אחרי שגם שם סתם את דבריו ולא הזכיר כלל לחבוב מצוה בענין זה. ועיין לקמן עמוד סו-סז שהראיתי שגם מדברי הטור מוכח שלא כדברי בעל מגן אברהם.

15　ספר מהרי"ל (לעיל, הערה 7), עמ' ר"י,ג, ובינתיים יצאו לאור הלכות ומנהגי רבינו שלום מנוישטט, מהד' ש' שפיצר, ירושלים תשל"ז והפסק מופיע שם בסימן ק"י.

16　הכוונה לשו"ת מהרי"ל, מהד' י' סץ, ירושלים תש"ם, סימן קל"ח, עמ' רל"ה.

אפשר לאמר כדברי הרב בעל מגן אברהם שיין ישן מצוה מן המובחר, שאם כן היעלה על הדעת שהר"ר מרוטינבורג אחד מגדולי חסידי אשכנז לא היה מדקדק במצות, אתמהה! ואל תשיבני שהרב בירך על יין מגיתו במקום שלא היה לו יין ישן, דא בורכתא,[13] שהרי אי אפשר לאמר שכך **נוהג** מהר"ר מרוטינבורג אלא על דבר שהיה רגיל בו ולא על דבר שאירע פעם אחת או שתיים. וגם אי אפשר לומר שבמקומו של הרב לא היה מצוי יין ישן, שהרי הוא בעצמו בתשב"ץ [סימן] שי"א כותב, וזה לשונו: "אבל **הכא שכל המלכיות מלאים יין**". וכבר ידענו שהרב דר בראשונה ברוטנבורג במדינת באייערן ואחר כך כשנתפס, דר במגדל ענזיסהיים בעלזאס, מדינות שיין נשפך בהן כמים. ומלבד זה בודאי לא היה נמנע בעל התשב"ץ או בעל המנהגים להוסיף שהר"ר מרוטינבורג נהג כן משום שלא היה לו יין מובחר למצוה. ומכל אלה מוכח שמעולם לא עלה על דעת בעל המנהגים לאמר, שלכן מברכין בליל ב' של ראש השנה על יין ישן משום שמין זה הוא מצוה מן המובחר, אלא כמו שפירש המהרי"ל טעם מנהג זה, והוא משום שכיון שבדעתו לשתות יין חדש יקדש עליו, כי ברכתו כוללת גם יין חדש ואילו ברכת יין חדש אינה כוללת יין ישן. והנה כבר ידענו שהמהרי"ם נהג להתענות בראש השנה (עיין הגהות מיימוניות, ראש הלכות שופר; תשובות מהר"ם, הוצאת בלאך, סימן נ"ד; [ותשב"ץ, סימן תקס"ו]) אבל קידש ואמר הטעם, משום שקידוש — על היין — מן התורה, וכיון שהתענה בראש השנה ולא היה שותה יין על שלחנו, לא חדש ולא ישן, לא היה נמנע מלקדש על יין חדש משום ברכת שהחיינו. וראיתי להעיר שבתשב"ץ שלפנינו בסימן ק"כ מובא בקצרה שמהר"ם היה רגיל להמתין מלשתות יין חדש עד ליל שני של ראש השנה ומברך שהחיינו לאפוקיה נפשיה מפלוגתא.[14] ולולא דברי בעל המנהגים היינו אומרים שהיה מנהגו לקדש על יין ישן ולברך שהחיינו על יין חדש, אבל דברי התשב"ץ כאשר מובאים בספר המנהגים מוכיחים שלשון התשב"ץ שלפנינו נתקצר מעט, וכוונתו שהר"ר היה מקדש על יין חדש, ומברך עליו שהחיינו. ובכתב יד של התשב"ץ משנת קמ"ו הנמצא באוצר הספרים של בית המדרש לרבנים בנוייורק הגרסא כמו שהיא בדפוס.

מלבד אלה עמודי עולם כמהר"ם, תשב"ץ ומהרי"ל שכפי אשר ראינו לא היו נמנעים מלקדש על יין חדש ואף שהיה להם יין ישן, עוד אחד מגדולי אשכנז נלוה עליהם, והוא ר' שלום מנוישטאדט, רבו של מהרי"ל ושל בעל תרומת הדשן ושל שאר גדולי הדור שבימיהם. וזה לשון מהרי"ל בראש

---

13 כלומר, דבר בורות או דבר הבדוי מן הלב. ראה כתובות ס"ג ע"ב וש"נ.

14 וציטוט זה מתשב"ץ מובא כאחד מהסעיפים בהגהה הנ"ל במנהגי ר' אברהם קלויזנר — לעיל, הערה 12.

מהרי"ל, וזה לשונו: **"מעשה שאמר מהר"י סג"ל** בליל שני דראש השנה **להביא יין חדש לבית הכנסת והיו מקדשין על יין חדש**...ושאלו את פי מהר"י סג"ל מאי שנא דבבית יעשו להיפך כדפירש לעיל. והשיב מהר"י סג"ל דשאני הכא **דיין החדש** עיקר משום התינוקות דלבם נגרר אחריו, אבל בסעודה יין ישן דעתם נוחה הימנו (עיין מגילה ט"ז, ב', "יין ישן שדעת זקנים נוחה הימנו", אבל עיין בדקדוקי סופרים במקומו שבספרים מדוייקים "ישן" ליתא, ונעלם מהמחבר דברי התוספות פסחים ק"ח, ב' בדבור המתחיל אחד חדש, שהביאו ראיה ממקום זה שבמגילה דיין ישן טוב מיין חדש), לכן מזומן הוא שם לברכה".[9] ומזה מוכח שלדעת המהרי"ל אין חשיבות ליין ישן על יין חדש אלא במקום שרוצה לשתות שניהם ואז צריך להקדים המין שברכתו כוללת וזה יין ישן, אבל במקום שאין רוצה לשתות אלא יין חדש, ובפרט בשאין לו אלא ממין זה, אין קדימה ליין ישן כלל, ולכן בבית הכנסת קידשו על יין חדש, כדי לעשות נחת רוח לתנוקות. ונדחים דברי הרב בעל מגן אברהם, שכתב שלכן המנהג לקדש על יין ישן בליל שני של ראש השנה ואף שיין חדש לפניו, משום שמצוה מן המובחר ביין ישן.

אבל לא בלבד שדברי בעל מגן אברהם נדחים מפני דברי המהרי"ל אלא גם מדברי בעל ספר המנהגים עצמו, והוא הרב ר' אברהם קלויזנר בעל המנהגים,[10] שמספרו או מספר תלמידו ר' אייזיק טירנא[11] הביא הרב בעל דרכי משה המנהג לקדש בליל ב' של ראש השנה על יין ישן ולברך שהחיינו על יין חדש. ובאלו שני הספרים הובא המנהג סתם בלשונו וכצורתו בשם "הגה" כאשר הוא במהרי"ל לעיל. במנהגי ר' אברהם קלויזנר [מובא המנהג] בלי שום טעם, אבל מיד אחר הגהה זו מובא מתשבי"ץ — הוא ספר תשבי"ץ הקטן לר' שמשון בר' צדוק אשכנזי תלמיד מהר"ם מרוטינבורג ולא התשבי"ץ הגדול לר' שמעון בר' צמח הספרדי! — פסק זה: "יין הבא מגיתו שפיר לקדש עליו דאמר רבא: סוחט אדם אשכול של ענבים ואומר עליו קידוש היום וכן הלכה וכן היה נוהג מהר"ם בליל שני של ראש השנה". ופסק זה ומנהג זה מובאים שם בב' מקומות, בדף ה', ב' ובח', ב' סוף העמוד.[12] ומזה נראה שאי

9   ספר מהרי"ל (לעיל, הערה 7), עמ' רע"ה.

10   מנהגי ר' אברהם קלויזנר, מהד' י' דיסין, ירושלים תשל"ח, עמ' רי"ט. רל"ג השתמש במהדורות ריווא די טרינטו, שיי"ט, דף ה' ע"א — ראה להלן.

11   מנהגי ר' אייזיק טירנא, מהד' ש' שפיצר, ירושלים תשל"ט, עמ' ק'. רל"ג השתמש כנראה במהד' ווארשא תרכ"ט, דף כ"ב ע"א.

12   מנהגי ר' אברהם קלויזנר, מהד' ריווא די טרינטו הנ"ל, דף ה' ע"ב ודף ח' ע"ב = מהד' דיסין הנ"ל, עמ' ט'. אבל עיין אצל דיסין בהערות 7-8 שיש גורסים "מהרי"א" במקום "מהרי"ם" ושהתשבי"ץ נזכר בכ"י אחד בלבד וליתא לפנינו.

משה לא פירש טעם מנהג זה, אבל לפי דעתו של ביצל מגן אברהם הטעם, "ואף על גב דמקדשין על תירוש כמו שכתוב סימן רע"ב, [סעיף] ב' מכל מקום יין ישן מצוה מן המובחר". וכבודו הגדול של הרב בעל מגן אברהם במקומו מונח, שנתן טעם פגום למנהג, משום שנעלם ממנו מקורו, [ואילו] היה לפניו ספר המנהגים או המהרי"ל כי אז בודאי לא היה חולק על עמודי ההוראה של האשכנזים, ושמדבריהם מוכח שלא בלבד שאין זה למנהג זה שום ענין למעלת יין ישן על יין חדש, אלא שבפירוש אמרו שטוב ויפה לקדש על יין חדש גם כשיש לו יין ישן. והנני מביא דברי הראשונים בלשונם כדי לברר את האמת.

וזה לשון המהרי"ל, הלכות ראש השנה: "יש פוסקים שיעשה כל הקידוש אכוס יין ישן ולא אתירוש דהא התירוש אינו מוציא את הישן מברכתו כדאיתא בירושלמי: 'בא לו יין ישן בתוך הסעודה יברך שנית אף על פי שכבר בירך על החדש', וכיון דיין הישן קובע ברכה לעצמו חשוב הוא ומוקדם לקידוש וכשמגיע זמן לומר אז יתפוס כוס יין חדש בידו".[7] והנה מה שהביא מהרי"ל מירושלמי ליתא לפנינו כצורתו, אבל בלי ספק נתכוון למה שאמרו בסוף פרק ו' ברכות ירושלמי [י ע"ד]: "יין ישן יין חדש צריך לברך", ולפני הרב היתה הגרסא לנכון כמו שהיתה לפני כמה מהראשונים: "יין חדש יין ישן צריך לברך". עיין לדוגמא תוספות שלנו ותוספות ר' יהודה חסיד[8] לברכות נ"ט, ב' ועיין דברי הראשונים המובאים באהבת ציון לראטנער במקומו. וצריך להוסיף על ציוניו, שבלי הלקט, ברכות קמ"ד [נ"ז ע"יא], שמביא דברי בעל העטור, עשרת הדברות, מצה ומרור עמוד 262 הוצאה חדשה, כתתקון: "יין חדש ויין ישן", ובעטור שם נשתבש ל"יין ישן ויין חדש". ודברי המהרי"ל ברור מללו שקדימת יין ישן על יין חדש הוא משום הברכה, שכיון שהוא נכון לשתות יין ישן בתוך הסעודה יקדש עליו שברכתו כוללת גם חדש ולא להפך, אבל אם אינו רוצה לשתות יין ישן בתוך הסעודה יכול לקדש על יין חדש. ועיין כעין זה בספר ראבי"ה, הוצאת מקיצי נרדמים, סימן קנ"ב, [חלק א'], עמוד 159, שאם הביא[ו] לו ב' מיני יין יברך על המין האחד שפוטר את השני, ודבריו מובאים בקצור בשבלי הלקט במקום הנסמן לעיל, והמוציא לאור ספר הראבי"ה לא העיר על דברי שבלי הלקט.

וכדי להוציא מדעת מתעקש, שיאמר כיון ששיין ישן ברכתו כוללת יותר מברכת יין חדש, לעולם יין ישן קודם ליין חדש, אביא גם סוף דברי

7   ספר מהרי"ל: מנהגים, מהד' ש' שפיצר, ירושלים תשמ"ט, עמ' רע"ד.

8   הכוונה לתוספות רבנו יהודה שירליאון, מהד' ניסן זק"ש, ירושלים תשכ"ט. בספר ברכה משולשת, ווארשא תרכ"ג, הספר מכונה תוספות רבנו יהודה החסיד.

תשובה

א. [שיטת בעל מגן אברהם וסתירתה]

כלל כללו רבותינו בעלי התלמוד דתירוש חמרא הוא, עיין יומא ע"ו ב',
וכן בירושלמי נדרים פרק ז', הלכה א' [מ' סוף ע"ב] אמרו: "התורה קראת
אותו — יין[4] — תירוש, 'תירושך' זה היין". ועל פי הכלל הזה השוו רבותינו
את מדותיהם ולא חלקו בין יין לתירוש, בין יין חדש לישן, ובין יין מגתו,
והוא יין קודם מ' יום, ליין של מ' יום, לא לענין קידוש ולא לשאר מצות
האמורות על הכוס, ואמרו "סוחט אדם אשכול של ענבים ואומר עליו קידוש
היום", וסוחט משמעו לכתחילה כמו שאמרו שם, בבא בתרא צ"ז, א' וב'. ולא
מצינו שום מחלוקת לא בבבלי ולא בירושלמי בהלכה זו, ולכן כל הפוסקים
הראשונים והאחרונים הביאוה להלכה ולמעשה בלי שום פקפוק כלל. והנה
בעלי התלמוד סתמו דבריהם ולא פרשו אם לכתחילה כאן משמעו לכתחילה
גמור ושאין בין יין חדש לישן ולא כלום, או שמצוה מן המובחר הוא לברך על
יין ישן אם יש לו משני המינים, ואפשר גם כן שמצוה היא להשתדל שיהיה לו
יין ישן לקידוש, אלא בשאין לו המין האחרון מקדש על יין חדש לכתחילה
ולא הטריחוהו לחזור בשבת אחרי היין המשובח. ולפי הכלל שדרך הפוסקים
לפרש ולא לסתום, הדעת נוטה שכל אלו אבות ההלכה בדורות שלאחרי
התלמוד, מהשאלתות ובעל הלכות גדולות עד השלחן ערוך ובעל המפה,
שהביאו דברי הגמרא "סוחט אדם" וכו', בלי להגביל ההיתר ולהפריש[5] בין
לכתחילה ולמצוה מן המובחר, דעתם שאין ליין ישן מעלה על יין חדש
וששניהם שוים.

"אחד היה אברהם"[6] הוא רבינו ר' אברהם בעל מגן אברהם על שלחן
ערוך אורח חיים שחיוה דעתו בפירוש בשני מקומות בספרו שמצוה מן
המובחר לקדש על יין ישן ולא על תירוש. וזה לשון הרב בסימן רע"ב, ב':
"יין מגתו: ומכל מקום מצוה" — מן המובחר — "בישן כמה שכתבתי
סימן ת"ר". ובמקום שרמז עליו מביא דברי דרכי משה בסימן ת"ר בשם
"מנהגים" שבליל ב' של ראש השנה אם יש לו תירוש לברך עליו שהחיינו,
יקדש על הישן וכשיגיע לשהחיינו יטול התירוש בידו. והנה הרב בעל דרכי

---

4   מילה זאת היא תוספת פירוש של רל"ג ויש להדגיש שכך מנהגו לאורך כל התשובה
      להכניס פירושים בין מקפים.

5   כלומר, להבדיל.

6   מליצה על פי יחזקאל ל"ג:כ"ד.

תשובה

בדבר יינות הכשרים והפסולים למצוה[1]

לוי בן מורנו הרב יצחק לבית **גינצבורג**
נין ונכד להגאון החסיד ר׳ אברהם אחי הגאון מווילנא

זכר כולם לברכה

שאלה

נדרשתי לאשר שאלוני רבים וכן שלמים לקבוע בדפוס תשובתי על
השאלה, אם נכון ויפה הוא לאמר קידוש והבדלה ושאר ברכות הנסדרות על
הכוס, על המשקה ״מהול ענבים״ ובלשון אנגלית גרייפ-יוס.[2] המשקה הזה
נעשה מענבים טובים ויפים, אלא שהיין היוצא מהם קודם שמתחיל לתסוס
מחממין אותו, ועל ידי החמימה[3] נפסד כוח האלקאהאלי שבו עד שלעולם
אינו משכר. וזאת תשובתי בעזר השם יתברך.

---

1   תשובה זאת נכתבה בתקופת האיסור על משקאות משכרים בארה״ב (prohibition).
למקור התשובה ולספרות עליה ראה החלק הלועזי של ספר זה, פרק ג׳, סימן ט״ז. בספר
המקורי שנדפס בנויארק, תרפ״ב יש הקדשה כדלהלן : ״ציון לנשמת דודי אלוף נעורי הרב
הגאון וכו׳ כמהו״ר אריה ליב ראשקעס זצ״יל ראב״ד דק״ק שניפישאק, פרוור ווילנא, בעל
ספר אבן לשם בדביר, נפטר לבית עולמו בירושלים תוב״ב ביום ד׳, י״ב לחדש שבט
ה׳תרע״יה״. לספרות על הרב ראשקעס, ראה המבוא הלועזי לספר זה, הערה 9.
מחמת אורך התשובה ניסינו למעט בהערות. בנוסח המקורי שיצא לאור בשנת תרפ״ב
השתמשו בכתיב חסר. באופן כללי השארנו את הכתיב החסר כמות שהוא, אבל בכל מקרה
של ספק כשהרגשנו שהדבר יבלבל את הקורא השתמשנו בכתיב מלא. מילים המוקפות
בסוגריים מרובעים הן מאיתנו.
2   כלומר, מיץ ענבים.
3   כלומר, החימום.

תשובה

בדבר יינות הכשרים והפסולים למצוה

מאת

לוי בן מורנו הרב יצחק לבית גינצבורג

נין ונכד להגאון החסיד ר' אברהם אחי הגאון מווילנא

זכר כלם לברכה

נויארק

במצות והוצאת כנסית הרבנים לחניכי בית מדרש הרבנים שבאמעריקא

תרפ"ב

שער המהדורה הראשונה של ה"תשובה בדבר יינות הכשרים"
שיצא לאור בניו יורק ב-1922

התשובות

הזרעה מלאכותית. ישראל חזני הגיה את החלק העברי של הספר והוכיח שוב ש״ישאלת חכם חצי תשובה״, מכיוון ששאלה שהוא רשם בגליון הכריחה אותי לפתור סוף סוף את בעיית הנוסחים השונים של התשובה על הזרעה מלאכותית.[30] חני דייס הגיהה את החלק הלועזי של הספר, ודני פינקל וצוות העובדים של ״לשון לימודים״ עיצבו את הספר בטוב טעם והביאו אותו לבית הדפוס.

פרופ׳ ישראל (איבן) מרקוס הסכים לפרסם את הספר בזמנו, בתוקף תפקידו כסגן נגיד בית המדרש לרבנים באמריקה. ד״ר שמואל גליק פיקח על פרסום הספר בירושלים, בתוקף תפקידו כמנהל הפרסומים העבריים של בית המדרש לרבנים באמריקה. פרופ׳ יצחק (איסמר) שורש, נגיד בית המדרש לרבנים, סידר תשלום עבור חלק מהוצאות הצילום, תמך בפרסום הספר ואף עזר לי ללבן את החשיבות ההיסטורית של התשובות. ואחרון אחרון חביב, עלי להודות לפרופ׳ אלי גינצבורג, בנו של רל״ג, שהוא דוגמא למופת של בן המכבד את אביו בחייו ובמותו (ראה קידושין ל״א ע״ב). הוא מימן חלק מההוצאות הראשונות, חלק איתי מזכרונותיו האישיים ועודד אותי לאורך כל הדרך מאז שכתבתי אליו לראשונה בקיץ תשמ״ז ועד היום. ועל כולם אני אומר : ״גדול המעשה יותר מן העושה״ (בבא בתרא ט׳ ע״א).

בסיכום, ברור שספר זה אינו כולל את **כל** תשובותיו של פרופ׳ לוי גינצבורג. דבר זה מוכח מעיון בפרק ז׳ של הספר המכיל שאלות שלא מצאנו להן תשובות. אולם החיפוש היסודי שנעשה על מנת לאתר חלק מאותן תשובות[31] מלמדנו שככל הנראה אותן תשובות כבר אינן קיימות. מכל מקום, ״לא עליך המלאכה לגמור״ (אבות ב׳ :ט״ז) ועל תשובותיו של רל״ג ניתן לומר : ״תם ולא נשלם״.

דוד גולינקין
בית המדרש ללימודי היהדות
ירושלים עיר הקודש
ראש חודש אלול תשנ״ו

---

30   ראה הסבר מפורט בחלק הלועזי של הספר, פרק ה׳, סימן א׳.
31   פרק ז׳, סימנים א׳, ג׳, ה׳ ו־י״ב.

שלום מנוישטט והמהרי"ל הוא כתב: "ואף ששלושה אלו כדאים המה לסמוך עליהם אפילו שלא בשעת הדחק, לא כך היא דרכה של תורה להורות הלכה על פי ספרי מנהגים במקום שיש לנו יתדות נאמנים בדברי הראשונים..." (להלן בחלק העברי, בתחילת סעיף ג'). לבסוף, רל"ג אמר בנאום בשנת 1921: "התלמוד, למרות שלעולם לא פורסם כקודקס הלכתי, הפך לקנה המידה הקובע (standard) של ההלכה... לאחר התלמוד אין שום סמכות במובן האמיתי של המילה" (פרק א', סימן ד').

בסיכום, גילינו כאן פן חדש של מפעלו התורני של פרופ' לוי גינצבורג. תגלית זו תורמת רבות להבנת גישתו של רל"ג להלכה, לביוגרפיה שלו, לתולדות הפסיקה הקונסרבטיבית, ולתולדות יהדות ארה"ב במחצית הראשונה של המאה הכ'.[29] אולם מעל הכל היא מציבה בפנינו דגם של חוקר תלמודי דגול שאינו מסתתר במגדל השן אלא יורד לעמו ומדריך אותו בבעיות ההלכתיות הסבוכות של העת החדשה. זהו דגם שלדעתי ראוי להערצה ולחיקוי.

* * *

פרופ' לוי גינצבורג לא זכה לראות את תשובותיו בדפוס ולכן נאלצנו להמציא שם עברי לספר זה. לבסוף, קראנו לו "שאלות ותשובות מענה לוי" על שם מחברו. באשר לשם המחבר המופיע בשער העברי, קראנו לו כך לאחר התייעצות עם בנו אלי כי כך כינה רל"ג את עצמו ב"תשובה בדבר יינות הכשרים והפסולים למצווה" שפורסמה על ידו בשנת תרפ"ב וכן בשער של תשובתו על הזרעה מלאכותית המתפרסמת לראשונה להלן וכן (בשינוי קטן) בפירושים וחידושים בירושלמי שהופיע בשנת תשי"א.

* * *

לבסוף, ברצוני להודות לכל אלה שסייעו בידי להוציא את הספר הזה לאור: על פי בקשתי, ד"ר ביילה שרגל סיפקה לי רשימה ראשונית של תשובותיו של רל"ג הנמצאות בארכיון של מסמכיו בספריית בית המדרש לרבנים באמריקה. דוד כהן והרב נחמה גולדברג צילמו את רוב התשובות בשבילי. חנה גולינקין, פיליפה בקל, אדוה הים, אירית באבד, דליה לב, חיה גולינקין, ומעל כולן מזכירתי אלן כהן, הקלידו את רוב הספר במעבד תמלילים. פרופ' מאיר רבינוביץ, ד"ר ג'רי שוורצברד וצוות הספריה של בית המדרש לרבנים באמריקה איפשרו לי לעיין בארכיון הנ"ל כשביקרתי בניו יורק. הרב דוד נובק היפנה אותי לרב אלן אייזר שסיפק לי חלק מהחומר על

---

29 לפרטים נוספים על עניינים אלה, ראה המבוא הלועזי של ספר זה, בפנים, על יד הערות 142-169.

ההלכתיות הכרוכות בדבר, הוא חושש שיהדות ארה״ב תנתק את עצמה
מכלל ישראל ולכן יש למנוע את השינוי הזה (פרק א׳, סימן ד׳; ופרק ג׳, סימן
י״ח).

בדיוקן שפירסם רל״ג על קרובו הגאון מווילנא נמסר שהגאון אמר: אל
תסתכל על דברי השלחן ערוך כמחייבים אם אתה סבור שהם חולקים על
התלמוד הבבלי.[27] ברור ממקומות רבים בתשובותיו שגם רל״ג האמין
בסיסמה זאת. בעיניו ההלכה נקבעת על פי התלמוד והראשונים ולא על פי
מדרשים, מנהגים מאוחרים או אחרונים.

בתשובתו על הזרעה מלאכותית הוא כותב בסוף השאלה: ״והרב השואל
האריך בחכמתו לפלפל בדברי האחרונים... ואולם באשר כן דרכי מעולם
לייסד דברי על דברי התלמוד והראשונים, נמנעתי מלהביא דבריו ולישא
וליתן בהם״ (להלן בחלק העברי של ספר זה). וכן הוא אומר בסוף אותה
תשובה: ״והנה די בכל אלה הדברים הנאמרים למעלה להוכיח להמעיין שלא
מצינו לא בתלמוד ולא אצל הראשונים יתד לפסוק עליו היתר בדבר חמור
זה״ (שם, סעיף י״ד). וקודם לכן באותה תשובה הוא דוחה את השימוש
באלפא ביתא דבן סירא כמקור הלכתי: ״ואיך שיהיה, אי אפשר להורות
הוראה מהגדה זו... הלא כבר אמרו בירושלמי פאה ב׳, ו׳ [י״ז ע״א]... ׳אין
למדין... מן ההגדות׳. ואם בהגדות של זמן התלמוד אמרו כך, קל וחומר בן
בנו של קל וחומר בהגדה זו שנמצאת רק באלפא ביתא דבן סירא שהוא ספר
מאוחר...״ (שם, סעיף ו׳). ובהמשך הוא כותב: ״אחרי שראינו שקשה לסמוך
בדבר חמור כזה על ההגדה שבספר בן סירא... נבוא אל העיון ונראה מה יאמר
התלמוד שמפיו אנו חיין״ (שם, סעיף ז׳).

גישה דומה מתבטאת בהיתר שלו בעניין שם הכלה כשם החותנת: ״אין
דבר בהלכה האוסר על איש להתחתן עם אשה ששמה כשם אמו״ (פרק ה׳,
סימן ב׳). כידוע, מנהג זה מבוסס על הצוואה המיוחסת לר׳ יהודה החסיד
ומשם הוא עבר לפתחי תשובה ופוסקים אחרים,[28] אבל בעיני רל״ג אין הוא
״הלכה״. גם תשובתו הנ״ל על מיץ ענבים מבוססת בעיקר על התלמוד
והראשונים וסותרת את שיטת המגן אברהם על פי עיון ודיוק בראשונים.
ואכן לאחר שהתיר את השימוש במיץ ענבים על פי ר׳ מאיר מרוטנברג, ר׳

---

27 Louis Ginzberg, *Students, Scholars and Saints*, Philadelphia 1928, p. 141.
בהערה שם, רל״ג רק מפנה לתשובה של ר׳ חיים מוולוז׳ין מבלי לציין מראה מקום מדויק.

28 צוואת ר׳ יהודה החסיד, סימן כ״ג בתוך ספר חסידים, מהד׳ מרגליות, ירושלים
תשי״ז, עמי י״ז-י״ח והערה ל״ג שם. והשווה בנימין אדלר, הנישואין כהלכתם, מהד׳ ב׳,
ירושלים תשמ״ה, עמי נ״ה-ס״ה.

פרופ' אלי גינצבורג, בנו של רל"ג, כתב פעם שאביו "חשש משינויי" בהלכה ובמקום אחר הוא דיבר על "שמרנותו הגדלה והולכת".[25] הערכות אלו דורשות תיקון לאור חלק מהתשובות המתפרסמות כאן. אכן, רל"ג היה שמרן בענייני תפילה ובית הכנסת, אבל הוא דן ברוב הנושאים לגופו של עניין ולעתים אף פסק לקולא. וכך, למשל, הוא התיר קבלת שבת באיחור כפי שהיה נהוג בהרבה קהילות בארה"ב (פרק ג', סימן ט"ו). הוא סתר את שיטת בעל מגן אברהם והתיר מיץ ענבים לקידוש כדי למנוע חילול השם שנגרם על ידי רבנים שהתעשרו ממכירת יין בימי "איסור המשקאות" (prohibition) — פרק ג', סימן ט"ז).[26] הוא התיר את השימוש ברדיו שהודלק לפני כניסת השבת (פרק ג', סימן י"ז). הוא התיר לאכול אפונה ושעועית בפסח כי אין הן בגדר קטניות (פרק ג', סימן י"ט). הוא התיר לשנות מנגינות בית הכנסת בהתעלמו מדברי המהרי"ל והרמ"א בנידון (פרק ג', סימן כ"א). במקרה שיהודי היה נשוי לגויה, הוא התיר לה להתגייר ולהישאר אשתו וכן לטבול בבגד ים שאינו הדוק (פרק ד', סימן י). רל"ג התיר לילדים אבלים להשתתף באסיפות ובשיעורי חובה במוסיקה (פרק ד', סימן כ"ו). הוא אסר לערוך חופה וקידושין בחול המועד; אבל התיר לעשות כך לחייל המפליג להילחם באירופה (פרק ה', סימן ז'-ח'). הוא גם עזר לפרופ' בועז כהן להכין "מינוי שליחות" לכתיבת גט במקרה שבעל יצא למלחמה וייעלם (פרק ה', סימן י"ג). ולבסוף, הוא התיר לנשים לשבת בוועד בית כנסת על אף התנגדותו של הרמב"ם ל"משימותי" לנשים (פרק ו', סימן ז').

מאידך גיסא, רל"ג לעתים אסר דבר לא מפני שהוא אסור על פי הדין אלא כדי לשמור על "רוח ההלכה" או למנוע מראית עין או חילול השם. ולכן הוא אסר על החזן ריצ'רד טאקר לעבוד בו-זמנית כזמר אופרה משום מראית עין (פרק ג', סימן א'). הוא אסר בניית בית כנסת בשבת על ידי קבלן נכרי למרות שאפשר למצוא לדבר פתרון הלכתי טכני (פרק ג', סימן י"ד). הוא הסכים שמותר לצבא ארה"ב להכריח חייל יהודי לגלח את זקנו במספריים כדי שיהודים דתיים לא ינסו להתחמק ממשרות צבאיים (פרק ד', סימן ח'). לבסוף, ומאותה סיבה, הוא התיר לכהן לשרת בצבא ארה"ב על אף החשש מטומאת המת (פרק ד', סימן כ"ד).

רל"ג גם דאג לאחדותו של כלל ישראל. בשתי הזדמנויות הוא התנגד להכנסת העוגב לבית הכנסת ובשני המקרים הוא הסביר שמלבד הבעיות

25   בספרו Keeper, עמ' 241-242 ובמאמרו Seminary Family, עמ' 125.
26   על פעילות זו היו מתבדחים: אל תקרי מ"אין יבוא עזרי" אלא מ"יין יבוא עזרי" — ראה הרב יעקב סונדרלינג, Five Gates, עמ' 113.

במטבע של העמידה, מן ההקדמה "התפלה", מן העריכה של פרקי תהילים
ושל "לכה דודי" ועוד. הם בעצמם היו מוכנים לכמה שינויים חיצוניים בלבד:

אין אנו מתעלמים מדרישת השעה למשוך את הנוער לבית הכנסת... אבל
לפי שעה מן הראוי הוא לשפר את החיצוניות של הסידור, להוסיף בסוף
התפילה תפילות בלשון המדוברת ואפילו לקרוא אחר כך (אחרי התפילה)
שנית את "שמע" באנגלית... (פרק ב', סימן ה').

בשנת 1946 פירסמה כנסת הרבנים סידור שנערך בידי הרב מוריס
סילברמן. הלה שלח עותק לרל"ג עם הבעת תודה על עזרתו, ורל"ג השיב:

אני מודה לך מקרב לב על ההקדשה שבה הודית לי עבור עצתי ועזרתי.
ברם הלוואי שעצתי היתה יעילה יותר. אז היו בסידור פחות השמטות
והוספות שאינני יכול להסכים להן (פרק ב', סימן ו').

בשנת 1949 נשאל רל"ג על פירושו של הביטוי "מי רגלים" בפיטום
הקטורת. בפתח תשובתו הוא כתב:

... מכתבך גרם לי עונג רב מכיוון שפעמים רבות נשאלתי על ידי קהילות
אם ניתן להשמיט חלק זה או אחר של הסידור. ולכן אני שמח במיוחד
שיש בקהילתך אנשים שעניינים להבין את הסידור ולא לשנותו (פרק ג',
סימן ה').

לבסוף, בשנת 1947, לאחר משא ומתן והיסוסים, התיר רל"ג ישיבה
מעורבת באזור האמצעי של קהילת "חיזוק אמונה" שבבלטימור כדי למנוע
את פירוק הקהילה, אבל לאחר מעשה הוא כתב לרב הקהילה:

לבי נוקפני אם צדקתי להתערב בסכסוכי הקהילה שלך. הלא תדע כי אני
אינני מאוהבי "חדשותי", ובייחוד נפשי מואסת בשינויי מנהגים שבבית
הכנסת... (פרק ג', סימן ט').[24]

---

24   לעוד פסקים מחמירים של רל"ג בעניייני בית הכנסת, ראה פרק ג', סימנים ד', י"א,
     י"ב וכן פרק ד', סימנים ד'-ה'.

הלכה שיפסוק הלכה ליהדות ארה״ב. אולם השעה לא היתה כשרה לכך, כי "בתי הכנסת המאוחדים" הירשו לחבריהם מידה גדולה של אוטונומיה, ואין סמכות בלי היכולת לאכוף אותה. ולכן הוא הציע להקים "ועד לפירוש ההלכה" (Committee on the Interpretation of Jewish Law) כפי שהוסבר לעיל. ואכן, ועד זה הוקם בשנת 1917 ורל״ג עמד בראשו עד שנת 1927 כאשר הוקם ועד חלופי מטעם "כנסת הרבנים".[21]

ברם, נשאלת השאלה, אם פסיקת הלכה היתה כה חשובה בעיני רל״ג, למה הוא לא פירסם את תשובותיו הרבות? אין על כך תשובה ברורה וחד-משמעית, אבל יש לציין שהוא כן פירסם או סיכם **חלק** מתשובות הוועד הנ״ל במאמרים ובדו״חות שנתיים שהופיעו בשנות העשרים.[22] באשר לרוב תשובותיו שלא פורסמו, יתכן שהוא לא רצה לפרסמן כי הן נכתבו, כאמור, באנגלית, ורמז לכך יש בעובדה שאת תשובתו הנ״ל על היינות הכשרים הוא פירסם, ושמא מפני שהיא נכתבה בעברית. מאידך, אולי הוא לא רצה לגזול זמן מעבודתו המחקרית ולכן הסתפק בכתיבת התשובות ולא בעריכתן לדפוס. לבסוף, יתכן שהוא נפגע מההחלטה ב-1927 להקים ועד חלופי ולכן הפסיק לפרסם את תשובותיו.[23]

על ידי בדיקת כל תשובותיו של רל״ג ששרדו, ניתן ללמוד הרבה על גישתו הכללית להלכה.

ראשית כל, הוא נטה להחמיר בענייני תפילה ובית הכנסת. בשנת 1945 פרסם הרב מרדכי קפלן את סידורו המהפכני *The Sabbath Prayer Book*. בחודש יוני של אותה שנה החרימה "אגודת הרבנים" האורתודוקסית את קפלן, ואחד מרבניה הצעירים אף שרף עותק של הסידור בפומבי. בחודש אוקטובר פירסם רל״ג, יחד עם אלכסנדר מרכס ושאול ליברמן, "גילוי דעת" בכמה עיתונים, בעברית ובלועזית, שבו התנגדו מחד לחרם ולשריפת הסידור אבל מאידך הביעו מורת רוח מהקיצוץ הגס בקריאת שמע, מהשינויים

---

21   על הוועד החלופי שהוקם בספטמבר 1927, ראה *PRA* 3 (1929), pp. 57, 151.

22   ראה הנספח של ספר זה.

23   הרב ישראל גולדשטיין נשא נאום בכנס השנתי של כנסת הרבנים בשנת 1927, שבו אמר: "זה דבר אחד להפנות שאלה ולקבל תשובה מפוסק. זה דבר אחר לגמרי לספק הזדמנות לדון הן בשאלה והן בתשובה בנוכחות עמיתים ולא בנוכחות המהממת של towering superior" (PRA 1 [1927], p. 36). אין ספק שהוא התכוון לרל״ג שאף היה נוכח באותו כנס — ראה שם, עמ' vii. על מאבקי הכח שהובילו להקמת הוועד החלופי, ראה מאמרי הנ״ל (לעיל, הערה 13), הערות 68-75.

הקונסרבטיביים בחו״ל שממשיכים לכתוב את רוב תשובותיהם באנגלית עד היום הזה.[18]

יש חשיבות גם להרכב השואלים. מתוך תשעים ושלושה שואלים, שלושים וששה היו רבנים, עשרים וארבעה היו ״בעלי בתים״, שבעה עשר היו יהודים שאינם מזוהים וששה עשר היו נוצרים. מרשימה זאת ניתן להסיק כמה מסקנות כלליות: א. מספרים אלה מצביעים על התעניינות בהלכה בקרב רבנים ו״בעלי בתים״ כאחד. ב. כששישית מתשובותיו של רל״ג נכתבו לנוצרים! זאת בוודאי הפעם הראשונה בהיסטוריה שפוסק כתב תשובות פורמליות לשאלותיהם של נוצרים. ג. מכאן אתה למד שפרט לציבור האורתודוקסי, הציבור הרחב בארה״ב — רבנים קונסרבטיביים ורפורמיים, ״בעלי בתים״ ונוצרים — ראו ברל״ג פוסק אחרון או דמות הלכתית בולטת שיש לפנות אליו כדי ליישב חילוקי דעות בין רבנים, בין רבנים ל״בעלי בתים״, או לקבוע את ״עמדת היהדות״ בנושא מסוים.

לבסוף, רל״ג קבע נוהג שנהוג עד היום בתנועה הקונסרבטיבית. בנאום שנשא בשנת 1917 בכנס השנתי של ״בתי הכנסת המאוחדים״ הציע רל״ג להקים ״ועד לפירוש ההלכה״ המורכב מחמישה חברים מלומדים כדי לייעץ לקהילות בכל מה שקשור לעניני הלכה ומנהג (פרק א׳, סימן ב׳). הצעה זאת אומרת דרשני. כלום היה רל״ג זקוק לעזרה? הרי היה הוא יכול לפסוק הלכה בעצמו וככל הנראה, הוא אכן כתב את **כל** תשובות הוועד בעצמו![19] יתכן שהוא רצה לשתף רבנים מוכשרים אחרים, או שרצה למנוע ביקורת על כך שבן אדם אחד יפסוק הלכה לתנועה שלמה. מאידך, יתכן שהוא הושפע על ידי התנועה הרפורמית שהקימה ועד הלכה דומה בשנת 1907.[20] ברם, תהא הסיבה אשר תהא, נוהג זה שנקבע על ידו ממשיך להתקיים עד עצם היום הזה.

לאחר הבנת החשיבות הכללית של תגלית זו, עלינו להסביר מה הניע את רל״ג להיות פוסק פעיל ולכתוב תשובות. אכן, אין צורך לנחש כי רל״ג הסביר את הדבר בעצמו בנאומו הנ״ל (פרק א׳, סימן ב׳). הוא מתלונן שם על ההפקרות הדתית השוררת בקרב יהודי ארה״ב כי ״איש הישר בעיניו יעשה״ (שופטים י״ז:ו׳): ״גאונים שהוכתרו על ידי בעלי מטבחיים, רבנים שהוסמכו על ידי סיטונאים, תיאולוגים שנקבעו על ידי בנקאים ועורכי דין, ואקדמאים מחוסרי תואר יש רק בארצנו״. הפתרון האמיתי הוא ועד **סמכותי** לעניני

18　כך מוכח מעיון במפתח שלי (לעיל, הערה 6).
19　כך מתברר מהדו״חות של ״הוועד לפירוש ההלכה״ הרשומים בנספח של ספר זה.
20　ראה לעיל, הערה 17.

פרופסורים שאכן עסקו בפסק הלכה ובהדרכה הלכתית לציבור הרחב: לוי
גינצבורג בדור הראשון, בועז כהן ומיכאל היגער בדור השני, סימור סגל
ויצחק גרשפילד בדור השלישי, ויעקב רוט ומאיר רבינוביץ בדור הרביעי.[12]
למסקנה זאת יש השלכות חשובות לגבי הדימוי העצמי של בית המדרש
לרבנים באמריקה בעבר ובהווה, אבל אכמ"ל.[13]

חידוש נוסף הוא שפת התשובות. כל התשובות של רל"ג, פרט לשתיים
המופיעות בחלק העברי של כרך זה, נכתבו באנגלית ויש להניח שזאת משום
שרוב השאלות נשאלו באנגלית.[14] כידוע, יש תקדימים בעבר לכתיבת תשובות
בשפות שונות: בארמית (הגאונים), בערבית (הגאונים, הרי"ף והרמב"ם),
ביידיש (ר' ישראל איסרליין),[15] ובגרמנית (רבנים אורתודוקסיים ורפורמיים
במאה הי"ט).[16] אבל רל"ג הוא אחד מהראשונים שכתב את **רוב** תשובותיו
באנגלית.[17] על ידי כך הוא קבע את הנורמה לכל ועדי ההלכה

---

12 לפרטים על פעילותם ההלכתית של מרצים אלה, ראה המבוא הלועזי של ספר זה,
הערות 119-122.

13 ראה את מאמרי "The Influence of Seminary Professors on Halakhah in the
Conservative Movement: 1902-1968" in: Jack Wertheimer, ed., *A History of the
Jewish Theological Seminary of America*, New York 1997 (in press) שבו אני מלבן
את הסוגיא הזאת.

14 אבל יש לציין שהתשובות באנגלית נדפסו במכונת כתיבה על ידי מזכיר ולכן נשתמרו
העתקים. מצד שני, ככל הנראה לא היה לרל"ג מזכיר לעברית ולכן יכול להיות שהיו תשובות
נוספות בעברית שנכתבו בכתב ידו ושלא נשתמרו.

15 ראה לקט יושר, חלק יורה דעה, ברלין תרס"ד, עמ' 19-20 לתשובה שלמה ביידיש;
והשוה ש"ז שזר, "גביית עדות בלשון יידיש בשאלות ותשובות", אורי דורות, ירושלים
תשל"א, עמ' 239-319 (אני מודה לידידי ד"ר אלחנן ריינר על הפניה זו) וכן יוסף בר-אל, מילון
יידיש עברית לשו"ת גדולי אשכנז, רמת גן תשל"ז.

16 לרבנים אורתודוקסיים, ראה ר' דוד צבי הופמן, שו"ת מלמד להועיל, חלק ב',
פרנקפורט ענ"מ תרפ"ז, סימן קי"ג, ועוד, וכן קובץ המגן על ברית מילה :R. Salomon
Abraham Trier, ed., *Rabbinische Gutachten über die Beschneidung*, Frankfurt am
Main 1843 (אני מודה לד"ר איירה רובינסון עבור ההפניה השניה). לרבנים רפורמיים ראה
Peter Haas in: Walter Jacob, ed., *Liberal Judaism and Halakhah*, Pittsburgh 1988 pp.
39, 43-52 שמתאר שני קבצים בפרוטרוט.

17 הרבנים הרפורמיים בארה"ב התחילו לכתוב תשובות באנגלית בשנת 1891 ובמיוחד
בשנת 1907 כשהם הקימו ועד הלכה רשמי והם ממשיכים לנהוג כך עד היום. לתולדות
הפסיקה הרפורמית, ראה האס הנ"ל, ;Walter Jacob, ed., *American Reform Responsa*
New York 1983, pp. xvi-xviii; Walter Jacob in: Walter Jacob and Moshe Zemer, eds.,
Progressive Halakhah: Essence and Application, Tel Aviv and Pittsburgh 1991,
pp. 87-105.

תשובותיו של רל״ג באופן שיטתי[6] ונתקיים בי המאמר ״יגעתי ומצאתי
תאמן״ (מגילה ו׳ ע״ב), כי גיליתי יותר ממאה תשובות שלמות או חלקיות
שנכתבו במשך ארבעים שנה (1913-1953).[7] תשובות אלו כלולות כעת בכרך
שלפנינו.

לפני שנסביר את מניעיו של רל״ג לכתיבת תשובות, כדאי להדגיש את
החשיבות הכללית של תגלית זו. בשנת 1986 נשא פרופ׳ יצחק (איסמר) שורש,
נגיד בית המדרש לרבנים באמריקה, נאום שבו טען בין השאר:

> בית המדרש לרבנים באמריקה ירש מבית המדרש לרבנים שבברסלאו
> מסורת שהסתלקה מהאחריות לתת הדרכה הלכתית לימיו. הדוגמא
> הכפולה של הראש ישיבה ושל הפרופסור הגרמני חברה יחד להעלות את
> האקדמאי בברסלאו או בניו יורק מעל לרמה של סתם ״מורה הוראה״...
> לא הורגשה שום סתירה בין הקדשת החלק הארי של תוכנית הלימודים
> ללימודה של הספרות הרבנית לבין ההתעלמות מצרכיה ההלכתיים של
> הקהילה בת-זמננו.[8]

אכן, אף אני הסכמתי לדבריו במאמר שפורסם בעברית ובלועזית, אלא
שהדגשתי בהערה שהיו שני יוצאים מן הכלל - פרופ׳ לוי גינצבורג ופרופ׳ בועז
כהן - שהיו פעילים בוועדי הלכה של התנועה הקונסרבטיבית ואף פירסמו
כמה תשובות.[9] ברם, עכשיו, לאור התגלית של כמאה תשובות של רל״ג ושל
כמה מאות תשובות של בועז כהן וחבורתו, ניתן להסיק ולקבוע כדלהלן:[10]
יתכן שהמרצים בבית המדרש לרבנים בברסלאו לא עסקו בפסק הלכה,[11]
אבל בכל דור ודור של מרצים בבית המדרש לרבנים באמריקה היו

---

6   על חשיבות הפרסום של תשובות קונסרבטיביות, ראה מה שכתבתי בספרי
An Index of Conservative Responsa and Halakhic Studies: 1917-1990, New York 1992,
p. 4 and note 12.

7   כמה מהפריטים אינם תשובות אבל נכללו בספר כי הם מלמדים על מעורבותו של
רל״ג בחיים ההלכתיים של יהדות ארה״ב.

8   *PRA* 48 (1986), p. 83.

9   דוד גולינקין, ״סדר יום הלכתי לתנועה״, עת לעשות, כרך ב׳ (תשמ״ט), עמ׳ 38 והערה
12, שהופיע בשינויים לאחר מכן בלועזית: David Golinkin, "A Halakhic Agenda for the
Conservative Movement", *Conservative Judaism* 46/3 (Spring 1994), p. 37 and
note 27.

10   הגעתי למסקנה זאת יחד עם פרופ׳ יצחק שורש בשיחה שהתקיימה בירושלים בכ״ב
בתמוז, תשנ״ב.

11   אבל יתכן שאף הם כתבו תשובות שלא התפרסמו.

מבוא[1]

פרופ' לוי גינצבורג (1873-1953)[2] ידוע כאחד מענקי המחקר התלמודי במאה הכ' וזאת בזכות יצירותיו הגדולות: שרידי ירושלמי, גאוניקה, אגדות היהודים, גנזי שכטר ופירושים וחידושים בירושלמי. אולם מעט מאד מודעים לכך שהוא היה פוסק חשוב בתנועה הקונסרבטיבית בארה"ב, ושבמשך תקופה של עשר שנים הוא היה הפוסק, בה"א הידיעה, של אותה תנועה.[3]

אמנם, הגר"ש ליברמן, רא"א פינקלשטין ואחרים, גמרו את ההלל על תשובתו של רל"ג ב"דבר היינות הכשרים והפסולים למצוה" שיצאה לאור בניו יורק בשנת תרפ"יב,[4] ולאחר מותו נדפסה תשובתו האחרונה על המחיצה בבית הכנסת,[5] אבל רוב תשובותיו לעולם לא נדפסו ונשארו בקרן זוית וכאבן שאין לה הופכין. ולכן לפני תשע שנים גמרתי אומר בלבי לחפש את

1   מבוא זה הוא עיבוד של הרצאה שהרציתי בקונגרס העולמי האחד-עשר למדעי היהדות בירושלים, בי' בתמוז, תשנ"ו, שהתפרסמה לאחר מכן בדברי הקונגרס העולמי האחד-עשר למדעי היהדות, חטיבה ג', כרך ראשון, ירושלים תשנ"ד, עמ' 251-258. למבוא מקיף יותר, ראה החלק הלועזי של ספר זה. לקיצורים הביבליוגרפיים המופיעים כאן, ראה רשימת הקיצורים בחלק הלועזי של ספר זה.

2   במבוא זה נכנהו "רל"ג". נכתבו עליו מאמרים והספדים למכביר וכן שני ספרים שלמים, ובראשם הביוגרפיה Keeper שנכתבה על ידי בנו אלי. לביבליוגרפיה שלמה, ראה המבוא הלועזי של ספר זה, הערה 1.

3   עובדה זאת הודגשה על ידי פרופ' אי"א פינקלשטין בנקרולוג שהופיע ב-PAAJR 23 (1954), p. li, וביתר שאת על ידי אלי גינצבורג בספרו הנ"ל, פרק עשירי, שאף ציטט מהרבה תשובות בהרחבה.

4   שאול ליברמן, הארץ, כ' בכסלו, תרצ"יד = מחקרים בתורת ארץ ישראל, ירושלים תשנ"א, עמ' 613-614 (אני מודה לפרופ' יעקב זוסמן מהאוניברסיטה העברית שהפנה את תשומת לבי למאמר זה); וא"א פינקלשטין במאמרו הנ"ל. תשובה זאת מתפרסמת שוב להלן בחלק העברי של ספר זה, והשוה לצד הלועזי, פרק ג', סימן ט"ז. כל ההפניות להלן מתייחסות לפרקי ספר זה ולסימניו.

5   Conservative Judaism 11/1 (Fall 1956), p. 39. אולם יש להדגיש שרל"ג כתב כמה תשובות על נושא זה ואי אפשר ללמוד על עמדתו האמיתית מתוך מכתב אותו בודד שפורסם. ראה פרק ג', סימנים ז'-ט'.

תוכן העניינים

מבוא   א

תשובה בדבר יינות הכשרים והפסולים למצוה   יג

תשובה בעניין הזרעה מלאכותית שנשלחה לרל״ג על ידי רב אלמוני   עט

תשובה בהלכות אישות (על הזרעה מלאכותית)   פה

* זהו התוכן של החלק העברי בלבד. לתוכן של הספר כולו, ראה בחלק הלועזי.

שאלות ותשובות
מענה לוי

מאת

לוי בן מורנו הרב יצחק זצ״ל לבית **גינצבורג**

בעריכת

דוד גולינקין

בית המדרש לרבנים באמריקה
ניו יורק וירושלים
תשנ״ו

ספר זה יצא לאור בעזרתה הנדיבה של הקרן לחקר התלמוד

על שם ר׳ לוי גינצבורג ז״ל

שאלות ותשובות מענה לוי